Historical Dictionary of Revolutionary China, 1839–1976

Map of China

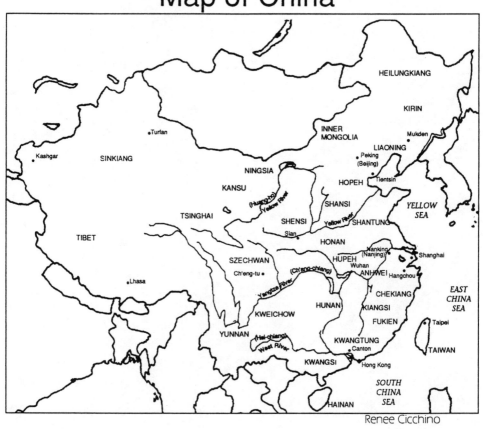

Renee Cicchino

HISTORICAL DICTIONARY OF REVOLUTIONARY CHINA, 1839–1976

EDITED BY

Edwin Pak-wah Leung

GREENWOOD PRESS

New York • Westport, Connecticut • London

Library of Congress Cataloging-in-Publication Data

Historical dictionary of revolutionary China, 1839–1976 / edited by
  Edwin Pak-wah Leung.
      p. cm.
    Includes bibliographical references and index.
    ISBN 0–313–26457–0 (alk. paper)
      1. Revolutions—China—History—Dictionaries.   2. China—
  History—19th century—Dictionaries.   3. China—History—20th
  century—Dictionaries.   I. Leung, Pak-wah, 1950–
  DS740.2.H57   1992
  951—dc20   91–15990

British Library Cataloguing in Publication Data is available.

Library of Congress Catalog Card Number: 91–15990
ISBN: 0–313–26457–0

First published in 1992

Greenwood Press, 88 Post Road West, Westport, CT 06881
An imprint of Greenwood Publishing Group, Inc.

Printed in the United States of America

The paper used in this book complies with the
Permanent Paper Standard issued by the National
Information Standards Organization (Z39.48–1984).

10 9 8 7 6 5 4 3 2 1

Dedicated to Professor Immanuel C.Y. Hsü
in commemoration of his retirement

CONTENTS

CONTRIBUTORS

Guy S. Alitto, History Department, University of Chicago

Robert J. Antony, History Department, Western Kentucky University

Gordon Bennett, Government Department, University of Texas

Gerald W. Berkley, Division of Humanities, University of Guam

John H. Boyle, History Department, California State University, Chico

Henry Y.S. Chan, History Department, Moorhead State University

Chan Man-hung Thomas, Centre of Asian Studies, University of Hong Kong

Chan Sin-wai, Department of Translation, Chinese University of Hong Kong

Maria Hsia Chang, Department of Political Science, University of Nevada, Reno

Parris H. Chang, Department of Political Science, Pennsylvania State University

Su-ya Chang, Institute of Modern History, Academia Sinica, Taiwan

Timothy Cheek, History Department, The Colorado College

Key Ray Chong, History Department, Texas Tech University

Kai-wing Chow, History Department, University of Illinois, Urbana-Champaign

Tse-tsung Chow, Department of East Asian Languages and Literature, University of Wisconsin, Madison

Edwin Clausen, History Department, Pacific Lutheran University

Loren W. Crabtree, History Department, Colorado State University

Kirk A. Denton, Department of East Asian Languages and Literatures, Ohio State University

Edmund S.K. Fung, School of Modern Asian Studies, Griffith University, Australia

K. K. Fung, Department of Economics, Memphis State University

Michael Gasster, History Department, Rutgers University

A. Tom Grunfeld, History Department, Empire State College, State University of New York

Chün-tu Hsüeh, The Huang Hsing Foundation (USA)

Tianji Jiang, Department of Philosophy, Wuhan University, China

Donald A. Jordan, History Department, Ohio University

Richard C. Kagan, East Asian Studies, Hamline University

Thomas L. Kennedy, History Department, Washington State University

Ilpyong Kim, Department of Political Science, University of Connecticut

Samuel S. Kim, Woodrow Wilson School, Princeton University

Janet Krompart, Library, Oakland University

D.W.Y. Kwok, History Department, University of Hawaii

Chi-kong Lai, History Department, University of California, Davis

Lau Yee-cheung, History Department, Chinese University of Hong Kong

Ta-ling Lee, History Department, Southern Connecticut State University

Steven A. Leibo, History Department, Russell Sage College

Edwin Pak-wah Leung, Department of Asian Studies, Seton Hall University

John Kong-cheong Leung, History Department, Northern Arizona University

Philip Yuen-sang Leung, History Department, California State University, Los Angeles

Marilyn Levine, Division of Social Science, Lewis and Clark State College

L. Eve Armentrout Ma, History Department, Mills College

Stephen R. MacKinnon, Center for Asian Studies, Arizona State University

Peter M. Mitchell, History Department, York University, Canada

Ramon H. Myers, Hoover Institution, Stanford University

Andrew J. Nathan, East Asian Institute, Columbia University

Terence T.T. Pang, Institute of Languages, University of New South Wales, Australia

Don C. Price, History Department, University of California, Davis

Tony Saich, Sinologisch Instituut, The Netherlands

Michael L. Schoenhals, Swedish Research Council for the Humanities and Social Sciences, Sweden

Peter J. Seybolt, History Department, University of Vermont

James D. Seymour, East Asian Institute, Columbia University

Richard Shek, Department of Humanities, California State University, Sacramento

Lawrence R. Sullivan, Department of Political Studies, Adelphi University

Lung-kee Sun, History Department, Memphis State University

Anthony Y. Teng, History Department, Rhode Island College

Wing-kai To, History Department, University of California, Davis

Jung-fang Tsai, History Department, College of Charleston

Shih-shan Henry Tsai, History Department, University of Arkansas

Stephen Uhalley, Jr., History Department, University of Hawaii

Hans J. van de Ven, Faculty of Oriental Studies, Cambridge University, England

Lyman P. Van Slyke, History Department, Stanford University

Arthur Waldron, History Department, Princeton University

James C.F. Wang, Department of Political Science, University of Hawaii at Hilo

Ke-wen Wang, History Department, St. Michael's College

William Wei, History Department, University of Colorado at Boulder

Byron Song Jan Weng, Department of Government and Public Administration, Chinese University of Hong Kong

Lynn T. White III, Politics Department, Princeton University

Odoric Y.K. Wou, History Department, Rutgers University

Tien-wei Wu, History Department, South Illinois University

Winston L.Y. Yang, Department of Asian Studies, Seton Hall University

Joseph K.S. Yick, History Department, Southwest Texas State University

Ka-che Yip, History Department, University of Maryland/Baltimore County

Won Z. Yoon, History Department, Siena College

John D. Young, Institute of History and Literature, Chu Hai College, Hong Kong

PREFACE

This dictionary represents the result of four years of hard work on my part as the editor: from designing the entire project at the very beginning stage; to selecting and inviting contributors who could write on entries of their respective areas of specialization; to administering the project and providing guidelines and instructions to the contributors; to editing all the entries and preparing the Chronology and Bibliography; and, in the final stage, preparing the Glossary and Index.

Over seventy contributors from all over the world participated in this dictionary project, making it a truly international academic endeavor. In addition, a number of senior scholars offered their assistance when called upon; they include Immanuel C.Y. Hsü of the University of California at Santa Barbara; Andrew J. Nathan of Columbia University; Samuel Chu of Ohio State University; Zhang Kaiyuan of Huazhong Normal University (China); Xiao Zhizi of Wuhan University (China); and Janet Krompart of Oakland University. My research assistants Yu-yuan Fei, Chun-fang Lai, and Sayinga Heye helped with some of the work. My wife Vera offered computer assistance. Seton Hall University provided two research grants. To all of them, I must record my appreciation.

I must also express my appreciation to Wuhan University where I was a visiting professor in May and June of 1989. While in China, I was able to collect a large volume of materials on or related to the Chinese revolutionary movements. Many of these materials were made possible because of a decision by China's State Education Commission in 1984 to approve a course on the "History of the Chinese Revolution, 1840–1956" for teaching on the college level. Since then, many textbooks, dictionaries, documentary studies, and reference materials on the subject have been made available or published. I found Tseng Fan-kuang's *Chung-kuo ko-ming shih piao-chieh* (Explanatory tables of China's revolutionary history, 1840–1956) particularly useful.

Also of use were Howard L. Boorman and Richard C. Howard's *Biographical*

Dictionary of Republican China (5 vols.) and Donald Kline and Anne Clark's *Biographic Dictionary of Chinese Communism, 1921–1965* (2 vols). But unlike the present dictionary, they deal only with biographies (many of which are now outdated), and neither covers the nineteenth century. As such, the present dictionary is more comprehensive in terms of its scope and treatment, for events, ideas, personalities, battles, organizations, and so on, are covered for the entire revolutionary period between 1839 and 1976.

The users of this dictionary should be aware that the Chinese revolutionary movements actually began in the nineteenth century, even though most of the existing reference books cover only the twentieth century. The Opium War (1839–1842) between China and Great Britain and the subsequent Chinese defeat had set the tone and background for the rise of Chinese revolutionary movements, the first being the Taiping Christian Revolution of 1851–1864. Dr. Sun Yat-sen's Republican Revolution started in the late nineteenth century and was carried over into the early twentieth century, to be followed by the Communist Revolution throughout the second half of the twentieth century. The socialist transformation in post–1949 China under Mao Tse-tung enabled the Chinese to enter into another revolutionary stage. The death of Mao and the conclusion of the Great Proletarian Cultural Revolution in 1976 ended the historical period of the Chinese revolutionary movements under study.

The appended Chronology of Revolutionary China is a skeleton of historical facts prepared to provide helpful and handy information. The Chronology permits a quick overview of the Chinese revolutionary movements. It can also be used to double-check and verify certain facts and/or dates. But most importantly, the Chronology serves to link the numerous and separate entries together so that collectively they can form a broad picture of revolutionary Chinese development in modern times.

The users of this dictionary should also find the cross-references (as marked by asterisks) useful in gathering more information from the many different relevant entries. Since each asterisk leads to another independent entry related to the same subject, the users of this dictionary can actually dig up a wealth of pertinent information by using the cross-references. They may also look for more information by turning to the readings as suggested by the separate "Reference" sections at the end of almost all the entries. An attempt has also been made to incorporate recent scholarship into this one-volume reference book by providing an updated and comprehensive Bibliography. It is hoped that these bibliographic suggestions can form the basis of further reading and/or research.

A note on the romanization system used in this dictionary is in order. The Wade–Giles system is adopted throughout the volume because scholars in the China field have used it widely since the nineteenth century. However, some scholars have recently begun to use the *Hanyu pinyin* instead of the Wade–Giles system. In order to meet this need, the Index uses both the Wade–Giles and the *Hanyu pinyin* systems. This combined Index should prove a convenience to the users of this dictionary.

A note on the various Chinese educational degrees also seems necessary here. Before its abolition in 1905, the civil service examination system was the traditional route for scholars to high office in the Confucian officialdom. The examination was customarily conducted on three levels: (1) the district level which conferred the *hsiu-ts'ai* (beautiful talent) degree, and the holder of this degree became the *sheng-yüan* (government student); (2) the provincial level which conferred the *chü-jen* (recommended man) degree, and the holder of this degree became eligible for an official appointment; and (3) the metropolitan examination in capital which conferred the *chih-shih* (advanced scholar) degree, with the three highest honors called *chuang-yüan, pang-yen,* and *t'an-hua,* respectively.

Finally, I want to thank Greenwood Press, especially executive editor Cynthia Harris, for inviting me to undertake this project. While it gave me a great opportunity to cooperate with a large number of international scholars in the past four years, the work has exhausted me both physically and mentally as it was done alongside my full-time teaching. In retrospect, had it not been for the constant support and encouragement of my family, this work would not have been completed on time.

Edwin Pak-wah Leung
Livingston, New Jersey

ABBREVIATIONS

CCP	Chinese Communist party
CPPCC	Chinese People's Political Consultative Conference
KMT	Kuomintang or Chinese Nationalist party
NPC	National People's Congress
PLA	People's Liberation Army
PRC	People's Republic of China
ROC	Republic of China

A

ALLEY, REWI (December 2, 1897–December 27, 1987): Communist sympathizer and prolific writer from New Zealand; supporter of the Chinese Communist movement.

Born into a farming family in Springfield, New Zealand, Rewi Alley, the third of seven children, was named after a Maori chieftain famous for his opposition to European rule. Alley spent an uneventful youth, graduating from Boy's High School in Christchurch and going into farming before he joined the New Zealand Army to fight World War I in France. Wounded twice in battle, he was invalided back home in 1919 and took up sheep ranching. Unhappy at his profession, and not very successful at it, Alley decided to opt for adventure and China looked the most adventurous to him. Selling everything he owned, he arrived in Shanghai on April 21, 1927.

Rewi Alley first landed a job as a fireman for the Shanghai Municipal Council in the International Settlement and eventually was promoted to chief factory inspector. When Alley arrived in China he was largely apolitical, but those early years in Shanghai (particularly his visits to the factories where he saw workers and young children in the most acutely desperate conditions) made him sensitive to the suffering he witnessed. This political awakening led to action as well as sympathy. On his vacations he worked for the China International Famine Administration, bringing relief to famine victims in Inner Mongolia and helping to reconstruct the banks of the Yangtze River after the devastating floods of 1931. On a personal level he adopted two Chinese orphans whom he raised and nurtured by himself, having never married.

Continuing politicization also led Alley to become involved with members of the Chinese Communist party* and non-Communist sympathizers, both foreign and Chinese. Alley's work for the CCP included harboring political fugitives, allowing his house to be used to store radio transmitters, laundering money, writing articles in leftist periodicals such as the *Voice of China*, and organizing secret meetings of foreign sympathizers to keep them abreast of the activities of the CCP and to recruit them to help the cause. Alley lived in Shanghai until 1938, following the Japanese invasion of China. In order to continue his work for the Chinese people, in collaboration with a few foreigners and Chinese he then established the Industrial Cooperative Movement, better known by its cable address, INDUSCO. The purpose of this group was to help the Chinese establish self-sufficient industrial cooperatives in villages free of Japanese rule. At one point as many as 3,000 cooperatives were functioning, employing tens of thousands of peasants and workers. INDUSCO had the support of the CCP as well as the Kuomintang government and many of China's most important businessmen such as H. H. Kung.* In 1943 Alley moved to Santan in rural Kansu Province where he took over the Pailie School, an experimental effort that combined academic study with practical training in industrial and agricultural subjects. By 1952 Alley had been responsible for training hundreds of boys who later as adults held important technical positions.

In 1952 Prime Minister Chou En-lai* invited Rewi Alley to Peking where he worked for the Asian Pacific Peace Liaison Committee. These committees had very few things to do; it was totally impossible for him to travel and write. But the final thirty-five years of his life were devoted to traveling throughout China and writing articles, books, pamphlets, translating Chinese poetry, and occasionally lecturing in Australia and New Zealand (1960, 1967, 1973). Alley wrote over seventy books and pamphlets and hundreds of articles and poems. He became, particularly in the 1970s and 1980s, an important source of information for journalists and academics visiting Peking. Alley was showered with honors in his native New Zealand, whose citizenship he had always retained. In China he was made an honorary citizen of the city of Peking and the province of Kansu.

REFERENCES: Rewi Alley, *Yo Banfa* (Shanghai, 1952); Rewi Alley, *At 90, Memoirs of My China Years* (Peking, 1987); Willis Airey, *A Learner in China: A Life of Rewi Alley* (Christchurch, 1970); Geoff Chapple, *Rewi Alley of China* (Auckland, London, and Sydney, 1980).

A. TOM GRUNFELD

ANARCHISM: One of the more protean *isms*, which appeared in China in the twentieth century.

Both the global nature and internal appeal of anarchism to humanity rather than to any particular nationality found truthful resonance in its Chinese form. Despite its many contradictory manifestations—political and apolitical, moralist and deviant, individualist and egalitarian, theoretical and terrorist, elaborate and simplistic—anarchism is richest and most instructive as a social philosophy of protest.

Chinese anarchism arrived via Japan at a time when the Chinese intellectual world had been expanded by the writings of Liang Ch'i-ch'ao,* Yen Fu,* and T'an Ssu-t'ung.* Five major works were translated in 1903: Murai's *Shakai Shugi*, Fukui's *Kinsei Shakai shugi*, Shimada's *Shakai Shugi Gaihyo*, Nishikawa's *Shakaito*, and Ohara's *Shakai Mondai*. The revolutionary Chang Chi (1882–

1947), then active in the Shanghai–Tokyo channels of radical action, produced what was perhaps modern China's first anarchist translation, *Wu-cheng-fu chu-i* (No-governmentism).

Chinese anarchism's first organized programs appeared in Paris and Tokyo. Leaders among the Paris group were Li Shih-tseng, the philanthropic Chang Ching-chiang, and Wu Chih-hui.* Chang set up a commercial enterprise in 1902 to provide work for Chinese youth arriving in Paris. In 1906 the group established the Imprimerie Chinoise, and its first publication was the *Shih-chieh* (The World), a pictorial. Its sister publication, the *Hsin shih-chi* (The New Century), appeared on June 22 of the same year, with an Esperanto title, *La Tempoj Novaj* and espoused the widest vision of revolution possible—a world made new by the universal laws of science (*kung-li*) and the tides of revolution. The Paris coterie pursued the teachings of Proudhon, Bakunin, and Kropotkin, whose *Mutual Aid* was the bible of these fervent and compassionate men.

In Japan, at the same time but independently, another Chinese anarchist group was formed. The *T'ien-i pao* (Journal of heaven's righteousness), which was chiefly the work of Liu Shih-p'ei and his wife Ho Chen, was the first Chinese serial publication on anarchism in Asia. The publication reflected accurately the shift from social democratic to anarchist thought, a worldwide movement between 1905 and 1907 attributable to the popularity of arachosyndicalism. In Japan the shift was largely the work of Kotoku Shusui, who had a great influence on overseas Chinese. This worldwide phenomenon explains how two unattached Chinese groups in different parts of the world could espouse more or less the same doctrines at the same time.

Liu Shih-fu (1881–1915), an ardent anti-Ch'ing radical before embracing anarchism, returned anarchism to Chinese soil. In 1912 Liu helped found the Conscience Society (Hsin she) and the Dawn Study Society (Hui-ming hsüeh-she). The Conscience Society, with its elaborate rules of stoical denial, was meant for personal renovation of the anarchist; the Dawn Study Society, which produced the *Hui-ming lu* (Journal of Crowing at Dawn, subtitled *Min-sheng*—Voice of the People), sought to propagate anarchism. In 1912 Liu, Lin Chun-fu, Mo Chi-p'eng, and Cheng Pi-an circulated some 10,000 copies of the Conscience Society's rules all over China. Other groups also organized anarchist societies: the Virtue-Promoting Society (Chin-te hui) of Li Shih-tseng, Wu Chih-hui, Wang Ching-wei, and Chang Chi; the Six-No's Society (Liu-pu hui) by Ts'ai Yüan-p'ei;* and the "Three no's and two each's" (no government, no family, and no religion; from each his ability and to each his need) of Chiang K'ang-hu. Shih-fu's group and publications were the most consistent and forceful. Even though he died in 1915, *Min-sheng* was effectively continued by Lin Chun-fu, Mo Chi-p'eng, Liu Shih-hsin (his younger brother), and Cheng P'ei-kang (his brother-in-law), and lasted through July 1921.

Anarchism captivated many minds between 1915 and the early 1920s. In 1918 another Chin-te hui (Society for Advancing Virtue) was formed in emulation of the 1912 group, with a membership of about 1,000. The young Mao Tse-tung* professed it while at Peking University. Around 1920 there were over twenty anarchist congregations in such places as Canton, Hupeh, Nanking, Shanghai, Shensi, and Szechwan. Eventually, in the early 1920s anarchism waned as communism waxed. The famed debate between Ou Sheng-pai and Ch'en Tu-hsiu* showed how Ch'en's disciplined ideology overcame Ou's idealism. That anarchism's visionary force never did die out can be seen in the continuing challenges to constituted authority, as well as in the novels of Pa Chin (Li Fei-kan), whose Chinese *nom de plume* is composed of the first syllable of Bakunin (*Pa*) and the last of Kropotkin (*Chin*).

REFERENCES: R. A. Scalapino and George Yu, *The Chinese Anarchist Movement* (Berkeley, Calif., 1961); D.W.Y. Kwok, "Die anarchistische Bewegung," *Chinas grosse Wandlung*, ed. Peter Opitz (Munich, 1972): 146–162; "Liu Shih-fu 1884–1915," *Die Sohne des Drachen*, ed. Peter Opitz (Munich, 1974): 160–169; Onogawa Hidemi, "Liu Shih-p'ei and Anarchism," *Acta Asiatica* 12 (1967): 70–99; *Wu-cheng-fu chu-i tsai Chung-kuo* (Anarchism in China), eds. Kao Chun, Wang Hui-lin and Yang Shu-piao (Hunan, 1984).

D.W.Y. KWOK

ANFU CLUB: A political faction in the Parliament of 1918–1920.

The Anfu Club, named after its headquarters on An-fu Lane in Peking, was a political faction founded by supporters of Prime Minister Tuan Ch'i-jui to contest the parliamentary elections of 1918. During the election, its role was to channel funds to candidates in the provinces to help them buy votes. These efforts were quite successful, so that the club initially controlled 342 of 470 seats in the new Parliament.

Once Parliament convened in August 1918, the club established an elaborate organization with five departments conducting numerous activities. It paid a monthly honorarium to its affiliated members of Parliament and so at first managed to maintain considerable voting discipline. The key initial issue facing the Parliament was the election of a new president. When Tuan Ch'i-jui threw his support to a senior bureaucrat, Hsü Shih-ch'ang,* the Anfu Club members voted for him as a bloc and contributed to his overwhelming election on September 4, 1918.

Thereafter, however, club discipline gradually declined, beginning with the defection of the allied Communications Clique from the Anfu camp over the issue of whom to elect as vice-president. Subsequently, the club split with the new president over his efforts to negotiate a peace agreement with the breakaway Canton-based government, fearing that the agreement would lead to the dissolution of the new Parliament. During the May Fourth Incident* of 1919, which was triggered by public opposition to provisions of the Versailles Peace Treaty confirming Japanese possession of the former German rights in Shantung, the Anfu group came under attack as pro-Japanese, although the group members' stance on the issue varied. The club eventually issued a public statement denouncing the Versailles Treaty, but this did little to improve its reputation in history.

In subsequent infights over the distribution of cabinet posts and other issues, the club's discipline weakened further. In the summer of 1920, war broke out between Tuan Ch'i-jui's so-called Anhwei Clique* and the Chihli Clique* of his rivals Ts'ao K'un* and Wu P'ei-fu.* The Chihli victory resulted in the dissolution of both the Parliament and the club.

The Anfu Club's leading figures were Hsü Shu-cheng and Wang I-t'ang. Hsü was a former military subordinate of Tuan Ch'i-jui. Wang was a protege who hailed from Tuan's home city, Hofei, Anhwei, and who had served as minister of interior in Tuan's cabinet in 1916.

REFERENCE: Andrew J. Nathan, *Peking Politics, 1918–1923: Factionalism and the Failure of Constitutionalism* (Berkeley, Calif., 1976).

ANDREW J. NATHAN

ANHWEI CLIQUE: Militarist factional coalition in the early Republic.

The Anhwei Clique grew out of Tuan Ch'i-jui's connections as a native of Hofei, Anhwei, his career as a Peiyang Army officer and instructor, and his prominence as a militarist-politician. During the late Ch'ing dynasty,* Tuan taught many of the military officer corps. As Yüan Shih-k'ai's* minister of war, he added bureaucratic and other civilian allies. On Yüan's demise in mid–1916, Tuan continued as premier and minister of war, consolidating his network of relations through extensive influence over military promotions, finances, and supplies throughout the 1916–1919 period. Lacking direct army command in a specific territorial base, Tuan nevertheless was one of the most influential central political figures in the post–1916 era.

Three of Tuan's policy orientations were critical to the Anhwei Clique's evolution and contributed heavily to the militarization of Chinese society and politics typical of this era.

1. China's entry into World War I: Tuan's tactics to secure China's entry into the European war precipitated his dismissal by President Li Yüan-hung* in late spring 1917. Eight pro-Tuan northern military governors refused to recognize any successor cabinet. The stalemate enabled Chang Hsün's Manchu restoration, which ended with Tuan's "liberation" of the capital and return as premier. The declaration of war on Germany followed on August 14. By year's end, Tuan was named commander of all forces slated for Europe, although no troops ever left Chinese soil.

2. Military reunification: In mid–1917, Tuan's affiliates controlled some ten provinces scattered strategically through most regions. To Tuan, these served to plan destruction of Sun Yat-sen's* republicans in the southeast and the independent militarists of the southwest. Tuan's rejection of negotiations toward the same ends alienated Feng Kuo-chang. An old Peiyang colleague, the acting president became the rallying point for the rival Chihli Clique.

3. The Japanese connection: From 1916 onward, Tuan accepted increasing Japanese financial loans and investments, especially when the declaration of war on Germany legitimized new militarization financed by the so-called Nishihara

loans. Tuan and his close associates dominated the resultant War Participation Army, which eventually melded into the clique's Northwestern Frontier Army.

In the aftermath of mid–1917, Tuan and his supporters sought to match their escalating military strength with a strong civilian political organization. This took the form of the Anfu Club,[*] and the Anfu Clique became a common synonym for the Anhwei Clique. The name alluded to Anhwei–Fukien, but it came more directly from the Peking street of the club's headquarters. The club and the clique were not regional phenomena so much as focuses for a web of military and civilian connections. Run by a Hofei associate, Wang I-t'ang and Tuan's ex-military aide, Hsü Shu-cheng, the club was the patronage center for the Anfu Parliament elected in the spring of 1918 to replace the original 1912 Parliament. By various tactics, Anfu-associated members held over 370 of the 470 seats. The cash subsidies and other amenities funneled through the club maintained these ties.

These two organizations—the Anfu Club and the Northwestern Frontier Army—became the operational base for Tuan's pursuit of policies that fragmented the old Peiyang unity. Entry into the European war greatly added to the Anhwei group's domestic military power, and others felt obliged to respond in kind. The insistence on military reunification alienated many who had hoped for peaceful negotiations. The Japanese connection proved a liability as popular nationalism, most notably in the famous May Fourth Incident[*] of 1919, responded to revelations of Tuan et al.'s collusion with Japanese designs in Shantung. These developments helped the rival Fengt'ien and Chihli militarists to gain the unity and strength to challenge Tuan's power in the Anhwei–Chihli War of July 1920.

That brief confrontation sealed the fate of the Anhwei Clique. Smaller than either of the two rival coalitions, the Anhwei group's less cohesive framework resulted in many units defecting to Chihli and Fengt'ien troops. Only Lu Yung-hsiang held out in Chekiang until wiped out in the autumn of 1924. Tuan Ch'i-jui retired to "study Buddhism," resurfacing briefly as provisional chief executive from late 1925 to early 1926. Eventual Fengt'ien's victory and Chang Tso-lin's determination to prevent any resurrection of the Anhwei Clique meant Tuan's return to private obscurity until his death a decade later.

REFERENCES: Howard L. Boorman and Richard C. Howard, eds., *Biographical Dictionary of Republican China*, Vol. 3 (New York and London, 1967–1971):330–335; Hsi-sheng Ch'i, *Warlord Politics in China 1916–1928* (Stanford, Calif., 1976); Andrew J. Nathan, "A Constitutional Republic: The Peking Government, 1916–1928," in *The Cambridge History of China*, vol. 12: *Republican China 1912–1949*, Part I, ed. John K. Fairbank (Cambridge, 1983):259–283; James E. Sheridan, "The Warlord Era: Politics and Militarism under the Peking Government, 1916–28," in ibid.: 284–321.

PETER M. MITCHELL

ANTI-COMINTERN PACT (1936): Agreement concluded on November 25, 1936, between Nazi Germany and Japan, and adhered to by Italy one year later.

The Anti-Comintern Pact contained neither a formal alliance nor specific military commitments, but it did represent an ominous rapprochement between the world's most aggressive nations. While such an agreement may have seemed attractive to military and civilian leaders in Japan, it backfired by causing the Soviet Union to strengthen Chinese resistance to the Japanese.

Prior to the conclusion of the pact, the Soviet position in the Far East had been ambiguous, promoting a united front to resist Japan, yet making tactical agreements with the Japanese to defend the national interest. The rise of fascism caused the Comintern's Seventh Congress (July–August 1935) to adopt a policy calling for a united front of all elements, classes, and nations against fascism. This position led the Soviet Union to see Chiang Kai-shek[*] as the only leader capable of uniting China within the immediate future. This policy shift was seen in the Chinese Communist party's[*] 1935 August First Declaration which, though still critical of Chiang, called for resistance to Japan. The pact of November 1936 must have further influenced the Comintern[*] to argue for a peaceful solution to the Sian Incident,[*] in which President Chiang-Kai-shek was kidnapped by his subordinates, and the subsequent release of Chiang Kai-shek in December.

The priority accorded by the Soviet Union to its national interest meant that Chiang lived with the constant fear that Moscow might reach an accommodation with Tokyo at China's expense. His nightmare was that the Soviets might recognize Japanese domination of Manchuria and northern China in return for Japanese recognition of Soviet control of Outer Mongolia and Sinkiang. This was no idle worry. After the Mukden Incident[*] (September 18, 1931), the Soviet Union had shown a marked willingness to come to terms with Japan, including its repeated proposals for a mutual nonaggression treaty, its accommodation with the new Manchukuo[*] regime, and its sale of the Chinese Eastern Railway to Japan in March 1935. The Soviet priority for national interest was reconfirmed in August 1939 when it signed the nonaggression pact with Germany, thus effectively terminating the Anti-Comintern Pact.

TONY SAICH

ANTI-JAPANESE BOYCOTT (1908): Chinese nationalistic movement.

In the history of modern China, the Chinese frequently resorted to the boycott as a means of passive resistance and patriotic protest against foreign imperialism. On February 5, 1908, a Japanese freighter, the *Tatsu Maru II*, was seized by Chinese gunboats in disputed waters off Macao because it was engaged in smuggling firearms into Kwangtung. Charging that the vessel had been seized in Portuguese waters and that the Chinese sailors had insulted Japan by striking its flag, the Japanese government demanded from China an apology, an indemnity, the release of the vessel, and the purchase of the cargo of firearms. The Ch'ing[*] government's capitulation to these demands angered the people of Canton who held mass meetings in protest. The Canton Merchants' Self-Government Society resolved to launch an anti-Japanese boycott on March 20. Supported by merchants, gentry, students, and the general public of Kwangtung, the boycott soon spread to Hong Kong, Singapore, Manila, Honolulu, Sidney, and other cities where Cantonese merchants were engaged in business. The boycott reflected an upsurge of Chinese nationalism against foreign imperialism. It also reflected the aspiration of the Chinese merchants to advance their interests against Japanese commercial competition.

The boycott provided the Pao-huang hui* (Emperor Protection Society) with an opportunity to expand its influence among the Chinese at home and abroad. Addressing boycott meetings of the Chinese community in Kobe, Japan, Liang Ch'i-ch'ao* bitterly denounced Japanese imperialism. Many Pao-huang hui constitutional reformers became boycott activists. They maintained close relations with the Canton Merchants' Self-Government Society. Based in Hong Kong were two leading Pao-huang hui members, Hsu Ch'in and Wu Hsien-tzu, editors of *Shang-pao*, who played an important role in promoting the boycott.

In contrast, many T'ung-meng hui* republican revolutionaries were opposed to the boycott. They asserted that the boycott could only do harm to both Chinese merchants trading with Japan and Chinese students studying in Japan. They argued that the best ways to enrich and strengthen China were the pursuit of knowledge, the development of industry, and the promotion of democracy and nationalism. They insisted that if there was to be a boycott, it should be directed against the Manchu government.

There were two major reasons why many T'ung-meng hui revolutionaries were opposed to the boycott. First, they saw the Pao-huang hui promotion of boycott as an expansion of the constitutional movement and hence an obstacle to the revolution in China. Second, the revolutionaries had a great interest in the Japanese vessels' smuggling of weapons into China. The boycott of Japanese goods could mean the discontinuation of the smuggling of firearms destined for the revolutionaries, who therefore were opposed to the boycott. But in opposing the boycott, the T'ung-meng hui revolutionaries actually ran against the current of the day. Chinese nationalism and anti-Japanese feelings were so intense, particularly in Kwangtung, that the boycott went on unabated.

The Hong Kong Chinese merchants trading with Japan suffered severe losses as a result of the boycott. They sought to renew their business by openly selling their commodities. News of the arrival of some thousands of packages of Japanese goods in Hong Kong warehouses aroused the anger of the boycotters. They selected Sunday, November 1, as the day for an attack on shopkeepers dealing in Japanese articles. Police intervention gave rise to riots. The colonial government seized the opportunity to punish a number of boycott activists. This action had an important effect in halting the boycott. Another important factor contributing to the end of the boycott was, ironically, the boycott riots organized by the radical activists from Canton. Because the riots had caused some death and injuries, had disrupted law and order, and had caused many stores and shops to close their doors for business, many merchants and shopkeepers began to take a dislike to the boycott. By January 1909 the anti-Japanese boycott had largely subsided. But a long series of anti-Japanese boycott movements were to break out in subsequent years. They played a crucial role in mobilizing the Chinese nation in support of nationalist objectives.

REFERENCES: C. F. Remer, *A Study of Chinese Boycotts* (Baltimore, 1933); and Jung-fang Tsai, *Hong Kong in Chinese History: Social Unrest in the British Colony, 1884–1913* (forthcoming), chapter 8.

JUNG-FANG TSAI

ANTI-LIN, ANTI-CONFUCIUS CAMPAIGN: An ideological campaign carried out in the Chinese press, late 1973–early 1975.

The campaign to criticize Lin Piao[*] and Confucius consisted of a wave of articles in the party-controlled Chinese press, written mostly by pseudonymous writing groups that attacked both the ancient sage Confucius and the recently deceased defense minister Lin Piao for their allegedly analogous retrogressive policies.

The campaign took the form of long articles scrutinizing various aspects of the thought of Confucius and his disciples, and placing their theories in historical context. The articles criticized the Confucians for resisting the progressive trend of history represented by the rising Ch'in dynasty. They claimed that Confucius tried to restore the slaveholding system, while the first emperor of the Ch'in represented the rising landlord class. Confucius stood for everything backward. He despised physical labor, opposed scientific research, opposed improvement in the status of women, and wished to keep China divided. By contrast, the first Ch'in emperor stood for everything progressive. He was the first ruler to unify China, following the progressive doctrines of legalism.

Similarly, the campaign argued, Lin Piao was a historically regressive figure, a counterrevolutionary revisionist who wished to restore capitalism in China. By contrast, Mao Tse-tung[*] stood for historical advance, the building of socialism in China, even though his methods might appear ruthless like those of the first emperor of the Ch'in.

Besides the historical analogy between Confucius and Lin, the campaign tried to establish a direct linkage by showing that Lin used Confucian terminology in some of his private writings. This was an extremely forced connection in view of the fact that Lin had been one of Mao's most radical supporters during the Great Proletarian Cultural Revolution.[*] The campaign seemed intended to explain how Lin could have turned against Mao in 1971, allegedly plotting a coup against him which ended in Lin's death in a plane crash. The idea was to show that Lin had never been a true progressive but was fundamentally reactionary.

Beyond this obvious message, the campaign was freighted with numerous other, often contradictory political implications that baffled Chinese and foreign observers at the time and remain obscure in retrospect. These were the late years of Mao's life when Mao was ill, the high tide of the Cultural Revolution had passed, and a battle over policy and the political succession raged behind the scenes between radical ideologues and bureaucratic moderates. Both sides used the campaign to advance their views, so that contradictory political messages were embodied in the Aesopian language of adjacent articles or even sometimes within one article. The issues addressed in this indirect way included those of whether officials purged during the Cultural Revolution should be restored to office, whether to promote scientific research and technical training, how much authority to give to technicians and intellectuals, how much emphasis to give to class struggle versus economic performance, whether to try to improve relations with the Soviet Union, and whether to allow increasing economic relations with the capitalist world. Both sides argued their positions by the tortuous method of attacking Confucius for supposedly taking the opposite stance on a historically analogous issue. The moderates used historical analogy to attack Mao's wife, Chiang Ch'ing,* and the radicals used it to attack the prime minister, Chou En-lai,* as part of the succession struggle.

The official media insisted that the campaign be carried on at the grass-roots level in the fashion that was standard in earlier political campaigns, through study and discussion of the documents in small groups, where the issues raised in the press would be related to problems and personalities in the local unit. However, local cadres and citizens largely ignored this campaign. They were exhausted from earlier mass campaigns, confused by the portrayal of the radical Lin Piao as a reactionary, and unable to understand and scholastic rhetoric and historical detail contained in the articles on Confucius. For a handful of intellectuals, the campaign provided an opportunity for deep study of Confucianism, which had been taboo for years. For the political system as a whole, it marked the exhaustion of the campaign model of mass political mobilization. There were several more campaigns before Mao's death—most prominently, one to study the theory of the dictatorship of the proletariat and one to study the novel *Water Margin* (an old novel about heroism)—but the failure of any of them to arouse a mass response signaled the bankruptcy of the Maoist model of politics.

REFERENCE: Merle Goldman, *China's Intellectuals: Advise and Dissent* (Cambridge, Mass., 1981).

ANDREW J. NATHAN

ANTI-RIGHTIST CAMPAIGN (or the Struggle Against the Bourgeois Rightists): A political movement to attack and destroy the "bourgeois rightists" in China, 1957–1958.

In 1956 the campaign to achieve Three Major Transformations (the socialist transformation of agriculture, handicrafts, and industry and commerce) had ended. When the leadership began formulating the party's new General Line, the party split over two different, major strategies. The strategy pushed by Liu Shao-ch'i* called for China's economic change through balanced sectoral development without violence and social disruption. Another strategy was shared by Mao Tse-tung* and his followers who made class struggle the "key link" to China's development, because they viewed social change as a battle between the ideologies favoring socialism or capitalism.

The Struggle Against the Bourgeois Rightist Campaign became a carefully planned attack to expose and eliminate all of Mao's opponents who suported the Liu Shao-ch'i approach.

On April 27, 1957, the Chinese Communist party* Central Committee decided to launch a rectification movement within the party to correct internal "bureaucratism," "subjectivism," and "sectarianism" among the membership. It appealed to the people outside the party to help the Communist party enact the program of having "all the people rectify the party." Then in May, Mao Tse-tung introduced his policy calling for "greater freedom to express views and to speak out freely" in order to encourage the people to feel free to express their criticisms of the party so that it could be reformed. In May and June, this new campaign had gained such momentum as to spin out of control, setting off a firestorm of antiparty sentiment by the populace. Infuriated and alarmed, Mao initiated a new tactic for his Anti-Rightist Struggle, by having the party and security bureau label and attack anybody who had dared to criticize the party as counterrevolutionaries.

On June 8, 1957, an editorial article entitled "What Is All This for?" appeared in the *People's Daily* (*Jen-min jih-pao*). This essay launched the first Anti-Rightist Campaign by attacking Chang Po-ch'un (1895–1969, chairman of the Chinese Farmers and Workers party, vice-chairman of the Chinese People's Political Consultative Conference*) and Lo Lung-chi (1898–1965, minister of the Department of Forestry and Industry, vice-chairman of the Chinese Democratic Alliance party) as the two biggest bourgeois rightists. This tactic was followed by mass arrests of cadres, intellectuals, and students.

Perhaps more than 550,000 people were labeled rightists during this campaign. Those people were stripped of the official titles they held and sent to camps for thought reform* through labor. Many intellectuals, unable to bear such humiliation, committed suicide.

On September 16, 1959, the Chinese People's Political Consultative Conference and the State Council issued new rules called the Decisions Concerning the Question of Handling Those Rightists Who Showed Signs of Having Reformed, which argued that such persons "will no longer be treated as bourgeois rightist elements, but will have their rightist cap removed." Until 1964, there were still more than 10,000 such individuals undergoing thought reform in prisons or labor camps. When the Cultural Revolution* started in 1966, those rightists without their "caps" were labeled as one of the "five types of black elements"; their persecution continued for another fifteen years.

REFERENCES: *A Comprehensive Glossary of Chinese Communist Terminology* (Taipei, 1978); Sung Cheng-t'ing, *Tang-tai kan-pu hsiao-pai-k'o* (Little encyclopedia of the present cadre) (Tientsin, 1986).

RAMON H. MYERS

AUTUMN HARVEST UPRISING: An abortive uprising staged by Mao Tse-tung* in Hunan in 1927.

Following the failure of the Nanchang Uprising,* the Chinese Communist party* held an emergency meeting on August 7 in Hankow and adopted ambitious revolutionary plans to put a stop to a succession of severe setbacks. These plans were collectively known as the Autumn Harvest Uprising and had a significant influence on the course of the Chinese Revolution. The CCP Central Committee passed a Resolution on a Plan for Insurrection in Hupeh and Hunan in the middle of August 1927 which was a detailed plan for peasant uprisings. The resolution called for a "thorough agrarian revolution" that would "confiscate all land . . . , kill all village bullies, bad gentry, and reactionaries and in towns to elect revolutionary governments, and disarm all except the workers and peasants."

The immediate goal of the Autumn Harvest Uprising was, therefore, to "overthrow the government of Wuhan and T'ang Sheng-chih and establish a genuine revolutionary government of the people." However, Mao Tse-tung played an important role in changing the Central Committee's resolution and adopted a more radical agrarian program, called for the immediate establishment of Soviets, and proposed that the date of the uprising be moved from September 10 to August 30, 1927.

The policy conflicts between the party's Central Committee and Mao were developed over the course of executing the Autumn Harvest Uprising. Mao was more radical than the Central Committee's official line and was a leftist; on the key issue concerning direct reliance on military force, however, the Central Committee accused Mao of rightist "military opportunism" for his greater reliance on available military forces than on the enthusiasm of the revolutionary masses. Mao accused party leaders of a "contradictory policy consisting in neglecting military affairs and at the same time desiring an armed insurrection of the popular masses." Thus, Mao placed himself in opposition both to the party's Central Committee and to the Comintern[*] policy line. Mao was suspended as an alternate member of the party's Politburo at the party's Central Committee meeting in November 1927 as the result of policy conflicts and the failure of the Autumn Harvest Uprising.

REFERENCES: Roy Hofheinz, Jr., "The Autumn Harvest Insurrections," *The China Quarterly* 32 (October/December 1967): 37–87; John E. Rue, *Mao Tse-tung in Opposition, 1927–1935* (Stanford, Calif., 1966); Arif Dirlik, *The Origins of Chinese Communism* (New York, 1989).

ILPYONG KIM

B

BATTLE OF HUAI-HAI (November 6, 1948–January 10, 1949): The second and the largest of the three decisive Chinese Communist campaigns to conquer Mainland China.

The battle of Huai-Hai (or Hsü-Pang, as the Nationalists call it) sealed the doom of the Kuomintang rule in the Central Plains and east China north of the Yangtze River. After the Chinese Communist conquest of Shantung on September 24 and especially of northeast China (or Manchuria) on November 2, 1948, Communist and Nationalist forces moved into the Hsuchow area, a strategic gateway to the KMT capital at Nanking and to the Yangtze River. Chiang Kai-shek* marshaled his best remaining troops for this confrontation. Mao Tse-tung,* determined to crush the main KMT forces north of the Yangtze River, sent the People's Liberation Army* into action under the command of Liu Po-ch'eng, Ch'en Yi, Teng Hsiao-p'ing,* Su Yü, and T'an Chen-lin, with the tactic of "encircling the point (i.e., the Nationalist concentration location) and beating the (KMT) reinforcements."

The Huai-Hai Campaign was a series of three battles. In the first battle (November 6–22, 1948) the KMT Army under Huang Po-tao clashed with Ch'en Yi's troops at Nienchuang, east of Hsuchow. The PLA attacked Huang's troops before they reached their assigned defensive position around Hsuchow. Simultaneously, Liu Po-ch'eng's forces rushed to Suhsien, located between Hsuchow and Pangpu, to prevent KMT reinforcements from assisting Huang's army. Trapped in Nienchuang, Huang's forces ran out of food and ammunition despite the Nationalist air drop of supplies. His troops succumbed to the tightening siege, and he committed suicide rather than surrender. The collapse of Huang's army weakened the KMT defense of Hsuchow and its connection with Pangpu in the south.

The battle of Shangtuichi (November 23–December 15, 1948), south of Suhsien, was an outgrowth of the first battle. Liu Po-ch'eng's forces, which had assembled in Suhsien, joined with Ch'en Yi's victorious armies to encircle the KMT Huang Wei's army at Shangtuichi. Again no rescuing breakthrough occurred, and the PLA destroyed the KMT armies. Huang Wei was captured.

The battle of Ch'inglungchi-Chenkuanchuang (January 6–10, 1949), southwest of Hsuchow, came out of the abortive KMT rescue of their troops at Shangtuichi. On November 29, 1948, three armies under Tu Yü-ming, vice commander-in-chief of the KMT Hsuchow Bandit Suppression Headquarters, moved toward Shangtuichi but were surrounded by the PLA in the Ch'inglungchi-Chenkuanchuang area on December 4. After destroying one KMT Army on December 6, the PLA completed the siege of Tu's armies by December 16, one day after the collapse of Huang Wei's forces. Then Mao Tse-tung ordered a lull in the campaign to give Lin Piao* time to prepare for the attack on Peiping (Peking) and to discourage Chiang Kai-shek from ordering Fu Tso-yi's* Peiping forces to leave the city to reinforce Tu's troops. On January 6, 1949, Lin Piao's armies were fully ready to attack Peiping, and Ch'en Yi and Liu Po-ch'eng began the assault on Tu's armies. Within four days, the Communist human sea tactics and overpowering artillery offensive routed the Nationalists, forced Commander Ch'iu Ch'ing-ch'üan to commit suicide, and captured General Tu.

The battle of Huai-Hai was over. In the five-day campaign the Communists destroyed or captured about half a million Nationalist troops. The KMT loss of the critical battle of Huai-Hai was responsible for the resignation of Chiang Kai-shek as president of the Republic of China* on January 21, 1949. Above all, the battle destroyed the last remnants of Chiang's best mechanized troops and created favorable conditions for the Communists' forthcoming crossing of the Yangtze River to capture Nanking and Shanghai, the KMT power bases.

REFERENCES: Chang Hsien-wen, ed., *Chung-hua min-kuo shih-kan* (A historical outline of the Republic of China) (Honan, 1985); Richard C. Thornton, *China: A Political History, 1917–1980* (Boulder, Colo., 1982); Wang Ch'ing-k'ui, ed., *Chung-kuo jen-min chieh-fang-chün chan-yi chi-ch'eng* (A compilation of the campaigns of the Chinese People's Liberation Army) (Peking, 1987).

JOSEPH K.S. YICK

BETHUNE, (HENRY) NORMAN (March 1890–November 12, 1939): Canadian doctor who worked in the Communist area in China.

Henry Norman Bethune was born in the small Ontario town of Gravenhurst and spent his childhood moving from town to town throughout Ontario, for his father, a Presbyterian minister, was assigned to different pulpits.

Young Bethune graduated from Owen Sound Collegiate in 1907 and spent the following two years working as a laborer and a teacher in a one-room schoolhouse. In 1909 he entered the University of Toronto only to leave two years later because he was bored. He returned to physical labor as a logger during the day, and he taught at Frontier College at night. He also worked briefly as a reporter for the *Winnipeg Tribune*.

In September 1912 Bethune entered medical school at the University of Toronto only to be interrupted by World War I for which he immediately volunteered in 1914. Serving in France as a stretcher-bearer, he was wounded at the battle of Ypres in 1915. He was sent back to Canada and completed his medical training, graduating in December 1916. Since the war was still on Bethune once again volunteered, this time as a lieutenant-surgeon in the Royal Canadian Navy, serving on the North Sea until the war ended in 1918.

After the war Dr. Bethune served a year as the senior medical officer of the fledgling Royal Canadian Air Force followed by three years of post-graduate medical studies in London. In 1924 he opened a private practice in Detroit, Michigan, but had a rough time, having to supplement his income by teaching prescription writing to medical students in the local university.

In 1926 Bethune discovered that he had tuberculosis in both lungs. He went to the Trudeau Sanitorium in Saranac Lake, New York, where he stayed for a year reading up extensively on the disease and even operating on his own lung. In 1928 his knowledge of and experience with tuberculosis led to an invitation to work with other prominent doctors in the field at the Royal Victoria Hospital in Montreal. There he became a well-known thoracic surgeon and a prominent member of the wealthy English-speaking society.

But Bethune was always restless; in addition, he was becoming angry at the disparity in health care available to low-income people and that which the wealthy could obtain. In his spare time he began treating the poor in Montreal at no charge. In 1935 he had an opportunity to visit the Soviet Union to attend an International Physiological Congress. Impressed with Soviet efforts to equalize health care, upon his return he became head of the Friends of the Soviet Union. These efforts led him to fight for a universal medical program in Canada and, eventually, to join the Canadian Communist party.

Bethune's involvement with the Communists drew his attention to the civil war in Spain, and in November 1936 he arrived in Madrid. Recalling lessons from his earlier war experiences, Bethune believed that more wounded could be saved if medical care were brought to them immediately in the field rather than having them transported to hospitals far behind the lines. Bethune developed the first mobile blood banks, which permitted more extensive medical care under combat conditions.

In June 1937 Bethune returned to Canada for a lecture tour through which he raised money for medical supplies for the anti-fascist cause in Spain. Although he missed the action and excitement of Spain, he yearned for yet newer experiences. Thus, when he heard that doctors were needed behind Communist lines in China, he volunteered immediately. Communist sympathizers in both Canada and the United States were raising money to send medical personnel and supplies to China. Bethune, along with a Chinese-speaking Canadian nurse, Jean Ewen, and an American doctor, Charles H. Parsons, were chosen to go to China. The three travelers arrived in China in late 1937. By then Japan had already invaded China, and communication and travel were extremely difficult. After several months, Bethune and Ewen (Parsons had been sent back) reached the Communist base in Yenan.

Bethune had never seen poverty such as he witnessed in Yenan, nor had he ever had to deal with such paucity of medical care. Given a team of five Chinese doctors, Bethune began to improvise mobile hospital units, traveling on horses and donkeys. He taught villagers to make medical supplies (splints and bandages) out of available material, and he developed blood donor groups. Working day and night, and operating under the most primitive conditions and often under gunfire, Bethune was forced to be constantly on the move. For the first time in his life, there in rural China, he was genuinely happy, feeling more valuable than ever before.

One day in Hopei Province Bethune cut himself while operating. Having no antibiotic and not taking the time to tend to it, he died of septicemia in the mountains of northern China.

Mao Tse-tung* praised Bethune for giving his life to the cause of the Chinese people; as a result, he is probably the most well-known foreigner in China today. Recently, the Bethune Memorial Hospital was established in Shihchiachuang where he worked half a century ago.

REFERENCES: Ted Allan and Sydney Gordon, *The Scalpel and the Sword: The Story of Doctor Norman Bethune* (Boston, 1952; revised, New York, 1971 and 1973); Jean Ewen, *China Nurse, 1932–1939* (Toronto, 1981); Roderick Stewart, *The Mind of Norman Bethune* (Toronto, 1977).

A. TOM GRUNFELD

BLACK GANG (*hei pang*): Metaphor applied to cultural and political dissidents, especially during ideological phases such as the Cultural Revolution.

To the Chinese people the color black has sinister, underhanded, clandestine, and even selfish dimensions. As a metaphor its imagery is strong; once summoned in the heat of political discourse, it cannot be returned to the bottle. "Black" is used to polarize. A "black line" is irredeemable, "black language" unspeakable, and "black books" worthy only of burning. "Black gangs" are beyond rehabilitation to acceptable political views; their members must be purged. The color red was the opposite metaphor during the Cultural Revolution* (1966–1976), symbolizing ideological orthodoxy, militance, and loyalty.

The term *gang* is also strictly a term of criticism; hence, the phrase "red gang" never occurs in Chinese political rhetoric. Most commonly, "black gang" was applied to figures in the spheres of culture, literature, and propaganda, or more pointedly to Chinese Communist party* authorities who protected "bourgeois intellectuals," but it occasionally was extended to any manner of dissident cabal. William Hinton even uncovered an episode in 1971 in which ousted village-level cadres, feeling confident, sloughed off the party propaganda team's label with Yankee Doodle-like defiance.

On the eve of the Cultural Revolution, in late 1965 and early 1966, the most prominent writers under political attack were Wu Han, Teng T'o, and Liao Mo-sha, the collective authors of the early 1960s "Three-Family Village," (*san-chia ts'un*), a series of articles in Peking municipal publications. The P'eng-Lo-Lu-Yang black gang who shielded them included Peking Mayor P'eng Chen,

People's Liberation Army[*] Chief-of-Staff Lo Jui-ch'ing, CCP Propaganda Department Director Lu Ting-i, and CCP Secretariat Office Director Yang Shang-k'un.
REFERENCES: Lowell Dittmer, *China's Continuous Revolution: The Post-Liberation Epoch, 1949–1981* (Berkeley, Calif., 1987); William Hinton, *Shenfan: The Continuing Revolution in a Chinese Village* (New York, 1983).

GORDON BENNETT

BLUE SHIRT SOCIETY (1932–1938): KMT secret organization.

The Blue Shirt Society was a secret organization within the Chinese Nationalist party[*] (Kuomintang) during the 1930s. Provoked by the Japanese invasion of Manchuria, a group of twenty young men founded the organization on March 1, 1932, in Nanking in order to "save the nation." All the founders were KMT members and graduates of the Whampoa Military Academy.[*]

Misnamed by outsiders as the Blue Shirts, the society considered itself to be the Chinese Renaissance Movement (Chung-hua fu-hsing yün-tung), organized in a series of concentric circles. Within the innermost ring was the 300-member Three People's Principles Earnest Action Society (San-min chu-i li-hsing she) charged with policymaking. The outermost ring of the movement consisted of public mass organizations, the largest of which was the Chinese Renaissance Society (Chung-hua fu-hsing she) with a membership of about 100,000.

Mistakenly characterized by some academics as a mimetic fascist movement, the Renaissance Movement was instead animated by a resolve to modernize China through the realization of the ideological program of Sun Yat-sen.[*] The movement believed that only through an aggressive program of economic and political development could China be saved and revitalized.

The agricultural policy of the Renaissance Movement centered on a land reform that included such features as cooperatives, reductions in land rent and land taxes, limitations on landholding, an equalization of land rights, land to the tillers, as well as collective farms. The movement sought to promote the industrialization of China through a mixed economy that combined state capital with private initiative.

For such an economic program to be implemented, a fundamental political restructuring was considered necessary. To begin with, a strong central government was needed, one that could wield effective authority over the national territory, unchallenged by either foreign imperialists or by domestic rivals of warlords and communists. Political restructuring also required the inculcation, through education, of a sense of nationalism among the Chinese, who had long been characterized by Sun Yat-sen as resembling "a tray of loose sand."

To facilitate and effectuate all of these objectives, the Renaissance Movement advocated emergency rule by a single party led by a charismatic leader. Not only did the crisis condition in China necessitate an authoritarian government, but also rule by the single party would create those economic and political prerequisites for a stable transition to the democracy that Sun Yat-sen had envisioned. The Renaissance Movement believed that the Kuomintang would be that single party—but only if it reformed itself. KMT members needed a renewal of their ideological commitment to Sun's Three People's Principles,* a purification of corrupt and elitist practices, as well as the cultivation of grass-roots support for the party among the nation's "toiling masses."

In effect, the Renaissance Movement was an effort at "catch-up" or delayed industrialization through the vehicle of a transitional authoritarian government. Ideologies and movements of delayed industrialization were common among the less developed nations in the nineteenth and twentieth centuries—a group that included Meiji Japan, fascist Italy, and countries that embraced Marxism-Leninism,* Kemalism, Gandhiism, Nasserism, as well as the ideology of Sun Yat-sen and the Renaissance Movement.

Among the Renaissance Movement's successes were four mass campaigns in the 1930s: the New Life Movement,* the National Voluntary Labor Movement, the National Economic Reconstruction Movement, and the National Military Education Movement. Despite its successes, the Renaissance Society was dissolved by an Extraordinary National Conference of the Kuomintang in March 1938. Together with two other KMT factions, the Renaissance Society was merged into a new entity: the Three People's Principles Youth Corps (San-min chu-i ch'ing-nien t'uan).

REFERENCES: Maria Hsia Chang, *The Chinese Blue Shirt Society: Fascism and Developmental Nationalism* (Berkeley, Calif., 1985); Maria Hsia Chang, " 'Fascism' and Modern China," *The China Quarterly* 79 (September 1979): 553–567; Teng Wen-i, *Mao-hsien fan-nan chi* (A record of risky adventures and hardships), vols. 1, 2 (Taipei, 1973).

MARIA HSIA CHANG

BLYUKHER (BLUECHER OR GALEN), VASILY KONSTANTINOVICH
(1892–1938): Chief Soviet military adviser to the Nationalists in Canton (1924–1927), known to the Chinese as Galen.

General Blyukher, son of a peasant family, was a revolutionary of outstanding military capabilities. He joined the Bolsheviks in 1916 and played an important role in organizing the Red Army in Petrograd in 1918. For his services during the civil war, he was four times awarded the Order of the Red Banner, the highest Soviet military decoration. In May 1921 he was appointed the Soviet Far Eastern Republic's minister of war.

In October 1924 Blyukher arrived in Canton to succeed General P. A. Pavlov as chief military adviser at Whampoa Military Academy,* at a time when Michael Borodin* was Stalin's man in China to assist the Nationalist revolution. Blyukher immediately began to direct the Whampoa troops, seeking to consolidate Kwangtung under the KMT which had formed a United Front with the Chinese Communist party.* He planned to move against the local militarist, Ch'en Chiung-ming, in what came to be known as the first Eastern Expedition. A precise and methodical man, Blyukher drew up detailed plans for the campaign. Although the Whampoa troops were small in size and inexperienced, they were highly motivated and of a much better quality than the enemy forces. In February 1925 two regiments of these troops fought the enemy under the most forbidding conditions. With the aid of the Soviet advisers, they routed Ch'en's forces which were many times their size, an accomplishment that confirmed Blyukher's faith in what a few well-disciplined and nationalistic troops could achieve in China. In his view, not only could Canton be held, but the whole of Kwangtung could be consolidated as well.

In June 1925 the Whampoa forces, executing another strategy developed by Blyukher, ousted the unreliable "guest troops" of Yang Hsi-min and Liu Chen-huan from Canton. Afterward, Blyukher returned to the Soviet Union for reasons of health, not being able to take part in the second Eastern Expedition that succeeded in dislodging Ch'en Chiung-ming's forces from Huichou in October and from Swatow in November. Chief-of-Staff Viktor P. Rogachev then acted as top military adviser until General N. V. "Kisanka" (Kuibyshev) arrived on November 1 as chief of the Soviet military mission. Blyukher returned to Canton in May 1926 at Chiang Kai-shek's* request. (Two months earlier, "Kisanka" and other Soviet military advisers had been sent home following the March 20 coup in Canton.) Chiang considered Blyukher's military experience vital to the success of the Northern Expedition,* and consulted with him frequently on matters of strategy and tactics.

As early as March 1925 Blyukher had discussed his plan for the Northern Expedition with Chiang, and in September, while on his way back to the Soviet Union, he developed it on paper. In his plan he called for part of the National Revolutionary Army (NRA) to remain behind, making a single thrust through Hunan toward Hankow, with forces deployed to protect Kwangtung from Fukien on the east, and other forces to protect the expedition's right flank from attack by Sun Ch'uan-fang in Kiangsi. Owing to the difficulty of coordination, the expedition was to begin only when all troops were in position. Chiang did not wholly agree with this strategy, for he envisaged a two-pronged attack that would assault the forces of Sun Ch'uan-fang and Wu P'ei-fu* at the same time. It took Blyukher some time to convince him that the NRA was not strong enough to fight both warlords simultaneously and that all efforts should be directed against Wu first. On June 23, shortly before the launching of the campaign, Chiang adopted Blyukher's proposal, but only for the time being.

While parts of the NRA, under General T'ang Sheng-chih, the Hunanese militarist recently converted to the KMT, drove toward Wuhan, Chiang turned his other forces toward the coast and into Kiangsi. When the eastern column of the NRA reached Nanchang in August, it met strong resistance. Lacking adequate weapons, reserves, and planning, Chiang was repeatedly repulsed with heavy losses. Although Blyukher disapproved of Chiang's course, he sought help from the forces that had taken Wuhan. With their assistance, some new equipment, and a few Soviet planes, Nanchang was captured in November.

Blyukher accompanied Chiang to Wuhan from Nanchang in January 1927. Returning to Nanchang in the following month, Blyukher was put to work on plans to capture Nanking and Shanghai. But when Chiang went to the battlefield on the evening of March 15, Blyukher did not go with him. The day before, Blyukher had left for Wuhan, angry that Chiang did not act on his plan which envisaged coordinated attacks on Shanghai from both outside (by the NRA) and inside the city (by local revolutionaries). What Chiang wanted to do was to drive on Shanghai by two routes, one down in the Yangtze and the other toward the northeast through Chekiang. Blyukher opposed this approach for both strategic and political reasons.

Blyukher's strategy was to use the Shanghai revolutionaries who had been awaiting the NRA for months. But by mid-March 1927 it was becoming apparent to him that Chiang had no intention of sharing victory and power in Shanghai with the local workers and Communists. Earlier, Chiang had refused to march on Shanghai on the ground that he was not prepared, even though the revolutionaries inside the city had risen up. Now Chiang was ready, but still he would not join hands with them. Feeling betrayed, Blyukher parted company with Chiang.

Chiang began a purge of the Communists as soon as he captured Shanghai. Then, in the summer of 1927, the Wuhan regime also announced its break with the CCP. Borodin and other Soviet advisers left China on July 27. Blyukher departed later, traveling via Shanghai and Japan. Back home he was made commander of the Soviet Far Eastern Army. He was executed late in the 1930s in a purge of the Red Army.

REFERENCES: O. Edmund Clubb, *China and Russia: The "Great Game"* (New York, 1971); Dan N. Jacobs, *Borodin: Stalin's Man in China* (Cambridge, Mass., 1981); C. Martin Wilbur, *The Nationalist Revolution in China, 1923–1928* (Cambridge, 1983).

EDMUND S. K. FUNG

BORODIN, MICHAEL (alias for Mikhail Markovich Gruzenberg, 1884–1951): Professional Communist revolutionary from Russia of Jewish origin; transcontinental Comintern agent and, as Moscow's man in China between 1923 and 1927, a deep influence on both nationalism and communism in China.

Born a shtetl Jew in imperial Russia's Pale, Borodin at the age of sixteen joined the Bund, or the General Jewish Worker's Union. Founded in 1896, the Bund, with its fluctuations between Jewish national identity and goals in traditional Marxist socialism, attracted numerous adventurous Jewish youth. By 1903, when Lenin returned from Siberian exile and attacked the Bund for its ineffectiveness, Borodin, now noted as a determined and skillful revolutionary activist, left the Bund to join Lenin's Bolsheviks. With his skills in organizing and smuggling, Borodin became increasingly useful to Lenin.

At first active in the Riga area for the 1905 revolution, Borodin went into foreign exile, first in England and then in America by 1907, all within a six-month period of revolution, going underground, imprisonment, and deportation by two countries!

In America Borodin worked summers in a factory, attended night school, published *The American Worker*, ran a school in Chicago, joined the American

Socialist party, and conducted revolutionary activities throughout this period. After the formation of the Comintern,* he was sent as agent to various countries, notably Mexico and England. In August 1922 he was arrested and jailed for six months in Glasgow. A shipment of precious stones, intended for Comintern activities and entrusted to him, was lost; Borodin was implicated throughout his travels until fellow-Comintern agent M. N. Roy* testified to clear him. With friend Leo Karakhan's intercession, Borodin's next sphere was China.

Borodin arrived in Canton on October 6, 1923, with wife Fanya and two sons, Fred and Norman. Although a practiced Comintern agent, Borodin instead came as a representative of the Soviet government to Sun Yat-sen,* who had met Adolf Joffe, a Comintern agent, in 1922 seeking aid in reforming his Nationalist party. The Sun–Joffe agreement provided for the inclusion of Communists as individual members of the Kuomintang. Distrustful of the Communists, Sun nevertheless was impressed by the "Bolshevistic vigor" in the Leninist party. Borodin's arrival resulted as much from Sun's wish for party invigoration as from Moscow's view at the time that the Chinese Revolution was better carried by Sun and cohorts than by the young Chinese Communist party.* Borodin's skill at managing different personalities and ambitions came into full play.

Amidst the stormy politics of Kuomintang reorganization, Borodin not only had to balance the left and right of the party, but also had to ensure the participation of the Chinese Communist party as individuals. Most importantly, he had to handle the strong-willed but at times equivocal Sun Yat-sen. All the while his real mission was, of course, to Bolshevize the KMT in ideology as well. The Manifesto of the First Congress of the reformed KMT was as much a triumph for Sun Yat-sen as it was for Borodin. Borodin managed to steer the KMT from a Western orientation, and, even though he failed to make it Communist, at least he helped strengthen its anti-imperialism.

This First United Front* lasted uneasily until 1927 Borodin participated directly in KMT–CCP relations. He and the Communist members dominated the propaganda division of the Whampoa Military Academy,* effectively extending Communist influence while appropriating the KMT left. Eugene Chen and Liao Chung-k'ai, KMT leaders, became close friends, in addition to ensuring KMT cooperation.

Borodin disagreed with Chiang Kai-shek's* plan for the Northern Expedition* to take place in the summer of 1926. Soviet arms support was not yet available, and he feared Chiang would seize the imperialist and warlord arsenals en route. The expedition would divide the KMT and CCP geographically as well, with Chiang in Shanghai and the left in Wuhan. Disaster came in the spring of 1927 when Chiang turned on the Communist worker unions in Shanghai. In April and May, Borodin and the Soviet advisers were burning papers and packing to leave Wuhan.

A motor caravan, organized by Eugene Chen's two sons, Percy and Jack, took Borodin, Anna Louise Strong,* and others across Mongolia to Moscow. Borodin was arrested during the Stalinist purges of 1936–1937 and died in a concentration camp in 1951.

REFERENCES: Dan N. Jacobs, *Borodin, Stalin's Man in China* (Cambridge, Mass., 1981); Vincent Sheean, *Personal History* (New York, 1934); Percey Chen, *China Called Me* (Boston, 1979); Chiang Yung-ching, *Pao Luo-t'ing yu Wuhan cheng-ch'uan* (Borodin and the Wuhan regime) (Taipei, 1963).

D.W.Y. KWOK

BOXER UPRISING (1900): Antiforeign and anti-Christian revolt.

On June 21, 1900, the Manchu court, under the leadership of Dowager Empress Tz'u-hsi,* declared war on all the foreign powers that had representatives in Peking. This rather foolhardy act had been set in motion by an antiforeign group that claimed both spirit-possession and physical invulnerability. Some ten days before the declaration of war, this assemblage, which came to be known in the West as the Boxers, had swarmed into the capital and burned churches and foreign residences, killed Chinese Christian converts, and exhumed the graves of foreign missionaries. They then began what was to be a fifty-five day siege of foreign legations in Peking. The end of this uprising was both swift and tragic. By the middle of August 1900, armies from seven foreign powers (German forces arrived later) had entered the capital and had begun wreaking a terrible revenge. In addition to killing many of the rebels, scores of innocent Chinese, who were either mistaken for Boxers or who just happened to be in the wrong place at the wrong time, were slaughtered. The foreign troops also engaged in a concomitant orgy of looting, rape, and arson. These punitive acts, and the subsequent Boxer Protocol, provided additional fuel for the revolutionary spirit that was festering in China.

Geographically, the Boxers' place of origin was the northwestern part of Shantung Province—an area characterized by flat land, cereal agriculture, dense population, and impoverished villages. The region was also prone to both human and natural disasters. In addition to the physical environment, the popular culture of the area contributed to the Boxer Uprising. The people of the northwest Shantung had a long tradition of heterodox religious sects, martial arts, and dramatic local opera. The heterodox practices included charms, spells, invulnerability, and spirit possession. Martial practices included boxing and swordsmanship. Most of the village operas focused on deities who were drawn from novels such as the *Romance of the Three Kingdoms*, *Journey to the West*, and *The Enfeoffment of the Gods*. When these three activities came together, the Boxers had their primary inspiration.

The rebellious energies of the Boxers were directed not at the Ch'ing dynasty,* but rather at the growing foreign threat and Christian aggressiveness. German Catholic missionaries were a particular target. Many of these individuals had been especially offensive in their intervention in secular disputes. There was also a link between German missionary activity and German imperialism in Shantung. In 1897 Germany had seized Chiao-chow Bay, on whose southeastern shore it proceeded to build the port city of Tsingtao. The German commercial and military presence that followed tended to further embolden the missionaries, who then became even more enmeshed in China's domestic politics.

Partially in response to the German incursion, and partially in reaction to the socioeconomic conditions in the region, especially the massive floods of 1898, the Society of Righteous and Harmonious Fists (I-ho ch'üan) or Boxers rose in northwest Shantung in the spring of 1898. Exactly who was responsible for the first Boxer group is unknown, but once begun the movement spread rapidly. Recruitment was relatively simple. Young men from one village would hear of the practice nearby and go to observe. They witnessed a simple ceremony that induced a trance, causing the youthful initiates to believe that they were possessed by a folk deity. This "Spirit Boxer" ritual then led to a conviction of invulnerability. Organizationally, the Boxers were essentially egalitarian. Each village's boxing group would have a leader, known as "Senior Brother-Disciple." Ordinary members knew each other as "Brother-Disciples." However, because the spirit ritual was so easily learned, and all who learned it became equally divinely possessed, all were, in fact, on the same level.

In the summer of 1899 the Boxers began to engage in acts of violence against Catholic missionaries in Shantung. Local government officials tended to look the other way, indicating, in effect, that they considered such action to be the work of ordinary villagers seeking their own way of countering Christian abuses of power. Soon the Boxers came to realize that they also enjoyed support from individuals high in the Ch'ing court, including the empress dowager. In response to this patronage, in early June 1900 Boxers began streaming into the national capital by the thousands. The tragedy that followed has already been noted.

The Boxer Protocol that officially marked the end of the uprising was signed by officials of the Chinese government and the representatives of some eleven foreign powers on September 7, 1901. Included in the document were provisions for the punishment of those considered most responsible for the rebellion; some 67 million pounds in indemnity; the stationing of foreign troops in China; and the suspension of civil service examination in forty-five cities for a period of five years. Military occupation and interruption of the traditional examination system played an extremely significant role in the Chinese Revolution of the twentieth century. The first served as a constant reminder of China's humiliation, and the second caused China's elite to look elsewhere for ways to assist their country in its time of need.

REFERENCES: David D. Buck, ed., "Recent Studies of the Boxer Movement," *Chinese Studies in History* 20 (1987); Joseph W. Esherick, *The Origins of the Boxer Uprising* (Berkeley, Calif., 1987); Liao Yi-chung, Li Te-cheng, and Chang Hsüan-ju, *I-ho ch'üan yün-tung shih* (History of the Boxer Movement) (Peking, 1981); Victor C. Purcell, *The Boxer Uprising* (Cambridge, 1963).

GERALD W. BERKLEY

C

CANTON COMMUNE (1927): A Communist-led urban uprising.

The Canton Commune (December 11–13, 1927) was the last and most spectacularly unsuccessful Communist-led urban uprising following the split between the Nationalists and Communists in the spring and summer of 1927. Thereafter, Communist activities were driven underground in the cities of China and forced into the countryside.

The background of the Canton Commune was the ruthless repression of the Communists, the labor movement, and leftists in general following the split between the Nationalists and Communists, beginning in April 1927. In the aftermath of the rupture, both the Comintern* and the central leadership of the Chinese Communist party,* now headed by Ch'ü Ch'iu-pai,* sought to retain an urban foothold against the superior forces of Chiang Kai-shek's* Nationalist armies and their regional allies. During the summer and early fall, uprisings in Wuhan, Nanchang, and Swatow were quickly suppressed.

In Canton, where the CCP had experienced much success under the First United Front,* the party still had a considerable presence in the fall of 1927. Moreover, disputes among Kwangtung and Kwangsi warlord cliques created an apparent power vacuum in the city. Encouraged by party and Comintern directives as well as by their own inclinations, party leader Chang T'ai-lei and Comintern representative Heinz Neumann planned an uprising to seize the city. A heavily infiltrated military cadet battalion was to be the spearhead, followed by a general mass rising among the laboring classes and ordinary city residents.

The uprising began two days earlier than planned because of fear that the warlord Chang Fa-k'uei might neutralize the cadet battalion. Although the Communists succeeded for a few hours in gaining control of the city and killing anti-Communists, mass support never developed. Two days later the insurrectionists were overwhelmed by Chang Fa-k'uei's forces. Foreign gunboats also shelled the city. Chang's forces and the police were even more violent than the Communists had been, killing thousands in retaliation for the hundreds slain by the rebels. Although many Communist leaders escaped, Chang T'ai-lei was among the dead.

In later years, persistent rumors suggested that the Canton Commune had been instigated by Stalin, whose China policy was under attack, in order to have some good news to report to the Fifteenth Congress of the Communist party of the Soviet Union. It now appears, however, that local leaders took much of the initiative for planning and carrying out the Canton Commune.

REFERENCES: Hsiao Tso-liang, "Chinese Communism and the Canton Soviet of 1927," *China Quarterly*, No. 30 (April-June 1967): 49–78; Harold Isaacs, *The Tragedy of the Chinese Revolution*, 2nd ed. rev. (Stanford, Calif., 1961); Benjamin Schwartz, *Chinese Communism and the Rise of Mao* (Cambridge, Mass., 1980).

LYMAN P. VAN SLYKE

CAPITALIST ROADER (*tsou-tzu-p'ai*): Rhetorical designation for the purge targets of the Great Proletarian Cultural Revolution.

The term *capitalist roader* entered Chinese politics on January 14, 1965, in the text of the Chinese Communist party* Central Committee's (CC's) "Some Current Problems Raised in the Socialist Education Movement in the Rural Areas" (summary minutes of a national work conference called by the CCP CC Politburo), known as the Twenty-three Points: "The crux of the current movement is to purge capitalist roaders in authority within the Party." Some capitalist roaders were said to be common people labeled as landlords, rich peasants, or counterrevolutionaries and other depraved elements, even people who through an oversight had not been identified as such. Others were said to be officials opposing socialism, including ranking officials in central departments.

As the Socialist Education Movement* (1962–1966) escalated into the Cultural Revolution* (1966–1976), the CCP Central Committee's Sixteen-Point Decision (August 1966), which was a blueprint of the Cultural Revolution, stated the "crux" of the new campaign to be "to purge the capitalist roaders in authority within the party." Beginning in the fall of 1966 former CC Vice-Chairman Liu Shao-ch'i* was used to personify the movement as China's number one capitalist roader.

In reality, the concept was an exceedingly primitive political artifice. Neither Liu at the top nor anyone more humbly positioned genuinely understood capitalism or seriously advocated moving China toward capitalism. Rather, the so-called capitalist roader opponents of Mao Tse-tung* were trying to protect party authority against threatening challenges from a charismatic leader pursuing a private agenda.

After the Cultural Revolution, the term disappeared from China's political lexicon.

REFERENCES: Lowell Dittmer, *Liu Shao-ch'i and the Chinese Cultural Revolution: The Politics of Mass Criticism* (Berkeley, Calif., 1974); R. C. Kraus, *Class Conflict in Chinese Socialism* (New York, 1981).

GORDON BENNETT

C.C. CLIQUE: A dominant faction in the KMT government under Chiang Kai-shek led by Ch'en Kuo-fu and Ch'en Li-fu.

Also known as the Organization Clique, the C.C. Clique was one of several factions that helped Chiang Kai-shek* maintain his dominant position in the Kuomintang government after 1927. The clique, which came into existence in June 1927, was led by Ch'en Kuo-fu and Ch'en Li-fu, brothers who had close ties with Chiang before his rise to power. They were nephews of Ch'en Ch'i-mei, a veteran of the revolutionary movement of the 1910s whom Chiang greatly admired. In 1926 Ch'en Kuo-fu became the head of the Kuomintang's Organization Department, which was to be the primary institutional base of the clique. His brother, Li-fu, was appointed director of the department's Investigation Division in 1928 and developed a strong party security apparatus. He then took over as secretary-general of the party's central headquarters in Nanking in 1929. In 1932 he succeeded Kuo-fu as head of the Organization Department and stayed in that post until 1936. These positions controlled by the Ch'en brothers were critical to the operations of the party. The Organization Department established and supervised party branches and organizations, controlled party membership and activity, and selected delegates to party congresses. Its party security apparatus directed an intelligence network that was responsible for internal stability and the prevention of anti-Kuomintang elements, especially Communists, from infiltrating into party organizations.

The clique maintained that only Sun Yat-sen's* Three People's Principles* was the fundamental basis of the Nationalist Revolution and the Kuomintang was the only party qualified and capable of leading the country. Chiang Kai-shek was the supreme leader of the revolution, the party, and the government, and there should be centralization of power. They were staunch anti-Communists and favored the revival of traditional moral values and ideals.

To broaden its base and support, the clique successfully extended its influence into the administrative machinery and various cultural and educational institutions in the 1930s. In 1933 Ch'en Kuo-fu became the governor of Kiangsu, and clique members gradually controlled the party organizational apparatus and provincial and county governments. They were also able to exert considerable influence in Chekiang and Anhwei and in the municipal government of Shanghai. The Ch'en brothers' control of the recruitment and training of new cadres was accomplished through their influence in the Central Political Academy, which was created from the former Central Party Academy in 1929. Ch'en Kuo-fu's power expanded further during the war years when in 1938 he became the head of the Third Department in Chiang Kai-shek's own personal staff (*shih ts'ung shih*). The department conducted all the government's top-level personnel management: it oversaw all personnel appointments, promotions, and punishments. During and after the war, the Ch'en brothers maintained their control over the security apparatus, organizing the Central Statistical Bureau which acted as a secret service to suppress opposition to Chiang.

The clique wielded considerable financial power through its domination of

Kiangsu's provincial Farmers Bank and the National Farmers Bank of China. In an attempt to influence the media, C.C. Clique members published a newspaper and a monthly journal and founded a publishing company. Members of the clique included mainly intellectuals, bureaucrats, politicians, and military officers. Although the reported membership of the group was only about 10,000, its importance was reflected in the number of clique members who were delegates to the Party Congress or elected to the Central Executive Committee. For instance, in 1931, 15 percent of the seventy-two newly elected members of the Central Executive Committee were members of the C.C. Clique.

The conservatism of its leaders, its ideological and policy positions, and the nature of its membership all combined to shape the C.C. Clique into a traditionalist right-wing power group. While it provided Chiang Kai-shek with a vehicle to dominate the party and government machinery, it also helped to push the Kuomintang farther and farther toward the path to becoming a conservative and ultranationalistic party preoccupied with its own political survival.

REFERENCES: Hung-mao Tien, *Government and Politics in Kuomintang China, 1927–1937* (Stanford, Calif., 1972); "Ch'en Kuo-fu," in *Chung-hua min-kuo ming-jen ch'uan* (Eminent figures in the Republic of China), vol. 1 (Taipei, 1984): 456–474.

KA-CHE YIP

CHANG CH'UN-CH'IAO (1917–   ): Member of the Standing Committee of the CCP Politburo; vice-premier of the State Council, PRC; one of the Gang of Four and purged in October 1976.

A native of Chü-yeh County, Shantung Province, Chang Ch'un-ch'iao began a lifelong career in political journalism and propaganda by publishing patriotic essays in the *Shantung Nationalist Daily News* in 1932. Between 1935 and 1937 he was active in leftist literary circles in Shanghai, where he joined the Chinese Communist party* in April 1936. After the outbreak of the Sino-Japanese War,* he moved to Yenan and the Communist-controlled areas of China, where he worked as a party propagandist throughout most of the 1940s.

By 1950 Chang had returned to Shanghai, and by 1954 he had become director of the organ of the Shanghai CCP Committee, the *Liberation Daily*. In 1958 he gained national fame as an ideological apologist of the Great Leap Forward.* In October 1958, at the direct suggestion of Mao Tse-tung,* the *People's Daily* reprinted his article "Eradicate the Ideology of Bourgeois Right" in which he advocated the wholesale abolition of so-called material incentives (i.e., various forms of remuneration according to labor), and the establishment of a quasi-military egalitarian supply system (i.e., a form of remuneration according to "need") as the means whereby China would be able to achieve the rapid transition from socialism to communism. In April 1959 he was elected to the Standing Committee of the Shanghai CCP Committee.

In the early 1960s, Chang established a close working relationship with Mao's wife Chiang Ch'ing,* whose attempts to reform the traditional Peking opera he actively backed as newly appointed director of the Shanghai CCP Propaganda

Department. Together with Yao Wen-yüan,* he had by 1965 become part of a small group of confidants on whom Mao relied to launch the Cultural Revolution* (1966–1976). In May 1966, he was appointed vice-director of the Cultural Revolution Small Group under the CCP Politburo and began to participate actively in high-level national politics.

In February 1967 Chang became chairman of the Shanghai Revolutionary Committee, a new body created to supersede the old municipal Party Committee. At the National Day celebrations in Peking in 1968, he ranked number seven among the party and government leaders present. In April 1969 the ninth CCP Central Committee elected him to its Politburo. In the early 1970s, while becoming more and more preoccupied with national affairs, he succeeded in retaining considerable control over Shanghai, turning the city into something of a private power base for himself, Chiang Ch'ing, Yao Wen-yüan, and Wang Hung-wen* (see Gang of Four*). In August 1973, at the First Plenum of the Tenth CCP Central Committee, he was made a member of the Standing Committee of the CCP Politburo.

In January 1975 Chang was appointed director of the People's Liberation Army* General Political Department and second vice-premier of the State Council. In this latter capacity he delivered a report on the revision of the constitution of the People's Republic of China* to the First Session of the Fourth People's Congress. In April 1975 he published "On Exercising All-Round Dictatorship Over the Bourgeoisie," in which he presented an authoritative Maoist theoretical justification for the praxis of the Cultural Revolution, as well as reiterated some of his own ideas from the time of the Great Leap Forward about the need to eradicate the "bourgeois right."

On October 6, 1976, four weeks after the death of Mao Tse-tung, Chang was arrested in what was essentially a palace coup by a coalition of senior government and military leaders opposed to the Cultural Revolution. Together with Chiang Ch'ing, Yao Wen-yüan, and Wang Hung-wen, he was accused of having attempted to use the Cultural Revolution to undermine the dictatorship of the proletariat in order ultimately to be able to restore capitalism in China. On January 23, 1981, at a major show trial, he was branded a counterrevolutionary and sentenced to death with a two-year reprieve (a punishment subsequently commuted to life imprisonment).

REFERENCE: Yeh Yung-lie, *Chang Ch'un-ch'iao fu ch'en shih* (History of Chang Ch'un-ch'iao's Rise and Fall) (Ch'ang-ch'un, 1988).

MICHAEL L. SCHOENHALS

CHANG CHÜN-MAI (Chang Chia-sen, in the West known as Carsun Chang, January 18, 1887–February 23, 1969): Democratic party political leader and philosopher.

Born into a relatively prosperous family in Pao-shan County, Kiangsu Province, in 1887, Chang had an early education that was the then common one of the Confucian classics taught by tutors. In 1901 his education changed to Western style when he and his younger brother, Chia-ao, were enrolled at the Institute of Modern Languages (Kuang fang-yen-kuan) in Shanghai. Graduating in 1902, he later attended various other Western-style schools in Shanghai and Nanking, and taught English at schools in Hunan. Like most students of the time, he read and was deeply influenced by the writing of Liang Ch'i-ch'ao.*

In 1906 Chang studied law and economics at Waseda University in Tokyo on a Chinese government scholarship. Liang Ch'i-ch'ao's own base of operations was also in Tokyo during this time; Chang initiated contact with Liang and became a strong supporter of his constitutional government blueprint for China as well as a lifelong disciple. Until the end of his life, Chang would maintain a fundamentally similar political position that envisaged a constitutional government as the keystone of a modern China.

When Chang returned to China in 1910, he was awarded a government civil service degree, and he became editor of the newspaper *Tientsin-Peking Shih-pao*. After the Wuhan Uprising at the end of 1911, Chang joined with Liang Ch'i-chao in publishing and writing for the journal *Yung-yen* (Justice). In January 1912 Chang joined with T'ang Hua-lung and others to establish the Group for Republican Construction (Kung-he chien-she t'ao-lun-hui) in Shanghai. In October of the same year, Chang and his brother Chang Chia-ao helped combine their separate political organizations—the Kung-ho chien-she t'ao-lun-hui and the Kuo-min hsieh-chin-hui—into a Democratic party (Min-chu-tang). The spiritual leader of the party was Liang Ch'i-ch'ao. The next month, as representative of this party, Chang went to Japan to bring Liang Ch'i-ch'ao back to China to head the party in person.

In early 1913 Chang left political life to further his studies in Europe, arriving in Germany in May. Until 1915 he studied political science and economics at the University of Berlin. During this sojourn he acquired both a doctorate in political science and the Western name "Carsun." In October 1915 he moved to London, where he wrote on European affairs for Chinese publications. Upon returning to China in April 1916, he immediately became involved with the political activities of Liang Ch'i-ch'ao's party and consequently obtained government posts. In 1918, as the complex Peking political situation became further involuted, Chang resigned his official post and began teaching at Peking University.

In December of that year, Chang left again for Europe as part of a semiofficial advisory delegation to the Versailles Peace Conference. Liang Ch'i-ch'ao led the group, which also included Ting Wen-chiang* and Chiang Fang-chen. Chang remained in Europe after the delegation returned to China, first studying philosophy under Rudolf Euken in Germany. He also had contact with the French Vitalist philosopher Henri Bergson and became familiar with European politics and systems of government while writing journalistic reports on them. On behalf of Liang Ch'i-ch'ao, Chang arranged for the German biologist-philosopher Hans Dreisch to lecture in China.

When Chang arrived back in Shanghai in January 1922, he accompanied

Dreisch as interpreter and again involved himself with Liang Ch'i-ch'ao's political activities. In February 1923 Chang himself lectured at Tsinghua University* on Philosophy of Life (*jen-sheng-kuan*) and set off the decade's most contentious public intellectual debate, later known as the Science and Metaphysics controversy. The major point of the lecture was that human life in its spiritual and moral dimensions cannot be guided by scientific laws of the material world, but instead required nonscientific intuition and recognition of free will. Geologist Ting Wen-chiang interpreted this as an assault on science and responded with an essay in which he sought to defend the value of science for human life and in education. Various prominent intellectuals joined in the debate in the next months.

At the end of 1923 Chang helped found a National Institute of Self-Government in Shanghai. It opened in 1924 with Chang as its president; he later changed the school's name to the National Institute of Political Science (Kuo-li cheng-chih ta-hsüeh). Consistently a champion for parliamentary democracy, Chang voiced opposition to the Nationalist party's concept of tutelage. In March 1927 the Nationalist Northern Expedition* reached Shanghai and immediately closed Chang's school. He persisted in publicly opposing the "political tutelage" of the Nanking government, and eventually he was placed under house arrest (the first of three times during his life that he was detained by the Nationalists). Chang left China in 1927. Returning in 1931, he resumed his political activities to promote democracy and constitutionalism.

In 1934 Chang formally announced the establishment of a National Socialist party (Kuo-chia she-hui-tang—which, unfortunately, was similar to the name of Adolf Hitler's party in Germany). As was the practice of any opposition party, it went in search of support among the independent power-holders who were opposed to Chiang Kai-shek's* Nanking government* (such as Yen Hsi-shan* in Shansi Province). That same year Chang moved to Canton under the patronage of yet another opponent of Chiang Kai-shek, Ch'en Chi-t'ang,* and established an academic base in another school, Hsüeh-hai shu-t'ang. With Ch'en Chi-t'ang's downfall, the school was abolished and Chang took refuge in Shanghai, where in 1936 he held the second national congress of his party. He was again elected general secretary.

In a continuation of the metahistorical cultural comparisons that Chinese intellectuals had begun during the May Fourth* era, Chang wrote *China's Culture Tomorrow* (Ming-jih chih Chung-kuo wen-hua). Like Liang Shu-ming's* more systematic 1921 work, *Tung Hsi wen-hua chi ch'i che-hsüeh* (Eastern and Western cultures and their philosophies), Chang's compared European, Indian, and Chinese cultures and advocated that China imitate or absorb modern Europe's scientific spirit and apply it to China's traditional culture.

As with all political independents and dissidents, the Japanese invasion in 1937 forced Chang and his party into cooperation with the Nationalist government. During this period Chang set forth his party's essential blueprint for China. It called for a form of state socialism, with state control of heavy industries, but strongly emphasized the role of the parliamentary system and constitutional guarantees of political freedoms.

In November 1939 in Chungking, Chang and five others joined Liang Shu-ming's initiative founding the Association of Comrades for Unity and Construction (T'ung-i chien-kuo t'ung-chih-hui). In 1944 this organization became the Democratic League (Min-chu t'ung-meng). Throughout its existence, the group attempted to maintain a liberal political middle ground between the Nationalists and the Communists and to mediate between the two major parties.

In the spring of 1945, the Chinese National government chose Chang as the Democratic League's representative at the founding meeting of the United Nations. During the meeting, Chang arranged with the leader of the Democratic Constitutional party to merge with his own party to form a new Democratic Socialist party.

As part of his politico-military maneuvering during the ensuing Nationalist-Communist civil war, on October 11, 1946, Chiang Kai-shek suddenly announced the convening of the long-awaited National Assembly for November 12. This left the Democratic League split over the question of boycott or participation. The league decided that participation in the assembly would compromise its neutral political position and so boycotted it. Chang, together with some members of his party, bolted the league and opted for participation in the assembly. Early in the next year, Chang's party disintegrated into factions, and the Democratic Constitutional party reconstituted itself as an independent organization.

At the end of April 1949, with the Chinese Communist armies victorious everywhere and the Nationalist cause lost, Chang left China, never to return. He spent most of the remainder of his life in the United States, writing several books on neo-Confucianism and a self-serving political autobiography, *Third Force in China* (1952). During the same two decades, he lectured extensively around the world on neo-Confucianism and democracy. He died in San Francisco in 1969.

REFERENCES: Carsun Chang, *The Third Force in China* (New York, 1952); Hsia K'ang-nung, *Lun Hu Shih yü Chang Chün-mai* (On Hu Shih and Chang Chün-mai) (Shanghai, 1948); Roger Baily Jeans, Jr., "Syncretism in Defense of Confucianism: An Intellectual and Political Biography of the Early Years of Chang Chün-mai, 1887–1923" (unpublished Ph.D. dissertation, George Washington University, 1974).

                                                                 GUY S. ALITTO

CHANG HSÜEH-LIANG (1901–   ): Warlord and leader of the Manchurian Army.

Chang Hsüeh-liang (alias Chang Han-ch'ing), popularly known as the Young Marshal, was born in Taishan County, Liaoning, on June 4, 1901, at a time when banditry was widespread in the northeast or Manchuria in the wake of the Boxer uprising.* His father Chang Tso-lin, leading some 300 bandits, received amnesty from the Ch'ing government* and was appointed a battalion commander. His mother Chao Shih was a daughter of a local landlord and died when the young Chang was only eleven years old. The elderly Chang, who had already achieved supremacy in the northeast, wanted Hsüeh-liang, the oldest of his fourteen children, to have all the benefits bestowed on a literate man and, therefore, put him into the care of several erudite Confucian scholars. However, the young Chang was not interested in traditional Chinese learning; instead, he was fond of Western sports and diversions such as driving an automobile and flying an airplane, and the Western way of life generally, and made some acquaintances with Western youths in Shenyang. He also began to sense how vulnerable the northeast was in the face of two imperialist neighbors—so much so that early in life he developed a strong sense of patriotism that characterized much of his life. Then he toyed with the idea of going to America to study medicine. To the surprise of his father, he later accepted the suggestion from his family that he enter the first class of the Military Institute with a major in artillery in 1919. For his intellect and diligence, he soon distinguished himself as the best student in his class and cemented a close friendship with his teacher Kuo Sung-ling who had exerted great influence on him.

After graduation from the Military Institute, at the age of twenty, Chang was made commander of his father's guards brigade. From that time onward, he with the help of Kuo Sung-ling had remarkable success in training troops and showed much prowess on the battlefield, particularly in the two wars between Chang Tso-lin and Wu P'ei-fu,* a northern warlord who was then dominating the Peking government. Like his father, Chang had charisma and was able to inspire the devotion of his subordinates, as well as the finesse to judge and control them (probably except for Kuo Sung-ling who staged a revolt against Chang Tso-lin in late 1925, that ended in failure). With most of the Northeastern Army under his command, Chang began to be called the Young Marshal, as his father was called the Old Marshal. With much reluctance, the Young Marshal fought the National Revolutionary Army during the Northern Expedition* launched by Chiang Kai-shek* in July 1926. He was not only tired of civil war but even grew more democratic in dealing with his subordinates.

When his father was assassinated by the Japanese in June 1928, the Young Marshal seemed to be well prepared to succeed him. But his succession to his father was not without challenge. At one stroke, he eliminated his enemies, Yang Yü-ting and Chang Yin-huai, thereby making himself undisputable leader in the northeast. Rejecting both inducement and pressure from Japan, he gave up his semi-independent status for the unification of China by joining the Nanking government.* On the other hand, he devoted himself to reconstructing the northeast: building railways, developing industries, and establishing private and public schools, especially the founding of the Northeastern University. He also drastically built up his air force and navy. All this Japan had viewed with alarm that apparently hastened its aggression against the northeast by launching the "September 18" incident in 1931, which resulted in the seizure of the whole northeastern provinces.

Once the Young Marshal joined hands with Chiang Kai-shek in 1929, he was increasingly involved in national affairs. In 1930, when Feng Yü-hsiang* joined by Yen Hsi-sheng* and Wang Ching-wei* fought against Chiang in a great civil war, it was the arbitration of the Young Marshal that saved Chiang from defeat. The next year, to answer Chiang's call for the suppression of Shih Yu-shan's revolt, he dispatched his crack troops to north China with his headquarters set up at Peking. The Japanese took this occasion to seize the northeast. For the loss of the northeast, the Young Marshal earned the ignominious title of non-resistant general. Unquestionably, it was based on Chiang's order and policy that the Young Marshal decided not to resist the Japanese. Still he cannot be exonerated for the wrong decision that caused the loss of the northeast to Japan. Following the loss of Jehol in early 1933, he resigned. Having cured his narcotic habit, he together with his Australian adviser William Donald went abroad on a European tour. In Europe, he was much impressed by the revival of Germany and Italy under fascism. Upon learning of the Fukien revolt in December 1933, he sailed for Shanghai, where he arrived in early January 1934.

Refreshed by his European tour, the Young Marshal regained his health and was filled with new ideas, particularly fascism. Once again he became Chiang's most favored and valuable partner, as his Northeastern Army would be used to suppress the Communists while his fascist ideology would bolster Chiang's aspiration to dictatorship. The Young Marshal reluctantly assumed responsibility for suppressing the Red Army and found Chiang's policy of ''internal pacification before resistance against external aggression'' contradictory to the best interest of the nation, whose enemy was none other than the Japanese. After suffering heavy losses of his army in fighting the Communist army, the Young Marshal began to seek new solutions to the national problem, with the result that he and the Chinese Communists formed an anti-Japanese united front, which was soon joined by General Yang Hu-cheng and his Northwestern Army by early 1936. Failing to persuade Chiang to change his policy by suspending the civil war and uniting the nation to fight Japan, the Young Marshal and General Yang staged the ''remonstration with military force'' (ping-chien) to put Chiang under house arrest in Sian on December 12, 1936. Two weeks later, having given verbal promise, Chiang was set free and returned to Nanking accompanied by the Young Marshal, who turned out to be a captive of Chiang. After over fifty years, the Young Marshal still lives in Taiwan under close watch by the government.

REFERENCES: Fu Hung-ling, Chang Hsüeh-liang ti cheng-chih sheng-ya (Political life of Chang Hsüeh-liang), trans. Wang Hai-chen et al. (Shenyang, 1988); Committee for Liaoning Wen-shih Tzu-liao, ed., Tsai tung Chang Hsüeh-liang hsiang-ch'u ti jih-tzu li (The days being together with Chang Hsüeh-liang) (Shenyang, 1986).

TIEN-WEI WU

CHANG HSÜN (1854–1923): Member of the Peiyang Clique who in a farcical attempt in 1917 failed to restore the Ch'ing dynasty to power in Peking.

During the 1880s and 1890s Chang Hsün had risen from a foot soldier to importance as a commander in Li Hung-chang's* Huai Army. In 1903 his old-style units were retrained, re-equipped with modern arms, and incorporated as the Front Division in the New Army,* which was one of six divisions comprising Yüan Shih-k'ai's* Peiyang or Northern Army. Between 1902 and 1903 General Chang Hsün's division acted as personal bodyguards for the Empress Dowager Tz'u-hsi* and afterward did other special duties tied to imperial family members in Manchuria. In the process Chang and his army became as loyal to the dynasty and the imperial family as they were to his new patron and commander, Yüan Shih-k'ai. Thus, in December 1911 Chang Hsün's division defended the dynasty against republican forces around Nanking. (Chang's division was stationed at the time near Hsuchow.) A month later, at Yüan Shih-k'ai's insistence, Chang became a reluctant petitioner in the process, forcing the dynasty's final abdication in March 1912. But Chang's troops never cut their queues and remained loyal to the dynasty. His division continued to be stationed at Hsuchow in northern Kiangsu Province, which became Chang's headquarters as inspector-general of the Yangtze Valley with sweeping powers. With the death of Yüan Shih-k'ai in June 1916, General Chang convened a series of conferences at Hsuchow attended by Peiyang Clique* commanders to discuss the political situation and how to maintain unity among clique members. By the end of the year, however, serious splits developed anyway, particularly between Premier Tuan Ch'i-jui and President Feng Kuo-chang. Eventually, a desperate Chang acted alone. In June 1917 he led his troops north from Anhui and staged a coup d'etat in Peking which restored the Ch'ing dynasty* and its last emperor, the teenager, P'u-i,* to power. Chang's restoration attempt lasted five days after a minimum of fighting demonstrated the hopelessness of his cause. Chang's pig-tailed troops beat a rapid retreat, cutting their queues and deserting their commander in comic opera fashion as described by foreign correspondents at the time. The episode ended Chang Hsün's career as a powerful militarist and Ch'ing loyalist. It also set off even fiercer competition among other militarists for national hegemony. The result was a miserable period of warlord rivalry which lasted at least until the completion of Chiang Kai-shek's Northern Expedition* in 1928. In the meantime, in 1923, Chang Hsün died a disgraced and forgotten figure, but remembered today for the restoration attempt of 1917.

STEPHEN R. MACKINNON

CHANG KUO-T'AO (1897–1979): Early leader of the Chinese Communist Movement.

A product of the May Fourth Movement,* Chang was one of the founders of the Chinese Communist party.* Born into a landed Hakka family on Kiangsi's border with Hunan, he received both classical and Western education by the time he left for Shanghai to prepare for engineering school. Chang experienced the urban culture of youthful radicals in China's caldron of change during the overthrow of the Ch'ing dynasty.* Entering Peking University in 1916, he enjoyed the innovative presidency of Ts'ai Yüan-p'ei,* who promoted freedom of inquiry and experimentation as being indispensable to China's modernization. Exposed to the New Culture of the trail-blazing faculty, Chang, as an elected student leader as well as in formal studies, developed great respect for both science and especially democracy. Teacher Ch'en Tu-hsiu's* scientific approach to strengthening China politically led Chang to Marxist readings under the guidance of librarian Li Ta-chao.* The pragmatism of philosopher Hu Shih prompted Chang to seek practical learning that could be taken to the masses to help reform China. His colleagues also focused Chang's attention on China's weakness against imperialism—especially that of Japan during World War I.

By the time of the May Fourth 1919 student demonstrations, Chang was educating the city illiterates and working in student government. His new sense of patriotic duty led him into the nationwide movement to resist Japan's takeover of former German holdings in Shantung. Lacking leverage against the warlords of North China, Chang and many fellow intellectuals were excited by the ideals of a socialist society and mobilization of revolutionary masses. However, he never lost his respect for intellectual freedom and the democratic process in problem solving. Elected to represent his university in a new Federation of Peking Students, he praised its parliament as a model for free discussions, but local warlords forced him to flee to Shanghai and later imprisoned him in Peking. The rapid changes taking place in revolutionary Russia impressed Chang, as did his teachers, Ch'en Tu-hsiu and Li Ta-ch'ao, who became Marxists in 1920. He was also struck by the sincerity of other Chinese activists such as Sun Yat-sen* and Wang Ching-wei.* Deciding that communism was the approach with the greatest impact on the needy in a backward society, Chang enthusiastically participated in the 1921 founding of the CCP in Shanghai in response to encouragement from the Communist International (Comintern).*

Elected to the initial Central Committee of the CCP, Chang represented the party at Comintern meetings in the Soviet Union where he was the only Central Committee (CC) member to interview Lenin. As a founder, Chang had approved the CCP constitution that required democratic discussion as well as minority subservience to the majority. He argued against the acceptance of a Comintern order to submit to the KMT party in what started out as an anti-imperialist revolutionary alliance in 1922 and ended with the absorption of the CCP into the KMT in the United Front of the National Revolution, which was fraught with potential for rivalry.

Chang worked on union organization matters within the National Revolution, from Shanghai to Hankow to Peking. He witnessed the bloody suppression of his railroad unions by Wu P'ei-fu* in 1923, and he enjoyed the expansion of the labor organization after the explosively anti-imperialistic May Thirtieth* episode against British and Japanese mills in Shanghai and Canton in 1925. During the KMT's Northern Expedition* in 1926, Chang's CCP cadre was successful in recruiting workers for their unions as well as members for the CCP in territories captured by the National Revolutionary Army from the northern warlords. Chang blamed the interference of Stalin and Comintern agents such as Michael Borodin* and M. N. Roy* in China's National Revolution for the bloody breakup of the CCP–KMT partnership in 1927, which also ended his hopes for a multiple-party system for China.

Forced into rural China after 1927 as rebels, Chang and the CCP leaders were ordered by the Comintern to set up soviet areas where guerrilla defense operations were possible. Chang directed enclaves in Hupeh, Szechwan, and Sikang among the Tibetans and other non-Chinese minorities. Never having embraced the idea of running soviets like independent "warlords," Chang became critical of what he saw as the increasingly autocratic style of Mao Tse-tung,* who had risen to top leadership status and resented Chang's independence. Chang felt that Mao was more concerned with his own power than with either the principles of the CCP or the national good during the Long March* to evade KMT suppression and then at Yenan. Anticipating his liquidation, Chang withdrew from the CCP in 1938 and later wrote a two-volume story of his experiences in the CCP, which reveals his nationalism and democratic idealism.

REFERENCES: Chang Kuo-t'ao, *The Rise of the Chinese Communist Party, 1921–1938*, 2 vols. (Lawrence, Kan., 1970–1971); C. Martin Wilbur, *The Nationalistic Revolution in China, 1923–28* (Cambridge, 1983).

DONALD A. JORDAN

CHANG PING-LIN (January 12, 1869–June 14, 1936): Classical scholar and a prominent figure in the anti-Ch'ing revolutionary movement, 1900–1912.

A complex and eclectic thinker, Chang Ping-lin was also a courageous activist and a highly unpredictable maverick whose seemingly contradictory ideas and sometimes impulsive actions earned him a reputation as an eccentric. Nevertheless, his numerous major and lasting contributions to learning are widely recognized, and he is commonly considered one of the leading scholars of his time. Although most commentators assign more weight to Chang's scholarly work than to his political activity, no less a figure than Lu Hsün* once wrote that "his contribution to the history of revolution is greater than to the history of scholarship." Nor was Lu Hsün the only prominent Chinese intellectual who acknowledged having been stirred by Chang's revolutionary work.

Like many others of his generation, Chang Ping-lin reacted strongly to China's defeat by Japan in 1894–1895, but his path to revolution was slow and winding. Chang had an inquiring, independent, and wide-ranging mind, ready to question anything and wedded to no orthodoxy or easily classifiable line of thought. At various times in the 1890s he associated himself with Yen Fu,* K'ang Yu-wei,* Liang Ch'i-ch'ao,* Li Hung-chang,* Chang Chih-tung, and Wang K'ang-nien, and he advanced ideas that drew on varying Chinese and Western sources. He veered this way and that on issues of reform, but despite certain differences with K'ang Yu-wei, Chang joined K'ang's Ch'iang-hsüeh hui* in 1895, praised K'ang's efforts in 1898, and sharply criticized the Empress Dowager Tz'u-hsi. Like K'ang, he fled China after the failure of the Hundred Days Reform,* going first to Taiwan and then to Japan. For a time in 1899 he worked with Liang Ch'i-ch'ao and continued to write in a reformist vein, but within a year he called on Li Hung-chang to "reject the sham court resolutely." Then he cut off his queue and further underlined his commitment to revolution by sending an anti-Manchu declaration to be published in a revolutionary journal.

From 1900 on, Chang threw himself into bold revolutionary writing and other activity. He also continued his classical studies, many of which appeared in the *National Essence Journal* (*Kuo-ts'ui hsüeh-pao*). He continued to draw on an ever-widening spectrum of sources for his political writings, spanning Chinese thought and many Western writers. He criticized traditional Chinese government and had harsh words for many aspects of China's past, but he also expressed reservations about Western democracy and its suitability for China. He wrote on virtually every facet of human existence. In a very short time he established himself as second to none among the intellectual leaders of the revolutionary movement. Many revolutionaries viewed him as their answer to K'ang Yu-wei, the only one of their number able to rival K'ang's scholarly credentials and to challenge his full range of ideas.

Early in 1902 Chang joined forces with Sun Yat-sen.* He also organized a major anti-Ch'ing rally in Tokyo. Soon thereafter he returned to China and was arrested and jailed in the *Su-pao* (a newspaper in Shanghai) case, a curious incident in which Chang displayed a certain urge to martyrdom. Chang wrote a number of revolutionary articles for the newspaper and was therefore arrested. The newspaper was also banned. Escaping a more severe sentence by an odd combination of circumstances, Chang served three years and emerged from prison to a hero's welcome in 1906. He went directly to Tokyo and became editor-in-chief of *People's Report* (*Min-pao*), the T'ung-meng hui's* official journal.

In some sixty-plus articles over the next two years, Chang Ping-lin almost singlehandedly turned the journal from what he regarded as a too narrowly based forum for debating Liang Ch'i-ch'ao to a more broadly conceived campaign for national rejuvenation. For Chang, the revival of China depended first and foremost on preserving and strengthening Chinese cultural identity, which he saw as threatened by both a growing tide of Westernization and the continuing domination of China by alien Manchus. He believed that a redefined and revived Chinese cultural identity was essential as a foundation for a modern Chinese nation.

Chang took upon himself the many-sided task of restoring to the Chinese people their lost confidence and self-respect, while also attacking foreign enemies. He wrote harsh and polemical condemnations of the Manchus, but he also wrote voluminously and in a more academic vein on Chinese history, philosophy, philology, and politics, attempting to work out a synthesis of ideas that might provide a basis for action. He condemned uncritical borrowing of foreign ideas and institutions, but he recognized the need for democratic government and the rule of law. Suspicious of strong government, he devoted years of his life to the problem of reconciling China's need for unity with its diversity, size, and fragmented polity.

In brief, throughout his life Chang Ping-lin dealt with the major issues of his time, both as an intellectual and a political activist. He changed his thinking and his political stands. He went into flights of mysticism and nihilism. He defies classification and has thus been variously interpreted by many different scholars.

He broke with Sun Yat-sen in 1907 and, although able to work with Sun for occasional brief periods in 1912 and 1917–1918, he remained at odds with him until Sun's death. He worked with Yüan Shih-k'ai* but also broke with him and spent three years under house arrest (1913–1916). He dealt with warlords and politicians of all stripes, worked for both a strong central government and a loose confederation of autonomous provinces, detested communism, and objected to the First United Front* but called on Chiang Kai-shek* to end the 1930s civil war in the name of resisting Japan. Through all this, Chang's central concern was to maintain China's integrity and bolster it with a vitally growing and distinctive Chinese cultural tradition. He embodied the modern Chinese search for a strong and progressive China that is also rooted in its own history.

REFERENCES: Hao Chang, *Chinese Intellectuals in Crisis: Search for Order and Meaning (1890–1911)* (Berkeley and Los Angeles, 1987); Michael Gasster, *Chinese Intellectuals and the Revolution of 1911: the Birth of Modern Chinese Radicalism* (Seattle, Wash., and London, 1969); Young-tsu Wong, *Search for Modern Nationalism: Zhang Binglin and Revolutionary China* (Hong Kong, 1989).

MICHAEL GASSTER

CHAO SHIH-YEN (other names: Kuo Fu, Ch'in Sun, Shih Ying, April 13, 1901–July 19, 1927): First secretary of the European branch of the Chinese Communist Youth Corps; a leader of the Shanghai Uprisings (1926–1927); editor, *Cheng-chih sheng-huo*, CCP Central Committee (1927).

During the early development phase of the Chinese Communist party,* Chao Shih-yen was one of the most important organizers on both the theoretical and practical level. Born in Yu-yang, Szechwan, in 1901, to a prosperous family, Chao Shih-yen was the youngest of five sons. During the New Culture Movement (1915–1920), Chao was to show his remarkable organizational proclivities. Attending the high school at Peking Normal University, where he was the representative for the May Fourth* Demonstrations, he also edited three newspapers. At the same time he was one of the youngest members invited to join the Young China Association, and he participated in the Work-Study Mutual-Help Corps. Chao was heavily influenced by his contacts with prominent leaders of the youth movement such as Li Ta-chao,* Tseng Ch'i, and Wang Kuang-ch'i.

In May 1920 Chao Shih-yen left for France under the auspices of the Diligent-Work Frugal-Study Movement. Working in the Creusot–Schneider factory system, Chao became involved with Chinese labor problems and joined a Marxist study group led by Chang Shen-fu. When the Work Study Movement went into decline, the impoverished Work Study participants looked to Chao, among several others for leadership. Throughout 1921 Chao Shih-yen, Li Li-san,* and Wang Jo-fei were to organize around the principles of mutual aid and self-sufficiency. However, after the expulsion of over 100 Chinese students in October 1921, Chao abandoned the Work Study principle and became a committed Communist. He became the key organizer of the Chinese Communist Movement in Europe. By the end of 1922 Chao Shih-yen led the formation of the European branch of the Chinese Communist Youth Corps and the Chinese Communist party. Among the ranks of these organizations, which covered France, Germany, and Belgium, were Chou En-Lai,* Chu Teh,* Li Wei-han, Ch'en Yen-nien, Nieh Jung-chen, Teng Hsiao-p'ing, Li Fu-ch'un, and Tsai Ch'ang.

At the end of March 1923, Chao led a Chinese contingent to Moscow, where he stayed for over a year, returning to China in July 1924. He spent his time in the Soviet Union learning Russian and attending meetings, including the Fifth Conference of the Communist International. Chao, who also knew English and French, was on demand for his translation skills. Upon his return to China, Chao worked under his former mentor, Li Ta-chao, in the Northern CCP Bureau. While in the north, Chao worked on labor organization (concentrating on Tientsin), Mongolian autonomy, translation projects, and editing the CCP theoretical journal, *Cheng-chih sheng-huo* (Political life). During this period Chao married another CCP member, Hsia Chih-hsu, and the couple both worked on the growing CCP mass movements. As an expert in labor agitation, Chao Shih-yen went to Shanghai in 1926, where he was a top coordinator of the three Shanghai Uprisings, which resulted in a workers' victory in March 1927. At the international press conference on March 25, 1927, Chao Shih-yen was one of three people announcing the victory. Within less than a month, the April Coup of Chiang Kai-shek* threw the Shanghai branch of the CCP into disarray. Chao Shih-yen decided to stay in the city, was captured on July 2, 1927, and was executed by decapitation on July 19, 1927.

Chao Shih-yen was one of the most brilliant early CCP leaders. He had sophisticated organizational and theoretical skills, together with a fierce intelligence. In the midst of rhetoric and agitation within CCP ranks about labor organization, Chao provided crucial leadership in genuinely inspiring Chinese workers. His successful organization of workers in Tientsin and Shanghai in the mid–1920s was an accomplishment unparalleled by later organizational attempts in Chinese urban areas. Chao knew the reality of factory labor from firsthand experience, but he could also articulate needs, analyze critically, and motivate by force of his personality, which from all accounts was charismatic. With the loss of Chao Shih-yen, the CCP lost a centrifugal force within the Chinese Revolution.

REFERENCES: *Chao Shih-yen hsuan-chi* (Selected writings of Chao Shih-yen) (Ch'engtu, 1984); P'eng Ch'eng-fu, *Chao Shih-yen* (Chungking, 1983); Tsinghua ta-hsüeh chung-kung tang-shih chiao-yü shih (Tsinghua University Faculty Research Unit on the history of the Communist party), comps., *Fu-fa ch'in-kung chien-hsüeh yün-tung shih-liao* (Documents on the travel to France Diligent-Work Frugal-Study Movement), 3 vols. (Peking: 1979–1980).

MARILYN LEVINE

CHAO TZU-YANG (1919–   ): CCP general secretary; PRC premier.

Chao Tzu-yang was born into a family of landlords and grain merchants in Hua-hsien County, Honan Province, in 1919 and received elementary and secondary education in his home province and the city of Wuhan. Joining the Communist Youth League in 1932, he became a Chinese Communist party* member in 1938. In the early 1940s he served successively as Communist party secretary of the Third Special District in the Hopei–Shantung Border Region and as Communist party secretary of the Lo-yang District in Honan Province.

After the establishment of the People's Republic of China* government in 1949, Chao held a series of posts in the South China Sub-bureau of the Central–South China Bureau of the CCP Central Committee until 1955 when he was elected to the People's Council of Kwangtung Province. Appointed first secretary of the Kwangtung Provincial Communist party in 1965, he was severely denounced as a "counterrevolutionary revisionist" and a "stinking element of the landowning class" during the early years of the Cultural Revolution* (1966–1976). It was not until 1971 that he returned to active service first as Communist party secretary of the Inner Mongolia Autonomous Region and later, concurrently, as chairman of the Revolutionary Committee of Inner Mongolia. Soon afterward he returned to Kwangtung as its Communist party secretary and was promoted to the position of first secretary. Elected to the CCP Central Committee by the Tenth CCP Congress in 1973, he became, in late 1975, the Communist party first secretary and governor of Szechwan, China's most populous province.

Chao's arrival in Szechwan became a turning point in his career. It was his five-year service there that built up his national reputation as a highly successful, pragmatic reformer. While in Szechwan, he increased, through bold and flexible programs, industrial output and raised agricultural production. These results were achieved through such innovative policies as rewarding workers on the basis of work rather than need and providing incentives based on free enterprise and market forces rather than on rigid quotas established by central authorities. In addition, factory managers were given much greater autonomy, and peasants were allowed to benefit from individual initiative. For such achievements as raising Szechwan's industrial output by 81 percent in three years, Chao was made a CCP Politburo member in 1979 and premier in 1980.

After he became premier, Chao, an economic experimenter, went even further by advocating any structure, system, policy, or measure that might stimulate the forces of production. In the early and mid–1980s China, under the leadership of Teng, Chao, and others, propelled itself from the bland egalitarian poverty of Maoism to the newfound consumerism of refrigerators, washing machines, and color television sets. During that period, China achieved some economic prosperity, and the average Chinese income more than doubled.

In sharp contrast to his earlier emphasis on ideological purity, class background, and socialist approaches as a conservative party leader in Kwangtung before 1975, Chao emphasized, after 1975, the need to stimulate the economy through the market mechanism and private initiative, and opening to the West. He even advocated a reduced role for the CCP in the government's day-to-day operations. He stressed that China, far from being well along on the road to socialist paradise, as Mao Tse-tung* had envisioned, was still in the primary stage of socialism, a condition of pronounced underdevelopment, which justified its adoption of capitalist practices.

In 1987, Chao replaced Hu Yao-pang as CCP general secretary and became first vice-chairman of the CCP's Military Commission. The growing student democracy movement in 1989 brought an end to Chao's career. He was dismissed from all his posts for his sympathy for the movement and for his refusal to go along with the hard-line leaders' demand for the military suppression of the pro-democracy drive. He was replaced by Kiang Tse-min as CCP general secretary in June 1989.

REFERENCES: Doak Barnett and Ralph N. Clough, eds., *Modernizing China: Post-Mao Reform and Development* (Boulder, Colo., 1986); Chao Tzu-yang, *China's Economy and Development Principles: A Report* (Peking, 1982); Chao Wei, *Chao Tzu-yang ch'uan* (Biography of Chao Tzu-yang) (Peking, 1989); Peter P. Cheng, *Marxism and Capitalism in the People's Republic of China* (Lanham, Md., 1989); Donald W. Klein and Anne B. Clark, *Biographic Dictionary of Chinese Communism, 1921–1965,* vol. 1 (Cambridge, Mass., 1971): 93–94; David Shambaugh, ed., "Zhao Ziyang's 'Sichuan Experience': Blueprint for a Nation," *Chinese Law and Government,* 15 no. 1 (Spring 1982): 3–126; Winston L. Y. Yang, "Zhao Ziyang," *Encyclopaedia Britannica 1988 Book of the Year* (Chicago, 1988): 86.

WINSTON L.Y. YANG

CH'EN CH'ENG (January 4, 1897–March 5, 1965): Nationalist general and political leader; governor of Taiwan; vice-president of the ROC on Taiwan.

Ch'en Ch'eng was born in the village of Kaoshih in Ch'ingt'ien hsien, Che-kiang Province. He was born the son of Ch'en Hsi-wen, a scholar and village schoolteacher who owned some land but was not considered wealthy. He enrolled in the Eleventh Normal School at Lishui in 1913, graduated in 1917, and entered the Hangchow provincial school of physical education from which he graduated in 1918. He enrolled in the eighth class of the Paoting Military Academy, artillery division, and joined the Kuomintang in 1920. He graduated in 1922 after seeing service in eastern Kwangtung as a member of the Third Regiment of the First (Kwangtung) Division. Ch'en joined the newly formed Whampoa Military Academy* in September 1924 and there formed an enduring relationship with Chiang Kai-shek,* then commandant of the academy. As a political ally and military commander in the many campaigns of the Kuomintang in the 1920s and 1930s, first against warlord armies and then against Communist forces, Ch'en rose to political and military prominence. Eventually, he became Chiang's second in command.

Ch'en was governor of Taiwan in 1949 when the Nationalists withdrew from the mainland. In 1954 he was elected vice-president of the Republic of China (ROC)* and reelected to that post in 1960. He also served as premier and president of the Executive Yuan 1950–1954 and 1958–1963. Ch'en Ch'eng resigned the premiership on December 15, 1963, as Chiang Kai-shek's son Chiang Ching-kuo* built up his own power to become premier in 1972 and president in 1978.

As president of the Executive Yuan, Ch'en worked with provincial governor K. C. Wu to execute a major land reform in Taiwan, a program often considered a model for other countries in Asia and elsewhere. His book *Land Reform in Taiwan* recorded that accomplishment as implemented by legislation in 1953.

Ch'en Ch'eng served in the Northern Expedition* of 1926 and participated in the capture of Shanghai and Nanking from the armies of Sun Ch'uan-fang. Ch'en served as guards commander at Chiang Kai-shek's headquarters and as commander of the artillery corps. Ch'en was one of a group of officers who traveled to Japan in 1930 to study Japanese military schools and methods of operation, and to visit local Chinese communities there.

In the early 1930s Ch'en Ch'eng served in a number of campaigns against the military forces of the Chinese Communists, notably in Kiangsi Province. He gained considerable military and political experience in fighting the Communists. Under his direction a compendium of captured Chinese Communist documents was published entitled *Ch'ih-fei fan-tung wen-chien hui-pien* (a collection of subversive documents of the Red Bandits). This work, reprinted in Taiwan in 1960, gave a detailed account of the history, organization, and operations of the Chinese Red Army in the early 1930s.

Throughout the 1930s, Ch'en Ch'eng continued as a close ally of Chiang Kai-shek in the military battles and political maneuverings that elevated Chiang to top Nationalist leader. Ch'en was one of the senior political and military officers detained by Chang Hsüeh-liang's* coup against Chiang Kai-shek in December 1936.

After the Sino-Japanese War* broke out in July 1937, Ch'en's military and political responsibilities expanded when he was asked to lead a variety of military training organizations and programs. In February 1939 he was appointed deputy director of the Guerrilla Training Class, and later he became head of the training section of the Central Training Corps, of which he was dean. In the early 1940s Ch'en's commands involved the defense of Yunnan and other areas in the joint American-Chinese operations coordinated by General Joseph Stilwell* against the Japanese.

As the civil war between the Communists and Nationalists flared up again following World War II, Ch'en Ch'eng was dispatched to Manchuria in 1947 to combat Communist operations. On his recommendation, the Nationalist government sent 90,000 additional troops to Manchuria, but Communist strength grew. Ch'en asked to be relieved of command on the grounds of a recurring stomach ailment.

In 1948 Ch'en went to Taiwan, was appointed chairman of the Taiwan provincial government, and also took command of the Taiwan garrison forces. As Communist forces gained strength on the mainland, he was assigned the task of making Taiwan a secure base for a Nationalist military retreat.

After Ch'en Ch'eng became vice-president of the Republic of China in the wake of the March 1954 elections, he was made head of the newly established Planning Committee for the Recovery of the Mainland. During his second term as vice-president, he visited the United States in July–August 1961 to build up goodwill for the Republic of China. In March 1963 Ch'en Ch'eng visited South

Vietnam and the Philippines on a similar mission. He died on March 5, 1965, of liver cancer.

REFERENCES: *Land Reform in Taiwan* (Taipei, 1961); Chiu Ch'i-ch'i, *Chi Chung-cheng Yung-chueh Yu I-sheng—Ch'en Ch'eng chuan* (Biography of Ch'en Ch'eng) (Taipei, 1985).

PARRIS H. CHANG

CH'EN CHI-T'ANG (1890–November 3, 1954): Regional militarist and ruler of Kwangtung, 1931–1936.

Born into a declining landlord family in 1890 in Feng-cheng, Kwangtung, Ch'en Chi-t'ang attended the Kwangtung Military School and the short-course military academy. Later, he joined the T'ung-meng hui.* In 1922 Ch'en became a battalion commander under Ch'en Ming-shu. During his dispute with Ch'en Chiung-ming, Sun Yat-sen* solicited the help of the Cantonese forces in the south and west of Kwangtung; Ch'en Chi-t'ang immediately rallied to Sun's side. In 1923 Ch'en served in the Third Brigade under Li Chi-shen, commander of the Kwangtung forces. Three times in 1925, he led his troops into Kwangsi to assist Li Tsung-jen and Huang Shao-hsiung in consolidating their power in the province. In this way, Ch'en was able to establish a long-term friendship with the Kwangsi Clique.

In the Northern Expedition,* Ch'en Chi-t'ang remained in Kwangtung to protect the rear. During this time, Ch'en never supported the Communist worker/peasant movement. In the spring of 1927, Ch'en made an "investigative trip" to the Soviet Union. He came back in June, resumed command of the Eleventh Division, and stationed his troops at the West River. In the Nanchang Uprising,* when Yeh T'ing and Ho Lung moved their troops down to Kwangtung, it was Ch'en who repelled them in the East River. Later, Ch'en lent his support to Li Chi-shen and drove Chang Fa-k'uei out of the province when Chang challenged Li's rule in Kwangtung. Ch'en was appointed leader of the Fourth Army and participated in the anti-Communist movement in Kwangtung. In 1929, when Li Chi-shen was imprisoned by Nanking for his implication in the Kwangsi revolts, Ch'en threw his support to Chiang Kai-shek* and was rewarded with the command of the Kwangtung forces. At the end of 1929 he sucessfully repelled the Kwangsi invasion of Kwangtung. And when Chiang Kai-shek withdrew his troops from Kwangtung during his conflicts with Feng Yü-hsiang* and Yen Hsi-shan,* Ch'en became the de facto ruler of the province.

When Hu Han-min* was arrested by Chiang Kai-shek, many Kuomintang leaders moved south to start an anti-Chiang movement in Canton. Ch'en then settled his differences with the Kwangsi leaders. In mid-1931, in opposition to Nanking, Ch'en, the Kuomintang leader, and the Kwangsi militarists jointly set up a new Nationalist government. After the outbreak of the Mukden Incident,* although outwardly agreed to unite with Chiang to fight against the Japanese, both Kwangtung and Kwangsi maintained their semi-independence. Together, these provinces established two separatist organizations: the southwest executive headquarters of the Kuomintang and the Southwest Political Council. Although Ch'en assisted Nanking in its extermination campaign against the Communists, in late 1934 he secretly negotiated a truce with the Red Army, allowing the Communists to pass through his line of blockade and flee the area.

Between 1931 and 1936, Kwangtung under Ch'en's rule experienced a period of stability. Ch'en devoted his time mainly to the development of the province. He built a large number of modern enterprises including the profitable sugar industry. Within ten years, total government investment in these enterprises climbed from CH $50,000 to CH $70 million. Private companies, which originally numbered only several hundred, also increased to over 2,000. Ch'en constructed the Pearl River Bridge and the Sun Yat-sen Memorial Hall. His government developed 4,000 *li* of roads in Kwangtung and 134 *li* in the city of Canton. Commerce in Canton was greatly revived. He encouraged land reclamation, set up agricultural research institutes, and developed water conservancy projects. By 1935 Kwangtung was able to cut its imported grain by half. His government also set up five model forestry centers and over ten fish breeding grounds. In the field of education, Ch'en not only strengthened the two major universities, Sun Yat-sen and Lingnan; he also built many professional schools and sent students abroad. During his rule, he revived neo-Confucianism, the worship of Kuan Yu and Yueh Fei, the study of geomancy, and fortune telling.

Conflicts betwen Nanking and Kwangtung intensified over the years; Ch'en and the Kwangsi Clique made use of the anti-Japanese sentiment in their attacks against Chiang. In June 1936 the two provinces put together an Anti-Japanese National Salvation Force to rebel against Nanking. But the scheme collapsed when the air force and some of his followers defected to Nanking. At the end, Ch'en was forced to step down; he left for Hong Kong and, later, Europe. During the Sino-Japanese War,[*] he joined the Nationalist government in Chungking, and, after the war, he was placed in charge of the development of Hainan Island. He retired with the Nationalists to Taiwan. Ch'en died in Taipei in November 1954.

REFERENCES: Ch'en Chi-t'ang, *Ch'en Chi-t'ang tzu-ch'uan kao* (Ch'en Chi-t'ang: An autobiography) (Taipei, 1974); *Kuang-tung shih* (A history of Kwangtung) (Canton, 1987).

ODORIC Y.K. WOU

CH'EN CHIA-KENG (TAN KAH-KEE) (1874–1961): Industrialist, patriot, and overseas Chinese leader.

A native of Chi-mei Village, T'ung-an County in Fukien Province, Ch'en Chia-kang was a rubber and shipping entrepreneur in Singapore who used his profits to found the renowned Amoy University and other schools in his native home and later became an influential political personality during both the war of resistance against the Japanese and the Chinese civil war. He was an outstanding example of overseas Chinese patriotism.

In 1890 when Ch'en was barely seventeen years of age, he made a trip to

Singapore, first dealing with the sale of rice and then establishing a pineapple plantation to supply fruit for the cannery business. In only a few years, Ch'en not only dominated the pineapple canning industry in Singapore, but also entered the rubber manufacturing business and shipping industry, both of which were extremely lucrative wartime undertakings. By 1917 he had become a millionaire and a powerful voice in the Southeast Asian Chinese community. But while Ch'en prospered, his motherland was suffering from imperialism and many deep-seated problems. Believing that his status as an overseas Chinese was intimately related to the fate of China, Ch'en, like many of his contemporaries, became active in the revolutionary movement against the Ch'ing dynasty.* He joined Sun Yat-sen's* T'ung-meng hui* in Singapore in 1907 and had his queue cut off in 1909 while raising hundreds of thousands of dollars to support the cause of republican revolution.

Ch'en firmly believed that the best way to help his motherland was by means of education. For this reason, he sent his younger brother home to establish the Chi-mei Normal School to train teachers. By the end of World War I, he had also established a school of marine production and navigation in Fukien. But the most important of all was the founding in 1921 of Amoy University. Ch'en personally contributed millions of dollars to the school and invited such prominent people as Ts'ai Yüan-pei* and Wang Ching-wei* to serve as directors of the board. In 1937 the Chinese government took over the institution.

Ch'en's businesses began to decline in the late 1920s, in part because of the Great Depression, and by 1931 he was forced to relinquish all his properties to the custody of trustees appointed by his creditors. But Ch'en continued to support Amoy University, and he also led a boycott campaign against Japanese goods. In 1928 he chaired a relief fund drive for Chinese war refugees in Shantung Province. At the time the Japanese occupied China's capital and started the carnage of the Rape of Nanking, Ch'en organized all the Chinese in Southeast Asia for a single objective: to resist Japanese aggression at all costs. In 1938 he was elected chairman of the Nanyang Overseas Chinese General Association for the Relief of War Refugees in China. Ch'en estimated that during the period 1939–1941, contributions from the Chinese in Southeast Asia averaged about U.S. $350,000 a month and that over 3,000 Southeast Asian Chinese went to China to assist in motor transport operation.

But when Ch'en toured China during 1940 he was disappointed in many of the government leaders he met. He witnessed corruption and bureaucratic problems in the Nationalist government that ultimately had a profound effect on his political views. On the contrary, during a visit to the Communist stronghold in Yenan, Ch'en was clearly impressed by the integrity and efficiency of the Communist leadership. In a statement issued on December 31, 1940, Ch'en openly criticized the Kuomintang in general and Governor Ch'en Yi of Fukien Province in particular. During the remainder of the war, he lived in disguise in several parts of Southeast Asia until August 1945 when the Japanese unconditionally surrendered. While hiding from the Japanese, Ch'en wrote his *Nan-chiao hui-*

yi-lu (Reminiscences of a Southeast Asian Chinese), totaling some 300,000 words.

During the civil war in China, Ch'en was won over by Mao[*] and the Communists. By the end of 1946 he published *Nan-chiao jih-pao* (The Southeast Asian Chinese Daily) which was to serve as the mouthpiece of the Chinese Democratic League in Malaya. Clearly, at this point in time, Ch'en could no longer reunify and lead the overseas Chinese. But when the People's Republic of China[*] was proclaimed on October 1, 1949, Ch'en found his name on the list of the Central People's Government Council. In May 1950 he published a collection of his writings about his impressions of new China. And for the next few years he was an important voice in either the Overseas Chinese Affairs Commission or the All-Chinese Federation of Overseas Returned Chinese. He died in Peking in 1961; prominent Communist leaders such as Chou En-lai[*] and Chu Teh[*] attended his funeral. A year later, the Chinese government issued an account of his life and the circumstances of his death. Today, Ch'en Chia-keng remains a legend in the overseas Chinese community of Southeast Asia.

REFERENCES: Ch'en Chia-keng, *Nan-chiao hui-yi-lu* (Reminiscences of a Southeast Asian Chinese) (Singapore, 1943); *Ch'en Chia-keng hsien-sheng chi-nien ts'e* (An Account of Ch'en Chia-keng's Life and the Circumstances of His Death) (Peking, 1962); and *Nan-chiao jih-pao* (The Southeast Asian Chinese Daily).

SHIH-SHAN HENRY TSAI

CH'EN KUNG-PO (October 19, 1892–June 3, 1946): Founding member of the CCP; KMT politician; collaborator during the Sino-Japanese War.

The only son of a disaffected military official under the Ch'ing[*] government, Ch'en as a teenager followed his father in participating in anti-Manchu activities in his home province of Kwangtung. After the arrest and imprisonment of his father, he managed to continue his education while helping to support his family.

The Revolution of 1911[*] improved the condition of Ch'en's family, and in 1917 he entered the prestigious Peking University. While not actively involved in the May Fourth Movement[*] of 1919, he was nevertheless influenced by the new ideological currents of the time. Shortly after his graduation from the university in 1920, Ch'en became an active member of the early Communist organizations in Canton. The following year he attended the founding meeting (i.e., the First National Congress) of the Chinese Communist party[*] in Shanghai. Ch'en, however, was troubled both by the disputes at the meeting and by the harassment from local police, and he left Shanghai before the meeting ended. In 1922, after Ch'en Chiung-ming's coup against Sun Yat-sen's[*] Canton government, the CCP leadership, which supported Sun, criticized Ch'en for his connections with Ch'en Chiung-ming. Angered by this accusation and dissatisfied with the party's interference in his personal plans, Ch'en announced his withdrawal from the CCP later that year. He then left for the United States for study.

Ch'en received an M.A. in economics at Columbia University in 1924, following the completion of a thesis entitled "The Communist Movement in China." At the invitation of Liao Chung-k'ai, he returned to China in early 1925 and soon was appointed to a number of important positions in both the Kuomintang and its government at Canton. When Liao was assassinated in August 1926, Ch'en succeeded him as head of the KMT's Peasant Department.

Ch'en became a follower of Wang Ching-wei[*] in the post–Sun Yat-sen power struggle within the Kuomintang and played a major role in Wang's Wuhan Regime[*] in 1927. From 1928 to 1930, while Wang was in exile in France, Ch'en led Wang's supporters in China to oppose the Nanking government under Chiang Kai-shek.[*] Their criticism of Chiang's conservative leadership won them the title the left KMT. In late 1928 Ch'en established the Society for the Reorganization of the Kuomintang (known as the Reorganizationists[*]) at Shanghai, which called for a return to the radicalism of the party's 1924 reorganization and supported Wang as the party's leader. The society was instrumental in instigating a series of political and military attacks on Nanking, culminating in the Enlarged Session opposition at Peking in late 1930. When Chiang crushed that last effort, Ch'en agreed with Wang's decision to dissolve the society and went into exile in Europe.

In early 1932 Wang decided to cooperate with Chiang in organizing a new government at Nanking. Ch'en followed Wang into this coalition and served as minister of industry under Wang's premiership. He held that position until 1935, when Wang was wounded by an assailant and forced to resign. Shortly after the outbreak of the Sino-Japanese War[*] in 1937, Ch'en toured Europe as a special envoy of the government in seeking international assistance for China's war effort. Returning to the country in early 1938, he was appointed head of the KMT's provincial branch in Szechwan.

When Wang decided to defect from Chungking and lead the peace movement later that year, Ch'en initially opposed the plan. He reluctantly followed Wang to Hanoi but refused to accompany Wang to Shanghai in negotiating a separate peace with Japan. Staying in Hong Kong for more than a year, he was finally persuaded by his loyalty to and affection for Wang to join Wang's collaboratist regime at Nanking in early 1940. For the next five years Ch'en served first as head of the regime's Legislative Yuan and then, after Wang's death in 1944, as chairman of the regime. Following Japan's surrender in 1945, Ch'en sought temporary refuge in Japan but was soon brought back to the country for trial. He was convicted of high treason and executed in Soochow in 1946.

REFERENCES: "Ch'en Kung-po," in Howard L. Boorman and Richard C. Howard, eds., *Biographical Dictionary of Republican China*, vol. 1 (New York, 1967); N. Lee, W.S.K. Waung, and L. Y. Chin, eds., *Bitter Smile: Memoirs of Ch'en Kung-po, 1925–1936* (Hong Kong, 1979); Shih Yuan-kao, "Ch'en Kung-po," in Huang Mei-chen, ed., *Wang wei shih han-chien* (Ten traitors in the Wang Ching-wei puppet regime) (Shanghai, 1986); C. Martin Wilbur, "The Variegated Career of Ch'en Kung-po," in Chün-tu Hsüeh, ed., *Revolutionary Leaders of Modern China* (Oxford, 1971).

KE-WEN WANG

CH'EN PO-TA (1904–September 20, 1989): Top ideological specialist among party radicals; political secretary and Marxist research assistant to Mao Tse-tung beginning at Yenan; developer of theory to justify the harsh party rectification after 1942, the quick collectivization of the mid–1950s, and the political defense of the Great Leap; main party monitor in the Chinese Academy of Sciences; chief editor of the CCP theoretical journal *Red Flag* upon its founding in 1958; head of the Cultural Revolution Small Group from 1966; purged for ultra-leftism in 1970.

Ch'en was born in Hui-an County, Fukien, as Ch'en Shang-yu. In his boyhood his parents, who are identified as poor peasants, moved southwest to Chi-mei on the mainland end of the causeway from Amoy Island. One of their motives may have been to facilitate their son's attendance at Chi-mei (Chip Bee) Normal School, financed by a Singapore tycoon. Upon graduation, Ch'en traveled briefly to Canton. By 1925 he enrolled in the Kuomintang (KMT)–Chinese Communist party (CCP)* United Front's Shanghai Labor University, whose faculty included Ch'ü Ch'iu-pai.* There he befriended Jao Shu-shih, an early Communist activist who later became a prominent Communist leader. Ch'en joined the CCP in 1927.

Ch'en received work as private secretary of KMT General Chang Chen, doing editorial and clerical preparation for the Northern Expedition.* When the Front collapsed in 1927, he fled to Shanghai, was arrested in Nanking, was jailed for a month, and then released on General Chang's recommendation. He soon renewed contacts with the party and departed for Moscow to attend Sun Yat-sen University.

Ch'en was afflicted with a stammer, and he had a heavy Fukien accent. He was short, and his personality was bookish. In Moscow he was affiliated with the minority branch faction of CCP students rather than with the main international faction that was more loyal to Soviet leaders. He was thus excluded from most local politics there—and in comparison with others, he learned more Marxism-Leninism.*

Returning to China in 1931, Ch'en married another Moscow student, Chu Yu-jen of Szechwan (whose sister had married CCP martyr and Politburo member Lo I-nung, a native of Mao Tse-tung's home town). He taught ancient Chinese history in Peking, making his name through articles he wrote as Ch'en Chih-mei and especially Ch'en Po-ta.* He also did underground party work at Tientsin. Ch'en engaged in disputes between revolutionary writers associated with Lu Hsün* who stressed class struggle and others who insisted that literature should serve current national needs. When the Sino-Japanese War* expanded in 1937, Ch'en went to Yenan, lecturing at the Central Party School and heading its China Problems Research Office. He soon became Mao's private secretary, finding apt quotations and putting Mao's ideas in proper Marxist terms. His calligraphy, reportedly taught by his elder brother Tun-yu, was reportedly "very beautiful," and this enhanced his prestige.

Ch'en claimed that dialectical materialism was the world's greatest cultural achievement, but it came in Chinese as well as Western forms. He insisted that modern plain speech (*pai-hua*), containing some Western loan words, could be made accessible to the Chinese masses and become common speech (*p'u-t'ung-hua*). Similarly, even Marxism could be localized. Ch'en relied not just on texts by Marx and Engels, but also on dialectical elements in ancient Chou philosophy. He liked Mo Tzu, whose notions about "appearance and reality" and "knowledge and action" (*ming shih, chih hsing*) seemed useful for contemporary problems. Ch'en was an academic, whereas Mao was a leader who often attacked Chinese traditions more broadly than did his secretary. But Ch'en phrased Maoism dialectically, as a Chinese national form of Marxism-Leninism, and this nicely suited Mao's political needs.

A few months after coming to Yenan in 1937, Ch'en published the first collection of Mao's writings (*Mao Tse-tung lun*). In the first anniversary issue of *Liberation Daily*, July 1, 1938, his article represented the Maoist faction and was set beside another essay from a student who had returned from the USSR. Ch'en participated avidly in the Rectification Campaign* after 1942. In 1944–1945 he drafted an official history of the party, stressing that Mao had consistently evolved the correct line from 1921 onward. (This official history was revised and published in the early 1950s.) Ch'en joined the Central Committee in 1945, becoming a full member by 1946.

After liberation, Ch'en's administrative duties broadened. For example, he joined the party's Rural Work Department in 1955 and the Politburo as an alternate in 1956. His policy interests also included defining China's position vis-à-vis the Soviet Union. Ch'en was the only high leader to accompany Mao on both the 1949 and 1957 journeys to Moscow. He first suggested the slogan "Let one hundred schools of thought contend." The term *People's Commune** was first published in his July 1, 1958, *Red Flag* inaugural article as editor. China's expanded cooperatives bore scant resemblance to the 1871 Paris Commune, but Ch'en was always much taken with the Paris precedent. In the fall of 1958, he proposed abolishing currency—an idea from which even Mao distanced himself. Along with Mao and Chang Ch'un-ch'iao,* Ch'en visited a Hopei commune that experimented with the free supply system. In 1962, when a plenum was called to reverse post–Leap* market policies, Ch'en gave the rural report.

By August 1966 Ch'en was named head of the Cultural Revolution Small Group. In this capacity, he led many Red Guard* rallies at Peking that autumn. By mid–1967, however, Mao needed to mend fences with an army in rebellion at Wuhan—and this meant a break with Ch'en's radicals. The autumn of 1967 saw a purge of the "ultra-left May 16 corps," removing Ch'i Pen-yü, Kuan Feng, Mu Hsin, Lin Chieh, and Wang Li—who were all members of Ch'en's CR Small Group and all on the staff of *Red Flag*. Ch'en survived, however, to help draft Lin Piao's* political report to the 1969 party congress. When Mao and Chou insisted on a less radical version, Ch'en resisted with Lin's support. The congress elected Ch'en one of the five Politburo Standing Committee members; this was the highest position of his career. At the August 1970 plenum, Ch'en again took a radical stance with Lin's apparent backing; about a month later, he was purged.

In 1980, when other top leftists in the Gang of Four* were also tried, a court sentenced Ch'en to eighteen years in jail. Because of sickness, he was released from prison at age eighty-four in October 1988. He died of heart failure at his home on September 20, 1989.

REFERENCES: Parris Chang, *Radicals and Radical Ideology in the Cultural Revolution* (originally entitled "The Role of Ch'en Po-ta in the Cultural Revolution") (New York, 1972); Roderick MacFarquhar, *The Origins of the Cultural Revolution*, 2 vols. (New York, 1974 and 1983); Raymond F. Wylie, *The Emergence of Maoism: Mao Tse-tung, Ch'en Po-ta, and the Search for Chinese Theory, 1935–1945* (Stanford, Calif., 1980).

                                                              LYNN T. WHITE III

CH'EN TU-HSIU (October 8, 1879–May 27, 1942): Founder of the *New Youth*; leader of the CCP between 1921 and 1927.

Ch'en Tu-hsiu was born in the town of An-ch'ing in Anhwei Province, in a family with substantial and growing commercial interests. In an unfinished autobiography that he began while in a KMT jail in 1937, Ch'en traced the beginning of his revolutionary career to his participation in examinations for the second level *chü-jen* degree in 1897, stating that the licentious behavior of the candidates and the filth of the examination halls revolted him. His writings of the turn of the century do suggest an acquaintance with the reformist thinking of the time, and it is certain that by 1901 Ch'en Tu-hsiu had established contact with various revolutionary figures. As a student in Japan, Ch'en committed his first clearly revolutionary act in 1903 when, together with others, he relieved the Ch'ing* official overseeing Chinese students in Japan of his queue. This was a serious insult to the throne as the obligatory queues were a symbol of submission to the Manchu ruling house.

Returning to China in 1903, Ch'en engaged in a variety of anti-Ch'ing activities. He assisted with the creation and publication of *The Citizens Daily* (*Kuomin Jih Pao*), the successor of the celebrated anti-Manchu periodical, the *Supao*, which had been closed down by the British in Shanghai in that year. In 1904 Ch'en Tu-hsiu founded *The Anhwei Vernacular* (*An-hwei Su-hua pao*), which is said to have been the largest vernacular periodical of the time, and formed the Warrior Yue Society, a small conspiratorial organization of militant revolutionaries, which sought to assassinate Ch'ing officials.

Not much is known about Ch'en Tu-hsiu's activities between 1904 and 1911. He seems to have continued his revolutionary commitments, and it is also clear that he stayed in Japan between 1907 and 1909, maintaining close friendships with exiled members of the National Essence School (*Kuo-ts'ui Hsüeh-p'ai*). Ch'en Tu-hsiu's thought before the 1911 Revolution* period was characterized by an apocalyptic anti-Manchuism, constitutionalism, and the cultivation of a strong moral sense.

After the 1911 Revolution Ch'en served as the personal secretary of Po Wen-wei, the military governor of Anhwei and a member of the Warrior Yue Society, and was in charge of education in the province. In 1913 Ch'en Tu-hsiu was forced to flee to Japan for his involvement in the Second Revolution* of 1913, which saw several military governors, including Po Wen-wei, declare their independence from Yüan Shih-k'ai.* Ch'en responded to his huge disappointment in the result of the 1911 Revolution by launching the New Culture Movement, bringing him nationwide fame for the first time. In the periodical that he founded to promote the movement, *The New Youth*—which at first carried the title of *Youth Magazine (Ch'ing-nien Tsa-chih)*—Ch'en advocated Western science, democracy, individualism, and the use of the vernacular. In a series of highly polemical articles, he inveighed against attempts, supported by Yüan Shih-kai, K'ang Yu-wei,* and others, to install Confucianism as China's state religion. He argued that basic Confucian ideas, including the idea of filial piety, were incompatible with the republican political order or with modern life. *The New Youth* soon became the vehicle by which a series of leading intellectuals, including Hu Shih,* Li Ta-chao,* and Lu Hsün* rose to national prominence as the heralds of China's enlightenment. Ch'en's growing prestige at this time translated into his appointment to the deanship of the School of Arts and Letters at Peking University in 1917.

Ch'en Tu-hsiu's turn toward Marxism-Leninism* in the summer of 1920 and his subsequent founding of the Chinese Communist party* took place when the conduct of China's republican parties, the behavior of local elites, rising warlordism,* and World War I made him skeptical about the virtues of republican institutions. In September 1920 Ch'en announced his support for Marxism-Leninism, and by late 1920 he had begun the building of the CCP with the help of agents of the Comintern.* He issued a CCP manifesto, initiated *The Communist Party Monthly (Kung-ch'an-tang Yue-k'an)*, and was urging acquaintances to set up CCP branches. At the First CCP Congress* of 1921, Ch'en Tu-hsiu was elected the party's leader, a position he retained until 1927.

Under Ch'en's leadership, the CCP developed into a mass party whose membership at its peak totaled nearly 60,000. Ch'en's association with the CCP gave it an immediate prestige and national standing that it would otherwise have lacked. His efforts to bring the various regional CCP branches into a centralized organization and his attempts to provide the CCP with an independent base in Chinese society outside the framework of the KMT were to prove of lasting significance. Ch'en was, however, also a highly controversial figure in the CCP who by 1927 had become widely disparaged as a willful and moody autocrat. He had become embroiled in vicious factional struggles, with one group of CCP members arguing that Ch'en had made an enormous error in refusing to take action against Chiang Kai-shek* after Chiang seized control of Canton on March 20, 1926, and curtailed CCP activity in the KMT and the Canton government. Internal CCP resentment of Ch'en, Stalin's need to find a scapegoat for his failed China policy, as well as the ambition of a young generation of CCP members led to Ch'en's downfall at the August Seven Emergency Conference of the CCP in 1927.

Ch'en was finally expelled from the CCP in 1929. In May 1929 local Chinese forces and Soviet troops clashed along the China Eastern Railway in Manchuria, which had been under Soviet control. The CCP Central Committee called on CCP members to support the Soviet Union, a development that prompted Ch'en to issue a strong protest. By this time he had also become involved in a Trotskyist opposition faction within the CCP, and in 1929 he published a Letter of Warning to all party members, in which he sought to demonstrate that he had been a consistent opponent of the KMT and in which he attempted to shift much of the blame for CCP disasters in the past onto the Comintern.* The Trotskyists never developed into a viable political force, and Ch'en's political career effectively ended in 1932 when he was imprisoned by the KMT.

Ch'en was released in 1937 as part of the agreement between the CCP and the KMT that led to the Anti-Japanese United Front. Negotiations for his reentry into the CCP remained fruitless, probably because of Comintern opposition. Ch'en Tu-hsiu died in a small town outside Chungking in 1942. Besides being an important political figure, he was a philologist of considerable repute, a productive poet, and a skilled calligrapher.

REFERENCES: Feigon Lee, *Chen Duxiu* (Princeton, N.J., 1983); Lin Mao-sheng, *Selected Articles by Ch'en Tu-hsiu* (Peking, 1984).

HANS J. VAN DE VEN

CH'EN YÜN (1905–): CCP labor and party organizer; Central Committee and Politburo member; party vice-chairman; government vice-premier; economic expert.

Ch'en Yün, born Liao Ch'en-yün, was a native of Ch'ing-p'u County, Kiangsu Province. Orphaned at four years of age, he was raised by relatives. Having received a primary school education, Ch'en became a worker at the Shanghai Commercial Press. In 1925 he joined the Chinese Communist party,* became a leading union organizer, and assisted Chou En-lai* in staging the three workers' uprisings in Shanghai during the Northern Expedition (1926–1928)*. When Chiang Kai-shek* purged the Communists, Ch'en fled to his home county and staged an ill-fated peasant uprising. He remained a leading member of the Kiangsu Party Committee and was catapulted into the Central Committee and then the Politburo in 1931 when the "Twenty-eight Bolsheviks"* purged the Li Li-san* faction from the leadership. Ch'en soon turned to security work in the party.

In 1933 the collapse of the CCP Party Center in Shanghai caused Ch'en to flee to the Kiangsi Soviet Republic*. He maintained an influence and rivaled Liu Shao-ch'i* in party work in the "white areas." In 1934 Ch'en participated in the Long March* as the Party Center's representative to the Fifth Red Army, and attended the Tsunyi Conference* that reaffirmed Mao Tse-tung's* leadership. In 1935 he was sent to Moscow to participate in Comintern* affairs, and he remained there until 1937. In that year, he went to Sinkiang briefly and then he flew to Yenan with Wang Ming* and K'ang Sheng. Acceptable to both Mao and Wang, Ch'en came to head the CCP Organization Department and played a key role in the Yenan Rectification Campaigns* in 1942–1944.

In 1940 Ch'en's life turned a new page when he assumed the new jobs of the head of the Central Committee's Finance and Economy Department and the director of the Border Regions' Finance Commission, which had been created to combat the KMT economic blockade. He continued his work in CCP financial and economic affairs in Manchuria after the end of the Sino-Japanese War,* and during the ensuing civil war, he led the takeover of Shen-yang. After the Communist victory, Ch'en was appointed vice-premier of the new regime and participated in Sino-Soviet negotiations throughout the 1950s. As the head of the government's Finance and Economy Commission, Ch'en also became China's economic tsar during the recovery period of 1949–1952. He solved the nationwide hyperinflation through centralized financial control. He took part in drafting the national constitution as well as the First Five-Year Plan. Despite the brief interlude when Kao Kang* served as the head of the State Planning Commission created in 1952, Ch'en remained influential over economic affairs until 1958, when differences with Mao began to surface.

Ch'en's major concerns were stability and balanced growth. He advocated concentration of resources, centralization of finance and banking, and a balanced budget. While supporting centralized planning, Ch'en also saw its limitations and consistently endorsed the use of market forces in agriculture, commerce, and parts of the light industry. In 1952 he regarded the attack on the capitalists during the Five-Anti Campaign* as excessive. While endorsing Mao's rural collectivization* policies, Ch'en opted for lower levels of collective ownership. Ch'en regarded collectivization as the best method for increasing agricultural yields. Meanwhile, he argued for a balance between demand and supply, purchasing power and consumer goods. Thus, he was less enthusiastic than some of his colleagues about a lopsided development of heavy industry in the First Five-Year Plan. He was also opposed to Maoist political campaigns when they jeopardized the economy.

In 1956 Ch'en became a vice-chairman of the CCP. The onset of the Great Leap Forward* in 1958 occasioned Ch'en's falling out of favor with Mao. With the campaign running into trouble, Ch'en returned to the scene briefly in March–May 1959 but stayed out of policymaking soon afterward until 1961. Although the post–Leap recovery adopted policies long advocated by Ch'en, he faded from view again in 1962. When the Cultural Revolution* commenced in 1966, Ch'en's place in the Politburo began to decline. He came under heavy wallposter attacks during the upheaval, but he managed to appear on certain ceremonial occasions. In the 1970s he also lost his vice-premiership and was appointed to a ceremonial position in the National People's Congress. Ch'en returned to the top leadership in late 1978, after the death of Mao and the fall of the Gang of Four.*

REFERENCES: David M. Bachman, Chen Yun and the Chinese Political System (Berkeley, Calif., 1985); "Ch'en Yün," in Donald W. Klein and Anne B. Clark, Biographic Dictionary of Chinese Communism, 1921–1965, Vol. 1 (Cambridge, Mass., 1971) I: 149–153; Nicholas R. Lardy and Kenneth Lieberthal, eds., Chen Yun's Strategy for China's Development: A Non-Maoist Alternative (New York, 1983).

LUNG-KEE SUN

CHENNAULT, CLAIRE LEE (1890–1958): American general; head of the American Volunteer Group or "Flying Tigers."

In 1937 the Texas-born Claire Lee Chennault, who had retired from the United States Air Force that year, was invited by Madame Chiang Kai-shek, China's national secretary for Aviation, to help reorganize the Chinese air force. Chennault became the chief instructor of the Aviation School in Hangchow and an adviser to Chiang Kai-shek.* When the Sino-Japanese War* broke out in 1937, he pressed President Roosevelt to help the Chinese air force which finally acquired 100 U.S.-financed P–40s in 1941. He also won approval to organize the American Volunteer Group or "Flying Tigers," with three squadrons of about 100 pilots. Initially, two squadrons were stationed at Kunming and one at Toungoo in Burma. After the Japanese occupied Burma, the third squadron was also moved to Kunming. Chennault was recalled to active duty after the United States entered the war, and he was appointed head of the China Air Task Force. Later, the Task Force was reorganized and became the Fourteenth Air Force with Chennault as its commander.

Even before 1942, the Flying Tigers had gained a reputation as effective hit-and-run fighters against the Japanese air force despite Japan's overwhelming superiority in the air. The Flying Tigers had frequent engagements with the Japanese in the Burma Campaign in the spring of 1942. They also provided tactical support for the Chinese infantry in the battles of Changsha, Chekiang, and Kiangsi.

Chennault believed that the war in China should be carried out largely from the air and that air power was the solution in the China theater. In October 1942 he outlined his plan to defeat the Japanese in a letter to Wendell Willkie, President Roosevelt's special representative. Chennault wanted to bring up his air strength to a total of 105 fighter aircraft of modern design, thirty medium bombers, and twelve heavy bombers. Such an air force would be maintained by an aerial supply line between India and China. With this force, Chennault proposed to cripple Japanese rail and river communications in China, to strike at Japanese shipping off the China seas, and eventually to commence bombing Japan proper with heavy bombers based in east China. He argued that the American air force could destroy Japan's major industrial centers at the Tokyo–Yokohama–Osaka area, thereby making it impossible for Japan to supply its armies with munitions of war.

Chennault's plan was endorsed by Chiang Kai-shek but rejected by General Joseph Stilwell,* commander of U.S. forces in the China–Burma–India theater and Chennault's superior. Instead, Stilwell preferred to emphasize the ground war against Japan and believed that a land supply route to China should be opened. In fact, Chennault was not on very good terms with Stilwell but was friendly to Chiang Kai-shek who shared Chennault's view that a costly land campaign to retake Burma was unnecessary and that the Japanese could be crushed after they had first been weakened by attack from the air. The disagreement between Chennault and Stilwell went beyond tactics to different perceptions of the Japanese threat in China. In April 1944, when Stilwell was scoring successes in Burma, Chennault was warning of massive Japanese troop movements in central China, and he pleaded for more supplies which he argued were needed to repel any Japanese air offensive. Stilwell, however, downplayed the importance of Chennault's reports, and Chennault never received adequate support for his operations. In the summer of that year, the Japanese successfully launched one of the most ambitious offensives in central China. Nevertheless, by the latter part of 1944, the U.S. Air Force had gradually gained the upper hand in the air war, and air power could now be directed against Japanese supply lines. Shortly before the end of the war, Chennault retired. During its years of operation, the Fourteenth Air Force had destroyed 2,600 Japanese aircraft and sunk or damaged over two and a half million tons of Japanese shipping.

Chennault returned to China in 1946 and founded the Civil Air Transport, a contract cargo carrier to carry supplies to the interior of China. He ardently supported Chiang Kai-shek when the civil war broke out. After Chiang's government moved to Taiwan, Chennault also left the mainland; he remained active with the Civil Air Transport until 1955. He died of cancer three years later.
REFERENCE: Robert L. Scott, Jr., *Flying Tiger: Chennault of China* (Westport, Conn., 1973).

KA-CHE YIP

CHIANG CH'ING (1913–May 14, 1991): Member of the Politburo of the CCP; married to Mao Tse-tung; one of the Gang of Four; purged in October 1976.

Chiang Ch'ing (her other names were Li Yun-ho and Li Chin, and her stage name was Lan P'ing) was born in the town of Chu-ch'eng, Shantung Province. She joined the Chinese Communist party* in 1933, while a member of the Seaside Drama Society in Tsingtao. Later the same year she moved to Shanghai, where she joined the city's community of leftist artists, literateurs, and bohemians. In Shanghai she acted in a number of films and plays, including Ibsen's *A Doll's House*.

In 1937 Chiang left Shanghai for Communist-controlled Yenan. There she met Mao Tse-tung,* whom she married in 1939. Because Chiang's political and personal past was regarded as somewhat murky (she was rumored to have been on intimate terms with members of the Kuomintang while in Shanghai and to have betrayed the CCP in order to get out of jail), the CCP leadership approved of the marriage only on the condition that Chiang refrain from involving herself in any kind of political work for the next thirty years. Aside from occasionally acting as Mao Tse-tung's personal secretary and playing a minor role in the Ministry of Culture's Film Guidance Committee in the early 1950s, Chiang had no significant role in Chinese politics or culture until the early 1960s, when she launched an attempt to reform Chinese opera along revolutionary lines.

Chiang's efforts to instill the traditional form of the Peking opera with a modern, socialist revolutionary content met with strong opposition from the

CCP's cultural establishment in Peking. It did, however, win the support of the party apparatus in Shanghai, where Chiang established a working relationship with the Propaganda Department Director Chang Ch'un-ch'iao* and the literary critic and essayist Yao Wen-yüan.* Another of Chiang's supporters at this time was the minister of defense, Lin Piao,* who in 1966 made her a consultant to the People's Liberation Army* in matters related to literature and the arts. During the Cultural Revolution,* the Chinese media referred to Chiang's eight so-called Revolutionary Model Operas as the pinnacle of revolutionary proletarian art.

In May 1966 Chiang was appointed vice-director of the Cultural Revolution Small Group under the CCP Politburo. Over the next few years she used her considerable power to mercilessly persecute old enemies who knew the truth about her life as a young actress in Shanghai, party leaders who in the 1930s had opposed her marriage to Mao, and cultural figures and officials who in the early 1960s had opposed her attempts to reform Peking opera. At the National Day celebrations in Peking in 1968, she ranked number six among the party and government leaders present. In April 1969 the Tenth CCP Central Committee elected her to its Politburo. She retained this position in August 1973, when the Eleventh CCP Central Committee held its first plenary session.

In the early 1970s, Chiang became deeply embroiled in factional politics within the highest echelon of the CCP. Together with Chang Ch'un-ch'iao, Yao Wen-yüan, and Wang Hung-wen* she formed a clique (see Gang of Four)* whose political program centered around the continuation of the Maoist policies and practices developed since the beginning of the Cultural Revolution. Her opposition consisted of a group of older politicians headed by Teng Hsiao-p'ing, who deeply resented everything the Cultural Revolution stood for. Chiang's main problem at this time would appear to have been her lack of a broad base of support within the party. The fact that she was surviving in politics was due largely to the tacit support given her by Mao Tse-tung.

On October 6, 1976, four weeks after the death of her husband, Chiang, together with the other members of the Gang of Four, was arrested. The political enemies she had made over the past decade now accused her of having attempted to use the Cultural Revolution to destroy the CCP and to usurp power for herself and her counterrevolutionary clique. On January 23, 1981, at a major show trial in Peking, she was branded an enemy of the state and sentenced to death with a two-year reprieve (a sentence subsequently commuted to life imprisonment). On May 14, 1991, Chiang Ch'ing committed suicide by hanging herself.

REFERENCES: Ross Terrill, *The Whiteboned Demon: A Biography of Madame Mao Zedong* (New York, 1984); Roxane Witke, *Comrade Chiang Ch'ing* (Boston, 1977).

MICHAEL L. SCHOENHALS

CHIANG CHING-KUO (1910–January 13, 1988): Eldest son of Chiang Kai-shek; minister of national defense; premier and president of the ROC on Taiwan.

Chiang Ching-kuo was born in Fenghua, in the coastal Cheking Province. He was the oldest son of Chiang Kai-shek* and his first wife, Mao Chieh-ju, an unschooled village girl who married Chiang in an arranged union.

The younger Chiang's long work in political and economic administration in China, combined with international experience arising from his twelve years of living and working in the Soviet Union as well as from his later diplomatic experience in negotiating with the Russians in the 1940s, helped prepare him to follow his father as leader of the Republic of China* on Taiwan. Both before and after his father's death on April 5, 1975, Chiang played an able and decisive role in guiding Taiwan through the adversity following the 1971 ouster of Taiwan from the United Nations and the widespread withdrawal of international recognition, including the United States' recognition of the People's Republic of China* in January 1979. Under Chiang Ching-kuo's leadership during this crucial period, Taiwan's rapid economic growth made it an important player in the world's economy as one of Asia's most prosperous newly industrialized nations.

Chiang Ching-kuo became premier in 1972. Incumbent vice-president Yen Chia-kan* retained his post in a succession plan that provided that after Chiang Kai-shek's death Yen would become ceremonial president with Chiang Ching-kuo holding real power as premier. Chiang Ching-kuo replaced Yen as president in 1978 and held that post until his death.

Chiang Ching-kuo was raised under the strict Buddhist discipline of his grandmother and educated in China, first at the Wushan School, Chekiang Province (1916–1917), and later in Shanghai at the Wan-chu School (1922–1924) and the Pootung Middle School (1925). He also studied under veteran republican revolutionary and classical scholar Wu Chih-hui* at a small private school in Peking.

In 1925 Chiang went to Canton to seek his father's permission to study in the Soviet Union. Chiang Kai-shek, then commandant of the Whampoa Military Academy,* had visited Moscow in 1923 in a mission for Sun Yat-sen* to secure Soviet military assistance for the Kuomintang. The younger Chiang and several other Chinese youths left for Russia by cargo ship in October 1925. Chiang Ching-kuo entered Sun Yat-sen University, established in Moscow that year to train Chinese revolutionary cadres. Chiang quickly learned Russian, wrote revolutionary articles for student publications, and even roused Moscow workers to applause with his revolutionary speeches. He joined the Communist Youth Corps in December 1925 and graduated from Sun Yat-sen University in April 1927. When the alliance between Chiang Kai-shek and the Chinese Communists broke down, Soviet authorities denied Chiang Ching-kuo's requests to return to China and assigned him to work in electrical and machinery factories near Moscow and in the Urals.

After spending almost twelve years in the Soviet Union and marrying an orphaned Russian girl named Faina, he returned to China with his wife and two children in 1937. He served in several posts in the Nationalist government, including high-level administration in Kiangsi Province. There he sternly cracked down on gambling, opium smoking, and prostitution, using secret police methods to consolidate his power. He was noted for his efforts in social and economic reform, including programs to implement his ideas on government administration.

The younger Chiang took on diplomatic responsibilities toward the end of World War II, when he used his experience in the Soviet Union to help negotiate agreements with Stalin which helped the Nationalist government reestablish political and economic control of China. Among these measures was an agreement for a postponed withdrawal of the Soviet military forces which had advanced to occupy Manchuria toward the end of World War II. This agreement helped prevent Mao Tse-tung's* Communists from moving in quickly to seize control of Manchuria.

After the war, Chiang Ching-kuo played a major part in stablizing the economic and political situation in Shanghai, where he earned a reputation for toughness by announcing drastic control measures, including the execution of black market speculators and the arrest of many merchants and bankers. He also assisted his father in directing the defense of the southwestern provinces as the Communists moved to take control in 1949.

Chiang Kai-shek appointed his son in 1950 to establish and direct the general political department of the Ministry of Defense of the Nationalist government in Taiwan. Chiang Ching-kuo achieved effective control of the secret police on the island. In August 1950 he was named one of sixteen members of a new central reform committee of the Kuomintang. He thus helped his father establish personal authority on Taiwan in the face of native Taiwanese revolt and demoralization within Kuomintang ranks.

Chiang Ching-kuo continued to serve as his father's trusted assistant. After 1950 he advanced steadily in influence. Operating largely in the shadows away from the public scene, by 1965 he rose to the top of a complex power pyramid composed of the armed forces and the security and intelligence agencies. In October 1952 Chiang was made a member of the new Central Committee of the Kuomintang and was given a seat on its ruling standing committee. His responsibility over political and security operations continued to rise.

In 1958 Chiang Ching-kuo was named minister without portfolio, and in 1960 he was named vice-minister of defense. In this post he supervised the new Nationalist guerrilla activity on the mainland aimed at destabilizing the Communist regime following the disastrous failure of the Great Leap Forward.* In 1965 Chiang Ching-kuo emerged visibly on the public scene when he was named minister of defense.

In 1969 the younger Chiang shifted from the Defense Ministry to a position as vice-premier in charge of overall economic policy. With this broadening of experience and outlook, he could truly be considered a "man for all seasons." After Chiang Ching-kuo took over as premier in June 1972, he pushed forward major programs to improve communications and industrial development. Chiang also cracked down on the island's flourishing corruption. He relaxed police repression and made major overtures toward the native Taiwanese population by increasing Taiwanese representation both in government organs and within the ruling Kuomintang party.

During his last years, Chiang instituted political reform, lifted the thirty-eight-year old martial law, permitted a multiparty system, and set in motion Taiwan's march toward democracy. He also lifted the ban on Taiwan residents' travel to Mainland China, allowing the reunion of divided families.

REFERENCES: Chiang Nan, *Chiang Ching-kuo chuan* (Biography of Chiang Ching-kuo) (Montebello, 1985); V. Vorontsov, "The Dictator's Heir," *Far Eastern Affairs*, No. 1, 1989 (Institute of the Far East, USSR Academy of Sciences).

PARRIS H. CHANG

CHIANG KAI-SHEK (October 31, 1887–April 5, 1975): Military general, statesman, and president of the ROC.

One of the two or three most important figures in twentieth-century Chinese history, Chiang Kai-shek presided over both the establishment of the Nationalist regime and its defeat on the mainland, and from the late 1930s on he enjoyed virtually supreme authority in the Kuomintang party and the government of the Republic of China* first on the mainland and then in Taiwan.

Born into a poor salt-merchant's family in Fenghua, Chekiang, Chiang attended military academies in Paoting and Tokyo, and joined Sun Yat-sen* at the time of the 1911 Revolution.* Rising quickly in the Kuomintang, Chiang was entrusted in 1924 with command of the Whampoa Military Academy* and the creation, with Soviet assistance, of a new party army.

Brilliantly judging the chaotic military situation in north China, Chiang launched the Northern Expedition* in 1926 and quickly brought the Kuomintang to national power. Simultaneously, he moved to end Soviet influence over the party, notably in the purge in 1927 of the Shanghai Communist underground. Chiang was convinced that communism posed a fatal threat to China, and he devoted his primary military attention to destroying it, even after the Japanese seizure of Manchuria in 1931.

Dissatisfaction with this approach led Chang Hsüeh-liang* to kidnap Chiang in December of 1936 (the Sian Incident*), releasing him only when agreement to an anti-Japanese United Front including the Communists had been reached. Full-scale war with Japan broke out in the following year, and in the early fighting Chiang resisted fiercely, committing and losing in the battle of Shanghai his finest German-trained divisions. The massive casualties of the war eventually destroyed both Chiang's personal power base and China's ability to resist, but Chiang, who withdrew China's government to the fastness of Chungking, refused to consider surrender. Wartime saw Chiang's prestige soar both internally and abroad (where his cultivated English-speaking wife Soong Mei-ling,* whom he had married in 1927, was a great asset).

The years after Japan's defeat, however, proved Chiang's undoing. The Northern Expedition* had been a bold stroke: by contrast, in the civil war* he fought cautiously. Stubborn as always, Chiang refused to compromise with the USSR over Manchuria, thus guaranteeing that Moscow would back the Communists. But in fighting this formidable foe Chiang was unwilling to entrust key commands to his ablest generals, preferring instead the politically trustworthy. As the war was lost, Chiang retreated to Taiwan in 1949 with the rump of the Republic of China government.

Politically, Chiang ruled Taiwan with an iron hand, crushing local aspirations for democracy and repeatedly purging his own followers. Yet at the same time he sought the advice and made the decisions (for educational and land reform, against import substitution policies, for domestic and foreign investment) that transformed Taiwan into a model of rapid and equitable economic and social development.

As yet without a proper biography, Chiang remains in many ways an enigma. Personally austere, deeply private, and without an ideology beyond nationalism, he elicited extreme and contradictory reactions from his contemporaries. Profoundly respected by his subordinates, and a human symbol during World War II of China's indomitable will to resist, Chiang was hated by the Chinese left, detested by General Joseph Stilwell* and certain other foreigners who worked with him, and widely blamed for the corruption and military ineptitude that brought down the Nationalist regime. Perhaps the contradictions are best reconciled by Donald Gillin's comparison of Chiang to a character in Greek tragedy: one who "when so many others were blind, foresaw an enormous catastrophe and made heroic efforts to prevent it, even though he sensed that he must fail, in part because of shortcomings in his own cause which he recognized but was helpless to eradicate."

REFERENCES: Hsi-sheng Ch'i, *Nationalist China at War: Military Defeats and Political Collapse, 1937–45* (Ann Abor, Mich., 1982); Parks M. Coble, Jr., "Chiang Kai-shek," in Ainslie T. Embree, ed., *Encyclopedia of Asian History*, vol. 1 (New York, 1988): 259–262; Lloyd E. Eastman, *The Abortive Revolution: China Under Nationalist Rule, 1927–1937* (Cambridge, Mass., 1974); Donald G. Gillin and Ramon H. Myers, eds., *Last Chance in Manchuria: The Diary of Chang Kia-ngau* (Stanford, Calif., 1989).

ARTHUR WALDRON

CHIANG MENG-LIN (January 26, 1886–June 19, 1964): Educator.

Chiang Meng-lin (often romanized Chiang Monlin) was born into a wealthy gentry family of Yüyao County in Chekiang Province. His father was something of a would-be inventor and entrepreneur who held financial interests in various Shanghai banks. His mother died when he was seven, one year after the beginning of his unusually long and varied education. After the standard few years of rote learning of the Confucian classics, Chiang was sent to Shaohsing in 1897 to attend the modern Chung-Hsi hsüeh-t'ang (Sino-Western School), whose faculty included Ts'ai Yüan-p'ei.* There he was first introduced to Western sciences and foreign languages. For the five years that followed the dissolution of the school in 1898, Chiang attended a French Catholic school in Shanghai, a Protestant missionary school in Hangchow, a student-run Kai-chin hsüeh-she (School of Reform and Progress), and finally the Chekiang Provincial College. In 1903 he wrote and passed the *hsiu-ts'ai* examination after which he entered Nan-yang kung-hsüeh (Nanyang Public School) in Shanghai. He remained there until August 1908 when, with family financial support, he was sent to study agriculture at the University of California at Berkeley.

Typical of May Fourth* intellectuals studying abroad, Chiang abandoned his practical studies for the humanities, in his case education (with minors in history and philosophy). During his four-year stay in Berkeley, Chiang met frequently with Sun Yat-sen* (who was in North America to raise funds for the T'ung-meng hui*) and was an editorial writer for Sun's *Ta-t'ung jih-pao*. After graduating, Chiang proceeded to Columbia University to pursue graduate work in education with John Dewey. His thesis, completed in 1917, was a comparative analysis of traditional Chinese and Western pedagogy. It was at Columbia that he began a long and close friendship with Hu Shih.*

Upon his return to China in 1917, Chiang became an editor with the Commercial Press. The following year he founded the *Hsin chiao-yü* (*New Education*), a journal whose purpose was ''to develop individuality and attain social progress'' through an approach that was a blend of Deweyian Liberalism and Mencian idealism. *New Education* was perhaps the most important educational journal of the May Fourth period. During this time Chiang met occasionally with Sun Yat-sen to discuss the economic reconstruction of China.

When the May Fourth Demonstrations broke out in 1919, Chiang Meng-lin temporarily replaced Ts'ai Yüan-p'ei (who had resigned in protest) as chancellor of Peking University. Chiang remained associated with Peking University (as teacher of education, dean of administration, and chancellor) until the end of the Sino-Japanese War* (1937–1945). During his first extended period as chancellor (1923–1927), Chiang found himself faced with the difficult political dilemma of assuaging growing student unrest and appeasing the government of the warlord Tuan Ch'i-jui. On March 18, 1926, the delicate balance collapsed: forty-six protesting students (six of whom were from Peking University) were slaughtered by soldiers of Tuan Ch'i-jui. When Chang Tso-lin's troops overtook Peking later that year, Chiang was informed that his life was in danger. He eventually fled Peking for the safety of Shanghai and his native Chekiang. After the forces of the KMT army captured Hangchow during the first half of the Northern Expedition,* Chiang was given several positions in the new provincial government of Chekiang (commissioner of education and member of the Central Political Council of the provincial KMT). In 1928 he was appointed president of the National Chekiang University, a position which, through the reorganized educational system, gave Chiang control of all educational matters for the province. In the same year he became minister of education for the newly established national government in Nanking. By December 1930 he resigned all government posts in order to return to Peking University where he remained as chancellor until 1937.

After the outbreak of the Sino-Japanese War, Chiang was instrumental in establishing the National Southwest Associated University (uniting Peking, Tsinghua, and Nank'ai universities), first in Ch'angsha and by May 1938 in Kunming. Chiang was one of three members of an executive committee administering the school.

With the end of the war, Chiang terminated his long association with Peking University and joined the KMT government as secretary general of the Executive Yuan, a post he held for two years. In 1948 he became chairman of the newly formed Joint Commission of Rural Reconstruction, a Sino-American project aimed at reorganizing and renovating agriculture in China. Chiang continued his work in agricultural reform in Taiwan until his death in 1964. In addition to rural reform, Chiang was involved in other large resource projects in Taiwan (i.e., Shihmen Reservoir) and was an outspoken advocate of birth control.

REFERENCES: Monlin Chiang, *Tides from the West* (New Haven, Conn., 1947); Sun Te-chung, "Meng-lin hsien-sheng ti sheng-p'ing yu chih-ch'ü" (Chiang Meng-lin's life and interests), *Chuan-chi wen-hsüeh*, vol. 2 (Taipei, 1964): 48–52.

KIRK A. DENTON

CH'IANG-HSÜEH HUI (Society for the Study of National-Strengthening): China's first study association after the Sino-Japanese War.

Founded by a handful of Chinese literati and scholar–officials, Ch'iang-hsüeh hui in Peking and Shanghai was the first study society that attempted to strengthen China after the Sino-Japanese War.* According to K'ang Yu-wei,* the purpose of the Ch'iang-hsüeh hui was to open the minds of the scholar-officials to new learning by which the country could be made strong and prosperous. Although it appears that a group of scholars in Peking such as K'ang Yu-wei, Ch'en Chih, and Shen Tseng-chih had already begun to discuss the formation of study societies by August 1895, Ch'iang-hsüeh hui was not formally inaugurated until mid-November 1895.

The publication of a periodical known as *Wan-kuo kung-pao* (*World Gazette*) by K'ang Yu-wei and Liang Ch'i-ch'ao* in August was only an initial effort to discuss current affairs. It was after support emerged from eminent figures in the scholar–official circles in Peking like Wen T'ing-shih that the thinking about study societies began to crystalize. By December the plan for a study society gradually evolved into the formation of a book publishing firm entitled Ch'iang-hsüeh shu-chü. The Book Depot published materials pertaining to current issues and reform ideas. In an attempt to provide educational facilities for the public, its operation also included the establishment of a museum, a library, and a reading room. Under the sponsorship of the Depot, the K'ang-Liang newssheet also began to improve its format, and its name was changed from *Wan-kuo kung-pao* to *Chung-wai chi-wen* (*Sino-Foreign* News). The membership of Ch'iang-hsüeh hui in Peking gradually expanded to include more than twenty eminent scholar–officials.

In Peking, however, Ch'iang-hsüeh hui achieved little success as an effective political organization. Personal and ideological disagreement among the membership seriously handicapped the solidarity and functioning of the society. There was reportedly a power struggle between K'ang Yu-wei and Wen T'ing-shih. There may also have been profound differences between K'ang and Chang Hsiao-ch'ien over the establishment of the publishing firm. In mid-October 1895 K'ang already decided to retreat and left Peking. However, the decisive attack on the Ch'iang-hsüeh hui was the impeachment of Wen T'ing-shih by the censor Yang Chung-i inspired by Li Hung-chang* in January 1896. Yang accused Wen and some members of the Censorate and the Hanlin Academy of organizing a faction to scheme for private profits and urged that the organization be banned immediately. Unable and reluctant to investigate the case, the throne finally shut down the Ch'iang-hsüeh hui project and reorganized the new publishing firm as a government-managed book depot. Ch'iang-hsüeh hui was thus a victim of the factional struggle of Peking officialdom.

After K'ang Yu-wei left Peking in mid-October 1895, he met with his former acquaintances like Liang Ting-fen and Huang Shao-chi, and they began to plan for the establishment of a Ch'iang-hsüeh hui in Shanghai. They received financial assistance and official patronage from Chiang Chih-tung and began to solicit the support of many scholar–officials. They also drafted a "preamble" and a set of regulations concerning the membership and activities of the association. They set up, first, a translation bureau to translate and publish books related to Western learning; second, a periodical concerning current affairs in China; third, a library of books on Chinese learning; and, finally, a museum or exibition hall for displays regarding Western culture. In January 1896 K'ang Yu-wei also planned a newspaper, entitled *Ch'iang-hsüeh pao*, without consulting the other organizers of the Shanghai Ch'iang-hsueh hui.

Ch'iang-hsüeh hui in Shanghai was ultimately undermined by the ideological differences between K'ang and the other members of the society. In the first issue of *Ch'iang-hsüeh pao*, K'ang identified 1895–1896 as the year 2737 after the death of Confucius. In traditional China, it was considered a treacherous act to change the reckoning of the year, for the year was supposed to be numbered according to the dynastic reign. K'ang's "Confucian era" in the society's publication led to the inevitable confrontation between K'ang Yu-wei and the other members of the study society. Chang Chih-tung was outraged and ordered Liang Ting-fen to announce that the *Ch'iang-hsüeh pao* had been an unauthorized publication of the society and that the periodical would be immediately suspended and the society would terminate operations.

The closing of the Ch'iang-hsüeh hui in Peking and Shanghai in early 1896 signaled the failure of the study associations. However, both attempts demonstrated the potential of study associations as a positive response among educated Chinese to national humiliation. They helped to create the intellectual climate for the reform movement that would flourish after 1895.

REFERENCES: Luke S.K. Kwong, *A Mosaic of the Hundred Days: Personalities, Politics and Ideas of 1898* (Cambridge, Mass., 1984): 94–103; Naito Shigenobu, "Kyo gakkai kiji" (On Ch'iang-hsüeh hui), *Tōyōshi kenkyū* (Journal of Oriental researches) 14, no. 4 (March 1961): 36–50; T'ang Chih-chun, "Wang Jang-ch'ing shih yü shou-cha chung kuan-yü Ch'iang-hsüeh hui te shih-liao" (Historical materials relating to Ch'iang-hsüeh hui in the correspondence of Wang K'ang-nien), *Wen-wu* 7 (1978): 60–67; T'ang Chih-chun, "Shanghai Ch'iang-hsüeh hui ho Ch'iang-hsüeh pao" (The Society for national-strengthening studies in Shanghai and the Journal of national-strengthening studies), *She-hui k'o-hsüeh* (Social sciences) 3 (1980): 114–124.

WING-KAI TO

CHIH-KUNG T'ANG (CHEE KUNG TONG): Triad society, Chinatown mafia, and revolutionaries.

A branch of the Triad Society, or the Hung League, Chih-kung t'ang was established in North America in the midnineteenth century by Chinese immigrants. The Triad Society is said to have been in existence in China during the seventeenth century with a goal of overthrowing the Ch'ing dynasty.[*] According to Liang Ch'i-ch'ao,[*] a large number of Hung League members emigrated overseas following the defeat of the Taipings[*] in 1864. Those who exiled themselves to America were largely the followers of a rebellious general, Ch'en Chin-kang of Kwangtung Province. It is believed that the first Hung League lodge in North America was founded in 1862 at Barkerville, Canada, and one year later the San Francisco Chih-kung t'ang came into existence. In subsequent years, more Hung League lodges sprang up in Chinese settlements in such Chinese communities as British Vancouver, Oregon, and Montana. By the 1880s the Hung League organizations were active not only along the Pacific Coast but also in such cities as Philadelphia, New York, Chicago, and St. Louis.

The machinery and methods of the secret societies in America were not greatly different from their counterparts in Canton. The extent of the secret societies' activities was wide but almost exclusively confined to Chinatowns. Their intergroup feuds, the notorious tong wars, were frequent, but by 1904 Chih-kung t'ang had become involved in Sun Yat-sen's[*] revolutionary activities. Sun enlisted the support of a secret society chief by the name of Huang San-te. He also drew up a constitution of the newly revamped Chih-kung t'ang and required that members register with the organization. Clearly, Sun had mustered an overseas Chinese secret society for his cause of Republican Revolution. As odd as it seemed to appear, Chih-kung t'ang of America was very effective in raising money to support Sun's activities. In 1910, for example, it raised more than $7,000 to meet expenditures of the armed uprising to take place at Tseng-nan-kuan. On June 18, 1911, Sun further molded the Hung League lodges into branches of his revolutionary organization, the T'ung-meng hui,[*] which he founded in Japan in 1905.

Sun drew up a set of regulations by which the so-called Hung League Subscription Bureau (Hung-men ch'ou-hsiang-chu) was to function as the ways and means committee of the revolutionary union. Within a few months, the Chih-kung t'ang of America had raised more than $400,000, which were channeled to support various revolutionary groups in China. Sun's travel expenses between October 10 and December 24, 1911, totaling about $3,000, also came from the subscription bureau account.

Unfortunately, Dr. Sun Yat-sen's relationship with America's Chih-kung t'ang began to deteriorate after the establishment of the Republic of China.* Those Chih-kung t'ang members who were waiting for rewards that Sun could not deliver were naturally disappointed. Others soon flirted with Sun's political rivals in China. Even Huang San-te, the chief, was bitter about the way the republican government treated him. Huang later wrote a reminiscence severely criticizing Sun Yat-sen, Hu Han-min, and the Kuomintang. Since the 1920s Chih-kung t'ang has ceased to be a significant political force.

REFERENCES: Feng Tze-yu, *Ke-ming i-shih* (Anecdotal history of the Revolution), vol. 2 (Taipei, 1965): 115–119, 4:26–37 and 140; Huang San-te, *Hung-men ke-ming shih* (Revolutionary history of the Hung League) (Los Angeles, 1936); Harold Z. Schiffrin, *Sun Yat-sen and the Origins of the Chinese Revolution* (Berkeley, Calif., 1968).

SHIH-SHAN HENRY TSAI

CHIHLI CLIQUE: The military group that controlled most of north and central China in the 1920s.

Taking its name from the capital district (today's Honan Province), the Chihli Clique had its origins in the Peiyang military system created by Li Hung-chang* and Yüan Shih-k'ai* in the late Ch'ing dynasty. Later, its leading figures were Feng Kuo-chang, and then Ts'ao K'un* and Wu P'ei-fu.*

As the successor, in effect, to the Ch'ing military establishment, the Chihli group was powerful and influential, and in 1924 it came very close to establishing dominance over all of China. It defeated successively the Anfu Clique* (1920) and the Fengt'ien Clique* (1922), but in 1924 in its showdown with Fengt'ien it was thrown into disarray by the defection and coup d'état of Feng Yü-hsiang.* Despite attempts to regroup in the Yangtze Valley, the clique effectively ceased to exist thereafter.

Given its size, internal tensions were to be expected in the faction, and they were clear between Ts'ao K'un and Wu P'ei-fu, and between the Northerners and the Yangtze Valley allies. After 1924, however, and with the rise of the Kuomintang, the issue became more political than regional and personal: whether to support Chang Tso-lin, the old adversary and a firm antirevolutionary, or Feng Yü-hsiang, who had betrayed the faction but who sympathized with the Nationalists. During the Northern Expedition* (1926–1928) what remained of the clique split along these lines, with the former group defending the Peking government, while the latter joined the Nationalist coalition. This development greatly helped the Kuomintang.

REFERENCE: Odoric Y.K. Wou, *Militarism in Modern China: The Career of Wu P'ei-fu 1916–39* (Folkestone, Kent, England, 1978).

ARTHUR WALDRON

CHIN-CH'A-CHI BORDER REGION: The major Communist base area in north China behind Japanese lines during the anti-Japanese war and the model for other resistance base areas as well as for social policies used in Shen-Kan-Ning.

Created in late 1937, the Chin-Ch'a-Chi administration survived severe Japanese repression and grew continuously from 1944. It was combined with two other bases in May 1948 to become the north China Base.

Following the Eighth Route Army's* engagement with the Japanese at P'ing-hsing Pass in September 1937, a portion of the 115th Division (merely 2,000 men) under General Nieh Jung-chen was sent to the mountainous region between Shansi and Hopei (centered at Wutai County, Shansi) to set up a base area. In a pattern followed by the other eighteen Communist base areas during the war, the Chin-Ch'a-Chi Military District was established on November 7, 1937, followed in January 1938 by the civilian administration, the Chin-Ch'a-Chi Resistance Base Area. Later that year, the Nationalist government recognized the administration (under its chair, Sung Shao-wen, a non-Communist), and the area became an official border region (the only Communist base area so recognized other than Shen-Kan-Ning*). Its capital was Fou-p'ing, Hopei. Until it briefly occupied Kalgan (Chang-chia-k'ou) in 1946, the border region controlled only the countryside and no major cities. The border region had three major subareas: Peiyueh (northwest Hopei), Central Hopei, and Hopei-Jehol-Liaoning. In October 1937 the Nationalist troops under Lü Cheng-ts'ao in south Hopei joined the Communists. In March 1938 troops of the 120th Division under Ho Lung extended the area's control to P'inghsi (west of Peip'ing).

The major achievement of the Chin-Ch'a-Chi Border Region was, in fact, survival—which it barely achieved. Japanese repression—its cleanup campaigns—was severe, particularly following the dramatic Hundred Regiments Offensive of late summer 1940. Between 1941 and 1943 the border region shrank considerably. After that, it grew to a maximum size of over one hundred counties and a population of about 25 million.

Social policies later adopted by the central Chinese Communist party* in Yenan were first developed in Chin-Ch'a-Chi between 1938 and 1941. P'eng Chen played a key role in developing such United Front versions of CCP policy, including rent and interest reduction, progressive taxation, new village governments (the "three-thirds" system limiting CCP representation to one-third), systematic guerrilla organization, and mobilization campaigns. These were codified in the August 1940 "Double Ten Program" of the Chin-Ch'a-Chi branch of the Politburo.

The social composition of north China was more complex than that in Shen-Kan-Ning. Tensions between landlords and peasants were not as clearcut as they were around Yenan. Thus, the party's first goal in Chin-Ch'a-Chi was to gain compliance among the rural elite in the face of Japanese attacks. This delicate balance of peasants, rural elite, and Japanese and puppet forces required the CCP in Chin-Ch'a-Chi to follow a moderate application of Rectification* and other party policies. By the end of the war the north China base areas were able to deliver to the CCP large areas of sympathetic and organized populations and a proven model of rural reform. After 1949 many of the senior cadres that had gained their administrative experience in the north China bases rather than in Yenan opposed Mao's utopian plans.

REFERENCES: Carl E. Dorris, "Peasant Mobilization in North China and the Origins of Yenan Communism," *The China Quarterly*, No. 68 (1976): 697–719; Kathleen Hartford, "Repression and Communist Success: The Case of Jin-Cha-Ji, 1938–1943," in Hartford and Steven M. Goldstein, eds., *Single Sparks: China's Rural Revolutions* (Armonk, N.Y., 1989): 92–127; Nieh Jung-chen, *K'ang-Jih mo-fan ken-chü ti—Chin-Ch'a-Chi pien-ch'ü* (A model anti-Japanese base area—the Chin-Ch'a-Chi Border Region) (n.p., 1939).

TIMOTHY CHEEK

CHINA REVIVAL SOCIETY (HUA-HSING HUI): Revolutionary organization against the Ch'ing dynasty.

The Hua-hsing hui was founded on February 15, 1904, in Hunan by Huang Hsing[*] for the explicit goal of overthrowing the Manchu dynasty. Among the many prominent members were men like Sung Chiao-jen,[*] Chang Shih-chao, Ch'en T'ien-hua, and others who later became key figures of the T'ung-meng hui.[*] Although the Hua-hsing hui was dominated by Hunanese students who had returned from Japan, from the very beginning it had strong ties with secret societies, especially with the Ko-Lao Hui,[*] whose members were said to have joined in many of the sub-branches of the Hua-hsing hui by the tens of thousands. The actual numbers might have been exaggerated, but it is significant that the Hua-hsing hui's organizational structure paralleled that of the Ko-Lao Hui, particularly in the area of the military chain of command. This probably reflected the primary goal of the Hua-hsing hui: to "kick out the Tartars" through assassinations of important Manchu officials. Huang Hsing, the top leader, was convinced that military uprisings and the patriotism of the Chinese people would surely topple the Manchu government.

Two plots were planned, one for November 1904, during the Empress Dowager Tz'u-hsi's[*] birthday celebrations, and another for early 1905. Ironically, despite elaborate safeguards to ensure the secrecy of their activities, Hunan provincial authorities learned about the precise uprising dates weeks before their execution. Both attempts failed miserably, and the main conspirators had to flee to Japan.

Huang Hsing soon realized that his fellow Hunanese followers must have the cooperation of other revolutionary groups, since everyone's main objective was to overthrow Manchu rule. In the summer of 1905, through Miyazaki Torazō's[*] efforts, Huang met Sun Yat-sen[*] for the first time in Tokyo, to discuss the possibility of the merger of Sun's Hsing-chung hui[*] and the Hua-hsing hui. Precisely what took place is still subject to extreme interpretations, but apparently a compromise was reached, and Huang decided to support Sun fully. Individual members of the Hua-hsing hui, however, were invited to join the proposed T'ung-meng hui in their private capacities. For all practical purposes, at this point, the Hua-hsing hui had ceased to exist.

Sun Yat-sen was elected *Tsung-li* (premier) of the new party on August 20, 1905. Historians generally agree that without the Hua-hsing hui's participation, the founding of the T'ung-meng hui would not have been possible. Since Sun's followers were mostly overseas Chinese and businessmen, the amalgamation ensured that Sun's revolutionary base could be enlarged to include intellectuals and army men (not to mention secret society members) within China. Not surprisingly, many scholars have insisted that without Huang Hsing and his Hua-hsing hui, Sun's revolutionary career would have turned out completely different.

The exact relationship between Sun and Huang will be forever debated by historians; lack of reliable source materials prohibit any kind of definitive observations. However, a closer look at the Hua-hsing hui's revolutionary program and ideology shows that it did not have any long-range goals for China other than the military defeat of the Manchus. The lack of any specific directions for development put into question the Hua-hsing hui's ability to sustain itself. Nevertheless, members did have rather different views on how China was to be transformed into a democratic republic. Some believed that individual provinces should gain independence first, before each and every one of them became a full member of the Chinese nation. Others felt that China must first be led by middle-ranking classes, those who were neither peasants nor members of the ruling factions. All thought that once the Manchus were eliminated militarily, China's problems would be quickly resolved.

Thus, after its unsuccessful uprisings, Huang Hsing became aware of Hua-hsing hui's limitations, and therefore decided to give wholehearted support to Sun's organization that had a broader political prospectus. However, although the Hua-hsing hui was short-lived, it did serve its purpose at the early stage of the 1911 Revolution* period. Without it, Sun's revolutionary activities might have been confined to the periphery of China proper. Even more importantly, most of the Hua-hsing hui leadership was to play vital roles in the history of republican China.
REFERENCES: Chün-tu Hsüeh, *Huang Hsing and the Chinese Revolution* (Stanford, Calif., 1961); Ta-ling Lee, *Foundations of the Chinese Revolution, 1905–1912* (New York, 1970).

JOHN D. YOUNG

CHINESE BOYCOTT (1905): Chinese rising nationalism, anti-American movement, and reaction to U.S. exclusions.

On May 10, 1905, the Shanghai Chamber of Commerce, under the leadership of Tseng Shao-ching, passed resolutions urging all Chinese in Shanghai not to buy American goods. Tseng sent telegrams to the chambers of commerce of twenty-two other treaty ports, calling on Chinese merchants to boycott American products unless the United States modified its immigration policy toward the Chinese. Tseng declared, "When our government proves itself unable to act, then the people must rise up to do so." In less than a month, this first antiforeign boycott spread throughout China, and it continued into 1906. It extended from Shanghai to Foochow, Amoy, and Canton in the south and to Tientsin and Peking in the north. It also penetrated into the central Yangtze Valley. Those who pushed the movement included intellectuals, students, urban professionals, labor leaders, educated women at home, and Chinese in the United States, the

Philippines, Hawaii, Singapore, Japan, and other places. It was indeed the largest antiforeign movement in China between the Boxer Uprising[*] of 1900 and the May Fourth Movement[*] in 1919.

The Chinese supporting the boycott objected to more than the provision of the American exclusion laws. They were particularly annoyed with the manner in which Chinese students, merchants, and other so-called exempt classes were treated. Several pervasive discriminations against the Chinese living in America had fueled the humiliation, frustration, and anger felt by Chinese at home and abroad. The rising Chinese nationalism helped ignite the anti-American movement.

When the boycott started, the Ch'ing[*] government tried to use the expression of public opinion to advantage in negotiations with the United States. Between August 12, 1904, and January 25, 1905, the Chinese minister to Washington, Liang Cheng, submitted two different drafts to the Roosevelt administration to replace the expired Gresham–Yang Treaty, but both were turned down. Meanwhile, the boycott activities were escalating and becoming more violent. The Ch'ing government then realized that the boycott could develop into another Boxer Rebellion. Consequently, it changed its stand and took measures to suppress the boycott.

On the other side of the Pacific, President Theodore Roosevelt publicly expressed his disapproval of abuses in the administering of the exclusion laws. Secretary of State John Hay, who was pushing for an Open Door policy in China, believed that the exclusion laws against the Chinese had become a major barrier to the extension of trade and cultural ties between the two countries. In June 1905, Roosevelt issued executive orders threatening to dismiss any immigration officials who mistreated Chinese who had proper documents.

The emotionally charged boycott was doomed to failure from its inception. The years 1905 and 1906 also saw a fierce rivalry between K'ang Yu-wei's[*] reformers and Sun Yat-sen's[*] revolutionaries. The boycott was the right kind of issue that helped to escalate their battle against each other. In general, the reformers represented the interests of the bourgeois class, while the revolutionaries were mostly young students and workers. This lack of coordination among the boycott leaders, as well as Ch'ing counter-boycott measures, greatly weakened the movement's strength.

Although the Ch'ing government refused to renew the Gresham–Yang Treaty, the United States unilaterally extended and reenacted all of the anti-Chinese exclusion laws, dictating the course of Chinese immigration until their repeal in December 1943. Nevertheless, the boycott movement had helped, to a great extent, arouse Chinese nationalistic sentiment.

REFERENCES: Chang Ts'un-wu, *Chung-Mei kung-yueh feng-ts'ao* (Agitation of the Sino-American Labor Treaty) (Taipei, 1965); John W. Foster, "The Chinese Boycott," *Atlantic Monthly* 97 (January 1906): 118–127; Chester Holcombe, "Chinese Exclusion and the Boycott," *Outlook* 81 (December 1905): 1066–1072; Delber L. McKee, *Chinese Exclusion Versus the Open Door Policy, 1900–1906* (Detroit, 1977).

SHIH-SHAN HENRY TSAI

CHINESE COMMUNIST PARTY (CCP): Vanguard of the Chinese Communist Movement and ruling party of the PRC.

Founded in July 1921 in Shanghai, the Chinese Communist party (Chung-kuo Kung-ch'an-tang) did not seize power until October 1949. In the early 1950s the party established control over the entire country, including Tibet, and formulated policies for developing the economy along socialist lines. Beginning in the late 1950s, the CCP also underwent considerable internal turmoil as top party leaders divided over fundamental political and economic issues, which ultimately provoked the assault on the party apparatus by Mao Tse-tung* during the Cultural Revolution* (1966–1976). Although the CCP was gradually reconstructed in the 1970s, Mao's death in 1976 left the new leadership of Teng Hsiao-p'ing* with an institution that had grown to over 40 million members, but that was still deeply divided on the political and economic direction of China's future.

The Struggle for Power, 1921–1949

The decision to form a Communist party in China was a response to domestic and international developments. These included the failure of the Chinese Republic, founded in 1912, to solve the internal political crisis fomented by powerful warlords and the government's inability to prevent the post–World War I Versailles conference from transferring Chinese national territory from German to Japanese control. The victory of the Bolsheviks in Russia also had a profound effect on Chinese intellectuals searching for an alternative model of political and state power. The Leninist party model was seen as a "modern" institutional structure with the capacity to mobilize society's resources, but without the debilitating weaknesses of Western parliamentary democracy.

Organizationally, the CCP initially reflected the influence of local study societies established in various cities by Marxist and anarchist intellectuals. Despite the adoption of a sophisticated institutional framework at its 1922 Second Congress, Communist party activity in the early years was highly decentralized, with considerable internal opposition, especially in Canton, to a highly centralized organization. The CCP's first leader, Ch'en Tu-hsiu,* thus refused the title of party chief (*tsung-li*) because, Chang Kuo-t'ao* later recalled, of the "many abuses it had brought to China." Instead, Ch'en preferred "the more democratic committee system . . . with a secretary elected from committee members to serve as coordinator," a role reflected in Ch'en's formal designation in 1922 as committee head (*wei-yüan chang*). Theoretically, ultimate political authority was exercised by a Central Executive Committee (later renamed the Central Committee in 1927), which appointed an executive standing committee, a Central Bureau, and a five-member Organizational Central Bureau.

Following the 1925 May Thirtieth Incident,* CCP membership expanded rapidly from under 1,000 to over 18,000 in 1926. The relatively autonomous study societies and regional party organizations were also replaced by a tightly knit, centralized structure based on vertical organizational principles. Along with the newly formed Organization and Propaganda departments and a Central Secretariat, the leadership established various secret organizations (*mi-mi chi-kuan*) and appointed special investigative personnel to enforce central authority. The party's grass-roots structure of cells (*hsiao-tsu*) and party corps (*tang-t'uan*) were also subject to greater central control.

The near destruction of the CCP's urban apparatus in April 1927 by the Nationalists in Canton and Shanghai had an equally profound impact on the party's institutional development. Further central control over the organization was strengthened by the introduction of basic Leninist principles of democratic centralism* (*min-chu chi-chung-chih*) and by the creation of a Politburo (*cheng-chih chü*) to "guide the political affairs of the entire country." At every level of the apparatus, power was concentrated in the standing committees—the executive arm of the larger party committees—which increasingly relied on investigation committees (*shen-ch'a wei-yüan-hui*) to subject the rank and file to intense perusal.

After Ch'en Tu-hsiu's dismissal, Li Li-san* assumed de facto control of the party in 1929–1930 and radically reorganized the apparatus to enhance his personal control. Combining party and mass organizations into single general action committees (*tsung hsing-tung wei-yüan-hui*), Li implemented a reckless strategy of political strikes and urban insurrections that brought the CCP even closer to complete destruction.

After Li Li-san's replacement by the Comintern* and the return to China of students trained in the Soviet Union (i.e., the Russian Returned Students, or Twenty-eight Bolsheviks*), the CCP shifted operations to the countryside. Although retaining the basic organizational structure established in the 1920s, changes were instituted to reflect the Communists' new rural environment and its military orientation. At an enlarged Politburo meeting in 1935, it was decided to "establish [Mao Tse-tung] in the leading position of the Red Army and the Party Center." While Chou En-lai* and the Russian Returned Student Chang Wen-t'ien were also accorded important decision-making authority, Mao clearly emerged as the CCP's preeminent leader. Steps were also taken to avoid independent power bailiwicks from emerging in the Red Army as a hierarchical structure of military-political committees, and CCP political departments were established to insure party control over the military.

By 1938 the Communist party structure of the war years was finalized at the Sixth Plenum held in Yenan after the completion of the Long March.* Ad hoc decision making was ended as party rules established clear lines of authority. The Central Committee was reaffirmed as the highest organ in political and organizational matters (except during the periodic party congresses), while standing committees were now subordinated to their respective party committees, reversing the 1927 decision cited above. The apex of the party consisted of the Politburo, the Secretariat, and a Central Bureau and central sub-bureaus. The latter two directed party activities through the hierarchical structure of party committees established at the region, prefecture, county, city, district, and branch levels. Six departments—organization, propaganda, war mobilization, popular movements, united front, and the Secretariat—were established at the central level with branches extending below. Overall, the Organization Department (Tsu-chih pu) and Secretariat (Shu-chi ch'ü) emerged as the most powerful instruments for controlling a membership that by 1942 had grown to over 800,000.

During the 1942–1944 party Rectification,* an even more elaborate organizational structure was developed. This included a Central Committee Office, a Party Committee for Managing Organs Directly Subordinate to the Central Committee, and the highly secretive Central Investigation Department (chung-yang tiao-ch'a pu) and Social Affairs Department. These were charged with investigating cadre loyalty and ferreting out Nationalist "spies." Under the influence of K'ang Sheng, this internal security apparatus carried out the first major internal party purge, which Mao ultimately terminated because of excessive killings and cadre suicides. Finally, Mao's position in the leadership was further enhanced by a March 1943 decision giving him the authority to "make final decisions regarding all problems discussed by the [three-member] Central Secretariat." Combined with the promulgation of the Mao personality cult, which began in 1942, the CCP and the "great leader" were now virtually indistinguishable. Yet, in upholding the supremacy of party committees over individual leaders in a 1948 speech, Mao also presaged the forthcoming clash between charismatic and institutional authority that would eventually split the CCP right down the middle.

The Chinese Communist Party in Power, 1949–1976

The CCP emerged from the 1945–1949 civil war* with an elaborate organization that quickly imposed its control over the entire country. From the central to the county (hsien) level, there were 6 central and 4 subcentral bureaus, 24 provincial committees, 17 regional committees, and 134 city and 218 area (ti-fang) committees. Total party membership in 1950 was 4.5 million (up from 3 million in 1948), with 80,000 full-time cadres forming the CCP's organizational core. As the CCP's role rapidly shifted from wartime mobilization (during both the civil and Korean wars), the need for professionally trained cadres increased dramatically. Meanwhile, the illiterate party veterans of the wars against the Japanese and Nationalists were now confronted with their own political obsolescence. Party rectifications in the early 1950s thus squeezed out 670,000 rural, uneducated members, while 910,000 more well-educated personnel were recruited into a party whose membership continued to expand to 6.2 million by 1953.

Party organization also reflected the imperatives of economic growth and management. Five new departments—industry, finance and trade, communication and transportation, political-legal, and agriculture—were thus established. Control over appointments and training of technical cadres was also decentralized, with a concomitant reduction in the Organization Department's authority. While Mao Tse-tung evidently supported such changes, the chairman showed increasing impatience with the deliberative process of decision making that emerged with the CCP's shift to economic management. In July 1955 Mao thus upset the gradualist approach to organizing rural cooperatives by announcing a socialist upsurge in the Chinese countryside.

From this point on, the issue of procedural and collective leadership (*chi-t'i ling-tao*) versus Mao's increasingly impulsive and individualistic leadership style would increasingly divide the party. While Mao's enormous charisma allowed him to prevail in most political standoffs, elliptical criticism of the chairman was expressed by relatively liberal CCP leaders, such as An Tzu-wen, who extolled the party committees, including the Central Committee, as the final sovereign body. Strengthened by the emphasis on collective leadership in the Soviet Union following Stalin's death, Chinese proponents of institutionalizing authority in the CCP won significant concessions from the chairman of the pivotal 1956 Eighth Party Congress. In addition to deleting "Thought of Mao Tse-tung*" from the party constitution, a more collective top leadership was created with the appointment of five vice-chairmen, the formal prohibition against leader cults, and a renewed emphasis in CCP decision making on such procedures as periodic congresses and utilization of formal agendas.

Yet, Mao was still able to circumvent the party with his personal charisma and the evident support of local party secretaries—the "little Maos," or "local despots"—who evidently admired his decisive leadership. Thus, without formal Central Committee or Politburo approval, Mao personally ordered the wide-open Hundred Flowers Campaign.* Speaking prior to a planned party plenum, Mao exhorted subordinates to "relay and implement" his proposals without formal authorization. "Being the first secretary, I will take charge of ideological work," Mao arrogantly asserted.

Then during the debate over the proposed Great Leap Forward,* Mao showed his contempt for institutional procedure by authorizing the formation of the rural communes before formal Politburo decisions. Mao also personally counter-manded central decisions on grain deliveries and production quotas. When P'eng Te-huai* responded at the now infamous 1959 Lushan* plenum by voicing sur-prisingly mild criticisms of the chairman's leadership style during the Leap, Mao countered by purging P'eng and launching a campaign against "rightist oppor-tunism." This action effectively silenced the entire organization and evidently created a basis for Mao's later decision to launch the Cultural Revolution. The relatively open and semilegal model of the party's decision-making structure outlined at the Eighth Congress was now effectively defunct.

Following the collapse of the Leap and Mao's retreat to the second front of decision making, CCP propaganda organs revived the Eighth Party Congress model. Throughout the early 1960s, "regularization" of party decision making through majority rule in party committees was reemphasized. A "moderate" leadership style was also advocated in place of the "tyrannical way" (*pa-tao*) criticized by the party intellectual Teng T'o in a Peking newspaper. In an obvious reference to the purge of P'eng Te-huai, the right of every party member to voice his or her views was defended, while Mao's tendency to rely on oral orders was indirectly criticized. With party membership at 17 million, central authorities also emphasized the recruitment of educated cadres. The increasingly leftward trend of the rural Socialist Education Movement* (1962–1966), however, effectively prevented the full substitution of expertise over "redness" in CCP ranks.

By 1964 Mao once again entered the political fray intent on eliminating political obstruction of his renewed effort to attempt yet another great leap. Detaching himself from central party leaders, the chairman mobilized youthful Red Guards* to attack veteran cadres whom Mao accused of "taking the capitalist road." As party ranks were decimated at all organizational levels, Mao supported the establishment of alternative political bodies to replace the Leninist structures of the CCP. In addition to the Revolutionary Committees*—which combined "good" party, government, and army cadres into a single but highly unwieldy organization—the regular structure of party committees was replaced by various party "groups" (tsu) dominated by the radical faction (tsao-fan p'ai).

At the April 1969 Ninth Party Congress, the unprecedented action was taken of naming Mao's successor—Lin Piao*—in the new party constitution. Yet, even as the last Revolutionary Committees were established in the provinces, Mao was already convinced that "rebuilding the party" was necessary to avoid civil war and social chaos. Although campaigns such as the notorious "cleansing of the class ranks" produced continued violence against party members, the CCP's conventional structure was gradually reestablished. Despite the protestations of Mao's radical supporters, especially his wife Chiang Ch'ing,* the radical experiment with alternative political forms, particularly the Revolutionary Committees, was terminated. Veteran cadres vilified during the Cultural Revolution, especially Teng Hsiao-p'ing,* were also gradually rehabilitated. Still, the presence of over 8 million party members recruited in the Cultural Revolution provided a social basis in the CCP for promoting such radical notions as "going against the tide"—a principle diametrically opposed to traditional democratic centralism.

The early 1970s witnessed a relatively open debate over the nature of the party in the post–Cultural Revolution era. Although Teng's veteran cadres advocated the restoration of conventional Leninist norms with renewed emphasis on maintaining tight control of recruitment and promotion, the radicals equated such moves with a restoration of the old regime. Using their control over propaganda organs in the 1973–1975 Anti-Confucian Campaign, the radicals also tried to secure the party's helm for Chiang Ch'ing after Mao's death. Yet, it was Teng Hsiao-p'ing who, relying on the political alliances built up over his years as party general secretary, ultimately won the political struggle for power following the chairman's death. By the early 1980s, however, even Teng was unsure whether he should simply return the CCP to the status quo ante of the early 1950s, or launch a dramatic process of political reform away from one-party dictatorship.

REFERENCES: Chang Kuo-t'ao, *The Rise of the Chinese Communist Party*, vol. 1 (Lawrence, Kan. 1971); *Chung-kuo Kung-ch'an-tang tsu-chih Shih tzu-liao Hui-pian* (Compilation of historical documents on the CCP's organization) (Peking, 1982); Roderick MacFarquhar, ed., *The Secret Speeches of Mao Zedong* (Cambridge, Mass., 1989).

LAWRENCE R. SULLIVAN

CHINESE NATIONALIST PARTY (KUOMINTANG OR KMT): The ruling party in the ROC from 1928 to the present.

The Kuomintang was the result of a reorganization by Sung Chiao-jen* in April 1912 of its predecessor, the T'ung-meng hui,* and the merging in August with four other political parties. After the so-called Second Revolution,* aimed at the overthrow of President Yüan Shih-k'ai* whose men had assassinated Sung in March 1913, the Kuomintang was outlawed. In July 1914 Sun Yat-sen,* then in exile in Tokyo, reorganized it as the clandestine Chinese Revolutionary party,* which pledged absolute loyalty to him. In 1916 it led the struggle against Yüan's Monarchical Movement until his death on June 6 of the same year.

On September 10, 1917, Sun set up the military government of the Republic of China* in Canton, with himself as the generalissimo, in opposition to the Peking warlord regime. In May 1918, however, the National Assembly in Canton adopted a law under which the generalissimo was to be replaced by a seven-man committee, thus depriving Sun of his authority in favor of the local warlords. Consequently, Sun was forced to leave for Shanghai. It was in Shanghai on October 10, 1919, that he announced the reorganization of the Chinese Revolutionary party as the Chinese Kuomintang. In November 1920 he returned to Canton to revive the military government and to use it as a base for China's reunification. But he remained dependent on the unreliable support of the local militarists, while the Kuomintang suffered from organizational weakness, internal strife, financial difficulties, limited mass support, and the lack of a party army.

Sun had sought in vain Western support of his revolutionary cause before he accepted the offer of Soviet aid in 1923 when the KMT entered into an alliance with Soviet Russia and the fledgling Chinese Communist party.* The first National Party Congress held in Canton during January 20–30, 1924, adopted a new constitution and a new political platform. Communists were admitted to the party as individual members in a marriage of convenience, with the Kuomintang as the senior partner. The party was reorganized along Soviet lines, assisted by the Comintern* and other Russian agents led by Michael Borodin.* Now reinvigorated, fortified by a powerful anti-imperialist ideology, and possessed of a highly indoctrinated and Russian-trained army, the Kuomintang appeared to be the only political party capable of ridding China of warlordism* on the one hand and foreign imperialism on the other.

The Northern Expedition* led to the establishment of the left-wing Wuhan Regime* at the beginning of 1927 and of the rival Nanking Regime on April 18. Led by Chiang Kai-shek,* the Nanking leadership immediately carried out a bloody purge of the Communists. Shortly afterward, the Wuhan Regime also began to suppress the Communists in Hupeh, thus putting an end to the United Front. The Wuhan Regime then dissolved itself, and the Northern Expedition went on to complete its task in the following year. On October 10, 1928, the National government was officially inaugurated in Nanking.

The Nationalist Revolution was designed to undergo three stages: first, military rule; second, political tutelage; and finally, constitutional government. In the event, Nationalist China was practically under military rule all the time, political tutelage became an instrument for keeping the Kuomintang in power as long as possible, and constitutional government was not effected until late 1947.

As a revolutionary party, the Kuomintang drew its support from the student and educated classes and enjoyed a large measure of popular support at the time of the Northern Expedition. Many of its leaders came from good socioeconomic backgrounds, although they did not necessarily represent the interests either of the landlords or of the commercial bourgeoisie. They were interested in a political rather than a social revolution. After 1928, as the revolutionary party became the government, it soon lost its capacity for change. Organizationally, the Kuomintang was similar to the Chinese Communist party, with its national and provincial congresses and committee structure, as well as party cells at the district levels. The Central Executive Committee with its Standing Committee and the Political Council were the highest decision-making bodies. The Leninist principle of democratic centralism,* adopted in 1924, remained in force after the split with the Communists.

Until his death in March 1925, Sun Yat-sen was the supreme leader whose Three People's Principles*—nationalism, people's rights, and people's livelihood—formed the basis of the party's ideology throughout its long history. After his death, the party was torn by factionalism: first, by conflicts between the left and the right (the Western Hills Faction*) with the military holding the balance of power, and then, after 1931, by rivalries among the various factions all of which pledged loyalty to Chiang Kai-shek, who, as chairman of the Military Affairs Committee, controlled the army. On March 29, 1938, Chiang was elevated to the exalted position of *tsung-tsai*, a position second in status only to that of *tsung-li*, which had been held by and was still reserved for the late Sun Yat-sen.

As the party came under the domination of the military, it was increasingly repressive. No political dissent was tolerated, and corruption among party leaders was rampant. The party was divorced from the masses, and for a considerable time it was attracted to the fascist ideology advocated in China by the pro-Chiang Blue Shirt Society.* Consequently, the leadership lost its ability and will to introduce the social, economic, and political reforms necessary to transform China into a modern nation-state. Meanwhile, it was preoccupied with the Communist problem, and yet it was unable to attack the problem at its roots or to eliminate the Communists by force of arms. A Second United Front* with the Communists was formed at the start of the war of resistance against Japan. But the civil war* was renewed as soon as the Japanese surrendered, and the government's ultimate—and ignominious—defeat forced the Nationalists to seek refuge in Taiwan in 1949. The Kuomintang has since ruled the island, which it still calls the Republic of China.

REFERENCES: Tuan-sheng Ch'ien, *The Government and Politics of China* (Cambridge, Mass., 1967); Hung-Mao Tien, *Government and Politics in Kuomintang China 1927–1937* (Stanford, Calif., 1972); Lloyd E. Eastman, *The Abortive Revolution* (Cambridge, Mass., 1974); also Eastman, *The Seeds of Destruction* (Stanford, Calif., 1984).

EDMUND S. K. FUNG

CHINESE PEOPLE'S POLITICAL CONSULTATIVE CONFERENCE (CPPCC): The "patriotic" United Front organization of the PRC.

Before October 1949 the CPPCC was the vehicle through which the Chinese Communist party[*] secured the support of various groups of people in preparation for the formal promulgation of the People's Republic of China[*] on October 1, 1949. Between that date and September 15, 1954, when the National People's Congress was convened on the basis of the first formal constitution of the new state, it was the PRC's parliamentary body. Since 1954, however, it has become a broad "patriotic" United Front organ, not the representative organ of power.

As a United Front organ, the CPPCC brings together the representatives of Communist and non-Communist constituencies in the population, excepting "the enemy," and functions under the CCP's leadership. For the Communist regime, it is useful for sizing up political forces in the country, identifying dissenting opinions, transmitting a policy and mobilizing wide-ranging support for a struggle, indoctrinating and reeducating certain elements, rewarding those who cooperate, controlling potential challengers, and legitimizing the CCP's rule.

The CPPCC must be distinguished from the Political Consultative Conference (PCC) held in Chungking during 1946. Unlike the PCC, which was held between the Kuomintang and the CCP, the CPPCC was first convened in 1949 by the CCP to unite all anti-KMT forces. Over 600 delegates representing fourteen political parties, nine geographical areas, six army units, sixteen "people's organizations," and some religious groups attended its first session from September 21 to 30, 1949. It gave birth to the PRC, organized the Central People's government and declared October 1 the new National Day. Three basic documents were formally promulgated, which became the legal basis of the new regime: (1) the Common Program of the CPPCC, (2) the Organic Law of the CPPCC, and (3) the Organic Law of the Central People's government of the PRC.

Because the CCP wanted the new government to appear as a coalition government of democratic parties, the Common Program was said to contain a set of principles supported by all parties and therefore governing their common effort. It spelled out the regime's program for the preliminary phase of revolution, that is, a New Democracy during China's transition from the semifeudal and semicolonial stage to the socialist stage.

In accordance with the Organic Law of the CPPCC, the Plenary Session elected a National Committee. A Standing Committee, composed of a chairman and a number of vice-chairmen and several members, was in turn elected from among the members of the National Committee. Provincial-level committees and standing committees were established as the National Committee saw fit.

The Second CPPCC National Committee held its first session in December 1954, three months after the NPC's first session was held. A constitution was adopted in place of the Organic Law of the CPPCC. It declared under General Principles that the CPPCC, no longer an organ of national power, "will continue to exist as an organization of the people's democratic united front for rallying all nationalities, democratic classes, democratic parties and groups, people's bodies, overseas Chinese, and other patriotic democrats." The Plenary Session of the CPPCC was discontinued, so that the structure of the CPPCC at each level was changed from three to two tiers. The National Committee was reorganized, and one honorary chairman, one chairman, several vice-chairmen, and a secretary-general were elected. Their terms of office were set at four years. In 1978 further amendments eliminated the post of honorary chairman, and the terms of office were extended to five years.

In the preamble of the 1982 constitution of the PRC, the CPPCC was formally given recognition as "a broadly representative organization of the united front, which has played a significant historical role and will continue to do so in the political and social life of the country, in promoting friendship with the people of other countries and in the struggle for socialist modernization and for the reunification and unity of the country." The Fifth CPPCC National Committee also adopted a new constitution at its Fifth Session on December 11, 1982. It echoed the new line of the Tengist reform and stipulated that the CPPCC should engage in internal political consultations and democratic supervision over the work of the government.

With the exception of the Fourth NPC, from 1959 on, the CPPCC has met yearly in conjunction with the NPC's yearly session. However, it remained not much more than a transmission belt of CCP policy. After 1979 and especially with the Sixth NPC during the five years from 1983 to 1987, there was a marked change. The Sixth CPPCC National Committee comprising 2,039 deputies was elected in June 1983. It gained significant stature as more and more deputies spoke up on national problems of the day. Noted personalities like Ch'ien Chia-chu and Hsü Sze-min who offered critical comments on prices, education, corruption, and other issues were widely acclaimed. The CCP leaders also promised to incorporate more leaders from the democratic parties at various levels of government.

The Seventh CPPCC National Committee was elected in 1988 and promised to be even more open and bold. This was true in 1988. However, the political atmosphere changed within the PRC after the June 1989 T'ienanmen Square Incident, as it had so often before, and dissenting opinion subsided.

REFERENCES: Chung-kung chung-yang tung-chan-pu yen-chiu-shi (Research unit, CPC Central United Front Department) and Chin-ling chi sheng kuang-po tien-tai (Editorial Department, The Voice of Chin-ling Broadcasting Station), eds., *Tung-i Chan-hsien*

Kung-tso Shou-ch'e (Handbook for United Front Work) (Nanking, 1986); Liang Ch'in, ed., *Ai-kuo Tung-i Chan-hsien Kai-lun* (An Introduction to the Patriotic United Front) (Changsha, 1987).

BYRON SONG JAN WENG

CHINESE REVOLUTIONARY PARTY: Revolutionary organization founded by Sun Yat-sen in 1914.

After the Second Revolution* failed to overthrow Yüan Shih-k'ai's* regime in August 1913, Sun Yat-sen* and fellow revolutionists fled abroad and formed a new party to continue their anti-Yüan endeavors. Officially founded in Tokyo, Japan, in July 1914 after about one year of preparatory work there, the Chinese Revolutionary party (CRP) was, in Edward Friedman's words, a "supra-Leninist organization. . . . a party based on a strategy of even greater centralized direction than Lenin's." Dr. Sun was determined to form a party centering around himself with the members' absolute obedience to him assured. Sun's previous frustrations caused by fellow revolutionaries who did not heed his decisions explained his assertion of party leadership, requiring each member to pledge absolute obedience to his person upon joining the party. Consequently, Huang Hsing* and some other veteran revolutionists never joined because of this requirement. Through the good office of Sun's Japanese acquaintances, he managed to secure a base in Japan for the CRP. Branches and sub-branches were subsequently set up in Southeast Asia, Hong Kong and Macao, South Africa, Australia and New Zealand, the United States, Canada, Hawaii, and Europe. The headquarters in Tokyo comprised five departments in charge of general, party, financial, military, and political affairs, respectively, with the branches and sub-branches under its direct supervision. In addition, a separate chain of military command was also set up with Sun as its generalissimo. The party was structured in such a way that it would function as a government once the revolution succeeded. In the party's constitution it was stipulated that the three-stage (military, political tutelary, and constitutional) revolutionary program would be strictly followed, and that the CRP would be China's sole ruling body before the institution of a full constitutional government. It also guaranteed CRP members and contributors of funds future political and economic privileges, respectively.

During its first two years of operation, the CRP fought alone against Yüan's dictatorship. With all revolutionary bases and strength in China lost and destroyed during the Second Revolution, it could operate mainly abroad and with limited resources. Its major activities included fund-raising, the propagation of revolutionary ideas, and military uprisings. About a dozen armed struggles occurred from January 1914 to December 1915, mostly along China's coastal provinces. Lack of sufficient funds accounted for most of their failures. Assassinations were also attempted, and in November 1915 CRP agents murdered Cheng Ju-ch'eng, Yüan's key general in the Shanghai region. Furthermore, beginning in May 1914 CRP published the monthly *Min-kuo tsa-chih*, or the *Republic Journal*, carrying

articles condemning Yüan's dictatorship and malpractices and revealing his conspiracy to restore the monarchy. Hu Han-min,* Tsou Lu,* and Chu Chih-hsin
were among the monthly's able contributors. Sun himself wrote about self-
government on the *hsien* or county level, enlightening the Chinese public on
exercising their political power. The cumulative effect of CRP's endeavors to
overthrow Yüan was considerable. When Ts'ai Ao* and the Republic-defending
army in Yunnan rose against Yüan's proclaimed monarchy on Christmas Day,
1915, they won support throughout most of China. Within six months, Yüan
fell from power and died. Indeed, the CRP had contributed to the nationwide
campaign by having done the groundwork with uprisings and by propagating
anti-Yüan messages during the two years of its lone struggle.

Yüan's demise in June 1916 and the subsequent, though short-lived, re-
installation of Parliament precluded CRP from wielding political power as originally planned. Sun wanted to initiate national reconstruction before the warlords
betrayed the Republic again by having the Parliament dissolved. Embarking on
his final attempt to save China and republicanism through his long years of
revolution, Sun reorganized the CRP, renaming it *Chung-kuo kuo-min-tang*, or
the Nationalist party of China (KMT), in 1919. The three-stage revolutionary
program was reiterated. Further reorganization took place in 1924 when Sun
struck an alliance with Soviet Russia, admitting members of the Chinese Communist party* into the KMT. The original CRP program remained the core of
the revolutionary goal, with its military stage nominally completed at the end
of the Northern Expedition* in 1928, and the political tutelary stage concluded
in 1947, when the Chinese constitution was promulgated. In retrospect, China
was again at the threshold of an extended revolution when the CRP was founded
in Tokyo in 1914.

REFERENCES: Wang Wei-ch'i, *Chung-hua ko-ming-tang chih yen-chiu* (A study on the
Chinese Revolutionary party) (Taipei, 1979); Edward Friedman, *Backward toward Revolution: The Chinese Revolutionary Party* (Berkeley and Los Angeles, 1974).

LAU YEE-CHEUNG

CH'ING DYNASTY (1644–1912): The last dynasty to rule China; founded in
1644 by Manchu conquerors; overturned in the Revolution of 1911, when the
Republic of China was established.

The Ch'ing dynasty was founded by the Manchus, a nomadic Jurched tribe
that lived in central Manchuria. In the late sixteenth century a chieftain named
Nurhaci (1559–1626) united all the tribes under his leadership. His most important innovation was the creation of a military and administrative organization
known as the Banner System, which laid the foundation for the conquest of
China in 1644. In the meantime, in 1636, the Manchus proclaimed the establishment of the Ch'ing (Pure) dynasty in their homeland. Their conquest of China
was facilitated by the collapse of the Ming dynasty (1368–1644) and by the
chaotic conditions in China brought on by widespread peasant rebellions. With
the aid of a Chinese general, Wu San-kuei (1612–1678), the Manchus were able

to defeat the rebels in northern China and capture the capital of Peking on June 4, 1644. Then on October 30, 1644, the Manchu Ch'ing emperor, Shun-chih (r. 1644–1661), was proclaimed emperor of China. After several more decades of fighting, the Ch'ing rulers finally consolidated their authority over all of China in 1683, when Taiwan was conquered and the last Ming loyalists were defeated.

The first four Ch'ing emperors, who reigned from 1644 to 1796, were capable rulers; China remained strong and prosperous under them. In politics the Ch'ing continued Ming administrative practices with only a few minor innovations. During the reign of the third emperor, Yung-cheng (r. 1723–1735), the throne became more despotic and the government more highly centralized. Besides consolidating their rule over China proper, the early Manchu rulers also expanded Chinese suzerainty over Tibet (1720), Turkestan (1759), Burma (1770), Vietnam (1789), and Nepal (1792). Internally, the years from the 1680s to the 1790s were years of general peace and prosperity, a time that later scholars have called the *Pax Sinica*. Taken as a whole, the Ch'ing period was one in which the traditional political, economic, and social institutions reached their full maturity, and the economy achieved a high degree of interregional integration and perhaps even the sprouts of capitalism.

By the start of the nineteenth century, however, the Ch'ing dynasty began to buckle under the weight of increasing internal and external problems. Over the century of the *Pax Sinica*, China experienced a phenomenal rise in population which created a set of serious political, economic, and social problems in which lay the roots of the nineteenth-century crisis. The waning of the dynasty was marked by economic stagnation, bureaucratic inefficiency, official corruption, military degeneracy, and mounting popular discontent. The White Lotus Rebellion (1796–1804) began a series of uprisings that reached a climax in the mid–1850s with the Taiping Rebellion[*] (1851–1864), the Nien Rebellion[*] (1853–1868), and Muslim rebellions in Yunnan (1855–1873), Shensi and Kansu (1862–1878), and eastern Turkestan (1864–1878). Although the Ch'ing was able to suppress these rebellions, the prestige of the dynasty was severely tarnished and the central government left greatly weakened.

The Ch'ing dynasty's internal problems were exacerbated by external pressures from the West. Not until the early nineteenth century did the West pose any serious threat to the Ch'ing. Led by Great Britain, the Western powers increasingly put pressure on China to open its doors to free trade and diplomatic equality. Ch'ing intransigence and the throne's insistence on suppressing the opium trade fueled misunderstandings and led to the Opium War (1839–1842). China's defeat was followed by further military defeats in the Arrow War (1856–1860), the Sino-French War (1884–1885), and the Sino-Japanese War (1894–1895). As a result, the Ch'ing dynasty was forced to accept a series of humiliating "unequal treaties" that gave foreign imperialists special privileges in China and further debilitated the dynasty's ability to rule.

In response to both the internal and external problems, in the last half of the nineteenth century China began to initiate modern reforms. The Self-

Strengthening Movement* in the 1860s and 1870s promoted the introduction of Western military technology as well as industrial development. These reforms, however, were insufficient in preventing China's defeat in the wars against France in 1884 and Japan in 1895. Afterward both within and outside the government reformers called for more extensive reforms. These efforts culminated in the Hundred Days Reform* (1898). Led by the radical Confucianist, K'ang Yu-wei* (1858–1927), and supported by the Kuang-hsü Emperor* (r. 1858–1908), these reforms would have completely revamped and modernized the old Ch'ing bureaucracy had they not been stopped by the Empress Dowager Tz'u-hsi* (d. 1908) and other conservatives at court. The emperor was placed under house arrest, and the reformers fled into exile or were arrested.

After the Boxer Uprising* (1900) had instigated foreign intervention, and China had once again suffered military defeat, the Ch'ing dynasty finally agreed to initiate serious reforms, including a constitutional monarchy and a national assembly. But the effort came too late and offered too little, for by now the growing discontent among the Chinese people had given rise to a revolutionary movement that called for the destruction of the Ch'ing dynasty and the establishment of a republic. The most important revolutionary leader was Sun Yat-sen* (1866–1925), who had formed a revolutionary party called the T'ung-meng hui* in 1905 and had helped to organize several uprisings against the dynasty in the first decade of the twentieth century. Finally, the end of the dynasty was signaled by the Wuchang Uprising on October 10, 1911, and the Republic of China* was proclaimed in Nanking on January 1, 1912. The abdication of the five-year-old emperor, P'u-i,* on February 12, 1912, ended not only the Ch'ing dynasty but also China's 2,000 years of imperial rule.

REFERENCES: Frederic Wakeman, Jr., *The Fall of Imperial China* (New York, 1975); Immanuel Hsü, *The Rise of Modern China*, 3rd ed. (New York, 1983); Ping-ti Ho, "The Significance of the Ch'ing Period in Chinese History," *Journal of Asian Studies* 26 (February 1967): 189–195.

ROBERT J. ANTONY

CHINGKANGSHAN PERIOD: An important period in Chinese Communist history when Mao Tse-tung retreated to the Chingkang Mountain and then established the Kiangsi Soviet Republic.

The Chingkangshan period (1927–1934) is commonly known as the Kiangsi Soviet period. It begins with the collapse of the CCP-KMT collaboration in July 1927 when the Chinese Communists left the Wuhan government. A series of rebellions like the Nanchang* and Autumn Harvest Uprisings* were executed, and the Canton Commune* was established in December 1927.

During the Kiangsi Soviet period, Ch'ü Ch'iu-pai* replaced Ch'en Tu-hsiu's* leadership. However, Li Li-san* controlled the Chinese Communist party's* policymaking machinery until the party's urban insurrection policy failed in 1930. This period has been characterized as the beginning of a strategy of guerrilla warfare from the rural base areas when Chu Teh* and Mao Tse-tung* linked up the scattered peasant armies to create the Fourth Red Army as well as the soviet base areas. At Chingkangshan in 1928 Communist leaders began to develop the techniques of the mass-line.* These developments later proved to be the most significant contribution to the success of the Chinese Revolution, which has been known as the Maoist strategy for rural revolution.

The revolutionary strategy in the countryside was to be fostered in order to link the rural revolution with the urban insurrection, thus crediting Mao with the originality of developing the mass-line and the strategy for rural revolution during the Kiangsi Soviet period. The critics of Mao's policy have argued, however, that the Comintern* in Moscow had adopted a similar policy line and had directed the Chinese Communist leaders to implement it, but the policy line was not transmitted to the rural base area. The question of whether or not Mao faithfully executed the Comintern policy has not been resolved among the scholars and specialists on the period, but it is generally agreed that Mao had developed his own strategy for rural revolution on the basis of the rural conditions that existed during the period.

The Chinese Soviet Republic (1931–1934) was established during this period by consolidating the scattered base areas and centralizing the Soviet system of government. Mao Tse-tung was elected chairman of the Chinese Soviet Republic on November 7, 1931, at the First National Congress of the Chinese Soviets, and was reelected to the same position at the Second National Congress in January 1934. However, Mao was not able to control the party's policymaking machinery and was thus in conflict with the Russian returned student leadership (the so-called Twenty-eight Bolsheviks*) that took control of the party's Central Committee at the Fourth Plenum in Shanghai in January 1931. The period is characterized by the continuing power struggle between the two major factions and the two policy lines; the Russian returned student group pushed for the leftist policy line, whereas the native revolutionary group led by Mao and the Red Army leaders in the rural base area took the line of rightist opportunism. The Kiangsi Soviet period ended with the collapse of the base areas and the beginning of the Long March* in October 1934.

REFERENCES: Arif Dirlik, *The Origins of Chinese Communism* (New York, 1989); Richard C. Thornton, *The Comintern and the Chinese Communists, 1928–1931* (Seattle, Wash., 1969).

ILPYONG KIM

CH'IU CHIN (*Tzu* Hsuan Ch'ing, Ching-hsiung; *Hao* Chien-hu nu-hsia, 1877?– July 15, 1907): Martyr of the 1911 Revolution; forerunner of the Chinese feminist movement; poetess.

Ch'iu Chin came from a scholarly family of Shanyin (Shaohsing), Chekiang. She was born and grew up in Amoy where her father, Ch'iu Shou-nan, a *chü-jen* degree holder, served as a legal secretary in the local government. In 1890 the Ch'iu family moved to Hunan. Six years later, Ch'iu Chin married Wang T'ing-chun, the son of a wealthy merchant family of Hsiang-t'an. She later gave birth to a son and a daughter.

An important change in Ch'iu Chin's life came when her husband bought an official post in Peking in 1902. There she became a friend of several talented women, particularly the calligrapher, Wu Chih-ying. Both Ch'iu and Wu were interested in the new literature, especially Liang Ch'i-ch'ao's *Hsin-min ts'ung-pao* (The new people's miscellany). Keenly aware of the weakness of China, Ch'iu Chin determined to leave her family to study abroad and dedicated herself to saving the country. In the summer of 1904 she met Shigeko, whose husband, Hattori Unokichi, was a professor at the Ching-shih ta-hsüeh-t'ang (Metropolitan Academy, the forerunner of Peking University). She took Shigeko's advice and traveled with the Hattori family to Japan for her education.

In Japan Ch'iu Chin at first attended a language school in Surugadai in the Kanda region and later transferred to Shimoda Utako's Vocational School for Girls in Kojimachi, Tokyo. Soon convinced that the Manchu regime must be overthrown for China's revival, she devoted most of her time to organizing anti-Ch'ing activities. In this period she advocated disseminating the revolutionary message to the public through speeches and writings. To this end she organized the Yen-shuo lien-hsi hui (Speech Practice Society) and the Kung-ai hui (Mutual Love Society). At the same time she contributed articles to the *Pai-hua pao* (Colloquial magazine) to champion the causes of anti-Manchuism and women's rights. She was also known for her patriotic poems. During the fall of 1904, she joined the Yokohama branch of the Triads headed by Feng Tzu-yu.

Ch'iu Chin returned to China in the spring of 1905. Through the introduction of T'ao Ch'eng-chang, she came to know Ts'ai Yüan-p'ei* and Hsü Hsi-lin, leaders of the Kuang-fu hui (Recovery Society). She probably became a member of the society at this time. Ch'iu Chin went back to Japan afterward. In early August she joined the T'ung-meng hui* in Tokyo and was appointed party head for Chekiang. In late November the Japanese Ministry of Education promulgated the more restrictive regulations governing Chinese students in Japan. Chinese students were divided in response to the new regulations. One group decided to compromise and remain in Japan. Ch'iu Chin was one of the other group who returned to China to participate in the revolution.

Early in 1906, Ch'iu Chin was back in China. She taught for some time at the Hsun-ch'i Girls School in Huchow, Chekiang, and left for Shanghai when summer vacation began. In Shanghai she helped raise funds for the Chung-kuo kung-hsüeh (Chinese Public Institute) and experimented with explosives. That winter she founded the *Chung-kuo nu-pao* (Chinese Women Magazine) for the promotion of women's rights in China. During this period she turned her attention to subversive activities. When the secret society members started a series of riots in P'ing-hsiang, Liu-yang, and Li-ling (Hunan-Kiangsi border) in December 1906, the Kuang-fu hui members met in Shanghai and planned to stage similar uprisings in Chekiang. In early 1907 Ch'iu Chin returned to Shaohsing. She worked in the Ta-t'ung hsüeh-t'ang (Ta-t'ung School), an institution founded by Hsü Hsi-lin for the training of radical students. Despite the suppression of the P'ing-Liu-Li rising, Ch'iu and Hsü continued their revolutionary endeavors.

Ch'iu Chin organized the Kuang-fu hui members in Chekiang into an army called the Kuang-fu chün (Recovery Army). The grand plan was that the secret society members would start uprisings in Kinhwa (Chin-hua, Chekiang) on July 19. Then Ch'iu Chin would lead her army to take Hangchow. Hsü would simultaneously occupy Anking, Anhwei. The plot was not carried out as planned, for the local authorities had obtained information about the conspiracy and had begun to take action against the revolutionaries. This forced Hsü to start the uprising in Anking on July 6, which resulted in his arrest and execution, even though he succeeded in assassinating the governor, En-ming. Ch'iu Chin did not give up after Hsü's death. By then the prefect, Kuei-fu, had found out more about the plot. He reported it to the governor. The governor dispatched an army to Shaohsing for her arrest. She was captured on July 13 and executed two days later. Ch'iu Chin's body was buried by her friend, Wu Chih-ying, on the shore of West Lake, Hangchow.

REFERENCES: Fang Chao-ying, "Ch'iu Chin," in Arthur Hummel, ed., *Eminent Chinese of the Ch'ing Period* (Reprint, Taipei, 1972): 169–171; Kuo Yen-li, *Ch'iu Chin nien-p'u* (A chronological biography of Ch'iu Chin) (Shantung, 1983); Mary B. Rankin, *Early Chinese Revolutionaries: Radical Intellectuals in Shanghai and Chekiang, 1902–1911* (Cambridge, Mass., 1971); Ono Kazuko, *Chinese Women in a Century of Revolution, 1850–1950*, ed. Joshua A. Fogel (Stanford, Calif., 1989).

HENRY Y.S. CHAN

CHOU EN-LAI (1898–January 8, 1976): First PRC premier and foreign minister; CCP vice-chairman; member of CCP Politburo since 1927.

Born of gentry parents in Huai-an, Kiangsu, in 1898, Chou En-lai was reared by uncles in Shanghai and Mukden during his teen years. He studied at Nankai Middle School and at Waseda University in Tokyo, and resided for a while in Kyoto. The May Fourth Incident* in 1919 brought him back to China, where he enrolled at Nankai University, although he devoted most of his time to political action. This included writing for and editing student publications and helping to establish the Chueh-wu she (Awakening Society), which became one of the several nuclei for the Chinese Communist Party* after its establishment in 1921. He was jailed for several months in early 1920 in Tientsin, but later that year departed for France in the work-study program, where he again spent most of his time engaging in political work among Chinese students. In 1922 he formally became a member of the CCP. He was also very active in the Kuomintang in Europe, and traveled to England, Belgium, and Germany.

In 1924 Chou returned to China, immediately assuming important posts in Canton. He served as occasional aide to Soviet military adviser Galen (General Vasily Blyukher*), but most importantly, Chou became head of the KMT's Whampoa Military Academy* Political Department. He distinguished himself in important political roles in the two military campaigns that secured Canton from the latent threat of warlord Ch'en Chiung-ming. In 1925 Chou married Teng Ying-ch'ao.* Following the Chung-shan Incident of March 1926, the first rupture in CCP–KMT relations, Chou was removed from his KMT posts. In the internal

CCP debate regarding an appropriate response to this mild KMT crackdown, Chou upheld the Comintern* line that advocated continued cooperation with the KMT. After the Chinese Revolutionary army* took Wuhan in late 1926, he was made head of the CCP's new Military Department. He played a prominent role in organizing the massive strike of March 21, 1927, in Shanghai that facilitated the city's seizure by Chiang Kai-shek's* army. He was fortunate to escape with his life when on April 12 Chiang suddenly smashed the CCP in Shanghai.

Chou then went to Wuhan where the CCP continued to carry out the Comintern line in working with the left-wing KMT. In Late April–early May 1927, Chou attended the CCP's Fifth Congress, at which time he became a member of the Central Committee and its Politburo. Soon afterward, the left-wing KMT also foreclosed on the Communists. Chou then became one of the organizers of the Nanchang Uprising* on August 1, 1927. In the aftermath of this disastrous operation, he came down with malaria, recuperating for a time in Hong Kong. In mid–1928 he attended the Sixth CCP Congress in Moscow, after which he was second in influence only to the powerful Li Li-san.* Chou was also elected a candidate member of the Executive Committee of the Comintern at its July-September 1928 Sixth Comintern Congress. He returned to China by late 1928, but in early 1930 he went back to Moscow as the effective head of the CCP delegation to the Comintern. That summer when the Chinese Red Army failed in its attempt to take and hold Changsha, Chou returned to China for the convening of the Third Plenum in September that was to target Li Li-san as the scapegoat. Chou waffled in his criticism of Li, and yet managed to be reelected to his positions at the next plenum in January 1931 after Li Li-san had been removed from power.

In 1931 Chou joined Mao Tse-tung* and Chu Teh* in Juichin, Kiangsi. Chou was elected to important political and military positions in the Chinese Soviet Republic. During this period he frequently opposed Mao, particularly on military matters, and for a time succeeded in overriding Mao. But the tactics Chou endorsed eventually resulted in the loss of the Soviet Republic. In January 1935, at Tsunyi* in Kweichow, Mao assumed effective command of the exodus from Kiangsi in what would come to be known as the Long March.* Once again, however, the agile Chou demonstrated that he could adjust to new leadership, and there ensued the collaboration with Mao that would last to the end of Chou's life.

Chou gained international attention when he negotiated the release of Chiang Kai-shek during the Sian Incident* of December 1936, and then the agreement for a Second CCP–KMT United Front.* He continued to act as liaison to the Nationalist government during the war of resistance against Japan. In the early postwar period he was the principal representative of the CCP in the unsuccessful efforts of American General George C. Marshall to mediate between the CCP and the KMT. He provided surrender terms to Nationalist Acting President Li Tsung-jen in early 1949, which, when rejected, led to the conclusive Communist military victory on the Chinese mainland.

By mid–1949 Chou turned his attention to participating in the formation of the impending new government for China, initially as vice-chairman under Mao of the reconstituted Chinese People's Political Consultative Conference,* which in turn formally established the People's Republic of China.* Chou became the premier (until his death) of the new government and its first minister of foreign affairs (until 1958). Thus, Chou was responsible for administering the government and was its chief diplomat in dealing with foreign governments; he devoted himself to both tasks with incredible energy and finesse for the next quarter century.

Chou gained international prominence again as a pallbearer at Joseph Stalin's funeral in March 1953, and his visit to Moscow contributed to a three-year honeymoon period of Sino-Soviet relations. He played an important role in bringing about the much-delayed 1953 armistice in Korea. In May 1954 he revealed his impressive diplomatic skills again at the Geneva Conference on Indochina. The following April saw his greatest triumph (prior to 1972) at the meeting of twenty-nine nonaligned nations in Bandung, Indonesia.

Chou's role in both the disastrous Great Leap Forward* of the late 1950s and in the chaotic Great Proletarian Cultural Revolution* beginning in 1966 was controversial inasmuch as he appeared to support Mao's radical policies, revealing considerable socialist zeal in doing so. In the 1960s, in particular, Chou decisively sided with Mao in the struggle against so-called revisionists and capitalist roaders,* including the relatively pragmatic Liu Shao-ch'i.* Yet, he used his negotiating skills to keep the government functioning during the Cultural Revolution and to protect many of his own, primarily, government cadres. However, his ability or willingness to protect others did not include his own adopted daughter, Sun Wei-shih, who was tortured to death by Red Guards.* At the Ninth Party Congress in April 1969, Chou was named party secretary general (Mao was chairman), and ranked third in the party hierarchy, after his chief rival, the now second-ranked Lin Piao* who had been named Mao's successor.

In the midst of China's protracted domestic political crisis, Chou played a major personal role in guiding China out of its isolation. He was highly successful in achieving rapprochement with the United States in 1972, in gaining admission to the United Nations in 1971, and in establishing or restoring diplomatic relations with a multitude of nations during the early 1970s.

Chou's diplomatic success sharpened the rivalry with Lin Piao, with whom Chou disagreed on both domestic and foreign policy issues. Chou then had a major role in the sudden demise of Lin Piao in September 1971. The militarily sagacious Lin had been no match for Chou politically. However, Chou's official explanation of the Lin Piao Incident, which he expounded at the Tenth Party Congress in 1973, was considered to be highly unsatisfactory, raising as many questions as it purported to answer. Nevertheless, his political position was strengthened at this congress. He was now number two in the party hierarchy.

Subsequently, as he sought to rehabilitate cadres that had been targeted during the early Cultural Revolution and to restore regular government, Chou was constrained to struggle with the radical Gang of Four*, including Mao's wife, Chiang Ch'ing.* The radicals, frustrated by Chou's adroit political maneuvering, attacked him indirectly in a widespread and intensive Criticize Confucius Campaign that eventually combined with a Criticize Lin Piao Campaign. Already exhausted by the extraordinary burdens of the Cultural Revolution, Chou soon weakened physically, if not mentally.

After being bedridden for many months, during which time he continued to work and was consulted, Chou died of cancer on January 8, 1976, at the age of seventy-eight. Teng Hsiao-p'ing,* whom Chou had made his expected successor, gave the funeral oration on January 15 in the Great Hall of the People. (Mao conspicuously absented himself from this simple ceremony.) In accordance with his request, Chou's ashes were scattered throughout China.

REFERENCES: *Selected Writings of Zhou Enlai*, vol. 1 (Peking, 1981); Kai-yu Hsu, *Chou En-lai: China's Gray Eminence* (Garden City, N.Y., 1968); Donald W. Klein and Anne B. Clark, *Biographical Dictionary of Chinese Communism*, vol. 1 (Cambridge, Mass., 1971): 204–219; David Wilson, *Zhou Enlai: A Biography* (New York, 1984).

STEPHEN UHALLEY, JR.

CHOU FO-HAI (1897–February 28, 1948): Founding member of the CCP; KMT theorist; collaborator during the Sino-Japanese War.

Born into an official family in Hunan, Chou displayed his talent and ambition early in his youth. He went to Japan for study in 1917, enrolling first in high schools and then in Kyoto Imperial University. While in Japan he became interested in Marxism and politics. In 1921 he returned to Shanghai to attend the founding meeting (i.e., the First National Congress) of the Chinese Communist party* and was elected the party's deputy leader.

Graduating from university in 1924, Chou went to Canton at the invitation of Tai Chi-t'ao to work for the reorganized Kuomintang. Although it was the heyday of the KMT–CCP United Front, Chou's position in the KMT and his new ideological orientation soon alienated him from his fellow Communists. Later that year he withdrew from the Chinese Communist party, and, under the influence of Tai, he became a fierce critic of the Communists. In late 1925 and early 1926 he participated in the formation of the Western Hills Faction,* an anti-CCP opposition within the KMT.

During the Northern Expedition* Chou briefly served at the Wuhan branch of the KMT's Central Military Academy, but he left for Shanghai when the Nanking–Wuhan split emerged in early 1927. He was quickly recruited by Chiang Kai-shek* into the Nanking regime, and from then on he became a loyal supporter of Chiang. The next year Chou published his book, *The Theoretical System of the Three People's Principles*, which firmly established him as a leading theorist of the KMT ideology in Chiang's camp.

In the early years of the Nanking government, when Chiang struggled to consolidate his power in the face of a series of political and military challenges, Chou was a trusted and able assistant to Chiang. For this service he was rewarded in 1931 with a membership in the Central Executive Committee of the KMT. From 1931 to 1933 Chou first headed the Education Department in the provincial government of Kiangsu, and then led the Department of Mass Training of the KMT. He was generally regarded as a member of the party's C.C. Clique.*

When the Sino-Japanese War* broke out in 1937, Chou was vice-head of the KMT's Department of Propaganda. While his official responsibility was to promote China's war effort, in private he was extremely pessimistic about the possible outcome of the war. In early 1938, with Chiang's approval, Chou sent Kao Tsung-wu, an official in the Foreign Ministry, to Hong Kong to seek opportunities for negotiating peace with Japan. Progress was made in Kao's effort, but Chiang's hesitation as well as the policy changes of the Japanese government soon led Chou to believe that Wang Ching-wei,* Chiang's arch-rival in the KMT, was the ideal person to lead the "peace movement." Later that year Chou arranged and accompanied Wang's defection from Chungking to Hanoi.

During the following fifteen months Chou was both Wang's principal adviser and representative in negotiating a separate peace with Japan, and the real architect of Wang's collaboratist regime at Nanking. When that regime was formally established in March 1940, Chou served as vice-head of its Administrative Yuan, finance minister, police minister, and president of the Central Reserve Bank. From 1940 to 1945 he was probably the most powerful person, other than Wang himself, in the Nanking Regime. Yet after the outbreak of the Pacific War, realizing that he was trapped in a lost cause, Chou secretly sought understanding from Chiang in Chungking. In 1944, following Wang's death, he became mayor of Shanghai while continuing to work for Chiang through Chiang's chief of intelligence, Tai Li.

Chou was arrested and sentenced to death shortly after the Japanese surrender. His sentence, however, was commuted to life imprisonment by Chiang. He died of illness in a Nanking prison in 1948.

REFERENCES: "Chou Fo-hai," in Howard L. Boorman and Richard C. Howard, eds., *Biographical Dictionary of Republican China*, vol. 1 (New York, 1967); Chang Yun, "Chou Fo-hai," in Huang Mei-chen, ed., *Wang wei shih han-chien* (Ten traitors in the Wang Ching-wei puppet regime) (Shanghai, 1986); Susan Marsh, "Chou Fo-hai: The Making of a Collaborator," in Akira Iriye, ed., *The Chinese and the Japanese* (Princeton, N.J., 1980): 304–327.

                                                                                    KE-WEN WANG

CH'Ü, CH'IU-PAI (January 29, 1899–June 18, 1935): CCP propagandist; CCP secretary-general; literary theoretician.

Ch'ü Ch'iu-pai was born into a declining gentry family in Ch'ang-chou in Kiangsu Province. His father, who appears to have been an amiable but irresponsible man with a predilection for occult Taoism and a liking for opium, dissipated the household's wealth and abandoned his family during Ch'ü's youth. In 1915 his mother, driven to despair, committed suicide. Despite the strained financial situation, Ch'ü Ch'iu-pai received a good education, attending primary and secondary school in Kiangsu, although impecunity forced him to withdraw from school prior to the final examinations. In 1916 he entered the tuition-free Russian Language Institute in Peking, a step that was to change his life. In Peking Ch'ü was marginally involved in the May Fourth Movement* and participated in Li Ta-chao's* Marxist Research Society.

In the fall of 1920, Ch'ü traveled to Moscow, having accepted an offer of the *Ch'en-pao*, a Peking daily, to serve as its Moscow correspondent. Out of his arduous, three-month long trip to Moscow through Manchuria and Siberia, Ch'ü produced *A Journey to the Land of Hunger* (in Chinese the word for Russia is homophonous with "the land of hunger") in which Ch'ü conceived of his journey as a spiritual one with the aim of discovering the meaning of the October Revolution, an event that he believed signaled the coming of a new age. In his dispatches to the *Ch'en-pao* during the next two years, Ch'ü continued to interpret events in the Soviet Union in this light.

In Moscow Ch'ü Ch'iu-pai joined the Chinese Communist party.* After his arrival, he frequently served as interpreter for CCP and KMT visitors to Moscow, acting as such during the December 1921 Congress of Toilers of the East as well as for the CCP delegation to the Fourth Comintern Congress a year later. During the congress, Ch'ü met Ch'en Tu-hsiu,* the CCP leader, and returned to China with him. With his knowledge of the Soviet Union and of the Russian language, Ch'ü played an important role in CCP propaganda affairs, editing and writing for *The Guide Weekly* (*Hsiang-tao Chou-pao*), the party's official organ, and *The New Youth* (*Hsin Ch'ingnien*), by this time a CCP periodical devoted to theoretical issues. He participated in the CCP's Third Congress of June 1923, which elected him as an alternate member of the Central Committee and appointed him to the Propaganda Committee. Ch'ü also taught at Shanghai University.

Following the March 20 Incident of 1926, in which Chiang Kai-shek* seized control in the KMT government in Canton, a split developed in the CCP between Ch'en Tu-hsiu and the CCP Kwangtung branch over policy toward the KMT. In September 1926 Ch'ü informed Ch'en that he endorsed the position of the Kwangtung branch, which was supported by Michael Borodin,* the Soviet adviser to the Canton government, of usurping the KMT from within. Thus began his campaign of opposition against Ch'en, which eventually led to his assumption of CCP leadership. The publication of a collection of previous writings and a collection of new essays in February 1927 was an important development in Ch'ü's rise to the top. In the two volumes Ch'ü asserted that the Ch'en Tu-hsiu leadership had brought disaster to the CCP because it failed to apply Marxism-Leninism* creatively to the Chinese situation, a theme that would dominate his writings from then on, and so had adopted policies inappropriate for the Chinese situation. He claimed for himself the mantle of orthodoxy.

No doubt with the crucial support of the Comintern,* it was at the August 7 Emergency Conference of 1927 that Ch'ü Ch'iu-pai became CCP leader, a position he retained for less than one year. The failure of the Autumn Harvest Uprising,* the Hai-lu-feng Soviet, and the Canton Commune,* as well as the harsh KMT suppression of the CCP during this period, doomed Ch'ü's policy of insurrection and the construction of soviets. The Sixth Party Congress of June–July 1928 replaced Ch'ü with Hsiang Chung-fa.*

Ch'ü Ch'iu-pai remained in the Soviet Union from 1928 to 1930. He served as chief of the Chinese delegation to the Comintern and became embroiled in a bitter struggle with Pavel Mif, director of the Comintern's China Commission. The Comintern sent Ch'ü back to China in 1930 in order to bring an end to the Li Li-san* line. Even though Li Li-san was removed from power, Ch'ü continued many of Li's insurrectionist policies. Ch'ü's second fall from power came when Mif replaced him and his supporters with his own appointees at the Fourth Plenum of January 1931.

It was only now, however, that Ch'ü secured an indelible place in the annals of the CCP. Living an underground life in Shanghai, he became the leader of the League of Left-wing Writers, conducting a great many polemics and developing a close friendship with Lu Hsün.* Ch'ü's major target of attack was the May Fourth Movement, which he believed had generated intellectuals who used a supposedly colloquial style and who claimed to contribute to the progress of China's society, but whose adoption of Western forms of expression had rendered them unintelligible to China's population. He called for a proletarian May Fourth Movement, urging leftist intellectuals to base themselves on art forms from the Chinese past and to strive to produce works that would contribute to the revolution, sacrificing artistic sophistication if need be. He singled out Chinese traditions in the visual and dramatic arts as especially suited for revolutionary propaganda.

Ch'ü left Shanghai for the capital of the Kiangsi Soviet, Jui-chin, in December 1933, where he served as commissar for education. Ch'ü did not join the Long March* and was captured by KMT troops in March 1935. In deep depression he wrote a final testament, "Superfluous Words," during his imprisonment in which he harshly condemned himself. He was executed on June 18, 1935.

REFERENCES: Paul Pickowitz, *Marxist Literary Thought in China: The Influence of Ch'ü Ch'iu-pai* (Berkeley, Calif., 1981); *Collected Works of Ch'ü Ch'iu-pai* (Peking, 1985).

HANS J. VAN DE VEN

CHU TEH (November 30, 1886–July 6, 1976): Founder of the Red Army; marshal; Politburo member; chairman, Standing Committee of the National People's Congress.

Born in I-lung hsien, Szechwan, to a tenant family that had earlier moved from Kwangtung, Chu Teh was raised with a knowledge of both the Szechwanese and Cantonese dialects. He attended middle school in Shun-ch'ing (later Nan-ch'ung) and then studied physical education at a higher normal school in Chengtu. In 1909 he enrolled in the new Yunnan Military Academy, where he secretly joined Sun Yat-sen's* revolutionary T'ung-meng hui* and the Ko-lao-hui* secret society.

While stationed in Kunming, Yunnan, Chu participated in the October 1911 Revolution,* and in the following year he joined the KMT. He also participated in the 1916 civil war against Yüan Shih-k'ai's* monarchical ambition. Chu spent the next few years in southwest Szechwan where he commanded a brigade of the Yunnan army on behalf of Szechwan governor Ts'ai Ao,* and lived the dissolute life of a petty warlord. In 1920 he returned to Yunnan where the following year he was appointed provincial commissioner of public security. A shift in the fortunes of warlord politics soon forced him to withdraw to the Szechwan–Tibet border area. By early 1922 he went to Shanghai where he was cured of the opium habit. Having already read revolutionary literature in recent years and greatly influenced by a friend, Sun Ping-wen, Chu now met with Sun Yat-sen and Ch'en Tu-hsiu,* although Ch'en responded coolly to his request for admission into the Chinese Communist party.*

Chu, now in his mid-thirties, went to Europe in late 1922. Soon after arriving in Berlin he met Chou En-lai* and joined the CCP. After studying both German and Marxism for several months, he attended lectures in 1923–1924 at the University of Göttingen, although he considered this work less useful than his visits to factories and other sites in various cities of Germany. In 1924 he edited the KMT *Cheng-chih chou-pao* (*Political Weekly*) in Berlin. After two brief arrests in 1925, he was soon deported to the USSR, where he then studied at the University of the Toilers of the East.

Chu returned to China just in time for the Northern Expedition* and played a useful role in that campaign by persuading powerful Szechwan warlord General Yang Sen to join the revolutionary cause. However, Yang Sen soon afterward turned on the Communists, and Chu narrowly averted arrest. Chu then went to Nanchang, Kiangsi, where a former student appointed him to important positions including chief public security officer and a deputy army commander. Thus, Chu Teh was strategically situated when the CCP, having been expelled by the KMT both in Shanghai in April and then in Wuhan in July 1927, staged the famous Nanchang Uprising* of August 1, 1927. In the aftermath of this disastrous event, Chu's forces were reduced to a few hundred poorly armed men.

By January 1928 his modest forces captured I-chang in southern Hunan, at which time they openly proclaimed themselves a Communist, rather than a KMT, military unit. In the spring of 1928 Mao* abandoned his precarious base at Chingkangshan* and joined forces with Chu. The combined force of about 10,000 men then reoccupied Chingkangshan where they now formally established the Fourth Red Army. In these difficult early months and years of the establishment of a base in the mountains (eventually centered at Juichin, Kiangsi, formally the seat of the Chinese Soviet Republic from November 1931), Mao and Chu forged a cooperative relationship, with Chu subordinate to Mao. Both men opposed the Li Li-san* line of fruitlessly attempting to take large cities during 1930, although they grudgingly complied for a time. Chu also sided with Mao during the Fu-t'ien Incident (a revolt directed against Mao) late that year. This was a critical juncture because it coincided with the imminent launching of the first of Chiang Kai-shek's* five annihilation campaigns against the Communist stronghold. Chu was preoccupied by these successive assaults, successfully turning them back until the Communists were forced to abandon the Kiangsi Soviet* in late 1934. At Juichin, Chu was made a member of the Politburo by 1934, although he may have been a member as early as 1931. He was also a member of the soviet's political cabinet and chairman of its Central Revolutionary Military Council. He was commander-in-chief of the famed Long March,* which relocated the Communists in Shensi a year later, although Chou En-lai was the chairman of the important party Military Affairs Committee at the beginning of the flight and was replaced in this post by Mao during the trek. Chu became a vice-chairman of this committee. After Mao resumed the Long March to Shensi, Chu remained for a time with Chang Kuo-t'ao,* giving rise to conflicting stories that Chu and Mao disagreed with each other for a time or that Chu was detained by Chang. Chu rejoined Mao in Shensi in the fall of 1936 and again assumed overall command of the Red Army.

Following the renewed cooperation between the CCP and KMT, Chu was named deputy commander of the Second War Zone and commander of the Eighth Route Army,* the redesignation of the Red Army. After the Japanese invasion of north China in July 1937, he was at the front much of the time until the end of 1939 when he was ordered back to Yenan where he spent the rest of the war against Japan. Here his attention was focused on measures to deal with the new state of siege laid on Yenan by the KMT and by pressure from the Japanese. Many American officials and journalists interviewed Chu after the establishment of the American Dixie Mission* in Yenan in 1944, and generally liked his unassuming manner and apparent lack of political dogmatism.

After the victory against Japan, and as the renewed civil war materialized despite the effort of the Marshall Mission* to avert it, the Communist military units were redesignated the People's Liberation Army,* with Chu continuing as commander-in-chief. Following the fall of Yenan in March 1947, Chu eventually relocated the headquarters in Hsi-pai-po Village near Shih-chia-chuang in southwest Hopeh ahead of Mao's arrival in May. The war was by now turning decisively in the Communists' favor, and much more quickly than either Mao or Chu had anticipated; victory came within the next several months. Chu was accorded a place of honor on Tiananmen when Mao pronounced the establishment of the People's Republic of China* on October 1, 1949.

During the 1950s and early 1960s, Chu was frequently active in the various high posts accorded him. He was regularly elected from Szechwan to the National People's Congress after its founding in 1954. In the same year he relinquished command of the PLA, and by 1959 he no longer had any formal military position other than his title of marshal. He was appointed chairman of the Standing Committee of the NPC in 1959, and was elected to the position in January 1965 and re-elected in January 1975. But during this tumultuous decade, Chu, in his eighties, mostly stayed clear of politics and was on hand for ceremonial occasions only. He died on July 6, 1976, at ninety years of age, six months after Chou En-lai and two months before Mao Tse-tung. Interestingly, he had been well enough to meet with visiting Australian Prime Minister Malcolm Fraser only a couple of weeks earlier (and after the infirm Mao was no longer seeing foreigners).

REFERENCES: *Selected Works of Zhu De* (Peking, 1986); Donald W. Klein and Anne B. Clark, *Biographic Dictionary of Chinese Communism, 1921–1965*, vol. 1 (Cambridge Mass., 1971): 245–254; Agnes Smedley, *The Great Road: The Life and Times of Chu Teh* (New York, 1956).

STEPHEN UHALLEY, JR.

CIVIL WAR, CHINESE (1945–1949): Period of the ultimate triumph of the CCP and the collapse of the KMT on Mainland China.

The Chinese civil war witnessed the victory of the Chinese Communist rural and urban revolutionary strategies and the bankruptcy of the Kuomintang rule in Mainland China. Chinese Communist historians refer to it as the Chinese People's War of Liberation or the Third Revolutionary Civil War. These years were the period of the culmination of Mao Tse-tung's* new democratic revolution, complicated by foreign involvement: American intervention in north China, Soviet invasion of northeast China (or Manchuria), and (seldom noted) the Japanese assistance to both the KMT and the Chinese Communist party.*

The Chinese civil war was fought in four stages. In the first stage, from August 1945 (the Japanese surrender) to June 1946, both the KMT and the CCP were engaged in an undeclared war and in peace talks. With American assistance and Japanese cooperation, the KMT recovered the major cities in central, east, south, and north China, which were urban islands in a Communist-dominated countryside. On the other hand, the Soviet forces swept into Manchuria and turned over to the CCP forces huge quantities of surrendered Japanese arms before permitting the KMT to recover the cities there in May 1946. The peace negotiations between Chiang Kai-shek* and Mao Tse-tung in Chungking from late August to early October 1945, and General George C. Marshall's mediation efforts from December 1945 to mid–1946 were abortive. The history of pre–1945 KMT–CCP conflict, the vast divergence of revolutionary aims, and the American support for the Nationalists could produce no peace or cooperation between the bitter Chinese antagonists. And the Marshall Mission* blocked an early KMT military solution when the Nationalists had about 3 million troops and the Communists about 1 million. Nevertheless, the corruption of the Nationalist takeover process alienated the populace, while the (underground) CCP preached ''peace, democracy and unity'' and used the students as the core of its political Second Front (as opposed to the military First Front in the countryside), thus neutralizing the KMT rule in urban areas. Above all, the failure of the KMT to conquer rural north China—the basic source of Communist strength—demonstrated the fundamental weakness of the KMT.

Stage two of the war lasted from July 1946 to June 1947. During this period, the Communists adopted a policy of strategic withdrawal and mobile warfare and allowed the Nationalists to extend deeply into north and northeast China and even to capture their wartime capital at Yenan. However, the Nationalist successes were hollow. The KMT garrisons (in the cities) were on the defensive, and they were hampered by rivalry between leaders and by Chiang Kai-shek's reluctance to delegate authority. In the KMT-controlled cities, the Communist underground instigated the students and intellectuals to engage in the U.S. Troops Quit China Movement and the Anti-Hunger, Anti-Civil War Movement; the KMT responded with ultimately ineffective repression. The result was to accentuate the Nationalist alienation from the urban intelligentsia. Besides, the continued economic mismanagement and corruption of the KMT officials aggravated its political and military problems.

Stage three of the war was the Communist limited counteroffensive from July 1947 to August 1948. In this period, the CCP smashed the KMT strategy of "clearing Central China, strengthening North China, and recovering Northeast China." By late summer of 1948 the Communist People's Liberation Army (PLA)* had cut off the Nationalist garrisons in Manchuria and linked together the Communist base areas in central and north China. Because of the Nationalist defeat, demoralization, and desertion, the PLA equaled the Nationalists in numbers of men and weapons. The tide of the war began to turn in favor of the CCP. In their cities, the KMT authorities still could not break up the Communist-instigated student movement. And the massive American aid to the KMT (about $2 billion) could not halt the galloping inflation, which destroyed the last remnant of urban support. With the military disasters and the loss of the allegiance of the students and the intellectuals, the days of the KMT were numbered.

The final stage of the war was the Communist general offensive from September 1948 to December 1949. In October 1948 the PLA completely routed the Nationalist troops in the battle of Liao-Shen (or Northeast) in Manchuria, which hastened the end of the Nationalist cause. In January 1949 the KMT also lost the major battles of Huai-Hai* (or Hsü-Pang) in central China and Ping-Tsin in north China. The military backbone of the KMT was thus gone. As the PLA advanced and ignored the KMT peace initiative, the Nationalists moved their capital from Nanking to Canton, then on to Chungking, and finally, in December 1949, to Taipei on Taiwan. The Communist conquest of Mainland China was complete. In March 1950 Chiang Kai-shek took over the reins of Nationalist power on Taiwan after Li Tsung-jen, the acting president, retired to the United States for medical treatment. In the meantime, on October 1, 1949, at Peking, Mao Tse-tung declared a new state—the People's Republic of China.*

REFERENCES: Chang Hsien-wen, ed., *Chung-hua min-kuo shih-kan* (A historical outline of the Republic of China) (Honan, 1985): 632–763; Hungdah Chiu, ed., *China: Seventy Years After the 1911 Hsin-Hai Revolution* (Charlottesville, Va., 1984); Immanuel C.Y. Hsü, *The Rise of Modern China* (Oxford, 1983); Suzanne Pepper, *Civil War in China: The Political Struggle, 1945–1949* (Berkeley, Calif., 1978).

JOSEPH K.S. YICK

COLLECTIVIZATION: Chinese Communist attempt to collectivize China, 1953–1957.

Collectivization involves the pooling of privately owned resources into a jointly owned production unit. Members of a collective derive their income from their labor contribution and not from ownership of nonlabor resources. Although collectivization was pursued in all economic spheres, it was mostly with agriculture that this process was associated.

Collectivization in agriculture was largely completed by 1957. This culminated a five-year three-step peaceful transition from individual ownership after land reform. In 1956 the average size of a collective had between 100 and 300 households. The collective was the basic unit of ownership, accounting, and distribution. In 1958 the basic unit of ownership, accounting, and distribution was elevated to the level of the commune with 4,000 to 5,000 households. Whereas the agricultural collective was organized purely for production, the commune combined the functions of production and government administration. After the setback in agricultural output in 1959 and 1960, the basic unit of ownership, accounting, and distribution was restored to the former collective, or even to the former brigade (twenty to forty households) under the collective. The former collective was renamed the production brigade, and the former brigade under the collective renamed the production team. This structure remained stable for almost two decades. Beginning in 1978, work was subcontracted to the work group (six to fifteen households) under the team to better match rewards with efforts. By 1983 the household became the dominant basis of subcontracting. With household subcontracting, the household's income no longer depended on the efforts of nonfamily members in the collective. Although land is still collectively owned, it can be assigned to the household for up to fifteen years.

Collectivization in China was a rare real-world experiment with a textbook development strategy commonly associated with R. Nurkse. He suggested that underemployed rural labor could be mobilized to build labor-intensive capital projects for agricultural development. But collectivization in China was intended not merely to be developmental but also extractive. The same power to mobilize surplus labor was also used to hold down rural consumption.

The failure to realize its developmental potentials was vividly demonstrated by the unprecedented growth spurts after work was subcontracted to the work group and the household in the 1978–1984 period. Not only were the output per capita of major crops increased, but also the agricultural basket of goods was more diversified. Many peasants got rich by starting businesses that required no special skills and little capital. This evidence suggested a serious prior misallocation of resources under collectivization.

This misallocation resulted from imposing a large-scale organization on a small-scale economy. Collectivization essentially reduced peasants to piece-rate laborers. It also substituted external for internal monitoring of labor efforts. Such a change would have been rational if farmwork had been standardized by machines and worker skills were specialized. Peasants would then become simple wage-earners charged with routine and specialized duties. But there were no machines to standardize work, and the peasants must still perform many nonspecialized duties. Moreover, effective external monitoring was hampered by the wide area over which farmwork was done. The results of poor efforts were often not immediately apparent. What is worse, the piece rate varied with the efforts of other members. Higher per worker output in units with more productive capital goods simply went to subsidize lower per worker output in units with less productive capital goods.

In short, collectivization simply added disincentives onto an unchanged technological base. That the base had remained intact was further evidenced by the dependence of the collective on the private sector. The collective must still depend on the household to supply (up to 50 percent) manure fertilizers from household pigs and to supplement (up to 30 percent) the meager collective income from household private plots. Thus, there was a constant competition for the same scarce resources between the collective and the private sector.

This competition led to repeated unsuccessful attempts to suppress the private sector, but collective pig husbandry was not cost effective. The elimination of private plots drastically reduced not only household cash income, but also the variety of diet and marketable sideline products. Each unsuccessful attempt to suppress the private sector was followed by an uneasy truce. Because collective management was held responsible to its superior for only the output of major food crops and not total (collective and private) income, it tended to hog more resources than it could effectively utilize.

Collectivization, however, did realize some development potentials. Collective management made it possible to reduce fragmentation of fields and to mobilize surplus labor for off-season capital construction. These capital improvements might well have contributed to the growth spurts after decollectivization. It should be pointed out, however, that much of the mobilized labor was wasted because of insufficient planning, inadequate complementary nonlabor inputs, and shoddy maintenance.

These developmental potentials were, of course, related to the collective's extractive potentials. Besides these collective investments in kind, the collective was able also to extract up to 30 percent of the gross collective incomes for the public accumulation fund. Collectivized production of major crops made it possible to extract larger marketable surplus at below-market prices. Judging from the poor output performance, it appears that these extractive powers failed to offset the disincentive effects of imposing a large-scale organization on a small-scale economy.

The absence of these extractive potentials under household subcontracting will test the long-term viability of a decollectivized economy. Already, there has been a substantial decline in state and collective long-term investment of all kinds. The higher peasant incomes have gone mostly into consumption and nonproductive investment.

REFERENCES: K. K. Fung, ''Output vs. 'Surplus' Maximization: The Conflicts Between the Socialized and the Private Sector in Chinese Collectivized Agriculture,'' *The Developing Economies* 12, no. 1 (1974): 41–55; Peter Nolan, ''De-collectivization of Agriculture in China, 1979–1982: A Long-term Perspective," *Cambridge Journal of Economics*, vol. 7 (1983): 381–403; Carl Riskin, *China's Political Economy: The Quest for Development Since 1949* (Oxford, 1987); Kenneth R. Walker, "Organization for Agricultural Production," in A. Eckstein, W. Galenson, and T. C. Liu, eds., *Economic Trends in Communist China.* (Chicago, 1968).

K. K. FUNG

COMINTERN (1919–1943): The Third Communist International.

From the Chinese Communist party's* foundation in 1921 until the Comintern's dissolution in 1943, the Comintern exerted a major influence on CCP policy. Comintern decisions were intended to guide CCP policy and to integrate it with the aims of the world revolution as decided by the Moscow-based organization. The Comintern had two main methods for ensuring these goals. First, it could send representatives to China. Second, it could work through local party members who were loyal to the Comintern's aims. To this end, the Comintern offered training programs for Communists from local parties. In addition, there was a permanent CCP mission to the Comintern in Moscow. Inevitably, friction occurred with those leaders who sought to maintain a more independent policy. As Comintern policy became identified with the Soviet national interest, the potential for such conflicts increased. Furthermore, as the Russian Communist party (Bolshevik) came to dominate the Comintern, internal party debates were exported to other Communist parties.

The origins of the First and Second United Fronts* between the CCP and the Kuomintang (1923–1927 and 1937–1945, respectively) reflect the impact of Comintern policy on the CCP. In 1920 at its Second Congress, the Comintern decided on a strategy of cooperation between Communist parties and national revolutionary movements. The precise application of this policy was worked out by Comintern representatives Maring* and Michael Borodin* often in opposition to the views of the local comrades.

The Second United Front was decided by a major shift in Comintern policy with implications for China. The Comintern's Seventh Congress (July–August 1935) adopted a new policy that called for a United Front of all elements, classes, and nations in the fight against fascism. This policy shift came primarily as a result of Soviet Russia's awareness of the increasing threat to its security posed by Germany and Japan. The new policy line was applied to China by Wang Ming,* the head of the CCP mission to the Comintern in Moscow. The August First Declaration (1935), issued in Moscow in the name of the CCP and the Chinese Soviet Republic, was a clear signal that the CCP was to make a strategic shift from civil war to a new United Front. The declaration claimed that it was the "sacred duty of everyone to resist Japan and save the nation."

The collapse of the First United Front in 1927 provides the first major occasion in which the China question became embroiled in Soviet party debates. The possibility of the CCP breaking with the Kuomintang left was hampered by the conflict between Stalin and Trotsky. It was impossible for Stalin to acknowledge the folly of continued cooperation. The subsequent leftward drift in CCP policy can also be attributed partly to debates in the Russian party. Having defeated Trotsky, Stalin turned his attention to Bukharin, whom he attacked for his "rightist, rich peasant line." In October 1929 the Comintern asserted that rightism was the greatest danger in the CCP and that a new revolutionary wave was about to roll in. This encouraged Li Li-san* in his insurrectionist line that all but destroyed the CCP as an organization.

Should policy go wrong, however, the Comintern was never to blame, and scapegoats were sought who had incorrectly applied policy. Thus, the failure of 1927 was blamed on the CCP leadership, and Ch'en Tu-hsiu* in particular, for not carrying out Comintern instructions among the masses. Similarly, while the Comintern refrained from criticism of Li Li-san while the strategy was in operation, as soon as it failed harsh condemnation followed, with Li being denounced as a Trotskyite.

With the dismissal of Li Li-san, from 1931 the Comintern tried to run its own CCP leadership directly through the group referred to as the Russian Returned Students. The period until 1935 saw the most direct effect of the Comintern over the Party Center in China. The Comintern representative, Pavel Mif, was able to maneuver his protégés Wang Ming* and Po Ku* into key leadership positions. Obsessed with ideological doctrines and basking in revolutionary enthusiasm, Po Ku, Comintern agent Otto Braun (Li T'e),* and their supporters lacked a profound insight into the political relations within which the CCP found itself. Neither could they balance this deficiency with an adequate experience in military command. The parallel growth of the red base areas, especially of the main base in Kiangsi, was producing a group of leaders independent of Soviet patronage. The Long March* provided this group under Mao Tse-tung* with the chance to consolidate power in the CCP and begin reducing Comintern influence.

Effective Comintern influence had long since disappeared when, on May 15, 1943, the dissolution of the Comintern was announced. Not surprisingly, it was greeted enthusiastically by the Maoist leadership who announced that this would strengthen the local Communist parties by making them "even more nationalized."

REFERENCES: Translation Group of the Institute of Modern History of the Chinese Academy of Social Sciences, *Kung-ch'an kuo-chi yu-kuan Chung-kuo ko-ming te wen-hsien tzu-liao* (Peking, 1981), vol. 1, 1919–1928 and vol. 2, 1929–1936; R. A. Ulyanovsky, ed., *The Comintern and the East* (Moscow, 1979).

                                                                                    TONY SAICH

COMMON PROGRAM (September 1949): A provisional "constitution" adopted by the CPPCC.

The Common Program (*Kung-t'ung Kang-ling*) was passed by the first session of the Chinese People's Political Consultative Conference.* This meeting was held in Peip'ing (soon renamed Peking) on the eve of the Chinese Communist People's Liberation Army's* victory in the civil war* (1945–1949). With over 600 delegates, including many non-Communists, the conference was considered more broadly "representative" of the Chinese nation than the Chinese Communist party.* According to an official CCP chronology, the meeting "acted on behalf of the National People's Congress" which did not formally convene until late 1954.

The full title of the document approved was the Common Program of the Chinese People's Political Consultative Conference (*Chung-kuo Jen-min Cheng-chih Hsieh-shang Hui-i Kung-t'ung Kang-ling*). It was drafted by the Chinese Communist party and presented to the conference by Chou En-lai.* Although various non-Communist "democratic parties and people's organizations" purportedly contributed to its drafting, the document was based on the CCP's basic policy line for the "transition period" decided at the March 1949 Second Plenum. The Common Program contained seven chapters and sixty articles that were not significantly amended or altered by the rubberstamping Consultative Conference.

The basic purpose of the Common Program was to lay out the broad national goals of the new government consistent with Mao Tse-tung's doctrine of New Democracy (*Hsin-min Chu-i*). Specifically, it "summarized the experiences of China's new democratic revolution and clearly stipulated that the People's Republic of China was a country led by the working class." It also declared China to be a "people's democratic dictatorship founded on the worker–peasant alliance." In the spirit of the New Democracy's United Front policies, the program emphasized unifying China's various classes and nationalities and "stipulated the election rights and powers of citizens and their political freedoms." Yet, as a harbinger of the harsh persecution of intellectuals and other social groups that would soon follow, the program singled out "reactionary elements, feudal landlords, and bureaucratic capitalists"—catch-all categories in which almost anyone could be arbitrarily placed—as targets of the new dictatorship. Despite the moderate tone of the program—especially in comparison to later CCP policies—this document began China's inexorable path to class warfare and political persecution which would peak in the Anti-Rightist Campaign* of 1957 and the devastating Cultural Revolution* in the 1960s.

The program also signaled the Communists' clear intention to create a unified and powerful state structure. After years of warlordism* and then civil war, the program promised a "unified military force, composed of the People's Liberation Army and the People's Public Security Bureau." It also committed the new government to establishing state control over the economy and "integrating" different sectors of the economy, such as agriculture, industry, and transportation.

Reflecting the Soviet experience, the program promised to "raise the people's cultural level, cultivate the nation's talent, and develop the scientific, cultural, and educational level" of the population. Equality and cooperation among all nationalities was also proclaimed as a national goal in the rather traditional terms of turning China into "a big family" (*ta chia-t'ing*). Finally, the Communist party's long-held opposition to imperialism was reaffirmed, especially to maintain China's independence and territorial sovereignty.

During the first five years of the People's Republic, the Common Program served as a "temporary constitution." It was formally replaced by the constitution of the Chinese People's Republic* adopted in 1954.

REFERENCES: Hung Ch'eng-hua et al., *Chung-hua Jen-min Kung-ho-kuo cheng-chih t'i-chi yen-ke ta-shih-chi, 1949–1978* (Chronology of developments in the political structure of the Chinese People's Republic) (Peking, 1987); Maurice Meisner, *Mao's China and After: A History of the People's Republic* (New York, 1986).

LAWRENCE R. SULLIVAN

COMMUNICATIONS CLIQUE: A group of bureaucrat/politicians in the late Ch'ing and early republican ministries and bureaus responsible for administering and financing modern communications.

As China entered the twentieth century, modern communications and the substantial finances involved provoked keen competition to control both that potential and that funding. Networks within the bureaucracy linked those involved in railway, telegraph, and similar communication projects, both to foster the cooperation necessary for sustained growth and to provide mutual protection against hostile outside political manipulation. The Communications Clique consisted of those who were engaged in politics to protect these networks and their supportive subsystems.

In late Ch'ing* times, the Ministry of Post and Communications oversaw expanding railway and telegraph systems financed largely through the Bank of Communications. A growing nucleus of able administrators made their careers within the ministry, the bank, and their associated agencies. Yüan Shih-k'ai* became a prominent mentor, and their mutually advantageous alliance continued into the early Republic.

The clique's pattern took shape during these years. Central in the group was a Cantonese, Liang Shih-i, who was involved with most railway development under the late Ch'ing. By establishing the Bank of Communications and numerous smaller private banks, he equally influenced much of China's early communications financing. The communications financing area also featured Chou Tzu-ch'i, another prominent clique leader. Educated in the United States, Chou became vice-minister of finance under Yüan Shih-k'ai's presidency, subsequently serving as both finance and communications minister in several cabinets. From a Shantung background, his childhood in Kwangtung equipped him with fluent Cantonese; this was a useful facility, for Liang Shih-i's circle was often referred to as the Kwangtung Clique. Such men made up the clique's top echelon, their cohorts being the bureau directors, the directors general, and the vice ministers of the communications infrastructure. They were little concerned with constructional issues, and their political interests were links to those in power to ensure continued development of the communications system.

In the early republican years, the clique's fortunes followed these linkages. After the 1911 Revolution,* Sheng Hsuan-huai's brief political control over communications forced Liang and Chou to go abroad until they were reinstated by Yüan Shih-k'ai. The clique's identification with Yüan required its leaders to flee abroad on his death in 1916. They recovered to play supporting roles in

Tuan Ch'i-jui's bid for power. In the 1918 Anfu election, some eighty to one hundred elected members were clique associates. Parliament, however, was not the clique's main arena: the Communications Clique's concern remained its influence at cabinet or medium- to high-level bureaucratic levels.

Some analysts distinguish the New Communications Clique of Ts'ao Ju-lin. Based in the same bureaucratic areas and often cooperative rather than competitive, this group's major distinction lay in a shared background in studies in Japan. Its members became closely associated with Tuan Ch'i-jui's financial negotiations with Japan. Correspondingly, its political fortunes plummeted with the rise of anti-Japanese nationalism, particularly after the May Fourth Movement[*] of 1919. Whether treated as part of the Communications Clique or as a separate entity, the eclipse of Ts'ao Ju-lin's circle prefaced the decline of the main clique's political prominence.

The clique's influence dissipated in the early 1920s. Earlier association with prominent figures had cost its members. Both Liang and Chou underwent temporary exile in 1911 and 1916. Both were briefly premier under Chang Tso-lin's influence, before becoming exiled victims of Wu P'ei-fu's[*] challenge of Chang's power in Peking in early 1922. Borrowing the talents of Li Ta-chao[*] and the infant Chinese Communist party,[*] Wu also effectively broke the clique's control network among the Peking–Hankow railway workers. After 1922, the clique had little coordinated force in Peking warlord politics.

Individuals remained influential by the nature of the bureaucratic infrastructure and the technological revolution that originally fostered the clique. A prominent clique member, Yeh Kung-cho was founder and first president of Chiao-t'ung University, an institution destined to be one of China's foremost engineering schools. Unlike the others, Yeh maintained connections with the Kuomintang, serving briefly with Sun Yat-sen's[*] Canton government in 1923–1924 and later in Sun Fo's[*] cabinet of early 1932. This postdated the clique's main political impact. Individuals representing communications technology remained influential, but only the unique political environment of the first two decades of China's twentieth-century revolution permitted or required them to coalesce into a distinct clique.

REFERENCES: Howard L. Boorman and Richard C. Howard, eds., *Biographical Dictionary of Republic China* (New York and London, 1967–1971) 1:429–431; 2:354–357; 4:31–33; Hsi-sheng Ch'i, *Warlord Politics in China 1916–1928* (Stanford, Calif., 1976); Andrew J. Nathan, *Peking Politics, 1918–1923: Factionalism and the Failure of Constitutionalism* (Berkeley, Calif., 1976).

PETER M. MITCHELL

D

DEMOCRATIC CENTRALISM (*min-chu chi-chung-chih*): A Leninist concept or system or set of principles guiding the organization and activities of party, state, and social organizations.

Democratic centralism is a concept of organizational structure and decision making employed by Communist parties throughout the world. In the Chinese Communist party* it is described as the "basic principle of the proletarian political party," providing a "dialetical unity of democracy and centralism." In theory, it insures both the widespread participation of all party members in CCP decision making and "iron discipline."

Lenin developed democratic centralism during the early years of the Bolshevik party. It figured prominently in Lenin's major writings on party organization where he contrasted this principle of decision making and discipline to the opposite extremes of bureaucratic centralism and anarchism. Unlike the latter two, democratic centralism purportedly provided for democratic participation of rank-and-file members, yet without the destructive consequences of an undisciplined mob. While reflecting Lenin's deep fear of spontaneity, it is also considered by contemporary Soviet historians to have been antithetical to Stalin's personality cult, which destroyed any semblance of democracy in the Soviet Communist party.

In its Soviet form, democratic centralism has four essential characteristics as outlined in recent Communist Party of the Soviet Union rules. (1) All leading bodies are elected; (2) party bodies must report periodically to their organizations and to higher bodies; (3) the minority is subordinate to the majority; and (4) the decisions of higher bodies are obligatory for lower bodies. In theory, democratic centralism allows substantial debate on policy issues (though within the general guidelines of official ideology and the party program) before formal decisions are taken. Afterward, however, all party members must follow strict discipline in implementing the decisions of the "majority." Throughout much of the

CPSU's history, the centralist component of the doctrine overwhelmed its democratic counterpart, especially under Stalin.

The Chinese Communist conception of democratic centralism is virtually the same. Reflecting recent experiences with Mao Tse-tung's* autocratic leadership, however, official descriptions of democratic centralism in China stress the necessity of collective leadership (chi-t'i ling-tao) and prohibitions against personality cults (ke-jen tsung-pai). The Chinese Communists also emphasize the "four obediences" (sze-ke fu-ts'ung) as a central component of democratic centralism. These stipulate that "party members must obey the organization; the minority is subordinate to the majority; lower levels obey higher levels; and party organs must unite with and obey the party center."

Although central to the Leninist party on which the Chinese Communist party was modeled, democratic centralism was not formally introduced into CCP organization until 1927. From 1921 to 1927, and particularly before 1925, the party was a loose amalgamation of study societies that had sprung up in Peking, Shanghai, and other cities. Under Ch'en Tu-hsiu's* leadership, central party organs were gradually created (e.g., an Organization Department), but controversies over the degree of party centralization (and Ch'en's own power) divided the CCP throughout its early years. It was not until the Communists' near destruction by the Nationalist coup in Shanghai in April 1927 that the CCP formally adopted democratic centralism as a party principle at the 1928 Sixth Party Congress. Not until the Seventh Party Congress in 1945 were the four obediences written into the CCP constitution.

Perversions of democratic centralism have, as in the Soviet Union, afflicted the CCP. While some party members overemphasized the democratic component and purportedly spawned anarchism in the CCP, others are accused of having gone to the opposite extreme and created pure centralism without a modicum of democracy. According to recent, post–Mao party histories published in the People's Republic of China,* the fragile balance of democracy and centralism was destroyed by "leftist" errors beginning in the late 1950s. This especially began with Chairman Mao's assault on P'eng Te-huai's* criticisms of the devastating Great Leap Forward* voiced at the 1959 Lushan Conference.* Contrary to the democratic guarantees of the Leninist principle, P'eng and other party leaders were effectively silenced, thereby destroying the CCP's "great tradition" in achieving both democracy and centralism. The Cultural Revolution* and other catastrophes rapidly ensued, for without democratic centralism, it is declared, the Communist party was incapable of producing "correct policies." With the destruction of democratic discussion and a sole emphasis on achieving centralism, other vital aspects of the CCP's correct structure, such as collective leadership (chi-t'i ling-tao) and the party committee system, suffered accordingly. Not until the 1978 Third Plenum and the triumph of Teng Hsiao-p'ing* were these traditions, including democratic centralism, purportedly restored.

REFERENCES: Ronald J. Hill and Peter Frank, The Soviet Communist Party, 3rd ed. (Boston, 1986); Tang ti sheng-huo chih-i shou-ts'e (Handbook on essential knowledge for party life) (1986); Kao Jui-lan, *Lun Min-chu Chi-chung Chih* (On democratic centralism) (no date).

LAWRENCE R. SULLIVAN

DIXIE MISSION (July 22, 1944–July 24, 1946): Informal name given to the U.S. Army Observer Group.

The Army Observer Group is so named because it was sent to the "rebel territory"—areas controlled by the Chinese Communists during the war of resistance against Japan. It was the first official contact between the United States and the Chinese Communists since 1938 and constituted a quasi-official recognition of the Chinese Communist party* by Washington. (The only official U.S. observer who had visited Yenan was Captain Evans Carlson of the Marine Corps. He visited this capital of the Communist territory in 1938.)

Attempting to build up direct contact with the United States, Chou En-lai,* the Communist representative in Chungking (the wartime capital of China), had requested several times since 1942 that Washington send observation missions to Yenan. Because of President Franklin D. Roosevelt's support of the Nationalist government, all the requests went unheeded. Meanwhile, a group of Foreign Service officers in Chungking, as represented by John S. Service,* John P. Davies, and Raymond P. Ludden, had reported extensively on the Communist movement as well as its value to the Allied cause. General Joseph Stilwell,* the commander of U.S. forces in China and Generalissimo Chiang Kai-shek's* chief-of-staff, had begun to recommend utilizing Communist troops against the Japanese since September 1943. After meeting with General Stilwell at the Cairo Conference (November 22–26, 1943), President Roosevelt became more receptive to the idea of contacting the Communists in order to increase the flow of intelligence about Japanese troops in north China and to use Communist forces against them. The success of the Japanese Ichigo Campaign (April to October 1944) strengthened the president's determination to send a mission to Yenan. He instructed Vice-President Henry Wallace, who visited Chungking in June 1944, to press for the issue. On June 23 the generalissimo finally agreed in principle to the dispatch of the Army Observer Group.

The mission, headed by Colonel David D. Barrett with John Service as its chief political reporter, included representatives from the Army, Air Corps, Navy, State Department, and Organization of Strategic Service (OSS). It had orders to gather information on weather as well as intelligence and the movement of Japanese forces in north China; to help U.S. pilots forced down in Japanese-held areas; and to evaluate the present and potential contribution of the Communists to the war effort. Treating the visit as the onset of the international United Front as well as the beginning of its diplomatic relations, Yenan gave the mission fullest cooperation.

Members of the mission reported their favorable impressions on the "Dixie Territory," as contrasted to the Nationalist-controlled areas. The political officers, Service in particular, repeatedly transmitted Mao Tse-tung's* idea of using

U.S. aid as a leverage to force Chiang to agree on a genuine coalition government. Mao even gave the impression that Yenan would rather deal with Washington than Moscow. Hence, Barrett recommended immediate military assistance to the CCP, and the OSS team went ahead to provide some training and equipment to certain Communist units for anti-Japanese operations. Both Barrett and the OSS, on their own initiatives, had drawn up separate plans of military cooperation with Yenan. The Communists often interpreted the enthusiasm of the mission members as signs of promise from Washington.

The Roosevelt administration was nevertheless more concerned with defeating Japan and averting a civil war in China. It had no intention of supporting the CCP. Ambassador Patrick Jay Hurley[*] therefore interpreted the Dixie Mission's proposals to cooperate with the Chinese Communists as attempts to sabotage his efforts to bring about a coalition government under the leadership of Chiang Kai-shek. All key members, including Colonel Barrett, Service, and Ludden, were subsequently removed from the mission. General Albert C. Wedemeyer,[*] successor to Stilwell as Chiang's chief-of-staff, also asserted control over all OSS clandestine, guerrilla, and intelligence activities by the Americans in China to prevent independent operations with the CCP.

The status of the Dixie Mission began to decline after Colonel Barrett was relieved in December 1944. He was succeeded by Colonel Morris De Pass, and then by Colonel Ivan Yeaton in July 1945, at which time the mission was renamed the Yenan Observer Group. Yeaton believed that Dixie's primary role should be to gather intelligence on a potentially hostile group for transmission to General Wedemeyer. In October 1945 Yeaton was informed that the Yenan Observer Group would soon be dissolved. He left Yenan on April 11, 1946. On July 24, 1946, the remnants of the group were moved to Shanghai, and the Dixie Mission was officially terminated.

REFERENCES: David D. Barrett, *Dixie Mission* (Berkeley, Calif., 1970); William P. Head, *America's China Sojourn* (New York, 1983); James Reardon–Anderson, *Yenan and the Great Powers* (New York, 1980); John S. Service, *Lost Chance in China* (New York, 1974).

SU-YA CHANG

E

EIGHTH ROUTE ARMY: The main CCP army during the anti-Japanese war and the early years of the civil war (1937–1947). Responsible for defending and expanding Communist-controlled areas in north China and promoting the party's social revolution.

With the renewal of the United Front between the Chinese Communist party* and the KMT following the start of the anti-Japanese war in July 1937, the CCP's Red Army was renamed the Eighth Route Army (*Pa-lu chün*). In September 1937 it was changed to the Eighteenth Army Group, but the earlier name continued to be used. The Eighth Route Army was commanded by Chu Teh,* with P'eng Te-huai* as deputy commander, Yeh Chien-ying* as chief-of-staff, and Jen Pi-shih as political commissar. In 1937 it totaled approximately 45,000 men. The army consisted of three divisions: the 115th (under Lin Piao* and Nieh Jung-chen), the 120th (under Ho Lung and Hsiao K'o), and the 129th (under Liu Po-ch'eng, with Teng Hsiao-p'ing* as its political commissar).

The Eighth Route Army was instrumental in establishing new Communist base areas in north China, as well as defending the CCP's original northern base, Shen-Kan-Ning.* During 1937 and 1938 the 115th (under Nieh Jung-chen) set up the Shansi-Chahar-Hopei or Chin-Ch'a-Chi base,* the 129th set up the Shansi-Hopei-Shantung-Honan or Chin-Chi-Lü-Yü base, and the 120th set up the Shansi-Suiyuan or Chin-Sui base. Later, forces from the 115th competed with KMT guerrilla forces for control of a Shantung base.

Never a modern fighting force, the Eighth Route Army was successful under extremely adverse conditions. It sustained a war of attrition (''guerrilla warfare'') against occupying Japanese and ''puppet'' Chinese forces in north China and defended (with less success in 1942–1943) the core areas of the Communists' base areas. (Shen-Kan-Ning, west of the Japanese lines, was never seriously attacked.) Most significantly, the army maintained admirable discipline and became a model for CCP goals of social revolution. This discipline and propaganda functions were ensured by the party's strict civilian control of the military through the political commissars at every level of the army (based on the Russian Soviet Army model). Thus, the Eighth Route Army was well received by local populations and did not contribute to leadership strife as did many of the KMT armies. (See, for example, the Nineteenth Route Army.[*]) By the end of World War II the Eighth Route Army had expanded to about 600,000 men and controlled most of north China outside the major cities. As the civil war[*] progressed, the army's name was changed in March 1947 to the People's Liberation Army.[*]

REFERENCES: Jacques Guillermaz, *A History of the Chinese Communist Party, 1921–49* (New York, 1972); William W. Whitson, *The Chinese High Command: A History of Communist Military Politics, 1927–71* (New York, 1973); Kathleen Hartford and Steven M. Goldstein, eds., *Single Sparks: China's Rural Revolutions* (Armonk, N.Y., 1989); *Pa lu chün tsung-pu ta-shih chi-lüe* (A brief account of the Eighth Route Army headquarters) (Peking, 1985); *Pa lu chün: Hui-i shih-liao* (Historical reminiscences of the Eighth Route Army) (Peking, 1988).

TIMOTHY CHEEK

F

FEBRUARY COUNTER-CURRENT (*Erh-yueh ni-liu*; also February adverse current of reversing verdicts, or restoration [*Erh-yueh fu-pi ni liu*]; 1967): The stage of the Great Proletarian Cultural Revolution between "January storm" and "March black wind" in which Mao Tse-tung made a necessary compromise with his opponents.

The main current in January 1967 was near-anarchic power seizures by rebel factions—the Cultural Revolution* at its most extreme. Province by province, power-holders taking the capitalist road were to be dragged out for criticism while rebel factions themselves assumed the mantle of authority.

The first power seizures established Paris communes (founded on the principles of the Marxist model) that were supposedly based on unity among rebel factions. These communes frightened Mao, who criticized them as hostile to all leadership; factional divisions on the rebel side widened. Quickly substituted were power seizures that established revolutionary committees based on three-sided coalitions of rebel factions, army, and "liberated" civil cadres. But the coalition form improved on the purely rebel form only slightly. By the end of January, thirteen provinces had announced power seizures, only four of which were recognized by the center; the rest were denounced as sham power seizures.

Officials under attack, sensing an opening as Mao Tse-tung's* side fell to quarreling internally, pressed their case. At a series of closed meetings in the capital, they protested emotionally that all of them were targeted by the Cultural Revolution, regardless of revolutionary background, loyalties, or performance. On February 15 Chou En-lai* extracted from Mao a promise to protect State Council members, and the same day Chou instructed rebel factions at one ministry first to clear all future attacks on the ministry with the center.

Mao bargained away concessions to Chou and aggrieved officials for the freedom to continue his Cultural Revolution. In late February and early March he eased up on officialdom, curbed the activities of rebel groups, and narrowed the movement's rhetorical focus. Now the overwhelming majority of cadres were said to be "good or very good," the campaign target was narrowed to "a small handful" of capitalist roaders,* detained members of much-criticized party work teams (summer 1966) were released, rebel groups were ordered to cease traveling about the country to link up with one another, rebel groups were denied access to confidential files and dossiers, and regional military commanders were instructed to "support the Left but not any particular faction." Even a third form of province-level power seizure, that by the Military Control Committee, was introduced.

Supporters of the Cultural Revolution tried to stem this "February counter-current" (their critical term) by arguing that it allowed officialdom to escape purge. They focused on the highest ranking purgee, Liu Shao-ch'i,* China's titular head of state who had been removed as a vice-chairman of the Chinese Communist party* in August 1966 for sending party work teams to coopt the nascent Cultural Revolution in schools before it got off the ground. Liu made a self-criticism to the party in October and, by one interpretation, saved China from civil war by not championing the opposition to Mao. Liu was "the number one person in authority taking the capitalist road" and also "China's Khrushchev." February counter-current pleas to rescue officials under attack even included pleas, ultimately unsuccessful, to reverse the verdict on Liu.

After February, Mao escalated and broadened the scope of the attack on Liu as he agreed to narrow the attack at lower levels. Mass factions that stood to gain from the Cultural Revolution were loath to accept the shift, largely ignored Liu, and lashed out at the February counter-current that ran against their interests.
REFERENCES: Lowell Dittmer, *Liu Shao-ch'i and the Chinese Cultural Revolution: The Politics of Mass Criticism* (Berkeley, Calif., 1975); Hong Yung Lee, *The Politics of the Chinese Cultural Revolution: A Case Study* (Berkeley, Calif., 1978).

GORDON BENNETT

FENG YÜ-HSIANG (1882–1948): Revolutionary militarist; warlord.

Feng Yü-hsiang was born in Hsing-chi, Hopei, in 1882. His father, Feng Yü-ting, a native of Ts'ao Hsien, Anhwei, was a low-ranking army officer and an upright man, and his mother, Yu Shih, gave birth to seven children, with Feng Yü-hsiang being the second. The family was so poor that Feng received only one and a half years of formal education before he joined the army at the age of fourteen in 1896. Owing to his giant physical structure and his incessant self-teaching efforts, he was promoted to battalion commander on the eve of the 1911 Revolution.* Together with Wang Chin-ming and Shih Ts'ung-yun, both battalion commanders, in response to the Wuchang Uprising of October 10, 1911, Feng staged an unsuccessful coup at Lan-chou, Hopei, that caused the death of Wang and Shih and his own dismissal from the army.

With the founding of the Chinese Republic, Feng started his military career anew. He found a patron in Lu Chien-chang. In 1914 Feng was promoted to regiment commander stationed outside of Peking; by then he had already distinguished himself in training troops and in accepting Christianity. Soon his regiment was expanded to a brigade, and Feng was assigned to move to Shensi to suppress banditry there.

Yet as a brigadier, Feng secretly opposed Yüan Shih-k'ai's* imperial adventure and later actively suppressed Chang Hsün's* imperial restoration. He was so bold and independent that in 1918, in defiance of Tuan Ch'i-jui's Peking government, he issued a manifesto advocating peace with Sun Yat-sen's* Canton government. He paid dearly for his daring. The desperate plight of his army was only relieved in 1921 when the Peking government, now under the control of the Hopei Clique led by Ts'ao K'un* and Wu P'ei-fu,* sent Feng's brigade to Shensi to suppress Ch'en Shu-fan of the Anhwei Clique.* His successful campaign against Ch'en was rewarded with the expansion of his brigade into a division, followed by his promotion to governor-general of Shensi. Feng seems to have been destined to be the ruler of northwest China, from which his army derived its name Hsipeichün (Northwestern Army).

In answer to the call of Wu P'ei-fu in the First Chih (-li)-Feng (-tien) War in 1922, Feng's army poured out of Tunkuan and marched eastward, in time to save Wu from being defeated by Chang Tso-lin. However, Wu failed to bestow the reward due to him, but allowed Feng's 30,000-man army to be settled at Peking, thus inadvertently making Feng the protector of the capital. At the outbreak of the Second Chih-Feng War in 1924, Feng had the best trained, if not the best equipped, troops of 34,000 men. Wu's failure to judge the man caused his downfall. While battle was raging in the front, Feng staged the "Capital Revolution." What ensued was an invitation to Sun Yat-sen to come north in order to consult with the newly formed triumvirate, Chang Tso-lin, Tuan Ch'i-jui, and Feng. One of the revolutionary deeds was to drive the "last emperor" out of the Peking palace. Rumors circulated that, in staging the coup, Feng had been inspired by the Japanese and that he had stolen treasures from the palace. Both rumors should be dismissed, as there is no evidence to support them, nor does reason militate for them.

After Sun's death at Peking on March 12, 1925, relations among the trio deteriorated rapidly, chiefly because the Manchurian warlord not only wanted to dominate north China but also even extend his influence in the Yangtze Valley. One of his major generals, Kuo Sun-ling, who served under Sun Yat-sen and became a confidant of Young Marshal Chang Hsüeh-liang,* son of Chang Tso-lin, after having reached a secret agreement with Feng Yü-hsiang, revolted against Chang Tso-lin on November 22, 1925. While Kuo's force marched toward Shenyang, Feng's army began to attack Tientsin. December 24, the day when Feng's army captured Tientsin, also brought the news that Kuo's force collapsed and that Kuo and his wife had been captured and killed. What followed was the Feng-Chang War, which was intermittently fought until the defeat of Feng's army at Nankou in late August 1926.

Feng had been on good terms with the Soviets at Peking since 1923. With the establishment of the Kuominchün (People's Army)* following his capital revolution, Feng got closer to the Soviets and the Kuomintang. From April 1925 to June 1926, Feng had received Soviet aid amounting to 11 million rubles, while sixty Soviet advisers were attached to his army. Out of desperation, Feng made a trip to Moscow and in the meantime joined the Kuomintang. At Moscow Feng was received by Stalin who promised him massive military aid in arms and ammunition which would be delivered at Urga. The sudden collapse of his army forced Feng to cut his trip short and immediately return to China. Within a few weeks after his arrival at Wuyuan, Suiyuan, in September 1926, Feng was able to rally his scattered forces into a strong army to coordinate with the National Revolutionary Army of the Northern Expedition.* His siding with Chiang Kai-shek* precipitated the downfall of the Wuhan government and its purge of the Chinese Communists. Nevertheless, Feng did join Chiang to bring the Northern Expedition to fruition, thus forcing Chang Tso-lin to return home in June 1928, when he was killed by the Japanese.

In 1930 Feng allied himself with Wang Ching-wei* and Yen Hsi-shan* to fight against Chiang. This "great central plain" war was probably the bloodiest civil war ever fought up to that time. Now Chang Hsüeh-liang became the arbitrator, as his support for Chiang Kai-shek not only brought the war to an end but also virtually terminated Feng's glorious career. Except for a brief episode of establishing an anti-Japanese Allied Army in Chahar in early 1933, Feng served as a titular vice-chairman of the Military Council, of which Chiang was the chairman, but maintained his popularity by voicing, sometimes vociferously, dissenting opinions from the Nationalist government. After the war, he visited the United States for a year. Finally, he decided to cast his lot with the Chinese Communists and return to China. Just before landing at Odessa in the Black Sea, he was killed by a fire in a movie theater aboard the Russian freighter *Pobeda* on September 1, 1948.

REFERENCES: James E. Sheridan, *Chinese Warlord: The Career of Feng Yü-hsiang* (Stanford, Calif., 1966); Chien Yu-wen, *Feng Yü-hsiang chuan* (Biography of Feng Yü-hsiang), 2 vols. (Taipei, 1982); Li Tai-fen, ed., *Kuominchün shih-kao* (Documents of the People's Army) (Peip'ing, 1930).

TIEN-WEI WU

FENG YÜN-SHAN (1815–1852): Founder of the God Worshippers Society; leader of the Taiping Revolution.

Born into a Hakka, or "guest people," family in 1815, in Hua County, Kwangtung, Feng Yü-shan was a cousin of Hung Hsiu-ch'üan,* leader of the Taiping Revolution.* When Hung began to preach his version of Christianity in 1843, Feng became one of his first converts. Having made little progress in Kwangtung, Feng suggested that they go to Kwangsi. After a short stay, Hung returned to Kwangtung; Feng chose to stay in Kwangsi and continued to spread Hung's teachings there.

Sometime during 1846 and 1847, Feng founded the God Worshippers Society,* recruiting many Hakka immigrants from Kwangtung. He taught them to worship God, and he attacked local superstitious practices. In the three years after 1844,

Feng was able to attract several thousand believers in about a dozen counties in Kwangtung and Kwangsi. On August 27, 1847, Hung Hsiu-ch'üan returned to Kwangsi and, to his surprise, discovered a large following acknowledging his supreme leadership. Feng helped Hung to mobilize the God Worshippers to destroy idols and temples. Such activities antagonized the local elite, including Wang Tso-hsin, who succeeded in arresting Feng with his own militia corps on December 28. During his imprisonment, Feng worked on a new calendar, clearly an attempt to make preparations for a political uprising.

When Feng was released in October 1848, he found that the God Worshippers Society had two new leaders. Yang Hsiu-ch'ing* and Hsiao Ch'ao-kuei* had used trances to establish their authority as the spokesmen for God and Jesus. Feng returned to Kwangtung in November to discuss the new situation with Hung. They decided to take advantage of the growing revolutionary situation in Kwangsi and conceded the de facto status of Yang and Hsiao. To prepare for an uprising, they wrote the T'ai-p'ing t'ien-jih (Taiping chronicle), which for the first time gave a political interpretation of Hung's dream during his delirium in 1837. The new account related that in the dream Hung was told that he was the second son of God, the younger brother of Jesus. More importantly, God conferred on Hung the title of Son of Heaven. This well-developed account was probably designed to reestablish Hung's authority over Yang and Hsiao.

On January 1, 1851, the God Worshippers gathered in Chin-t'ien and raised their banner against the Manchus. Hung Hsiu-ch'üan declared the founding of the T'ai-p'ing t'ien-kuo, the Heavenly Kingdom of Great Peace, and assumed the title of Heavenly King. In September 1851 the Taipings captured the city of Yung-an. Hung conferred new titles on the core leaders, and Feng Yün-shan was made South King.

Feng had great organizational abilities. He was responsible primarily for creating the basic structure of the political and military organizations of the Taipings. He wrote several works, including the T'ai-p'ing chün-mu for military organization, the T'ai-p'ing t'iao-k'uei for military discipline, and the T'ai-p'ing kuan-chih for bureaucratic structure and recruitment. Feng's military organization was built on the model of the Chou-li, and he owed many of his strategies to his familiarity with the military operations described in the popular novel Water Margin. The calendar Feng created during his imprisonment was promulgated as the official calendar of the Taiping kingdom in February 1852.

Hardly had the Taipings settled in Yung-an when the Ch'ing forces began to lay a strong siege to the city. On April 5, 1852, the Taipings broke the siege, but as they passed Ch'üan-chou city on May 25, Feng was wounded. He died in June. The loss of Feng resulted in the rise of Yang Hsiu-ch'ing to a supreme position overshadowing Hung's.

REFERENCES: Chung Wen-tien, "Feng Yün-shan," in T'ai-p'ing t'ien-kuo jen-wu (Leaders of the Heavenly Kingdom of Great Peace) (Kwangsi, 1984); Su Hsiang-pi, "Lun T'ai-p'ing t'ien-kuo yün-t'ung ti tien-chi jen Feng Yün-shan" (On the founder of the Taiping movement Feng Yün-shan), in T'ai-p'ing t'ien-kuo jen-wu lun-chi (Collection of essays on leaders of the Heavenly Kingdom of Great Peace) (Fukien, 1984): 93–115; Hsing Feng-lin and Hsing Feng-wu, "Lun Feng Yün-shan" (On Feng Yün-shan), in *T'ai-p'ing t'ien-kuo shih hsüeh-shu t'ao-lun hui lun-wen hsüan-chi* (Selected essays of the symposium on the study of the history of the Heavenly Kingdom of Great Peace) (Peking, 1981): 518–551; Yu-wen Jen, *The Taiping Revolutionary Movement* (New Haven, Conn., 1973).

KAI-WING CHOW

FENGT'IEN CLIQUE: The military group in the 1920s based in Manchuria, loyal to Chang Tso-lin, and patronized by the Japanese.

With the Chihli Clique* the Fengt'ien Clique was a prime contender for power in China during the mid–1920s. The name comes from Fengt'ien, today's Chilin Province, and the seat of power of Chang Tso-lin (1872–1928). Chang, a man of little education who rose from bandit to general, had by the late 1910s consolidated his grip on Manchuria. Styling himself *Ta-shuai* ("Old Marshal"), he thereafter moved to strengthen his military and political influence in China proper.

Chang's clique combined uneasily his own followers, his son Chang Hsüeh-liang* and his circle, as well as Japanese, White Russians, Britons, and other foreigners. He fought three major wars: in 1920 Fengt'ien allied with Chihli in a successful struggle against the Anhui group, but was devastatingly defeated by Wu P'ei-fu* in 1922 in the first Chihli-Fengt'ien War. Thereafter Chang reorganized and modernized his armies, and greatly expanded his arsenal at Mukden [Shen-yang]. Feng Yü-hsiang's* coup in the autumn of 1924 effectively delivered China from Peking to Shanghai into the Old Marshal's hands, but occupying the new territories overextended his forces and upset his Japanese sponsors, who wanted him to serve as watchdog in Manchuria. A major rebellion in 1925 by his top subordinate, Kuo Sung-ling, was suppressed only with Japanese assistance. Chang, however, remained the most powerful figure in north China until he was ousted by the Nationalists.

Chang was killed in June 1928 by the Japanese as he retreated to Manchuria from Peking ahead of the Nationalists. His son made peace with the Nationalists, but continued to use Fengt'ien Clique connections.

REFERENCES: Hsi-sheng Ch'i, *Warlord Politics in China 1916–1928* (Stanford, Calif., 1976); Gavan McCormack, *Chang Tso-lin in Northeast China, 1911–1928: China, Japan, and the Manchurian Idea* (Folkestone, Kent, England, 1977).

ARTHUR WALDRON

FIRST CONGRESS OF THE CHINESE COMMUNIST PARTY (July 1921): Ch'en Tu-hsiu was elected first general secretary; the twelve delegates representing fifty-seven members included Mao Tse-tung and Chang Kuo-t'ao.

Heir to the May Fourth Movement,* the Chinese Communist party* introduced a completely new element into Chinese political life. Unlike other political parties such as the Kuomintang that looked to Europe and the United States for ideological, financial, and moral support, the Chinese Communist party drew its inspiration from Russia's October Revolution, the social-economic analysis of Marxism, and Lenin's concept of the party as the vanguard of the revolution.

The First Congress of the Chinese Communist party was held secretly at a girls' school in the French Concession of Shanghai in July 1921. The beginnings were meager and unpropitious. Twelve delegates, including Mao Tse-tung* and Chang Kuo-t'ao,* represented fifty-seven members. The two leaders, Ch'en Tu-hsiu* and Li Ta-chao,* were absent but were credited as the co-founders. Fearing discovery, the group fled the school and finished the Congress on a boat on a scenic lake near Shanghai. Historical documentation on this Congress is limited.

The first issue before the Congress concerned the relationship of the party to the Third Communist International (Comintern),* an international Communist organization reestablished by Lenin to help operatives establish communism worldwide. Party members were deeply divided on what role the Comintern should have in the party. Right-wing representative Li Han-chun, "the Marxist theorist," argued for independence from the Comintern, calling for limits on its influence in the party's activities in China. Li also objected to the immediate adoption of the Bolshevik constitution. He felt that most members lacked a sufficient knowledge of Marxism to engage in political activity, and he recommended that party members go abroad to study Marxism, the German Social Democrats, and various socialist constitutions in order to adopt suitable models for China. Li argued that the party would fulfill its goals and duties with a less centralized party structure.

Li's proposals were countered by Liu Jen-ching, a left-wing activist who wanted the party to pursue a more revolutionary line. Liu argued for the immediate adoption of the policies of class struggle and the dictatorship of the proletariat. Liu was suspicious of intellectuals and believed that the party should strive to make itself a party of the true proletarians. Eventually, the leftist faction was able to obtain support for its position from party members, but the division between the two factions remained until the Second Congress in 1922.

The second issue was the role of the Chinese peasant and the proletariat in the revolution. Ch'en Tu-hsiu, the former dean of Peking University and leader of the May Fourth Movement, used the European-Marxist model to construct his revolution in China. He expressed disdain for the peasant masses and placed his revolutionary expectations on the role of the urban proletariat. On the other hand, Li Ta-chao, a librarian at Peking University and mentor to Mao Tse-tung, romanticized the importance of the peasantry. Li urged the youth of China to travel to the villages and release the revolutionary energies of the peasantry.

The third issue was more threatening to the organizational stability of the party. Most representatives displayed little or no commitment to the party centers. Two members of the Congress, Ch'en Kung-po* and Chou Fo-hai,* refused to give party obligations priority over their personal careers and left China to continue their education in Japan and the United States, respectively. Because of the relative safety of the International Concessions, the party's central office was established in Shanghai. But Ch'en Tu-hsiu, even though elected general secretary of the party, initially remained in Canton and Li Ta-chao stayed in Peking. The result was a poorly coordinated and structured party organization. Personality problems also exacerbated the absence of tight structural organization. Li often complained about Ch'en Tu-hsiu's behavior. Chen had temper tantrums when his instructions were not carried out to his specifications.

Confronted with a high attrition rate, leadership problems, and organizational chaos, the First Party Congress failed to achieve its goals. The Second Party Congress accomplished what the First Congress failed to carry out: it instituted reforms to stabilize the party, and it increased membership in Shanghai, Wuhan, Canton, and Changsha. The party placed itself under the direct control of the Comintern. Only three members from the founding congress attended the Second Congress of the Chinese Communist party.

REFERENCES: Jean Chesneaux, Françoise Le Barbier, and Marie-Claire Bergère, *China: From the Revolution to Liberation* (New York, 1977); Arif Dirlik, *The Origins of Chinese Communism* (New York, 1989); Harold Isaacs, *The Tragedy of the Chinese Revolution* (London, 1938).

                                                                              RICHARD C. KAGAN

FIRST UNITED FRONT (1923–1927): First KMT–CCP collaboration against warlords and imperialists.

The First United Front refers to the earlier of two periods of alliance between the Chinese Communist party* and the Nationalist party. The alliance evolved in 1922 and 1923, and was formally announced at the first Congress of the Kuomintang in January 1924. It lasted until April 1927, when Chiang Kai-shek* and the KMT turned their guns on the Communists in what they called party purification.* To the CCP, this was "the white terror."

Shortly after its establishment in July 1921, the CCP joined the Communist International (Comintern* or CI) and pledged obedience to its leadership. Early CI representatives in China, following Lenin's strategy of affiliation with local nationalist parties, overruled initial resistance by CCP leaders such as Ch'en Tu-hsiu* to an alliance with Sun Yat-sen's* Kuomintang. At Sun's insistence, members of the CCP joined the KMT and agreed to obey his orders. This formula was called "the bloc within," that is, a bloc of CCP members within the KMT. The most influential of these early CI agents was Maring* (pseudonym of Hendricus Sneevliet).

The alliance proceeded fairly well until Sun Yat-sen's death in March 1925. Despite opposition from the KMT's right wing (the Western Hills Faction*), CCP members occupied important positions within the KMT, particularly in labor, peasant, and organization departments. The alliance was also successful in consolidating the revolutionary base in Kwangtung Province. Meanwhile, the most famous of the Soviet advisers, Michael Borodin* (pseudonym of Mikhail Gruzenberg), was exercising much influence over Sun Yat-sen. Sun's death, however, touched off a destabilizing power struggle within the KMT, and the radical currents of the May Thirtieth Incident (1925)* led to rapid growth in the CCP's numbers and influence.

Although Chiang Kai-shek utilized Comintern and CCP allies to defeat his rivals for power in the KMT, he was deeply concerned about the power of the left. Thus, on March 20, 1926, Chiang staged a partial coup against the CI and the CCP, the so-called *Chung-shan* gunboat incident, severely curtailing their influence. Nevertheless, the Comintern insisted on maintaining the alliance, in part because Stalin, under attack by Trotsky for his China policy, could not admit the possibility of error. Thus, the CCP now aimed to use the alliance to strengthen Chiang's liberal rivals within the KMT, the so-called KMT left-wing. This group included Wang Ching-wei,[*] among others.

In July 1926 Chiang initiated the long-awaited Northern Expedition[*] to unify China, thus fulfilling Sun Yat-sen's dream. Although the CI and the CCP knew that this would further add to Chiang's power, they could not oppose it without being branded counterrevolutionaries. The Communists did much to assist the victorious march toward the Yangtze, and joined with their left KMT allies in establishing government and party headquarters in the Wuhan cities. Meanwhile, Chiang Kai-shek's military headquarters was located in Nanchang. Thus, by early 1927 the movement had two heads, neither of which was in control of the other. Conflicting orders continued to come from Moscow, from the CI, and from the CCP center, on the one hand, urging more radical policies in order to mobilize workers and peasants, and on the other hand toning down extremist demands that threatened to break up the United Front. The CCP, it seemed, could neither advance nor retreat.

Meanwhile, Chiang was carrying on delicate behind-the-scenes maneuvers with the foreign powers and major financial interests in Shanghai. In effect, he presented them with two options: either support him or risk chaos and the Communists. Reassured by their signals, he entered Shanghai, which had been delivered to him by a rising of the CCP and its labor unions, still loyally following the orders of their own party.

On April 12, 1927, party purification began, carried out mainly by Shanghai's mafia, the Green Gang. Thousands of Communists, leftists, labor leaders, and intellectuals were killed or arrested, to be executed later. Similar repression soon erupted in other cities where Chiang's influence prevailed.

For a few months, the CCP continued its United Front alliance with the left KMT in Wuhan, but in June and July this collaboration also broke down, and the Communists were hounded from nearly all their previous strongholds. Party membership fell from over 60,000 in early April to less than 10,000 at year's end. Ch'en Tu-hsiu was made the principal scapegoat for these failures and was expelled from all his positions in the CCP.

Out of the ruins of the First United Front, the KMT sought to extend its control as the recognized government over all of China. Meanwhile, the CCP struggled to survive and to fashion a more successful revolutionary strategy.

REFERENCES: Harold Isaacs, *The Tragedy of the Chinese Revolution*, 2nd ed. rev. (Stanford, Calif., 1961); Benjamin Schwartz, *Chinese Communism and the Rise of Mao*, paperback ed. (Cambridge, Mass., 1980); C. Martin Wilbur, *The Nationalist Revolution in China, 1923–1928* (London, 1983); C. Martin Wilbur and Julie Lien-ying How, *Missionaries of Revolution: Soviet Advisers and Nationalist China, 1920–1927* (Cambridge, Mass., 1989).

LYMAN P. VAN SLYKE

FIVE-ANTI (*WU-FAN*) CAMPAIGN: A campaign to eliminate bribery, tax evasion, theft of state property, cheating on government contracts, and theft of state economic intelligence.

Shortly after assuming power in 1949, the Communist government of China nationalized much of the urban sector of the economy. It took control of most commerce and industry formerly owned by foreigners and formerly controlled by the bureaucrat-capitalists—that is, by officials in the recently vanquished Nationalist (Kuomintang) government. At the same time, it allowed a continuation of private ownership of the economy owned by the national bourgeoisie— those indigenous entrepreneurs attached neither to the government nor to foreign enterprise. In late 1950 and throughout 1951, the national bourgeoisie flourished. Official government figures indicate that in 1951 private industrial establishments grew by 11 percent, their personnel by 11.8 percent, and their production value by 39 percent. Private commercial firms grew by 11.9 percent, their personnel by 11.8 percent, their wholesale volume by 35.9 percent, and retail volume by 36.6 percent. Profits in that year exceeded that taken in any of the twenty-two years of Nationalist government control. In 1952 the government claimed that much of that profit was obtained illegally and that many entrepreneurs were avoiding tax payment. An especially damaging criticism was that illegal business activities were subverting Chinese efforts in the Korean War (1950–1953), even to the extent that manufacture and sale of phony and dangerous products were causing unnecessary casualties. The new socialist government was also concerned that such rapid growth of the private sector of the economy would subvert its collectivist aspirations.

In late 1951 the Central Committee of the Communist party began a mass Three-Anti Campaign[*] against waste, corruption, and bureaucratism to counter "bourgeois corrosion" in the party and government. Within a few weeks, this led to a secondary campaign, the Five-Anti, aimed specifically at the national bourgeoisie and designed to address problems said to be endemic among them— bribery, tax evasion, theft of state property, cheating on government contracts, and theft of state economic intelligence. The Five-Anti Campaign was officially launched on January 26, 1952, by a directive from the Party Central Committee, and it was refined by subsequent directives from the Central People's government in March and April: "Standards and methods for dealing with industrial and commercial firms in the 'Five-Anti' campaign," and "Regulations for punishing corruption in the People's Republic of China." To remedy the somewhat unstructured, chaotic proceeding of the early phase of the campaign, Chairman Mao Tse-tung,[*] in a speech published on April 21, distinguished five principles for dealing with businesses and five categories of firms, based on their degree of compliance with the law. The five principles were: to be lenient with past offenders, strict with future ones, lenient with the majority, and strict with the minority; lenient with those who confess and strict with those who resist; lenient with industry and strict with commerce; lenient with ordinary commercial firms and strict with speculators. The five categories of firms were: law-abiding; basically law-abiding; semi-law-abiding, semi-law-breaking; seriously law-breaking; and completely law-breaking.

As is usual in such campaigns, the masses were mobilized to denounce transgressors. Workers accused managers and owners, and customers accused shopkeepers. Businessmen were organized in small groups to criticize themselves and each other. Following practices refined in cadre rectification campaigns, they were obliged to read documents defining correct ideology and to write autobiographies in which they revealed past transgressions. In such campaigns, the party always discovered excesses such as the use of coercion by overzealous cadres to obtain confessions, many of which later proved to be false; drew hasty and rash conclusions; and was too inclusive in accusations of wrongdoing. At the height of the Five-Anti Campaign many businesses went bankrupt, and hundreds of suicides were reported. In an effort to bring the campaign under control, the State Council in June published its Decision on Resolving Several Problems in the "Five Anti" Campaign. It called for a cautious assessment of the actual situation and review of verdicts, observing the principle of being strict in struggle, but lenient in resolving problems. The final assessment, based on statistics drawn from eight major cities at the end of the campaign, was that 10 to 15 percent of the firms investigated were law-abiding; 50 to 60 percent were basically law-abiding; 25 to 30 percent were semi-law-abiding and semi-law-breaking; 4 percent were seriously law-breaking; and 1 percent was completely law-breaking.

The party considered the campaign a great success. It netted the state treasury approximately $1.25 billion, and it considerably weakened the bourgeoisie, "establishing favorable conditions for the socialist transformation of capitalist enterprise." That process was accomplished over the course of the first Five-Year Plan, 1953–1957. Private enterprise would not be tolerated again until the 1980s.

PETER J. SEYBOLT

FIVE ENCIRCLEMENT AND SUPPRESSION CAMPAIGNS (1930–1934):
KMT military efforts that successfully suppressed the Central Soviet base area in Kiangsi Province and forced the Chinese Communists to undertake the Long March.

Chiang Kai-shek's* First Encirclement and Suppression Campaign (December 19, 1930–January 3, 1931) called for a simultaneous advance on the Central Soviet base area from different directions by three Nationalist Army corps (consisting of approximately 100,000 men) that would envelop and annihilate a numerically inferior Red Army located in Ning-tu and Chi-an counties, Kiangsi. Meanwhile, the Communist Red Army relied on a strategy of "luring the enemy deep,'' allowing Nationalist Army units to enter the base area. Because Lu Ti-p'ing's Nationalist expeditionary force consisted mainly of warlord coalitions with conflicting interests, the implementation of the Nanking government's plan was seriously impaired. Using superior military intelligence and mobility, the Red Army was able to mass its forces on some of the Nationalist Army units and defeat them in detail.

Chiang's strategy for the Second Encirclement and Suppression Campaign (April 1–May 30, 1931) was similar to the first, calling for the simultaneous advance of several columns to surround and destroy the Red Army in the area of Ning-tu County. The Nationalist expeditionary force was doubled in size and ordered to ''proceed steadily step by step'' to avoid the earlier trap of being isolated and surrounded by the Red Army. Ho Ying-ch'in's* Nationalist armies were defeated. Once again, warlordism* and factionalism made mutual coop-eration between Nationalist Army units difficult and was the principal reason for their defeat.

In order to deal with the persistent problems of warlordism and factionalism in the expeditionary forces, Chiang mobilized men and units that were personally loyal to him for the Third and Fourth Campaigns. Again, the Nationalist Army was defeated. Their defeats were due less to the presence of military factions, which continued to be a factor, than to causes external to the campaigns themselves. The Third Encirclement and Suppression Campaign (July 1–Sep-tember 20, 1931) was adversely affected by two developments: the Canton Secessionist Movement (May 1931), which challenged Chiang's control of the country, and the Mukden Incident* (September 18, 1931), which resulted in Japanese control of Manchuria. The Fourth Encirclement and Suppression Cam-paign (January 1–May 29, 1933) was halted in the face of Japanese aggression in north China.

After the Third Campaign, Chiang also sought to pacify the rural population through a policy described as ''Three Parts Military and Seven Parts Politics.'' In practice, the policy proved to be mainly a continuation of his military approach by various political means. Socioeconomic reforms such as the cooperative societies movement and the New Life Movement* were of low priority. Instead, the emphasis was on controlling the rural population through a redesigned and reinvigorated administrative apparatus. Such measures as the Administrative Inspectorate system, which included the *pao-chia* system, bypassed the provincial administration and allowed the Nationalists to have direct access to the peasantry. They also tried to extend their authority into the countryside through various police agencies and official militia units. However, none of these security forces proved to be effective. Only local militia under the leadership of the rural elite achieved any results. Under pressure from the Nationalists above and the Com-munists below, the rural elite eventually threw their lot in with the Nanking government. In retrospect, it is evident that the support of the rural elite was an essential element in the last Nationalist campaign.

Ultimately, the Fifth Encirclement and Suppression Campaign (October 16,

1933–October 14, 1934) succeeded because Chiang Kai-shek abandoned the discredited strategy of enveloping the elusive Red Army and adopted a strategically offensive but tactically defensive approach. This method of attack called for a stringent economic and communications blockade, consisting chiefly of blockhouses and trenches around the Central Soviet, that destroyed the self-sufficiency of the base area. This steadily contracting wall of stone and steel was built and guarded by 800,000 soldiers and countless civilians. Contrary to the accepted view, the blockade–blockhouse strategy was developed by Nationalist leaders themselves rather than by German advisers attached to Chiang. The new strategy synthesized and integrated parts of earlier Nationalist programs employed against the Communists.

REFERENCES: *Chiao-fei chan-shih* (Military history of exterminating the bandits), 6 vols. (Taipei, 1967); Ts'ao Po-i, *Kiangsi su-wei-ai chih chien-li chi-ch'i peng-k'uei, 1931–34* (The Kiangsi Soviet: its establishment and collapse, 1931–34) (Taipei, 1969); William Wei, *Counterrevolution in China* (Ann Arbor, Mich., 1985).

WILLIAM WEI

FIVE PRINCIPLES OF PEACEFUL COEXISTENCE: PRC's principles of conducting relations with other countries.

Although the concept of peaceful coexistence is of Leninist origin, it was not until 1954 that Peking advanced its own adaptation in the form of the Five Principles of Peaceful Coexistence (FPPC): (1) mutual respect for sovereignty and territorial integrity; (2) mutual nonaggression; (3) mutual noninterference of internal affairs; (4) equality and mutual benefit; and (5) peaceful coexistence. The Five Principles, also known by its Indian name *panch shila*, were first embodied in the Sino-Indian Treaty (April 29, 1954) concerning trade and communications between India and the Tibet region of China. On June 18, 1954, the principles were ceremoniously confirmed in a joint declaration that Premier Chou En-lai[*] signed with Prime Minister Nehru of India and also in Chou's joint declaration the next day with Prime Minister U Nu of Burma. In his report to the Central People's Government Administrative Council on August 11, 1954, Chou reaffirmed that the FPPC would apply to China's relations with all Asian nations and to international relations in general. China's first (1954) constitution incorporated the FPPC. Moreover, in the course of China's debut at the first Third World conference held in Bandung, Indonesia, in April 1955, Chou added more elements to the FPPC and succeeded in having most of his seven principles incorporated into the ten principles adopted by the conference.

Since 1954, the Five Principles have recurred, with varying degrees of consistency, in Chinese policy pronouncements as the fundamental norms for international relations. In addition, they have often been touted as evidence of continuity in China's principled foreign policy. Far from being the normative guide to action, however, an instrumental conception of the FPPC has remained the central underlying thread of continuity of Chinese foreign policy. Even as a set of fundamental principles, the Five Principles have followed, rather than guided, Peking's changing foreign policy needs and goals in that they have always been applied in a manner that both reflects and effects the shifts in Chinese foreign policy. In short, the Five Principles have a rather checkered history.

During the formative period of 1954–1958, the FPPC served as a normative rationale for breaking out of U.S.-imposed isolation and containment by creating an opening bridge to greater cooperation with India and Burma and to establishing diplomatic relations with Afghanistan, Nepal, Egypt, Syria, Yemen, and Ceylon (Sri Lanka), all of which had different social and political systems from China's. From 1958 to 1963 the Five Principles fell by the wayside as a casualty of China's growing conflicts with India over Tibet and the unresolved territorial dispute; with the United States over the Taiwan Strait; and with the Soviet Union over the issues of war and peace. Although Moscow and Peking agreed on the necessity for peaceful coexistence, they disagreed sharply on its specific meaning and application. For Peking the Five Principles apply no less within the socialist world; for Moscow they apply only to state relations between the two contending systems.

Peking's dual-adversary policy vis-à-vis the two superpowers, coupled with its revolutionary clarion call in the Third World, in the remaining part of the 1960s could not be easily reconciled with the cooperative spirit of the FPPC. From 1970 to 1982 anti-hegemonism (anti-Sovietism) served as the cardinal principle and operational guide of Chinese foreign policy. The 1972 Shanghai Communiqué formalizing the Sino-American rapprochement incorporated the FPPC as a thinly disguised form of anti-Sovietism, just as the reference to the FPPC in the preamble of the 1975 constitution was aligned with the objective to "oppose the imperialist and socialist-imperialist policies of aggression and war and oppose the hegemonism of the superpowers." With the inauguration of an independent and peaceful foreign policy in 1982, the Five Principles have regained the status they enjoyed during the heyday of the mid–1950s, but with new twists and interpretations. In both nature and scope, the Five Principles have become globalized, providing the basic norms governing all types of state-to-state relations, East–West, North–South, South–South, as well as East–East (intersocialist). The current (1982) constitution also places the FPPC in a new context, which emphasizes Peking's positive and cooperative relationship with the rest of the world.

The significance of the FPPC lies not so much in the conceptual originality as in the acceptance of modern principles of international law and relations as a way of competing with Western nations on an equal footing, or even beating them at their own game. The Five Principles also mark the beginning of Peking's Third World policy. As such, they constitute a departure from, or at least a drastic reinterpretation of, the "lean-to-one-side" aligned policy of 1949–1953, based on the growing recognition of the insufficiency of the Sino-Soviet alliance. Although adapted from Leninism as well as from the principles of the U.N. Charter (Article 2), the Five Principles nonetheless represent a first significant step in China's own search for its national identity and for control of its national destiny in the international system. Because of the prominence of the legitimation problem in light of China's long isolation from the international community and the still unsettled two-China question, "principles" play an important legitimating role in Chinese polity. The broad generality and wide elasticity of the FPPC define the outer limits of the permissible, making it possible for Peking to be "firm in principle but flexible in tactics" to accommodate new needs and the requirements of its expanding relations with the world at large.

REFERENCES: Jerome A. Cohen and Hungdah Chiu, *People's China and International Law*, 2 vols. (Princeton, N.J., 1974); James C. Hsiung, *Law and Policy in China's Foreign Relations* (New York; 1972); Samuel S. Kim, *The Third World in Chinese World Policy* (Princeton, N.J., 1989).

SAMUEL S. KIM

FOUR FUNDAMENTAL PRINCIPLES: Principles introduced by Teng Hsiao-p'ing in order to define the limits of dissent and protest in Chinese society and the CCP.

The Four Fundamental (or Cardinal) Principles (*Szu-hsiang Chi-pen*) were first enunciated by Teng Hsiao-ping[*] at a March 1979 Politburo meeting that followed the Chinese Communist party's[*] suppression of the Hsi-tan Democracy Wall Movement that had broken out in 1978. The Four Principles call on all Chinese to "uphold the socialist road; uphold the dictatorship of the proletariat; uphold the leadership of the Chinese Communist Party; and uphold Marxism-Leninism[*] and Thought of Mao Tse-tung."[*] Overall, they provide hard-line, orthodox leaders in the Communist party with an ideological carte blanche for persecuting any individuals, including party members, who advocate significant political reform and human rights.

Since 1979, China's leaders have periodically invoked the Four Principles to justify political repression and cultural conservatism. Although always cited as official ideology even during times of great relaxation and openness in the press and cultural circles, the government's reliance on the Four Principles was especially pronounced in periods of retreat from political reform. This was true during the so-called Anti-Spiritual Pollution Campaign in the mid–1980s and the subsequent attack on bourgeois liberalism following Hu Yao-pang's[*] dismissal as CCP general secretary in 1987. The Four Principles are also now a central part of the Communist orthodoxy imposed on China following the military crackdown against the popular democracy movement in June 1989.

From the orthodox Chinese Communist point of view, "upholding socialism and the CCP's dictatorship" are essential to combat the penetration of Western pro-capitalist and democratic ideas into China. Similar to nineteenth-century Chinese conservatives who attempted to "use" (*yung*) Western techology while maintaining the essence, or "body" (*t'i*), of traditional Chinese culture, Teng has introduced modern economic principles and technology into China while trying to avoid the inevitable cultural and political influences of the outside world. The contradictions intensified when the party exhorted its members to "liberate their thought" (*chieh-fang szu-hsiang*) from the "evil" leftist influences of the radical Gang of Four.[*] Contrary to the intention of orthodox leaders,

such *pronunciamentos* seemingly encouraged learning from the democratic capitalist world, which is why Teng Hsiao-p'ing had a difficult time differentiating
bourgeois liberalism from liberation of thought.

Official CCP documents thus warn CCP members against being influenced by
the wave of capitalist ideas on freedom (*tzu-ch'an chieh-chi tzu-yu-hua szu-
ch'ao*) and capitalist standards of morality and literature and art. One document
complained that "in the party there are certain comrades who not only don't
recognize the dangers of this wave, but even go so far as to encourage more of
it." Such warnings were undoubtedly aimed at supporters of Hu Yao-pang and
those relatively liberal party members at universities and research institutes, such
as the Chinese Academy of Social Sciences, where support for dramatic political
change in the direction of democratic liberalism is strong. Even before the spring
1989 demonstrations, Chinese Communist leaders expressed alarm over the active role some party members were taking in street demonstrations and other
popular protests. Once party members applied their considerable organizational
skills to mobilizing the population for political change, it was obvious that the
old guard's grip on power would be seriously threatened.

REFERENCES: Lowell Dittmer, *China's Continuous Revolution: The Post Liberation
Epoch, 1949–1981* (Berkeley, Calif., 1987); *Tang Shih Chih-shih Chen-wen-lü* (Tidbits
of knowledge about party history) (1988).

LAWRENCE R. SULLIVAN

FOUR MARTYRS OF HUNG-HUA KANG (*Hung-hua kang ssu lieh-shih*):
Wen Sheng-ts'ai (1870–1911), Lin Kuan-tz'u (1883?–1911), Ch'en Ching-yueh
(1870?–1911), and Chung Ming-kuang (1881–1915).

Revolutionaries died in three separate assassination missions in Canton: Wen
Sheng-ts'ai versus Fu-ch'i on April 8, 1911; Lin Kuan-tz'u and Ch'en Ching-
yueh versus Li Chun on August 13, 1911; and Chung Ming-kuang versus Lung
Chi-kuang on July 17, 1915. They were buried at Hung-hua kang (Red Flower
Hill) in the eastern suburb of Canton.

The four martyrs shared a common social background. All were Cantonese,
and all came from peasant families. Wen Sheng-ts'ai, Ch'en Ching-yueh, and
Chung Ming-kuang were *hua-ch'iao* (overseas Chinese[*]) who had lived in the
Nanyang (Southeast Asia) for some years. It was in Southeast Asia that they
joined the T'ung-meng hui.[*] When the revolutionaries in southern China suffered
repeated failures, their overseas comrades returned to Canton to promote the
revolutionary cause by assassination and self-sacrifice. Wen and Chung were
individual assassins. As members of the Chih-na an-sha-t'uan (China Assassination Corps), Lin and Ch'en cooperated in their mission against Li Chun.

Wen Sheng-ts'ai was a miner in Perak, Malaya. After the T'ung-meng hui
opened a reading center at Perak in 1907, he became interested in the anti-
Manchu movement in China and joined the revolutionary organization. When
news of the suppression of the New Army[*] uprising (February 1910) and the
failure of Wang Ching-wei's[*] attempt on the prince regent (April 1910) reached

Perak, he decided to play the role of assassin in the revolutionary movement. Wen returned to Canton in early 1911. He opted for individual action, without notifying other revolutionaries who were busy preparing for an uprising in April. Wen carried out the assassination on April 8. The occasion was an aircraft demonstration performed by Feng Ju, a Chinese aviator from the United States. Many officials were invited to attend the show. Wen waited in a teahouse near the place of demonstration. As a procession of official palanquins passed the teahouse in the afternoon, Wen rushed out and fired his pistol repeatedly at one of them, instantly killing a Manchu general named Fu-ch'i inside. He was arrested and beheaded a week later.

Wen's success alarmed the local authorities in Canton. This in part contributed to the failure of the uprising on April 27. In the summer of 1911 revolutionaries resorted to assassination to remove two of their chief enemies, namely, Li Chun, the admiral of the Pearl River fleet, and Chang Ming-ch'i, the acting governor-general of Kwangtung and Kwangsi. The operation was planned and executed by members of the Chih-na an-sha-t'uan.

The assassination corps was organized by Liu Ssu-fu, Hsieh Ying-po, Ch'en Chiung-ming, and Li Hsi-pin in the wake of the fiasco of the New Army uprising. Their plot against the prince regent in August 1910 aborted when one of their members defected to the government in northern China. In July 1911 an attack group was formed for the assassination of Li Chun and Chang Ming-ch'i. Lin Kuan-tz'u was one of the assassins. Ch'en Ching-yueh, a teacher in Perak, returned to Canton in time to join the group. Twice they changed the plan because they found it unlikely to succeed. Later, they learned that Li Chun used to enter the city by way of the Shuang-men-ti. On August 13 Lin disguised himself as a peddler and waited near the Yung-ch'ing Gate, while Ch'en and two other members hid nearby. At noon when Li and his entourage approached the Yung-ch'ing Gate, Lin cast two bombs at them. The admiral and some of his guards were wounded. The other guards killed Lin Kuan-tz'u on the spot. Ch'en Ching-yueh was caught later and decapitated on November 7, 1911.

Chung Ming-kuang's attempt on Lung Chi-kuang, a loyal supporter of Yüan Shih-k'ai,* occurred in the warlord years. Lung's forces occupied Canton in August 1914. Once in control, Lung suppressed the revolutionaries ruthlessly. He further enraged the Cantonese by ordering a lantern procession to celebrate Yüan's acceptance of Japan's Twenty-one Demands. Chung Ming-kuang, a schoolteacher in Singapore, just returned home from visiting his family in 1915. Having witnessed Lung's atrocity, he deemed it his responsibility to get rid of the warlord. A strong sense of revolutionary dedication pervaded the five letters that he wrote one month before the mission. He advocated self-sacrifice for the salvation of the people. His friend Ch'iu Han-miao, leader of a workers' assassination group, offered him financial and material support. On July 17 when Lung Chi-kuang paid a visit to his brother during a flood in Canton, Chung threw a bomb at him. It killed seventeen members of his bodyguard. Lung received only a foot wound. Chung Ming-kuang was executed the next day.

Wen Sheng-ts'ai, Lin Kuan-tz'u, Ch'en Ching-yueh, and Chung Ming-kuang were interred at Hung-hua kang after their execution. In 1918, Dr. Sun Yat-sen's* army regained control of Canton. The Nationalist government built a tomb to honor the sacrifice of the four revolutionaries. A stone tablet with inscriptions was added in 1924. The tribute to the martyrs was complete when Tsou Lu* edited and published an account of their lives and deeds in 1927.

REFERENCES: Li Hsi-pin, "Ch'ing-mo Chih-na an-sha-t'uan chi-shih" (An account of the China Assassination Corps in the late Ch'ing period), in *Kuang-tung wen-wu t'e-chi* (A special collection of materials relating to Kwangtung) (Canton, 1948): 17–23; "Lung Chi-kuang," in Howard L. Boorman and Richard C. Howard, eds., *Biographical Dictionary of Republican China*, vol. 2 (New York, 1968): 455–457; Edward Rhoads, *China's Republican Revolution: The Case of Kwangtung, 1895–1913* (Cambridge, Mass., 1975); Tsou Lu, *Huang-hua kang ssu lieh-shih chuan-chi* (A biographical account of four martyrs at Red Flower Hill) (Shanghai, 1927).

HENRY Y.S. CHAN

FOUR MARTYRS OF WAN-SHENG YÜAN (*Wan-sheng yüan ssu lieh-shih*): Chang Hsien-p'ei (1892?–1912), Huang Chih-meng (1891?–1912), Yang Yü-ch'ang (1885?–1912), P'eng Chia-chen (1888–1912).

These four revolutionaries were members of the Ching-Chin T'ung-meng hui (the Peking–Tientsin branch of the T'ung-meng hui*) who died in assassination missions in Peking. Chang Hsien-p'ei, Huang Chih-meng, and Yang Yü-ch'ang lost their lives in the plot against Yüan Shih-k'ai* on January 16, 1912, while P'eng Chia-chen died in the mission against Liang-pi on January 26, 1912. They were buried at Wan-sheng yüan (Garden of Ten Thousand Animals, currently the Peking Zoo) in the western suburb of metropolitan Peking.

The Ching-Chin T'ung-meng hui was organized by Wang Ching-wei* on December 1, 1911. At the suggestion of Wang and Li Shih-tseng, an assassination department was formed for the removal of officials who obstructed the progress of the revolution. The four martyrs belonged to this department, and Yüan Shih-k'ai was one of their targets. The revolutionaries were suspicious of Yüan's intention in the peace negotiations. They planned to get rid of Yüan in early December. Wang Ching-wei counseled patience, and the assassination department agreed to shelve the plan. The situation changed in January 1912. Yüan forced T'ang Shao-yi,* head of the government's peace delegation, to resign. Members of the Ching-Chin T'ung-meng hui were arrested in Tungchow, Shensi. The assassination department decided to take action without delay.

The assassins had earlier learned that Yüan Shih-k'ai would drive from his office to the palace to present a memorial to the empress on January 16. Four attack groups were organized for the operation. The first two groups hid, respectively, in a tea-shop and a restaurant near the Tung-hua Gate. The third group waited outside the Tung-an Market. The fourth one was a mobile unit for reconnaissance and support to other groups. At 11:15 A.M. Yüan returned from the palace after the imperial audience. As his carriage passed the Tung-hua Gate, Chang Hsien-p'ei and his comrades threw down four bombs from the tea-shop,

killing twelve guards. Yüan got away unhurt. His guards searched the surrounding area and arrested ten assailants. Chang, Huang, and Yang were executed
after interrogation. Yüan released the rest under the pressure of foreign correspondents in Peking.

Both Huang Chih-meng and Chang Hsien-p'ei came from Kweichow. Chang's
father was a Ch'ing* official. In the spring of 1911 Chang left his home town
to study in a military institution at Peking. Huang Chih-meng had earlier graduated from a military academy and worked as a surveyor in the capital. Yang
was a Szechwanese and a lecturer in the Paoting Normal School.

The attempt on Yüan's life strengthened his position in the government. It
showed that he was the enemy of the revolutionaries. But he and the cabinet
had presented a memorial to the imperial court urging abdication of the emperor.
A court conference was summoned to discuss the memorial. A small group of
Manchu nobility strongly objected to the proclamation of a republic. Led by
Liang-pi and T'ieh-liang, they formed the Tsung-she tang (Manchu Clique)
pledging to protect Manchu interests. P'eng Chia-chen volunteered to remove
Liang-pi.

P'eng was born into a Szechwanese official family. He graduated from the
Chengtu Military Institute with distinction. Hsi-liang, the governor of Szechwan,
sent him to Japan on a study tour in 1905. P'eng served in the Szechwan Army
as an officer after his return from Japan in 1906. In 1909 he moved to Yunnan.
The next year he followed Hsi-liang to Manchuria. In Tientsin P'eng joined the
Ching-Chin T'ung-meng hui, and he assigned himself the task of assassination.

P'eng spied on Liang-pi's house and found that it was well guarded. He faked
an invitation to lure Liang-pi out but without success. Then he asked his friends
in Manchuria to send a false telegram to Liang-pi, giving Liang-pi the impression
that his friend, Ch'ung-kung, would pay him a visit in Peking. On the evening
of January 26, P'eng entered Liang-pi's mansion with Ch'ung-kung's name card.
To his disappointment, Liang-pi was not at home. He was about to leave. Then
he saw Liang-pi's carriage coming from a distance. P'eng waited at the front
gate and threw a bomb at Liang-pi when he stepped out of his carriage. P'eng
was killed in the explosion; Liang-pi died two days later. An atmosphere of fear
gripped the capital after the incident. Most leaders of the Tsung-she tang left
Peking hurriedly. That hastened the abdication of the emperor which spelled the
end of the Ch'ing dynasty.

For his contribution to the revolution, Dr. Sun Yat-sen,* the provisional president of the Chinese Republic, conferred on P'eng Chia-chen posthumously the
title of *ta chiang-chün* (Great General). Sung Chiao-jen* and other T'ung-meng
hui members buried the four martyrs at Wan-sheng yüan with formal ceremonies
in July 1912. The next month a tombstone with inscriptions was erected to
commemorate the heroic deeds of the four revolutionaries.

REFERENCES: Jerome Ch'en, *Yüan Shih-k'ai* (Stanford, Calif., 1972); Ch'en Yao-tsu,
"Wan-sheng yüan ssu lieh-shih ying-tsang chi" (an account of the burial of four martyrs
at the Garden of Thousand Animals) in *Ko-ming hsien-lieh hsien-chin chuan* (biographical

writings of the martyrs and pioneers in the revolutionary movement) (Taipei, 1965); Hu O-kung, *Hsin-hai ko-ming pei-fang shih-lu* (An account of the 1911 Revolution in northern China) (Shanghai, 1948); Shang Ping-ho, *Hsin-jen ch'un-ch'iu* (Spring and autumn annals: 1911–1912) (reprint, Taipei, 1962).

HENRY Y.S. CHAN

FOURTH RED ARMY: Communist army located in central China, ca. 1937–1950.

The Fourth Red Army, more commonly known as the New Fourth Army, originated among approximately 20,000 Communist party members who remained in south and central China following the departure of the Chinese Communist party* on the Long March* in the mid–1930s. At first, it was controlled by Communist leaders who only nominally accepted Mao Tse-tung's* leadership of the party. It played a key role in the relations between the Kuomintang and the Communist party, since the New Fourth Army Incident* of January 1941 in effect destroyed what remained of the Second United Front* between the Nationalists and the Communists.

The Fourth Red Army emerged out of the political maneuvering surrounding the Sian Incident* of December 1936, which led to the Second United Front and the opening of the Sino-Japanese War* in July 1937. Wang Ming,* leader of the "international" group within the Communist party, argued in 1937 that the Communists should join a United Front against fascist aggression in order to prevent Japanese domination of China. By the end of 1937, Mao Tse-tung and other party leaders accepted this position. Wang also gained approval for the creation of new regional party organizations. Two of these organizations were the Yangtze Bureau, located in Wuhan and controlled directly by Wang, and the Southeast China Bureau, located in Nanchang and controlled by Hsiang Ying as secretary. The Southeast Bureau's military arm was the Fourth Red Army.

Until late 1937 when the Fourth Red Army was formed, about 10,000 men had operated against the Kuomintang in rural areas scattered from Wuhan to Shanghai and south to Hainan Island. They were the survivors of the 20,000 military and political activists who remained behind in some fourteen separate pockets when the main forces of the Red Army embarked on the Long March. There was little coordination among these groups because of Kuomintang pressure, although Hsiang Ying was the nominal commander and Ch'en Yi was the political commissar. But the army took on new organizational strength after October 1937, when the Kuomintang authorized the creation of the New Fourth Army as part of the United Front agreements.

Between late 1937 and the end of 1940, the army grew rapidly, increasing from 12,000 to 135,000 regulars. As the army expanded numerically, it moved into new areas of central and east China, creating Kuomintang misgivings and resulting in numerous clashes between Communist and Nationalist troops. This resulted in discussions between the Kuomintang and the Communist party, and in an agreement in June 1940 that required the Fourth Army to withdraw from central and east China. Most of the Communist troops complied, but the New

Fourth Army's headquarters unit of about 9,000 men, under the command of Hsiang Ying and Yeh T'ing, did not. It appears that Hsiang Ying wanted to remain in the area to preserve his independence from Mao's leadership.

Instead of moving north, Hsiang Ying's unit moved to the southwest. On December 9, 1940, the Kuomintang set a final deadline of the end of 1940 for all the Communist troops to withdraw north of the Yangtze River. When the New Fourth Army's headquarters unit refused, the Kuomintang attacked it on January 4, 1941, and a bitter ten-day battled erupted in which the Communists were nearly annihilated. Hsiang Ying and other high-ranking personnel were killed, and only 1,000 troops survived.

This incident effectively climaxed the deterioration of the Second United Front. On January 17, 1941, the Kuomintang issued orders that the New Fourth Army should be disbanded. But Mao appointed a new command staff on January 22, and the 90,000 remaining troops were reorganized under the control of Liu Shao-ch'i[*] and Ch'en Yi. A new Central China Bureau was created under Mao's firm control, and the Fourth Army became an important part of the civil war strategy against the Kuomintang.

The Fourth Red Army is important to the history of the Communist Revolution for at least three reasons. First, it played a key role in Mao's victory over Wang Ming and the Moscow-oriented leadership within the Communist party. Second, the demise of the Second United Front between the Communists and the Kuomintang was ensured by the New Fourth Army Incident. Third, the activities of the army in the central Yangtze area created a Communist base area that was important in the eventual victory of the Communists in the civil war,[*] 1945–1949.

REFERENCES: James P. Harrison, *The Long March to Power; A History of the Chinese Communist Party, 1921–1972* (New York, 1972); Tetsuya Kataoka, *Resistance and Revolution in China; The Communists and the Second United Front* (Berkeley, Calif., 1974); Richard C. Thornton, *China, the Struggle for Power, 1917–1972* (Bloomington, Ind., 1973); Lyman P. Van Slyke, *Enemies and Friends: The United Front in Chinese Communist History* (Stanford, Calif., 1967).

LOREN W. CRABTREE

FU TSO-YI (June 27, 1895–April 19, 1974): Top Nationalist general in north China; minister of water conservancy and electric power in the PRC.

Fu Tso-yi was born in Jungho County, Shansi Province, in 1895, and he was educated at the Paoting Military Academy. In 1918 he entered the military service of Yen Hsi-shan[*] in Shansi. After Yen Hsi-shan joined the Kuomintang in 1927, Fu was ordered to capture and hold Chochow, midway between Peking and Paoting. Fu's heroic defense of Chochow for three months (October 12, 1927–January 12, 1928) was hailed throughout China as a remarkable achievement in the best military tradition. In 1930 he joined the coalition of Yen Hsi-shan, Feng Yü-hsiang,[*] and Wang Ching-wei[*] against Chiang Kai-shek.[*] After the demise of this anti-Chiang coalition, Fu became governor of Suiyuan in late 1931. From 1932 to the outbreak of the Second Sino-Japanese War[*] (1937–1945), Fu suppressed the local bandits in Suiyuan, fought the Japanese aggressors in the Great Wall region (Jehol and Chahar provinces), and routed the pro-Japanese Inner Mongolian leader Te Wang (Demchug donggrub) in battle in Suiyuan. The great victory at Pailingmiao in the Suiyuan's War of Resistance, in November 1936, cleared the province of Japanese and their (Mongol) puppet armies and catapulted Fu to national fame. By then Fu had become a member of the Central Executive Committee of the KMT. During the war (1937–1945), Fu served successively as senior commander in the Second, Eighth, and Twelfth War Zones.

After the Japanese surrender in August 1945, Fu was charged with recovering Suiyuan, Chahar, and Jehol. His haste in restoring authority in Suiyuan, his power base, also aimed at containing the Communist activities there. After the failure of the peace talks at Chungking and in the Political Consultative Conference, the KMT launched a general offensive against the Communists in north China in June 1946. Fu's forces captured several points on the Peip'ing–Suiyuan Railway and lifted the siege of Tatung in Shansi. In October 1946 he took Kalgan (Changchiakou) from the Communists. In March 1947 the Twelfth War Zone became the Kalgan Pacification Public Office, with Fu as the director. He emphasized the policy of "20 percent military, 30 percent politics, 50 percent economics." By mid–1947 the KMT offensive failed, and the Communists started their advance against the Nationalists in various parts of China.

On December 3 Fu became the commander-in-chief of the North China Bandit Suppression Headquarters, while his troops were defensively confined to the Peip'ing–Tientsin–Paoting area and Tangshan. Fu's armies won a major battle in East Hopei in August 1948, the most brilliant one in the two-year campaign against the Communists; however, it turned out to be his final success. In late October Fu, by the order of Chiang Kai-shek, attempted to score a miracle by capturing Shihchiachuang and Hsipaipo, where the Communist Central Committee was stationed. However, because of the information provided by an underground Communist working in Peip'ing, the Communist Central Military Affairs Committee knew Fu's plans and repulsed the "surprise" assault. In early December the Communists destroyed Fu's 11th Army Group in Kalgan and the 35th Army, 105th Army, 106th Army, and a part of the 16th Army Group at Hsinpaoan. Fu then had only one division in Peip'ing and some troops in Suiyuan; his military backbone was broken. His grand plan to consolidate his troops in Peip'ing–Tientsin collapsed; he could only sit still in Peip'ing and wait.

It was in this grave military situation that the underground Communist party in Peip'ing carried out the most brilliant move of its United Front tactic, resulting in the peaceful seizure of the city. Fu's daughter Fu Chü (or Fu Tung-chü), an underground Communist, began to work on her father, while several prominent figures including Fu's teacher, fraternal brothers, colleagues, and friends also influenced him. He finally decided to surrender to the Communists. On December 17 Fu established informal contact with the field headquarters of Lin Piao's* Communist forces. On January 15 Tientsin, Fu's last escape route, fell to the Communists. On January 21, 1949, Fu sent his representative secretly to sign an agreement with his former enemies. One day later the peace agreement was publicly announced. Peip'ing fell into Communist hands after a forty-two-day siege (December 13–January 22). The conclusion of the Peip'ing–Tientsin Campaign represented the KMT loss of north China. Fu also persuaded his subordinate generals in Suiyuan to surrender to the Communists in September 1949. Fu, a man of "understanding of the times," had become a traitor to the KMT.

After the establishment of the People's Republic of China,* Fu became the minister of water conservancy, a member of the National Committee of the Chinese People's Political Consultative Conference* and a member of the People's Revolutionary Military Council. Mao Tse-tung* awarded him the Liberation Medal, first class, in September 1955. In 1958 Fu became the minister of water conservancy and electric power but resigned the post in 1972. He died in Peking in 1974.

REFERENCES: Howard L. Boorman and Richard Howard, eds., *Biographical Dictionary of Republican China*, vol. 2 (New York, 1968): 47–51; Cheng Wei-shan, *Ts'ung Huapei tao Hsipei* (From north China to the northwest) (Peking, 1985); *Chung-kung tangshih chien-ming tz'u-tien* (A concise dictionary of the Chinese Communist party's history), vol. 2 (Peking, 1987): *Fu Tso-yi sheng-p'eng* (The life of Fu Tso-yi) (Peking, 1985).

JOSEPH K.S. YICK

FUKIEN REBELLION (1933): A short-lived military revolt by Nationalist officers against their government.

On November 20, 1933, Ch'en Ming-shu and other officers of the Nationalist government's Nineteenth Route Army* rebelled against the authority of Chiang Kai-shek* and one day later established an opposition People's Revolutionary government at Foochow in the coastal province of Fukien. The rebellion gained the support—some say the reluctant support—of the popular general Ts'ai T'ing-k'ai, hero of the year's previous battles with the Japanese at Shanghai. Eugene Ch'en, diplomat and protégé of Sun Yat-sen,* was the most senior Nationalist official to associate himself with the insurgent regime.

The dissidents, unhappy with the generalissimo's policy of "first pacification, then resistance," called for a relaxation of the anti-Communist annihilation campaigns that were underway at the time and demanded a more vigorous resistance to the Japanese encroachment into China. The rebels also announced a series of ambitious social reforms, including nationalization of the land.

The Fukien rebels counted for support for their cause from two sources, both of which were hostile to Chiang Kai-shek's leadership. It was hoped that allies would emerge from the ranks of the various surviving warlord armies—including those of Feng Yü-hsiang,* Han Fu-chu, and Yen Hsi-shan.* Although preliminary contacts had been made with these generals, the support never materialized. A general from distant Ninghsia was the only warlord to declare support for the Fukien rebels—and it came too late to be of any significance. The radicalism of the Fukien Regime's political agenda was an important factor in discouraging support from warlord generals.

A second source of potential help for the Fukien rebellion was the Communists.

The Fukien rebels began negotiating the details of an alliance with the Communists in neighboring Kiangsi Province in the spring of 1933 and had in fact reached a preliminary understanding with them in October, a month before the rebellion was launched. In this agreement the Fukien authorities promised to cease hostilities against the Communists, release political prisoners, and cooperate with the Communists in a United Front against the Japanese and Chiang Kai-shek.

The Communists, however, failed to implement the agreement and on December 5, 1933, broke with the rebels. The rebellion and its Nineteenth Route Army were thus left to face Chiang Kai-shek's armies alone. The generalissimo diverted troops from his fifth annihilation campaign against the Communists and in short order overwhelmed the rebels by using both ground troops and his newly acquired air power.

The Foochow government disbanded in mid-January 1934 less than two months after the rebellion had begun, and the rebels formally surrendered on January 23, 1934. Remnants of the Nineteenth Route Army fled into Kwangtung to be absorbed by that province's powerful chief, Ch'en Chi-t'ang.* The leaders of the rebellious Nineteenth either escaped to Hong Kong or went into temporary European exile. The episode marked the last time there was an organized military resistance to Chiang Kai-shek from within the Nationalist movement.

The most puzzling historical legacy of the Fukien incident centers on the failure of the Communists to follow through on their preliminary agreement to support the Fukien rebels. Controversy on this point has endured down to the present time. It is paramount to remember that at the time of the rebellion the Communist party did not speak with one voice. While Mao Tse-tung's* star was on the rise, he had not consolidated his power over the party's central political apparatus which at the time of the Fukien Rebellion was following the so-called Wang Ming* line associated with Mao's rivals. Both sides were later to interpret the Fukien revolt in such a way as to discredit the other. Whereas Mao later claimed that it was his rivals who had been responsible for erroneously abandoning the Fukien rebels, there is compelling evidence that Mao also regarded the rebels as counterrevolutionaries unworthy of support.

REFERENCES: Tso-liang Hsiao, *Power Relations within the Chinese Communist Movement, 1930–1934* (Seattle, Wash., 1961); John E. Rue, *Mao Tse-tung in Opposition, 1927–1935* (Stanford, Calif., 1966); Laszlo Ladany, *The Communist Party of China and Marxism, 1921–1985: A Self-Portrait* (Stanford, Calif., 1988).

JOHN H. BOYLE

G

GANG OF FOUR: CCP Politburo faction composed of Chiang Ch'ing, Chang Ch'un-ch'iao, Yao Wen-yüan, and Wang Hung-wen; rose to power during the Cultural Revolution; purged in October 1976.

Mao Tse-tung* reportedly was the first to use the expression "Gang of Four" to refer to Chiang Ch'ing* and her closest political associates. In the winter of 1974–1975 Mao repeatedly warned his wife, Chang Ch'un-ch'iao,* Yao Wen-yüan,* and Wang Hung-wen* not to alienate themselves from the other members of the Chinese Communist party* Politburo by "forming a 'Gang of Four.' "

As a political phenomenon, the Gang of Four was in a sense Mao's own creation. His Cultural Revolution* was the political movement that catapulted the members of the "gang" to positions of power. Chiang had not participated in politics at all prior to 1966; Chang and Yao were local propaganda officials in Shanghai; and Wang was a Korean War veteran who since 1953 had been employed in a Shanghai textile mill. The only thing the four had in common was their willingness to support Mao's Cultural Revolutionary endeavors, and for this they were amply rewarded. By 1969 Chiang, Chang, and Yao had been made members of the CCP Politburo, and Wang a member of the CCP Central Committee. By 1973 Wang had been made a vice-chairman of the party and Chang a member of the Standing Committee of the Politburo.

The Gang of Four exerted their greatest influence on political events in China on the national level in the early 1970s, after the demise of Defense Minister Lin Piao.* From 1972 to 1976, with Mao Tse-tung's blessing, they masterminded a series of nationwide political campaigns aimed at "consolidating the dictatorship of the proletariat" and "defending the glorious fruits of the Great Proletarian Cultural Revolution." The most important of these campaigns were the P'i-Lin, P'i-K'ung (i.e., Criticize Lin Piao and Confucius) Movement, the Movement to Study the Theory of the Dictatorship of the Proletariat and Criticize Bourgeois Right, the Movement to Study the Novel *Water Margin* and Criticize Sung

Chiang, and the Movement to Beat Back the Right Deviationist Wind to Reverse Correct Verdicts. In one form or the other, all the movements were attempts to wrestle power from the hands of political foes who opposed the Cultural Revolution. The latter two movements in particular were directed specifically against the main enemy of the Gang of Four, Deputy Premier Teng Hsiao-p'ing.*

Virtually all the political power wielded by the members of the Gang of Four derived from their unique relationship with Mao Tse-tung. Chiang Ch'ing in particular did not enjoy broad popular support or, unlike Teng Hsiao-p'ing, the backing of significant segments of the CCP or the People's Liberation Army.* This fact made the Gang of Four extremely vulnerable. In the spring of 1976, widespread dissatisfaction with the Cultural Revolution erupted in a number of popular incidents in various parts of China. The most important of these incidents, the T'ienanmen demonstrations* in Peking, was used by the Gang of Four—supported by a dying Mao Tse-tung—to force the demotion of Teng Hsiao-p'ing from all his posts inside and outside the CCP. This major political victory would be the Gang of Four's last, however. Mao's death on September 9 spelled the beginning of the certain end for the forces inside the CCP who aspired to carry on the Cultural Revolution without Mao.

On October 6, 1976, the 8341st Military Unit headed by Mao's former bodyguard Wang Tung-hsing arrested the Gang of Four. Among the senior CCP and PLA leaders who had plotted their arrest were Hua Kuo-feng,* who succeeded Mao as chairman of the party. On January 23, 1981, the Gang of Four and the followers of Lin Piao were tried by a special court in Peking and found guilty of having attempted to usurp state power. Chiang and Chang were sentenced to death with a two-year reprieve, Wang to life imprisonment, and Yao to twenty years' imprisonment.

REFERENCES: David Bonavia, *Verdict in Peking: The Trial of the Gang of Four* (London, 1984); *Huan "Si-jen-pang" I Lao You-p'ai-ti Ben-lai Mien-mu* (Restore the original rightist facade of the "Gang of Four") (Peking, 1976)—includes an excellent bibliography of some 800 writings and speeches by members of the Gang of Four.

MICHAEL L. SCHOENHALS

GIQUEL, PROSPER MARIE (1835–1886): Naval construction engineer; educational administrator; foreign military adviser and modernizer in China.

Among those who believe China's modern transformation has been linked to its relationship with the outside world, Giquel's role in modern Chinese development is well appreciated.

The French naval officer's role in China almost exactly paralleled the history of nineteenth-century Sino-Western interaction. Born in Lorient, France, Giquel first arrived in China as a member of the Anglo-French expeditionary force of the Arrow War (1856). Later, he went on to become a member of the Sino-foreign Canton occupation police and eventually commissioner of the Chinese Maritime Customs service at Ningpo.

Although active in the Taiping Revolution* as an organizer and commander of the Sino-French Ever-Victorious Army that fought alongside Tso Tsung-t'ang in Chekiang Province, Giquel is best known as the European director of the Foochow Dockyard, an ambitious effort begun by Tso and led by Shen Pao-ch'en to transfer the knowledge necessary from the West to build and operate a Western-style fleet of gunboats. During his tenure as European director of the dockyard (1866–1874), Chinese students built fifteen steam gunships of various sizes and carried out naval training missions as far away as Singapore. Although criticized at times for producing wooden ships at a time when naval technology was rapidly turning to iron hulls, Giquel and his Chinese superiors nevertheless saw the dockyard more as an evolving educational establishment rather than as a producer of state of the art naval technology.

As a diplomatic and military aide to the Chinese, Giquel was deeply involved in efforts to deal with the Sino-Japanese Crisis over Taiwan (1874) and the Ili Crisis (1881), and he finally worked secretly with Tseng Chi-tse to help end the Sino-French War of 1884–1885. More significant than his diplomatic activities was his role in leading and directing the several Sino-European Educational Missions that regularly left China during the 1870s and 1880s for study in Europe, especially France and Great Britain. These missions, which paralleled the better known efforts of Yung Wing to arrange American Educational Missions, were in fact considerably more successful. Conceived more as "graduate" studies than as the more preliminary efforts of Yung Wing's charges, the missions, helped by more receptive European attitudes, survived even the outbreak of open warfare between France and China in 1884. By 1886 students were again arriving in France.

Giquel was awarded the Imperial Yellow Jacket—a high honor rarely bestowed on foreigners—by the emperor of China for his contributions to China's naval development.

REFERENCES: Steven A. Leibo, *Transferring Technology to China: Prosper Giquel and the Self-Strengthening Movement* (Berkeley, Calif., 1985); Prosper Giquel, *A Journal of the Chinese Civil War, 1864*, ed. Steven A. Leibo (Hawaii, 1985).

STEVEN A. LEIBO

GOD WORSHIPPERS SOCIETY (1846–1851): Religious organization established by the Taiping leaders before the revolution.

Founded by Feng Yün-shan* in 1846–1847, the God Worshippers Society provided the basic network of organization for the political uprising of the Taiping Revolution* that broke out in Chin-t'ien, Kwangsi, in January 1851. It began as a religious congregation when Feng Yün-shan, after becoming a convert of Hung Hsiu-ch'üan,* went to Kwangsi to preach Hung's version of Christianity in 1845. Being a literatus and eloquent in speech, Feng acquired a favorable reputation by curing diseases, drafting petitions for litigation, and probably participating in a tax resistance movement. In three years Feng was able to attract a large body of believers from many villages in Kuei-p'ing and Kuei-hsien counties, who shared his ethnic background—Hakka, or "guest people," from Kwangtung. Members of the society were instructed to worship the Christian God and to destroy Confucian and Buddhist idols.

On August 27, 1847, Hung Hsiu-ch'üan returned to Kwangsi and, to his surprise, discovered a large following of over 2,000 acknowledging his supreme leadership. Hung began to mobilize his followers to destroy idols and temples, including the image of Confucius. Such activities provoked a member of the local gentry, Wang Tso-hsin, who arrested Feng with his own militia corps on December 28. Feng remained in prison from January to October 1848. After Feng was released in late 1848, he found that Yang Hsiu-ch'ing* and Hsiao Ch'ao-kuei* had taken over the leadership of the God Worshippers through the use of trances in which they were possessed by God and Jesus, respectively. In the fall of 1849, Hung and Feng returned to Kwangsi and planned to mobilize the God Worshippers for a political uprising.

In the late 1840s Kwangsi was extremely unstable. Numerous groups of local outlaws and roving bandits plagued the countryside. There was also an influx of armed mercenaries previously hired to strengthen the defense of Kwangtung during the Opium War.* As a result of the shift of trade from Canton after the Opium War, large numbers of unemployed laborers from Kwangtung poured into Kwangsi. Many became bandits. Some were hired by local elite families as their own militia corps. Sporadic popular uprisings organized by secret societies such as the T'ien-ti hui rose and fell. Government control was precarious. People were driven to join better organized groups for protection and mutual help. The God Worshippers Society was able to serve some of these needs.

In early 1850, or at the latest mid–1850, Feng and Hung informed the top leaders of all the branches of the God Worshippers Society of a plan for a political uprising to be held in Chin-t'ien, Kwangsi. From July through the end of the year, God Worshippers in different places were instructed to sell their family properties and march to Chin-t'ien. In mid–1850 the God Worshippers grew dramatically as a result of the defeat of the Hakka people in an unprecedentedly large-scale armed feud with the "local" people. On January 1, 1851, the God Worshippers under Hung Hsiu-ch'üan, Feng Yün-shan, Yang Hsiu-ch'ing, Hsiao Ch'ao-kuei, Wei Ch'ang-hui,* and Shih Ta-k'ai* gathered in Chin-t'ien and raised the banner of revolt against the Manchu government. Hung declared the founding of the T'ai-p'ing t'ien-kuo, or the Heavenly Kingdom of Great Peace. Since all members of the Taiping Kingdom worshipped God, there was no longer any need to maintain the original structure of the God Worshippers Society.

REFERENCES: Wang Ch'ing-ch'eng, " 'Pai Shang-ti hui' shih-lun'' (On the God Worshippers Society), in *T'ai-p'ing t'ien-kuo ti li-shih he ssu-hsiang* (The history and thought of the Heavenly Kingdom of Great Peace) (Peking, 1985): 43–64; idem, "Chin-t'ien ch'i-i chi'' (An account of the Chin-t'ien uprising), in ibid.: 65–163; Han Yung-pao, "Lüeh-lun Feng Yün-shan'' (A short essay on Feng Yün-shan), in *T'ai-p'ing t'ien-kuo shih lun-wen hsüan* (Selected essays on the history of the Heavenly Kingdom of Great Peace) (Peking, 1981): 1052.

KAI-WING CHOW

GORDON, CHARLES G. (CHINESE) (1833–1885): Foreign military adviser/ commander of the Ever-Victorious Army against the Taiping Revolution.

Charles "Chinese" Gordon was once regarded as perhaps the most influential Westerner in nineteenth-century China. More recently, however, scholarship has dramatically reevaluated the significance of his activities. Gordon first saw military action during the Crimean War. By 1860, during the Second Opium War, he took part in the Anglo-French effort to capture Peking and in 1863 he succeeded Frederick Townsend Ward* (1831–1862) as commander of the Ever-Victorious Army (EVA), a Sino-foreign military contingent that helped gentry militia commanders like Li Hung-chang* defeat the Taiping* kingdom. Under Gordon's command, the EVA helped capture the cities of Taitsang and Soochow. His work was well appreciated by the Ch'ing* government, and Gordon was the first foreigner to be awarded the prestigious Imperial Yellow Jacket as a reward for his services. Although he later helped advise the Chinese during the Ili Crisis, a border crisis between China and Russia in the early 1880s, his last years were spent in Africa where he died during the Mahdi Uprising. Gordon was certainly among the best-known of the English officers who served in nineteenth-century China, but a better appreciation of the activities of gentry militia leaders like Tseng Kuo-fan* has considerably lessened our appreciation of the importance of his activities in ending the Taiping Christian Revolution of 1851–1864.

REFERENCES: Richard J. Smith, *Mercenaries and Mandarins* (Millwood, N.Y., 1978); Andrew Wilson, *The Ever-Victorious Army* (Edinburgh and London, 1868); Bernard Allen, *Gordon in China* (London, 1933); William J. Hale, *Tseng Kuo-fan and the Taiping Rebellion* (New Haven, Conn., 1927).

STEVEN A. LEIBO

GREAT LEAP FORWARD (1958–1960): Chinese Communist attempt to increase economic output.

The Great Leap Forward (GLF) was a desperate attempt by the Chinese leadership to correct the structural imbalance created by overemphasis on heavy industry in the First Five-Year Plan (1953–1957) period. The movement sought to increase output and capital accumulation in the labor-intensive agricultural sector by mobilizing underemployed resources so that the capital-intensive industrial sector could continue its fast growth. Hence, the graphic slogan of "walking on two legs" arose. This bootstrap strategy was supposed to enable China to catch up with Britain in the output of steel and other industrial products within fifteen years. These goals necessitated an eightfold increase in steel output, an average annual rate of some 15 percent. They would be achieved by putting politics in command.

This unconventional approach had its rewards and perils. The rewards were the phenomenal jumps in reported outputs overnight. According to even downwardly adjusted official data in 1958, the output of food grains rose in one year by 35 percent, cotton by 28 percent, steel by 81 percent, and coal by 108 percent.

Most of these increases turned out to be statistical exaggerations reported under intense political pressure.

Such fantastic claims would have been easily dismissed in normal times—but the times were anything but normal. Major institutional shakeups were overtaking the rural areas. Agricultural collectives consisting of only 100 to 300 households each in 1956 were reorganized overnight into communes with 4,000 to 5,000 households each in 1958. Being the basic unit of ownership, accounting, and distribution, the commune could mobilize all the resources under its disposal. To release underemployed female labor, it established communal kitchens to centralize the cooking of meals and communal nurseries to centralize the day care of children. To tap off-work and off-season labor, it abolished all private plots and confiscated all domestic livestock. More than 100 million peasants in late 1957 and early 1958 were mobilized to build water conservancy projects. Some 60 million people were organized to build more than 1 million backyard blast furnaces to smelt iron and steel. In addition, millions of "new" factories and workshops processed output from agriculture and produced capital goods for agriculture.

The perils of "politics in command" were the feverish actions based on these incredible claims. The initial food grain output of 375 million tons (cf. 195 million tons in 1957) reported in 1958 lulled Mao* into reducing the sown area in 1959 and transferring a large number of peasants (over 20 percent of the agricultural labor force in 1958) into capital construction and nonagricultural activities. National overusage of food grains was widely practiced in 1958. Higher state procurement quotas then followed even as the actual output declined in 1959 and 1960. These claims also accelerated the indiscriminate application of unproven farming techniques.

The chaos created by the Great Leap Forward was unnecessarily prolonged because Mao was reluctant to give up his cherished dreams. In mid–1959 the Chinese leadership was already aware that the output figures were inflated and agriculture was in disarray. The Eighth Plenum of the Party Central Committee even approved the downward transfer of the power of ownership, accounting, and distribution from the commune to the brigade (the former collective). But internal power struggle prevented its implementation until one year later.

The upheavals brought by the Great Leap Forward can best be gauged by its demographic impacts. For China as a whole, the net fertility loss in this period amounted to 90 percent of a normal year's births. Excess mortality was about twice a normal year's total deaths. Fertility decline and mortality increase at least in 1958 and the early part of 1959 cannot be attributed to food shortage. Instead, fertility decline can be largely explained by the physical separation of husbands from wives, the increased divorce rate, and the postponement of marriages necessitated by the large population migration and hectic work pace. Mortality increase can be attributed to the disruption of traditional family care for infants and the elderly and overconsumption produced by communal kitchens.

The Great Leap Forward was thus a big gamble that lost. Food grain output in 1959 and 1960 was, respectively, 13 percent and 27 percent below that of pre-Leap 1957. Even though industrial output increased by 3.8 percent per year, decline in agricultural output dragged the national income growth rate to a negative 3 percent per year for the period.

There is an ongoing debate on whether the failure was a result of unfortunate circumstances or leadership folly. Admittedly, natural disasters were worse than normal. In many provinces, however, the output decline can be largely or entirely attributed to a decrease in sown acreage. A large labor drain from agriculture certainly contributed to the output decline. What weak and inexperienced labor that was left behind was demoralized by the excessively egalitarian remuneration system. What is worse, much of the labor drain was wasted in producing useless products and unusable capital projects. The withdrawal of Soviet aid certainly did not help, but since it did not come until 1960, it had little to do with the agricultural fiasco.

Pragmatism took over after the Great Leap Forward. Communal kitchens, nurseries, and backyard blast furnaces were disbanded. Private plots were restored. Sown acreage was returned to pre-Leap levels. The labor drain from agriculture was reversed. State procurement quotas of major food crops were adjusted downward, and the team-based three-level collective structure remained unchanged for almost two decades. But the extractive powers of the collective continued. Off-season capital construction projects were still pursued, though at a more feasible pace. The powers of the collective to dictate cropping mix, to siphon off marketable surplus, to redistribute income, and to put aside investment funds were firmly exercised especially in the Cultural Revolution* (1966–1976) period. Although the output of chemical fertilizers and tractors rose rapidly from a low base, there was no major redirection of state investment to agriculture. As a result, output of food grain and cotton barely kept ahead of population growth. This meager result was obtained party by diverting land more suited for other agricultural activities to food grain production.

REFERENCES: Chu-yuan Cheng, *China's Economic Development—Growth and Structural Change* (Boulder, Colo., 1982); Victor D. Lippit, "The Great Leap Forward Reconsidered," *Modern China* 1, no. 1 (1975): 92–115; Roderick MacFarquhar, *The Origins of the Cultural Revolution*, vol. 2 (New York, 1983); Xizhe Peng, "Demographic Consequences of the Great Leap Forward in China's Provinces," *Population and Development Review* 13, no. 4 (1987): 639–670.

K. K. FUNG

GREAT PROLETARIAN CULTURAL REVOLUTION (1966–1976): An ideological crusade launched by Mao Tse-tung, as well as a power struggle between the Maoists and Liuists, leading to the greatest upheaval in Chinese Communist history. No event in contemporary China has had as profound an impact on China's development as the Cultural Revolution.

China's gigantic upheaval during 1966–1976, known as the Great Proletarian Cultural Revolution, can best be viewed from the themes that China scholars employed to explain its origin and causes. There is, first of all, the power struggle thesis which states that a basic cleavage existed within the Chinese Communist top leadership (particularly between Mao Tse-tung* and Liu Shao-ch'i*) over the development policies to be pursued and that at some stage this policy cleavage over strategy and priority became intertwined with a power struggle which, in essence, obscured the importance of the policy conflict among the leaders. Factional dispute and unresolved dissension among top party leaders were also closely related to the rise of the party's bureaucratic tendencies. From that perspective, the Cultural Revolution was an ideological crusade launched to prevent the gradual erosion of the revolutionary spirit espoused fervently by Mao and his radicalized supporters. Moreover, the upheaval was an attempt to resolve the central question of the nature of the Chinese Communist society by the Maoists, who had faith in voluntarism, which, among many other things, stresses the importance of human will and the transformation of values. Other themes that explain the upheaval are the desire of Chairman Mao and others to prevent the resurgence of elitism and special privileged classes in the advancement toward an egalitarian society, the need to develop the politics of activism to "restart the engine of mobilization," the appropriate role of the culture and of the intellectuals in a revolutionary society, and, finally, the necessity for China to develop a mass mobilization and participation model for community action and responsiveness. The U.S. escalation in the Vietnam War and the deterioration of Sino-Soviet relations may have served as a catalyst for the policy debate among the leaders. Prolonged dissension among the top leaders ultimately raised the crucial question of political succession to an aging Mao.

The Cultural Revolution was officially launched on August 8, 1966, when the Eleventh Session of the Eighth Central Committee approved a sixteen-point guideline for conducting a thorough revolution. However, some nine or ten months before approval of the guidelines, a literary debate developed over a play: "Hai Jui Dismissed from Office"—a historical allegory. Mao's supporters claimed the play had been presented to vindicate Marshal P'eng Te-huai* who was purged by Mao in 1959 over policy differences. The literary debate was followed by mass criticism that led to purges of top party and military leaders. University and high school students then organized themselves as Red Guards* and served as Maoist storm troopers to disrupt and dismantle established party and government organizations and activities. For the first months of 1967, China was the scene of a gigantic spectacle of big-character posters, slogans, and endless processions and meetings in a sea of portraits of Mao and banners. Feuding student groups created chaos and violence that brought all party functions and government activities to a standstill. By January 1967, the anarchical situation had reached such alarming proportions that the military had to be called in to quell the riots and violence in the cities caused by rampaging students. China then entered into a period of military control and supervision that lasted well into the mid–1970s.

No one knows exactly how many party members and intellectuals were persecuted and tortured by the Red Guards and radicals. In many cases it was sufficient merely for the accused to be labeled rightist or counter-revolutionary. The denounced and their relatives were subjected to beatings, imprisonment, loss of jobs, and banishment to rural areas to do menial labor. During the 1981 trial of the Gang of Four,* it was revealed that 729,511 people had been persecuted, including a number of high-ranking party and state officials. Of that group, 34,000 died. Other official figures indicated that political persecution was even more widespread. In 1978 more than 300,000 victims of false accusations and persecution were rehabilitated and exonerated. In 1980 some 13,000 overseas Chinese were found to have been wrongly accused of crimes against the state. Teng Hsiao-p'ing* estimated that as many as 2.9 million people had been victims of persecution during the decade of the Cultural Revolution.

There seems to be no question that the Cultural Revolution was not only a gross policy error in the name of ideological purity but also a dark page in the Chinese Communist party's* history. It was a "civil war" and a "catastrophe" that decimated the ranks of the experienced veteran cadres. Furthermore, a large percentage of China's intellectuals—educators, scholars, and scientists—were uprooted from their institutions and their talents wasted on menial work in the countryside. Finally, the Cultural Revolution failed to produce any long-term fundamental institutional changes. Most of the changes instituted during the Cultural Revolution have been rejected or abandoned since 1977.

REFERENCES: Thomas W. Robinson, *The Cultural Revolution in China* (Berkeley, Calif., 1971); Ahn Byung-joon, *Chinese Politics and the Cultural Revolution: Dynamics of Policy Processes* (Seattle, Wash., 1976); William Hinton, *Shenfen: The Cultural Revolution in a Chinese Village* (New York, 1983); Nien Cheng, *Life and Death in Shanghai* (New York, 1987).

JAMES C.F. WANG

H

HO KAI (HO CH'I, SIR KAI HO KAI) (1859–1914): Barrister, doctor, teacher, reformer, and civic leader.

Born in Hong Kong on March 12, 1859, Ho Kai was the son of Ho Fu-t'ang, a rich proprietor and preacher affiliated with the London Missionary Society. Educated at the Government Central School in Hong Kong, Aberdeen University, St. Thomas' Medical and Surgical College, and Lincoln's Inn in Great Britain, Ho Kai returned to Hong Kong in 1882 with degrees in law and medicine and an English wife named Alice Walkden. In 1887 Ho Kai built the Alice Memorial Hospital to commemorate his now deceased wife and to provide free care for Chinese patients. He was also a major founder of the Hong Kong College of Medicine for the Chinese in 1887, where he taught physiology and medical jurisprudence. The future revolutionary, Sun Yat-sen,* was Ho Kai's student at the college from 1887 to 1892, much inspired by the doctor's liberal ideas.

One of Hong Kong's most prominent Chinese residents, Ho Kai was nominated by the colonial authorities to serve on the Sanitary Board and the District Watch Force Committee. He was also named justice of the peace, and was appointed by the governor to serve on the Legislative Council (in fact merely an advisory body) from 1890 to 1914. Ho Kai became a leading spokesman of the Chinese community in Hong Kong, which often looked to him for advice in its dealings with the colonial government; and the government often consulted him in its transactions with the Chinese community. In recognition of his loyal service, the British Crown bestowed knighthood on him in 1912.

Ho Kai was a man of dual loyalties. His vision and interest went beyond the British colony of Hong Kong. In 1887 Ho Kai and his scholarly friend Hu Li-yüan* jointly published an article urging the Chinese government to make institutional reforms along Western lines. They forcefully challenged the "self-strengtheners' "* narrow focus on the adoption of Western techniques alone. Subsequently, Ho and Hu co-authored six more essays advocating governmental reforms. Both men were inspired by Western classical liberalism as formulated by the liberal thinker John Locke, the Enlightenment philosophers Adam Smith and Montesquieu, and the Utilitarians Jeremy Bentham and John Stuart Mill. Impressed by Britain's wealth and power, Ho and Hu came to value Britain's liberal tradition which stressed individual rights, free trade, industrialism, and constitutionalism. They advocated British liberal political institutions and the capitalist economic system as models for China. A striking characteristic of their reform program was its equation of the merchants' interests with the nation's interests, its strong emphasis on the development of commercial capitalism as the road to the nation's wealth and power, and its demands of political power for the merchants and overseas Chinese businessmen.

Ho Kai became an active supporter of the republican revolutionaries, conspiring with them against the Manchu government in China. He helped to draft the Hsing-Chung hui proclamation to foreign powers on the eve of the abortive Canton plot in October 1895. Again, during the national crisis of 1900 when eight foreign powers sent expeditions to north China to suppress the Boxers,[*] Ho Kai became actively involved in the revolutionaries' vain attempt to use the good offices of Governor Henry Blake to persuade Li Hung-chang[*] to declare the independence of Kwangtung and Kwangsi under British protection. However, unlike Sun Yet-sen[*] who sought every opportunity to engage in an armed uprising, Ho Kai always sought to rely on Western powers' (especially British) intervention to help "regenerate" China in the Western image. As a spokesman of the marginal Chinese merchants in Hong Kong with economic ties to foreign capitalism, Ho Kai could only hope to reform China in collaboration with foreigners within the framework of imperialist domination in China.

Although the Ch'ing dynasty[*] was overthrown in 1911, the Kwangtung revolutionary government led a precarious existence, lacking in financial resources. Again, Ho Kai was eager to help in his peculiar way. He sought in vain to persuade Governor Henry May to give financial aid to the Canton government in return for British supervision of Canton government expenditure and administration.

Ho Kai died in 1914, carrying to his grave his dream of China's "regeneration" under British tutelage.

REFERENCES: G. H. Choa, *The Life and Times of Sir Kai Ho Kai* (Hong Kong, 1981); Jung-fang Tsai, "The Predicament of the Comprador Ideologists: He Qi (Ho Kai, 1859–1914) and Hu Li-yuan (1847–1916)," *Modern China* 7, no. 2 (April 1981): 191–225.

JUNG-FANG TSAI

HO YING-CH'IN (1890–October 21, 1987): Minister of war (1930–1944); chief-of-staff (1938–1944) and commander-in-chief of the Chinese Army (1944–1946); chief Chinese delegate to the United Nations' Military Advisory Committee (1946–1948); chairman of the Strategy Advisory Committee in Taiwan (1950–1958).

Born into a land-owning family in Hsin yi District in Kweichow Province,

Ho Ying-ch'in received a military education at an early age. He first studied in the provincial military primary school in Kweiyang in 1901 and then went on to the military secondary school in Wuchang. In 1908 he was sent by the Ministry of War to study at the Shimbu Gakko in Japan and, in the following year, was admitted to the Shikan Gakko. After the outbreak of the Revolution of 1911,* he returned to China, joining the revolutionary forces in Shanghai and, in 1913, serving as a battalion commander in the Kiangsu Army. Following the collapse of the so-called Second Revolution,* he went back to Japan to complete his studies, graduating in the summer of 1916.

In the next few years, Ho led an active military life in his home province, serving as dean of the Kweichow Military Academy and commander of the Fifth Mixed Brigade of the Kweichow Army, and holding various other positions, including police chief in Kweiyang. He advocated political reforms in Kweichow, which caused him the hostility of the conservatives who sent him fleeing to Yunnan in 1922. He survived an assassination attempt on his life in Kunming, but had to go to Shanghai for further medical treatment.

Early in 1924, he went to Canton to take up an appointment as chief instructor at the newly founded Whampoa Military Academy.* In September 1925 he participated in the campaign against militarist Ch'en Chiung-ming in Fukien. During the Northern Expedition* which followed, he was in Chiang Kai-shek's* camp vis-a-vis his Nationalist rivals who had established themselves in Wuhan. When Chiang was forced to resign his posts in August 1927, Ho remained loyal to him, repulsing all the attacks by the recalcitrant warlords. For all this, Ho was duly rewarded early in 1928 when Chiang resumed his military and political posts and appointed Ho governor of Chekiang and chief-of-staff of the newly reorganized First Group Army. Ho had since become one of Chiang's most trusted military officers.

With the inauguration of the National government in October 1928, Ho was made a member of the State Council. Furthermore, at the Kuomintang's First National party Congress in January 1929 he was elected to the Central Executive Committee and the Central Political Council. But it was in the military field that he was to distinguish himself. As minister of war, he directed Chiang's field headquarters at Kaifeng, Canton, Chengchow, and Wuhan against the forces that rebelled against Nanking in 1929–1930.

Ho's most important task was to deal with the Chinese Communists who had established themselves in the border areas of Kiangsi and Hunan. In February 1931 he was appointed director of Chiang's anti-Communist headquarters in Nanchang. But he failed in his first attempt in June, after which Chiang resumed personal command of the "extermination campaigns." Another campaign in September was postponed as soon as it started, owing to the Mukden Incident* and the Manchurian crisis.

When Jehol Province was occupied by the Japanese Army in March 1933, Ho was appointed chairman of the Peking branch of the Military Affairs Commission, with the responsibility of negotiating a cease-fire. The result was the much-criticized Tangku Truce of May 31, which did nothing to stop the Japanese aggression. On June 10, 1935, the humiliating Ho-Umezu Agreement (Lieutenant-General Umezu Yoshijirō was the commander of the Japanese north China garrison) was concluded. The revelation of the terms of the secret agreement, which included the withdrawal of Nationalist troops from Hopei Province, the abolition of the local Kuomintang organs, and the prohibition of anti-Japanese activities throughout China, gave rise to student demonstrations in many places. Subsequently, Ho returned to Nanking, after the Peking branch of the Military Affairs Commission had been abolished.

During the war of resistance following the Marco Polo Bridge Incident,* Ho served as chief-of-staff. Between 1942 and 1944, he developed a rivalry with Lieutenant-General Joseph W. Stilwell,* commander of the United States forces in the China–Burma–India theater and Allied chief-of-staff to Chiang Kai-shek. Chiang also had difficulty working with Stilwell and had him recalled by President Roosevelt on October 19, 1944. Meanwhile, Ho was deprived of his war portfolio which he had held for fourteen years, although he stayed on as commander-in-chief of the Chinese Army.

On September 9, 1945, Ho formally received the Japanese surrender in Nanking from General Ōkamura, commander-in-chief of the Japanese force in China. But his political fortunes were beginning to fall because of opponents within the government. When the wartime Military Affairs Commission was replaced by a new Ministry of National Defense in June 1946, the new portfolio went to Pai Ch'ung-hsi,* and the post of chief-of-staff to Ch'en Ch'eng.* Ho took little consolation in his appointment, in October of that year, as chief Chinese delegate to the United Nations' Military Staff Committee and chief of the Chinese Military Mission to the United States. He returned to Nanking in March 1948 and later succeeded Pai Ch'ung-hsi as minister of defense, but not before the government found itself in a most precarious position in the civil war* with the Communists. In March 1949, Ho became president of the Executive Yuan following the resignation of Sun Fo,* in the administration of Acting President Li Tsung-jen. He resigned in less than three months. Before the year was over, he joined Chiang Kai-shek in Taiwan, serving as chairman of the Strategy Advisory Commission.

In his later years, Ho played an active part in the World Moral Rehabilitation Movement, in connection with which he visited a number of European countries that recognized the People's Republic of China.* In 1982 he was made chairman of the Promotion Committee of the Grand Alliance for China's Reunification through the three Peoples' Principles. He died in Taipei in 1987.

REFERENCE: Howard L. Boorman and Richard C. Howard, eds., *Biographical Dictionary of Republican China,* Vol. 2 (New York, 1968).

EDMUND S. K. FUNG

HONG KONG INSURRECTION (1884): Riots directed against Europeans in Hong Kong.

During the Sino-French War (1884–1885), a wave of hostility to foreigners swept the southern provinces of China from Chekiang to Yunnan. Hong Kong was not immune to this anti-imperialist movement. On September 18, 1884, a strike broke out in the shipyards in protest against the presence in Hong Kong of a French warship that had taken part in the attack on Foochow. Soon many cargo boat people also joined the strike. When the colonial authorities fined ten boat people for refusing to work for the French, nearly all the boat people staged a strike on September 30. For several days, all work of loading and unloading cargo in the harbor came to a halt. Cargo-carrying coolies on shore also joined the strike. When some cargo coolies sought to prevent the jinricksha and chair coolies from working for foreigners, the police intervened, which in turn led to street riots. The crowd attacked Westerners in the streets. The Sikh constables fired into the crowd. One street coolie was found dead, and many were wounded. The British military authorities had to send two companies of troops to help suppress the unrest. By October 6, order had been restored, though sporadic attacks on Europeans continued to occur after that date.

The insurrection in 1884 was complex in nature, a number of causes and circumstances converging to cause the strike and riots. The Canton mandarins issued proclamations exhorting the Chinese along the coast to patriotism and warning them against working for the French. As most Chinese in Hong Kong had relatives or property on the mainland, fear of mandarin retaliation was an important factor that initially caused many people in Hong Kong to refuse to work for the French. But other factors were also at work. The French attacks and threats of attacks on various points along the coast had provoked anti-French patriotic feelings among all classes of people in Hong Kong. Disregarding the Chinese feelings, however, the colonial government prosecuted the local Chinese newspaper editors for publishing mandarin proclamations exhorting people to patriotism. It also imposed fines on ten boat people who refused to work for the French. This was an important factor that set off the labor strike.

All these events occurred in a social context of general poverty and misery among the working coolies. The strike then spread to most sectors of the working population because many coolies faced the threat of a heavy fine and the loss of a whole month's earnings. Concerned about their livelihood and morally indignant at the fines, coolies became politically activated. By late September many workers had not only refused to work for the French, but had gone on strike protesting against the colonial authorities' repressive measures. In fact, such measures had inflamed the people's initial anti-French sentiment into an anticolonial and anti-imperialist movement with a nationalistic overtone.

The strike and riots were led by head boatmen, head cargo coolies, coolie housekeepers, and the Triad societies. The Triads engaged in a wide variety of acts, ranging from petty crimes to patriotic actions against foreign imperialism. The Canton mandarin authorities sought to enlist the Triads to fight against France by promising them material rewards and by appealing to their anti-imperialist patriotism.

In 1884 anti-French patriotic sentiments were prevalent among all classes of

Hong Kong Chinese. However, the Chinese merchant elite did not take the leadership in the popular protest movement. With strong economic ties to Western capitalism, merchants desired law and order in the colony. Sympathetic with the boat people who were fined by the colonial government for refusal to work for the French, the merchant elite sought to mediate between the striking coolies and the government to restore peace and order to the colony. But the elite did not regard coolie strikes and riots as "legitimate" expressions of patriotism.

The events of 1884 in Hong Kong are significant, not only for what they revealed about the nature of British rule and social tensions in the colony, but for what they also demonstrated about the capacity of the Hong Kong masses to become politically activated. The colony's populace showed some vague awareness of China as a nation-state at war with the French. Sun Yat-sen,* then a young student in Hong Kong, was much inspired by the striking workers' patriotism.

REFERENCES: Lewis M. Chere, "The Hong Kong Riots of October 1884: Evidence for Chinese Nationalism," *Journal of the Hong Kong Branch of the Royal Asiatic Society* (*JHKBRAS*), 20 (1980); Elizabeth Sinn, "The Strike and Riot of 1884—A Hong Kong Perspective," *JHKBRAS* 22 (1982): 65–98; Jung-fang Tsai, "The 1884 Hong Kong Insurrection: Anti-Imperialist Popular Protest During the Sino-French War," *Bulletin of Concerned Asian Scholars* (January–March 1984): 2–14.

JUNG-FANG TSAI

HSIA-FANG (Send down): A device periodically employed by the CCP in political campaigns to reinvigorate ideological commitment as well as resuscitate Mao Tse-tung's ideal of the "mass-line."

The *hsia-fang* was first used in the Communist base area in Yenan in 1941–1942; it was then known as *hsia-hsiang* (to the village). At that time, students, intellectuals, and cadres were sent down to live and serve in the countryside. The practice of *hsia-fang*, however, is not exclusive to villages: individuals could also be sent down to work in factories.

In theory, *hsia-fang* was designed to achieve the following objectives. In the first place, the isolated and relatively primitive villages would receive an infusion of outside skills and talent. Those who were sent down would educate the local cadres and villagers, study native conditions, and assist the local cadres in their tasks. *Hsia-fang* would also reduce rural isolation by linking the countryside with the central authorities. Not only would the outsiders communicate to the villagers party policies and objectives, but through *hsia-fang* the party presumably would also gain a better understanding of local problems and performance. In this manner, the centuries-old alienation between the city and the countryside, between urban elites and untutored peasants, could be overcome.

A final objective of *hsia-fang* is to reform bureaucrats, officials, and intellectuals in general by having them perform manual labor. According to Mao,* true knowledge was derived from practice rather than from abstract academic learning. Intellectuals were suspect because their exclusive engagement in mental labor precluded a genuine comprehension and appreciation of the lives of the toiling masses. Through *hsia-fang*, however, intellectuals and bureaucrats would eat, live, work, and talk with the masses. In this manner, not only would the elitism and arrogance of intellectuals and officials be eradicated, but true knowledge could also be acquired from the masses. The working masses, for their part, would no longer be intimidated by technology, intellectuals, and officialdom.

Since its initiation in the early 1940s, the Chinese Communist authorities have periodically reinstituted *hsia-fang*. As an example, *hsia-fang* featured prominently in the Anti-Rightist Campaign[*] of 1957–1958 in which 1.3 million intellectuals and cadres were sent down for physical labor. At the peak of the Cultural Revolution[*] in 1966–1968, some 10 million were sent down. Between 1949 and 1965, an estimated 40 million students participated in *hsia-fang*. More recently, *hsia-fang* was revived in the aftermath of the bloody suppression of the pro-democracy movement in T'ienanmen Square of June 4, 1989. Once again, university students are sent down for labor reform in the factories, while cadres and skilled personnel are sent down to villages in the service of the "massline."[*]

REFERENCES: James Pinkney Harrison, *The Long March to March: A History of the Chinese Communist Party, 1921–72* (New York, 1972); Franz Schurmann, *Ideology and Organization in Communist China* (Berkeley, Calif., 1966); Mark Seldon, "The Yenan Legacy: The Mass Line," in A. Doak Barnett, ed., *Chinese Communist Politics in Action* (Seattle, Wash., 1969).

MARIA HSIA CHANG

HSIANG CHUNG-FA (1888–1931): Secretary-general of the CCP, 1928–1931.

All accounts agree that despite a nearly three-year stint as Chinese Communist party[*] leader, Hsiang was a minor figure in CCP history. At the Sixth Congress of June–July 1928, Pavel Mif, head of the Comintern's[*] China Commission, arranged Hsiang's election to the chairmanship of the CCP Central Committee as a compromise candidate at a time of intense factional rivalries within the CCP. Hsiang had the advantages of a worker background and active participation in the labor movement; thus, he made a suitable CCP leader at a time when the Bolshevization of the CCP and the promotion of members from proletarian origin to important CCP positions were party policy. Following a CCP security breakdown in Shanghai in April 1931, Hsiang was arrested by the KMT, and executed shortly afterward in June.

Hsiang was born in Shanghai, but at some point moved to Wuhan where he earned his living as a sailor and dock worker. He joined the CCP in 1922 and with a distinct talent for mobilizing and communicating with workers, he quickly rose in the CCP labor movement hierarchy in Hupeh. He first served as vice-chairman of the labor union of workers in the Han-yeh-p'ing Industrial Complex, and in 1926 Hsiang became general commander of the Wuhan Workers Pickets as well as head of the Workers Department of the Wuhan government of the KMT left wing. At the Fifth CCP Congress of April–May 1927 he was elected

to the CCP Central Committee. During his tenure as CCP leader, Hsiang Chung-fa was overshadowed by Li Li-san[*] and the so-called Twenty-eight Bolsheviks.[*]
REFERENCES: *Important Events and People in CCP History* (Shanghai, 1984); Tso-liang Hsiao, *Power Relations Within the Communist Party* (Seattle, Wash., 1961).

                                                                          HANS J. VAN DE VEN

HSIAO CH'AO-KUEI (d. September 1852): West King of the Taiping Revolutionary government from December 25, 1851.

Hsiao Ch'ao-Kuei, probably of Hakka ancestry, was a peasant from Lu-lu-t'ung in the Wu-hsuan District of Kwangsi Province. After the death of his first wife Yang Yün-chiao, a relative of the Taiping East King Yang Hsiu-ch'ing,[*] Hsiao married Hung Hsüan-chiao, a younger sister of Taiping Heavenly King Hung Hsiu-ch'üan.[*]

In the 1840s, while residing in the Kuei-p'ing District of Eastern Kwangsi, Hsiao was baptized a Christian by Hung Hsiu-ch'üan, leader of the God Worshippers Society[*] which was a Christian evangelical and revolutionary organization. Hsiao established his position in the society as a divine spokesman, claiming to have been so designated by Christ during an earthly visit. In the summer of 1849, Hung and his associate Feng Yün-shan[*] named Hsiao and three others deputies. The following year, they elevated Hsiao to a position of operational control of the society's armed forces with personal command of a large army, a move calculated to counterbalance the mounting influence of the ambitious deputy Yang Hsiu-ch'ing.

Coercive measures by government forces against village strongholds of the God Worshippers in the Kuei-p'ing District in 1850 led to a successful uprising by God Worshippers at the village of Chin-t'ien in early 1851. Hsiao is reported to have led a force of 500 which dispersed the government army of 3,000 under the command of I-k'o-pu-tan, whom Hsiao personally decapitated. Shortly thereafter Hung proclaimed his dynastic intentions by announcing the establishment of the T'ai-p'ing T'ien-kuo (the Heavenly Kingdom of Great Peace). A new designation of military responsibilities placed Hsiao in charge of the Taiping Forward Army.

After the uprising at Chin-t'ien, Taiping forces advanced northward by a circuitous route to occupy the walled city of Yung-an, approximately 75 kilometers northeast of Chin-t'ien, on September 25, 1851. There, Hung established the Taiping court and government and conferred on Hsiao the title of West King, one of four subordinate kings named for the four cardinal points of the compass. An imperial army of more than 30,000 held Yung-an under siege until the night of April 5, 1852, when the Taipings slipped out from the east side of the city. A few days later on April 7, as they marched northward toward Kweilin, an imperial army commanded by Manchu General Wu-lan-t'ai fell on their rear guard, slaughtering approximately 2,000, mostly noncombatants. A retaliatory strike led by Hsiao Ch'ao-kuei resulted in several thousand imperial casualties and the death of four general officers. Wu-lan-t'ai himself narrowly escaped death. On April 19, Hsiao ambushed Wu's forces as they approached Kweilin. Wu was mortally wounded by artillery fire. The main force of the Taiping military held Kweilin under siege from April 17 until May 19 when they abandoned the city and proceeded northward taking Hsing-an and Ch'uan-chou in northeastern Kwangsi. From there, they crossed into Hunan and captured the district city of Tao-chou on June 12.

At Tao-chou, Hsiao and East King Yang Hsiu-ch'ing jointly issued a proclamation calling on all Chinese to rise up, rid China of Manchu misrule, and establish peace and prosperity in the name of God. The Taipings occupied Ch'en-chou in southern Hunan on August 17, whence Hsiao led a light infantry strike force through difficult terrain in eastern Hunan, arriving in the suburbs of Changsha on September 11. After an initial victory over the imperial forces outside the city wall, Hsiao's small force arrived at the wall to find the gates closed. Defense of the city had been hastily organized by Provincial Governor Lo Ping-chang and some 8,000 militia. Hsiao stationed his small force at the South Gate and the Small West Gate. Cannon fired from the south tower in the city wall forced the Taiping troops to take cover. The following day ostentatiously wearing the insignia of his royal rank, Hsiao led his forces into battle and was promptly struck down by the fire of imperial gunners. Hsiao died from his wounds later in September. He was survived by his widow Hung Hsüan-chiao and a son, Yu-ho, who inherited his title.

Hsiao Ch'ao-Kuei's death opened the way for the uncontested rise of the personally ambitious East King Yang Hsiu-ch'ing. Hsiao was known for his loyalty and fearlessness in battle. His fearlessness explains his foolhardy self-exposure during the siege of Changsha, which resulted in his untimely death and deprived the revolutionary movement of his leadership.

REFERENCES: Chien Yu-wen, *T'ai-ping T'ien-kuo Ch'üan-shih* (Complete history of the Heavenly Kingdom of Great Peace), vol. 1 (Hong Kong, 1960): 135, 420–428; Jen (Chien) Yu-wen, *The Taiping Revolutionary Movement* (New Haven, Conn., 1973); Ts'ai Kuan-lo, ed. *Ch'ing-tai ch'i-pai ming-jen chuan* (Biographies of seven hundred famous people of the Ch'ing period), vol. 3 (Peking, 1984): 1868–1870.

THOMAS L. KENNEDY

HSÜ SHIH-CH'ANG (October 23, 1855–June 6, 1939): Protégé of Yüan Shih-k'ai and president of China from 1918 to 1922.

Although his forebears originally hailed from Tientsin, Hsü Shih-ch'ang was born and grew up in Honan. Not much is known about his early life, except for the fact that he was poor and made his living as a *yamen* clerk or a family tutor. In 1879 he met Yüan Shih-k'ai,[*] and the two became sworn brothers and lifelong friends. Through Yüan's financial assistance Hsü was able to go to Peking to take the imperial examinations. His career immediately took a turn for the better as a result of the trip. He became a *chü-jen* in 1882, a *chin-shih* in 1886, and a Hanlin compiler in 1889.

When Yüan Shih-k'ai was in charge of training the New Army[*] in Chihli, Hsü Shih-ch'ang, despite his civilian background, served as Yüan's chief-of-staff. Thus began his long and intimate association with the Peiyang Military Clique.* Through this connection, Hsü was eventually promoted to be acting president of the Board of War and grand councillor. In 1906 he was sent on a special mission to Manchuria, which had just served as the battleground for Japan and Russia. The purpose of his trip was to study the region and to recommend measures that would strengthen China's influence there. As a result of his survey and comprehensive study, some far-reaching reforms and reorganization in the northeast were instituted. Hsü was appointed governor-general of the entire region.

In the final years of the Ch'ing dynasty,* Hsü remained a prominent figure in the metropolitan bureaucracy, despite his close association with Yüan Shih-k'ai, who had temporarily fallen from favor with the court. In fact, it was Hsü who played the critical role in Yüan's reinstatement by persuading the regent to the infant Hsüan-t'ung emperor to recall Yüan from his involuntary retirement to deal with the situation after the Wuch'ang Uprising in October 1911. It was also through Hsü that Yüan presented his conditions to the Manchu court to resume power. After making the arrangements for the abdication of the last emperor of the Ch'ing dynasty, however, Hsü took the calculated move to retire from public life in an ostensible show of loyalty to the dynasty.

In 1914, when Yüan Shih-k'ai succeeded in eliminating all opposition to his de facto rule of China, he persuaded his old friend Hsü to come out of retirement to serve as his secretary of state, a largely ceremonial post. In 1915, however, when Yüan's monarchical aspirations became all too apparent, Hsü again shrewdly withdrew from government. Yüan died in 1916 when his dream of becoming China's next emperor ended in fiasco. His two lieutenants, Tuan Ch'i-jui and Feng Kuo-chang, began a bitter fight to control the government. Hsü came to be seen by many as the only elder statesman within the Peiyang Clique who could serve as mediator between the two militarists. In 1918, when Feng's term as president expired and Tuan chose to manipulate the situation behind the scene, Hsü was elected president of China and assumed the post on October 10, 1918.

Hsü's presidency was filled with controversy. The southern government never recognized its legitimacy. It was further rocked by a burgeoning Chinese nationalism that manifested itself most dramatically on May 4, 1919, when news of the Versailles Treaty provisions reached home and caused massive demonstrations in Peking. Although he initially reacted harshly to the student demonstrators, Hsü was later forced to renounce the treaty and to accept the resignation of his negotiators. But Hsü's greatest failing was his inability to control the warlords. When the Chihli Army won a decisive victory over the Fengt'ien troops and Hsü was found to be dispensable, he was forced out of office in 1922.

During the period from 1922 until his death in 1939, Hsü devoted himself to the promotion of scholarship and culture. He sponsored the compilation of various literary and philosophical collections, the most notable of which was the *Ch'ing-*

ju hsüeh-an (The scholarship of Ch'ing Confucians). He was also instrumental in the publication of the complete Taoist canon (*Tao-tsang*) since the Ming dynasty.

REFERENCES: Howard L. Boorman and Richard Howard, eds., *Biographical Dictionary of Republican China*, vol. 2 (New York, 1968): 136–140; Liu Shao-t'ang, ed., *Min-kuo jen-wu hsiao-chuan* (Biographical sketches of republican China), vol. 3 (Chuan-chi wen-hsüeh, 1980): 132–134.

RICHARD SHEK

HU CH'IAO-MU (1905–   ): Conservative political theorist, and political figure influential before and after the Cultural Revolution.

Hu was born in Yensheng, Kiangsu, into a family of wealthy landowners. His father had once been a member of the National Parliament in Peking. Hu Ch'iao-mu attended middle school in Yangchou. He studied physics in Tsinghua University,* 1930–1932, and while there was active in the Communist Youth League.

Although Hu did not join the Chinese Communist party* until 1935, for years he had been doing pro-Communist propaganda work in Shanghai, and he continued doing this work until the outbreak of war with Japan. He then left for Yenan, where he was put in charge of press work, and with Chiang Nan-hsiang he co-edited *Chinese Youth*. He spent the period of KMT–CCP alliance in Sian operating a youth training school. After the alliance broke up, he returned to Yenan (1937). In 1938 he became dean of the Mao Tse-tung School for Young Cadres, and he also became secretary of the Political Affairs Committee, headed by Mao.*

Though not a highly educated man, Hu had received more schooling than most party leaders. Thus, he was able to provide a modest intellectual basis for party policies. He was publishing works of history (of varying reliability) as early as 1934. In 1951 he published the book *Thirty Years of the CCP*, of which almost 3 million copies appeared by the end of 1952, and which stood for years as virtually the official party history. He was also actively involved in the preparation of Mao's selected works (though there is some question about the extent of his involvement in the radical volume 5), and *Selected Correspondence of Mao Tse-tung* (1983).

Hu played an important role in journalism and cultural affairs. He established the New China News Agency, and was director of it for about a year prior to October 1949. On the eve of the establishment of the People's Republic of China* in 1949, Hu became director of *People's Daily*, until the end of 1950. He was chairman of the Preparatory Committee of the National Federation of Journalists from July 1949 to September 1954. Around 1950 he became the Government Administrative Council's director for press administration, a post he held until August 1952. He was secretary-general of the party's Cultural and Education Committee between October 1949 and November 1952. In 1955 he became a member of the Department of Philosophy and Social Science at the Chinese Academy of Science (CAS). In 1959 Hu appears to have promoted the publication of Wu Han's controversial play "Hai Jui Upbraids the Emperor." This play came under attack on the eve of the Cultural Revolution,* heralding the storms that would follow.

In 1962 Hu was dismissed as Mao's political secretary (which he had been since 1941), though it is still not clear to what extent there was a falling out between the two. Beginning in January 1, 1965, the *People's Daily* began devoting a large amount of space to Hu's poems, on which the media lavished much praise. This was a remarkable departure from the tradition that the poetry of Mao alone should be given great prominence, and it demonstrated both Hu's unusual position in the party and the extent to which the media were now ignoring Mao. In 1966 Hu came under attack (particularly by Chiang Ch'ing,* with whom he had been on bad terms since 1950) and lost his remaining posts. In January 1967 he was humiliated by the Red Guards* and denounced as a "Three Anti element" and a follower of Liu Shao-ch'i* and Teng Hsiao-p'ing.* However, he was not a major target during the Cultural Revolution,* and he seems to have passed these years relatively uneventfully.

After about 1973, Hu's fate would be tied to that of the pragmatists. With Hu Yao-pang,* he drew up a program that would be criticized as "restorationist." Among other things, they wanted to revive the CAS (over which, as it turned out, Hu would preside from March 1978 intermittently until August 1982). In 1975, on Teng Hsiao-p'ing's instructions, Hu tried (unsuccessfully) to establish a new theoretical journal to compete with the leftist *Red Flag*. During the 1976 campaign against Teng, Hu Ch'iao-mu proved much more compliant than Hu Yao-pang and Teng. He not only confessed his errors, but he also apparently criticized Teng. This proved a major tactical error, and his political recovery was slower than that of the others.

Still, his position as theoretician could not be filled by anyone else, and before long he was restored to his position as spokesman for the new leadership in matters of political theory. His first major post–Cultural Revolution article appeared in October 1978. From then on his star rose steadily. After the Twelfth Party Congress he was admitted to the Politburo (1982), with responsibility for such important questions as Hong Kong.

For Hu, economics seems to have been more religion than science, and his views on the subject are bewildering. On the one hand (as he pointed out in 1978), the laws of economic development were independent of human will and consciousness; on the other hand, these laws determine will and consciousness. He would quote Lenin regarding economics being independent of human will, and Mao to the effect that the laws of economics are unknowable, and then warn of the danger of "acting blindly in accordance with the will of superior officers and taking things for granted" and ignoring the laws of economics. The common denominator seemed to be that Hu implicitly opposed leftist economics (though he generally upheld Maoism in name). The "laws" that Hu claimed were in reality merely statements of current policy (such as the need for planned development and for defining value in terms of inputs rather than market forces) and of the need to uphold the policies of the leaders ("the unity of interests among the state, enterprise and individual"). This led Hu to conclude that it was necessary to follow party leadership, but also (after the Cultural Revolution, at least) that China had something to learn from the experience of Western capitalist countries. On the other hand, as late as 1978 he was anachronistically quoting Stalin's depression-era remarks regarding the crises to which capitalism was allegedly prone.

Thus, there is no little irony in the fact that Hu was a victim of the Cultural Revolution. He was always a staunch proponent of class struggle and was a rigid proponent of authoritarianism. Although he opposed the fragmenting tendencies of the Cultural Revolution, he fought hard against the liberal popular in the late 1970s and 1980s. Hu was somewhat xenophobic, worrying about foreign organizations "secretly plotting terrorist activities" as part of class struggle. In opening up to the world, China must open up to the world with caution, always distinguishing between friends and "wolves."

Hu was usually able to tailor his ideological pronouncements to fit the leaders' needs at any given time. During the era of Teng Hsiao-p'ing, he became a major conservative influence. In 1979 he said that sociologists need not necessarily adhere to Marxist approaches. But soon he made it clear that he saw no value in free discourse. What really seemed to matter for him was that there be uniformity of thought. Otherwise, people would go off in different directions, and "our rank-and-file would not be able to march forward." In 1981 he declared that anyone who openly advocated absolute freedom of speech, publication, assembly, and association "is a representative of bourgeois ideology." He inveighed against "endless debates on fundamental political questions." What mattered to him was "the freedom of the Party as a whole, the army as a whole, the nationalities as a whole, to unite as one and build a new socialist life."

During the early 1980s, Hu was active in the field of reform of the legal system. Although a new constitution did result from such efforts, little progress was made in the direction of rule of law. His main interest seems to have been to develop "laws" applying to economic activities. Sometimes he seemed to confuse law with theoretical laws. Thus, people who did not follow the law of "to each according to his work" would be punished. He was strongly in favor of imprisoning as "counterrevolutionaries" those who expressed opposition to the socialist system, and he rejected the notion that such views are appropriate for debate in the media.

For a few years after his restoration to influence, Hu moved cautiously on the subject of intellectuals, avoiding positions that would be redolent of his soft-on-leftism past. But this would change. Beginning by the early 1980s he stood at the forefront of the campaigns against bourgeois liberalization and spiritual pollution. He was much more vehement on these subjects than was Hu Yao-pang, and his views were perhaps excessive even for Teng (or at least it proved expedient for the latter to let people believe this).

Hu's conservativism made him unpopular with intellectuals. True, this fact was of apparent concern to him, and in the mid–1980s he is said to have occasionally shown private contrition to writers such as Wu Chu-kuang, Shu T'ing, Liu Pin-yen, and especially Wang Meng. But this did not help him in what was probably his last intellectual battle. This was over the question of whether alienation is peculiar to capitalist systems or can also occur under socialism. Here he came head-to-head with his intellectual superior, protégé Wang Jo-shui. Wang Jo-shui was a proponent of the idea that there is alienation under socialism, and he was a critic of such features of the political order as personality cults.

Hu Ch'iao-mu found himself very much on the defensive. The arguments in his famous 1984 speech "On Humanism and Alienation" were rather lame. "The proletarian dictatorship (which we call the people's democratic dictatorship, and has nothing to do with fascist terror) is an indispensable condition for the transition to a classless society." He went on to ridicule the belief (which had become increasingly common) "that any problems, big or small, may be solved by holding popular elections and acting in accordance with the will of the majority." Although Hu's essay received widespread de rigueur praise, it is doubtful that very many people found Hu's counter-arguments compelling. Calling Wang a "utopian" who denied the need for authority was an obvious distortion of the man's views. Anyway, Hu had to admit to the existence of China's social ills and the need at least for "socialist" humanism. Although the liberals were temporarily silenced after the appearance of Hu's essay, Wang Jo-shui never felt the need to confess any errors.

Hu's political career was generally characterized by loyalty. In the 1980s the beneficiary of this loyalty was Teng Hsiao-p'ing. Still, Hu remained loyal to Mao's memory—however Mao may have felt about him. During the brief chairmanship of Hua Kuo-feng,[*] Hu constantly cited Mao in speeches. To the end, he defended his thought as "a complete scientific theory," and he was able to undercut much of the revisionist historical thinking about him.

REFERENCES: Chu Yuan, "The Crisis of Hu Ch'iao-mu," *Cheng-ming*, No. 82 (August 1984): 50–53; Hu Ch'iao-mu, "Act According to Economic Laws, Step up the Four Modernizations," *People's Daily* (October 6, 1978); *Thirty Years of the Communist Party of China: An Outline History* (Westport, Conn., 1973).

                                                        JAMES D. SEYMOUR

HU FENG AFFAIR (1955): Incident of the purge of Hu Feng, later escalated into a nationwide campaign against antiparty elements by the CCP.

Hu Feng (1903–1985), a leading Marxist literary critic and writer, was purged in 1955 by the Chinese Communist party[*] for his independent approach to literature and to the role of the writer in a socialist society.

Hu was born in I-tu hsien in southern Hupeh, and his original name was Chang Ku-fei. He joined the Communist Youth League in 1925 in Nanking, but he never became a member of the Communist party itself. In 1934 in Shanghai, Hu joined the League of Left-Wing Writers and became one of Lu Hsün's[*] leading disciples.

After the establishment of the Chinese Communist regime in 1949, Hu Feng assumed leadership positions in newly created mass organizations. These included the All-China Federation of Literary and Art Circles, the All-China Association of Literary Workers (which later became the Union of Chinese Writers), as well as the Culture and Education Committee of the East China regional government. In 1954 Hu was made a deputy from Szechwan to the First National People's Congress and was appointed to the editorial board of *Jen-min wen-hsüeh* (*People's Literature*), an important party literary magazine.

As early as the 1930s, Hu's independent views on literature had brought him into periodic conflict with party authorities. In 1954 he once again found himself at variance with party orthodoxy. In July of that year, Hu submitted a statement entitled "Views on Literary Questions" to the party's Central Committee in which he criticized the party for its intellectual sterility. Dissenting from the official party position on literature, Hu argued that the writer should have the freedom to express his deepest emotions without party control or ideological remolding. Literature should not merely portray the officially proscribed classes, but should describe the lives of all men. The criteria of evaluation for literature should be apolitical, governed solely by the merits of the individual writer.

All of this was in direct opposition to the orthodox view on literature and art as it was established by Mao in a speech in Yenan in 1942. According to Mao, there was "no such thing as art for art's sake." Instead, "art and literature are subordinate to politics." The guiding principle for art and literature should be that of "socialist realism": Writers should present things as they should be and not as they are.

The Communist party responded to Hu Feng's statement with a massive nationwide campaign. Although no credible evidence ever existed that his ideas were anti-Marxist in principle or that he really intended to subvert or sabotage the Communist government, Hu was declared to be a bourgeois reactionary and was derided as "an imperialist dog of the United States and Chiang Kai-shek." Private correspondence between Hu and his followers was published, and his views were distorted into those advocating an overthrow of the Communist party. In 1955, despite his undertaking of a self-criticism, Hu Feng was stripped of all his posts. In July Hu and other members of his "clique" were arrested and imprisoned as counterrevolutionaries.

The campaign against Hu did not end with his arrest but was enlarged in scope and intensified so that even a humble peasant in a remote area of Inner Mongolia was ferreting out latent "Hu Fengism." That campaign would become the harbinger of a full-scale assault on Chinese intellectuals in the Anti-Rightist Campaign[*] of 1957–1958.

REFERENCES: Merle Goldman, "The Chinese Communist Party's 'Cultural Revolution' of 1962–1964," in Chalmers Johnson, ed., *Ideology and Politics in Contemporary China* (Seattle, Wash., 1973): 249–251; James Pinkney Harrison, *The Long March to Power:*

A History of the Chinese Communist Party, 1921–72 (New York, 1972); Howard Boorman and Richard Howard, eds., *Biographical Dictionary of Republican China*, Vol. 2 (New York, 1968): 155–158.

MARIA HSIA CHANG

HU HAN-MIN (October 26, 1879–May 12, 1936): Republican revolutionary, statesman, and socialist thinker.

Born into a petty semiofficial family in Pan-yu County, Kwangtung, Hu Han-min started his revolutionary career in 1905 when he joined the T'ung-meng hui.* As editor of its organ *Min Pao* (People's Journal), Hu championed republicanism and explained the organization's social program of land nationalization and regulated capitalism. Based in Southeast Asia and Hong Kong, Hu helped Dr. Sun Yat-sen* to organize uprisings in the southwestern border provinces of China. He was instrumental in the T'ung-meng hui's capture of Kwangtung in November 1911 and the subsequent founding of the Republic of China.* He took part in the Second Revolution* against Yüan Shih-k'ai's* dictatorship before joining the Chinese Revolutionary party* founded by Dr. Sun in Tokyo in 1914 in continuing the anti-Yüan endeavors. During the May Fourth* period, Hu published on China's cultural heritage and the present socioeconomic crises, using historical materialism as his analytical framework. Searching for a solution to China's crises, Hu synthesized traditional Chinese and modern Western social ideals, stressing *jen* or benevolence in formulating socioeconomic policies. In achieving a bright future for humankind, Hu believed that the play of class struggle in social progress should be avoided.

In overthrowing warlordist rule following Yüan's demise in June 1916 and expelling their foreign imperialist backers, the reorganized Kuomintang joined hands with the Chinese Communist party* in 1924. Subsequently, the rapidly increasing Communist strength alarmed the KMT old guards, who accused the CCP of sabotaging their party. Hu's cautious approach to the "alliance" and growing CCP influence led to suspicion between him and Michael Borodin,* the Russian adviser to Dr. Sun and a seasoned Bolshevik. Hu was stripped of power in Canton's revolutionary regime after Sun's death in March 1925. He later traveled to Moscow as Canton's ambassador following the assassination of Liao Chung-k'ai in August the same year.

Hu's meeting with Joseph Stalin and other Soviet leaders while in Moscow confirmed his earlier reservation about the KMT–CCP "alliance." Back in Canton in April 1926, Hu presented to his KMT colleagues a critical view of the Russian motive in forging the "alliance" and adopted an anti-Communist stance. One year later, Hu and other KMT leaders purged the Communists, and there followed a long, bitter power struggle between the two revolutionary parties.

In mid-1928 China entered into the political tutelary stage of revolution under the auspices of the KMT when the Northern Expedition* brought about nominal unification of the country. As the first president of the Legis-

lative Assembly of the Republic of China,* Hu vigorously applied Dr. Sun's
Three People's Principles* to legislation on land, civil affairs, and local self-
government among other areas. He was determined to uproot the bureaucratism, capitalism, and militarism then plaguing China, admonishing government officials against corruption and bribery and urging them to heed the
party doctrine and Sun's Principles in making the best possible endeavors
for the interest of people.

Meanwhile, heated exchanges between Hu and Chiang Kai-shek* over promulgating a provisional constitution strained their relationship, resulting in
Chiang putting Hu under house-arrest in March 1931. Hu was set free after the
Mukden Incident* in September the same year, when the Japanese Army invaded
Manchuria. He lived most of his remaining years in Hong Kong, where he edited
and published the *Three People's Principles Monthly*, condemning the nonresistance policy adopted by the Nanking government, its total negligence of the
people's economic hardship, and its ineffectiveness in suppressing the Communist insurgency. Deepening Japanese invasion drew the Chinese leaders together and a United Front was achieved in the face of foreign threat. Hu was
elected chairman of the central executive committee of the KMT in December
1935. However, he died in Canton in the following May before assuming the
position.

REFERENCES: David Peter Barrett, "Socialism, Marxism and Communism in the
Thought of Hu Han-min" (Ph.D. thesis, University of London, 1978); Chiang Yung-
ching, *Hu Han-min hsien-sheng nien-pu* (A chronological biography of Mr. Hu Han-
min) (Taipei, 1978).

LAU YEE-CHEUNG

HU LI-YÜAN (1847–1916): Merchant, writer, reformer, revolutionary sympathizer.

Born in San-shui, Kwangtung, Hu Li-yüan was the son of a merchant
who became associated with the Taiping* rebels, and therefore had to flee
China and take his family to Hong Kong in the 1850s. At the age of ten,
Hu Li-yüan began to study English with Wu T'ing-fang, who was five years
Hu's senior and a student at St. Paul's College. In 1862 Hu enrolled in the
Hong Kong Government Central School (later known as Queen's College),
where he was later appointed as a Chinese assistant, teaching Chinese until
the 1870s.

Well versed in Chinese classics and literature, Hu aspired to enter a Chinese
official career. But he failed at least twice in the Chinese civil service examinations, which contributed to his later denunciation of the uselessness of the
eight-legged essay examinations (style of writing that was required for the
Chinese civil service exam). With excellent command of both Chinese and
English, Hu served from 1879 to 1881 on the translating staff of Wang T'ao's
newspaper *Hsun-huan jih-pao*. In 1885 he helped found the journal *Yueh-pao*.
Hu also assisted a group of English businessmen in developing British North
Borneo. Back in Hong Kong, he was associated in business with Wong Tsik-

hing, comprador to Messrs. Douglas Lapraik and Company. Hu also worked in his brother's Fat Ki Coal Shop; his trip to Japan in July 1893 was probably related to the coal business.

Hu's reformist thought was shaped by his commercial background in the colonial environment of Hong Kong and by his experience in Japan, where he stayed for nearly two years during the Sino-Japanese War* (1894–1895). He was deeply impressed by a strong sense of nationalism among the Japanese in time of war against China. He concluded that the Meiji constitution and parliamentary institution made Japan invincible in war.

A staunch patriot, Hu was gravely concerned about imperialism in China. As early as 1887, in the aftermath of the Sino-French War (1884–1885), he had co-authored with the barrister Ho Kai (Ho Ch'i)* an essay calling on the Chinese government to make institutional reforms along Western lines. Hu was particularly prolific in the years 1895–1900. Hu and Ho Kai jointly published six more reformist essays that established their fame as reformers. They exposed the corruption and oppression of China's gentry-dominated ruling bureaucracy. They insisted that merchants were the backbone of the nation, commercialism was the road to the nation's wealth and power, and private enterprise was the best way to develop China's economy. They also advocated the creation of representative institutions and a responsible cabinet, with a Ministry of Commerce taking the leading position in government. They demanded that merchants and overseas Chinese businessmen should be placed in politically responsible positions in China. In short, IIu Li-yüan and Ho Kai's reformist essays reflected a perspective from the merchants and intelligentsia in Hong Kong.

A collection of Hu and Ho's essays was reprinted in Shanghai in 1901 under the title of *The True Meaning of the New Government* (*Hsin-cheng chen-ch'uan*). Subsequently, Hu wrote many more articles and poems, advocating freedom and people's rights against Manchu tyranny in China. All these were included in the posthumous *Complete Works of Mr. Hu Li-yüan* (*Hu I-nan hsien-sheng ch'uan-chi*).

Hu Li-yüan sympathized with the republican cause and befriended revolutionaries in Hong Kong such as Hsieh Tsuan-t'ai. Hu was on the Manchu suspect list in connection with the revolutionaries' abortive plot to attack Canton on January 28, 1903. He rendered strong support to the "Queue-Cutting Society" organized in 1910 by Dr. Kuan Hsin-yen, advocating the removal of the pigtail imposed on the Chinese by the Manchu rulers. In a mass demonstration in Hong Kong on December 4, Hu was one of the six old gentlemen who led several hundred people in removing their queues.

Hu Li-yüan's offspring have maintained prosperity in Hong Kong. His oldest son, Heng-sheng, was a comprador to the Butterfield and Swire Company. The second son, Heng-chin, became a lawyer after receiving a law degree from the University of London in 1913. Hu Li-yüan's grandson, Hu Pai-ch'uan (the Honorable Dr. P. C. Woo), also a lawyer with a degree from London, was until his retirement in the late 1970s a director of the Butterfield and Swire Company and a member of the Hong Kong Executive Council appointed by the governor.

REFERENCE: Jung-fang Tsai, "Syncretism in the Reformist Thought of Ho Kai (Ho Ch'i, 1859–1914) and Hu Li-yüan (1847–1916)," *Asian Profile* 6, no. 1 (February 1978): 19–33.

JUNG-FANG TSAI

HU SHIH (December 17, 1891–February 24, 1962): Cultural critic and educator.

Hu Shih was born in Shanghai in 1891, the only son of his father Hu Ch'uan's third marriage. Hu Ch'uan, a holder of the *hsiu-ts'ai* degree, served in a variety of minor offices in the civil service until his death in 1895 when his son was only four. Hu Shih had been taken back the previous year to the family's native village, Chi-hsi, in Anhwei Province to begin schooling in the classics, a task to which he showed an unusually keen interest and precocity. At the age of nine, Hu Shih experienced something of a rebirth, with the discovery of traditional vernacular fiction which he devoured hungrily. In 1904 at the age of thirteen he was sent to Shanghai to supplement his traditional education with study in mathematics, foreign languages, and the natural sciences. From 1906 to 1908 Hu attended the Chung-kuo kung-hsüeh (China National Institute), a hotbed of revolutionary activity. Although he did not join the T'ung-meng hui,* which recruited among the institute's students, he was a frequent contributor of iconoclastic articles (written mostly in the vernacular) to the *Ching-yeh hsün-pao* (The Struggle), the institute's journal. In 1908 striking students withdrew from the institute to organize an independent school under student administration; lacking funds, Hu was forced to drop out and support himself for the next two years by teaching English. His thought at this time was shaped by readings in democracy and cultural dynamism by Liang Ch'i-ch'ao* and the Social Darwinist writings and translations of Yen Fu.*

In 1910 Hu Shih sat for and passed the Boxer Indemnity scholarship examination which enabled him to study in the United States. Hu's seven years of overseas study began in the agriculture college at Cornell University, but within two years he abandoned these practical studies to pursue his true interest in comparative philosophy, in which he completed a B.A. in 1914. After a year of graduate study in philosophy at Cornell, Hu Shih transferred to Columbia University to study experimentalism with John Dewey. His doctoral dissertation, completed in 1917, was a historical analysis of logic in traditional Chinese philosophy. During his final year of study in the United States, Hu's vernacular poems and polemical articles began to be published in *Hsin ch'ing-nien* (*New Youth*). Most notable was his 1917 "Tentative Proposals for the Reform of Literature" (*Wen-hsüeh kai-liang ch'u-i*) which launched the vernacular movement.

Hu Shih returned to China in 1917 to take up a position in the Philosophy Department of Peking University. At this time he was a frequent contributor to

New Youth and a leading voice in May Fourth* cultural iconoclasm. In 1920 he broke with the increasingly radical and politicized Ch'en Tu-hsiu,* editor of *New Youth* and dean of the College of Arts at Peking University, but he continued to participate in the major intellectual debates of the 1920s as the dominant voice for liberal skepticism. In the ''Problems and Isms'' debate of 1919, Hu warned against an overzealous adherence to ideologies blinding one to tangible social problems. In the debate on science in 1923, Hu was with Ting Wen-chiang,* a leading supporter of the continued applicability of the Western scientific method to China's problems, thus opposing a conservative reaction that exploited the European postwar spiritual collapse as a justification for a return to a more Chinese (traditional) ''philosophy of life.''

In 1927 Hu Shih returned from a year of lecturing abroad to settle in Shanghai. He taught philosophy at Kuang Hua University and became president of the China National Institute, which had been made a university since the days when he had attended it as a student. In 1928 Hu helped found *Hsin-yüeh* (*Crescent Moon*), a journal devoted to literary and political issues of the day. He wrote articles (for which he was suspended from his university presidency in 1930) critical of the growing dogmatism of the KMT. At the invitation of Chiang Meng-lin,* Hu Shih was brought back to Peking University as its dean of the College of Arts. From 1932 to 1937 Hu Shih was editor of a widely read journal, *Tu-li p'ing-lun* (*Independent Critic*), which promoted democracy (in the face of rising authoritarianism, nationalism, and the reactionary New Life Movement*) and continued his liberal faith in the intellectual as independent social critic.

Hu Shih left China shortly after the outbreak of the Sino-Japanese War* to which he lent only reluctant support. From 1938 to 1942 Hu was the Chinese ambassador in Washington. Even after his dismissal (a casualty of worsening Sino-American relations), Hu stayed on in the United States, lecturing and attending conferences (including the founding of the United Nations in 1945). He returned to China in 1946 to become chancellor of Peking University and in the fall of the same year was instrumental in drafting a Chinese constitution, a long-held ambition. Rumors that he would soon become president of the Republic proved unfounded, but Hu was elected to the National Assembly in 1947. With the defeat of the KMT in 1949, Hu Shih chose to return to the United States, where he pursued scholarly interests. In 1958 Chiang Kai-shek* personally selected him to head the Academia Sinica, a post he held until his death in 1962. No apologist for the KMT, Hu Shih continued his role as social critic by lending support to the journal *Tzu-yu Chung-kuo* (*Free China*), which was suspended for its criticism of the KMT.

In addition to his prodigious writings on such topical subjects as feudal customs, Ibsen's individualism, language reform, experimentalism, and democracy, Hu Shih must also be remembered as one of the champions of modern research methodology which he applied in his own investigation of Chinese philosophy and his highly acclaimed work on traditional vernacular fiction. Hu Shih was

one of the principal shapers of the cultural dimension of the May Fourth Movement and throughout the republican period was the leading voice of liberal
humanism. He consistently promoted democracy, constitutionalism, and the notion of the intellectual as disinterested social critic, ideas for which he was
fiercely criticized, in absentia, during a political campaign in the People's Republic of China* in 1954–1955.
REFERENCES: Min-chih Chou, *Hu Shih and Intellectual Choice in Modern China* (Ann
Arbor, Mich., 1984); Jerome Grieder, *Hu Shih and the Chinese Renaissance: Liberalism
in the Chinese Revolution 1917–1937* (Cambridge, Mass., 1970); Li Ao, *Hu Shih p'ing-
chuan* (Hu Shih: A critical biography), 2 vols. (Taipei, 1964).

KIRK A. DENTON

HU YAO-PANG (1915–April 15, 1989): CCP general secretary.

Born into a peasant family in Liu-yang, Hunan Province, in 1915, Hu Yao-
pang joined the Children's Corps during the Autumn Harvest Uprising* in 1927
and began his involvement in Communist youth work in 1933 by his association
with the Communist Youth League's Central Bureau in the Central Soviet area
in Kiangsi.* A veteran of the Long March* (1934–1935), he was appointed head
of the Organization Department of the Communist Youth League and a member
of the league's fifteen-member Central Committee in 1935.

Attending the Anti-Japanese Military and Political Academy (K'ang-ta) in
north Shensi in 1936, Hu became the director of the Organization Division of
the General Political Department, Eighteenth Army Corps in 1941. During the
Sino-Japanese War* (1937–1945) and in the postwar years when the Chinese
Communist party* forces were fighting against the Nationalist Army led by
Chiang Kai-shek,* Hu was an active political officer in Liu Po-ch'eng's Second
Field Army. Early in 1949 he served as a vice-chairman of the Taiyüan Military
Control Commission under General Hsü Hsiang-ch'ien's command to manage
the city's military and civil affairs.

In 1949–1952 Hu worked closely with Liu Po-ch'eng and Teng Hsiao-p'ing*
first to capture Szechwan from the Nationalist forces and then to rule Szechwan
and the southwest region of China in a number of capacities. In late 1952 Hu
was transferred to Peking to head the Communist Youth League. In the late
1950s and early 1960s he distinguished himself for his dominance over the affairs
of the league, which became his power base. The league produced many younger
leaders, many of whom emerged in the 1980s as leading figures committed to
the promotion of the modernization drive. After his transfer to Peking, he began
active participation in a variety of CCP and People's Republic of China* government programs, having been first elected to the National People's Congress
and its Standing Committee in 1954 and to the CCP Central Committee in 1956.
Under the blessing of Teng Hsiao-p'ing, Hu became even more active and visible
in the early and mid–1960s. A rising star in Chinese politics, he delivered
important speeches and published major articles on various occasions. In 1965–
1966 he served briefly as acting first secretary of the Shensi Provincial Communist
party.

Hu's career came to an abrupt end at the beginning of the Cultural Revolution[*] in 1966 when he, Teng Hsiao-p'ing, and many others were purged. Attacked in 1967 by the radical Red Guards[*] as a member of Liu Shao-ch'i's[*] antiparty clique, Hu did not reappear in public until 1972. He resumed his activities after Teng Hsiao-p'ing returned to power in 1973 but was purged again by the radicals following the death of Premier Chou En-lai[*] in January 1976. Upon Teng's return to power for the second time in July 1977 after the downfall of the radical Gang of Four,[*] Hu became an important member of Teng's team of reform-minded officials who led the modernization drive in the post-Mao years. In 1981 he replaced Hua Kuo-feng,[*] Mao Tse-tung's[*] handpicked successor, as chairman of the CCP Central Committee. As Teng's heir-apparent, he was elected later to the newly created position of general secretary of the CCP, the highest post in the CCP structure, to work together with Premier Chao Tzu-yang[*] to carry out Teng's reform programs.

In January 1987 Hu was dismissed from his post as CCP general secretary for his liberal political views and for his failure to suppress the growing student democracy movement. It was Hu's death on April 15, 1989, that triggered weeks of massive protests in April and May when throngs of over 1 million students and others filled the streets of Peking and occupied T'ienanmen Square, a symbol of China's political power, to protest the growing official corruption and to demand democratization, a cause with which Hu had been identified. After seven escalating weeks, the protests came to a sudden end. In the early hours of June 4, the tanks of the People's Liberation Army[*] moved toward T'ienanmen and fired on the crowds, killing hundreds and wounding thousands to suppress the democracy movement. A shocking massacre had taken place in Peking, and a decade of reform was in shambles.

A self-taught party veteran, Hu was known for his simple way of life, demanding style, liberal views, pragmatic policies, explosive energy, and quick intelligence. He made important contributions to the preparation of younger leaders for China and to China's modernization drive in the 1980s.

REFERENCES: A. Doak Barnett and Ralph N. Clough, eds., *Modernizing China: Post-Mao Reform and Development* (Boulder, Colo., 1986); Hu Yaobang, *An Interview with Hu Yaobang*, ed. Lu Keng (New York, Hong Kong, 1985); Donald Klein and Anne Clark, *Biographic Dictionary of Chinese Communism, 1921–1965*, vol. 1 (Cambridge, Mass., 1971): 383–385; Winston L.Y. Yang, "Hu Yaobang," *Encyclopaedia Britannica 1982 Book of the Year* (Chicago, 1982): 78–79; Yang Zhong Mei, *Hu Yaobang: A Chinese Biography* (trans. William A. Wycoff), ed. Timothy Cheek (Armonk, N.Y., 1988).

WINSTON L.Y. YANG

HUA KUO-FENG (b. 1921): Premier of the PRC and chairman of the Central Committee of the CCP, successor to Mao Tse-Tung.

Hua was born in 1921 in Chiao-ch'eng County in Shansi Province. Not much else is known of Hua's childhood or early experiences except that he came from a poor peasant family that, owing to a natural calamity when he was a child, had to flee to northern Shensi. Hua "joined the revolution" when the Communist

forces entered the northwestern region of Shansi Province after the Long March,*
that is, around 1936, which would put Hua at about fifteen years of age. In 1945
Hua became the secretary of the Chinese Communist party's* Chiao-ch'eng
County Committee and was promoted two years later to be secretary of the Yang-
ch'ü County Party Committee and political commissar of the local Communist
forces.

In the summer of 1949, Hua joined the work teams sent by the Red Army
south to do political work in support and followup of the Communist thrust
toward southern China. Hua's destination was Hunan, where, in August of that
year, he became secretary of the CCP Committee of Hsiang-yin County. Here
Hua launched a vigorous land reform campaign and won the acclaim of Huang
K'e-ch'eng and Wang Shou-tao in the Hunan Provincial Party Committee for
his campaign against "local tyrants" and landlords. In the autumn of 1951, he
was transferred to the posts of Hsiang-t'an County secretary and political commissar of the People's Armed Forces Department in Hunan. With encouragement
from Chou Hsiao-chou, who became Hunan provincial party secretary in 1953,
Hua promoted the agricultural cooperativization campaign and, simultaneously,
the campaign to suppress counterrevolutionaries in the Hsiang-t'an area. He set
up many production mutual aid teams, which were the preliminary forms of
agricultural cooperatives, and by early 1955 these had escalated to agricultural
producers' cooperatives (APCs). During 1954 and 1955 there was some debate
within the CCP leadership over the intensity and level of agricultural cooperativization. Mao Tse-tung* ultimately stood firm that, in line with what he propagandized as "an upsurge of socialism in the countryside," the policy of
increasing the scope (and escalating the level) of cooperativization from primary-
level cooperatives to higher level cooperatives must be pushed forward. Hunan
Province became an "exemplary" region in this regard, and by March 1955
there were over 12,000 agricultural producers' cooperatives in the province, with
almost 5,000 in the Hsiang-t'an area alone. Since 1954, Hua had been the CCP
party secretary for the Hsiang-t'an special district, with jurisdiction over twelve
counties. He would hold this position until 1963, marking a most important
stage in his political career.

Hua's strategy of agricultural cooperativization was distinguished by two characteristics. First, he emphasized the massive and rapid organization of a large
number of primary level APCs, thus eventually putting pressure on the need for
organizing higher level cooperatives. Second, he paid a great deal of attention
to investigative work. That Hua's efforts caught the eye of Mao Tse-tung is
evident in the prominence of material reported from the Hsiang-t'an area in the
book *The Upsurge of Socialism in China's Countryside*, which became the
handbook for the cooperativization campaign. Mao himself wrote prefaces and
commentaries for this book, which was published in 1955. Of the forty-four
regional reports included in the abridged version of the book published in 1956,
six came from Hunan Province, and of these five dealt with the situation in the
Hsiang-t'an area. Hua compiled three of these and for each Mao had written

laudatory "editorial notes." Moreover, in November 1955 the CCP magazine *Hsüeh-hsi* (Study) published a special edition on agricultural cooperativization which incorporated Mao's own essay, "On the Question of Agricultural Cooperativization," and other Central Committee directives and documents, in addition to three reports from special district party secretaries, one of which was Hua's. Hua emphasized the need to rely on the poor peasant in the campaign, and he criticized the "latent capitalist tendencies" of cadres that felt that cooperativization had to rely on the "middle peasants." This approach fell completely in line with Mao's class theory and analysis of the class distinctions in the rural revolution. In 1957 Hua was promoted to alternate party secretary of Hunan Province.

In 1958 Mao launched the Three Red Banners Campaign* (i.e., promoting the People's Communes,* the Great Leap Forward,* and the General Line). Hua wrote a series of essays based on the investigative report on P'ing-chiang County, which were published in Hunan newspapers. This work was again praised by Mao. After the Lushan Conference* in September 1959, at which the P'eng Te-huai-Huang K'e-ch'eng faction was criticized and purged, Hua was nominated to be Hunan provincial party secretary, and doubled as vice-chairman of the Hunan Provincial People's government.

In the next few years, Hua continued to work on rural revolution in Hunan Province. His major achievements were the installation of a model project of the campaign to "Emulate Ta-chai in Agricultural Development" in the Mao-tian area and the massive irrigation project in Shao-shan.

During the Cultural Revolution* period, Hua's position in Hunan was consolidated. He was nominated by Chou En-lai* to the position of deputy group leader of the preparatory committee to organize the Hunan Provincial Revolutionary Committee in September 1967, and when the Revolutionary Committee was established in April 1968 he became its second deputy chief. In October of that year he attended the Twelfth Plenum of the Eighth Central Committee of the CCP in Peking, at which Liu Shao-ch'i* was criticized. Hua was appointed to read the investigative report on Liu at the plenum. Then, in April 1969, Hua was elected to the Ninth Central Committee of the CCP. By the end of 1970, Hua had become the acting chairman of the Revolutionary Committee of Hunan Province and virtually the top-ranked official in Hunan. With the purging of Lin Piao* in September 1971, Hua's position rose even further.

Transferred to Peking in November 1971, Hua was appointed secretary of a special group, operating out of the State Council under Chou En-lai, which investigated the Lin Piao affair. Meanwhile, he continued to hold the positions of the head of the Hunan Revolutionary Committee and first secretary of the Hunan Provincial Party Committee (which was the first to be reconstituted after the Cultural Revolution). In August 1973 he was reelected to the CCP Tenth Central Committee and was made a member of the Politburo. In Jaunary 1975 he was elected by the Fourth National People's Congress to vice-premiership of the State Council and as minister of public security.

Hua's final step of ascendance to his highest position of power began in April 1976 when Mao nominated him to take the place vacated by Chou En-lai, who had died in January of that year, as premier of the State Council of the People's Republic of China.* At the same time, the Politburo ratified Mao's nomination of Hua also as first vice-chairman of the CCP Central Committee. Then, in October that year, quite immediately after Mao's death, Hua had the Gang of Four* (i.e., the top leaders of the Cultural Revolution, namely, Mao's wife Chiang Ch'ing,* Chang Ch'un-ch'iao,* Yao Wen-yüan,* and Wang Hung-wen*) arrested, and Hua became the chairman of the CCP Central Committee and the chairman of the Central Military Council. These supreme positions were reconfirmed at the First Plenum of the CCP's Eleventh Central Committee in August 1977, and he was reelected to the premiership in March 1978 at the First Session of the Fifth National People's Congress. With the rise to power of Teng Hsiao-p'ing* in 1978, and especially Teng's triumph at the Third Plenum of the Eleventh Central Committee in December of that year, Hua's leadership had been eclipsed, and he became a figurehead announcing policies made by a collective leadership. Hua was divested of his premiership at the Third Session of the Fifth National People's Congress in September 1980, and he retired formally as chairman of the CCP Central Committee at the Sixth Plenum of the Eleventh Central Committee in June 1981 (at which time he also stepped down from the chair of the Military Affairs Council). Finally, he lost the vice-chairmanship of the party and his position in the Politburo at the Twelfth CCP National Congress in September 1982, but he remained a member of the Central Committee.

REFERENCES: Wolfgang Bartke and Peter Schier, *China's New Party Leadership: Biographies and Analysis of the Twelfth Central Committee of the Chinese Communist Party* (Armonk, N.Y., 1985): 120–121; Wolfgang Bartke, *Who's Who in the People's Republic of China* (Armonk, N.Y., 1981): 122–123; *Chung-kung jen-ming-lu* (Biographies of Chinese Communists) (Taipei, 1978): 751–755; Ting Wang, *Hua Kuo-feng Chi Teng-kuei ho hsin ch'i te i-tai* (Hua Kuo-feng, Chi T-kuei and a new generation) (Hong Kong, 1977).

JOHN KONG-CHEONG LEUNG

HUANG HSING (October 25, 1874–October 31, 1916): Revolutionary leader and co-founder of the ROC.

Huang Hsing was born in Shanhua (now Changsha), Hunan, of an educated family who was descendants of Huang T'ing-chien, a noted poet of the Sung dynasty. He received a traditional education and earned a *sheng-yüan* degree before going to Japan for normal school education in 1902. There, he was active in patriotic and anti-Manchu student activities.

After returning to China in June 1903, Huang taught at the Ming-te School in Changsha. In November he organized the Society for the Revival of China for the purpose of overthrowing the Manchu dynasty. After the abortive attempt to capture Changsha the following year, he fled again to Japan.

In 1905 Huang joined with Sun Yat-sen* in establishing the T'ung-meng hui* in Tokyo. The founding of this revolutionary organization was a milestone in the history of the Chinese Republican Revolution. For the first time various independent anti-Manchu groups were united under the complementary leadership of Sun and Huang.

Between Sun Yat-sen's exile following the failure of his revolutionary attempt in 1895 and December 1911, ten weeks after the outbreak of the Wuchang Uprising, Sun stepped on his native soil only once—an overnight stay on the Chinese side of the Sino-Vietnamese border in December 1907. His major contributions were propaganda, organization, and fund-raising abroad. On the other hand, Huang Hsing was an intellectual in charge of military affairs. He was in and out of China at the risk of his life to organize and conduct military campaigns against the Manchus, the most famous one being the Canton Revolution of March 29, 1911.

After the outbreak of the Wuchang Uprising on October 10, 1911, Huang arrived at Wuchang to take up the command of the revolutionary army, defending Hankow and Hanyang. Although the two cities were eventually lost, fifteen provinces were able to secede from the empire during the two major battles of the Republican Revolution.

When the Republic of China* was established with the capital at Nanking in January 1912, Huang Hsing served concurrently as the minister of war and chief of general staff. He exercised predominant power in the government except in matters of finance and foreign affairs, which were personally handled by Provisional President Sun Yat-sen. When Sun resigned the next month, recommending that Yüan Shih-k'ai* be made provisional president, the Nanking government ceased to exist. Huang remained in Nanking as the resident general with supreme administrative and military authority during the transitional period. In June he resigned from the post and began to develop interests in mining, industry, railroads, and party politics.

For all practical purposes, the assassination of Sung Chiao-jen in March 1913 ended the first brief attempt at party politics in the history of China. The subsequent Second Revolution* against Yüan Shih-k'ai failed, and Huang and other revolutionary leaders were exiled to Japan. He left Japan for the United States in July 1914, partly because he was opposed to Sun Yat-sen's dictatorial demands that members of the newly established Chinese Revolutionary party* be loyal and obedient to Sun personally.

During his sojourn in the United States, Huang Hsing observed with keen interest the American democratic system, and continued to engage in propaganda and fund-raising activities against Yüan Shih-k'ai. Having stayed in the United States for nearly two years, he returned to Japan in April 1916 and went to Shanghai in June, shortly after the death of Yüan Shih-k'ai. On October 31, 1916, Huang died of a stomach hemorrhage at the age of forty-two.

Although Huang left no political writings, his political thought can be found in his numerous speeches and statements made during the first years of the Republic. The significance of his role in the Republican Revolution was not fully understood in the West until the 1960s, and it was not until the 1980s that

numerous objective studies on Huang Hsing began to appear on the mainland of China.
REFERENCES: Chün-tu Hsüeh, *Huang Hsing and the Chinese Revolution* (Stanford, Calif., 1961); Chün-tu Hsüeh, ed., *The Chinese Revolution of 1911: New Perspectives* (Hong Kong, 1986); Chün-tu Hsüeh, co-ed., *Huang Hsing hsin-lun* (Essays on Huang Hsing: new perspectives) (China, 1988); Chün-tu Hsüeh, ed., *Revolutionary Leaders of Modern China* (New York, 1971).

CHÜN-TU HSÜEH

HUANGHUAKANG UPRISING (April 27, 1911): The most famous and heroic series of abortive attempts to overthrow the Ch'ing dynasty.

This uprising, like several others before it, was planned and executed by the T'ung-meng hui.[*] It came as a result of Sun Yat-sen's[*] reinvigorated and successful fund-raising efforts in Penang (Malaya) in the fall of 1910. Formulated by Huang Hsing,[*] Chao Sheng, and others, it called for an assault force of 500 men to attack Canton, and, when successful, the attack would supposedly trigger ripple disturbances in other places such as Hunan, Hupeh, and Kiangsi.

The conspirators made their way back to Hong Kong and Canton in preparation for the uprising, which was originally scheduled to take place on April 13, 1911. Drawing on the lessons learned from previous failures, Huang and Chao decided to decentralize their operation. Each team leader was made aware of, and responsible for, only one aspect of the attack, so that in the event of capture by the authorities, none could jeopardize the entire plot. This, as it turned out, proved to be a fatal mistake for the revolutionaries.

As the time for the uprising approached, more than thirty branches of the operation congregated in Canton, some coming from the provinces along the Yangtze River. The attack targets included the governor-general's office and the provincial naval headquarters, and the assault force was increased to 800 men. The operation, however, never materialized as planned. In the first place, the needed weapons and ammunitions did not arrive on time or were delivered in much smaller quantities than expected. The government made matters more difficult for the rebels by putting tight controls over the munitions distributed to the New Army[*] troops, thereby depriving them of a valuable source of arms. Second, Sun Yat-sen's activities in Malaya in the previous year had been reported to Kwangtung's governor-general Chang Ming-ch'i, who was therefore in a state of high alert. Finally, a revolutionary named Wen Sheng-ts'ai had, on his own, assassinated a Manchu official in Canton on April 8. As a result, martial law was declared, additional soldiers were brought in, and house-to-house searches were initiated.

Huang Hsing was unable to enter Canton until April 23. The following two days saw several branches of the operation being discovered and some revolutionaries arrested. Huang had no choice but to postpone further the planned uprising, much to his chagrin. But on April 26 he learned that the soldiers newly transferred to guard the city were in fact sympathetic to the revolutionary cause. He therefore ordered the execution of the plan on the following day.

By 5:30 P.M. on April 27, 1911, the rebels finally began their assault, but with only half the force that was originally planned because of the repeated delays and the suddenness of the decision to attack. Huang Hsing's men managed to breach the defense at the governor-general's office. But they discovered that Chang Ming-ch'i had dug a hole in his back wall and escaped to the provincial naval headquarters of Admiral Li Chun. They therefore followed in hot pursuit. As they approached the naval offices, they ran into a group of city guards commanded by one Wen Tai-hsiung. Wen was summoned by the admiral to protect his offices, but was in fact a revolutionary himself who had planned to attack the Admiralty along with the others. To avoid detection of his scheme, Wen ordered his men not to put on their white armbands to reveal their identity as rebels until the last minute. Unfortunately, Huang Hsing was not aware of the fact that Wen had joined the revolutionaries and, seeing that he had no identifying armbands, opened fire and summarily killed him. The two revolutionary groups then exchanged fierce gunfire, not realizing that they were comrades, until both sides were dispersed. Meanwhile, Huang Hsing was pinned down by overwhelming firepower from government troops. He finally escaped by hiding in a private residence, only to discover that he had lost several fingers in the fierce battle.

Governor-general Chang and Admiral Li also escaped death and capture, because of the lack of coordination among the rebels. The revolutionaries suffered yet another heartbreaking defeat, with over eighty of their most dedicated members dead. Seventy-two of the martyrs were later buried at the Yellow Flower Mound (Huanghuakang), thus giving the operation its famous name, the Huanghuakang Uprising. Even though this uprising ended in failure, its heroism served to awaken the majority of the Chinese to the necessity of revolution. A mere six months later, the successful Wuch'ang Uprising broke out, bringing an end to the last imperial dynasty in China.

REFERENCES: Chün-tu Hsüeh, *Huang Hsing and the Chinese Revolution* (Stanford, Calif., 1961); Li Chien-nung, *The Political History of China, 1840–1928* (Stanford, Calif., 1956).

                                                                                        RICHARD SHEK

HUI-CHOU (WAICHOW) UPRISING (October 1900): The second attempt by Sun Yat-sen to overthrow the Ch'ing dynasty.

The failure of the Reform Movement in 1898 forced Sun Yat-sen[*] into direct competition with the reformers headed by K'ang Yu-wei[*] and Liang Ch'i-ch'ao[*] who, as fugitives from the Manchu court, now intruded into his territory. The reformers were recruiting and raising funds among the same pool of people (overseas Chinese merchants, students, and secret society members) with whom Sun had been associating since he founded his Hsing-Chung hui (Revive China Society[*]) in 1895.

While the two groups did not share identical political philosophies or tactics, they nevertheless maintained close contacts with each other, partly because of some reformers (such as Liang Ch'i-ch'ao and Pi Yung-nien) who were gradually leaning toward revolution, and partly because of Sun Yat-sen, who was naively open-minded and gullible. By the summer of 1900, the debacle of the Boxer Rebellion* and the subsequent eight-nation invasion of Peking convinced both the reformers and the revolutionaries that the time was ripe for some military action against the ruling Manchu government. Maverick reformers under T'ang Ts'ai-ch'ang and Lin Kuei planned their action at Hankow, Tat'ung, and Anking in September, while Sun Yat-sen plotted his second attempt at revolution in Hui-chou, Kwangtung, in October. T'ang and Lin's movement was crushed before it was carried out, owing to K'ang Yu-wei's failure to remit the necessary funds and the discovery of the plan by Governor-general Chang Chih-tung.

Sun's planned uprising fared better, at least initially. Its target was Hui-chou, a town situated to the east of Canton along the East River. The assault force was composed of Hsing-Chung hui members, secret society operatives, and even some Japanese volunteers, under the command of Cheng Shih-liang. Sun directed the entire operation from Taiwan, where he had earlier founded a branch of his Hsing-Chung hui. A particularly noteworthy aspect of the planning was its tacit blessing by the Yamagata government in Japan and the promised support of the Japanese governor of Taiwan. Sun had been cultivating his Japanese contacts ever since his narrow escape in London in 1896, and those efforts seemed to be bearing fruit.

Sun Yat-sen left Yokohama on September 28, 1900, for Taiwan, his first trip there. On October 8, ten days after his arrival in Taipei, the uprising was executed at Hui-chou, as planned. It was a spectacular success, with the rebels taking a district magistrate captive as they advanced toward Canton. Sun was prepared to cross the Strait and enter the mainland to provide further reinforcement, when a totally unexpected hitch to his operation appeared. He had counted on the supply of ammunitions from the Japanese governor in Taiwan, General Kodama Gentaro. At the critical moment, however, General Kodama was unable to deliver the support as promised. In fact, his home government in Japan had prevented him from doing so. The Yamagata administration had just been replaced by a new government headed by Itō Hirobumi, who was adamantly opposed to further Japanese intervention in the Chinese revolutionary movement. As a result, the Hui-chou Uprising ended in failure for lack of reinforcement. A Japanese volunteer by the name of Yamada Yoshimasa (Ryosei), along with others, perished in this event.

The suppression of the Hui-chou Uprising did not end individual acts of heroism, however. On October 26, a twenty-two-year-old revolutionary by the name of Shih Chien-ju attempted to assassinate the governor-general of Kwang-tung, Te-shou, by bombing. This plot also failed, and Shih was martyred.

Because of the proximity of the events in Hankow and in Hui-chou, Sun Yat-sen was now mentioned along with K'ang Yu-wei by the imperial government as its most hated enemy. Overnight, Sun gained much notoriety, even respectability, in China. His equal billing with the "former teacher of the emperor" finally brought him to the center stage of Chinese politics. Another insurrection was planned at Hui-chou in June 1907, but it pales in significance when compared with this earlier one.

REFERENCES: Li Chien-nung, *The Political History of China, 1840–1928* (Stanford, Calif., 1956); Li Yün-han et al., *Min-kuo-shih erh-shih chiang* (Twenty lectures on the history of the Republic) (Yu-shih wen-i, 1976).

RICHARD SHEK

HUNDRED DAY REFORM (*Wu-hsü pien-fa*, June 11–September 21, 1898): The last-ditch effort by the Throne to reform China toward the very end of the nineteenth century.

By early 1898 the need for immediate and fairly extensive reform in China was recognized throughout the realm, a need precipitated by a series of humiliating diplomatic setbacks and outright military defeats suffered at the hands of the imperialist powers. The most serious psychological blow to China was dealt by Japan, its former tributary state, which defeated China in several naval battles in 1894–1895. A sense of national crisis prevailed throughout the empire, prompting scholars and officials, both within and without the government, to search for solutions to the country's predicament.

The clamor for meaningful and fundamental change had actually been gathering momentum since the Self-Strengthening* period, coming from different quarters. Already in the early 1860s Feng Kuei-fen (1809–1874) had suggested in his *Chiao-pin lu k'ang-i* (Protests from the Chiao-pin Studio) that, in addition to emulating the military superiority of the West, China should learn about Western advances in science, education, political organization, and agricultural technology. Feng's views were echoed by others such as Kuo Sung-tao* (1818–1891), Wang T'ao (1828–1897), and Cheng Kuan-ying (1842–1923), who unanimously urged reforms in government administration, taxation, and legal structure.

Another impetus for reform came from a number of enlightened Protestant missionaries, who tried to reach out to China's educated class with something more than the traditional Christian message of salvation. Innovative figures such as Timothy Richard of Great Britain and Young J. Allen of the United States pushed for material and institutional changes in China through publications (such as the *Wang-kuo kung-pao* or the *Globe Magazine*, later renamed *Review of the Times*) and study societies (such as the Kuang-hsüeh hui or the Society for the Diffusion of Christian and General Knowledge among the Chinese*). They made considerable impact on the generation of scholars and officials in the 1880s and 1890s.

Prominent officials in the central bureaucracy, such as Weng T'ung-ho (1830–1914) and Sun Chia-nai (1827–1909), and in the provinces, such as Governor-general Chang Chih-tung (1837–1909) and Governor Ch'en Pao-chen (1831–1900), were all in favor of reform in administration and education. Chang Chih-tung's *Ch'üan-hsüeh p'ien* (Exhortation to Learning), published in the summer of 1898, best reflected the attitude toward reform held by these influential officials. It insisted on a Chinese moral base that could be supplemented, but never supplanted, by Western science and technology. It was a position that even the court, including the emperor and the Empress Dowager Tz'u hsi,* would endorse.

Into this general atmosphere of reform-mindedness stepped K'ang Yu-wei* (1858–1927), a zealous and eccentric scholar from Kwangtung. Though without any official status, K'ang and his associates agitated for reform through petitions (e.g., the Ten Thousand Words Memorial signed by over 1,000 *chin-shih* candidates in 1895), unsolicited memorials, study societies (e.g., Ch'iang-hsüeh hui or the Society for the Study of National Strengthening*), and newspapers (e.g., *Shih-wu pao* or the *Chinese Progress*). Urging the Kuang-hsü Emperor* to model himself after Peter the Great of Russia and the Meiji emperor of Japan, K'ang proposed (1) abolition of the eight-legged essays and revision of the examination system; (2) establishment of a Government Institutions Bureau (Chih-tu chü) and the creation of twelve new bureaus that potentially could replace the existing Six Boards; (3) organization of local people's affairs bureaus throughout the empire; (4) establishment of a parliament and a national assembly; and (5) adoption of a constitution.

On June 11, 1898, the Kuang-hsü Emperor officially made public his commitment to reform by promulgating an edict that exhorted all his subjects to support change and to learn things from abroad, while maintaining their Chinese cultural base. This was followed by more than forty other decrees over the next three months, all issued in rapid succession. The stampede of reform edicts fell into several categories. In education, the hated eight-legged essay in the examinations was abolished, an Imperial University in Peking was approved, modern schools were founded in the provinces, and vocational institutions in mining, agriculture, and industry were created. In government administration, sinecure posts and even some governorships were eliminated, administrative procedures were simplified, and communication channels between the Throne and the people were widened. For the national economy, a sound annual national budget was to be prepared by the Board of Revenues, a Central Bureau of Agriculture, Industry, and Commerce was created, and private enterprise was encouraged.

During those hectic summer months, a deluge of proposals advocating reform in every conceivable area poured in from all segments of society, including unsophisticated commoners and arch-conservatives. This frenzy of activities came to an abrupt end when the empress-dowager regained control of the government through a coup d'état on September 21.

The failure of the Hundred Day Reform has often been blamed on the reactionary empress dowager and her vindictive henchmen who ruthlessly suppressed the idealism of the emperor and his chief adviser K'ang Yu-wei. Yet a critical examination of the records reveals that the empress dowager was not opposed to all reforms and that the policies of the Hundred Days were not as radical as popularly believed. During the height of the reform period, the emperor ordered the wide circulation and discussion of two works—Feng Kuei Fen's *Chiao-pin lu k'ang-i* and Chang Chih-tung's *Ch'üan-hsüeh p'ien*. Both works, it should be emphasized, advocated only selective and controlled changes. Nor was K'ang Yu-wei's role as central as heretofore accepted. Many of his proposals never received imperial consideration or adoption, including those calling for the creation of a parliament and the promulgation of a constitution. He did not have direct access to the emperor; much less was he in daily contact with him. The Hundred Day Reform suffered from a lack of methodical planning and careful coordination, and K'ang's presence in the capital alienated many sympathizers to the reform effort, because many of them could not agree with his scholarship and personality. Overall, the Reform in the summer of 1898 was closer in spirit to the Self-Strengthening Movement than K'ang's radical ideals.

REFERENCES: Hao Chang, "Intellectual Changes and the Reform Movement, 1890–98," in *The Cambridge History of China*, vol. 11, Pt. 2, ed. John K. Fairbank and K. C. Liu (Cambridge, 1980); Chao-ying Fang, "*Wu-hsü pien-fa*," *Journal of Asian Studies* 17 (1957): 99–105; Immanuel C.Y. Hsu, *The Rise of Modern China* (London, 1970); Luke S.Y. Kwong, *A Mosaic of the Hundred Days: Personalities, Politics and Ideas of 1898* (Cambridge, Mass., 1984).

RICHARD SHEK

HUNDRED FLOWERS: The occasional party policy permitting certain intellectuals greater latitude in expressing themselves.

The full phrase, "let a hundred flowers bloom, let a hundred schools contend" (*pai-hua ch'i-fang, pai-chia cheng-ming*), has its roots in the ancient Chou period, and is often abbreviated "double hundred." The slogan is particularly associated with the period from mid–1956 to mid–1957, but it was revived on various other occasions. It never signaled that generalized free speech was to be permitted; rather, it indicated that "proper" intellectuals were to be accorded greater respect and allowed more latitude in their work. The leniency applied particularly to the professional class; it did not benefit those who, though they might be knowledgeable and deep-thinking people, were not classified as "intellectuals" by the party. Whenever "hundred flowers" remained in effect, such intellectuals were exempted from thought reform,* did not need to spend much time in ideological study, and instead were encouraged to hold their own nonpolitical forums. Amateurs and cadres were told to take a back seat to the experts.

The 1956–1957 thaw was heralded by a speech by Chou En-lai* on January 14, 1956, in which it was admitted for the first time that the party's handling of the intellectuals had been defective. "Certain unreasonable features in our present employment and treatment of intellectuals and, in particular, certain sectarian attitudes among some of our comrades towards intellectuals, have . . . handicapped us in bringing the existing powers of the intelligentsia into full play." Chou argued that Communists should have more confidence in the intellectuals, who had made "colossal political advances" and could be trusted. He called for more appropriate work assignments and a more rational promotion system.

On May 2, Mao Tse-tung* made a pronouncement of his own, in which he called for permitting the hundred flowers to bloom. That speech was not published, but it was summarized later in the month by propaganda director Lu Ting-i, who said: "We stand for freedom of independent thinking, of debate, and creative work; freedom to criticize and freedom to express, maintain and reserve one's opinions on questions of art, literature or scientific work." That may have implied that politics and economics was off limits. People were at first very cautious. The party continued to urge intellectuals to speak out, and many of them were enrolled into the party during the year following Mao's speech. The hitherto satellite "democratic parties" grew phenomenally during this period. The Communists promised these groups of intellectuals that "long-term coexistence and mutual supervision" would be practiced, and most of them did indeed begin to act independently.

The most famous pronouncement on the subject of hundred flowers came from Mao on February 28, 1957. It had a remarkably liberal ring to it. Not only would freer speech facilitate the flourishing of the arts and sciences, he said, but it would also indirectly raise the strength and vitality of the Chinese Communist party.* Even when freedom of speech was abused, healthful benefits would accrue. Mao likened the struggle against wrong ideas to a person's being vaccinated; one is healthier after having fought off the few germs that have been placed in the system. While wreckers of the socialist program need not be tolerated, it was not desirable to ban the expression of incorrect ideas. "It is not only futile but very harmful to use crude and summary methods to deal with ideological questions among the people ... You may ban the expression of the ideas, but the ideas will still be there." Furthermore, in the original version of the speech (but not in the version later made public), Mao indicated that political pluralism was not just a matter of tactics, and that there would be independents even in the ultimate stage of communism after the party and state had withered away.

Even with this exhortation, for a number of weeks caution remained the watchword among intellectuals. A major break came in April, however, when the Communist party's long-promised internal Rectification Campaign* was formally launched. In a departure from earlier rectifications, non-Communists were invited to assist the party in the campaign. It was chiefly the politically oriented intellectuals, such as those in the democratic parties, who took advantage of the occasion afforded. Indeed, these groups led the "blooming and contending," with intellectuals in cultural, technical, and business circles involved only to a minor degree. As was later explained by Teng Hsiao-p'ing* (who would lead the counterattack against intellectuals), "The rightists in the various democratic parties functioned as the core of the rightist attackers because the people had granted them a certain political status and they could make use of their positions to issue orders and enlist followers."

Finally, in May, political criticism came in torrents, and much of it was reported in the press. Now, not only "official intellectuals," but also students and others complained about the bureaucratism, party sectarianism, party domination of the government, official lawlessness, unfair treatment of intellectuals, and the naive friendship with the Soviet Union. Among the most outspoken intellectuals were Chang Po-chün (head of the Peasant's and Worker's party, who now advocated a bicameral legislature), Lo Lung-chi (vice-chairman of the Democratic League, who wanted this party to become an opposition party), and Chang Nai-ch'i (vice-chair of the National Construction Association, who challenged the whole concept of reeducating the bourgeoisie).

The leadership was hearing more criticism than it expected or could tolerate. On June 8, the *People's Daily* carried an editorial called "What Is This For," in which it was said that Hundred Flowers had proven to be of no value. Soon, the intellectuals who had spoken out were making "confessions." Some were not contrite enough, however, and fell victim to the Anti-Rightist Campaign.* Many spent decades in prison.

Scholars have debated whether Mao was sincere in wanting freer expression, or whether Hundred Flowers was a trap to expose secretly unreformed intellectuals. The truth may lie somewhere in between. He doubtless believed that most intellectuals supported the new order, but he must have been aware, too, that he might have been wrong and that Hundred Flowers would be a good way to find out.

In the wake of the failure of the Great Leap Forward* and of the perceived need to mobilize the experts to rebuild the economy, the authorities attempted to stimulate a second "blooming and contending" in 1961–1962. After the experience of 1957, however, most nonparty intellectuals remained silent or parroted the official line. One of the more outspoken was the novelist Pa Chin, but even his article on the need for writers to be bold did not exceed party guidelines. The only notable political criticism now came from various officials in charge of propaganda, some of whom criticized the Great Leap and the glorification of Mao Tse-tung. Among those who published dissenting works at this time were Teng T'o, Wu Han, and T'ien Han. They usually wrote in Aesopian language, intended for the cognoscenti, not the masses.

REFERENCES: Merle Goldman, "The Unique 'Blooming and Contending' of 1960–1962," *China Quarterly*, no. 37 (January 1969): 54–83; Roderick MacFarquhar, *The Hundred Flowers* (London, 1960); Roderick MacFarquhar, *The Origins of the Cultural Revolution* (New York, 1974); James D. Seymour, *China's Satellite Parties* (Armonk, N.Y., 1987), chapter 5.

JAMES D. SEYMOUR

HUNG HSIU-CH'ÜAN (January 1, 1814–June 3, 1864): Leader of the Taiping Revolution and Heavenly King of the Taiping Kingdom.

Hung Hsiu-ch'üan was born into a Hakka farming family in Hua-hsien, Kwangtung. From 1828 to 1843 he went to Canton four times to take the civil service examinations. In the fall of 1833 he received a set of religious tracts called "Good Words Exhorting the Age" (*Ch'üan-shih liang-yen*), written by Liang A-fa, a Chinese Christian convert. The next year the Ch'ing* government banned the tracts because of their heterodox teachings.

In 1837 after failing the examination again, Hung, intensely frustrated and angry, fell ill. In delirium he dreamed that he had a curious meeting with God. Following another abortive attempt at passing the examination in 1843, Hung read the tracts again and came to understand the dream as a revelation from God. He was instructed to teach people to worship God and destroy idols. In April 1844 he and Feng Yün-shan,* his cousin and one of his first converts, began to preach but made little progress in Kwangtung and Kwangsi. In November, Hung left Kwangsi, and for two years he devoted his spare time to the writing of tracts at home while continuing to work as a private tutor.

In March 1847, Hung went to Canton to seek instructions in the Bible but failed to obtain baptism from Rev. Issachar J. Roberts (1802–1871), an American missionary. He returned to Kwangsi in July. He was surprised to find that Feng Yün-shan had founded the God Worshippers Society* (Pai Shang-ti hui), whose some 2,000 members recognized Hung as their supreme leader. Greatly encouraged, Hung set out publicly to destroy idols and temples, which resulted in Feng's arrest and in Hung's departure for Kwangtung. In their absence, the God Worshippers Society came under the control of two newly emerged leaders, Yang Hsiu-ch'ing* and Hsiao Ch'ao-kuei,* who represented themselves as earthly spokesmen of God and Jesus, respectively, through the exploitation of local religious belief in spirit possession. Hung and Feng decided to concede Yang and Hsiao's de facto status, and wrote the *T'ai-p'ing t'ien-jih* (Taiping Chronicle). This work for the first time gave a political interpretation of Hung's dream, claiming that God conferred the title "Son of Heaven" on Hung, his second son, and ordered him to cleanse the earth of evils.

On January 1, 1851, the God Worshippers convened in Chin-t'ien, Kwangsi, and Hung Hsiu-ch'üan declared the founding of the T'ai-p'ing t'ien-kuo, the Heavenly Kingdom of Great Peace, and assumed the title of T'ien-wang, or Heavenly King. In September the Taipings* captured the city of Yung-an. Hung conferred new titles of "wang," or King, on the core leaders. On March 19, 1853, the Taipings captured Nanking, which Hung made the capital of his new kingdom. Hung thereafter became even more devoted to his faith, leaving the administration and military campaigns to Yang Hsiu-ch'ing. Yang's power grew even greater, and so did his arrogance. In 1856 rivalry between Yang Hsiu-ch'ing and Wei Ch'ang-hui* erupted into a bloody struggle, which resulted not only in their own deaths but also the departure of Shih Ta-k'ai,* who left with the best troops of the Taipings.

To fill the leadership vacuum, Hung promoted young commanders, Li Hsiu-ch'eng* and Ch'en Yü-ch'eng, to command the Taiping forces. Hung's suspicion of rebellion led him to depend increasingly on his relatives, especially his two brothers, Hung Jen-fa and Hung Jen-ta, and later on his cousin, Hung Jen-kan.* Hung Hsiu-ch'üan's continued lack of interest in administration and practice of nepotism prevented him from creating an effective political leadership. Despite several major victories over the imperial forces, the lack of centralized planning weakened the Taipings considerably. The Taipings' desperate attempt to resist the encirclement by Ch'ing forces under Tseng Kuo-fan[*] and Li Hung-chang[*] collapsed in 1864. On June 3, 1864, Hung Hsiu-ch'üan died of a lingering disease before Nanking was captured by the Hunan Army in July.

REFERENCES: Wang Ch'ing-ch'eng, "Lun Hung Hsiu-ch'üan ti tsao-ch'i ssu-hsiang chi ch'i fa-tsan" (On the development of the early thought of Hung Hsiu-ch'üan), in *T'ai-p'ing t'ien-kuo ti li-shih he ssu-hsiang* (The history and thought of the Heavenly Kingdom of Great Peace) (Peking, 1985): 1–42; Su Hsiang-pi, "Lun Hung Hsiu-ch'üan" (On Hung Hsiu-ch'üan) in *T'ai-p'ing t'ien-kuo jen-wu lun-chi* (Collection of essays on leaders of the Heavenly Kingdom of Great Peace) (Fukien, 1984): 25–54; Tsou Sheng-ch'eng, " 'Ch'üan-shih liang-yen' yü Hung Hsiu-ch'üan tsao-ch'i ti tsung-chiao ssu-hsiang" ("Good Words Exhorting the Age" and the early phase of Hung Hsiu-ch'üan's religious thought) in *T'ai-p'ing T'ien-kuo shih-shih shih-lun* (A study of historical events of the Heavenly Kingdom) (Shanghai, 1984): 14–37.

KAI-WING CHOW

HUNG JEN-KAN (February 18 or 20, 1822–November 23, 1864): Chief-of-staff of the Taiping Revolution.

Hung Jen-kan was a cousin of Hung Hsiu-ch'üan,[*] leader of the Taiping Revolution.[*] He was born into a Hakka, or "guest people," family in Hua County, Kwangtung. He became one of Hung Hsiu-ch'üan's first converts in 1843. In March 1847 he and Hsiu-ch'üan went to Canton to study the Bible under an American Southern Baptist missionary, the Reverend Issachar J. Roberts (1802–1871).

When the Taiping Revolution broke out in Chin-t'ien, Kwangsi, in 1851, Hung made several abortive attempts to join it. In 1853 he went to Hong Kong to study Christianity with the Reverend Theodore Hamberg (1819–1854), and later he worked for the London Missionary Society as catechist and preacher. During his stay in Hong Kong, he sought knowledge of all sorts—about astronomy, medical science, geography, calendrical calculations, and the political, economic, and social conditions of European countries.

In April 1859 Hung finally reached Nanking. He arrived at a time when Hung Hsiu-ch'üan desperately needed someone to revitalize the revolutionary movement in the wake of the coup of 1856 that decimated the Taiping leadership. Hung Jen-kan was rapidly promoted to the position of chief-of-staff (*chün-ssu*) and prime minister, and the title "Kan Wang," or "Shield King," was bestowed on him. To deal with a wide range of political and military problems, Hung Jen-kan submitted to Hung Hsiu-ch'üan his reform proposals, entitled "Tzu-cheng hsin-pien" (New treatise for aid in government). These recommendations called for a restoration of the authority of the central government and strict control over official appointment, promotion, and demotion. The knowledge he attained during his stay in Hong Kong helped him to put the Taiping regime in a world perspective. In his "Tzu-cheng hsin-pien," he proposed that modern means of communication be set up—railroads, highways, postal services, and shipping lines. He also proposed that industries and mining be developed and that modern banks be set up to facilitate trade. But for him the revitalization of the Taipings' religious faith and the correction of their erroneous teachings were essential to resolving the Taipings' problems.

Having no real basis of power within the Taiping bureaucracy, Hung Jen-kan failed to gain support from the loyal king, Li Hsiu-ch'eng.* Li was the most able military commander after 1857, who took offense at Hung's meteoric rise. Nonetheless, in January 1860 Li supported Hung's strategy for breaking up once again the Imperial Great Camp on the southern bank of the Yangtze River under Ho-ch'un and Chang Kuo-liang. After the Ch'ing encampment was broken up, Hung devised a plan for a further military expedition aimed at taking Kiangsu, including Soochow and Shanghai.

Since June 1860, the Ch'ing forces under Tseng Kuo-fan* had laid siege to An-ch'ing. Hung and other leaders strove to break up the encirclement, but they failed to obtain Li Hsiu-ch'eng's cooperation and the city fell in September 1861. Hung Hsiu-ch'üan was infuriated and temporarily stripped Hung Jen-kan of all titles and ranks. From the second half of 1862 on, Hung Hsiu-ch'üan depended increasingly on Li Hsiu-ch'eng's military defense of Nanking, and Hung Jen-kan's role was further reduced. In 1863 when Hung Hsiu-ch'üan sensed the imminent capture of Nanking by the Hunan Army under Tseng Kuo-ch'uan, he made Hung Jen-kan the regent for his son, Hung Fu. Hung Hsiu-ch'üan died in June 1864, and Hung Jen-kan left Nanking before it fell; he escaped to Shih-ch'eng, Kiangsi, where he was seized on October 9. He was executed on November 23.

REFERENCES: Hsü Hsü-tien and Ma Ta-cheng, "Lun Hung Jen-kan ko-hsin ssu-hsiang ti hsing-ch'eng chi ch'i li-shih ti-wei" (On the formation and historical significance of the reform ideas of Hung Jen-kan), in *T'ai-p'ing t'ien-kuo shih lun-wen chi* (Kwangtung, 1983): 325–349; Su Hsiang-pi, "Lun Hung Jen-kan chi ch'i hsin-cheng" (On Hung Jen-kan and his new policies), in *T'ai-p'ing t'ien-kuo jen-wu lun-chi* (Collection of essays on leaders of the Heavenly Kingdom of Great Peace) (Fukien, 1984): 209–240; Lu Yao, "Lun Hung Jen-kan" (On Hung Jen-kan), in *T'ai-p'ing t'ien-kuo shih lun-wen hsüan* (Selected essays on the history of the Heavenly Kingdom of Great Peace) (Peking, 1981): 1106–1128; S. Y. Teng, "Hung Jen-kan, Prime Minister of the Taiping Kingdom and His Modernization Plans," *United College Journal* 8 (1970–1971):87–95.

KAI-WING CHOW

HURLEY, PATRICK JAY (January 8, 1883–July 30, 1963): Army general, lawyer, businessman, statesman, and ambassador to China.

Born in Choctaw, Indian Territory (Oklahoma), Hurley was awarded a law degree from George Washington University in 1913 and was married to Ruth Wilson in 1919. He served as secretary of war in the Herbert Hoover administration (1929–1933), ambassador to New Zealand in 1942, and personal representative of President Franklin D. Roosevelt to Moscow in 1942 and to the Middle East, China, and the Teheran Conference in 1943. In September 1944 he undertook his most significant mission as Roosevelt's personal representative, and later, as ambassador to China. He resigned his China post on November 27, 1945, and remained active in Republican politics, running unsuccessfully for a New Mexico Senate seat three times. He also became interested in mining projects, particularly uranium, during the 1950s until his death in Santa Fe in 1963.

In April 1944 Japan launched the Ichigo Offensive and wiped out airfields in southeast China. Attempting to prevent the collapse of the Nationalist resistance, General Joseph W. Stilwell,* the commander of U.S. forces in China and Generalissimo Chiang Kai-shek's* chief-of-staff, suggested that he be authorized to command all Chinese, including Communist, forces. Roosevelt made the demand to Chiang, who in turn suggested that the president send a personal emissary to discuss the proper terms. Hurley was selected for the task. Unlike other "China hands" in Chungking, Hurley lacked the experience and knowledge regarding China prior to his assignment. His only advantage was that he had made a favorable impression on both Stilwell and the generalissimo during his trip to Chungking in November 1943, while he was sent to China to invite Chiang Kai-shek to the Cairo Conference (November 22–26, 1943).

Hurley's immediate task was to mediate the differences between Stilwell and Chiang, but he interpreted his ultimate mission as that of attaining the unification of all Chinese military and political groups under the leadership of Chiang Kai-shek. Failing to perceive the complexity behind the Chiang–Stilwell quarrel, Hurley was impressed by the generalissimo's willingness to cooperate and by the general's abrasiveness. Consequently, he sided with Chiang in demanding Stilwell's recall. Then he took upon himself the task of mediating the conflict of the Nationalists and the Communists. To implement Washington's policy of averting a civil war in China, he pushed both sides to compromise and organize a coalition government.

The animosity and mutual distrust between the Communists and the Nationalists proved to be deeper than Hurley had comprehended. The negotiations between the two advisories were conducted on and off in Chungking throughout Hurley's tenure in China without any concrete agreement. The Nationalists insisted that the integration of Communist forces into a unified national army should proceed while planning of the reorganization of the government was underway. The Communists, on the other hand, were by no means willing to hand over their military forces until their political power was secured through a genuine coalition government. Moreover, after decades of power struggle, the ultimate goal of both parties was to eliminate the other and control all of China, which made the U.S. goal unattainable and Hurley's task impossible.

Hurley's mediation was complicated by the controversy between the ambassador and other U.S. representatives, especially career diplomats such as John S. Service,* John P. Davies, George Atcheson, and Raymond Ludden—the "China hands" from the State Department. During the course of his mediation, Hurley became more and more a partisan of the Nationalists since he was convinced that Chiang was indispensable if the United States wanted a united, democratic, pro-U.S. China. He believed that if the Communists had no hope of receiving outside assistance, they would be more inclined to make concessions.

He therefore worked to secure Stalin's promise of no assistance to the Communists and resisted stubbornly the pleas to grant U.S. aid to the Communists.

The China hands, on the other hand, were convinced that the Communists would prevail in the power struggle. Fear that a Communist victory might result in the expansion of Soviet influence in China, they urged Washington to extend its aid to the Communists. They reasoned that to strengthen the Communists through U.S. assistance not only would expedite the defeat of Japan but would also force Chiang Kai-shek to be more conciliatory regarding a coalition government.

Supported by Roosevelt and his successor, President Harry S Truman, Hurley's position prevailed and all those who opposed him were eventually removed from their China assignments. However, Hurley failed to bring about a coalition government in China. On November 27, 1945, an angry Hurley resigned in public, claiming that Communist agents within the U.S. government had undermined his peace efforts. Historians blamed his removal of the embassy staffs and his resignation charges for initiating the purge of the China hands that peaked during the McCarthyist era.

REFERENCES: Russell D. Buhite, *Patrick J. Hurley and American Foreign Policy* (Ithaca, N.Y., 1973); William P. Head, *America's China Sojourn* (New York, 1983); Don Lohbeck, *Patrick J. Hurley* (Chicago, 1956); Michael Schaller, *The U.S. Crusade in China, 1938–1945* (New York, 1979).

SU-YA CHANG

I

IRON AND BLOOD SOCIETY (T'ieh-hsüeh hui): Revolutionary organization in northern China and Manchuria, 1907–1912.

This clandestine organization first appeared as a patriotic society at the height of the Russo-Japanese War (1904–1905) in Manchuria and was known as the K'ang-o t'ieh-hsüeh hui (Resist-Russia Iron and Blood Society). The aims of the society, according to Ting K'ai-chang, one of its founders, were to organize students, soldiers, and bandits against the Russian aggressors in northeast China. In 1905 Ting K'ai-chang and Ting Tung-ti turned their attention to the capital area and set up an organization known as the Chiu-ming chün (Life-saving Army) at Changkiakow (Chang-chia-k'ou, Hopei). As elaborated in its declaration, the Chiu-ming chün was formed to save the life of China and its people. But its programs, ranging from abolition of the civil service examination to formation of a constitutional government, were reformist in nature. Ting K'ai-chang joined the T'ung-meng hui* in 1906. The next year he organized an anti-Ch'ing association called the Pei chen-wu she (Northern Military Revival Society) at Yingkow, Manchuria. With the support of Ting Tung-ti and Huang Chi-lung, Ting K'ai-chang expanded the organization and renamed it the T'ieh-hsüeh hui.

The T'ieh-hsüeh hui represented one of the early forms of the revolutionary party in twentieth-century China. It was basically a traditional secret society with a revolutionary program. While radical intellectuals from Chihli (Hopei), Honan, Hupeh, and Shantung provided the leadership, most of its members were from the lower class, particularly the northeastern bandits. Of the two revolutionary goals, the members were more interested in the anti-Manchu cause than in republicanism. Anti-Manchuism in fact formed the common bond tying members of different regions together. But regionalism and personal loyalty remained the major organizational weaknesses. There was little party discipline. The rules and rituals of secret societies were generally observed. Revolutionary propaganda was spread in the traditional way. People were usually invited to watch a classical drama played on a makeshift stage in a temple. After the show came revolutionary speeches and recruitment of new members.

Like the Kuang-fu hui (Recovery Society), the T'ieh-hsüeh hui advocated the subversive tactics of military uprisings and terrorism. According to Ting K'ai-chang, four regional armies known as the T'ieh-hsüeh chün (Iron and Blood Army) were organized. In addition, there were assassination units. In 1911 the society boasted of a total fighting force of 95,000. One of the plans was to start an uprising in Peking on October 17, 1911, when most of the metropolitan army would be shifted to Kaiping and Luanchow for the autumn maneuvers. The T'ieh-hsüeh chün in Manchuria and other regions would rise simultaneously after the eruption in the capital. Their plan was disrupted by the sudden outbreak of the Wuchang mutiny (October 10), for the Ch'ing government had canceled the maneuvers on October 13.

As the battle between the revolutionaries and the Ch'ing Army raged in Wuhan, Li Yüan-hung,[*] the military governor of Hupeh, commissioned Hu O-kung (leader of the Kung-ho hui, another revolutionary organization in northern China) to meet with Ting K'ai-chang at Tientsin to form a Ko-ming lien-ho hui (United Revolutionary Association). Thereafter, members of the T'ieh-hsüeh hui and the Kung-ho hui (Republic Society) fought side by side against the imperial army in northern China. From November 1911 to January 1912 the T'ieh-hsüeh chün played an important role in a series of abortive uprisings in Changkiakow, Peking, Luanchow, and Tungchow. In the same period Huang Chi-lung led an assassination team against Huang Huai-ching, the Ch'ing military commander in Tientsin. The plot ended in failure. Many members joined the Ching-Chin T'ung-meng hui (the Peking–Tientsin branch of the T'ung-meng hui) after its formation on December 1, 1911. In early 1912 Ting K'ai-chang reorganized the society under the name of Peiyang T'ieh-hsüeh hui (Iron and Blood Society of the Northern Oceans) and prepared to start a new wave of uprisings in northern China. It was a futile effort because the abdication of the emperor on February 12, 1912, temporarily put an end to the revolutionary war. Ting K'ai-chang disbanded the armies of the Peiyang T'ieh-hsüeh hui afterward. He lived in retirement, while some of the former members joined the Kuomintang (Nationalist party) under Sung Chiao-jen's[*] leadership.

REFERENCES: Hu O-kung, *Hsin-hai ko-ming pei-fang shih-lu* (An account of the 1911 Revolution in northern China) (Shanghai, 1948); Ting K'ai-chang, "Hsin-kai ko-ming shih-ch'i ti T'ieh-hsüeh hui" (The Iron and Blood Society during the period of the 1911 Revolution), *Chin-tai shih tzu-liao* (Materials on modern history), No. 2 (1955): 22–31; Chang K'ai-yüan et al., *Hsin-hai ko-ming shih* (A history of the 1911 Revolution), vol. 3 (Peking 1981): 155–189.

HENRY Y.S. CHAN

K

K'ANG YU-WEI (March 19, 1858–March 31, 1927): Reformer and philosopher best known for his participation in the Hundred Day Reform of 1898.

A native of Nan-hai County in Kwangtung, K'ang Yu-wei has been ranked among a small coterie of Cantonese who had a large influence on national politics in late Ch'ing* China. The others include Hung Hsiu-ch'üan,* leader of the Taiping Revolution,* and Sun Yat-sen,* leader of the revolutionary movement that finally brought an end to China's imperial system.

Born into a family of local prominence, K'ang received most of his early schooling from his paternal grandfather, a scholar of considerable erudition. According to his own recollection, K'ang was a child prodigy gifted in literary skills. He also aspired to be a sage in the traditional mold. Supremely confident of his moral and intellectual superiority, he took it upon himself to save the world and to alleviate the suffering of the masses. During the first twenty years of his life, K'ang Yu-wei steeped himself in traditional studies, which included the classics, history, neo-Confucian works, Buddhist and Taoist texts, and, of course, poetry and examination essays. After 1879, however, his travels to Hong Kong and Shanghai opened his eyes to Western learning; he was deeply impressed with the orderliness and efficiency of these two cities influenced by the West. He began to read widely all available works in translation on Western science and politics, incorporating the knowledge he gained thereby into his program for reform and modernization of China.

K'ang's vision required nothing short of the total transformation of Chinese polity and society, made necessary by his perception that without it China would not survive as a nation in the modern world. His argument for reform was buttressed by his ingenious reinterpretation of the Confucian tradition. He first sought to separate authentic Confucianism from the millennia-old state orthodoxy by asserting, through his New Text scholarship, that it was the Old Text forgeries of the philosopher Liu Hsin (ca. 46 B.C.–23 A.D.) that gave Confucianism its authoritarian and obscurantist bent. This explanation of the purported distortion of the Confucian teaching was outlined in his *Hsin-hsüeh wei-ching k'ao* (A study of the forged classics of the Hsin period), completed in 1891. Next, K'ang Yu-wei advanced the theory that Confucius himself was actually a bold innovator who relied on the authority of an imagery past to put forth his vision for a new age. In his *K'ung-tzu kai-chih k'ao* (A study of Confucius as a reformer), published in 1896, K'ang tried to show that change, not stagnation, was inherent in the Confucian tradition. This radical reappraisal of Confucianism as intrinsically progressive and modern earned for K'ang both ardent admirers and determined detractors.

But it was China's humiliating defeat in the Sino-Japanese War of 1894–1895[*] that finally thrust K'ang into the political limelight. In Peking for the last of his several tries for the highest level of the civil service examinations, he became the leader of over 1,000 provincial graduates gathered there when he drafted the celebrated "Ten Thousand Words Memorial" on their behalf to protest the terms of peace with Japan and to call for fundamental changes in the government. Subsequently, he also organized study societies and published newspapers to propagate his reform proposals.

Meanwhile, the Kuang-hsü emperor[*] had been won over by the arguments for reform. On June 11, 1898, he issued the famous decree that inaugurated the Hundred Day Reform.[*] K'ang Yu-wei was granted an imperial audience on June 16 and was appointed a secretary in the Tsungli Yamen to assist in the reform efforts. His involvement in this movement has been a subject of debate among historians. Most historians, relying primarily on K'ang's own accounts, see him as the mastermind of the entire operation, constantly giving advice and guidance to the emperor. Others, examining the records with a more critical eye, view his role as more peripheral.

In any event, the Hundred Day Reform came to an abrupt end with the Empress Dowager Tz'u-hsi's[*] coup d'état on September 21. K'ang was forced to flee China, but his younger brother and five other reformers were arrested and executed. While in exile, K'ang became an avid world traveler for the next two decades, circumnavigating the globe three times and visiting over thirty countries in four continents. He also founded the Pao-huang hui[*] (Emperor Protection Society), with branches in North America and Southeast Asia. His unfailing loyalty to the Kuang-hsü Emperor[*] brought him into direct competition with Sun Yat-sen's revolutionary camp, which worked toward the complete overthrow of the Manchu regime. K'ang did attempt one abortive armed uprising in the summer of 1900, but its purpose was to rescue the emperor from his stepmother, not to start a revolution.

K'ang's faith in the monarchy never wavered, even after the premature death of the Kuang-hsü Emperor in 1908 and the establishment of the Republic in 1912. Indeed, it was this lingering attachment to the imperial system that prompted him to participate in the farcical attempt in 1917 to restore the last Manchu emperor to the throne. K'ang increasingly found himself an anachronist in republican China. In the twilight of his life, he devoted himself to astronomical studies and utopian dreams, two subjects he had explored in his youth during the 1880s. He died a solitary man in Tsingtao, Shantung, away from relatives and friends.

REFERENCES: Hao Chang, *Chinese Intellectuals in Crisis: Search for Order and Meaning, 1890–1911* (Berkeley, Calif., 1987); Kung-ch'uan Hsiao, *A Modern China and a New World: K'ang Yu-wei, Reformer and Utopian, 1858–1927* (Seattle, Wash., 1975); Luke S.K. Kwong, *A Mosaic of the Hundred Days: Personalities, Politics, and Ideas of 1898* (Cambridge, Mass., 1984); Jung-pang Lo, ed. and trans., *K'ang Yu-wei: A Biography and a Symposium* (Tucson, Ariz., 1967).

RICHARD SHEK

KAO KANG (1905–August 1954): Chinese Communist guerrilla leader in northern Shensi area; top official in northeast China; State Planning Commission chairman; Politburo member.

Kao Kang was born in Hengshan, northern Shensi Province, in 1905. He studied at Yülin Middle School; influenced by Communist instructors, he joined the Socialist Youth League. In 1926 he joined the Chinese Communist party[*] and entered Chungshan Military Academy, established by the warlord Feng Yü-hsiang.[*] Among Kao's instructors were Liu Chih-tan and Teng Hsiao-p'ing.[*] After the collapse of the First Nationalist-Communist United Front in mid-1927, Feng suppressed the Communists at the academy and throughout Shensi. In 1928, after the abortive Weihua Uprising led by Liu Chih-tan, Kao and Liu were assigned by the Communist party to spread propaganda and to infiltrate Nationalist units in Shensi and Kansu. In late 1932 they joined their guerrilla forces with remnants of the Twenty-fourth Red Army to form the Twenty-sixth Red Army. Kao served as political commissar of the Forty-second Division of the Twenty-sixth Red Army. After a defeat east of Sian, the Twenty-sixth Red Army moved to central Shensi and the Kansu border. Under pressure from hostile warlords, however, Liu and Kao shifted to northern Shensi, which was loosely controlled by warlord Ching Yueh-hsiu. By the spring of 1935 a Shensi–Kansu soviet regime had been established, with headquarters at Wayaopao, and Kao had become vice-chairman of the Northwest Revolutionary Military Council and political commissar of the General Front Command.

In the summer of 1935 Hsü Hai-tung's Twenty-fifth Red Army arrived in Shensi from the Hupeh-Hunan-Anhwei (O-yü-wan) Soviet Area and joined the Shensi forces to form the Fifteenth Army Group. Kao became director of the Political Department of this army. Soon after the arrival of some Communist Central Committee members at Wayaopao, a power struggle erupted; Liu and Kao, the top local leaders, were imprisoned and charged with deviation from the party line. When Mao Tse-tung[*] and the central leadership reached northern Shensi in October 1935, they ordered Liu and Kao's release to bring about a semblance of unity between the "central" faction and the local leaders. Kao was then made political commissar of the Army Group.

After Liu's death in combat in April 1936, Kao emerged as the leading Shensi

Communist. He served as secretary of the North Shensi Provincial Committee and commander of the Shensi–Kansu–Ninghsia (Shen-Kan-Ning)* Border Region's Peace Preservation Corps. During the wartime period (1937–1945), Kao was secretary of the party's Committee for the Shen-Kan-Ning Border Region and of the Central Committee's Northwest Bureau. This second position gave Kao the power to help Mao purge Wang Ming's* International Group. During the Rectification Movement* in 1942, Mao spoke highly of Kao. He stated: "I came to Shensi five or six years ago, yet I cannot compare with comrades like Kao Kang in my knowledge of conditions here or in my relations with people of this region. No matter what progress I make in investigation and research, I shall always be somewhat inferior to the northern Shensi cadres." The 1943 directive, entitled "Summation of the Experience of the Northwest Bureau's High-Ranking Conference," also extolled Kao for pursuing "a correct line" and condemned Wang Ming as a "sectarian."

At the Seventh Party Congress in April 1945, Kao was elected a member of the Central Committee and the Politburo—a spectacular rise for a Shensi cadre. In the civil war* period (1945–1949), Kao served as second secretary of the Northeast Bureau and deputy commander and deputy political commissar of the Northeast Military Region. He was a major leader in the war of liberation in the region. By mid–1949 Kao had become secretary of the Northeast Bureau, commander and political commissar of the Northeast Military Region, and chairman of the Northeast People's government. Kao was the only regional leader to be a vice-chairman of the Central People's Government Council from 1949 to 1954. In November 1951 he also became a vice-chairman of the People's Revolutionary Military Council. To undercut Kao's growing power, Mao transferred him to Peking to take the new post of chairman of the State Planning Commission, after the November 1952 meeting of the Central People's Government Council. In August 1954, purged in a power struggle with Mao and other senior leaders, Kao reportedly "upheld his erroneous standpoint" and "committed suicide as an ultimate betrayal of the Party."

The fall of the Kao Kang-Jao Shu-shih Antiparty Clique in February 1954 was attributed to the following causes: (1) Kao's theory of two parties stated that the party of the revolutionary bases and army should prevail over the party of the white (Nationalist-controlled) areas; (2) being a leading cadre in the first party, Kao desired to replace Liu Shao-ch'i* and Chou En-lai,* who had spent much time in the white areas and occupied the very posts to which he aspired: vice-chairman of the party and premier of the state; (3) Kao regarded his northeast region as an independent kingdom; (4) Kao's separate trade agreement with the Soviet Union in July 1949, which gave the Soviets extensive rights in northeast China, was proof of his "illicit relations with foreign countries"; and (5) Kao and Jao (east China regional leader), in opposition to the Maoist group, demanded preferential treatment for northeast and east China in the allocation of economic resources. In April 1955, eight months after Kao's suicide, Teng Hsiao-p'ing, general secretary of the party, led the official attack against Kao and Jao at the Fifth Plenum of the Seventh Party Congress.

REFERENCES: Howard L. Boorman and Richard Howard, eds., *Biographical Dictionary of Republican China*, vol. 2 (New York, 1968): 233–235; *Chung-kung tang-shih chien-ming tz'u-tien* (A concise dictionary of the Chinese Communist party's history), vol. 2 (Peking, 1987): 862; Donald W. Klein and Anne B. Clark, *Biographical Dictionary of Chinese Communism*, vol. 1 (Cambridge, Mass., 1971): 431–436; Richard C. Thornton, *China: A Political History, 1917–1980* (Boulder, Colo., 1982).

JOSEPH K.S. YICK

KIANGSI SOVIET REPUBLIC: Government established by the Chinese Communists in Kiangsi in 1931–1934.

The Chinese Soviet Republic (1931–1934), commonly known as the Kiangsi Soviet Republic, was proclaimed by the First National Soviet Congress at Juichin, Kiangsi Province, on November 7, 1931. Following the breakdown of the CCP–KMT United Front in 1927, the Chinese Revolution was carried out on two fronts: the urban revolution under the policy of military insurrections, which was implemented in the forms of the Nanchang Uprising* (August 1, 1927); and the Canton Commune* (December 11, 1927). The other revolutionary line was to establish the rural bases in Kiangsi–Hunan border areas which would foster the model of the rural revolution in China.

When the First National Soviet Congress was convened in Juichin, Kiangsi, on November 7, 1931, the Chinese Soviet Republic consisted of seven large soviet areas: Central Area, West Fukien, Hunan–Anhwei Border, Hunan–Kiangsi Border, Northeast Hunan–Hupeh–Kiangsi, Western Hunan–Hupeh Border, and Hainan Island. An official report of the Chinese Soviet Republic at the time of its First Congress claimed that the territorial bases of the soviet comprised approximately 300 *hsien*, scattered in eleven provinces of the eighteen provinces of China at the time. This was estimated at one-sixth of the area of China proper. The total population within the soviet areas, according to the same source, was more than 60 million.

The structure and function of the Kiangsi Soviet Republic was modeled after the Soviet Union's system of government, which was established after the Bolshevik Revolution on November 7, 1917. The soviet (meaning the council of people's deputies) system of government was organized at the provincial, *hsien* (county), *ch'ü* (district), and *hsiang* (town) level, and the organizational principle of the government was based on the concept of democratic centralism.* However, the organizational principles were not uniformly implemented at the local level owing largely to the blockade of the KMT Army as well as to the Five Encirclement Campaigns* that the KMT government carried out to exterminate the Chinese Communists.

The Kiangsi Soviet Republic collapsed in October 1934 when the Central Committee of the Chinese Communist party* and the central government decided to take the Long March* in order to break the encirclement of the KMT Army.

The First National Congress of the Chinese Soviet Republic had more than 600 deputies representing Red Army units, the National General Labor Union, and the major soviet areas, except the Oyüwan Soviet area, where the Oyüwan

Soviet government held its Second Congress simultaneously. The First National Congress established a Provisional Central Soviet government at Juichin and elected a Central Executive Committee of sixty-three men as the supreme authority between sessions of the national soviet congresses, which were to be held every two years. The executive committee in turn elected Mao Tse-tung* as its chairman and Hsiang Ying and Chang Kuo-t'ao* as vice-chairmen. A Council of People's Commissars (cabinet), headed by the same three men, was created as the top executive body. Its other commissars included Chu Teh,* chairman of the Revolutionary Military Council; Hsiang Ying, commissar of labor; Teng Tzu-hui, commissar of finance; Ch'ü Ch'iu-pai,* commissar of education; Ho Shu-heng, commissar of the procuracy; and Wang Chia-hsiang, commissar of foreign affairs. Mao Tse-tung and his followers controlled this government, but the Russian Returned Students, the so-called internationalists, gradually assumed more and more control over governmental and military affairs as well as the party machinery in the soviet areas.

The Second National Congress of the Chinese Soviet Congress was convened in Juichin, January 22 to February 1, 1934. The Russian Returned student leadership controlled the elections, in contrast to the First National Congress elections, which were held at township, district, county, and provincial levels. Mao, chairman of the Central Soviet government, made the principal report on the work of the Central Executive Committee since 1931. Reports were also made by Chu Teh on the Red Army, by Lin Po-sh'ü on the economy, and by Wu Liang-p'ing on soviet construction. A minor revision of the Construction of the Chinese Soviet Republic was passed by the Second National Congress, and major changes were made in the composition of the Central Soviet government.

Some 693 deputies, 83 alternates, and 1,500 observers from as far away as Manchuria, Korea, and Indochina attended and elected a new Central Executive Committee of the Second National Congress which consisted of 175 members and 36 alternates. The new executive committee included only 32 of the 36-member executive committee which was elected at the First National Congress, thus adding 143 new members which included Ch'in Pang-hsien (Po Ku)* and Chang Wen-t'ien (Lo Fu).* Mao was reelected chairman of the Central Executive Committee and Chang Kuo-t'ao and Hsiang Ying vice-chairmen. Mao's authority was curtailed as the seventeen-member Presidium was created as a standing committee of the Central Executive Committee. When the Council of People's Commissars (the cabinet), the executive arm of the Central Executive Committee, was elected, Chang Wen-t'ien replaced Mao as its chairman, thus diminishing Mao's power considerably. Only three former commissars or chairmen were reelected: Wang Chia-hsiang for foreign affairs, Chu Teh for the Revolutionary Military Council, and Ch'ü Ch'iu-pai for education. In addition, several new commissars were appointed. Thus, an attempt by the Russian Returned group to control the Central Soviet government began sometime in 1933, and the power struggle between the Maoists and the internationalists continued throughout the Long March.

REFERENCES: Ilpyong Kim, *The Politics of Chinese Communism: Kiangsi under the Soviets* (Berkeley, Calif., 1973); Trygve Lötveit, *Chinese Communism, 1931–1934: Experience in Civil Government* (Lund, Sweden, 1973); Derek J. Waller, *The Kiangsi Soviet Republic: Mao and the National Congresses of 1931 and 1934* (Berkeley, Calif., 1973).

ILPYONG KIM

KO-LAO HUI (Elder Brother Society): Secret society active in the nineteenth and twentieth centuries.

The Ko-lao Hui (Elder Brother Society) probably emerged along with the T'ien-ti Hui (Heaven and Earth Society) and the Pai-lien Chiao (White Lotus Sect) when Ming loyalists went underground to form or join secret organizations by which to continue their fight against the Ch'ing. Geographically, the Ko-lao Hui began in western China, in either Szechwan or Kweichow. The main vehicle for the society's expansion into the Yangtze Valley appears to have been Tseng Kuo-fan's* Hunan Army. One estimate puts some 30 to 40 percent of new peasant recruits in Tseng's army as Ko-lao Hui members. When the Hunan Army disbanded, these former soldiers, soon bored with the quiet life in the villages and craving the travel and excitement they had known in military service, ventured into the cities along the Yangtze and proceeded to recruit merchants and artisans into the society. Well-to-do persons joined the Ko-lao Hui to protect their possessions. As a result of these recruitment efforts, during the last fifty years of the Ch'ing dynasty,* the Ko-lao Hui became the predominant secret society in central China.

Organizationally, the Ko-lao Hui appears to have had a loose network with no single headquarters or leader. Individual units or cells, located throughout central China, wove themselves into the fabric of Chinese society. A chief dragon head (*cheng lung-t'ou*) led each lodge (*t'ang*), with numerous officers serving under his authority. Each society applicant was required to have a Ko-lao Hui sponsor and to undergo an initiation ceremony that consisted of taking a blood oath of loyalty. There was also an elaborate system of hand and body movements by which members identified themselves.

The Ko-lao Hui were anti-Manchu, but as was true of many other secret societies, they were too dispersed, too loosely organized, and too enmeshed in the existing political system to be the leading force in the drive to oust the Ch'ing. This is not to say, however, that their activities are not noteworthy. They are.

In 1870 and 1871 the Ko-lao Hui engaged in uprisings in several districts in Hunan. The primary motivating factor appears to have been social and economic malaise. In 1891 the Ko-lao Hui fomented anti-Western riots in the lower and middle Yangtze. This activity was designed to put the Manchu government in a difficult position by antagonizing the foreign powers. In the summer of 1900 dissident literati recruited a large Ko-lao Hui army in Hunan and Hupeh for an attempted revolt against the Ch'ing court.

In 1904 Huang Hsing* prepared for his Hua-hsing hui (China Revival Society)* revolt by mobilizing a Ko-lao Hui force for the insurrection at Changsha. Although detected and suppressed, this endeavor engendered more anti-Ch'ing sentiment within the society. This additional hostility manifested itself in December 1906 in the P'ing-Liu-Li uprising. This massive antigovernment uprising occurred along the Hunan–Kiangsi border. Tactics utilized by the Ko-lao Hui in this adventure included such guerrilla techniques as insuring rapid mobility by carrying only minimal supplies and using crack marksmen to guard their rear during a retreat. Finally, suppressed by government armies from four provinces, this revolt cost the Ko-lao Hui much of their political vitality in central China.

Given this fact, is it not surprising that the Ko-lao Hui did not play a leading role in the 1911 Revolution,[*] despite some assertions to the contrary? To be sure, the society was active in aiding the T'ung-meng hui[*] in occupying several towns and cities in Szechwan. The Ko-lao Hui provided a similar service in Canton and Sian, but to credit the society with any sort of leadership in the Republican Revolution is a bit excessive. During the Second Revolution[*] of 1913, when the Kuomintang tried to rise against Yüan Shih-k'ai,[*] the Ko-lao Hui also reportedly provided troops with which to attack the general from the west.

In addition to providing assistance to the Nationalists, the Ko-lao Hui had links with the Chinese Communist party.[*] Several well-known Communist personalities, including Chu Teh,[*] Wu Yü-chang, Liu Chih-tan, and Ho Lung, were highly placed in the society. Chu had joined the Ko-lao Hui in Szechwan in 1911 and had risen to become a dignitary. He even credited the society with the idea of the cell system of organization that was utilized by both the Nationalists and the Communists. Wu, who also joined the society in Szechwan, was, at some point, elected a "Great Elder." Liu, one of the founders of the soviet in north China prior to the Long March,[*] was an "exemplary member" of the Ko-lao Hui. And Ho, whose father had been a reknowned leader in the society, supposedly inherited this prestige. Ho Lung's rank and fame in the Ko-lao Hui were such, according to one source, that he could enlist an entire society lodge into the People's Liberation Army.[*]

Mao Tse-tung[*] was apparently not a member of the Ko-lao Hui, but he thought very highly of its revolutionary virtues. In 1936 he wrote an appeal to the society in which he attempted to forge a connection between the anti-Ch'ing nationalism of the Ko-lao Hui and the anti-Japanese nationalism of the Chinese Communist party. Mao's missive ended with a spirited call to "Let the Ko-lao Hui and the whole of the Chinese people unite to strike at Japan and to restore China!"

REFERENCES: Hirayama Shū, *Chung-kuo pi-mi she-hui shih* (History of secret societies in China) (Shanghai, 1912); Charlton M. Lewis, "Some Notes on the Ko-lao Hui in Late Ch'ing China," in Jean Chesneaux, ed., *Popular Movements and Secret Societies in China 1840–1950* (Stanford, Calif., 1972); T'ai-ch'u Liao, "The Ko-lao Hui in Szechwan," *Pacific Affairs* (June 1947); T'ao Ch'eng-chang, "Chiao-hui yüan-liu k'ao" (Origins of the societies and sects) in *Hsin-hai ko-ming* (1911 Revolution), vol. 3 (Shanghai, 1957).

GERALD W. BERKLEY

KU WEI-CHÜN (known in the West as Wellington Koo, January 29, 1888–November 15, 1985): China's premier diplomat in the early twentieth century; served as ambassador to England, France, the United States, the League of Nations, and the United Nations.

Born in Chia-ting, Kiangsu, of an affluent family with holdings in Shanghai, Ku attended Western-style schools in the Shanghai area, graduating from St. John's Academy (later University) in 1908. That year he went to the United States where, after spending one year at Cook Academy in upstate New York, he entered Columbia University. Upon graduation from college, he entered the graduate program at Columbia in political science, earning both M.A. and Ph.D. degrees. His Ph.D. dissertation, *The Status of Aliens in China*, was published by Columbia University Press in 1912.

During his student years Ku was extremely active in extracurricular activities, serving as editor of the *Columbia Daily Spectator*, as the manager of the *Columbian*, the school yearbook, and as president of the Chinese Students Alliance of the Eastern States. He was later elected national president of that organization, in which capacity he first met T'ang Shao-yi.*

Upon returning to China in May 1912, Ku was briefly the English-language secretary of President Yüan Shih-k'ai* and the cabinet. The next month Ku married the third daughter of T'ang Shao-yi, T'ang Mei. In 1913 he was appointed councilor in the Foreign Ministry. In 1915 Ku was appointed the Chinese minister to the United States and Cuba. He was extremely successful as a diplomat, and Yale University awarded him an honorary LL.D. degree in 1916. Near the end of 1918, his wife was carried off by influenza, and he then returned to China.

In January 1919 Ku was a member of the Chinese delegation to the Paris Peace Conference which ended World War I. He played a significant role in the handling of the Shantung question and the final decision to refuse to sign the resulting Treaty of Versailles because it transferred Germany's treaty rights to Japan. While in Paris, Ku was one of the representatives of the ''minor states'' that developed the League Covenant, and he represented China at the first meeting of the League of Nations Assembly, in November 1920. At the end of the year Ku married Huang Hui-lan, the daughter of the wealthy overseas Chinese from Java, Oei Tiong Ham (Huang T'ai-yuan).

In October 1921 Ku served as a member of the Chinese delegation to the Washington Conference, which presented China's Ten Points, including the definition of China as a territorial and an administrative entity with the right to participate in international conferences affecting its interests. From November through February 1922, Ku was instrumental in negotiating a settlement with Japan which returned sovereignty of parts of Shantung to China. In August of that same year, Ku was appointed minister of foreign affairs. Ku's first important mission in this new post was negotiations with the USSR to establish diplomatic relations, arbitrate the Chinese Eastern Railway question, and resolve the status of Outer Mongolia. Negotiations with Soviet representative Adolf Joffe began in September, just as the Wang Ch'ung-hui* cabinet fell and Ku resigned. Ku then became acting foreign minister in Kao Ling-wei's cabinet and retained the post through the abdication of the presidency by Li Yüan-hung* and its assumption by Ts'ao K'un.* When Ku became involved in the tricky negotiations resulting from the Lincheng Incident in which several foreigners were kidnapped by a bandit in Shantung, he assigned Wang Cheng-t'ing responsibility for continuing negotiations with the USSR.

In March 1924 Wang signed an agreement with the Soviet envoy Leo M. Karakhan which provided for the immediate establishment of formal diplomatic relations with the USSR but allowed the Soviet Army to remain in Outer Mongolia. The cabinet refused to ratify the agreement, and Ku repudiated Wang's signature. In May, however, Ku signed essentially the same agreement because of Soviet intimidation. In July 1924 Ku became acting premier of China. In October Feng Yü-hsiang* staged a coup in Peking which forced Ku to resign and flee to Weihaiwei. Later he joined his wife in the foreign concession in Tientsin.

In May 1926 Ku returned to politics by accepting the portfolio of finance in the W. W. Yen cabinet. Yen, however, was soon driven out of Peking by Chang Tso-lin. In a new cabinet formed in June, Ku became acting premier and minister of foreign affairs. He resigned a year later. When the Nationalist Northern Expedition* reached Peking in June 1928, its leaders issued orders for Ku's arrest as an official of Chang Tso-lin's regime. Ku escaped again to Weihaiwei, and from there to France and Canada. In 1929 Ku was in Mukden where he became associated with the Young Marshal, Chang Hsüeh-liang.* After allying himself with Chiang Kai-shek,* Chang induced Chiang Kai-shek to cancel the arrest order for Ku. In December 1931 Ku became minister of foreign affairs in the Nanking government.*

In 1932 Ku became the Chinese representative at the League of Nations. In Geneva he stated China's indictment of Japanese seizure of Manchuria in late 1931. The Lytton Commission's final recommendations were rejected by both China and Japan. In July he helped Nanking's minister of finance, Tse-Ven Paul Soong,* to obtain League of Nations technical cooperation for public health efforts. During 1935–1936 he was China's chief delegate to the League of Nations Assembly.

Ku remained in Europe for several years where he represented China at several international conferences. With the German occupation of France and the establishment of the Vichy Regime that year, Ku was appointed the Chinese ambassador to Great Britain, where he was active in the negotiations that resulted in the relinquishment of British extraterritorial rights in China and the Sino-British Lend-Lease Agreements of 1944.

In San Francisco in June 1945, Ku signed the Charter of the United Nations on behalf of China, and he was the Chinese delegate to the United Nations Preparatory Commission. In May 1946, Ku became Chinese ambassador to the

United States, in which capacity he endeavored to obtain American aid for the Nationalist government during the civil war[*] with the Chinese Communists. After the Communists drove the Nationalists from the mainland to refuge in Taiwan, Ku continued to push for U.S. aid for the Nationalist government. He helped negotiate the U.S.–China Mutual Defense Pact in 1954.

In 1956 Ku resigned his ambassadorship, and in January 1957 he was elected to complete the term of Hsu Mo on the International Court of Justice. He assumed office at The Hague in May and was reelected for a full ten-year term in October. He served as vice-president of the court from 1964 until 1967. That year he returned to New York where he lived with his third wife, Yen Yu-yun, until his death.

Ku's accomplishments in the field of international diplomacy won him many honors, including more honorary degrees from Columbia, St. John's, Aberdeen, Birmingham, and Manchester universities. He made significant contributions to the formation of the League of Nations and the United Nations and notably strengthened China's international position prior to 1928, when the "national" government in Peking actually represented only the militarists currently controlling the city itself.

REFERENCES: Hui-lan Koo, *Hui-lan Koo: An Autobiography as Told to Mary Van Rensselaer Thayer* (New York, 1943); Robert T. Pollard, *China's Foreign Relations, 1917–1931* (New York, 1933); William Tung, *V. K. Wellington Koo and China's Wartime Diplomacy* (New York, 1977).

GUY S. ALITTO

KUANG-HSÜ, EMPEROR (August 14, 1871–November 14, 1908): The ninth emperor of the Ch'ing dynasty (r. 1875–1908).

Emperor Kuang-hsü was the second son of Prince I-huan. His personal name was Tsai-tien. He was chosen at the age of four by his aunt, Empress Dowager Tz'u-hsi,[*] to succeed Emperor Tung-chih, who died without an heir in 1875. Because Tsai-tien was the nearest prince to Tz'u-hsi by blood, this guaranteed T'zu-hsi's control over the infant emperor. On January 15, 1875, it was officially announced that Empress Dowager Hsiao-chin (or T'zu-hsi) and Empress Dowager Hsiao-chen (Tsai-tsin's natural mother) would be the co-regents until Emperor Kuang-hsü was of age. Reportedly, this act was a blunt violation of the dynastic laws of succession; nonetheless, it was carried out without objection.

Kuang-hsü was therefore raised under the total domination of Tz'u-hsi, and he learned to fear the empress early on. When Kuang-hsü came of age in 1887, T'zu-hsi insisted on retaining power until 1889, when she "retired" to her Summer Palace outside Peking. However, all important state papers still went to her for approval, and key government appointments could not be made without her authorization.

Although Kuang-hsü was a weak emperor, he was reportedly "intelligent, studious, and well-informed on a variety of subjects." He was inquisitive and possessed a fairly open mind about national and international affairs. He was particularly interested in new ideas introduced to China in the nineteenth century by Westerners. For instance, Kuang-hsü was the first Ch'ing emperor to study English.

Immediately after the humiliation China suffered in the Sino-Japanese War* of 1894–1895, Kuang-hsü became immensely concerned with the plight of China and wanted to do something to avert its demise. At this time, a young and dynamic scholar, K'ang Yu-wei,* attracted the emperor's attention. K'ang Yu-wei had repeatedly sent memorials to Kuang-hsü expressing his concerns over the impotence of the government, calling for the urgent reform of the government to avert the danger China faced. When Kuang-hsü's imperial tutor, Weng T'ung-ho, supported K'ang Yu-wei's ideas in early 1898, Kuang-hsü became more eager to pursue K'ang's suggestions for reform. After January 29, 1898, K'ang Yu-wei was even granted the special right of having his memorials reach the emperor without obstruction or delay by court officials. With this power, K'ang became more aggressive. Through February and May of 1898, K'ang made it clear in his memorials to Kuang-hsü that reforms had to comprise (1) a national polity under Kuang-hsü's leadership modeled after Peter the Great of Russia and Emperor Meiji of Japan, (2) a comprehensive reorganization of the national government based on the new ideas of new talents (i.e., reform-minded intellectuals like K'ang himself); and (3) provincial governments with the authority to initiate the necessary changes according to national needs.

Finally, on June 11, 1898, Kuang-hsü issued an imperial decree for a general governmental reform (now known as the Hundred Day Reform*), which lasted exactly one hundred days ending September 20, 1898, when Empress Dowager T'zu-hsi rushed back to the Court in Peking after hearing about the details of the reform. ''Imprisoning'' Emperor Kuang-hsü and expelling K'ang Yu-wei from the Court, T'zu-hsi resumed control of the government. Emperor Kuang-hsü once again became nothing more than a figurehead ruler and was placed under total surveillance by T'zu-hsi.

China went through more humiliations after Empress Dowager T'zu-hsi regained control, both internally and externally. Emperor Kuang-hsü had little power to prevent any of them. The fate of the Ch'ing dynasty* was doomed. It seemed that Kuang-hsü lived his life under the shadow of T'zu-hsi; even his official death announcement on November 14, 1908, came a day before that of Empress Dowager T'zu-hsi. Kuang-hsü was succeeded by his nephew, Emperor Hsüan-tung (or P'u-i*), who became the last emperor of the Ch'ing dynasty.

REFERENCES: Immanuel C. Y. Hsü, *The Rise of Modern China*, 4th ed. (New York, 1990); Arthur W. Hummel, *Eminent Chinese of the Ch'ing Period* (Washington, D.C., 1943); Frederic Wakeman, Jr., *The Fall of Imperial China* (New York, 1975).

ANTHONY Y. TENG

KUNG, HSIANG-HSI, CHAUNCEY (better known as H. H. Kung, 1888–August 15, 1967): Financier; minister of industries; finance minister and vice-premier of the ROC.

Born into a pawnbroker-turned-banker family in Taiku, Shansi, Kung was a direct descendant of Confucius of the seventy-fifth generation. He attended missionary school before studying at the North China Union College near Peking in 1896. After the Boxer Rebellion,* he mediated with Westerners and missionaries on behalf of his province. Duly impressed, the imperial court sent him to study in the United States, and he attended Oberlin College in Ohio of his own choice. He graduated in 1906 with a B.A. and completed an M.A. at Yale in 1907. Back in Taiku, he served under General Yen Hsi-shan* to reform the economy. He married in 1910, but his wife died in 1913.

During the 1911 Revolution,* Kung commanded the volunteers of Shansi. In 1914 he married Soong Ai-ling. When Dr. Sun Yat-sen* set up his government in Kwangtung, he became the finance commissioner of the Kwangtung Province, finance minister and minister of industry of the Nationalist government. During the Northern Expedition* of 1926, he successfully negotiated with Generals Feng Yü-hsiang* and Yen Hsi-shan to accept Chiang Kai-shek's* nominal leadership. In 1927 Kung became minister of industry, commerce, and labor of the Nanking Regime. Together with his wife, he persuaded his brother-in-law Tse-ven Soong* to accept Chiang's offer of the finance ministership. His wife was allegedly the directing force in forging the alliances between the Four Big Families of Soong, Kung, Chiang, and Chen and maintained close touch with the Green Gang boss, Tu Yueh-sheng. This was a decisive factor in Kung's policies in the Finance Ministry, and they amassed a huge family fortune. As minister of industry, he accomplished little in China's industrialization.

In 1932, Kung was appointed special commissioner to study Western industrialization, visiting the United States, Germany, and Japan. To forge close links with Hitler and Mussolini, he purchased U.S. $25 million in weapons from Germany and succeeded in obtaining the U.S. $2 million remaining of Boxer indemnities owed to Italy for the purchase of Fiat war planes. In 1933 he succeeded T. V. Soong as finance minister and vice-premier. During his term of office, China's economic conditions deteriorated, with the cost of living rising twenty-five times. To boost government finance, Kung passed the savings bank law in July 1934, requiring all banks to invest 25 percent of their assets in government bonds or securities, to be held in trust by the Central Bank. The policy tied the banks and financiers to the government, reducing their autonomy and limiting their lending capacity to agriculture and industry. He also increased the ceiling on bank investment on bonds from $13 million to $173 million in 1934. He further alienated the banks in 1935, when the government announced the takeover of the Bank of China and the Bank of Communications, putting the Kungs and the Soongs on the boards of the nationalized banks. The rising foreign exchange value of the silver currency threatened the deficit financing of the regime. Belatedly, Kung imposed an embargo on silver and exempted the Central Bank from the 10 percent export tax. This policy, together with the monopoly in gold trading, kept the Central Bank and the Treasury in good shape for a short time. As the United States remained unconciliatory on silver policies, China finally went off the silver standard and issued the paper currency, *fa-pi*, in 1935. Kung's expectations of foreign currency support and optimism to balance the budget in eighteen months were short-lived. The *fa-pi* soon devalued to almost nothing, because of Chiang's huge military expenditure and rampant corruption. He was able to give the government another breathing spell in 1936 by consolidating loans and the government bonds structure. However, irregularities were common in his financial reports; for example, receipts and payments for 1936 and 1937 were not published in the Finance Ministry's Annual Reports.

After the fall of Nanking in 1938, Kung became premier when Chiang temporarily gave up all offices. In 1943, in a desperate attempt to control inflation which had gone wild because of his printing press approach to solve government deficits, Kung introduced price fixing, resulting in the withdrawal of vital food supplies from the market. He also asked for a loan of U.S. $50 million in gold from the United States to check inflation. In 1944 he was targeted for attack by the Ko-hsin (Reform) Group, which caused Chiang to transfer his favor to the C.C. Clique* and to reinstate Soong. As a result, he left China for one year from June 1944.

Theodore White commented that Kung's one desire was to stay in office and be liked by others. In contrast with Soong, Kung was very Chinese and conservative and possessed less knowledge of modern banking and finance. After Chiang Kai-shek's retreat to Taiwan, Kung never assumed any official posts again. He was actively involved with personal business and welfare throughout his life. In 1966 he stepped down from the directorship of the Bank of China. He died in August 1967. T. V. Soong, his brother-in-law, was conspicuously absent from his funeral.

REFERENCES: Sterling Seagrave, *The Soong Dynasty* (London, 1985); Howard L. Boorman and Richard C. Howard, eds., *A Biographical Dictionary of Republican China* (New York, 1968); Arthur N. Young, *China's Nation-Building Effort, 1927–1937: The Financial and Economic Record* (Stanford, Calif. 1971).

TERENCE T.T. PANG

KUO SUNG-TAO (April 11, 1818–July 18, 1891): Reformist and first Chinese minister to Great Britain.

Kuo Sung-tao, also known as Yün-hsien or Yu-ch'ih lao-jen, was born in Hsiang-yin County, Hunan Province. He received a Confucian education at home and was with Tseng Kuo-fan* and Liu Jung at the Yueh-lu Academy, where he absorbed a special brand of Sung neo-Confucian philosophy and the learning of "statesmanship for practical use" (*ching-shih chih-yung*). In many of his writings, Kuo expressed his interest in Chang Tsai (1020–1077), Ch'eng Hao (1032–1085), and Ch'eng Yi (1033–1108). Chang and the Ch'eng brothers opposed the political reform movement in the Northern Sung. They are nonetheless well known as scholars who delved into the questions of truth and reason. Kuo also held the early Ch'ing thinker, Wang Fu-chih (1619–1692), in high esteem. As an admirer of Wang Fu-chih, Kuo stressed the intellectual flexibility needed to cope with the ever-changing world.

Kuo earned the *chin-shih* degree in 1847 and was nominated as a compiler of the Hanlin Academy. In 1852 when the Taiping* forces invaded Hunan, it was through Kuo's effort that Tseng Kuo-fan was persuaded to organize local forces for war against the Taipings. Kuo also proposed the establishment of a naval fleet for the Yangtze River. In order to finance Teng's Hsiang Army, Kuo supported the *likin* (inland transit dues) tax. He served in a *likin* bureau that collected merchandise taxes to support Tseng's military campaign.

Kuo later filled a number of official posts. In 1858 he was ordered to Peking to take up an appointment as secretary-tutor in the Hanlin Academy. This position gave him an opportunity to meet important Manchu princes and influential officials. He became an adviser of Shu-shun, who was influential at the Hsienfeng court. In 1862, on the recommendation of Li Hung-chang,* Kuo was appointed grain intendant of the prefectures of Soochow and Sung-chiang. Later, Kuo was promoted to salt controller of the Liang-huai region. He served as acting governor of Kwangtung Province between 1863 and 1866. He seems to have been an extremely competent provincial administrator. However, he was dismissed from office, having been unexpectedly impeached for political reasons by Tso Tsung-t'ang* in 1866. After eight years out of office, Kuo was summoned to Peking in 1874 for appointment. He was appointed judicial commissioner of Fukien in 1874, but within a few months he was made an acting vice-president of the Board of War and a minister in the Tsungli Yamen.

In the aftermath of the Margary Affair (1875) and the Chefoo Convention (1876),[1] Kuo was appointed minister to England. He thus became the first Chinese resident envoy to the Western world. In 1878 he was appointed minister to France, but in the same year he was ordered back to China. His outspoken criticism led to disputes with Tso Tsung-t'ang and others. His extremely enlightened views on foreign affairs, formulated during his ambassadorship, caused the ruin of his official career. After his return to China, he retired from political life, taught in Ch'eng-nan Academy in Changsha, and spent his last years reading and writing.

Kuo Sung-tao was remarkable for his courage and conviction—qualities that caused him considerable trouble. As a reformist intellectual, he was outstanding, but he was too far ahead of his contemporaries. He was deeply concerned with the fate of China and seriously jeopardized his career by the sincerity and fearlessness with which he expressed his views on China's institutional reform to a conservative, unsympathetic, and unreceptive bureaucratic audience. Kuo's descriptions of the power and prosperity of Western nations (especially England) were greeted by Chinese readers with protests. Ho Chin-shou accused Kuo of telling lies about England and wishing to subjugate China to England. In his diary entitled *Hsiang-yi-lou jih-chi*, Wang K'ai-yün pointed out that "We Hunanese feel very ashamed to be associated with Kuo." The printing blocks of Kuo's diary *Shih-Hsi chi-ch'eng* were ordered by imperial decree to be destroyed. As the attacks on him reached their climax, Kuo's ancestral temple was destroyed by a mob. Prior to the 1890s, only a few distinguished reformers could appreciate Kuo's reform ideas and act on them. The outcome of Kuo's attacks on traditional

Chinese culture was a tragedy. Reflecting on his own life, he regarded himself in the following way: "half accomplished in scholarship, half successful in official career; in one lifetime, how many aspirations have been fulfilled?"

NOTE

1. After British vice-consul Augustus Margary was killed along the Chinese-Burmese border, the Chefoo Convention was concluded to settle the case, and an apology was dispatched to Britain.

REFERENCES: David Hamilton, "Kuo Sung-tao: A Maverick Confucian," *Papers on China* 15 (December 1961): 1–29; Kuo T'ing-Yee et al., *Kuo Sung-tao hsien-sheng nien-p'u* (A chronological biography of Kuo Sung-tao) (Taipei, 1971); J. D. Frodsham, *The First Chinese Embassy to the West: The Journals of Kuo Sung-t'ao, Liu Hsi-hung and Chang Te-yi* (Oxford, 1974); Chi-kong Lai, "The Theory of Statecraft of Kuo Sung-tao" in *Proceeding of the Conference of the Theory of Statecraft of Modern China* (Taipei, 1984): 509–530; Owen Wong, *A New Profile in Sino-Western Diplomacy: The First Minister to Great Britain* (Hong Kong, 1987).

CHI-KONG LAI

L

LEA, HOMER (December 17, 1876–November 1, 1912): Amateur writer on military affairs and supporter of the Chinese reform and revolution.

Homer Lea was born in Boulder, Colorado, in 1876 to a family that had moved west after the Civil War. His grandfather, Dr. Pleasant John Graves Lea, a physician, was the father of ten children, most of whom were active on the side of the Confederacy and dispersed west of the Mississippi after the war. One of his uncles, Joseph C. Lea, a captain in the Confederate Army, became a founder of the New Mexico Military Academy at Roswell. The nephew was so proud of his military family background that he later claimed direct family ties to General Robert E. Lee, the Civil War hero.

During his school days at Los Angeles High School and Stanford University Homer Lea developed a keen interest in military affairs by studying military history and strategy of the great wars, especially the Civil War. When the Spanish-American War started in 1898, he wanted to join the army but was rejected because of his physical defects, including a hunchback and chronic eye disease. Thus, he joined the California National Guard cavalry troop instead. Since the hostilities ended so quickly, he did not go to the war, nor did he get any military training. He returned home to Los Angeles to cure his recurring eye disease instead of continuing his education at Stanford. While at home, he pursued a military career by involving himself with the Chinese reformists in California.

When the Hundred Day Reform* of 1898 failed in China, T'an Shu-pin (Tom She Bin), president of the Pao-huang hui* in San Francisco, commissioned Lea to go to China in the summer of 1900 to deliver funds to the reformist forces on behalf of K'ang Yu-wei,* to rescue the imprisoned Emperor Kuang-hsü* from Empress Dowager Tz'u-hsi,* and finally to organize and direct the reformist troops in south China. But there is little evidence about his activities in China, although he claimed to have lifted the siege in Peking with the American expeditionary contingent during the height of the Boxer Rebellion* in 1900. He returned to California in April 1901 via Japan where he had discussed the reform of China with a leading Japanese politician, Ōkuma Shigenobu. From this time on, he continued to have ties with the Chinese reformists in America. In the summer of 1903, Liang Ch'i-ch'ao* visited him in Los Angeles. As a result, Lea established the Western Military Academy in 1904 and trained the Chinese cadets to send them to China in case of need. Lea not only became a military adviser to the reformists, but he also ran the Imperial Chinese Reform Army which he had created for them. When K'ang Yu-wei came to America to inspect the reformist activities in 1905, Lea began to have trouble with him because of differences of opinion on the military and financial operations for the Pao-huang hui. K'ang was criticized for delegating the leadership of the Imperial Chinese Reform Army from Lea to another American, General Richard A. Falkenberg, and for mismanaging public funds raised from the Chinese in America by investing them in Mexico for his own personal gains. K'ang and Lea's relations subsequently cooled.

Being disappointed in K'ang, Lea paid more attention to Sun Yat-sen's* revolutionary cause in 1908–1912. Together with other American plotters such as W. W. Allen and Charles B. Boothe, Lea tried to help Sun. In 1910 Lea and Sun worked on the forthcoming revolution in China. Lea planned to raise funds from American supporters and to coordinate military strategy with Chinese collaborators in America. But nothing came of his plans. When the Chinese Revolution occurred in Wuchang in October 1911, Lea joined in the traveling party of Sun Yat-sen. Prior to his departure for Europe, he had married his longtime secretary, Ethel Powers, who was a divorcee from Tennessee. They decided to honeymoon in Europe. On the way to Europe, Lea personally tried to persuade American officials such as Elihu Root and Philander Knox in Washington to help Sun diplomatically and financially. While in London and Paris, Lea also tried to obtain economic aid and diplomatic recognition from the respective governments on behalf of Sun Yat-sen. He had met many influential bankers in England and France for the loan. Although he did not get funds for Sun's revolutionary government, he was successful in lifting the ban on Sun's entry to the British territories. After stopping by in Hong Kong, Sun's entourage arrived in Shanghai on Christmas Eve, 1911. Lea attended Sun's presidential inauguration on January 1, 1912, in Nanking. Soon thereafter, Sun had to give up the presidency in favor of Yüan Shih-k'ai.* Lea used all means to prevent Yuan from assuming the presidency, but in vain. Lea fell ill and returned to California in April and died of hemiplegia there in November 1912 at the age of thirty-six. He had devoted his short adult life to the cause of the Chinese reform and revolution continually but unsuccessfully.

As an amateur writer, Lea published many obscure articles and three books. One of these works, *Valor of Ignorance* (1909), predicted the forthcoming Japanese attacks on the United States. As a result, when the Pearl Harbor attack became a reality in 1941, the book was an instant best seller and became one of the required readings for the high-ranking military officials at war colleges.

REFERENCES: Eugene Anschel, *Homer Lea, Sun Yat-sen, and the Chinese Revolution* (New York, 1984); Key Ray Chong, *Americans and Chinese Reform and Revolution* (Lanham, Md., 1984); C. M. Wilbur, *Sun Yat-sen: Frustrated Patriot* (New York, 1976).
                                                                                                    KEY RAY CHONG

LEI FENG (1940–1962): Chinese Communist model of a socialist man.

Born in November 1940, Lei Feng was a peasant soldier from Hunan Province who was held up by Mao Tse-tung[*] to be a youthful paragon of Maoist virtues, one who exemplified the Chinese Communist ideal of the new socialist man. Those virtues included courage, humility, sacrifice, love of and identification with the common people, and, above all, unquestioned loyalty and devotion to the Communist party.

Quoted as having said that "Man is happiest when he contributes everything of himself to the cause of liberating mankind," Lei Feng epitomized the qualities of the new socialist man which the Communist party sought to imprint on the Chinese people. The party insisted that selfishness and individualism were not universal traits, but only those of the bourgeoisie. Under the proper guidance, workers, peasants, and soldiers would no longer be motivated by selfish desires but would instead become devoted to the community.

Portrayed by the party as having sacrificed his life for the revolution, the real Lei Feng died unheroically in August 1962, crushed by a fallen telegraph pole. He left a diary that idolized Chairman Mao. What followed was a nationwide propaganda campaign instigated by the Communist party to "learn from Lei Feng." Lei's diaries, greatly embellished, were published across China as the chronicles of a perfect Communist life. Promoted by the official media, exhibitions, and textbooks, the image of Lei was that of a humble soldier, a good Samaritan who helped old ladies across the road, chopped firewood for the crippled, and repeated every day the slogan: "I love the motherland, the people, and the party." As such, the campaign preceded what was to become the mass idolatry of Mao during the Great Proletarian Cultural Revolution (1966–1976).[*]

Chinese and Western historians believe that Lei Feng was largely a creation of Mao's imagination, a symbol of Maoist ideology invented for imitation and indoctrination. In the wake of the bloody suppression by the People's Liberation Army[*] of the pro-democracy movement in T'ienanmen Square on June 4, 1989, the Chinese Communist party[*] has reinvoked the memory of Lei Feng. March 4, 1990, was proclaimed to be Lei Feng Day and the entire year to be the Year of Lei Feng. Leading intellectuals sympathetic with the pro-democracy movement, such as Fang Li-chih and Liu Pin-yen, were criticized by the regime for having "maliciously attacked and uglified Lei Feng's spirit." Finally, in an effort to regain public trust and esteem, soldiers and members of the public security apparatus are enjoined, once again, to "learn from Lei Feng" by serving the people.

REFERENCES: Merle Goldman, "The Chinese Communist Party's 'Cultural Revolution' of 1962–64," and John Israel, "Continuities and Discontinuities in the Ideology of the

Great Proletarian Cultural Revolution,'' in Chalmers Johnson, ed., *Ideology and Politics in Contemporary China* (Seattle, Wash., 1973).

MARIA HSIA CHANG

LI HSIEN-NIEN (1906–   ): Top-ranking cadre of the CCP with experience in military and economic affairs (finance and state planning); member of the CCP Politburo; vice-chairman of the Central Committee of the CCP; deputy premier of the State Council of the PRC; president of the PRC (1983–   ).

Li Hsien-nien is a native of Huang-an County (now known as Hung-an) in eastern Hupeh Province. He came from a poor peasant family and did not receive much formal education. In his youth he worked as a carpenter. Li spent a brief time as a soldier in the Nationalist forces that entered Hupeh during the Northern Expedition* in 1926. When the split between the Communists and the Nationalists took place in 1927, Li returned to Huang-an County as an operative in the Communist Young Pioneers. Together with others who would also become prominent Communists, such as Hsü Hai-tung and Cheng Wei-san, Li worked at organizing peasants and developing guerrilla bands in eastern Hupeh. In 1928 he became a member of the Chinese Communist party* and served as a district commissar in the trade unions of the Huang-an District for the CCP. In 1930, he became an instructor in the Red Guard,* and in the following year, he was elected chairman of the small Soviet government of Huang-an County.

Li's entrance into the mainstream of the CCP military command began in 1931. In that year, top Communist leaders Chang Kuo-t'ao* and Ch'en Ch'ang-hao joined the command of the Oyüwan (Hupeh-Honan-Anhwei) Soviet which Hsü Hsiang-ch'ien had established. The same year saw significant reorganization in the military and government structure of the Communist Soviet system. In November 1931 the Fourth Front Army was formed, under Hsü's command, and Li, by now commanding a considerable local force, joined the Fourth Front Army as a regiment political commissar and then division political commissar. Under attack by the Nationalist forces, the Fourth Front Army moved westward out of the Oyüwan base and into northern Szechwan in 1932 and 1933. At this time Li became the political commissar of the Thirtieth Army.

In the summer of 1935 the forces under Hsü Hsiang-ch'ien and Chang Kuo-t'ao rendezvoused with the Communist troops under Mao Tse-tung* and Chu Teh* in western Szechwan. As a result of a rift between Mao and Chang, the Long March* split, with Chang taking his forces into western Sikang and eventually eastern Kansu. Li went with Chang, although the bulk of his Thirtieth Army went with Mao more directly to northern Shensi. After being in eastern Kansu for the better part of 1936, Chang's forces went further westward and northward into the Kansu corridor, ultimately reaching Chiu-ch'uan. When Hsü Hsiang-ch'ien and others turned back toward Shensi, Li was left in command. Suffering repeated defeats at the hands of Nationalist general Hu Tsung-nan and the warlord Ma Pu-fang, the Communist forces under Li's command in this region became decimated as they pushed northward in two detachments. In the spring of 1937, Li reached the Kansu-Sinkiang border, with barely 700 men. There he was sheltered by the Soviet forces and by the local warlord Sheng Shih-ts'ai. In December of that year, Mao sent Ch'en Yün* to Ti-hwa, the capital of Sinkiang, to arrange for the transportation of Li's men to Yenan, in northern Shensi, where by this time Mao had established a viable base.

Thus, in late 1937 Li entered the Anti-Japanese Military and Political University in Yenan. In late 1938, when Wuhan fell to the Japanese, Li was sent back to Hupeh to reorganize resistance guerrillas and became the commander of the Hupeh-Honan Assault Column, a major Communist military unit in central China. These forces in east central China were subsequently organized into the New Fourth Army, of whose fifth column Li became commander. After the so-called New Fourth Army Incident* of January 1941, and in the subsequent reorganization, Li became commander of the fifth division. In June 1945, at the Seventh Congress of the CCP, Li was elected to the Central Committee.

After the Japanese surrender in August 1945, Chu Teh ordered Li to manage the surrender of the Japanese troops in Honan and Hupeh. Instead, the Japanese surrendered to the Nationalist forces, and skirmishes between the Communists and Chiang Kai-shek's* troops in the following months in this region forced Li to withdraw to northern Hupeh. After the collapse of the Communist-Nationalist truce that had been negotiated by U.S. Special Envoy George C. Marshall in June 1946, Li took part in the Communist forces' attempts to "liberate" the southern Shensi, Hupeh, and Honan region. In 1948 Li was deputy commander of the Central Plains Military Region under Liu Po-ch'eng and was political commissar of the Second Field Army when that was established in the winter of 1948–1949. When Wuhan fell to Lin Piao's* Fourth Field Army in May 1949, Li became deputy commander under Lin and the chief CCP official in the Hupeh region. In May 1949 he became the governor of Hupeh and commander and political commissar of the Hupeh Military District, and secretary of the Hupeh Provincial Committee of the CCP.

At the time of the founding of the People's Republic of China,* Li was appointed to the People's Revolutionary Military Council, a national post, while holding his regional positions. In February 1950, when the Central-South Military and Administrative Committee was established and replaced the provincial governments in the central and southern provinces of China (Honan, Hupeh, Hunan, Kiangsi, Kwangtung, and Kwangsi), Li became a ranking member of this powerful institution, and a member of its Finance and Economics Committee. He held these, and similar, positions through the reorganization of the Central-South Military and Administrative Committee as the Central-South Administrative Committee in 1953. Meanwhile, in February 1952, he also became mayor and party secretary of Wuhan. In June 1954 Li became deputy chairman of the Finance and Economics Committee of the Government Administrative Council (GAC) under Ch'en Yün and minister of finance of the GAC. In these early years of the PRC, Li embarked on and cultivated a second career as an economic administrator, while he spent most of his time in the Wuhan region. In September

1954 the government structure of the PRC was reorganized, with the formation of the State Council to take the place of the GAC. Li then became a vice-premier of the State Council and minister of finance. He was also a member of the State Defense Council. In November of that year, he was nominated director of the Fifth Staff Office of the State Council, which was in charge of trade and financial affairs. From 1954 onward, Li was primarily a national officer in Peking. His position in the party apparatus was enhanced in September 1956 when he was elected a member of the Central Committee of the CCP, and, at the First Plenum of the Eighth Central Committee, he was elected to the Politburo for the first time. In 1958 Li was appointed a secretary of the party's Central Secretariat. Meanwhile, throughout the 1950s and early 1960s, Li retained his top government positions in the State Council and in October 1962 added the position of vice-chairman of the State Planning Commission, the government's top body in strategic long-term national planning.

In the early phase of the Cultural Revolution,* Li was briefly criticized by the leftists but was not seriously affected. However, during the period of the Cultural Revolution when power was preempted by Lin Piao* and other Maoist leftists, and with the Red Guard Movement dominating almost every aspect of life in the PRC, government was in total chaos, and government positions, even party positions such as those that Li held, were essentially meaningless. Indeed, for this period, and through the period of the Gang of Four,* Li's activities were confined to little more than a litany of official overseas visits and meetings with foreign state guests in China, inspection tours, and the like—essentially ceremonial functions. The only significant note to make here is that Li managed to maintain his positions (in 1972 the State Planning Commission was abolished) and ride out the storm of those ten years—largely, it seems, because he retained the trust of Mao Tse-tung.

After Mao's death in September 1976, and under the premiership and party chairmanship of Hua Kuo-feng,* Li and other veteran cadres became politically active again. With the decimation of the ranks of old, top-ranking party cadres in the Cultural Revolution period, those that remained standing played major roles in the post–Mao era. Li, in particular, was one of the key people in overthrowing the Gang of Four. He was one of Hua's chief allies in the coup of October 6, 1976, and one of five people who attended the secret meeting held the previous day at the headquarters of the People's Liberation Army* that plotted the swift steps to bring down Chiang Ch'ing,* Chang Ch'un-ch'iao,* Wang Hung-wen,* and Yao Wen-yüan.* (The others attending were Hua Kuo-feng, Wang Tung-hsing, Ch'en Hsi-lien—commander of the Peking garrison—and Yeh Chien-ying.*) With the Gang of Four purged, the post–Mao party leaders began to reconstruct Chinese politics and government.

Although he did not take overt steps in the power struggle between Hua Kuo-feng and Teng Hsiao-p'ing* in 1977, except as a mediator and as an advocate for a smooth transition, Li was clearly an ally of Teng and played a part in Teng's rehabilitation. It was to cultivate the support of Li and Yeh, among other top leaders, that Hua agreed in 1976 to the rehabilitation of Teng, to be openly considered in 1977 and that took effect at the Third Plenum of the Tenth Central Committee in July 1977. In August 1977 Li was elected to the Eleventh Central Committee of the party, and at the First Plenum of the Eleventh Central Committee, he was elected a vice-chairman of the Central Committee and member of the Politburo. This made him effectively one of the top five leaders of the CCP. In March 1978 he was reelected as vice-premier of the State Council.

In July 1979 Li was appointed vice-chairman of the State Financial and Economic Commission, a post he held until March 1981. In August 1980, at the Third Plenum of the Fifth National People's Congress, the Teng faction reached the peak of power in this early post-Mao era. Hua Kuo-feng resigned as premier and later that year offered to resign also as party chairman. At the time of the Sixth Plenum of the Eleventh Central Committee in June 1981, the transition of power was complete. Since then, it has been Teng Hsiao-p'ing in charge, although he did not assume what might have sounded as supreme titles. These he left to others, and Li was elected as state chairman, or in the new nomenclature, president of the People's Republic of China, in June 1983. Nonetheless that has remained essentially a titular role.

REFERENCES: Wolfgang Bartke, *Who's Who in the People's Republic of China* (Armonk, N.Y., 1981): 197; Wolfgang Bartke and Peter Schier, *China's New Party Leadership: Biographies and Analysis of the Twelfth Central Committee of the Chinese Communist Party* (Armonk, N.Y., 1985): 139–140; *Chung-kung jen-ming lu* (Biographies of Chinese Communists) (Taipei, 1978): 176–182; Donald W. Klein and Anne B. Clark, *Biographic Dictionary of Chinese Communism, 1921–1965*, vol. 1 (Cambridge, Mass., 1971): 499–504.

JOHN KONG-CHEONG LEUNG

LI HSIU-CH'ENG (d. August 7, 1864): Military leader of the Taiping Revolution.

Li was the most important military leader of the Taiping Revolution* after 1857. Born into a poor family in Hsin-wang Village in T'eng County, Kwangsi, he became a member of the God Worshippers Society.* In September 1851 he joined the Taipings. After the Taipings established their capital in Nanking in 1853, Li Hsiu-ch'eng's exceptional ability in military leadership won him several rapid promotions. In 1854 he was promoted to Twentieth Commander after his successful defense of the city of Lu-chou. What truly distinguished Li as a talented military leader was the battle to release Chenkiang from Ch'ing encirclement in February 1856.

The Taiping Revolution was at a turning point in September 1856 when internecine strife between the kings of the Taipings resulted in the killing of the East King, Yang Hsiu-ch'ing,* and his rival, the North King, Wei Ch'ang-hui.* With the departure of Shih Ta-k'ai,* the Assistant King, in May 1857, the Taiping leadership collapsed. In order to fill the vacuum of leadership, Hung Hsiu-ch'üan,* the Heavenly King, promoted Li and Ch'en Yü-ch'eng to take charge of military affairs, serving under Meng Te-en, for whom Li had no respect.

Despite the lack of political leadership, the new military leadership of Li and Ch'en proved to be effective in resisting attacks by imperial forces. After the success of the joint effort to defeat the Hunan Army in Anhwei and to break up the siege by imperial forces at Nanking in the last two months of 1858, Li felt sufficiently confident to submit a memorial to Hung calling for strict enforcement of the laws against bribery and of the regulations for promotion and punishment. Hung was infuriated and deprived Li of his ranks. But Li was able to win the support of court officials, and Hung subsequently restored Li to his duties.

Li's trouble with Hung Hsiu-ch'üan continued to grow, however, when Hung Jen-kan,[*] a cousin of Hung Hsiu-ch'üan, arrived in Nanking in April 1859 and rapidly received important positions. Nonetheless, in January 1860 Li supported Hung Jen-kan's strategy for breaking up once again the Imperial Great Camp on the southern bank of the Yangtze. Riding on the crest of victory, he took Hangchow, and in May he captured Tan-yang, Soochow, Ch'ang-chou, Chia-ting, and Chia-hsing. Li proved his political pragmatism as he sought the co-operation of landlords and promoted trade in Kiangsu and Chekiang by allowing them to serve as local officials. In the meantime, from August 1860 to January 1862 he made three abortive attempts to capture Shanghai. Li's discontent with Hung's leadership led to defiance. In late 1861 he failed to carry out his assignment of providing relief to the siege of An-ch'ing. Its loss was a heavy blow to the defense of Nanking.

As the Hunan Army strengthened its siege of Nanking in June 1863, Hung Hsiu-ch'üan ordered Li back to defend Nanking. In his absence, the Huai Army under Li Hung-chang[*] and the Ever Victorious Army under Charles G. Gordon[*] began to attack the Taiping stronghold in Soochow. Despite his efforts after his return to Soochow in July, Li failed to resist the imperial forces, which by December had gained control of most of Kiangsu except Nanking and other small pockets of Taiping resistance. After Soochow was captured by Li Hung-chang's forces in December 1863, Nanking was in great danger. On June 3, 1864, Hung Hsiu-ch'üan died of a lingering disease. His son, a sixteen-year-old boy, ascended the throne as the "Young Heavenly King." On July 3, the Hunan Army broke the defense. Li was able to break out of the city and escaped with the new king and a thousand men. He was captured on July 22, 1864 and was executed by Tseng Kuo-fan[*] on August 7.

After Li was taken captive by Tseng, he wrote a confession, *Li Hsiu-ch'eng kung-chuang* (The confession of Li Hsiu-ch'eng), which recounts the history of the Taiping Revolution. Whether he exaggerated his own contributions and what his motives were in writing the confession remain highly controversial issues among scholars.

REFERENCES: Su Hsiang-pi, "Lun Li Hsiu-ch'eng" (On Li Hsiu-ch'eng), in *T'ai-p'ing t'ien-kuo shih hsüeh-shu t'ao-lun hui lun-wen hsüan-chi* (Selected essays of the symposium on the study of the history of the Heavenly Kingdom of Great Peace) (Peking, 1981): 572–594; Chung Wen-tien, "Li Hsiu-ch'eng," in *T'ai-p'ing t'ien-kuo jen-wu* (Leaders of the Heavenly Kingdom of Great Peace) (Kwangsi, 1984): 375–404; C. A. Curwen, *Taiping Rebel: The Deposition of Li Hsiu-ch'eng* (Cambridge, 1977).

KAI-WING CHOW

LI HUNG-CHANG (posthumous title, Wen-chung, February 15, 1823–November 7, 1901): Statesman and diplomat in late imperial China.

Li Hung-chang was born on February 15, 1823, in Ho-fei, Anhwei, to a scholar class family. His father, Li Wen-an, was a *chin-shih* degree holder of 1838. Li Hung-chang received a good education and passed the provincial examination in 1844. He, too, became a *chin-shih* degree holder in 1847 and was appointed to the Hanlin Academy in 1850 as a compiler, a prestigious academic position for a scholar.

Li's government career began when he was asked to participate in the suppression of the Taiping Uprising* (1851–1864) in his home province of Anhwei in 1853. Li joined the staff of Governor Tseng Kuo-fan* in 1858 and began a long association with Tseng, his mentor and friend. In 1862 Li was named acting governor of Kiangsu. It was during this assignment that he began his lifelong association with Europeans in China. Shanghai, the capital of Kiangsu, had become the center of European activities in China, where many Western mercenaries such as the Ever Victorious Army were employed by locals to defend the city from the Taiping forces.

After the defeat of the Taipings in 1864, Li was appointed acting governor-general of Nanking. He was also ordered to participate in the suppression of the Nien Rebellions* (1851–1868). In 1867 Li was named the governor-general of Hupeh and Hunan.

From 1870 to 1895 Li Hung-chang received numerous honors and promotions because of his distinguished performance. He was given the title of a first-class earl with the designation of *su-i*, the hereditary rank of *ch'i tu-yu*, and named grand tutor to the heir apparent. Li was also named the associate grand secretary of the government, the grand secretary of the government, and the high commissioner of trade for the North Ocean.

It was the position of the high commissioner of trade for the North Ocean (to which Li was appointed in 1879) that made Li Hung-chang aware of the importance of modernization and industrialization in China and the importance of employing Western specialists to help develop China. As trade commissioner, Li himself had to implement many industrialization projects, such as the construction of the first railway in China (1876), the first telegraph lines (1865, 1880, 1881), the Kiangnan Shipyard (1876), the Kiangnan Arsenal (1876), the China Merchant's Lines (1872), and the Tientsin Military Academy (1885).

Li Hung-chang's diplomatic career did not begin until 1870 when he was chosen to investigate the Tientsin Massacre and negotiate with France for the compensation of those involved in the incident. Shortly afterward, Li was called to negotiate with Japan for a treaty that was signed on July 21, 1871. The Margary Affair of 1875 also required Li to bargain with Sir Thomas Wade, the British minister in China, and to conclude the Chefoo Convention on September 13, 1876.

Even though Li Hung-chang's diplomatic skills made him "the most experienced diplomat" in the Ch'ing court at the time, his signing of the 1885 Treaty of Tientsin and the 1895 Treaty of Shimonoseki greatly discredited his abilities. In dealing with the French over the Treaty of Tientsin, China lost control over Indochina, while negotiations with the Japanese in 1894–1895 resulted in China's loss of Taiwan and the Pescadores. These failures were not, however, due to Li's lack of diplomatic skill; the cause, rather, was the weakness of the government that he represented. But Li took the blame on both occasions. Subsequently, he was relieved of most of his governmental positions and sent into semiretirement.

Li was called back by the emperor and appointed China's emissary at the coronation of Tsar Nicholas II of Russia in 1896, which made Li the first high Chinese official ever to visit Europe. From Russia, Li went to Germany, the Netherlands, Belgium, France, Great Britain, and the United States.

The outbreak of the Boxer Rebellion* in 1900 saw Li Hung-chang's final diplomatic service for the Ch'ing court. Aged and physically weak, Li was summoned by Empress Dowager Tz'u-hsi* to represent China in negotiations of the Boxer's Protocol in 1901 with the West, which was finally signed on September 7, 1901. By then, the Ch'ing dynasty* had already reached its lowest point, and the republican revolutionary movement, led by Dr. Sun Yat-sen,* was raging in south China. The end of the Ch'ing was near. Li died two months later on November 7, 1901, at the age of seventy-eight.

REFERENCES: Immanuel C.Y. Hsü, *The Rise of Modern China*, 4th ed. (New York, 1990); Arthur W. Hummel, *Eminent Chinese of the Ch'ing Period* (Washington, D.C., 1943); Lei Lu-ch'ing, *Li Hung-chang Hsin-Chuan* (New biography of Li Hung-chang), (Taipei,1983).

ANTHONY Y. TENG

LI LI-SAN (originally Long-chih; aka Li Min-jan, Li Ch'eng, Li Ming, Po Sheng; pen-names Po-shan, Po-san; 1899–1967): Early Chinese Communist leader educated in France; known for labor-organizing skills; led the Chinese Communist party from 1928 to 1930 with what came to be known as the Li Li-san line.

Beyond being known as the son of an improverished country teacher of Liling Country in Hunan, little is known of Li Li-san's family and early life. After a short spell as a teacher, he went to Peking in the summer of 1919 to join the May Fourth Movement.* There he enlisted for the work-study project and set sail for France in December 1919.

Working in various factories, Li soon distinguished himself as an activist leader. He, Chao Shih-yen,* Li Po-chien, and others formed labor study groups. In 1921 he went to Paris to join Chou En-lai,* Ts'ai Ho-sen, Ch'en Yi, and others in forming, among labor and student groups, the Chinese Communist Youth League. The league became a branch of the Chinese Communist party.* The French authorities soon deported Li and others for excessive agitation, especially in their efforts to seize the University of Lyons.

In the winter of 1921, Li joined the CCP in Shanghai and worked in the Secretariat of the newly formed China Trade Union under the leadership of

Chang Kuo-t'ao.* Soon after he was sent with Liu Shao-ch'i* to work in Anyuan, Kiangsi, to organize coal workers in the Han-yeh-p'ing mines. His skill led to signal success in 1924, when the mines were closed down. Back in Shanghai, Li quickly took a leading role in the May Thirtieth Incident* of 1925. He founded and led the Shanghai General Union, and he was inextricably linked with every major strike in Shanghai. In March 1926 he was the All-China Federation of Labor's representative to the Communist International Federation of Trade Union in Moscow. Upon return to China, he was elected vice-chairman of the All-China Federation and did labor work in Hupeh Province.

In April 1927 the Fifth National Party Congress in Wuhan elected Li a member of the Central Committee and the Politburo. After the Nationalist–Communist split, Li, Ch'ü Ch'iu-pai,* and others at Kiukang planned the Nanchang Uprising* that met with a bad fate on August 1. Earlier, in July, Li, Chou En-lai, Chang T'ai-lei, Li Wei-han, and Chang Kuo-t'ao had formed the temporary Standing Committee of the Politburo which replaced Ch'en Tu-hsiu's* leadership. The Nanchang and Swatow failures drove the leadership, Li included, to Hong Kong. Then came the Canton Commune* of December 1927 in which Chang T'ai-lei perished. Li became the party chairman for Kwangtung.

In 1928 Li began to reach the height of his power. In April he was elected to the Communist International Federation of Trade Unions. In June he was reelected to the Politburo at the Sixth Party Congress meeting in Moscow. Returning to China, Li exerted influence in numerous spheres of party activity. Even though Hsiang Chung-fa* was the general secretary, Li exercised de facto power. The "Li Li-san line" emerged in 1929. Essentially, the line was to conduct military uprisings in urban centers by organized urban proletariats with the aid of the Red Army. By 1930, the party apparatus branded this line as leftist deviationism just as Ch'en Tu-hsiu had earlier been a rightist opportunist. In September, following a Comintern* directive, Chou En-lai and Ch'ü Ch'iu-pai led in stripping Li of all his posts. In January 1931 Wang Ming* and others stripped him of his Central Committee membership. A fifteen-year sojourn in Russia followed, for correction and readjustment of views as required by the Comintern. Li became a carpenter, a mechanic, and a dockworker, and entered the Lenin Institute for reeducation. He was a representative at the Communist International Trade Union in the mid–1930s, and in 1935 he was named Chinese section head of the Comintern Workers' Publishing House. In 1938 he was accused by Soviet internal security as a Japanese spy, and he spent twenty-one months in jail, after which he returned to his former job at the publishing house.

Reelected to the Central Committee in 1945, Li returned to China in January 1946. He became active in party and labor work in the northeast, becoming vice-chairman of the All-China Federation of Labor in 1948. Difficulties with the leadership once again caused him to confess his former mistakes at the Eighth Party Congress in September 1956. He became publicly obscure after that, and he suffered further abuse during the Cultural Revolution.* He died an accused man in 1967 but was posthumously exonerated in March 1980. He had a son named Li Jen-tsun. His third wife was a Russian named Liza.

REFERENCES: Howard Boorman and Richard Howard, eds., *Biographical Dictionary of Republican China*, vol. 2 (New York, 1968): 310–312; Donald Klein and Ann Clark, *Biographic Dictionary of Chinese Communism*, 2 vols. (Cambridge, 1971); Wang Yung-chun and Liu Chien-kao, eds., *Chung-kuo hsien-tai jen-wu chuan* (Personalities of contemporary China) (Szechwan, 1986): 287–290.

D.W.Y. KWOK

LI TA-CHAO (October 6, 1888–April 28, 1927): Propagandist of Marxism-Leninism, librarian of Peking University, and founding member of the CCP.

Born in 1888 in Lo-ting County in Hopei Province, Li Ta-chao was brought up by his grandparents after his father and mother died in his early childhood. In 1904 his grandfather also passed away, but he dedicated part of his estate to provide for Li Ta-chao's education. Having received a traditional schooling until then, Li enrolled at the prefectural middle school in 1905 where he received some education in Western subjects, and from 1907 until 1913 he studied at the Peiyang College of Law and Political Science in Tientsin.

It was the 1911 Revolution* which drew Li for the first time into politics. He joined the pro-Yüan Shih-k'ai Pei-yang Legal and Political Study Society and began to publish articles in its magazine. Before long, however, Li came to oppose Yüan Shih-k'ai's* rule. In 1913 he expressed support for constitutionalism and associated himself with the Progress party, the Chin-pu-tang, of Liang Ch'i-ch'ao.* T'ang Hua-lung, one of the party's leaders, became Li's patron. With T'ang's assistance Li spent three years in Japan after 1913 studying political economy at Waseda University in Tokyo.

In Japan Li's constitutionalist commitments deepened, in part because of his reading of John Stuart Mill, Montesquieu, and Voltaire. He also became acquainted with various nationalist revolutionaries, including Chang Shih-chao, and in 1914 and 1915 he published articles denouncing Yüan Shih-kai's attempts to concentrate power in his own hands and to emasculate representative political institutions.

Li returned to China in the summer of 1916, throwing himself into politics, initially on the side of the constitutionalists. He served as secretary to T'ang Hua-lung and edited a constitutionalist daily in Peking. However, in October Li Ta-chao broke with the constitutionalists when T'ang Hua-lung and Liang Ch'i-ch'ao refused to let him publish an article critical of Tuan Ch'i-jui, the warlord who had come to control Peking following Yüan's failed effort to establish himself as emperor.

Following his departure from the constitutionalist camp, Li's thought radicalized in the sense that he abandoned the hope that political change could be achieved in an evolutionary way. He also became far more hostile to China's traditional culture. He developed contacts with New Culture Movement leaders, joining the editorial board of *The New Youth* (*Hsin Ch'ing-nien*) in January 1918 and becoming librarian and professor of economics and history at Peking University the following month.

Li Ta-chao was one of the first Chinese intellectuals to announce his support for the October Revolution in July 1918. Li pictured the revolution as an event that heralded the birth of a new age in which the people of all countries would demolish national boundaries, oppressive political institutions, and exploitative economic relations. He placed the October Revolution in the context of World War I, arguing that it constituted the victory of the common people against their governments, which, he believed, had plunged the world into a period of unparalleled violence and destruction and which therefore raised questions about the superiority of Western democratic forms of government. In his articles about Marxism-Leninism[*] and the October Revolution, Li developed a nationalistic interpretation of Marxism, in which economic determinism had little significance and which carried pronounced voluntaristic and populist features. In casting Marxism-Leninism in this way, Li showed consistency with his earlier thinking. He had been greatly influenced by Bergson's idea of the free will of individuals as a shaping force in history, and he had formulated a chiliastic conception of change, arguing that a new China was about to be born out of the ashes of the old society.

Li Ta-chao was involved in the founding of the Chinese Communist party,[*] organizing Marxism study societies at Peking University and supporting various leftist student groups. However, he left the day-to-day management of CCP institutions to others, although until his death he remained the preeminent CCP member in north China. Li's numerous connections in China's political world were important to the early CCP. He was instrumental in bringing about the ill-fated cooperation between the CCP and the warlord Wu P'ei-fu,[*] which resulted in the first large CCP-led worker strike, only to be ruthlessly suppressed by Wu. Li Ta-chao also was a promoter of the KMT–CCP United Front, working hard to smooth relations between the two parties. After 1925 he supported CCP collaboration with Feng Yü-hsiang,[*] a warlord who had rebelled against his patron, Chang Tso-lin, and who hinted that he was desirous of a relationship with Moscow.

Following the death of Sun Yat-sen[*] in March 1925, the CCP–KMT relationship in Peking deteriorated, and Feng Yü-hsiang's power rapidly declined. On March 18, 1926, Li and other left-wing and KMT figures led a large demonstration against a Japanese ultimatum to the Peking government demanding the withdrawal of Chinese forces from the Taku forts near Tientsin, where they were not supposed to be according to the Boxer Protocol. The demonstration led to many casualties as the police opened fire, and an arrest warrant was issued for Li, who took refuge in the Soviet Embassy. Chang Tso-lin occupied Peking in December 1926 and raided the Soviet Embassy. Captured during the raid, Li Ta-chao was executed on April 28, 1927.

REFERENCES: Maurice Meisner, *Li Ta-chao and the Origins of Chinese Marxism* (New York, 1977); Li Ta-chao, *Collected Works of Li Ta-chao* (Peking, 1984).

HANS J. VAN DE VEN

LI T'E (Otto Braun, circa 1896–1974): Adviser from the Comintern to the CCP from 1933 to 1937, and the only known foreign participant to complete the Long March.

Otto Braun's name seldom appears in the pages of Chinese history on the Long March,* yet he was the only known foreigner to participate in the Red Army's Long March through China. Appointed by the Third Communist International (Comintern)* in 1933 as a military adviser to the Central Committee of the Chinese Communist party,* Braun advised Po Ku,* the leader of the pro-Stalin faction of the CCP. This pro-Moscow group was dubbed the faction of the Twenty-eight Bolsheviks.* Its members had been students in Moscow and had joined the Soviet branch of the Communist party. They promoted Stalin's policies by attacking Mao Tse-tung,* the Chinese Trotskyists, and Chang Kuo-t'ao.* Braun also devised military tactics against the Nationalist forces of Chiang Kai-shek.*

While his background is sketchy and contradictory at times, it is known that Braun was raised in Germany and fought in the German Army during World War I. He later served as a revolutionary agent in South America and Spain. Because of his participation in the street battles in Munich in April 1919, he was arrested and sentenced to death for being a Communist agent. Following his escape from prison, Braun fled to the Soviet Union where he attended the Frunze Military Academy for training in tactics and strategy.

After his appointment by the Comintern to advise the CCP, Braun entered China to assist the revolutionary movement. He was unfamiliar with the culture, language, history, or the conflict. For Braun, the CCP's struggle against the Nationalist government was a struggle to overthrow bourgeois European governments rather than an attempt to solve China's problems. Initially, Braun's orthodox Marxism-Leninism* dictated that all foreign revolutionary parties should work for world revolution, even if this commitment hindered the National Revolution. Later, with the failure of revolutions in Europe and the growing isolation of the USSR, Braun adopted Stalin's argument that the Comintern should mobilize foreign governments to protect the Soviet Union. Both policies resulted in minimizing and sometimes even harming the revolutionary movement in China.

When Braun arrived in Kiangsi, he quietly took over the command of the Revolutionary Military Commission in April 1934. As a strategist, Braun rejected numerous attempts by Mao to change the Red Army's tactics from positional to guerrilla warfare. He ridiculed Mao and others who opposed his tactics for their lack of knowledge of military matters. The Chinese hated Braun for his arrogance and short temper, as well as for his constant womanizing. Ironically, Braun's tactics of positional warfare resulted in the disastrous defeat of the Red Army at the battle of Kuangchang, located near the Fukien-Kiangsi border. Red Army losses were staggering: 4,000 soldiers were killed and 20,000 wounded. Braun overestimated the resources of the Red Army's Soviet base and misjudged the strength of the Red Army in immobile warfare. Compounding his errors of self-confidence, he underestimated the offensive capability of Chiang Kai-shek's air force and the morale of the Nationalists' fighting forces.

Desperate to stem the high casualty and desertion rate, and to raise their own troop morale, the top leaders of the Red Army convened a meeting at the Pai Mansion in Tsunyi* on January 15, 1935. The outcome of this conference had a profound impact on the leadership and direction of the Chinese Communist Revolution. The leaders of the CCP discussed the military setbacks from Chiang's Fifth Encirclement Campaign.* Mao's supporters blamed the disastrous outcome on Po Ku and Braun's positional warfare strategy. Braun insisted that his plans were sabotaged by Mao, who wanted to gain control over the army. Unable to defend his strategy in the Chinese language, Braun helplessly watched Mao's supporters make all military decisions with Mao. A resolution was drafted, and it placed the blame of Kuangchang on Braun and others who supported the Comintern position of revolutionary struggle.

In 1937, with the Long March completed and Mao's new policies established in Yenan, Braun attempted to leave China for the Soviet Union. But his departure was postponed when Wang Ming (Ch'en Shao-yü)* advised him to stay because purges were taking place in Moscow. Otto Braun finally left for Moscow in 1939 and dropped out of sight until the Sino-Soviet split in 1960. He re-emerged in his final days to write anti-Mao propaganda; he became a living symbol of the ideological and political differences between China and the Soviet Union.

REFERENCES: Dieter Heinzig, "The Otto Braun Memoirs and Mao's Rise to Power," *China Quarterly* 46 (April/June 1971): 274–288; Richard C. Kagan, "The Comintern, the 28 Bolsheviks, and the Alumni of Sun Yat-sen University," *International Review of History and Political Science* 11, no. 1 (February 1974); John E. Rue, *Mao Tse-tung in Opposition* (Stanford, Calif., 1966); Edgar Snow, *Red Star over China* (New York, 1968); Helen F. Snow, *My Years in China* (New York, 1984); Dick Wilson, *The Long March 1935* (New York, 1971).

RICHARD C. KAGAN

LI YÜAN-HUNG (1864–1928): Troop commander in Wuchang prior to the 1911 Revolution; reluctant leader of 1911 Revolution military forces; twice president of the Republic of China.

Son of an army officer who fought for the Ch'ing during the Taiping Revolution,* Li Yüan-hung was first a naval cadet in the Tientsin Naval Academy (graduating 1889) and then chief engineer on a modern cruiser. His ship was ordered north during the Sino-Japanese War of 1894–1895* but hit a coral reef and then was sunk by the Japanese. Li escaped by floating in a life belt for three days until washed ashore, and then ended his naval career.

Later in 1895, Li entered the staff of Governor-General Chang Chih-tung as an engineer and, after Chang sent him to Japan for training, as troop commander. In 1906 Li became first commander of the Twenty-first Mixed Brigade of the New Army* in Hupeh, stationed near Wuchang. Revolutionary organizers were active in his brigade. Each time one was brought to his attention, Li cashiered him but evidently did not have him arrested.

When the 1911 Revolution* began on October 10 with a mutiny in the Hupeh Army at Wuchang, no major revolutionary leaders were present. Needing a figurehead of at least moderate stature, the revolutionaries forced Li at gunpoint to assume titular command of their forces, possibly encouraged by Li's reputation for sensitivity to Han nationalism. For three days Li refused to assume his new command, but once he did, he was anxious to retain control. In late October, when a revolutionary government was inaugurated in Hupeh, Li secured the top post of military governor (*tu-tu*).

In November 1911, three groups were vying for control of the country: revolutionaries, dynastic loyalists, and a group willing to cashier the imperial system but wanting an authoritarian, even militaristic, government. Personal ambition was an important consideration, particularly in the third group. Li Yüan-hung lay between the revolutionaries and the authoritarian militarists.

Yüan Shih-k'ai,* the authoritarian militarist par excellence, decided not to use his armies against the revolutionaries if they would make him president of a republic of China, while in the revolutionary camp, Li Yüan-hung competed with more committed revolutionaries such as Huang Hsing* and Sung Chao-jen.* Li favored making Yüan Shih-k'ai president. Overawed by Yüan's military strength and desiring to retain Li's support, in December 1911 the revolutionaries made Li one of two vice-presidents of the T'ung-meng hui* and agreed to Yüan as president. Yüan succeeded to the office in March 1912. Li became vice-president, but refused to leave Wuchang for Peking when the new government moved there for fear of leaving his power base. In 1913 the failure of the Second Revolution* weakened Li and forced him to agree to move to Peking. There, Li found himself honored but powerless.

Yüan Shih-k'ai died in June 1916, and Li Yüan-hung assumed the presidency. A power struggle soon developed between now-President Li and the premier, the warlord Tuan Ch'i-jui. Matters came to a head in the spring of 1917 over the issue of China's entry into World War I on the Allied side. Tuan chose to strongarm Parliament to force China to join the Allies. Li dismissed Tuan, wrongly expecting support from other militarists such as then Vice-President Feng Kuo-chang. Instead, Tuan called on provincial military governors to declare independence, and eight of them did. Li fell back on the support of the conservative general Chang Hsün,* who neutralized Tuan's influence but then tried to restore the Ch'ing,* forcing Li to dissolve Parliament. Chang eventually failed, but by the time matters had been settled, Li had been forced out as president, Tuan was once again premier, and Feng Kuo-chang had become president.

In April 1921, southern revolutionaries associated with Sun Yat-sen* established a rival government in Canton under the direction of the Nationalist party. Early in 1922 Sun tried but failed to unify the country. Instead, the Chihli Clique* of northern warlords (including Feng Kuo-chang and Wu P'ei-fu*) reestablished a semblance of national unity. The Chihli Clique then offered to reseat the Parliament dismissed in 1917 and invited Li Yüan-hung to resume the presidency. Li stipulated that regional armies must be drastically reduced and military governorships abolished. The Chihli Clique agreed, and Li resumed the presidency in May 1922, but his two conditions were never fully met. Li remained president until May 1923 when he found himself on the wrong side of another warlord quarrel precipitated by the near-bankruptcy of the central government and disagreements between Wu P'ei-fu and the warlord Feng Yü-hsiang.* Li was hounded from office by hired ''citizen protesters'' and disobedient police (whose pay was in arrears); he fled to Shanghai, resigning from the presidency. He spent the rest of his life in retirement, and died in June 1928.

REFERENCES: Howard L. Boorman and Richard Howard, eds., *Biographical Dictionary of Republican China*, vol. 2 (New York, 1968); Vidya Prakash Dutt, ''The First Week of Revolution: The Wuchang Uprising,'' in Mary Clabaugh Wright, ed., *China in Revolution: The First Phase, 1900–1913* (New Haven, Conn., 1968): 383–416; Edward S.G. Li, *Life of Li Yüan-hung* (Tientsin, 1925); K. S. Liew, *Struggle for Democracy: Sung Chiao-jen and the 1911 Chinese Revolution* (Berkeley, Calif., 1971); James E. Sheridan, *Chinese Warlord: The Career of Feng Yü-hsiang* (Stanford, Calif., 1966).

L. EVE ARMENTROUT MA

LIANG CH'I-CH'AO (February 23, 1873–January 19, 1929): Leading journalist, political thinker, and politician of the late Ch'ing and early Republic.

Liang was born in Kwangtung Province and at first followed the normal course of training in the Confucian classics, seeking to win a degree in the imperial examinations and join the bureaucracy. He passed the provincial (*chü-jen*) examination. But an encounter with the iconoclastic reformist thinker K'ang Yu-wei* in 1890 changed Liang's life. He became K'ang's disciple and then a fellow-leader and theorist of the Reform Movement of 1898.

When the reform effort failed, Liang fled to Japan, where until 1912 he published a series of influential political journals, especially *The New Citizen*, which broke circulation records of its time with a circulation of 14,000. His thinking showed the influence of his exposure, through Japanese translations, to the classics of Western thought as well as to a mixed list of contemporary European and Japanese authors. Liang's voracious appetite for theory and his facility with the pen made him perhaps the most influential early twentieth-century Chinese thinker.

Liang's thought was protean. From 1898 to 1903, his writings tended to favor revolution. Drawing on the Social Darwinism so popular worldwide in his day, he argued that the Chinese people were losing out in a struggle for survival among the races. They needed a highly participant, democratic society in order to mobilize all their energies for the common national good. But after visiting America in 1903 and seeing both the corruption of American democracy and the backwardness of the Chinese communities there, Liang argued that China needed an enlightened despot in order to modernize. He said China's culture was still too backward for democratic institutions to be successful until after an extended period of tutelage. During 1905–1907 Liang carried out a polemic in his journal against the journal of the rival pro-revolutionary T'ung-meng hui* headed by Sun Yat-sen.*

Although chiefly a political writer, Liang was also active in political organizations. During his time in exile he worked with, then broke with, his mentor K'ang Yu-wei's Emperor Protection Society (Pao-huang hui).* In 1907 he organized a society called the Cheng-wen she to support the constitutionalist movement then developing in China. Although still in exile, Liang became the intellectual patron of the constitutionalist movement.

After the outbreak of the 1911 Revolution,[*] Liang returned to China both to continue his career as a writer and publisher, and to participate in party politics. He was a leader of the Progressive party that supported Yüan Shih-k'ai[*] in the Parliament of 1913–1914, and he served as minister of justice and in other high governmental posts. He broke with Yüan over Yüan's effort to make himself emperor, and he helped coordinate the successful revolt against Yüan led by his former student, Ts'ai Ao.[*] After Yüan's death, Liang returned to Peking and organized the Association for Constitutional Research; the association was not actually a research organization but a political group that became known as the Research Faction. As an influential power broker, Liang again served briefly in the cabinet in 1917, this time as minister of finance.

After Liang resigned this post, he devoted the remainder of his life to intellectual pursuits. He promoted Chinese knowledge of Western thought through translation projects and invitations to foreign lecturers. He taught at Nankai University and lectured at other universities, and he published a number of important scholarly works on Chinese intellectual history and other subjects.

REFERENCES: Hao Chang, *Liang Ch'i-ch'ao and Intellectual Transition in China, 1890–1907* (Cambridge, 1971); Philip C. Huang, *Liang Ch'i-ch'ao and Modern Chinese Liberalism* (Seattle, Wash., 1972); Joseph R. Levenson, *Liang Ch'i-ch'ao and the Mind of Modern China*, 2nd rev. ed. (Berkeley, Calif., 1970).

                                                                ANDREW J. NATHAN

LIANG SHU-MING (October 18, 1893–June 24, 1988): Philosopher, social and political activist.

Born into an impoverished metropolitan official's family in Peking, Liang Shu-ming was educated in a variety of Peking "Western-style" schools until his graduation from Shun-t'ien Middle School in 1911. During his teenage years he was philosophically a Benthamite utilitarian and politically a liberal democratic advocate of British-style parliamentary government. When the Wuhan Uprising occurred in October of that year, however, he joined the underground Tung-meng hui[*] and was involved in planning violent terrorist acts. After the establishment of a republic in 1912, Liang worked as a reporter for the party newspaper, *Kuo-min-pao*, until the reorganization of the party into the Kuomintang in 1913. At that time he underwent a profound spiritual crisis that led to two suicide attempts and a desperate "conversion" to Buddhism; he became a devotee of the Wei-shih school as well as a celibate vegetarian. His father Liang Chi, a radical reformer in his time, opposed both his son's revolutionary activity and his renunciation of marriage, but refused to intervene.

In 1916 Liang's first published article on Buddhism attracted the attention of the newly appointed chancellor of Peking University, Ts'ai Yüan-p'ei,[*] who appointed him professor of Indian philosophy, despite the fact that Liang had never attended college. In November 1919, his father, Liang Chi, committed suicide out of "loyalty to the emperor" and other traditional values of Chinese culture. This traumatic event influenced Liang greatly. The following year Liang became interested in the question of traditional Chinese culture and Westernization, which at the time was a prominent topic of public discussion. He also publicly abandoned Buddhism for Confucianism. As a first act of his new persona, Liang married Huang Ching-hsien, a Peking Manchu who subsequently bore him two sons.

In 1921 his book *Tung Hsi wen-hua chi ch'i che-hsüeh* (Eastern and Western cultures and their philosophies) created a sensation and made Liang a national figure as a new type of an intellectually sophisticated cultural conservative who prized traditional Chinese ethical values in the teeth of the prevailing antitraditional cultural revolution espoused by the intellectual elite of the New Culture and May Fourth movements.

In the book, Liang explained life itself as expressions of a cosmic Will, which, in its individual expressions, makes demands on the environment and overcomes obstacles to fulfillment; "culture" was the way in which the human expressions of the Will resolve the contradictions between their demands and obstacles to them in the environment. He posited three ideal cultural types—expressions of three distinct directions of the Will—represented by the West, China, and India. The Western direction was forward, an unending Faustian struggle to subdue the external world, but never attaining satisfaction and contentment; the Chinese direction was a sideways compromise of harmonization with the environment, but gaining true contentment and happiness; in Indian culture, the Will is turned backward on itself seeking its own negation, as human consciousness achieves the final enlightenment. Each of the directions should have succeeded the other at the appropriate stage of human evolution, but the primeval sage creators of Chinese and Indian cultures had somehow transcended their own time and prematurely set the direction of the culture at higher levels before their societies were prepared materially. These cultures now appeared backward, compared to Western culture, but were actually on a different track altogether. Liang argued that the West, having already adequately attended to primal wants and material welfare, was about to enter into the era of the second direction (Chinese culture). China, Liang advised, should therefore accept and absorb Western culture in order to satisfy primal human wants, but should simultaneously revitalize and invigorate its own traditional culture and attitude toward life.

When he published the book, Liang had not yet worked out the institutional and organizational means for the cultural revival he prescribed. In 1924 Liang resigned from Peking University to head a middle school in Shantung. There he began the first of many educational experiments aimed at creating a young intelligentsia who was both a Confucian paragon of virtue and altruism devoted to serving the people and proficient in the new modernizing knowledge of the West. For the next few years he was active in experimental educational work in several provinces, gradually integrating his theory of Chinese cultural rebirth with a practical method.

By 1929 Liang had "awakened" to his final solution to China's cultural dilemma—rural reconstruction—by which means China would give birth to a new world civilization that possessed both the material advantage of Western modernization and the spiritual contentment and happiness of traditional Chinese culture. Liang quickly began to integrate a new version of his metahistorical theories and his educational experiments with specific rural reform measures. He joined with several other intellectuals interested in rural reform in founding a school for the training of cadres in Honan Province, the Village Government Institute (Ts'un chih hsüeh-yüan). The next year, with Chiang Kai-shek's[*] victory over Feng Yü-hsiang[*] and the Kuomintang occupation of Honan, the school was immediately closed. Chiang rewarded Feng's erstwhile lieutenant and current Honan governor, Han Fu-ch'ü, for his timely sellout to the KMT side with the governorship of Shantung Province. Han had seen the value of rural work and invited Liang and his comrades to reestablish their school in Shantung forthwith. The resulting Shantung Rural Reconstruction Institute (Shan-tung hsiang-ts'un chien-she yen-chiu-yüan) began operations in 1931, training several levels of cadre for rural work as well as governing the county in which it was located, Tsou-p'ing, and another experimental county, Ho-tse. Liang became a national leader of the rural reform movement, providing it with a philosophical foundation and articulating its theory in his books and articles. He specifically rejected the Western and Soviet paths to modernization, and was critical of the Nationalist government's as well. By the time the war broke out in 1937, all Shantung counties had institute graduates working in them, and half of Shantung's counties had rural reform programs in place.

With the Japanese invasion, Liang's Shantung projects came to an end. The Nationalist government appointed him to the Supreme Defense Council, and he went with the government to Chungking in 1938. He was active in promoting conscription reform, but the government proved to be uncooperative. Dissatisfied with this powerless public role, Liang spent many months making two trips behind enemy lines in north China. He also visited Yenan in January 1938, encouraged that the Communists seemed to have abandoned their radical policies. There he spent a week in intense discussions with Mao Tse-tung[*] (with whom he had become acquainted in 1919) on the nature of Chinese society, culture, and the future. Liang's observatory expeditions into occupied China had convinced him that a new KMT–CCP civil war was imminent. Upon his return to west China in late 1939, he immediately set to work in creating an independent "third force" to interpose itself as mediator between the two major parties. His organization, the T'ung-i chien-kuo t'ung-chih hui (Association of Comrades for National Unity and Construction), was an alliance of the small liberal democratic parties composed of noted intellectuals and their followings. The KMT did not welcome its participation in politics. In order to give the association a public voice, Liang secretly decamped to Hong Kong, where in October 1941 he began to publish a newspaper, *Kuang-ming pao* (Light). The Japanese occupation of Hong Kong in December forced Liang to flee back to China, this time to Kweilin, where, in January 1944, he married his second wife, Ch'en Shu-fen. (His first wife had died in 1935 in Tsou-p'ing.)

In 1944 the association was reorganized as the Min-chu t'ung-meng hui (Democratic League) under which name it still exists, after a fashion, in China today. With the end of the war in 1945, Liang became secretary general of the Democratic League, and for a year and a half devoted himself exclusively to arbitrating the differences between the Nationalists and Communists. In October 1946, seeing that further attempts at negotiation would be useless, he retired from political life to the countryside near Chungking. During this time he wrote and published *Chung-kuo wen-hua yao-i* (The essence of Chinese culture), which proved to be his last major work for the next thirty-five years.

After the establishment of the People's Republic of China[*] in 1949, Mao Tse-tung prevailed on him to return to Peking. Liang refused Mao's offer of an official position in the new government, which offended Mao greatly and created a fissure in their hitherto close relationship. Liang did accept a position on the Standing Committee of the Chinese People's Political Consultative Conference.[*] Mao also commissioned Liang to inspect land reform in various areas of the country, which he did during 1950 and 1951. During this period Mao often invited Liang to his home for private discussions in the evening. At a meeting of several hundred top government and party leaders in 1953, however, Liang pointedly criticized party policies, arguing that they had resulted in an enormous gap in living standards between the urban workers and the peasantry. Perhaps because he knew Liang's criticism to be accurate and because Liang dared to speak for the peasantry, Mao responded with a public tirade against him, and never saw him privately again. Liang was the target of a mass criticism campaign during 1955 and 1956. Throughout, he steadfastly refused to change his "erroneous" political opinions and philosophical ideas, although he did conscientiously study Marxism-Leninism.[*]

In August 1966, at the very onset of the Cultural Revolution,[*] students from a neighboring school (Red Guards)[*] invaded his home, "struggled" against him, burned his library, family heirlooms, and furniture, beat his wife, and occupied his house. For the next decade and a half, Liang lived in one small room in poverty and isolation. Although he continued to ponder his philosophical ideas, he did not finish his last book manuscript, *Human Life and the Heart/Mind* (*Jen-sheng yü jen-hsin*), until 1979. His wife died that year after several years as an invalid. In 1980 the Chinese People's Political Consultative Conference[*] gave him a modern apartment where he lived quietly until his death in 1988 at age ninety-six.

Liang's other important books include *Chung-kuo min-tsu tzu-chin yün-tung chih tsui-hou chueh-wu* (The final awakening of the Chinese people's self-salvation movement) (1931); *Hsiang-ts'un li-lun* (Theory of rural reconstruction) (1936); and *Liang Shu-ming chiao-yü lun-wen chi* (Liang Shu-ming's collected essays on education) (1935). His collected works were assembled and edited by his son P'ei-k'uan after his death. When asked by his English-language biographer in 1980, if, from the perspective of extreme old age, he had discovered errors in writings, he thought for several minutes, and then replied that he had misunderstood the concept of "instinct" (*pen-neng*) in his 1921 book.

REFERENCE: Guy S. Alitto, *The Last Confucian: Liang Shu-ming and the Chinese Dilemma of Modernity* (Berkeley, Calif., 1979).

GUY S. ALITTO

LIN PIAO (1907–1971): Communist leader; defense minister of the PRC; designated successor to Mao.

Lin Piao was born into a well-to-do merchant family at Huangkang, Hupeh Province, in 1907. His father owned a cloth-dyeing factory. Lin attended high school at Wuchang, the provincial capital of Hupeh. While at high school in 1925, he joined a satellite organization of the Chinese Communist party* and took part in the May Thirtieth* Movement of that year. In that October, he entered the fourth class of the Whampoa Military Academy,* from which he graduated in 1926, just in time to join the Northern Expedition.* He served as a platoon leader and later a company commander in Yeh T'ing's independent regiment under Chang Fa-k'uei. It was then that he became a full-fledged member of the CCP. He took part in the Nanchang Uprising* staged by the CCP following the split between the Kuomintang left and the CCP at Wuhan in July 1927.

Having suffered further setbacks in Kwangtung, Lin followed Chu Teh* to join forces with Mao Tse-tung* to form the Fourth Army* in the Chingkang Mountain, bordering Hunan and Kiangsi, in May 1928 with Chu as army commander and Mao as political commissar. Soon Lin rose to regiment commander but was pessimistic about the future of the Chinese Revolution, as seen in a letter Mao wrote to him in early 1930. Lin fought well in the anti-Chiang Kai-shek* Encirclement and Suppression Campaigns* throughout the Kiangsi period, 1928–1934. He rose to commander of the First Group Army in 1932, when P'eng Te-huai* commanded the Third and Tung Chen-tang the Fifth, the three being the only Red Army in the Kiangsi Soviet.*

At the end of Chiang's fifth campaign against the Communists in Kiangsi, the Communists were forced to set out on the Long March* in October 1934. During the Long March, Lin's First and Peng's Third Group armies bore the brunt of assaults from the pursuing forces of the KMT until they successfully made a rendezvous with the Fourth Front Red Army from northern Szechwan led by Chang Kuo-t'ao* and Hsü Hsiang-chien in June 1934. The Chang-Mao split caused by personality conflict and strategic differences led to Mao's moving northward independently with Lin's and P'eng's armies. Almost a year to the day after they left Kiangsi, the Long Marchers settled at Paoan in northern Shensi, where they built anew the Soviet base with some scattered Communist guerrillas having survived there.

The suspension of the civil war between the CCP and KMT created by the Sian Incident* in December 1936 facilitated the rapprochement between them and made possible the formation of a United Front against Japan. Barely had the Japanese launched the Lukouchiao Incident on July 7, 1937 than China was united to fight an all-out war of resistance against Japan. Then the Red Army was organized into the Eighth Route Army* with three divisions, the 115th, 120th, and 129th, commanded by Lin Piao, Ho Lung, and Liu Po-ch'eng, respectively.

Lin Piao's fame cannot be separated from his victory over the Japanese Army at the battle of P'inghsing Pass. On September 23–30, 1937, Lin's 115th Division scored a major victory by ambushing a Japanese convoy escorted by a force of over 1,000 men, all of whom were killed except one who was taken prisoner. Unquestionably, it was the first great victory in north China since the war, but the 115th Division also had suffered heavy losses of nearly 1,000 men dead or wounded. Although Lin's victory greatly boosted the morale of the Chinese Army and saved the CCP from the allegation that the Eighth Route Army had evaded engagement with the enemy, it could not have saved the battle of P'inghsing Pass, which ended with another Chinese defeat.

After sustaining an injury in Shansi in the fall of 1939, Lin went to the Soviet Union for recuperation and never again took an active command in the war with Japan.

Being always Mao's man, Lin sided with Mao in all his intraparty struggles from the Fut'ien Incident in 1930 to the Cultural Revolution.* With the advent of V-J Day, Lin was sent to northeast China, where he drew recruits and reinforcements from various Communist-held bases, reorganized the puppet troups of Manchukuo,* received Japanese warehouses and military equipment, and was aided by the friendly Soviet occupation forces. As a result, he forged a strong Communist force that was able to defeat the American-equipped forces of Chiang Kai-shek in the northeast, which ultimately led to the collapse of Chiang's regime in the mainland.

Lin's northeastern army was later reorganized into the Fourth Field Army, a term that is still used today. With the People's Republic* inaugurated in 1949, Lin became the top-ranking leader in the CCP hierarchy. At the outset of the Korean War, Lin was the commander-in-chief of the Chinese Volunteer Force and soon was wounded and relieved by P'eng Te-huai. At the Lushan Conference* in the summer of 1959, P'eng fell into disgrace when he criticized Mao's policies on communes and the Great Leap Forward.* Lin then replaced P'eng as defense minister, thus becoming second only to Mao in the Chinese military establishment.

In launching the Cultural Revolution, Mao and his wife Chiang Ch'ing* turned to Lin for support, without whom it is questionable whether the movement could have been initiated, sustained, and developed as it had. Conversely, Lin, by advocating the "politics in command" and the cult of the Thought of Mao Tse-tung* and by holding the "Little Red Book" of Mao's quotations, exploited the Cultural Revolution to his own advantage. Not only did he consolidate his power in the People's Liberation Army* but also his succession to Mao was assured by a statutory guarantee in the CCP constitution adopted by the Ninth Congress in April 1969.

By then, however, the honeymoon between the Mao-Chiang and Lin factions was over. At the CCP Second Plenum held at Lushan in midsummer 1970, Ch'en Po-ta,* Mao's longtime secretary and chairman of the Cultural Revolution Group, supported Lin Piao in Lin Piao's bid for chairmanship of the state, a position vacated by Liu Shao-ch'i.* Lin's ambition was blocked by Mao himself, for fear that Lin might become a threat to his power. Failing to come to terms with defeat at Lushan, Lin resorted to conspiratorial activities as evidenced by a document known as the Outline of Project 571. As recent reports have revealed, at the height of his power, Lin built palace and underground headquarters by the West Lake at Hangchou, coupled with the holding of a beauty contest for choosing a "queen" for his son Lin Li-kuo, the engineer of Project 571.

At any rate the relationship between Lin and Mao deteriorated apace. Probably as a result of his feelings of insecurity in his dealings with Mao and driven by his wife and followers' impatience to assume power, Lin acceded to a conspiratorial design for an armed coup d'état and the assassination of Mao. When that attempt failed, Lin and his family made a hasty flight out of the country, but his airplane crashed near Undur Khan, Outer Mongolia, on September 13, 1971.

The melodrama of Lin Piao did not come to an end with his death, simply because he had been the chairman's comrade-in-arms for nearly half a century and had been designated his heir apparent. His conspiracy against Mao and his failure not only constituted a disgrace of Lin himself, but also revealed Mao's failure. Hence, a rectification movement was needed to criticize Lin's thought and deeds. The Anti-Lin, Anti-Confucius Campaign* went far beyond what its title implied. Aside from criticizing Lin, the movement was an innuendo attack on Chou En-lai,* Teng Hsiao-p'ing,* and even Hua Kuo-feng,* and was not concluded until the death of Mao.

REFERENCES: Hong Yung Lee, *The Politics of the Chinese Cultural Revolution* (Berkeley, Calif., 1978); Tien-wei Wu, *Lin Biao and the Gang of Four* (Carbondale, Ill., 1983); Kao Kao and Yen Chia-ch'i, *Wen-hua ta ke-ming shih-nien shih* (A ten-year history of the Cultural Revolution) (Tientsin, 1986).

TIEN-WEI WU

LITERARY REVOLUTION (New Literature Movement, or the Plain Language Literature Movement, 1910s–1920s): A movement that promoted spoken Chinese for literary writing and for a new humanistic and realistic literature.

Before the second decade of the twentieth century, all formal Chinese writing, including literary works in both prose and poetry, were composed primarily in the classical and literary language (*wen-yen*), which is not spoken. Although after the Sung–Yüan period most of the traditional fiction and part of drama were written in the vernacular or plain language (*pai-hua*), they were not recognized as serious literature. Often such formal literature was also heavily permeated with moral principles and sometimes written in a verbose ornate style. They were hardly understood by the common people.

By the end of the nineteenth century and the early twentieth century, however, a few young intellectuals already started to publish a few journals in plain language, and a few authors mentioned a "poetry revolution" and a "literary revolution" without much action. In 1915 Huang Yüan-yung, a famous journalist, suggested "the promotion of a new literature," and Ch'en Tu-hsiu,* in the *New Youth* monthly he edited, also suggested a Chinese literature of "realism" and "naturalism." But pure literature, except part of fiction and drama, and practical writing in general were still composed in the classical language. Moreover, the above suggestions for a change were scarcely noticed by the public until Hu Shih,* then a student in the United States, wrote Ch'en a letter that was published in the monthly on October 1, 1916. Since the summer of 1916 Hu Shih had argued with his fellow students for a vernacular poetry. In the letter Hu said that, if a literary revolution in China was intended, eight changes should be made: "(1) Do not use allusions; (2) Do not use clichés; (3) Do not care about parallelism (Get rid of paralleled prose and the regulated poetry); (4) Do not avoid colloquial words and speech (Do not regret for writing poems and lyrics in plain language); (5) It is necessary to seek and follow grammar. (The above are for a revolution in literary form.) (6) Do not moan and groan without being ill; (7) Do not imitate the ancients, what one writes must reflect oneself; (8) One's words must have substance. (The above are for a revolution of spirit.)" Of the eight suggestions, the most important one was the fourth—that is, use of colloquial words and plain language for writing. With Ch'en's encouragement, Hu also wrote an article titled "Some Humble Suggestions for the Reform of Chinese Literature," which appeared in the January 1, 1917, issue of *New Youth* monthly. In the article Hu expanded the eight principles and declared that the existing Chinese literature in the vernacular should be regarded as the "standard" literature. The vernacular, not the classical or literary language, he said, would be the fit medium for creating a "living literature." A year later Hu put the above eight suggestions all in negative terms—thus the famous so-called "eight-don'ts-ism."

Ch'en Tu-hsiu published Hu's article with great enthusiasm; to further support and strengthen Hu's suggestions, in the February issue Ch'en also published an article of his own with the bold title "On the Literary Revolution." He stated, "The promotion of a literary revolution has been mushroomed for a not short length of time, and the foremost in the vanguard, who first raised the revolutionary banner, is my friend Hu Shih. I am willing to brave the enmity of all the pedantic scholars of the country, and hoist the great banner of the 'Army of the Literary Revolution' in support of my friend." Ch'en said that on this banner should be written his "three principles of the Revolutionary Army: (1) overthrow the carved and obsequious literature of the aristocracy, and establish the plain and expressive literature of the people; (2) overthrow the stale and extravagant classical literature, and establish the fresh and sincere realistic literature; (3) overthrow the obscure and difficult literature of the hermit and the recluse, and establish the plain-speaking and popular social literature." The article approved the folk tradition of the *Book of Poetry* and the *Song of the South*, the Yün drama, and the traditional vernacular fiction, but attacked the time-honored principle that "literature is a vehicle for conveying the Tao" (*wen i tsai tao*), the *fu* rhapsody, and the traditionalist poetics of the Ming dynasty. It also persuaded Chinese writers to follow Western examples, such as Hugo, Zola, Goethe, Hauptmann, Dickens, and Wilde.

Hu and Ch'en's articles immediately attracted the attention of other scholars and writers, including Ch'ien Hsüan-t'ung and Liu Fu. They attacked the older writers who had clung to the traditional literary tenets, calling them the "black sheep of the T'ung-ch'eng school" (*T'ung-ch'eng miao-chung*) and "demons of the *Wen-hsüan* learning" (*Hsüan-hsüeh yao-yeh*).

By 1918 the new Chinese literature developed into its natal period. From January of that year on, *New Youth* was published completely in the vernacular, which was later to be called the national language (*kuo-yü*), a term that returned students had used in 1906. Most of the poems in Hu Shih's pioneering work, *A Book of Experiments*, published in 1920, were composed in 1918. Leading reformers, such as Liu Fu, Lu Hsün,* Shen Yin-mo, Yü P'ing-po, Chou Tso-jen, Chu Tzu-ch'ing, K'ang Pai-ch'ing, Ch'en Tu-hsiu, Li Ta-chao,* Liu Ta-pai, Lo Chia-lun, and Fu Ssu-nien, all joined in writing vernacular poems by this time. Lu Hsün published his first significant vernacular short story, "The Diary of a Madman," in the May 1918 issue of *New Youth*. The works of Ibsen, Strindberg, Andersen (Northern Europe), of Dostoyevsky, Kuprin, Tolstoy (Eastern Europe), as well as the modern Greek Ephtaliotis and the Pole Sienkiewicz, were translated into a written Chinese vernacular influenced by the grammar and style of the original European languages.

But the spread of the new literary movement did not reach wider circles until 1919, when the May Fourth Movement* was on the rise. The students established and widely circulated a great number of publications that were usually in the vernacular language. The new thought reform* and political protest also made the intellectuals more acceptable to the literary revolution. Therefore, the passive opposition from older writers such as Lin Shu and Ku Hung-ming who used the classical language for writing was hardly heard by younger intellectuals.

After the initial success of the new literature, the young writers organized several literary groups. One of these groups was the Society for Literary Studies (*Wen-hsüeh yen-chiu hui*), established on January 4, 1921. Under the influence of Chou Tso-jen and Mao Tun, the society first advocated a "literature of humanity" and later introduced a number of writings by European, Russian, and American authors, mostly with realistic or naturalistic approaches. On the other hand, in the summer of 1921 a group of Chinese returned students from Japan, such as Kuo Mo-jo, Yü Ta-fu, T'ien Han, Chang Tzu-p'ing, and Ch'eng Fang-wu, established the Creation Society (Ch'uang-tsao she). They first advocated "art for art's sake," the development of the self, unrestricted expression of emotion, and freedom of organization. But many of them drifted to a kind of revolutionary romanticism after the middle of the 1920s and gave up their earlier individualistic ideas. They adopted revolutionary literature as their battle cry. The Society for Literary Studies also split into groups. The brothers Lu

Hsün and Chou Tso-jen went on to found the Thread-of-Talk Society (Yü-ssu she), insisting on realism and humanism, whereas Hsü Chih-mo, Hu Shih, Wen I-to, and Liang Shih-ch'iu organized the Crescent Moon Society (Hsin-yüeh she) advocating symbolism. After 1928, the Creation Society entered its third period, propagating proletarian literature. Then in 1930 the influential League of Leftist Writers (Tso-i tso-chia lien-meng) was established under the leadership of Lu Hsün but actually under the control of the Chinese Communist party.* Against this group stood another group promoting nationalistic literature, led by Huang Chen-hsia, Wang P'ing-ling, Shao Hsün-mei, and others. There were also writers and poets, such as Shih Chih-ts'un and Tai Wang-shu who espoused modernism. Before the outbreak of the Sino-Japanese War* in 1937, literary controversies often became political, and through the 1930s and 1940s leftist writings almost dominated China's new literaure, although they might not necessarily be the best.

REFERENCES: Tse-tsung Chow, *The May Fourth Movement: Intellectual Revolution in Modern China* (Cambridge, Mass., 1960); C. T. Hsia, *A History of Modern Chinese Fiction, 1917–1957* (New Haven, Conn., 1961); Amitendranath Tagore, *Literary Debates in Modern China, 1918–1937* (Tokyo, 1967); Bonnie S. McDougall, *The Introduction of Western Literary Theories into Modern China* (Tokyo, 1971); Leo Ou-fan Lee, *The Romantic Generation of Modern Chinese Writers* (Cambridge, Mass., 1973); Merle Goldman, ed., *Modern Chinese Literature in the May Fourth Era* (Cambridge, Mass., 1977.)

TSE-TSUNG CHOW

LIU JEN (c. 1909–October 26, 1973): CCP and government official; leader of Communist underground struggle in urban north China prior to 1949.

Liu Jen was born in Yuyang County, Szechwan Province, in 1909. He joined the Chinese Communist party* in 1927 and conducted underground workers' movements in Shanghai, Wuhan, and (under the leadership of P'eng Chen* and Liu Ning-i) in Peip'ing (Peking), Tientsin, and Tangshan. He was arrested by the Kuomintang authorities in Tientsin in 1930 but was released two years later. From 1933 to 1935 Liu conducted an underground soldiers' movement and mass work in Changchiakou, Inner Mongolia, and Peip'ing, encouraging local KMT armies to join the Anti-Japanese Anti-Chiang Kai-shek United Army. Afterward he studied in the Soviet Union for about two years. At end of 1937 he returned to Yenan and became the secretary-general of the CCP Central Party Academy. In late 1938 he served as the deputy director of the Organization Department and the secretary of the Urban Work Committee of the CCP Central Committee (CC) Chin-Cha-Chi (Shansi-Chahar-Hopei) Sub-bureau. Later, he was the director of both the Urban Work Department and the Enemy Work Department of the CCP CC Chin-Cha-Chi Central Bureau.

During the wartime period (1937–1945), the underground CCP in Peip'ing, Tientsin, and other cities in north China acted in accordance with (1) Mao Tse-tung's* guiding principles of having "well-selected cadres working underground, accumulating strength and biding its time there" (1939); and (2) Liu Shao-ch'i's* theoretical and practical teachings on the Communist urban work in the enemy-occupied territories (1936–1937). However, Liu Jen was the Communist leader most responsible for the growth and consolidation of the CCP in Peip'ing and Tientsin. He carried out the policy of creating well-qualified cadres working in concealment inside the city, contacting, educating, and allying with the progressive elements for the purpose of complementing the military strategy of the anti-Japanese war of resistance in the countryside. Before the civil war* (1945–1949) started, he had already sowed the "red seeds" in Peip'ing and Tientsin. Liu Jen fulfilled the idea that "dispatching one person and developing one person amounted to planting a time bomb in the heart of the enemy."

In 1948 Liu was the deputy director of the Organization Department and the director of the Urban Work Department of the CCP CC North China Bureau. In October 1948 he informed the CCP Central in Hsipaipo Village, Hopei, of the Peip'ing KMT plot of capturing the Communist headquarters. The KMT "surprise" assault on the village was thus repulsed. Above all, Liu made a major contribution to the successful conclusion of the Peip'ing pattern in the Communist conquest of Mainland China—that is, "to compel enemy troops to reorganizing peacefully, quickly and thoroughly into the People's Liberation Army* in conformity with the latter's system." The peaceful occupation of Peip'ing in January 1949 was Liu's crowning success in the urban strategy of the Chinese Communist Revolution. After the establishment of the People's Republic of China,* Liu held a number of important posts in Peking (Peip'ing): director of the Organization Department of the CCP Peking Municipal Committee (1949), deputy secretary of the CCP Peking Municipal Committee (1950), second secretary of the CCP Peking Municipal Committee, and chairman of the Peking Municipal Committee of Chinese People's Political Consultative Conference* (1955), alternate member of the Eighth CCP CC (1956), political commissar of the Peking Garrison Command (1960), secretary of the Secretariat of CCP CC North China Bureau (1961), and first political commissar of Peking Garrison Command (1964). From 1949 to 1965 Liu contributed to the construction and transformation of Peking from a consumer city to a producer city. In 1966 he became one of the first victims of the Great Proletarian Cultural Revolution.* He was replaced by Wu Teh in early June in his most important post—secondary secretary of the CCP Peking Municipal Committee. Liu was arrested by the Red Guards* in December 1966. His tragic death in prison in October 1973 was probably due to his close connection with Liu Shao-ch'i,* P'eng Chen, and Liu Ning-i.

REFERENCES: *Mien-huai Liu Jen t'ung-chih* (Reminiscing Comrade Liu Jen) (Peking, 1979); *Chung-kung tang-shih chien-ming tz'u-tien* (A concise dictionary of the Chinese Communist party's history), vol. 2 (Peking, 1987): 666; Donald W. Klein and Anne B. Clark, *Biographical Dictionary of Chinese Communism*, vol. 1 (Cambridge, Mass., 1971): 595–596; *Chinese Communist Who's Who*, vol. 2 (Taipei, 1971): 42.

JOSEPH K.S. YICK

LIU SHAO-CH'I (November 24, 1898–November 12, 1969): The CCP's main organization man; ranked directly after Mao Tse-tung from about 1945 until

August 1966; second to none in day-to-day CCP administration; described by colleagues as a taciturn, disciplined, hard-working Communist; purged by the Cultural Revolution as China's Khrushchev; chief organizer and symbol of party bureaucratism.

Liu was born the son of a rich peasant and primary school teacher in Ning-hsiang County, Hunan. This area is near the provincial capital Changsha and near the home town of Mao Tse-tung,* who was five years older than Liu. After prolonged study, apparently under his father's tutelege, Liu entered the local school in 1913. Two years later, he was already active in politics, join-ing a movement against Yüan Shih-kai's* partial acceptance of Japan's Twenty-one Demands. By mid–1916, he was admitted to the middle school that his county ran in Changsha. He soon joined a military study society, which the local warlord dispersed, sending Liu back home for further reading on his own. After several such episodes by 1920 Liu traveled to Shanghai and in 1921 joined the China Socialist Youth League. He was chosen as one of the first Chinese to study in Moscow, at the University of the Toilers of the East. By the winter of 1921, he became a member in Russia of the newly formed Chinese Communist party.*

Liu's time at university was brief, but he studied throughout his life. In 1922 he returned to organize Shanghai workers and then to assist Mao Tse-tung in their native Hunan and among miners at An-yuan in western Kiangsi. A strike brought better conditions for the workers. In 1925–1926, Liu orga-nized in Shanghai, Canton, Hong Kong, and (when the Northern Expendi-tion* reached there) Wuhan. The collapse of the First United Front* sent Liu into hiding, again to Moscow for the CCP's Sixth Congress, to Shanghai, and in late 1932 to the Kiangsi Soviet* at Juichin. Liu and Mao were close in Kiangsi; they both opposed the political claims of other Russian Returned Students. When the CCP had to leave the south, Liu became one of the Long Marchers.*

At Yenan, Liu sometimes lived in a cave next to Mao's, writing lectures on *How to Be a Good Communist*, the manual about party discipline that first came out as a pamphlet in 1939. When the cult of Mao began, Liu emphasized that a Communist's obedience was to the party, not to any individual—but that Mao's good policies entitled him to allegiance. In 1942, when Mao's title as party chairman was much publicized, Liu remarked, "What is a chairman? I have never heard people in the Soviet Union calling Lenin Chairman Lenin." He told a 1947 meeting, "There is no perfect leader in the world." Yet Liu agreed with Mao on many policies, and he largely administered the 1940s Rectification Campaign,* even while his manner remained more self-effacing and detached (see MacFarquhar and Dittmer for more on the enigmatic Liu–Mao relationship). Liu relied on careful procedures and education to create an enthusiastic party.

Liu's organizational policies stressed the need to separate dissident leaders from their constituencies, sending them for education but then restoring them to lower positions. He reportedly originated the idea that urbanites periodically be "sent down" (hsia-fang).* He applied this policy to himself and his family, who sometimes left cities for brief stints of agricultural labor. He was less radical than other top leaders about rapid collectivization*—and in October 1955 criticized himself for this reticence. Liu gave the longest speech at the Party Congress in 1956, a watershed time as the CCP assumed more administrative work after the transition to socialism. His government counterpart, Premier Chou En-lai,* also spoke about the need for more efficiency—a theme that Liu downplayed, perhaps because he was more hopeful that socialist planning could effectively replace markets. Liu thought of bureaucratism as a common fault of the government, not of the party, because of its members' training and loyalty. Thus, ordinary people could criticize the state, whereas the party did not need this check.

The Great Leap Forward* was formally launched at a May 1958 Party Congress, with full support from both Liu and Mao. As the Leap faltered, Liu headed the "first line of leadership." In April 1959 he presided at a National People's Congress that elected him chairman of the Republic (and of the National Defense Committee, which met in the next month). Although Mao and other civilian leaders supported Liu's succession as head of state, Defense Minister P'eng Te-huai* apparently felt Marshal Chu Teh* deserved the job. After P'eng was dismissed in 1959, Liu (along with Lin Piao* and others) made speeches in effect defending Mao's prestige. The Party Propaganda Department had nonetheless mandated that newspapers print Liu's and Mao's pictures, equal in size and side by side, on national day.

Toward the end of 1959, an inflammation of Liu's shoulder and elbow forced a month's sick leave on warm Hainan, where he called a conference to study China's troubled economy. Liu worked collegially with Chou and Mao for many years. He also cooperated with Teng Hsiao-p'ing* and especially with P'eng Chen,* who may have been his only close personal friend among the leaders. Liu's virtues of reliability, loyalty, and work served the party as a whole in the early 1960s, when his career peaked. In 1962 *How to Be a Good Communist* was serialized in the *People's Daily*; then it was republished as a book. Liu's life remained a model of asceticism and incorruptibility that characterized (ideally but not actually) the whole CCP. He often scolded his own children for not being stoic enough.

As radicals associated with Mao and Lin stepped up their critique of Liu's administered revolution during the mid–1960s, Liu apparently accepted their long-term goals and was slow to perceive their interest in political confrontation. By early June 1966, however, Liu and Teng sent work groups to lead the Cultural Revolution* in Peking universities and schools. In early August Liu was criticized at a plenum that reorganized the party's leading organs and demoted him from second to eighth place on public rosters. Attacks against him, often from supporters of Lin Piao, continued at a work conference in October, as Red Guard* posters excoriated his policies and followers. By the end of 1966, Liu's position became nearly irrelevant as the party he treasured was destroyed at all levels by social forces much broader than either his immediate followers or his rivals had envisioned.

On July 18, 1967, Mao was outside Peking, and Chiang Ch'ing,* K'ang Sheng, and Ch'en Po-ta* organized a struggle meeting against Liu Shao-ch'i and his wife Wang Kuang-mei. Liu's health and spirits were severely weakened by coercive harangues throughout 1968. The Twelfth Plenum, in October, received a Criminal Investigation Report on the Renegade, Traitor, and Strike-breaker Liu Shao-ch'i. The plenum passed a resolution that "forever expelled" Liu from the party to which he had devoted his life. Even though he was severely ill, Liu was transferred to a jail in Kaifeng on October 17, 1969. He was denied medical care and died by November 12.

Liu's posthumous rehabilitation, long rumored, did not become official until February 29, 1980, when the Central Committee reinstated his name. On May 17, a memorial service was held in Peking's Great Hall of the People. Numerous exhibits honored Liu, and his *Selected Works* were published. Some Chinese dissidents also hold him in esteem, despite his administration of manipulative campaigns, because he was victimized by Mao. Footage of his family spreading his ashes on the sea is seen in the last episode of the famous 1988 documentary, "River Elegy." Liu's life showed a deep tension between egalitarian ideals and party discipline.

REFERENCES: Lowell Dittmer, *Liu Shao-ch'i and the Chinese Cultural Revolution: The Politics of Mass Criticism* (Berkeley, Calif., 1974); Hsü Kuan-san and He Ling-jen, eds., *Liu Shao-ch'i yü Liu Shao-ch'i lu-hsien* (Liu Shao-ch'i and his line), (Hong Kong, 1980); Liu Shao-ch'i, *Collected Works*, 3 vols. (Hong Kong, 1968–1969); New China News Service Correspondents' Society and CCP Central Archive, eds., *Kung-ho-kuo chu-hsi Liu Shao-ch'i* (Liu Shao-ch'i, Chairman of the Republic) (Peking, 1988); Roderick MacFarquhar, *The Origins of the Cultural Revolution,* 2 vols. (New York, 1974 and 1983).

LYNN T. WHITE III

LO FU (CHANG WEN-T'IEN) (1900–1976): CCP propaganda head (1931–1935); general secretary, CCP (mid–1930s); CCP Central Committee, Politburo; ambassador to the Soviet Union (1951–1955).

Lo Fu (Chang Wen-t'ien) was born on August 30, 1900, in Nan-hai, Kiangsu. Although a member of the Twenty-eight Bolsheviks,* Lo Fu also had other important personal linkages that made him acceptable in the mid–1930s as the general secretary of the CCP. A talented and precocious student, Lo Fu studied at various private and public schools in Wu-sung and Nanking. Under the influence of the New Culture Movement, Lo Fu aspired to travel to other countries in his studies and was able to travel to Japan and the United States in his early twenties. During this period, he had joined several youth groups including the Young China Association and the Creation Society. In the early 1920s, Lo Fu wrote several short stories, poems, essays, a short novella (*On the Road*), and began a series of translations. After he formally joined the CCP in 1925, Lo Fu left for the Soviet Union where he attended Sun Yat-sen University. While in

Moscow, he aligned himself with Wang Ming* and the clique known as the Twenty-eight Bolsheviks.

In 1930 Lo Fu returned to China, where along with Wang Ming, Po Ku,* and others he obtained high positions after the downfall of Li Li-san.* In 1931 he helped direct Central Committee affairs with Po Ku in Shanghai. With the retreat to the Kiangsi Soviet* in 1933, Lo Fu became head of the CCP Propaganda Department, and editor of the Chinese Communist party* newspaper, *Tou-cheng* (The struggle). Lo Fu served as a major writer and theorist within the CCP. He had not only a broad background in theoretical training, but also an increasing amount of practical experience. Between 1931 and 1974 he wrote over seventy essays.

Lo Fu was an important leader within the Kiangsi Soviet. He had organizational affiliations in common with leaders like Mao Tse-tung* (Young China Association), he had not limited his foreign experience to the Soviet Union (like Wang Ming and Po Ku), and he had been an important literary figure during the New Culture Movement. Thus, besides his outstanding facility in the Russian language, and his strong backing as a member of the Twenty-eight Bolsheviks, Lo Fu was ideally cast as a transitional leader in the mid–1930s, when the Communist International was too strong, CCP political factions still abounded, and Mao Tse-tung was too weak to take the sole reins of CCP leadership. In January 1935 Lo Fu was elected general secretary of the CCP. Historians have not yet determined when power passed to Mao Tse-tung, but the consensus is that Lo Fu came increasingly under the sway of Mao's control after 1935.

During the Sino-Japanese War* and the ensuing civil war* with the Kuomintang, Lo Fu contributed in the areas of propaganda and theoretical training in Yenan, and performed organizational work for the Northeast Administrative Committee in Manchuria from 1945 to 1950. After 1949 he was very active in the development of foreign relations for the People's Republic of China.* Between 1951 and 1955, he served as the ambassador to the Soviet Union, where he helped negotiate the initial treaties of friendship and concrete programs of support. He also officially accompanied Chou En-lai* on several diplomatic ventures, including the Geneva Conference of 1954. In 1959, after the Lushan Conference,* because of factors such as CCP factional struggles and the increasing pressures of the Sino-Soviet relationship, Lo Fu was unofficially "retired." Criticized during the Cultural Revolution,* Lo Fu nonetheless continued to write about the progress of socialism in China until his death in 1974.

Lo Fu was an important leader in the Chinese Revolution. Having a wide array of affiliations ranging from the Young China Association to the Twenty-eight Bolsheviks, as well as an ability to express himself in several languages and forms of writing, Lo Fu was able to serve as the party secretary at a time when compromise was still needed, but difficult. In addition to his seeming status as a "compromise candidate," Lo Fu also contributed to CCP organizational, propaganda, and theoretical development. During the crucial consolidation of the PRC, after 1949, Lo Fu further expanded his role by serving in the area of foreign affairs. Several years after his death, attention focused on Lo Fu, now called by his original name, Chang Wen-t'ien, for both his early literary efforts and his later political writings. Perhaps because of his participation in important episodes of CCP history, besides his wide-ranging affiliations and activities, Lo Fu, unlike several others of the Twenty-eight Bolsheviks, has not become a target of historical politics.

REFERENCES: Otto Braun, *A Comintern Agent in China, 1932–1939* (Stanford, Calif., 1982); *Chang Wen-t'ien tsao-nien wen-hsüeh tsuo-p'in hsien* (selections from the early works of Chang Wen-t'ien) (Peking, 1983); *Chang Wen-t'ien hsüan-chi* (selections from the writings of Chang Wen-t'ien) (Peking, 1985).

MARILYN LEVINE

LONDON KIDNAP (October 11–24, 1896): Famous kidnap incident that firmly established Sun Yat-sen's revolutionary credentials.

After the failure of his Canton plot in October 1895, Sun Yat-sen[*] had an unexpected reunion with his former teacher, Dr. James Cantlie, in Hawaii. Apparently not progressing satisfactorily with his anti-Manchu activities in Hawaii, Sun decided to accept Cantlie's invitation to visit London. On October 1, 1896, Sun arrived for the first time in what was probably the leading city of the world. Sun visited the more famous sites, but on October 11, while on his way to Cantlie's residence, Sun was "enticed" (to use his own word) into the Chinese Legation on Portland Place. There he was kept against his will for twelve days, during which time the legation's secretary, Sir Halliday Macartney (1833–1906), prepared for Sun's extradition back to China.

Other than tossing notes out of his bedroom window, Sun used every possible means to pressure some of the legation workers to inform Cantlie and Dr. Patrick Manson, another of his medical instructors at the Hong Kong College of Medicine for the Chinese, of his plight. Sun knew very well that once he was taken off British soil, his life would no longer be his own. A message was finally delivered, and without hesitation, the two physicians alerted Scotland Yard, the Foreign Office, and the British press of Sun's abduction. By then, the incident was quickly turning into a diplomatic debacle. Meanwhile, Sun continued to send notes to his former mentors. In one note Sun stated, "I was born in Hong Kong. I went back to interior of China about four or five years of age. As legally a British subject, can you get me out by that?" Eventually, after a series of serious protests lodged by the Foreign Office, and the public outcry generated by most of the leading British press, Sun was released.

Sun freely gave interviews to British reporters, detailing his ordeal. In early 1897 he published an account of his detention, entitled *Kidnapped in London*. Some historians speculate that the work might have been authored by Cantlie, but there is no evidence to support this view. It is likely, however, that Sun did receive editorial assistance during his writing. At any rate, the incident boosted Sun's confidence. His account was available in Shanghai and Tokyo, and the

Hong Kong *China Mail* spoke of him as a "remarkable man" with "most enlightened views on the undoubtedly miserable state of China's millions." Indeed, the experience must have left a permanent imprint on Sun's personality, who was by now convinced that his destiny was inseparable from that of the fate of a New China which he would help to create.

While the significance of the kidnap on Sun's revolutionary career seems clear enough, it is important to note that some historians are skeptical of Sun's "capture" at the entrance to the Chinese Legation. There is evidence to show that Sun had ventured into the legation before his kidnap to get some information on the lives of his fellow Cantonese living in London. In other words, Sun was taking unnecessary risks, and he was therefore probably deliberately exposing himself to danger. However, it can be argued that, although Sun knew he had a price on his head, he felt that the Manchu representatives in London would not dare take any drastic actions against him. Whatever Sun's real intentions may have been on that fateful Sunday morning may never be known, but Sun grasped the opportunity and carefully exploited the incident for his revolutionary goals. He attempted to get an endorsement for his cause from the well-known missionary Timothy Richard (1845–1919), although to no avail, and he made friends with several "sympathizers," such as Rowland J. Mulkern, a British soldier who later took part in Sun's Hui-chou (Waichow) Campaign* of 1900.

On March 1, 1897, Sun published an article entitled "China's Present and Future: The Reform Party's Plea for British Benevolent Neutrality" in the *Fortnightly Review*, in which he called for the "entire overthrow of the present utterly corrupt regime." Some scholars have suggested that Sun had probably invented the existence of a Reform party, but new evidence uncovered by this author in Macao suggests that Sun did organize some kind of political group before his trip to Tientsin to petition Li Hung-chang;* his group was reported in a newspaper called *Ching-hai Ts'ung-pao*, published in Macao between 1892 and 1894. At any rate, what is important is that after the London kidnap, Sun began to publicize his revolution to an international audience, an approach that dominated his revolutionary program until his last days.

REFERENCES: Harold Z. Schiffrin, *Sun Yat-sen and the Origins of the Chinese Revolution* (Berkeley, Calif., 1968); Lo Chia-lun, ed., *Kuo-fu nien-p'u ch'u-kao* (Chronological biography of Sun Yat-sen, first draft), 2 vols. (Taipei, 1958); *Ching-hai Ts'ung-pao* (*Macao Miscellany*) (Macao, 1892–1894).

JOHN D. YOUNG

LONG MARCH (October 1934 to October 1935): A 6,000-mile military retreat from Kiangsi to Shensi to escape the Fifth Encirclement Campaign by Chiang Kai-shek's Nationalist forces; participants included Mao Tse-tung, Chou En-lai, Chu Teh, Lin Piao, Ch'in Pang-hsien (Po Ku), and Teng Hsiao-p'ing.

On October 16, 1934, 100,000 Red Army soldiers (plus several dozen women) abandoned their military base and broke through Chiang Kai-shek's* military blockade of Kiangsi. This military maneuver was the beginning of a 6,000-mile journey that became known as the Long March. (In Chinese, the Long March is known as the Long Campaign.) Before ending in Shensi a year later, the Red Army would cross over some incredibly difficult terrain, including eighteen mountain ranges and twenty-four rivers while under attack by Nationalist and other hostile forces. The Long March was truly one of the great human accomplishments in the Chinese Communist Revolution. The exploits of the Red Army became legendary. The most famous episodes included the crossing of the Tatu River under a hail of enemy fire; making alliances with minority groups by drinking chicken blood, marching through inhospitable swamps without sufficient supplies, and promoting the revolutionary spirit against seemingly hopeless conditions.

The decision to march resulted from the Nationalists' Fifth Encirclement Campaign* to annihilate the armed forces of the Chinese Communist party.* Advised by two German military officers, Alexander von Falkenhausen and Hans von Seeckt, General Chiang Kai-shek directed his troops to surround and cut off the Red Army, killing 4,000 Communist soldiers and wounding 20,000 at the battle of Kuangchang on the Fukien–Kiangsi border.

Red Army leaders decided that their only recourse for survival was to evacuate from the Kiangsi Soviet* base and regroup at another base to be designated at a later time. Wounded soldiers were left behind under the care of local villagers. Another 6,000 soldiers stayed behind to prevent Chiang's army from closing in on the retreating forces. Eventually, these soldiers were overrun by the Nationalist forces, and most of the survivors were either imprisoned or executed.

Mao Tse-tung,* a commander of the First Front Army, challenged the party's military leadership and its tactics. Mao's ideological and military rivals within the party were known as the Twenty-eight Bolsheviks,* a group of Communist Chinese trained and educated in the Soviet Union. Of these rivals, few had any combat experience, and most of them relied on the strategy of the Comintern military adviser, Otto Braun (Li T'e).*

Mao's first criticism of the party's military leadership and battle strategy came after the terrible losses suffered at the Hsiang River. Mao blamed the high losses on Braun's strategy of having the army fight in parallel columns protecting the noncombatants in the center but exposing the army to enemy fire. Mao proposed that his First Front Army would be better off changing its destination to Kweichow where the enemy was weak instead of marching battle-worn soldiers 250 miles to the Shangchih Soviet area. Mao's forces successfully subdued the notorious Kweichow warlord, Hou Chih-tan. Subsequently, Red Army leaders held a conference at Tsunyi* on January 8, 1935, which produced not only the most significant document of the Long March but also the most important leadership changes.

The objective of the Tsunyi Conference was to concentrate on the poor military tactics that led to the disastrous defeats. Po Ku,* leader of the CCP, opened the meeting with an analysis of Chiang's Fifth Encirclement Campaign, blaming the retreat on Chiang's numerical and firepower superiority over the Red Army.

With the exception of other Twenty-eight Bolsheviks, few accepted Po's argument. Mao exposed the political and military mistakes committed by the party center. Mao's criticism was followed by Chu Teh's* attack on Otto Braun and Po Ku, for their tactics of positional warfare.

Support for the Twenty-eight Bolsheviks disappeared: Mao's election to the Central Military Commission signaled the abandonment of the Stalinist belief in the priority of an urban revolution. Mao's ascendance resulted in the pursuit of economic, political, and military self-sufficiency. After the Tsunyi Conference, Mao's goal was to march to northern China to establish a rural base to promote guerrilla warfare against the Japanese and the Chinese warlords.

Mao faced another political showdown over the direction and long-term objectives of the Red Army. Chang Kuo-t'ao,* commander of the Fourth Front Army, disagreed with Mao's strategy. After a series of tense meetings, both men agreed to a compromise by dividing their armies into two columns and heading in separate directions. Mao's column headed north for Shensi to engage in anti-Japanese guerilla warfare, while Chang's column of 60,000 men headed to Szechwan to wait out the war. Chang, however, was unable to secure a base in Szechwan, and after a series of tactical blunders, he withdrew his remaining force of 10,000 to Shensi in 1936.

After liberation in 1949, the Long March would take on new meaning for Mao and the Communist party. Mao made the Long March a symbol of the miracle of the revolution. When he asks, rhetorically, what is the significance of the Long March, he answers, "the Long March is the first of its kind in the annals of history, that it is a manifesto, a propaganda force, a seeding machine. Since Pan Ku divided the heavens from the earth and the Three Sovereigns and Five Emperors reigned, has history ever witnessed a long march such as ours?" For Mao, the Long March was a divine revelation predicting the success of the Chinese Communist Revolution.

REFERENCES: Jerome Ch'en, "The Communist Movement 1927–1937," *The Cambridge History of China: Republican China 1912–1949*, Part 2 (London, 1986); Jerome Ch'en, "The Resolution of the Tsunyi Conference," *China Quarterly* 40 (October/December 1969): 1–38; Mao Tse-tung, *Selected Works*, Vol. 1 (Peking, 1964); Dick Wilson, *The Long March 1935* (New York, 1971).

RICHARD C. KAGAN

LU HSÜN (CHOU SHU-JEN) (September 15, 1881–October 19, 1936): Professor of Chinese literature; prominent short story writer; essayist; social critic.

Born in 1881 into a family of commercial and minor-official background in Shao-hsing, Chekiang, Chou Shu-jen, along with his brothers Tso-jen and Chien-jen, received a traditional Chinese education in early childhood. After the family's decline and the death of his father in 1897, Chou Shu-jen went to Nanking in 1898 and enrolled in the Kiangnan Naval Academy. In the following year he transferred to the Academy of Railroads and Mines. During these years he read many translated books of Western science, political philosophy, sociology, and literature. After graduation he went to Japan, first in Tokyo for language study

(1902–1904) and then in Sendai Medical School (1904–1906). In 1906 he decided to become a "physician of the soul" rather than a "physician of the body," and returned to Tokyo to study literature.

Lu Hsün returned to China in 1909 serving first as a teacher and later as principal of a local school in his home town, Shao-hsing. After the Revolution of 1911,* he joined the Ministry of Education of the new Republic at Nanking. Later he moved to Peking to be a professor of Chinese literature at Peking University. During these years, Lu Hsün not only established himself as a scholar but also emerged as the most influential writer.

Lu Hsün published his first short story, "A Madman's Diary," written in vernacular Chinese, in the May 1918 issue of *Hsin Ching-nien* (*New Youth*). The story, known as a "declaration of war" against Chinese tradition, and the first short story in the history of modern Chinese literature, attacked the traditional family system and the Confucian society as oppressive and "cannibalistic." Another story, "The Story of Ah Q," published in 1921, again created a big stir. Written in a satirical style, the story revealed, through the thoughts and actions of Ah Q, an illiterate, poverty-stricken village outcast, the inferiority and inadequacies of old Chinese culture in a modern age.

In the years between 1918 and 1926 Lu Hsün wrote more than two dozen short stories, which were published in two collected volumes, "Na-han" (Call to arms), which appeared in 1923, and "P'ang-huang" (Hesitation), which appeared in 1926. Written in a terse, realistic style, these stories, according to Lu Hsün, were based "almost entirely on the lives of unfortunate people living in a sick society" and were intended to stimulate social reform.

At the same time, Lu Hsün also produced scholarly commentaries and systematic studies of classical Chinese literature and early Chinese fiction. His "Chung-kuo hsiao-shuo shih-lüeh" (Brief history of Chinese fiction) is a commendable work frequently cited by later students of Chinese fiction. In addition to creative writing, university teaching, and research, Lu Hsün was also a political and social critic, writing polemic and critical essays for magazines such as *Yü-ssu* (Thread of talk) and *Hsien-tai p'ing-lun* (Contemporary critic). The Warlord government responded to his criticisms by forcing him to leave Peking in 1926. After a short stay at Amoy University, he moved to Chung-shan University in Canton. After 1927, he settled down in Shanghai until his death on October 19, 1936.

While still in Shanghai, Lu Hsün became increasingly sympathetic toward the Communist Revolution. Although he was not a Communist himself, some of his younger friends like Jou Shih and Feng Hsüeh-feng had close connections with the Chinese Communist party.* In 1930 he participated in preparations for the establishment of the League of Left-Wing Writers. In 1933 he served on the executive committee of the China League for Civil Rights, a group that was anti-Kuomintang but primarily non-Communist. Throughout his final years, he continued to antagonize the Kuomintang through his laconic yet powerful essays. However, he also quarreled with many Communist writers, maintaining an independent and unyielding spirit. Despite his controversies with the Communists, Lu Hsün was accorded high status by Mao Tse-tung[*] soon after his death in 1936. Mao said, "Lu Hsün was the greatest and most militant standard-bearer of the new cultural force. He was the supreme commander in China's cultural revolution; he was not only a great man of letters, but also a great thinker and a great revolutionary."

REFERENCES: Leo Ou-fan Lee, *Voices from the Iron House* (Bloomington, Ind., 1987); C. T. Hsia, *A History of Modern Chinese Fiction* (New Haven, Conn., 1971); Shao Po-chou, *Lu Hsün yen-chiu kai-shu* (Studies on Lu Hsün: An introduction) (Wuhan, 1957).

PHILIP YUEN-SANG LEUNG

LUSHAN CONFERENCE (1959): Important CCP meeting in which Mao Tse-tung had to give up his state chairmanship to Liu Shao-ch'i.

The Communist party leadership was retreating from the excesses of the Great Leap Forward[*] (GLF) throughout the first part of 1959. The intraparty conflicts centering around this issue eventually came to a head in an enlarged Politburo meeting from July 2 to August 1, followed by the Eighth Plenum of the Eighth Central Committee, August 2–16, held at Lushan, Kiangsi.

Mao Tse-tung[*] began the conference by raising the issue of the "disproportions" in the economy caused by the GLF, and he proposed a reversal of the priorities of heavy industry, light industry, and agriculture. Mao even endorsed Ch'en Yün's[*] priority of solving the problem of supply and demand over "basic construction." Two opposing views concerning the GLF and the communes coexisted. The opposition was represented by the defense minister, P'eng Te-huai.[*] Having inspected the sorrowful conditions of the peasants in his home town in Hunan, as well as Kiangsi, Anhwei, and Hopei, P'eng had openly criticized Mao in an enlarged Politburo meeting in Shanghai in March and April. During the Lushan Conference, P'eng continued his criticism in the "North-western Group" discussions, July 3–10. He even challenged Mao's personality cult.

P'eng then summed up his views in a "letter of opinion" to Mao on July 14. While affirming the "achievements" of the GLF, it pointed out its extravagance, which had caused dislocations in the economy and had generated social tensions. It particularly referred to the problems created by communal ownership, the communal mess-hall, the indigenous blast furnaces, and "putting politics in command." According to P'eng, these "leftist" errors, which were usually more immune to criticism than "rightist" errors, were expressions of "petty-bourgeois fanaticism."

On July 16, Mao circulated copies of P'eng's letter. It was openly supported by Huang K'e-ch'eng, Chou Hsiao-chou, and Chang Wen-t'ien (Lo Fu)[*] and struck a sympathetic chord in many. Chang actually supplemented it with a long speech to his small group meeting on July 21. On July 23, Mao in a speech suggested that P'eng was a rightist succumbing to "the pressure of imperialists and the bourgeoisie." Mao forced the "middle-of-the-roaders" to choose sides by raising the issue of "unity," and he threatened to "go to the countryside to lead the peasants and overthrow the government." Leaders like Liu Shao-ch'i,[*] Chou En-lai,[*] and Chu Teh[*] were compelled to take Mao's side. They did it also to win concessions from him to tone down the GLF. As a result, the whole meeting turned into a struggle against P'eng's "antiparty clique."

Mao set the keynote for the Eighth Plenum on August 2 by openly naming Chang Wen-t'ien and turning the ongoing critique of leftist excesses into a struggle against rightist opportunism. P'eng was forced to undertake self-criticism which listed his mistakes of past and present. On August 7, before the meeting was over, the Party Center issued a directive to the whole party to launch a campaign against rightism at all levels. The plenum concluded on August 16, with Mao having the final words, describing the struggle at Lushan as "a class struggle."

The plenum passed two resolutions. One concerned "the antiparty clique" headed by P'eng Te-huai, adjudicating its activities as "purposive, prepared, planned and organized," and "a continuation and development of the antiparty alliance of Kao Kang[*] and Jao Shu-shih." P'eng, Huang, Chang, and Chou were relieved of their government posts but retained their respective membership or alternate membership of the Central Committee or the Politburo. The resolution lowered the planned production targets for steel, coal, food, and cotton for the year 1959. The total investment in "basic construction" was also lowered.

At the Lushan Conference, Mao used P'eng Te-huai's criticism of him to turn an ongoing critique of the GLF into a drive against the "right," by threatening to split the party. He eventually made this threat real in the Cultural Revolution[*] of the 1960s, when a greater part of the party leaders turned opposition. Mao did it with the help of Lin Piao,[*] who replaced P'eng as defense minister after the Lushan Conference.

REFERENCES: Jürgen Domes, *P'eng Te-huai: The Man and the Image* (Stanford, Calif., 1985); Union Research Institute, *The Case of Peng Teh-huai, 1959–1968* (Hong Kong, 1968).

LUNG-KEE SUN

LUSHAN CONFERENCE (1970): Important CCP meeting in which Mao Tse-tung broke his relationship with Lin Piao.

During the Cultural Revolution,[*] Marshal Lin Piao[*] emerged as Mao Tse-tung's[*] successor, a position officially confirmed by the new party statutes passed by the Ninth Party Congress in April 1969. However, the rebuilding of the party that began in the same year signaled the end of the pervasive "military control" required by the chaos of the Cultural Revolution. The Sino-Soviet armed clashes over Damansky Island in March also compelled China's leadership to reassess its foreign policy, with Premier Chou En-lai[*] emerging as the advocate of rapprochement with the United States. Chou's rising influence, backed by Mao, might have threatened Lin's position. He probably did not see the Soviet Union as China's chief enemy, or otherwise perceived a massive military buildup as an alternative to detente with America. The return to "normalcy" and the erosion of the power of the left might also have caused Ch'en Po-ta,* the propaganda chief, to decide to throw in his lot with Lin Piao.

Tensions between Mao and Lin became evident from March to July of 1970, when the two wrangled over the issue of whether to preserve the office of the state presidency in the revised constitution to be ratified by the upcoming Fourth People's Congress. Mao reiterated his opposition four times, to no avail. The issue was raised again at the Second Plenary Session of the Ninth Central Committee held at Lushan, Kiangsi, from August 23 to September 6. The agenda of the conference included the draft of the revised state constitution, the Fourth Five-Year Plan, and military buildup in preparation for a possible war.

The current official story describes what transpired at the Plenary Session as following: On the first day, Lin Piao, in his speech, presented a "discourse on genius" under the pretext of praising Mao, without previously consulting Mao. On August 24 Lin Piao's coterie—consisting of his wife Yeh Ch'ün, Ch'en Po-ta, Wu Fa-hsien, Li Tso-peng, and Ch'iu Hui-tso—promoted, in their respective small-group discussions, the "discourse on genius" materials approved by Lin Piao. Ch'en Po-ta spread rumors in his "northern China" group, to the effect that there were people who were opposed to Mao assuming the state presidency. The northern China group even issued Brief Bulletin No. 2, publishing his talk, thus sowing confusion among many who attended the conference. On August 25 Mao called an enlarged Politburo Standing Committee meeting. It decided to terminate the discussions of Lin Piao's speech in all groups, recalled Brief Bulletin No. 2, and ordered Ch'en to clear himself. Afterward, Mao talked to Lin personally. Chou talked to Wu, Li, and Ch'iu, ordering them to clear themselves to the Party Center. At that moment, a key member of Lin Piao's gang, the chief of general staff, Huang Yung-sheng, had just arrived from Peking. Upon hearing what was happening, he immediately destroyed his own speech draft, which he had prepared according to Lin's wishes. Mao later recollected that the conspirators' "coup" during the conference "went on for two-and-a-half days" before it was stopped. On August 31, Mao published an article, "An Opinion of Mine," exposing the hoax of the "discourse on genius." The conference discussed Mao's article, criticized Ch'en, but made no reference to Lin Piao.

The plenum approved the Draft of the Revised Constitution of the People's Republic of China. It also resolved to propose to the Standing Committee of the People's Congress to prepare for the convening of the Fourth People's Congress at an "appropriate time." It ratified the State Council's reports on the economy and the Central Military Commission's report on military buildup. It was decided that the investigation of Ch'en Po-ta was to be continued, but—according to Mao's later statement—at the end of the conference, "to protect Vice-Chairman Lin no conclusions concerning individuals were reached," in spite of the fact that "this Lushan Conference was again a struggle between two headquarters."

After the conference, Mao proceeded to undermine Lin Piao's power. In reaction, Lin planned a military coup, which was abortive, leading to his attempted flight to the Soviet Union and his death in a plane crash in Mongolia on September 13, 1971.

REFERENCES: Y. M. Kau, ed., *The Lin Piao Affair: Power Politics and Military Coup* (White Plains, N.Y., 1975); Jaap van Ginnekan, trans. Danielle Adkinson, *The Rise and Fall of Lin Piao* (New York, 1977).

LUNG-KEE SUN

M

MANCHUKUO (1932–1945): Puppet state created by the Japanese in Manchuria.

Manchukuo or the state of Manchus was the puppet state established in Manchuria on March 9, 1932, by the Japanese Kwantung Army officers following the Mukden Incident* (September 18, 1931), which they had engineered. P'u-i,* the last of the Manchu emperors who had been deposed in 1912, was made chief executive of the state. The capital city was established in Changch'un, which was renamed Hsinking or "New Capital." In order to obtain more positive support from the Manchus for the Japanese activities in Manchuria, the Japanese Army, on March 1, 1934, gave P'u-i the more elevated title of emperor, with a reigning name of K'ang-te (Tranquility and Virtue). The Manchu state ceased to exist at the end of World War II in August 1945, when Japan surrendered to the Allied Powers, and it subsequently reverted to China.

Manchukuo, with an area of 380,000 square miles, consisted of four provinces (Liaoning, Kirin, Heilungkiang, and Jehol). The Manchu state contained a population of about 30 million—about 5 million Manchus, over 20 million Chinese, 800,000 Koreans, 230,000 Japanese, 150,000 White Russians, and the rest of them, Mongols and others. The Manchu state was bounded on four sides—the Soviet Union in the north, northeast, and northwest, Mongolia in the west, Chosen or Korea in the southeast, and China in the southwest. The country was rich in natural resources. The most important minerals were coal and iron deposits. Some of the major crops included soybeans, millet, corn, wheat, barley, and oats. These natural resources in Manchuria and the strategic location of the region were the chief sources of fierce international conflicts among rival powers (Japan, Russia, and China) as manifested in the Sino-Japanese War of 1894–1895* and the Russo-Japanese War of 1904–1905.

The Japanese penetration into Manchuria began with the Sino-Japanese War. As a result of the victory, Japan gained the Liaotung Peninsula, only to be forced out by the international pressure of the Triple Intervention (1895) organized by Russia. Meanwhile, Russia secured from China the leased territory of Liaotung in 1898 and the right to construct the Chinese Eastern Railway across Manchuria connecting railway lines between Vladivostok and the Trans-Siberian Railway. Russia also obtained the right to construct the Southern Manchurian Railway, which connected Port Arthur with Changch'un, just north of Mukden. Following the Japanese victory in the Russo-Japanese War, Japan gained much of the Russian interest in Manchuria, including the leased territory of Liaotung and the Southern Manchurian Railway. In 1906 Japan created the Kwantung Army to guard the leased territory of Liaotung (the Japanese renamed it Kwantung) and the Southern Manchurian Railway zone. The leased territory was placed under the control of the governor-general of the Kwantung Province who was concurrently serving as the commander of the Kwantung Army. Later, in 1919, the office of the governor-general was transferred to a civilian administrator, and his office was moved to Mukden from Port Arthur.

Upon the completion of the Northern Expedition* in 1928, the Kuomintang government in Nanking embarked on a vigorous campaign to recover national rights and interests. The Kuomintang government proclaimed that Manchuria was an integral part of Chinese territory, and consequently the leased territory of Liaotung and the Southern Manchurian Railway should be restored to China. In the midst of the rising tide of Chinese nationalism, the Kwantung Army officers were becoming very apprehensive. It was increasingly self-evident to them that the realization of Chiang Kai-shek's* objective of achieving a strong unified country in China was very near. They feared that the Japanese position and interest in Manchuria were threatened and that there were no other options but to take an immediate action to create a Manchu state in order to forestall the Chinese nationalist objective of achieving unification. The Kwantung Army officers therefore plotted the Mukden Incident and created Manchukuo in March 1932. In fact, the creation of Manchukuo was the brainchild of the two staff officers of the Kwantung Army—Colonel Itagaki, Seishirō, the senior staff officer, and Lieutenant Colonel Ishiwara Kanji, the operations officer. Both officers believed that Japan had to take over Manchuria for the survival of the Japanese Empire. They believed that it was imperative that Japan establish a major strategic base in Manchuria against the Soviet Union, that it develop a powerful industrial base in Manchuria for Japan's preparations for a possible war with the Soviet Union, and that it maintain an outlet for Japan's surplus population, which was sharply increasing at the rate of 1 million annually. Manchukuo, therefore, was to serve the urgent needs of the Japanese Empire and was to be strictly controlled by the Japanese Kwantung Army.

Immediately following the creation of Manchukuo on March 9, 1932, Japan and Manchukuo signed the Manchukuo–Japan Protocol which recognized the independence of Manchukuo, but in actuality, the commander-in-chief of the Kwantung Army, who was concurrently Japanese ambassador to Manchukuo, would control all matters (economic, political, diplomatic, and military) relating to Manchukuo. P'u-i was completely powerless. He was to be "guided" by Japanese advisers who were attached to all departments of the government. Each Manchu minister had a Japanese vice-minister who would administer all department affairs. The Manchu people were not permitted any voice in governmental affairs. Such was the nature of the government of Manchukuo under the Japanese Kwantung Army.

REFERENCES: A. C. Brackman, *The Last Emperor* (New York, 1975); F. C. Jones, *Manchuria Since 1931* (London, 1949); E. B. Schumpeter, *The Industrialization of Japan and Manchukuo, 1930–1940* (New York, 1940).

WON Z. YOON

MANDATE OF HEAVEN: Ancient Chinese political concept that legitimized dynastic rule.

The concept of Mandate of Heaven (*t'ien-ming*) is deeply rooted in Chinese tradition and the popular mind, having first appeared at the start of the Chou dynasty (1123–249 B.C.). In imperial China it was the chief justification for rulers to maintain their power, and also for rebels in their struggle to topple dynasties. Those in power concerned themselves with perpetuating the heavenly mandate, while those trying to acquire power claimed that they were acting on behalf of Heaven (*t'ien*). Both legitimacy and the right to revolt, therefore, were based on this concept of Mandate of Heaven.

The basis for the whole concept of Mandate of Heaven rests on that of Heaven itself. Ever since the Chou dynasty, Heaven has been considered the supreme deity and moral force in the universe, and thereby the chief source for dynastic legitimacy. Yet the Mandate of Heaven was not thought of as irrevocable, but rather as transferable. This idea of transferability of the heavenly mandate is expressed repeatedly in the classics, especially in the Book of History and the Book of Songs. For example, the Book of Songs explicitly states: "The Mandate of Heaven is not forever." Heaven, in other words, was not bound to any single dynasty. It viewed rulers according to objective, universal criteria of behavior. Dynasties lost the mandate because of gross ritual and moral failings. Various omens and signs—such as celestial portents, droughts, floods, bureaucratic corruption, and social upheavals—preceded the fall of a dynasty and indicated that the mandate had been withdrawn.

It was Mencius (372–289 B.C.) who developed the idea of the people's right to rebel against corrupt and evil rulers. Like Confucius, Mencius also emphasized that good government was primarily ethical government. The rule of a truly moral king was characterized by his benevolence toward his subjects. Mencius stressed the well-being of the people. In fact, the Mandate of Heaven manifested itself only through the acceptance of a ruler by his people. As Mencius explained, "Heaven sees as the people see; Heaven hears as the people hear." He declared that when a ruler failed to be a good ruler, he no longer had the right to rule and the people had the right to overthrow and even to kill him. In this way Mencius made the concept of heavenly mandate fundamentally an expression of the people's satisfaction. He made the people the ultimate standard for judging government, and what is more, he made man the standard for Heaven itself.

The concept of Mandate of Heaven was a common and persistent theme among most rebel movements throughout the history of imperial China. Many rebels made repeated references to Heaven, and their movements often carried banners with such slogans as "Realize the Way for Heaven" (*t'i-t'ien hsing-tao*). As an old Chinese saying observes, the successful rebel becomes king, but the loser a mere bandit. Success in overturning a dynasty and establishing a new one was an absolute sign of Heaven's approval. This "change in mandate" was called *ko-ming*, a traditional Confucian term that has been adopted in the twentieth century by modern political movements to mean "revolution."

REFERENCES: Harlee G. Creel, *The Origins of Statecraft in China*, vol. 1 (Chicago, 1970); Benjamin I. Schwartz, *The World of Thought in Ancient China* (Cambridge, Mass., 1985); Frederick W. Mote, *Intellectual Foundations of China*, 2nd ed. (New York, 1989); Vincent Y.C. Shih, *The Taiping Ideology* (Seattle, Wash., 1967).

ROBERT J. ANTONY

MAO TSE-TUNG (December 26, 1893–September 9, 1976): One of the founders of the CCP; leader of the CCP from 1935 to his death in 1976.

Mao Tse-tung was one of the major leaders of Chinese history, and his life was distinguished both by notable successes in the face of formidable obstacles and by policies that brought tremendous calamaties to his country and people.

Mao was born in Shao-shan, Hunan Province. His parents attained the status of rich peasants by the time he became a teenager, but he knew personally the physical labor of a farm family during his formative years. He received a traditional primary education but subsequently ran away from home in order to continue into middle school. By 1911 he moved to Changsha and after a short half-year stint in the army and some independent study, enrolled at age nineteen in what would soon be the Hunan First Normal School. Mao was an activist student and heavily caught up in the excitement of this early May Fourth*period. He taught in a night school for illiterate workers and with a friend helped establish the Hsin-min hsüeh-hui (New People's Study Society), which would subsequently become one of the nuclei of the Chinese Communist party.* Following his graduation in 1918, Mao took a position in Peking University's library, where he became involved with other activist students and was influenced by Li Ta-chao,* the university librarian and radical historian. In this period, Mao, though an ardent nationalist, was still open to various ideas and schools of thought from abroad. He went to Shanghai in early 1919 and then returned to Changsha soon after the May Fourth Incident. He helped organize a Hunan student organization, but two of his publication ventures, successively the *Hsiang-chiang p'ing-lun* (*Hsiang River Review*) and the student newspaper, *Hsin Hu-nan* (*New Hunan*), were closed down by the authorities. Mao was then compelled to flee Hunan after involvement in a student strike aimed at the provincial governor. He traveled to Peking and then to Shanghai, where he met with the leading intellectual Ch'en Tu-hsiu,* who would become the first chairman of the CCP. Mao was able to return to Hunan later in the summer of 1920, where he became head of the primary school attached to the Hunan First Normal School. He married Yang K'ai-hui, the daughter of progressive Professor Yang Ch'ang-chi with whom Mao was close. Mao opened a radical bookstore, and soon after the arrival of Comintern* agent Gregorü Voitinsky in China, he established a Communist cell and a Socialist Youth League branch in Changsha.

In July 1921 in Shanghai, Mao became one of the founders of the CCP which at the time had only about sixty members throughout the country. He returned to Changsha as secretary of the newly formed CCP Hunan Committee. Among a number of activities, Mao now helped establish the Self-Education College in Changsha, which was to train many who would later become Communists, and he helped organize workers at the Anyuan mines in Kiangsi Province. Mao was elected to the Party Central Committee for the first time at the Third Party Congress in Canton in June 1923, and he directed the party's Organization Department. In keeping with the CCP–KMT policy of cooperation, Mao attended the Kuomintang's First Congress in January 1924 in Canton. He then was given various posts in the KMT organization, including secretary of its Organization Department and alternate member of its Central Executive Committee, eliciting criticism from some party comrades that he was excessively cooperative with the KMT.

In late 1924 Mao recuperated from an illness in Hunan, following which he personally spent some months investigating the situation in the countryside, an enlightening interlude that ended in late 1925 when he had to flee to Canton. Mao continued for a time to have influential positions within the KMT, including service on the credentials committee for the Second KMT Congress and de facto leadership of the KMT Propaganda Department. After losing the latter position following the warship *Chung-shan* incident in March 20, 1926, Mao became director of the sixth class of the Peasant Movement Training Institute in Canton. In December 1926, in defiance of party chairman Ch'en Tu-hsiu's directive, Mao told a conference of peasant delegates in Changsha of the importance of the peasant issue, spurring them on to intensified revolutionary action.

Following further rural investigation near Changsha, Mao wrote one of his best known reports in March 1927, calling the peasant movement "a colossal event." By now Mao was firmly persuaded that the party needed to harness this great social force. But most of his comrades remained conservative on this issue, and for this reason Mao left the party's Fifth Congress before its conclusion. That meeting was held after Chiang Kai-shek's*coup against the CCP in Shanghai in early April 1927, but within three months what remained of the CCP–KMT alliance in Wuhan was terminated as well. This experience and the military engagements that ensued in the months and years that followed confirmed Mao in the belief that "political power grows out of the barrel of a gun." He was responsible for part of the ill-fated Autumn Harvest Uprising* in September– October 1927. He then led some of the survivors of this campaign to the mountainous terrain between Hunan and Kiangsi provinces. In the spring of 1928 he was joined at Chingkangshan* by reinforcements led by Chu Teh.* The merged Chu–Mao forces ultimately established a base centered on Juichin in southeast Kiangsi. Mao worked assiduously to politicize his troops and to improve their interrelationships with the civilian population. His counsel in this regard was best articulated at the Ku-t'ien Conference in December 1929 and was often referred to subsequently.

Mao avoided cooperating fully in the costly ill-conceived initiatives of the Li Li-san* line which aimed to capture major cities in 1930. Instead, he continued to preside over the Communist forces in the countryside where Chinese communism's gravity of power had clearly shifted. Following the establishment of the Chinese Soviet Republic in late 1931, Mao held two of the top positions in government and an influential role in the military. However, he lacked influence in the party apparatus which was dominated by the returned students faction (or Twenty-eight Bolsheviks),* and his position steadily eroded. In addition, Mao was replaced by Chou En-lai* as chief army political commissar. Mao sharply disagreed with many policies that were implemented during this period, and he seems to have lost almost all authority by the time of the Soviet Republic collapse under the onslaughts of Chiang Kai-shek's* final Encirclement Campaigns.*

During the flight of the Communists from Kiangsi, at a conference in Tsunyi,* Kweichow, Mao assumed effective leadership of what would come to be known as the Long March.* Through brilliant maneuvers, he turned what had been a debacle into an orderly campaign that traveled over 6,000 miles, much of it over exceedingly tortuous terrain. Although the personnel losses were tremendous by the time the remnants of the retreat reached Shensi a year after the breakout in Kiangsi, the feat was a notable symbolic achievement.

Mao used the years in Yenan, where his new headquarters was established in 1936, to good effect. A new United Front with the KMT was agreed to in 1937, facilitated by the Sian Incident* of December 1936 and necessitated by Japan's massive invasion of north China in July 1937. But this cooperation basically ended by late 1938 when Japanese offensive operations ceased and the Nationalist Army reimposed a blockade on the Communists. However, despite opposition from both Nationalist and Japanese, the Communists managed to expand control over disparate territorial bases and their respective populations. Furthermore, Mao used these years to consolidate his political position. The *cheng-feng* or Rectification Campaign* of 1942–1944 served this purpose, indoctrinating the party along the lines of his thinking. Thus, Mao triumphed over the political challenge of the returned students faction, and he enjoined the CCP to accept his ideas with regard to adjusting Marxist-Leninist ideology to meet the circumstances and needs of the Communist Revolution in China. Mao's victory within the party was confirmed at the Seventh Party Congress held between April and June of 1945. Mao married (in 1939) a former Shanghai actress, Lan P'ing, whom he renamed Chiang Ch'ing,* while in Yenan. To do so, he had to set aside Ho Tzu-chen, whom he had married in 1931, sometime after Yang K'ai-hui, Mao's former wife, had been killed.

By the end of the war of resistance against Japan in August 1945, the Communist forces had expanded tremendously since their arrival in Yenan some eight years earlier, and they had good morale and discipline. But Mao's military was still overwhelmingly outnumbered by the Nationalists so that the CCP was amenable to suggestions of a political settlement with the Nationalist government. Hence, Mao was more willing initially than was Chiang Kai-shek to talk and later to cooperate with the Marshall Mission* in 1946 that sought to prevent renewed civil war in China. However, it proved impossible to resolve the deep differences and suspicions that divided the two sides, and war broke out in earnest as 1946 wore on. The war then followed the three stages that Mao predicted, and the third stage, that of positional warfare with large armies, came to a conclusion even more quickly than he, or anyone, anticipated.

Mao proclaimed the establishment of the People's Republic of China* in Peking on October 1, 1949. He went to the Soviet Union in late December 1949 and stayed until March 1950, the visit culminating, after hard bargaining, in a Sino-Soviet Treaty* on February 14, 1950. The new government restored the economy with some success by 1952. The initial policies of the new regime were intended to be moderate, under the banner of New Democracy. But such moderation was severely affected by and eventually abandoned partly as a result of China's entry in late 1950 into the Korean War, during which Mao lost a son. China was heavily influenced by the Soviet Union in the course of the 1950s.

In September 1956 the Eighth Party Congress celebrated the party's apparent success in many undertakings, including the amazingly rapid collectivization* of agriculture and the socialization of industry and commerce throughout the country. But divisions began to appear between Mao and many of his comrades. Against the wishes of the majority of party leaders, he insisted on programs such as the Hundred Flowers* thaw of 1956–1957 and the 1957 Rectification Campaign,* and his initiatives culminated in the terrible 1957 Anti-Rightist Campaign* that would cause great suffering for many intellectuals for decades and detracted from Mao's credibility among both party members and intellectuals. Then in 1958 Mao instigated the Great Leap Forward* and the radical communization of agriculture that resulted in incredible losses of life (later acknowledged by the Chinese government) and suffering for the Chinese people. As the situation worsened, Mao decided in the fall of 1958 not to be a candidate again for state chairman. The following July at a party plenum in Lushan,* he survived a serious challenge inspired by the forthright criticism of his policies by P'eng Te-huai.* But Mao's radical policies contributed to the further deterioration of relations with the Soviet Union, which finally terminated its aid programs in 1960.

Mao's policies were now systematically reversed, and China gradually recovered from the disastrous post–Leap depression. But Mao viewed the recovery policies with apprehension and grew increasingly frustrated because of his diminishing power and resentful because he was being ignored and even ridiculed by party intellectuals. In 1962 he began to emphasize the need for class struggle. He insisted on a Socialist Education* Program that yielded considerable opposition and little results. Neutralized by opponents, that is, a veritable political machine led by Liu Shao-ch'i* and Teng Hsiao-p'ing,* Mao countered by reforming the People's Liberation Army (PLA)* to his taste, which he would use when necessary in the developing power struggle. This task was facilitated because Mao's trusted lieutenant, Lin Piao,* had replaced P'eng as defense minister in 1959.

Unable to get his way in the ''watertight kingdom'' of Peking, Mao went to Shanghai where in November 1965 he initiated the opening gambit (by authorizing the publication of a critical review of a play that had been used earlier to criticize him) of what would become the Great Proletarian Cultural Revolution.* By the following summer, at the Eleventh Plenum of the Eighth Central Committee, this ill-fated campaign was formally underway, the purpose of which was to take to task those in authority alleged to be revisionists and capitalist roaders.* Following Mao's own ''Bombard the Headquarters'' wallposter, Chinese youth, now organized as Red Guards,* traveled about the country at will, participating in monster rallies in Peking during the fall of 1966 at which Mao would appear, and generally created havoc. By the end of 1966 the attention shifted to the provinces, spreading chaos throughout the country. Beginning in early 1967, government bodies everywhere were gradually displaced in ''power seizures'' by revolutionary committees, comprising of cadres ostensibly loyal to Mao, representatives of new revolutionary mass organizations, and military representatives. The army had to be called in to side with Mao's leftists in these struggles, but in the confusion it did so only selectively as it tried to preserve order at the same time. Mao's principal antagonist, Liu Shao-ch'i, was persecuted to death. The Cultural Revolution was essentially spent by the time of the Ninth Party Congress in April 1969, although following Mao's death it would be said that it had lasted for a decade.

In the early 1970s, Mao dramatically shifted China's foreign policy radically, ending the country's isolation and improving relations first with the United States and subsequently with most other countries around the world. Dubbed ''Mao's Revolutionary Line in Diplomacy,'' the change was necessitated largely by China's perceived threat from the Soviet Union. Its success was partly marred for Mao by the Lin Piao Incident of September 1971, when Lin, previously Mao's chosen successor (and constitutionally designated as such), allegedly attempted to assassinate Mao. This incredible development did further incalculable damage to Mao's credibility.

While the rehabilitated government sought to regularize governance once again by the early 1970s, Mao continued to insist on radical mobilization campaigns to assure the continuity of his revolutionary ideals, although fewer and fewer Chinese understood what it was that he sought to achieve. He died on September 9, 1976.

REFERENCES: *Selected Works of Mao Zedong*, vols. 1–5 (Peking, 1967–1977); Donald W. Klein and Anne B. Clark, *Biographical Dictionary of Chinese Communism*, vol. 2

(Cambridge, Mass., 1971): 676–688; Stephen Uhalley, Jr., *Mao Tse-tung: A Critical Biography* (New York, 1975).

STEPHEN UHALLEY, JR.

MAO TUN (SHEN YEN-PING) (July 4, 1896–March 27, 1981): Novelist; literary and art critic; minister of culture.

Born into a gentry family of T'ung-hsiang, Chekiang, in 1896, Shen Yen-ping (original name Shen Te-hung) received his early education in Hu-chou, Chia-hsing, and Hang-chou. At the age of seventeen, he went to Peking and attended the Preparatory College of Peking University. Three years later, in 1916, he began working at the Commercial Press, first as a proofreader, and then as a translator and editor. In 1920, already an emerging young writer, Shen and some of his writer friends such as Cheng Chen-to, Yeh Sheng-t'ao, and Hsü Ti-shan, founded the Literary Study Society (Wen-hsüeh yen-chiu-hui), which advocated realist literature and literature with a social purpose. Shen was editor (1921–1923) of the *Short Story Monthly* (*Hsiao-shuo yüeh-pao*), one of the most influential literary publications in China. After a short stint as a teacher at a Communist-controlled girls' school in Shanghai, he joined the left-wing Kuomintang government under Wang Ching-wei* in Chungking. After the Kuomintang purge of the Communists in 1927, Shen returned to Shanghai and devoted most of his time to creative writing.

To hide his true identity, Shen began to use the pen-name Mao Tun. Between September 1927 and June 1928, Mao Tun completed three stories, known as the trilogy of "Eclipse" (*Shih*): "Disillusion" (*Huan-mieh*), "Vacillation" (*Tung-yao*), and "Pursuit" (*Chui-Ch'iu*). The trilogy depicted the life and values of the revolutionary youth, decadent bourgeois, and intellectuals during the period of the Northern Expedition.* In 1930 Mao Tun became a founding member of the League of Left-Wing Writers. But his national fame came only after the publication of his novel *The Twilight* (or "Midnight," *Tzu-yeh*) in 1933. An impressive and realistic study of the complex life of Shanghai during the depression of the 1930s, *The Twilight* depicts the exploitation and ruthlessness of capitalist society and confirms the Communist thesis that capitalism is a dead-end road in China.

In 1936 Mao Tun joined Lu Hsün,* Hu Feng, and other writers who formed the Chinese Literary Workers Association, which called for People's Literature for the National Revolutionary Struggle. His works in this period included some excellent short stories such as "Spring Silkworm" and "The Lin Family Shop." In May 1940 Mao Tun went to Yenan where he lectured at the Lu Hsün Institute. In 1941 he went to Hong Kong via Chungking, and he published another novel, *Putrefaction* (*fu-shih*), which was again sympathetic to the Communist cause and against the Kuomintang. In 1942 Mao Tun moved to Chungking where he served under Kuo Mo-jo on the cultural work committee of the political training board of the National Military Council. After the Sino-Japanese War,* Mao Tun and his wife toured the Soviet Union in 1947, and upon his return he founded the pro-Communist *Fiction Monthly* (*Hsiao-shuo yüeh-kan*) in Hong Kong in 1948. After the Communist takeover in 1949, Mao Tun went to Peking and was elected vice-chairman of the All-China Federation of Literary Workers (later the Writers' Union) with Kuo Mo-jo as chairman. Soon afterward he was appointed minister of culture. In 1954 he was elected a deputy to the First National People's Congress.

During the Hundred Flowers Campaign* in 1957, Mao Tun in his official capacity as minister of culture attacked the conformity of the Communist literary product, but he was removed from office as minister of culture. Like other writers he also suffered during the Cultural Revolution.* He reemerged as vice-chairman of the Chinese People's Political Consultative Conference* in 1976 after the downfall of the Gang of Four.* In 1979 he was also selected chairman of the Writers' Union. Mao Tun died on March 27, 1981, at the age of eighty-five.

REFERENCES: C. T. Hsia, *A History of Modern Chinese Fiction* (New Haven, Conn., 1971); Mao Tun, "The Road I Travelled," *Chinese Literature*, No. 7 (July 1981): 7–39; Leo Ou-fan Lee, *The Romantic Generation of Chinese Writers* (Cambridge, Mass., 1973).

                                                          PHILIP YUEN-SANG LEUNG

MARCO POLO BRIDGE INCIDENT (July 7, 1937): Incident leading to Japan's full-scale invasion of China.

The Marco Polo Bridge Incident, also called the China Incident, took place on the night of July 7, 1937, when the Japanese troops conducting field exercises were fired on by Chinese troops at Lukouchiao (the Marco Polo Bridge) on the outskirts of Peking. After an exchange of fire, the Japanese company commander discovered that one of his men was missing. The Japanese then approached the local Chinese military authorities in the nearby city of Wanping and requested that a Japanese search party be permitted to enter the city. When refused, the Japanese troops attacked and occupied Wanping on the night of July 8. This incident and subsequent developments touched off the Second Sino-Japanese War,* which eventually led to Pearl Harbor on December 7, 1941. Neither Japan nor China made any formal declaration of war until December 7, 1941, when Japan formally declared war on China. China responded with the same declaration on the next day. The war lasted until August 14, 1945. Several fundamental changes resulted from eight years of the Sino-Japanese War. (1) The Japanese Empire was completely shattered by the Allied powers and the most dreadful effect of the atomic bomb. (2) The Chinese Nationalists were utterly weakened and destroyed by the Japanese beatings, from which they never recovered. The Nationalists were eventually pushed out of Mainland China to Taiwan. (3) The Chinese Communists gained the chance they needed to strengthen their army and party during the war, which were the major factors in the Communists' ultimate victory over the Nationalists in 1949 and in establishing a fully sovereign state, free from foreign imperialism for the first time since the 1840s.

Did the Japanese have the right to conduct military maneuvers at the Marco Polo Bridge? From the legal point of view, they did not. Article IX of the Boxer Protocol of 1901 provided for twelve places where the foreign powers could hold military maneuvers. The Marco Polo Bridge was not one of them. Who fired the first fateful shot at the Marco Polo Bridge? It was certainly not the Japanese. The first shot might have been fired accidentally either by a Chinese soldier or by the Communists in the area who intended to provoke a full-scale war between the Japanese and the Chinese Nationalists. But it was not engineered by the Japanese Army as in the case of such earlier incidents as the assassination of Chang Tso-lin (April 1928) or the Mukden Incident* of September 1931, which was engineered by the Kwantung Army officers. In fact, the Japanese military commander of the North China Army and the key officers of the Army General Staff earnestly tried to settle the incident locally. Furthermore, Konoe Fumimaro and other civilian government officials in Tokyo were in complete agreement, at the time of the incident, with the nonexpansionist view held by General Ishiwara Kanji (chief of the Operations Division of the Army General Staff) and General Tada Shun (vice-chief of the Army General Staff). The "nonexpansionists" maintained that Japan should not risk war with China because Japan's archenemy was the Soviet Union, that the war with the Soviet Union had to be well prepared for through a series of five-year plans, and that Japan should wait for a showdown with the Russians until 1952, when Japanese industry would reach its high peak. Consequently, they adopted a policy of nonexpansion and local settlement.

On July 11, however, upon receiving the information that Chiang Kai-shek* had dispatched four army divisions to north China, which was in violation of the Ho-Umezu Agreement of 1935, the expansionists pressed Ishiwara and Tada to send reinforcements to north China. The expansionists led by Sugiyama Gen (war minister) urged an all-out attack against Chiang Kai-shek who, they feared, might use this incident as a pretext for retaking Manchuria. Japan's quick knockout blow against China was to bring a quick settlement. Ishiwara, however, authorized the reinforcement order, hoping to stop an endless war of retribution. On the same evening, when he was informed of a truce agreement arranged by the local commanders of both sides, Ishiwara canceled the orders of mobilization of three divisions which had been authorized on July 10. But problems of implementing the local truce agreement caused another exchange of fire at Langfang on July 25, which turned into a major war. The Japanese took Peking on July 28 and Tientsin on July 30. The fighting spread into Shanghai on August 13, and the city was seized by the Japanese on November 12. Japan occupied Nanking on December 13, hoping that Chiang Kai-shek would sue for peace if the capital was seized. But Chiang simply moved the capital to Chungking on December 20. When victory was not immediately apparent, and in order to win over the Chinese popular support, Japan established, on March 30, 1940, a puppet regime in Nanking headed by Wang Ching-wei.* But Japan's effort to gain the Chinese support was futile.

The Nationalist government and the Chinese Communist party* patched up their relations after the Sian Incident* (December 1936), which resulted in es-

tablishing a United Front against Japan. They seemed to have a cordial relationship during the initial phase of war, but the KMT government was alarmed by the CCP's rapid growth in strength in Yenan (the wartime capital of the CCP) and in other CCP territorial bases in north China. The war gave Mao Tse-tung[*] much needed time to restructure the party and the army. In January 1941 KMT–CCP relations deteriorated when the KMT forces attacked the CCP's New Fourth Army,[*] capturing its commander, Yeh T'ing. During the Pacific War, the KMT–CCP relations worsened. In order to put up stiffer resistance against Japan, the U.S. government made vain efforts to achieve closer KMT–CCP unity through the Wallace Mission (June 1944) and the Hurley Mission (November 1944). The KMT–CCP conflict remained unsolved until 1949, when the CCP overthrew the KMT. Totally exhausted by skyrocketing inflation, economic distress which alienated the majority of people, and serious loss of fighting capacity (the KMT suffered 1.3 million dead and 1.8 million wounded during eight years of war), the KMT had no other choice but to leave the mainland and retreat to Taiwan.
REFERENCES: James B. Crowley, "A Reconsideration of the Marco Polo Bridge Incident," *Journal of Asian Studies* 22, no. 3 (May 1963): 277–291; David Lu, *From the Marco Polo Bridge to Pearl Harbor* (Washington, D.C., 1961); James Morley, *The China Quagmire* (New York, 1983).

WON Z. YOON

MARING (SNEEVLIET), HENDRICUS (b. Holland, May 13, 1883–April 12, 1942): Comintern representative in China, 1921–1923.

Maring played the major role in bringing about cooperation between the Chinese Communist party[*] and the Kuomintang. Personally chosen by Lenin, Maring arrived in Shanghai in April 1921 charged with the task of exploring the possibility of setting up a Comintern[*] Bureau in the Far East. Influenced by discussions at the Comintern's Second Congress (1920), he took the view that the national and colonial question was the key to the future development of the world revolution. His experiences in the Dutch Indies made him realize the importance of cooperation with the national bourgeoisie. Furthermore, his early experiences in the Dutch labor movement made him realize the power of organized labor.

Maring attended the First Congress of the CCP (July–August 1921) and was critical of the hostility expressed at the Congress toward cooperation with the Nationalist movement and the exclusive focus on the working class that was adopted. Following the Congress, he proposed the establishment of a National Labor Secretariat (August 1921) to coordinate work, drafted its declaration, and had it translated into Chinese.

Maring, disappointed with the Communist party's work, at the end of 1921 turned his attention to establishing relations with the Nationalist movement. In December 1921, he met with Sun Yat-sen[*] in Kweilin. He had mixed feelings about Sun and was particularly worried about what he termed his militarism and his belief in a quick military solution to the problems facing him. However, the power of organized labor displayed during the Hong Kong seaman's strike (January–March 1922) impressed him. He was also impressed by Kuomintang support for the strike and thought that the strike's leadership was in its hands.

In July 1922 Maring went to Moscow to report on his first year. He proposed that Communist party members be persuaded to join the Kuomintang and to concentrate activities in Canton where the party could organize openly under Kuomintang protection. He justified this tactic of entryism on the grounds that the Kuomintang was not a true bourgeois party but rather an amalgam of four different groups: a leading intelligentsia partially oriented toward socialism; rich Chinese capitalists living overseas; soldiers of the southern army; and the workers. This anticipated the Stalinist conception of the four-class bloc.

Although the Comintern endorsed Maring's tactic in August 1922 and January 1923, it was clear that powerful forces in Moscow were opposed to his ideas. Comintern members such as Karl Radek, G. I. Safarov, and Grigorii N. Voitinsky were worried that such a tactic would stifle independent work among the proletariat and the peasantry. They saw a greater potential for the Communist party to develop its own independent power base. This opposition found support within the Communist party, the main proponent being Chang Kuo-t'ao.* In August 1922 Maring forced his ideas on the party leadership, but disputes continued until the Third Congress (June 1923). By this time, Wu P'ei-fu's* brutal suppression of the railway workers' strike in north China (February 1923) made most party members aware of the fact that the proletariat was not strong enough to wage a revolution by itself and needed allies. As a result, a majority at the Congress went along with Maring's ideas.

Despite this success, Maring had made many enemies and was not returned to China after his mandate ran out in August 1923. Many of the Chinese Communists were offended by what they saw as his high-handed manner. Powerful enemies remained in the Comintern. Furthermore, Maring's criticisms of Sun Yat-sen's policies had caused relations between the two men to become strained. Finally, Maring himself had consistently expressed his desire to be given other work in the Comintern apparatus. Until March 1924, he worked in the Comintern's Far East Department in Moscow after which he returned to Holland. He remained active in Dutch left-wing politics until his execution by the Nazis in 1942.

REFERENCES: Tony Saich, *The Origins of the First United Front in China: The Role of Sneevliet (Alias Maring)* (Leiden, 1990); Tony Saich and Fritjof Tichelman, "Henk Sneevliet: A Dutch Revolutionary on the World Stage," *The Journal of Communist Studies* 1, no. 2 (June 1985): 170–194; *Ma-lin tsai Chung-kuo te yu-kuan tzu-liao* (Materials concerning Maring in China) (Peking, 1980).

TONY SAICH

MARSHALL MISSION (December 20, 1945–January 8, 1947): The United States' last attempt to mediate the conflict between the Nationalists and the Communists in China.

The United States wanted a unified, pro-U.S. China after World War II in order to counterbalance the Soviet Union in the Far East. In November 1944

Ambassador Patrick Jay Hurley[*] began to arbitrate the power struggle between the Kuomintang and the Chinese Communist party[*] for fear that a civil war would result in the expansion of Soviet influence in China. When Hurley resigned on November 27, 1945, President Harry S Truman immediately appointed General George C. Marshall, the organizer of victory in World War II, to continue the ambassador's task. The announced goal of Marshall's mission was to arrange for an immediate cease-fire, to be followed by broadening the basis of the one-party government. The CCP responded enthusiastically to Marshall's appointment. Immediate civil war would be disadvantageous to the CCP since it remained inferior militarily. Besides, the CCP was pleased with Washington's placing the reorganization of the government ahead of the integration of forces. The KMT, though it opposed Marshall's arbitration, had no choice but to accept it because it needed U.S. aid.

Marshall's prestige and the anti-civil war sentiment in China had produced the initial success of his mission. On January 10, 1946, a cease-fire agreement was announced. Then the Political Consultative Conference (PCC) met from January 10 to January 30, and reached agreement on the following issues: the reorganization of the national government; a program to establish constitutional government; revision of the 1936 draft constitution; membership of the proposed National Constitutional Assembly which would adopt the revised constitution; and reorganization of government and the Communist armies under a unified command. On February 25, the Military Subcommittee of the PCC announced an army reorganization agreement that provided for massive troop reduction on both sides and the integration of Communist forces into a unified national army.

Unfortunately, soon both parties breached the political and military accords. The KMT was unwilling to grant the CCP equal political power, whereas the CCP resisted the integration of its armed forces. The truce was neglected while both parties rushed to expand their military control in Manchuria and in north as well as south China. Marshall was able to exert a temporary cease-fire from June 7 to the end of that month. Chiang Kai-shek[*] said it would be the last time he would attempt to resolve his differences with the Communists through negotiations. Full-scale war broke out because no agreement was reached when the cease-fire expired on June 30. However, since no one was willing to admit failure, desultory rounds of inconclusive negotiations continued for six more months. By the end of 1946, both sides had determined that they had more to gain on the battlefield than at the conference table. Marshall finally announced the failure of his mission and returned to Washington on January 8, 1947, to assume the position of secretary of state.

Marshall considered the greatest obstacle to peace in China was the almost overwhelming suspicion with which the Nationalists and the Communists regarded each other. Among the other important factors which he cited for the breakdown of negotiations were the opposition of the dominant group of the Nationalist reactionaries, the efforts of the extreme Communists to produce an economic situation that would facilitate the overthrow or collapse of the government, and the dominating influence of the military in China.

Historians have cited other factors that contributed to the failure of the Marshall Mission. The most often stressed point is the pro-Nationalist bias of the U.S. mediator. Washington was not indifferent to the terms of the settlement since it could not accept a Communist victory. Continued U.S. military and economic assistance to the KMT made it difficult for Marshall to convince the CCP of his impartiality and sincerity. Hence, the CCP intensified its attacks on the United States for strengthening the KMT, thereby encouraging it to seek a military solution to the conflict. In response, Washington placed an embargo on the shipment of arms and ammunition to China from August 1946 to May 1947. But the ban did not pacify the CCP owing to the following announcement of a U.S. decision to sell $900 million worth of war surpluses to the Nationalists. Thus, it failed to reverse the tide of a civil war. It merely served to increase the resentment of both sides to U.S. intervention.

One historian has pointed out that decades of strife and mistrust should be read as an indication of each party's intention to eliminate the other if given the chance. The greatest failure of the Marshall Mission, therefore, was that the Americans should ever have assumed their mediation might actually influence the course of the conflict.

REFERENCES: *The Complete Records of the Mission of General George C. Marshall to China, December 1945–January 1947*, microfilm, 50 reels (Washington, D.C., 1988); Steven I. Levine, "A New Look at American Mediation in the Chinese Civil War: The Marshall Mission and Manchuria," *Diplomatic History* 3, no. 4 (Fall 1979): 349–375; George C. Marshall, *Marshall's Mission to China: December 1945–January 1947*, 2 vols. (Arlington, Va., 1976); Forrest C. Pogue, *George C. Marshall*, vol. 4, *Statesman, 1945–1959* (New York, 1987).

SU-YA CHANG

MARXISM-LENINISM: The principle that in the transition from capitalism to communism the bourgeois democratic republic should be scrapped and replaced by the revolutionary dictatorship of the proletariat.

Lenin regarded this principle as the sole criterion for demarcating real Marxism from opportunism, revisionism, and bourgeois thinking. Lenin said: "The theory of the class-struggle was not created by Marx, but by the bourgeoisie before Marx and is, generally speaking, acceptable to the bourgeoisie. He who recognizes only the class-struggle is not yet a Marxist; he may be found not to have gone beyond the boundaries of bourgeois reasoning and politics. . . . A Marxist is one who extends the acceptance of class-struggle to the acceptance of the dictatorship of the proletariat. Herein lies the deepest difference between a Marxist and an ordinary petty or big bourgeoisie" (Lenin, *State and Revolution*, p. 30).

The acceptance or rejection of the dictatorship of the proletariat is, therefore, the demarcation line between the Marxism-Leninism of the Third International and the Marxism of the Second International, and between the European Social-Democratic parties and the Communist parties all over the world.

There are three main theses in Lenin's theory of the state:

1. The state is a special organization of force; it is the organization of violence for the suppression of some class. No matter what form it takes, every state is an apparatus of class repression. A democratic republic is such an apparatus just as much as a monarchy.

2. According to Marx, "The working class cannot simply lay hold of the ready-made state machinery and wield it for its own purpose" (Marx and Engels: *Manifesto of the Communist Party*, p. 7). In other words, the proletariat must not attempt to transfer the bureaucratic and military machinery from one hand to the other, but must break up, shatter the "ready-made state machinery." This is the principal lesson of Marxism for the tasks of the proletariat in relation to the state during a revolution; just this lesson has been distorted by the prevailing Kantskyist interpretation of Marxism, according to Lenin. What is to replace this machinery is "the proletariat organized as the ruling class," the establishment of democracy, according to the Communist Manifesto. It is, in other words, the dictatorship of the proletariat.

3. The dictatorship of the proletariat is still a state, but a "transitional state," according to Lenin. Democracy is transformed from capitalist democracy into proletarian democracy. It is still a state, but the organ of suppression is now the majority of the population, and not a minority. And, once the majority of the people itself suppresses its oppressors, a "special force" for suppression is no longer necessary. In this sense the state begins to wither away.

The above theory of the state is the core doctrine of theoretical Marxism-Leninism. Based on this theory, Lenin and his disciples denounced any socialist who did not advocate the utter destruction of the democratic republic, but instead tried to utilize the "more or less complete democracy" (Lenin) of this form of the bourgeois state to further the tasks of socialist revolution as a petty bourgeois opportunist or revisionist.

Under the guidance of this theory, all Communist parties that professed Marxism-Leninism when ascending to power abolished every remnant of the bourgeois democracy in order to strengthen the dictatorship of the proletariat. What appears now is not "the very simple organization of the armed masses" (ibid., p. 75) replacing any special force of suppression, but a huge security system and an army of secret police appearing in the wake of the victory of the proletariat. Victims of this complicated military machine would not be any real enemy, but dissidents among the people. Then it turns out that it is again a ruling minority suppressing the powerless majority for the sole purpose of safeguarding an ever-lasting reign for itself. Examples are not difficult to find.

On the other hand, most Western European Marxist-Leninist parties have one after the other abrogated this slogan in recent years and begun wholeheartedly to engage in parliamentary activities. Some of them have even participated in the bourgeois cabinets.

We may conclude that, while in the advanced capitalist countries Marxism-Leninism seems to be impractical as a guide to revolutionary strategy and tactics, in the less developed and underdeveloped countries, when put into practice, it might bring about unexpected or unintended consequences that are precisely the opposite to "the establishment of democracy" as solemnly declared in the *Communist Manifesto*.

REFERENCES: K. Marx and F. Engels, *The Manifesto of the Communist Party* (London and New York, 1932); V. I. Lenin, *The State and Revolution* (Wesport, Conn., 1978); F. Engels, *The Origin of the Family, the Private Property, and the State* (London and New York, 1933).

TIANJI JIANG

MASS-LINE: A theory defining correct leadership and procedures for maintaining close relations between leaders and followers.

The classic formulation of the mass-line of the Chinese Communist party[*] is found in a resolution passed by the Politburo of the Central Committee on June 1, 1943. Entitled "Concerning Methods of Leadership," the resolution states in part:

In all the practical work of our Party, all correct leadership is necessarily "from the masses, to the masses." This means: take the ideas of the masses (scattered and unsystematic ideas) and concentrate them (through study turn them into concentrated and systematic ideas), then go to the masses and propagate and explain these ideas until the masses embrace them as their own, hold fast to them and translate them into action, and test the correctness of these ideas in such action. Then once again concentrate ideas from the masses and once again go to the masses so that the ideas are persevered in and carried through. And so on, over and over again in an endless spiral, with the ideas becoming more correct, more vital and richer each time. Such is the Marxist theory of knowledge.

This statement, attributed to Party Chairman Mao Tse-tung,[*] is an application of the epistemological principles and practical methods that he articulated in his essay "On Practice" in 1937 to the populism that had characterized his leadership style for many years. The mass-line was a formula for resolving the innate contradiction between leadership and the masses. It posits that leadership is legitimate only insofar as its policy formulations are derived from intimate knowledge of the needs and desires of the masses, and in turn, that policy implementation is undertaken by the masses. At the same time, there is an insistence on the role of a guiding elite. Mao's populism does not permit democratic decision making by the masses.

Epistemologically, the mass-line follows the methodology prescribed for attaining "correct" knowledge laid out in "On Practice." The premise of that essay is that cognition proceeds in stages. It must begin with sensory perception of the objective, material world. That corresponds to the mass-line stage of the masses—gathering the scattered and unsystematic ideas of the common people. In the next stage, the cognitive theory, the brain sorts out and categorizes the various sense perceptions and, through reflection, makes judgments and inferences. This is the conceptual stage, the stage of rational knowledge. It corresponds to the mass-line prescription of "concentrating" the ideas of the masses through study and systematizing them. That is what makes theory and policy possible. The third stage in the theory is practice. Practice mediates between theory and reality, turning one into the other; through work, one can intimately observe the empirical situation, making possible the formulation of correct ideas, which, when put into practice, makes possible the transformation of the empirical situation. This corresponds to the mass-line requirement that ideas be explained to the masses and implemented by them. The process is perpetual, moving to ever higher stages of knowledge and transformation of reality.

The mass-line, in defining correct leadership, provides the standards for assessing incorrect leadership. Bad leaders are those who do not do empirical investigation. They do not solicit the ideas of the masses prior to making policy, and thus they commit the error of idealism. That is, their ideas are not derived from or commensurate with objective reality. The worst sort of idealists are dogmatists. They often commit the error of commandism—the forceful propagation of unrealistic, unpopular ideas.

At the other extreme of poor leadership from commandism is tailism, a term that refers to leaders who do not take the step of concentrating and systematizing the ideas of the masses and pushing them to the level of theory and policy formulation. Their narrow empiricism is said to make them lag behind the masses instead of leading them.

It is generally felt that the mass-line formulation served the Communists well in their struggle to attain power in China and transform its institutions. It provided a methodology for cadre work, and it helped maintain a close relationship between the leadership and the common people in a system that does not permit the people to choose their leaders. It is somewhat ironic, however, that Chairman Mao Tse-tung became the principal violator of the mass-line principle that he himself had formulated. His commandist insistence on unpopular collectivization* in rural areas and the disastrous policies of the Great Leap Forward* and Cultural Revolution* are evidence that the mass-line eventually had little influence on his own leadership style.

REFERENCES: Mao Tse-tung, *Selected Works of Mao Tse-tung*, vol. 3 (Peking, 1965): 163–176; Mark Selden, *The Yenan Way* (Cambridge, Mass., 1971).

PETER J. SEYBOLT

MAY FOURTH MOVEMENT (1919): A student and intellectual movement of great cultural and sociopolitical significance.

The name of the movement derived from the student demonstration in Peking on May 4, 1919, against the Chinese government's foreign policy and Japan's aggressive action against China. But the scope of the movement extended far beyond the initial protest. Its origin may be traced back either to 1915, when the Chinese intellectuals' patriotic feelings were spurred after Japan presented its Twenty-one Demands to China, and when the influential *New Youth* monthly was established, or to 1917, when a new literature and new thought revolution started to be promoted. The movement may be considered to have lasted either to 1921, when student movements somewhat declined, or to 1924, after many students joined in a political and military struggle against the Peking government.

The cultural and political impact and influence of May Fourth, however, extended to the 1930s and even the present and perhaps may last into the future too.

The immediate cause of the student protest involved the settlement made during the Versailles Peace Conference in Paris after World War I. Under Japanese pressure the Great Powers decided to award Japan the Chinese territory in Shantung Province and other privileges that Germany had seized from China by force in 1898. The Peking government under the control of warlords failed to raise strong objections. A day after the alarming news from Paris reached China, on May 3, 1919, more than 3,000 students from thirteen colleges and universities in Peking gathered in T'ienanmen Square in the south of the Imperial Palace demanding resistance to the Japanese aggression and punishment of three pro-Japanese officials: Ts'ao Ju-lin, minister of communications, Chang Tsung-hsiang, minister to Japan, and Lu Tsung-yü, Chinese director of the Chinese-Japanese Exchange Bank and a former minister to Japan. After the mass meeting, the students marched to the Legation Quarters, asking the Allies—Great Britain, the United States, France, and Italy—to support justice. Thereafter, they paraded to Ts'ao Ju-lin's home, where they found Chang and beat him into insensibility. Ts'ao escaped in disguise, but his house was burned down. The police arrested thirty-two students at the scene.

The incident provoked wide intellectual and popular support for the students. Mass student demonstrations took place in more than 200 cities in over twenty-two provinces in the ensuing month. On June 3 and 4 the government made mass arrests of 1,150 students in Peking, preceding, coincidentally, a more serious event seventy years later. The arrests aroused further indignation in all the cities and resulted in mass strikes of merchants, industrialists, and workers in Shanghai on June 5. Other cities were going to follow suit. Two days later the government gave in. On June 8 all arrested students were released, and on the next day the three pro-Japanese officials resigned. This was followed by the resignation of the prime minister and China's refusal to sign the peace treaty with Germany in Paris.

In the months following the May Fourth Incident, the students carried their patriotic campaign all over the country by holding mass meetings, making public speeches, and boycotting Japanese goods. More significantly in the long run, with their publication of over 400 magazines established in 1919, the students and young intellectuals vigorously spread the Literary Revolution and the New Culture Movement, both of which had been proposed in 1916–1917. Therefore, a new literature, written in the vernacular instead of the classical language and characterized by realism, romanticism, and social criticism, arose as a consequence. Western ideas, in the name of science and democracy, were enthusiastically promoted. Various doctrines, such as liberalism, John Dewey's pragmatism, Bertrand Russell's social and political philosophy, anarchism, and later many kinds of socialist ideas, were exalted. The Chinese tradition, particularly Confucianism and its ethical principles and practices, was severely attacked. A new spirit of skepticism and iconoclasm was on the rise. The young intellectuals generally believed that only through criticism and reevaluation of Chinese traditional thought and custom could a "new culture" and the modernization of China be achieved. This was also known as the "new thought tide."

As a result of the movement, the decline of the traditional ethics and family system accelerated; the emancipation of women gathered momentum; a vernacular "new literature" emerged; the press and popular education made progress; and, most importantly, the modern intelligentsia became a major factor in China's subsequent political developments. The movement spurred the reorganization of the Kuomintang and the birth of the Chinese Communist party* and other political groups and fostered some of the conditions favorable to a coalition between these two major parties for the overthrow of the Peking Regime. The movement also provided inspiration and impetus for all later major student movements in China and among overseas Chinese students.

Furthermore, interpreting and evaluating the movement became controversial in political, intellectual, and historical circles. The Kuomintang generally regarded it as a youths' patriotic movement, whereas the Chinese Communist party following the Maoist line interpreted it as an "anti-imperialist and antifeudal bourgeois-democratic revolution." But many of the independent scholars and historians considered it a Chinese Renaissance, a Chinese Reformation, or a Chinese Enlightenment.

REFERENCES: Tse-tsung Chow, *The May Fourth Movement: Intellectual Revolution in Modern China* (Cambridge, Mass., 1960); Tse-tsung Chow, *Research Guide to the May Fourth Movement, 1915–1924* (Cambridge, Mass., 1963); Chou Ts'e-tsung (Chow Tse-tsung), *Wu-ssu yün-tung shih* (History of the May Fourth Movement) (Taipei, 1989); Wen-han Kiang, *The Chinese Student Movement* (New York, 1948); P'eng Ming, *Wu-ssu yün-tung shih* (History of the May Fourth Movement) (Peking, 1984); Vera Schwarcz, *The Chinese Enlightenment: Intellectuals and the Legacy of the May Fourth Movement of 1919* (Berkeley, Calif., 1986).

TSE-TSUNG CHOW

MAY 7 CADRE SCHOOLS: Schools set up during the Cultural Revolution (1966–1976) for the reeducation of cadres and intellectuals; located mostly in the countryside as state-run farms.

The name "May 7" originated from the letter Mao Tse-tung* wrote to Lin Piao* on May 7, 1966. The letter was written after Mao had read a report submitted by the General Logistics Department of the Central Military Commission of the Chinese Communist party* Central Committee on further improving agricultural and sideline production of the army units.

In the letter Mao said that as long as there was no outbreak of world war, the army should be a large school. Even if there were to be a third world war, it would still be a large school. Besides fighting in battles, the army could also perform other jobs. In the army, one could study politics, military techniques, and cultural skills. The army would engage in agricultural and sideline production as well as set up small and medium-sized factories to produce products that the army needed and for exchange with the state at equal values. The army could conduct mass mobilization work to forge closer integration with the masses. It would also be ready to participate in the Cultural Revolution* struggles to criticize the bourgeois class. Hence, military work and study, military work and agricultural production, military work and industrial production, military work and civilian work could all be combined together. With appropriate coordination and with priorities, the army of a few million could make a very substantial contribution in all spheres.

In the same fashion, the workers would take up, besides their main responsibility of industrial production, the study of military work, politics, and cultural skills, and take part in the "Four-cleanups" movement (see Socialist Education Movement)* and criticism of the bourgeois class. In localities where conditions allowed, as in the Ta-ch'ing oilfield, workers should also engage in agricultural and sideline production.

The peasants, while they devoted most of their time to agricultural production (including activities in forestry, husbandry, sideline, and fishery), should also study military work, politics, and cultural skills, and set up small factories in the name of collectives when and where conditions permitted. They were to criticize the bourgeois class too. Students should follow the same example to take up other activities along with the focus on studying at schools. Staff in commerce, services, and state and party administration should do so if conditions allowed.

The letter reflected Mao's stand against excessive division of labor in society. Just as during the Great Leap Forward* when he endorsed the establishment of People's Communes* to represent a new form of social and political integration in the countryside, he wanted to see the blurring of occupational boundaries as a means of overcoming social division of labor, which might be politically divisive and linked to the capitalist legacy. The letter was not a personal letter to Lin Piao. It was written just prior to his "May 16 instruction" that triggered off the Cultural Revolution. Together with the "May 16" instruction, it may be seen as representing Mao's ideas about the destruction of the old regime and the establishment of the new one.

Mao's letter and the original report of the General Logistics Department were issued as part of a central document on May 15, 1986, one day before the May 16 instruction.

On August 1, 1966, the *People's Daily* published an editorial to call on the nation to become one large school of Thought of Mao Tse-tung.* The ideas came directly from Mao's May 7 letter.

The policy or institutional implications of Mao's May 7 instructions were not realized until 1967 when revolutionary committees replaced preexisting party and state organizations and the new political regime strove to implement every revolutionary idea of Mao's.

After then May 7 factories, May 7 schools, May 7 universities, May 7 hospitals, and the like were inaugurated or renamed.

On October 4, 1968, the *People's Daily* reported that the Heilungkiang Provincial Revolutionary Committee, the first provincial committee of its kind, organized a large number of cadres to work in the countryside on May 7 that year. The committee had set up a farm in Ch'ing-an County for this purpose and named it the May 7 cadre school.

The *People's Daily*'s report was accompanied by an editor's note, which signified the central Politburo's approval of the issue reported. In the note, it gave Mao's latest instruction. Mao said that it was an excellent chance for cadres to receive reeducation by going down to the countryside to labor. He suggested that apart from those incapacitated by senility, sickness, or physical handicap, all cadres should be sent down to labor. Even cadres with responsibilities should be organized to take turns in being sent down to labor in groups. After the publication of the *People's Daily*'s report and Mao's instructions, May 7 cadre schools were set up all over the country in the form of farms for cadres and intellectuals. Some of the schools were also called October 4 cadre schools after Mao's October 4 instruction of published in the *People's Daily*.

After the Ninth Party Congress in 1969, the May 7 cadre schools in many cases served as the institution for reeducating cadres that had been criticized and removed from offices, and in preparing them for return to duty after differing periods of political persuasion and laboring in the field. The hardship in working in the May 7 cadre schools was well known, but mainly because the cadres had not been accustomed to hard labor related to agricultural work and the political depression brought on them by the alleged political mistakes they had committed.

Many of the cadre schools were set up by individual party and state organizations for their own cadres. In some cases cadres took turns coming down to labor in the farms of the cadre school without being reprimanded. Therefore, the May 7 cadre schools may generally be regarded as remand centers similar in some aspects to labor reform camps run by the public security departments.

The institution was gradually abolished when most of the cadres were rehabilitated in the early 1970s and finally after the closing of the Cultural Revolution era with the arrest of the Gang of Four* in 1976.

CHAN MAN-HUNG THOMAS

MAY THIRTIETH INCIDENT (1925): The killing of student demonstrators by British-led police in Shanghai that touched off nationwide protest.

The mid–1920s was a period of heightened nationalism in China. The nationalistic sentiments were directed mainly against foreign imperialism and Chinese warlords. In particular, the perceived domination of China and the mistreatment of Chinese by foreign powers often provoked impassioned outbursts of nationalism, which in turn were violently suppressed by foreign powers. By the mid–1920s there were frequent strikes at foreign-owned factories and student demonstrations in major cities. The May Thirtieth Incident (*wu-san tsan-an*, literally the May Thirtieth Atrocious Incident) in Shanghai, involving British-controlled police killing Chinese students and civilians on May 30, 1925, was one of the most notorious cases.

After the founding of the Chinese Communist party[*] in 1921 and the revitalization of Sun Yat-sen's[*] Kuomintang as a result of the KMT–CCP United Front in January 1923, nationalism grew rapidly in China. In collaboration with the KMT, members of the CCP were busy organizing workers and peasants to fight for national salvation. Under the leadership of the CCP and often with the help of university students, the labor movement spread quickly. The movement had strong anti-imperialist overtones and was directed mainly against foreign-owned factories and mills in China. In early May 1925, some 280 delegates representing unions from throughout the country met in Canton and organized a National General Labor Union. This new organization was dedicated to the militant goals of organizing strikes to paralyze foreign-controlled factories in the cause of national salvation. In Shanghai, students at Shanghai University were encouraged to take active part in the labor movement. It was a strike at a Japanese-owned textile mill that led to the May Thirtieth Incident.

Chinese workers at this cotton-weaving mill first struck in February 1925, protesting low wages and poor working conditions. Mediation by the city's Chamber of Commerce and other civic bodies produced a preliminary settlement, which the Japanese owners subsequently rejected. When the workers went on a second strike, the Japanese owners closed down the plant. On May 15, the striking workers sent eight representatives to renew negotiation with the management. Japanese guards at the plant barred their entry, and the confrontation led to bloodshed. The armed guards opened fire, killing one and wounding seven. The British-dominated Municipal Council of Shanghai not only failed to bring to justice the Japanese guards but also arrested a number of Chinese workers on charges of disturbing the peace and order. Labor leaders and university students immediately began large-scale demonstrations, demanding punishment of the culprits and release of the arrested.

On May 22, a large number of students and workers held a public memorial service in the International Settlement for the slain worker and paraded afterward. More demonstrators were arrested. This triggered an even larger demonstration a week later. On May 30, more than 3,000 people, including students from eight Shanghai area universities, rallied on Nanking Road, Shanghai's business center, to protest British and Japanese atrocities. The angry crowd then pressed on the Lousa Police Station where the arrested students were held. The British officer, Inspector Everson, ordered his constables to fire into the demonstrators. Four demonstrators were killed, and eight more died later of wounds. Several dozens more were wounded, and some fifty students were arrested.

The May Thirtieth Incident provoked a nationwide outrage. Demonstrations and strikes took place in at least twenty-eight cities. Antiforeign riots broke out in many places. Funds poured into Shanghai from all over the country and from overseas Chinese to support the strikers. In December of the same year, the Shanghai Municipal Council, under mounting pressure, finally fired the British police inspector-general and his lieutenant and paid 75,000 *yuan* to the families of the victims. The May Thirtieth Incident was a nationwide protest; it aroused public opinion everywhere against the "unequal treaty" system imposed on China by foreign powers.

REFERENCES: Wen-han Kiang, *The Chinese Student Movement* (New York, 1948); Pao Tsun-peng, *Chung-kuo chin-tai ch'ing-nien yün-tung shih* (A history of youth movement in modern China) (Taipei, 1953).

TA-LING LEE

MIYAZAKI TŌTEN (TORAZŌ) (December 6 (?), 1870–December 6, 1922): Japanese political activist and Sun Yat-sen's closest confidant and collaborator.

Born in the village of Arao (present-day Arao City), Kumamoto Prefecture, in 1870 as the youngest of eleven children to Miyazaki Nagazo, Miyazaki Tōten pursued a political career to advance the cause of liberty and people's rights, as did many discontented fellow samurai during the Meiji era. His family was so poor that only five children (three sons and two daughters) survived to adulthood. The family strongly influenced the young Miyazaki. The poor father was proud of the old samurai family and taught swordsmanship for a living. The mother taught the children that they should live only for the sake of courage and honor. Hachiro, one of the brothers, advocated liberty and human rights; he joined in the antigovernment forces of Saigō Takamori and died during the Satsuma Rebellion of 1877. The father died when the young Miyazaki was eleven. The surviving brothers followed the family tradition.

Their early education and experiences also shaped the course of their lives. Exposed to many Western liberal ideas, they all became Christians and political activists. For example, the young Miyazaki studied under Tokutomi Ichiro, a writer and socialist, through whom he had learned about democracy, justice, morality, and the French Revolution. Later, he studied further at Waseda and several other foreign language schools in Tokyo and elsewhere. Converted to Christianity, he admired its democratic government and liberal creeds and practiced them for the benefit of people in the world, especially in China and Asia. He feared that Western imperialism would slowly destroy China and the yellow races. Thus, he became aware of Asian problems.

All the Miyazaki brothers returned home from Tokyo and witnessed the grinding poverty and the unjust burdens the tenants were forced to bear. Tamizo devoted his lifetime to the problem of land and devised a solution based on Henry George's single tax theory, which also influenced Sun Yat-sen.* Yazo and his young brother, hoping to save China and Asia, both set off for Shanghai in 1891 but returned home empty-handed after four years. While at home, Tōten married, but soon he left home again.

After a brief flirtation with the Korean issue in 1894, Tōten's next plans centered on Siam in 1895–1896. He visited Siam twice to work through the Chinese community, to help the Siamese government reform and ward off imperialism, and to develop the immigration of Japanese farmers. Again nothing came of these plans. To push the Siam question further, he met Inukai Kowashi, and as a result of their meeting, Miyazaki abandoned the project in Siam. Inukai in turn gave Miyazaki and Hirayama Shū secret government orders and funds to investigate and contact various secret societies that could promote reform in China. This was the beginning of his life's work with K'ang Yu-wei[*] and Sun Yat-sen. On July 23, 1897, his party arrived in Hong Kong and visited Macao and Canton to investigate the Hsing-chung hui[*] and contacted K'ang and Liang Ch'i-ch'ao.[*] As a result of this trip, Inukai and Miyazaki became close friends. In the summer of 1898 Miyazaki translated Sun's *Kidnapped in London* into Japanese and published it to make the revolutionary Sun known to the Japanese. Miyazaki also brought K'ang Yu-wei to Japan in late 1898 on Inukai's orders. Miyazaki and Inukai had tried unsuccessfully to bring Liang Ch'i-ch'ao and Ch'en Shao-pai together in the spring of 1899 to Tokyo.

Miyazaki contributed directly to the Chinese Revolution in the following events. Together with Ucnido Ryohei and Kiyofuji Koshichiro, he negotiated with Li Hung-chang[*] about the independence of Kwangtung and Kwangsi in 1900, but failed because of Li's rebuff.

In the same year the Hui-chou (Waichow) Uprising,[*] planned by the Japanese and Chinese, failed to launch attacks from Taiwan because of betrayal by the Japanese. Discouraged, Miyazaki did not involve himself in Chinese affairs for a time. Instead, he wrote his autobiography which he called *My Thirty-three Years' Dream* in 1902. This book promoted Sun's revolution in Japan more than before. In July 1904 Miyazaki introduced Sun Yat-sen to Huang Hsing,[*] Sung Chiao-jen,[*] Chang Chi, Ch'en Yu-jen, and Ch'en T'ien-hua to discuss the Chinese Revolution. On August 20, 1905, the T'ung-meng hui[*] was formed in Tokyo through Miyazaki, Hirayama Shu, and Kayano Chochi. Sun was elected president and Huang vice-president. In September 1906 the *Kakumei hyoron* (the Revolutionary Review), published with the help of Miyazaki and other Japanese, stressed the importance of the Chinese and Russian revolutions, appealing to the Japanese for help. In 1907 the T'ung-meng hui fell apart because of disagreements over ideological and financial matters. But Sun gave Miyazaki powers of attorney to raise funds for the purchase of arms and supplies for the Chinese Revolutionary Army in Japan. At this time Sun was planning to attack south China from the Vietnam border, but he was not successful in the end.

After the 1911 Revolution,[*] Miyazaki attended Sun's presidential inauguration in January 1912 in Nanking and subsequently prevented the revolutionary forces from fighting Yüan Shih-k'ai[*] by force; the Japanese government asked Miyazaki to persuade Sun Yat-sen and Huang Hsing. During the subsequent Chinese Revolution, however, Miyazaki continued to support the revolutionary forces in the south by providing them refuge in Japan. Nonetheless, Sun was well aware of the Japanese military's intentions, trying to divide and rule China, that is, playing the south off against the north. In March 1921 Miyazaki met Sun in Canton for the last time and tried to explain changing public opinion in Japan. Sun was not convinced of Miyazaki's explanation. Miyazaki died soon thereafter in Tokyo.

Miyazaki and Sun shared similar ideas about China and Asia, ranging from racism to religion. Sun collaborated with Miyazaki largely to get Japanese aid for his revolution. But Miyazaki's aid turned out to be more moral than material. Thus, both directly and indirectly he helped the Japanese military and capitalists more than he had intended.

REFERENCES: M. B. Jansen, *The Japanese and Sun Yat-sen* (Cambridge, Mass., 1954); Miyazaki Tōten, *My Thirty-Three Years' Dream* (Princeton, N.J., 1982).

KEY RAY CHONG

MOSCOW-PEKING AXIS: A Sino-Soviet alliance as the result of the agreement concluded by the PRC and the USSR in 1950.

After nine weeks of behind-the-scenes negotiations in Moscow, Mao Tsetung[*] and Joseph Stalin concluded six agreements, including the Treaty of Friendship, Alliance, and Mutual Assistance[*] on February 14, 1950. Thus, the forging of the Moscow–Peking Axis resting on military, political, ideological, and economic cooperation was completed more than four months before the outbreak of the Korean War on June 25, 1950. Mao had to go through another protracted "struggle" to prod the skeptical Stalin, who did not particularly want such an alliance with China at the time, to conclude an alliance system largely on Soviet terms. Peking's request for economic aid was on the order of U.S. $3 billion, but Mao managed to get only U.S. $300 million. Only through its intervention in the Korean War, as Mao later recalled, did Peking demonstrate, to Stalin's satisfaction, China's credibility as a trustworthy alliance partner. The Korean War (1950–1953) congealed the Moscow–Peking Axis on a foundation of shared values and shared fears.

The Sino-Soviet alliance, based on a thirty-year treaty, can be said to have lasted about eight years (1950–1958). The life cycle of the alliance was subject to the dynamics of military, economic, and ideological factors as perceived, interpreted, and acted on by the leaders in Moscow and Peking. As in any alliance system, the relative roles and positions of the partners vis-à-vis each other in the context of the changing world situation shaped the course of alliance politics. As a weaker but "realistic" partner, Peking always found itself in the twin dilemmas of "abandonment and entrapment," which it attempted to resolve with the duality of dependency when necessary and independence when possible. If Mao was more insistent than Stalin in the formation of this axis, Mao can also be said to have been more culpable than Khrushchev for its rupture.

Having already adopted the lean-to-one-side policy as the first basic foreign policy line of New China, Peking clearly perceived that it needed such an alliance for political, economic, and strategic reasons. The dire economic conditions, the perceived need for a protective shield against American intervention, the lack of a viable "third road," and the requirement of a new regime for international recognition and legitimation—all these factors constituted a necessary and sufficient condition for Peking to assume the role of a supplicant in the formation of this asymmetrical alliance system.

During the "golden years" (1953–1957) of the alliance, the scope of Soviet economic, technological, and nuclear aid was considerable, especially given the state of the Soviet economy in the 1950s. In the 1950s more than 10,000 Soviet specialists had been sent to China, while some 10,000 Chinese engineers, technicians, and skilled workers, and about 1,000 advanced scientists had received further training in the Soviet Union. In the wake of Stalin's death, many of the strings imposed by Stalin on Soviet aid were removed on Moscow's initiative. At least up to Khrushchev's de-Stalinization speech at the Twentieth Congress of the Communist party of the Soviet Union in 1956, Peking's publicly proclaimed policy was one of setting in motion a tidal wave of learning from the Soviet Union. Two months after the Korean armistice was concluded in July 1953, post–Stalinist Russia offered aid for the construction or renovation of 141 industrial enterprises. In September and October 1954, Khrushchev, Bulganin, Mikoyan, and others made their first post–Stalin foreign visit to Peking, concluding several important aid agreements with Mao. Between 1955 and 1958 six agreements related to the development of China's nuclear science, industry, and weapons program—including the New Defense Technical Accord of October 15, 1957, in which Moscow agreed to supply Peking a prototype atomic bomb and missiles as well as related technical data—were completed. Moscow's assistance had met Peking's critical needs when there was no alternative source of support, laying the foundations for economic recovery after decades of foreign invasion and civil war.

Here we find Khrushchev resisting—and yielding to—Chinese pressures for more aid with the plea that the Soviet Union was still "hungry and poverty-ridden from the war" and Mao demanding—and resenting—more Soviet help. Paradoxically, the rise of substantial Soviet aid in the post-Stalin years was a consequence of China's increased independence and greater political and ideological leverage in Communist intrabloc politics. Yet such a relationship with an uneven distribution of costs and benefits could not go on too long. By 1959 Moscow, in Peking's eye, had failed to meet expected alliance obligations (indeed, litmus tests) in the Taiwan Strait crisis, the Sino-Indian conflict, and a united front against American imperialism. Symbolically and strategically, the "perfidious" Soviet letter of June 20, 1959, in which Moscow called off the 1957 Defense Technical Accord, marks the rupturing of the "spinal cord" of the Moscow–Peking Axis. All subsequent attempts to put the alliance back on track proved to be of no avail.

The collapse of the Sino-Soviet alliance system has reinforced the traditional Sinocentric values of autonomy, self-reliance, and independence. Never again would China enter into such an alliance system. Even at a time of acute security needs, China would prefer more flexible and less formal means of security alignments (a form of a united front strategy) to binding security alliance pacts that could prove once again to be inimical to China's status, sovereignty, and security. Herein lies the historical significance of the Moscow–Peking Axis.

REFERENCES: Howard L. Boorman et al., *Moscow-Peking Axis: Strengths and Strains* (New York, 1957); Allen S. Whiting, " 'Contradictions' in the Moscow-Peking Axis,"

Journal of Politics 20, no. 1 (February 1958): 127–161; O. Edmund Clubb, *China and Russia: The "Great Game"* (New York, 1971); John Wilson Lewis and Xue Litai, *China Builds the Bomb* (Stanford, Calif., 1988).

SAMUEL S. KIM

MUKDEN INCIDENT (September 18, 1931): Japanese attack in Manchuria and beginning of World War II.

The Mukden Incident, also called the Manchurian Incident, took place on the night of September 18, 1931, on the outskirts of Mukden in Manchuria, when a bomb explosion displaced railway tracks of the Southern Manchurian Railway owned by the Japanese. The Japanese alleged that Chinese troops blew up the Japanese railway. Actually, the explosion was engineered by staff officers of the Kwantung Army who used the incident as a pretext for the conquest of Manchuria and the establishment of the Japanese puppet state of Manchukuo.* The incident touched off the Sino-Japanese conflict which led to the Marco Polo Bridge Incident* (July 7, 1937) and, eventually, to Pearl Harbor (December 7, 1941). In fact, the Japanese invasion of Manchuria shattered the Nationalist government's objective of achieving a unified China and weakened the Kuomintang, which ultimately led to the victory of the Chinese Communists in 1949.

The officers who plotted the incident were Colonel Itagaki Seishirō (the senior staff officer) and Lieutenant Colonel Ishiwara Kanji (the operations officer). These officers believed that Japan's conquest of Manchuria was essential for the survival of the Japanese Empire. They wanted to establish a major strategic base in Manchuria against the Soviet Union. They also wanted to control economic resources in Manchuria which were vital for Japanese industry and for preparing for a possible war with the Soviet Union. The Japanese officers were increasingly apprehensive about the Japanese interest in Manchuria, when Chiang Kai-shek* completed the Northern Expedition* and established the Nationalist government in Nanking in 1928. They feared that a strong unified China might upset the status quo in Manchuria, subsequently jeopardizing the Japanese interest in the region. Under these circumstances, the Japanese officers wanted to take immediate action to forestall the Chinese movement toward the complete unification and recovery of national rights in Manchuria.

Although the Mukden operations were carried out without the direction of the Army General Staff in Tokyo, the high command gave tacit approval for the action. With the approval of General Shigeru Honjo, the commander-in-chief of the Kwantung Army, the staff officers ordered their troops to launch an attack on Chinese garrison barracks in Mukden. Immediately following the occupation of Mukden, the Japanese troops swept quickly all over Manchuria. Changchún was taken on September 19, Antung on the 20th, and Kirin on the 21st. Five months later, the Japanese took most cities, driving Chinese troops out of Manchuria. The advancing troops met little resistance from the Chinese since Chiang Kai-shek ordered Marshal Chang Hsüeh-liang*, the commander of the Chinese forces in Manchuria, to withdraw his troops from Manchuria. Chiang believed that the Chinese troops were not yet prepared for a foreign war with Japan since he was seriously hampered by domestic enemies, especially the Chinese Communists. Chiang decided that he must first pacify China before fighting the Japanese.

Having completed the conquest of Manchuria, on March 9, 1932, the Kwantung Army established the puppet state of Manchukuo* (the state of Manchus). P'u-i,* the last of the Ch'ing emperors who had been deposed in 1912, was brought to Hsinking (New Capital) from Tientsin and was made chief executive of the state. Two years later, on March 1, 1934, P'u-i was installed as the emperor of Manchukuo.*

Initially, the Japanese civilian government under Reijirō Wakatsuki was opposed to the military action in Manchuria. The government tried to keep the military under control but found itself helpless. The Wakatsuki cabinet finally fell on December 11. When the next cabinet under Tsuyoshi Inukai took over, it could do no better. Inukai was subsequently assassinated by an ultranationalist naval officer on March 15, 1932. Two navy cabinets that followed from 1932 to 1936 tried hard to curb the army's activities in Manchuria, but nothing much was accomplished.

While the Kwantung Army was still engaging in aggressive operations in Manchuria, the Chinese government appealed to the League of Nations and the U.S. government. The Chinese government hoped that international pressure might halt the Japanese invasion. In February 1933 the league's Lytton Commission, after investigating the situation in Mukden, condemned Japan as the aggressor. Japan responded by withdrawing its membership from the league in March 1933. Meanwhile, the U.S. government strongly reminded Japan that the United States would not recognize any territorial changes brought about by force in Manchuria. The Japanese turned a deaf ear to these warnings. Although there was one possible way of checking the Japanese—employing economic sanction—the Powers, including the United States and Britain, would not use it. No government in the world would be able to stop the Japanese aggression in Manchuria.

The Mukden Incident caused a critical setback for the League of Nations, from which it never recovered. The incident also showed that any attempt to impose international pressure on Japan without using any apparatus for enforcing collective security was useless against the Japanese aggressors. Consequently, the Japanese Army's aggressions in China continued until Pearl Harbor.

REFERENCES: F. C. Jones, *Manchuria Since 1931* (London, 1949); Sadako Ogata, *Defiance in Manchuria: The Making of Japanese Foreign Policy, 1931–32* (Los Angeles, 1964); Mamoru Shigemitsu, *Japan and Her Destiny* (New York, 1958).

WON Z. YOON

N

NANCHANG UPRISING (1927): Communist revolt following the breakdown of the first KMT–CCP United Front.

In early 1927 the Northern Expeditionary* forces led by the KMT–CCP United Front split into two rival camps. At Wuhan the Chinese Communists and left-wing leaders of the Kuomintang continued to uphold the United Front, while Chiang Kai-shek* and his followers organized their own regime at Nanking and terminated the United Front with a bloody purge. In mid-July the KMT leadership in Wuhan, worrying about its own survival in the face of expanding Communist power, also turned against the Chinese Communist party.*

The CCP immediately decided on a policy of armed uprisings in the four provinces of Hunan, Hupeh, Kiangsi, and Kwangtung. It hoped especially to seize control over Wuhan's Second Front Army under Chang Fa-k'uei, since the Communists commanded many of its units. In late July Chang's army, participating in Wuhan's Eastern Expedition against Nanking, arrived in Kiangsi. From July 19 to 22, CCP leaders including T'an P'ing-shan, Li Li-san,* and Chou En-lai* met with the Communists in Chang's army at Kiukiang and agreed on a plan of mutiny at Nanchang, the provincial capital of Kiangsi. A few days later the CCP leadership and Comintern* representatives in Wuhan, hesitant to break with Chang at this time, sent Chang Kuo-t'ao* to Nanchang to halt the plan. The plotters, however, ignored Chang's message.

In the early morning of August 1, the pro-Communist troops at Nanchang, led by the Twentieth Corps under Ho Lung (not yet a CCP member) and the Twenty-fourth Division under Yeh T'ing, revolted and took over the city. Chang Fa-k'uei, attending a KMT meeting at Lushan, was caught by surprise. About half of the Second Front Army participated in the revolt; they were joined by Chu Teh's* units from the local forces in Kiangsi. In order to assume an appearance of legitimacy, the revolters established the Central Revolutionary Committee of the KMT and claimed to continue the KMT–CCP United Front. Among the thirty-one listed members of the committee were eight KMT leaders who had not been involved in the uprising. The actual leadership of the uprising, however, lay firmly in the hands of a few Communists, notably T'an P'ing-shan, Liu Po-ch'eng, and Chou En-lai.

The revolters occupied Nanchang for four days before heading for Kwangtung. During the following weeks of the southward march, over one-third of the original 21,000 men were lost to illness and desertion. After entering Kwangtung, they briefly occupied Ch'aoan and Swatow, but they were soon attacked by KMT forces loyal to Nanking. The revolters were outnumbered and outequipped; assistance from the local peasant armies added little to their strength. In late September they suffered disastrous defeats at the hands of Ch'en Chi-t'ang's* Kwangtung Army. By early October the entire revolting force disintegrated in the area of Hai-feng and Lu-feng. Most of its leaders escaped to Hong Kong and Shanghai, while some remnants, led by Chu Teh, later joined Mao Tse-tung* in the Chingkang Mountains in Kiangsi.

The CCP leadership criticized the uprising at the time for its failure to carry out land revolution and class struggle. After 1949, however, the People's Republic* exalted this event, and the date of the uprising was recognized as the founding date of the Red Army.

REFERENCES: Hsiao Tso-liang, *Chinese Communism in 1927: City vs. Countryside* (Hong Kong, 1970); Wang Chien-min, *Chung-kuo Kung-ch'an-tang shih-kao* (A draft history of the Chinese Communist party), vol.1 (Hong Kong, 1974); C. Martin Wilbur, *The Nationalist Revolution in China, 1923–1928* (Cambridge, 1983).

KE-WEN WANG

NANKING GOVERNMENT (1928–1937): Chinese Nationalist government in Nanking under President Chiang Kai-shek.

The National government of the Republic of China* was formally established in Nanking on October 10, 1928, with Chiang Kai-shek* as president. It was a five-power government consisting of the Executive Yuan, the Legislative Yuan, the Judicial Yuan, the Examination Yuan, and the Control Yuan. It was a single-party rule during a period of political tutelage on which the Nationalist Revolution entered in 1928. It set itself the task of national reconstruction after a decade of warlord destruction.

Although it was the most modern administration China had ever had, offering the best hope for China at the time of formation, the Nanking government proved unequal to the task of nation-building. From the start, it was weak as a central government, lacking the full authority and powers necessary for performing its functions and duties. It effectively controlled less than one-third of the country, its writ being confined to Nanking, Shanghai, and a few provinces in the lower Yangtze Valley. Until 1931, it was a coalition of the military and the right wing of the Kuomintang. The warlords, Yen Hsi-shan* and Feng Yü-hsiang,* revolted against it in 1929–1930, while the leftists who called themselves the Reorganizationists* attempted to break away.

In the spring of 1931 Hu Han-min,* leader of the right, was put under house arrest because of his differences with Chiang Kai-shek over the provisional constitution. This triggered another anti-Chiang movement in Canton in May. A renewal of civil war was averted only by the Japanese aggression following the Mukden Incident.* In December Chiang resigned from all his posts in the government in accordance with an agreement reached earlier with the Canton Regime. Wang Ching-wei,* the leader of the left, was then appointed president of the Executive Yuan. But Chiang staged a comeback early in 1932, becoming chairman of the powerful Military Affairs Committee in March. This enabled him to form a new coalition with Wang, which lasted until December 1, 1935, when Wang stepped down from the government because of ill health after an attempt on his life. Chiang's power was further increased when he took over as president of the Executive Yuan.

The Nanking government enjoyed a monopoly of power in the name of political tutelage. No opposition parties were allowed, and no political dissent was tolerated. But the Communist insurgency remained the single most serious domestic problem for the authorities. Between 1930 and 1934, five extermination campaigns against the Communists were launched, the last one forcing them into the historic Long March.* As opposition to Chiang grew, the government became more and more repressive, maintaining its position by coercion and the skillful use of bribery, "silver bullets" diplomacy, and propaganda that played on the treachery of subordinate generals. Political tutelage did not to come to an end in 1936 as had been promised, and constitutional government was not effected until 1947 after the constitution of the Republic of China had been adopted and promulgated the previous December.

The Nanking government was a dictatorship formed by Chiang Kai-shek, who presided over a ramshackle regime comprising numerous vested interests, diverse elements, and political factions. It failed to establish the rule of law. Personal relations and loyalty to Chiang rather than government institutions determined much of what could be done. Consequently, corruption and graft were commonplace, which, combined with factionalism, political instability, and incessant civil war, prevented the government from introducing the social, political, and judicial reforms necessary for national reconstruction. Nowhere was this failure more manifest than in the area of land reform, with the result that the lot of the rural masses was little improved during the period of Nationalist rule.

In foreign affairs, the Nanking government pursued a moderate policy in regard to the revision of the "unequal treaties." Negotiations with the great powers between 1928 and 1931 led to the recovery of tariff autonomy, the return of the leased territory of Weihaiwei, and the retrocession of several foreign concessions and settlements. Furthermore, an extraterritoriality treaty would have been concluded with the British government but for the threat of renewed civil war and the Japanese invasion of Manchuria. The movement for the abrogation of the unequal treaties was called to a halt at the end of 1931.

The biggest external problem for the Nanking government was Japanese aggression. Indeed, the most criticized aspect of Nanking's foreign policy was its unwillingness to fight the Japanese as soon as the Manchurian crisis came to a head. Choosing to trade space for time, Chiang regarded the Chinese Communists as a more serious threat than the Japanese invasion, believing that once the internal enemy had been eliminated the government would be much better placed to repel the external foe. This policy of nonresistance caused widespread antigovernment sentiments among opposition groups and patriotic students, seriously undermining Nanking's credibility as a champion of Chinese nationalism. As the Japanese Army occupied Jehol and Chahar provinces in 1933, a revolt occurred in Fukien Province, and a People's Revolutionary government was set up in Foochow in October, pledging to overthrow Chiang and to fight the Japanese. The rebellion collapsed in January 1934, but anti-Japanese and antigovernment sentiments continued to grow. Eventually, the government decided to fight the Japanese in December 1936, but not before the Japanese had established a zone of autonomous provinces in north China, or before Chiang was kidnapped by General Chang Hsüeh-liang* in Sian.*

Despite its failures in the social and economic spheres, the Nanking government made some remarkable achievements in the areas of fiscal reform, communications, education, and industrial development. These reforms were not easy. National reconstruction was a formidable task in this vast and divided country, and the government's efforts were not helped by the Communist insurgency and the Japanese aggression.

REFERENCES: Hung-Mao Tien, *Government and Politics in Kuomintang China, 1927–1937* (Stanford, Calif., 1972); Lloyd E. Eastman, *The Abortive Revolution* (Cambridge, Mass., 1974); Immanuel Hsü, *The Rise of Modern China*, 3rd ed. (New York, 1983).

EDMUND S.K. FUNG

NANKING MASSACRE (1937): Massive killing of Chinese by the Japanese in Nanking during the war of aggression against China.

The Japanese aggression against China since the September 18 Incident in 1931 had continued to grow until the outbreak of the Lukouchiao (Marco Polo Bridge)* Incident on July 7, 1937, when the Chinese people decided to launch an all-out war of resistance against Japan. On August 13, 1937, Japan opened a southern front at Shanghai, in which Chiang Kai-shek's* Nationalist forces put up a stiff resistance by holding the Japanese Shanghai Expeditional Army under the command of General Matsui Iwane at bay for almost three months. Not until their flank was threatened by the landing of Japan's Tenth Army at Hangchou Bay did they withdraw from Shanghai, which fell to the enemy on November 9.

The next phase of the war was the battle of Nanking, the Chinese capital, which was defended by thirteen divisions numbering around 150,000 men. For the attack on Nanking, the Japanese Army was reorganized into the Central China Front Army under Matsui's command, which consisted of the original Shanghai Expeditional Army now under a newly appointed commander, Prince Asaka Yasuhiko, and the Tenth Army still under the command of Lieutenant General Yanagawa; the former had the Third, Ninth, Eleventh, and 101st divisions with the 101st left to garrison Shanghai, and the latter had the Fifth, Sixth, Eighteenth, and 114th divisions. The assaulting force separated into three routes and marched toward Nanking: the eleventh, thirteenth, and sixteenth divisions of the right wing moved westward along the Shanghai–Nanking Railway; the central army of the third and ninth divisions marched along the Nanking–Hangchou Highway; and the left-wing army of the sixth, eighteenth, and 114th divisions and Kunisaki's detachment of the fifth Division marched along a line from Kuangte and Hsuan-cheng leading to Wuhu on the Yangtze, sixty miles west of Nanking.

Tang Sheng-chih, a former warlord and rival of Chiang Kai-shek, volunteered to assume the command for the defense of Nanking. On December 9, Japanese airplanes flew over Nanking and dropped thousands of leaflets in Chinese declaring that "the Japanese troops exert themselves to the utmost to protect good citizens and enable them to live in peace, enjoying their occupations."

In the middle of November 1937, after the Shanghai Refugee Shelter had taken in 450,000 Chinese refugees, foreign residents in Nanking established the International Committee for the Nanking Safety Zone and negotiated with both the Chinese authorities and the Japanese Embassy for support. On December 1, Ma Ch'ao-chün, mayor of Nanking, gave the committee the ruling responsibility for the 3.86 square mile Safety Zone, centering around the American Embassy and the University of Nanking, just opposite the Japanese Embassy.

By December 8 Japanese forces had taken most of the strategic positions of the outer defense of Nanking. On the morning of December 13, the Japanese first seized the west gate; other gates fell in quick succession. By 11:00 A.M. some Japanese soldiers entered the Nanking Safety Zone, and in front of G. A. Fitcher, deputy secretary-general of the zone, killed twenty refugees, thus commencing the wanton massacre, rape, looting, and burning that China would suffer for the next two months and beyond.

There were twenty-eight cases of large-scale massacres involving the deaths of more than 190,000 capitulated soldiers and civilians. The most horrendous such incidents took place at Ts'ao-hsieh-chia, where 57,400 people were killed; at Hsiakuan (40,000 killed); at Yentzuchi (50,000); at Paotashih (30,000); and at Shangsingho (28,700).

The most shocking individual murders were those reported by the Tokyo *Nichi-nichi shimbun* newspaper on December 4, 1937: "Contest to Kill First 100 Chinese with Sword Extended When Both Fighters Exceed Mark." Recently, *Asashi Shimbun* reprinted an entry of a Japanese soldier's diary written at Nanking:

Today we again beat the innocent Chinese half-dead, then pushed them into the ditch, and had their hairs lighted so as to see them lingering to die. For the sake of passing away time, everybody does the same to amuse himself. If this happened in Japan, it would have created a great uproar, but here at Nanking it would be simply like killing a dog or cat.

In like manner, 150,000 Chinese perished at Nanking. When the mass and individual murders are combined, the conservative figure stands at over 340,000 killed.

Japanese commanders also encouraged their men to rape the Chinese women. Lieutenant General Tani Hisao himself, in additon to killing some Chinese, raped a dozen women at Nanking. An American missionary, James MacCallum, testified that "there were at least 1,000 raping cases every night." Another foreigner testified that one-third of the raping took place during daytime. All told, 80,000 raping cases were reported.

One Japanese soldier wrote home that "in my half year at the front, about the only two things I have learned are rape and robbery—the looting by our armies is beyond imagination." According to one survey made in March 1938, 62 percent of the buildings outside the city of Nanking and one-third of those inside it were burned. Most of those burned had been systematically stripped of their contents. The total losses of buildings and contents were estimated at U.S. $836 million (1938 value) and the family losses at $136 million, thus bringing the combined property losses to about $1 billion.

The German Embassy in Nanking reported to Berlin that "the Japanese army was a bestial group; the crime was not committed by this or that Japanese, but by the entire Japanese Imperial Army, a bestial machine being in operation." Indeed, none of these crimes would have been possible without the acquiescence and even the approval of the Imperial Headquarters at Tokyo. Barely had the Great Nanking Massacre subsided when Generals Matsui and Yanagawa and Prince Asaka were given an imperial audience on February 26, 1938, at which they were rewarded by Emperor Hirohito. Each was given a pair of silver vases embossed with the imperial chrysanthemum. Shortly after the war Yanagawa died, and Matsui along with Lieutenant General Tani was executed by the International Military Tribunal for the Far East. Lieutenant General Prince Asaka, however, for reasons unexplained by the Tribunal, was not even prosecuted. Nor were other division commanders under Matsui, including Generals Fujita, Yoshizumi, Yamamura, Ogishiyo, and Nakajima and Brigadier Sasaki, whose deeds in Nanking made them eminently qualified as Class A war criminals.

REFERENCES: H. J. Timperley, ed., *Japanese Terror in China* (New York, 1938); Akira Fujiwara, *Shinpan Nankin tai giyakusatsu* (new edition of the Great Nanking Massacre) (Tokyo, 1989); Committee for Compiling Materials of the Great Nanking Massacre, ed., *Ch'in Hua Jih-chün Nanking ta tu-sha tang-an* (Archival documents relating to the great Nanking massacre) (Nanking, 1987).

TIEN-WEI WU

NATIONAL PROTECTION ARMY: Army organized in 1915–1916 by Ts'ai Ao in Yunnan Province to oppose Yüan Shih-k'ai's Monarchical Movement.

The National Protection Army (*Hu-Kuo chün*) was founded by a romantic young New Army* officer, Ts'ai Ao,* who first emerged as an important figure in Yunnan Province during the 1911–1912 Republican Revolution. Ts'ai had been educated and radicalized by Sun Yat-sen's* movement in Japan during the previous decade. Yüan Shih-k'ai* brought Ts'ai Ao to Peking in 1912 to serve in the Ministry of War. His radical organizing activities soon landed him in prison. Ts'ai Ao was released in mid-July 1915, at which time he headed for Yunnan. In the fall he reorganized old and recruited new units into a National Protection Army of 10,000 men. Ts'ai was also in touch with Liang Ch'i-ch'ao* and may have had some Japanese financial assistance as well. Ts'ai's sole purpose in raising the army was to stop Yüan Shih-k'ai's Monarchical Movement as it began to take form in Peking by supporting a declaration of independence or succession by Yunnan Province. In part through Ts'ai Ao's efforts and in part through the refusal of Yüan's generals to support the Monarchical Movement, Yüan Shih-k'ai gave up his campaign for emperor and then resigned the presidency in May 1916. On the surface, the National Protection Army succeeded, and Ts'ai Ao became a national hero. The tyrant Yüan Shih-k'ai was forced to resign in disgrace, and the cause of parliamentary democracy was saved. On another level, however, the army failed. The overthrow of Yüan Shih-k'ai caused the unraveling of centralized authority and inaugurated a long, debilitating warlord era. This era lasted at least until 1928, and it was more destructive of Chinese polity and society than the excesses of Yüan Shih-k'ai. In the battered history of Chinese democracy, however, Ts'ai Ao and his National Protection Army still have an honored place.

STEPHEN R. MACKINNON

NATIONALISM: The political assertion of the primacy of national goals; in China used in contrast to stress on culture, region, or social ideology.

Although China has possessed both a unified state structure and a well-defined culture longer than most other polities, the search for nationhood of the sort that developed in nineteenth-century Europe has proved both a dominant and elusive goal in the twentieth century.

Before the modern period, notions of Chinese identity hinged on loyalty to the family, clan, and emperor, in particular as understood through the culture and values of Confucianism, which were conceived of as having universal rather than specifically national validity. Only in the late Ch'ing dynasty* did clear forerunners of nationalist ideas, such as the concept of a national essence (*kuo-ts'ui*), begin to appear. At the same time the Manchu ruling house began increasingly to be considered alien to the Chinese race (*min-tsu*). Both words appear to have been borrowed from Japan, and reflected the gradual adoption by Asian cultures of Western European notions of nationhood.

Truly European-style nationalism may perhaps be said to have appeared in China only at the time of the May Fourth Movement* of 1919, although it was paradoxically blended with an iconoclastic desire to destroy the Chinese past and adopt wholesale all things Western, which might seem the antithesis of the nationalistic impulse. With the May Thirtieth Movement* of 1925, nationalism gained great strength, and nationalistic bidding wars having clear domestic purposes (familiar in other parts of the world) became a standard feature of Chinese

political competition. This was particularly clear during the Northern Expedition*
and the early years of the Nationalist government, as well as in the early 1930s
when the Communists and Nationalists competed for the mantle of nationalism
in the struggle against Japan. An influential work by Chalmers Johnson attributes
the Communist victory in 1949, at least in part, to the mass nationalism of
peasants mobilized in wartime, which he contrasts to the elite nationalism of
earlier periods. Scholars regularly stress the nationalism of the People's Republic
of China,* evident, for example, in its eventual repudiation of its ideological
alliance with the Soviet Union.

Yet nationalism is an elusive concept, not easily applied. In labeling some
Chinese as nationalists, are we suggesting that others loved their country less?
The term regularly proves either too inclusive ("everyone is a nationalist") or
too narrow ("only X is an authentic nationalist") to be of much analytical, as
opposed to polemical, use. The Chinese have many other loyalties that may
overlap with or overshadow those to the nation, especially regional identifica-
tions. Furthermore, the content of Chinese nationalism appears variable and
contradictory. Do nationalists cherish distinctively Chinese traditions, or do they
repudiate them as the New Culture Movement did? How can nationalism be
reconciled with the cosmopolitan and internationalist doctrines of Marxism-
Leninism?*

In the period since the death of Mao Tse-tung* in 1976, the issue of what it
means to be Chinese and to love China (i.e., to be a nationalist) has once again
become highly contentious, and in many cases, the debate has paralleled that of
the May Fourth era. China clearly has a remarkable unity, but whether that unity
can (or should) ever take the form of the Western nation-state and its associated
doctrine of nationalism remains to be seen.

REFERENCES: Charlotte Furth, ed., *The Limits of Change: Essays on Conservative
Alternatives in Republican China* (Cambridge, Mass., 1976); Chalmers A. Johnson,
*Peasant Nationalism and Communist Power: The Emergence of Revolutionary China
1937–1945* (Stanford, Calif., 1962); Tu-ki Min, *National Polity and Local Power: the
Transformation of Late Imperial China* (Cambridge, Mass., 1989); Arthur Waldron,
"Theories of Nationalism and Historical Explanation," *World Politics* 37, no. 3 (April
1985): 416–433.

ARTHUR WALDRON

NATIONALIZATION OF RAILWAYS: Movement that contributed to the
demise of the Ch'ing dynasty in 1911.

The Ch'ing government announced the nationalization of the railways in Peking in May 1911. The policy caused widespread opposition in the provinces.
The issue was indicative of the popular resentment against foreign encroachment,
the increasing power of local gentry and merchants, and the distrust of Peking
by the provinces. The local people saw the policy, backed by massive foreign
loans, as another sign of Peking caving in to foreign pressure at a time when
there was a nationalistic movement to recover rights from foreign powers. The

railway controversy further alienated the provinces from the central government and paved the way for the revolution that ended the Ch'ing dynasty* in 1911.

In the last decade of the nineteenth century, the slow-moving modernization drive in China quickened its pace. Railway construction, which conservative forces had so strongly resisted, became a national craze in the 1890s. Lack of funds and the absence of strong national leadership, however, resulted in many lines being built with foreign loans and under foreign control. In the heightened nationalism following China's humiliation after the Boxer Rebellion,* a wave of sentiment to recover rights from foreign control swept the land. Public feelings on this issue were so strong that Peking bowed to the outcry, allowing the provinces to recover railway rights from foreign companies. A prominent case was that of the Hankow–Canton Railway, a north–south trunk line through the provinces of Hupeh, Hunan, and Kwangtung from the Yangtze Valley to the southern coast.

The American-owned China Development Company had acquired the right to build the line in 1898. After complicated negotiations, Chang Chih-tung, governor-general at Hankow, redeemed the right from the American-owned company in 1905 for $6.75 million, through a loan from Hong Kong. He allowed the three provinces to build the section of the line within their respective borders. The people of Szechwan were given the right to build a westward extension of the line into their province. The next step was to raise money to finance the construction.

Under the leadership of local gentry and merchants, private companies were formed to sell low-priced shares to the public. Before long, it became clear that the localities not only had woefully inadequate financial resources, but also lacked the management skills to run the newly formed companies. Hunan and Kwangtung fell far short of meeting the cost; Szechwan was further plagued by corruption and embezzlement by company officials. With the project stalled, Peking decided to nationalize all railway trunk lines in May 1911. The decision prompted widespread opposition in the provinces. Provincial assemblies, which represented gentry and merchant interests, led the opposition. The fight over the control of railways thus became a struggle between central control and local autonomy, an idea whetted by almost a decade of growth of local power in the face of Peking's decline. Worse still, the Peking government secured huge loans from a four-power (Britain, France, Germany, and the United States) banking consortium. To the provinces, this was reverting back to foreign control. The struggle was thus turned into a crusade to prevent further "sellout" to foreign powers.

Local leaders organized the Pao-lu hui (Railway Protection Club), mobilizing large nationalistic crowds. They held public demonstrations and organized petition drives, often leading to conflicts with the local authorities. The disturbances became most serious in Szechwan, where open fighting between civilians and troops occurred in September 1911. To restore order there, the Peking government sent in troops from Hupeh Province. The New Army* units in the Wuchang area that had received orders to go were heavily infiltrated by the revolutionaries who had been plotting an uprising for some time. Fearing that the departure of more units would weaken their ranks, the revolutionaries decided to strike first. They launched the Wuchang Uprising on October 10, 1911, which sparked the revolution that was to end the Ch'ing dynasty.

REFERENCES: En-han Lee, *China's Quest for Railway Autonomy, 1904–1911: A Study of the Chinese Railway-Right Recovery Movement* (Singapore, 1977); Li Kuo-chi, *Chung-kuo chao-ch'i te t'ieh-lu ching-ying* (Early history of Chinese railway development) (Taipei, 1961).

TA-LING LEE

NEW ARMY: Late Ch'ing modernized army with some of its members turned revolutionaries.

The New Army (*Hsin-chün*) began appearing in China around the turn of the twentieth century. Equipped with modern arms and schooled in current military strategy and tactics, these new armies differed from the Chinese military forces of previous eras in both motivation and makeup. The earlier armies were often composed of vagrants seeking little more than food and shelter, who were led by officers who frequently specialized in embezzlement. Neither the officers nor the troops were provided much in the way of formal military training. In contrast, the new armies often required that their recruits be from settled peasant families of the province; that their neighbors and their clan and village heads vouch for them; and that they be examined by a foreign doctor before being accepted into service. The officers who led these enlistees were mostly graduates of recently established military academies.

China's first modern military academy was established at Tientsin in 1885 by Li Hung-chang.* Shortly thereafter Yüan Shih-k'ai* set up his military school at Paoting. The real impetus behind formal military training in China, however, came in 1904, when the Commission for Army Reorganization (Lien-ping-ch'u), which had been established in late 1903, provided formal regulations for military training at four different levels. Each province in China was to establish a three-year elementary military school. Two-year, midlevel military schools were to be formed in Chihli, Shensi, Kiangsu, and Hupeh. In Peking, there was to be both a senior military academy as well as a military college. In addition, Japan's new military academies provided an alternative to these Chinese military schools.

Officers trained in these schools, both in China and abroad, were almost inevitably from the gentry or bourgeoisie. Before the Sino-Japanese War of 1894–1895,* these individuals would have been candidates for the traditional civil service examination. After China's rather ignominious defeat, however, many of them were awakened to their country's dire plight.

Both the Boxer Uprising* of 1900 and the abolishment of the examination system in 1905 further increased the number of those who had reached the conclusion that drastic action was necessary if China was to survive as a nation. After coming to the realization that Manchu reforms were too little and too late to allow China to withstand the external threat, many of these Chinese nationalists became anti-Ch'ing revolutionaries. After graduating from the military schools

as newly commissioned officers, they became the core of an expanding revolutionary activity in the new armies.

In two provinces, Kwangtung and Hupeh, the revolutionary undertakings of
the officers and men of the new armies are particularly noteworthy. In the
Kwangtung Army, thanks to the efforts of individuals such as Chao Sheng,
Huang Hsing,* Hu Han-min,* and I Ying-tien, a revolutionary organization was
created which planned a revolt for February 10, 1910. Unfortunately, the attempted uprising was quickly suppressed at a substantial cost in human lives.
In addition to the casualties, which included I Ying-tien, about 1,000 New Army
forces fled to avoid punishment.

The significance of this event, other than the attempted revolt, is that provincial
officials, literati, merchants, and peasants alike rose in support of the New Army
troops that had deserted. Arguing that these were men from good families who
had acted out of patriotism, they forced the governor-general of Kwangtung to
show leniency and permit the return of the deserters to their native places under
controlled conditions. This involvement demonstrated the support that the New
Army revolutionaries in Kwangtung enjoyed among the various segments of the
population.

The revolutionary center for the Hupeh Army was Wuhan. As early as 1904
a revolutionary nucleus organized for the specific purpose of staging a revolution
was founded in the New Army of Hupeh. It was entitled the Institute for the
Diffusion of Science in an effort to avoid suspicion from Ch'ing loyalists; nevertheless, the efforts of the organizers were foiled, and the institute was destroyed.
However, several organizations with the same goal, consisting of lower ranking
officers, noncommissioned officers, and soldiers from the rank-and-file, followed. Finally, in January 1911, a group calling itself the Literary Institute
emerged. Drawing on earlier experiences with revolutionary propaganda, this
New Army organization flourished, and on October 10, 1911, it staged a revolutionary uprising that succeeded in bringing down not only the Hupeh government, but the entire Ch'ing dynasty* as well.

REFERENCES: Yoshihiro Hatano, "The New Armies," in Mary C. Wright, ed., *China
in Revolution: The First Phase, 1900–1913* (New Haven, Conn., 1968); Ralph L. Powell,
The Rise of Chinese Military Power, 1895–1912 (Princeton, N.J., 1955).

GERALD W. BERKLEY

NEW FOURTH ARMY INCIDENT: A clash between Communist and Nationalist armies during the Sino-Japanese War, December 1940–January 1941.

The New Fourth Army Incident must be understood in the context of the
Second United Front* period during which it occurred. (An earlier United Front,
1923–1927, had brought about CCP–KMT reconciliation aimed at a common
assault on warlord power.) The term *Second United Front* refers to a program
of cooperation negotiated between the Communist forces under Mao Tse-tung*
and the Nationalists under Chiang Kai-shek.* This program was based on several
agreements reached by representatives of the Chinese Communist party* and

the Kuomintang in the months following the Sian kidnapping incident* of December 1936. Its principal object was the cessation of the Civil War in the interest of a vigorous and cooperative CCP–KMT resistance to the Japanese aggressor.

One of the most important features of the Second United Front was the KMT's authorization of the Communists to organize two large field armies. The first was the Eighth Route Army* headquartered at Yenan in the north. The second, organized shortly after the Sino-Japanese War,* began in July 1937 and was designated as the New Fourth Army; it was assigned to operate in central China in the region of the lower Yangtze River. Yeh T'ing was appointed as its commander.

The spirit of cooperative effort did not last long. Both parties to the United Front were interested not only in resisting Japan but also in expanding the areas under their control in unoccupied China. In general, it was the Communists who were more successful in this enterprise, and by the summer of 1939 friction between the two parties had reached the stage of armed clashes as the KMT sought to check Communist expansion. Still, both sides sought to minimize the friction until October 1940 when the two Communist field armies linked up, thus dramatically heightening the need for countermeasures by the KMT. In response, General Ho Ying-ch'in,* KMT minister of military affairs, ordered both armies to evacuate recently gained positions. In early December the generalissimo personally ordered the New Fourth Army to withdraw from southern portions of Anhwei and Kiangsu provinces by December 31.

The events of the next few days constitute the New Fourth Army Incident, which is sometimes referred to as the South Anhwei Incident, the most serious breach of the United Front to this time.

Exactly what happened remains clouded by controversy. The Nationalists claim that the Communists were defying the evacuation instructions, whereas the Communists insist that they were in the process of loyally obeying orders when KMT forces attacked them. In any case, there was a major confrontation between KMT forces and the New Fourth Army in which the CCP suffered about 9,000 casualties and was driven from its positions; KMT forces also incurred heavy casualties. Lyman Van Slyke, a recognized authority on the United Front period, asserts that the attack was ''clearly an act of retribution for defeats inflicted on KMT armies a year earlier.'' The Communist commander, Yeh T'ing, who had long enjoyed good relations with the KMT, was arrested and imprisoned for the duration of the war. On January 17, Chiang Kai-shek declared the New Fourth Army dissolved for insubordination, though in actual fact it was soon reorganized (under Ch'en Yi) and went on to rebuild its strength, though not in the area to the south of the Yangtze River.

While details of the clash remain uncertain, the more important significance of the incident seems clear. The CCP gained an enormous propaganda victory from the incident by presenting themselves as martyred patriots to the cause of anti-Japanese resistance. In a frequently quoted summation of the import of the

New Fourth Army Incident, Chalmers Johnson wrote that "No single event in the entire Sino-Japanese War did more to enhance the Communists' prestige *vis-à-vis* the Nationalists than the destruction of the New Fourth Army headquarters while it was 'loyally following orders.' "

REFERENCES: Yung-fa Chen, *Making Revolution: The Communist Movement in Eastern and Central China, 1937–1945* (Berkeley, Calif., 1986); Chalmers Johnson, *Peasant Nationalism and Communist Power: The Emergence of Revolutionary China, 1937–1945* (Stanford, Calif., 1962; 2nd rev. ed., 1966); Lyman Van Slyke, "The Chinese Communist Movement During the Sino-Japanese War, 1937–1945," in John K. Fairbank and Albert Feuerwerker, eds., *The Cambridge History of China*, vol. 13 (Cambridge, 1986).

JOHN H. BOYLE

NEW LIFE MOVEMENT: Movement launched by the Nationalist government in the 1930s to achieve China's modern transformation.

Originating as a movement to enhance the Nationalist effort to reconstruct and rehabilitate the areas in Kiangsi newly recovered from the Communists in early 1934, the movement soon became a nationwide attempt to revitalize the population morally and spiritually. Launched by Chiang Kai-shek* in a speech at Nanchang, Kiangsi, on February 19, 1934, the immediate purpose of the movement was to boost the morale of the Nationalist soldiers and to mobilize the masses behind the government. Two days later, the Nanchang New Life Movement Promotion Association was established. In March, Chiang urged the expansion of the movement beyond Kiangsi, and promotion associations were quickly established in other provinces. On July 1, these organizations were placed under the supervision of the Nanchang New Life Movement Promotion Association, which became the Central Association with Chiang Kai-shek as its chairman. The headquarters at Nanchang directed the movement in the country and overseas through a hierarchy of associations extending all the way down to the *hsien*.

Ideologically, the New Life Movement combined traditional Confucian doctrines, Christian character-building ethics, and military ideals into a system of thought that was viewed as a viable alternative to Marxism-Leninism* and other foreign ideologies. These ideas, properly inculcated and practiced by the people, would, it was claimed, create a revitalized, socially conscious, and disciplined population ready to work and sacrifice for the nation. At the core of the revived Confucian morality were the four cardinal virtues of *li* (propriety), *i* (righteousness), *lien* (integrity), and *ch'ih* (sense of shame), redefined to make them applicable to a modern society. *Li* meant regulated attitude and adherence to social rules and disciplined behavior; *I* was the outward manifestations of *li* and denoted right conduct; *Lien* meant the ability to distinguish right from wrong; and *Ch'ih* stood for conscience. The observance and practice of these four principles would help the population achieve the three desirable modes of life: cultural, productive, and militarized.

The cultural mode of life was characterized by selflessness toward others, voluntary services, constant self-improvement, and the abandonment of superstitions. The productive mode of life was characterized by frugality, the habit of saving, a spirit of cooperation, the wise use of time, the purchase of native goods, and a respect of public property. Militarization was to be attained through military training in schools, a spartan life-style that excluded smoking, drinking, and dancing, obedience toward superiors and respect for the law, and developing the habit of regularity and cleanliness. Specifically, the movement stipulated ninety-six rules to guide individual behavior. These rules encouraged people to eat quietly, to lace their shoes, to refrain from spitting in public, and to observe certain standards of orderliness, personal hygiene, and decorum. The adherence to these standards of personal behavior would, it was believed, transform an individual's inner self and, for the country as a whole, would result in a rejuvenated population joined in united action.

The actual implementation of these ideas, however, was confined mainly to the two immediate goals of promoting orderliness and cleanliness. Sanitary and public health measures such as street cleaning and inspection of bathhouses and restaurants were carried out. In some areas, the police and boy scouts were used to enforce the correct behavior of the citizens. In Kiangsi, a Special Movement Force composed of young officers was set up to promote the movement, especially in the pacification of areas recovered from the Communists. They organized local defenses, maintained order, and carried out mass education and political warfare against the Communists. Outside Kiangsi, the movement became more urbanized, with most of the promotion associations established in urban centers. The movement grew rapidly during the first year of its existence, but by the third year, interest in the movement sharply declined among the population and lower level officials. The direction of the movement was turned over to Madame Chiang Kai-shek. The outbreak of the Sino-Japanese War[*] in 1937 greatly altered the movement's thrust to emphasize its military aspects in China's struggle for survival while the civilian aspects became less and less evident.

The major weakness of the movement was its failure to address the critical issue of improving the people's material life in the campaign to revitalize their spirit. The movement, promoted through paternalistic methods, never developed into a mass movement as the Kuomintang had intended.

REFERENCES: Samuel C. Chu, "The New Life Movement Before the Sino-Japanese Conflict: A Reflection of Kuomintang Limitations in Thought and Action," in F. Gilbert Chan, ed., *China at the Crossroads: Nationalists and Communists, 1927–1949* (Boulder, Colo., 1980): 37–68; Arif Dirlik, "The Ideological Foundations of the New Life Movement: A Study in Counterrevolution," *Journal of Asian Studies* 34, no. 4 (August 1975): 945–980; *New Life Centers in Rural Kiangsi* (Nanchang, 1936).

KA-CHE YIP

NEW TIDE SOCIETY (Hsin-Ch'ao-She): A literary organization established in 1918 during the May Fourth era.

This organization was founded in 1918 by a group of student leaders from Peking University, notably Fu Ssu-nien, Ku Chieh-kang, Hsü Yen-chih, and others, for the purpose of promoting the new cultural movement after 1917, mainly through the publication of a monthly magazine called the "New Tide" (*Hsin-ch'ao*, with an English title "Renaissance"). The initial membership of the society was twenty-one, and well-known professors of Peking University, Ch'en Tu-hsiu,* Li Ta-chao,* Hu Shih,* and Chou Tso-jen, were advisers of the society. Fu Ssu-nien was elected editor-in-chief of the magazine and Lo Chia-lun, editor. The monthly adopted three guiding principles—a critical spirit, scientific thinking, and reformed rhetoric. Other members of the society included K'ang Pai-ch'ing, Mao Tzu-shui, Sun Fu-yüan, Yeh Sheng-t'ao, and Fung Yu-lan—all Peking university students from literature, history, and philosophy departments. Although the Hsin-ch'ao was a small organization (its membership never exceeded forty-one) and lasted only a few years (it stopped functioning in 1922 and the last issue of the monthly was published in March 1922), the society had a profound impact on the young generation of Chinese in the May Fourth* era. Most of its members were active leaders in the May Fourth Incident (1919) and thereafter played important roles in the intellectual and social development of modern China.

REFERENCE: Tse-tsung Chow, *The May Fourth Movement: Intellectual Revolution in Modern China* (Cambridge, Mass., 1950); Fu Lo-ch'eng, *Fu Meng-chen hsien-sheng nien-p'u* (Chronological biography of Dr. Fu Ssu-nien) (Taipei, 1964); Immanuel Hsü, *The Rise of Modern China* (New York, 1983).

PHILIP YUEN-SANG LEUNG

NIEN REBELLION: Anti-Ch'ing revolutionary movement of the 1850s and 1860s.

The Nien Rebellion, which has been somewhat overshadowed by the Taiping* Rebellion, falls both within the pattern of peasant rebellion of premodern China and the more recent revolutionary movements of the nineteenth and twentieth centuries. Motivating factors that the Nien shared with their peasant rebellion forerunners included incompetent and/or corrupt officials who neglected their duties, economic hardship, and general insecurity in society. To this list the Nien and some of their contemporary and subsequent revolutionary movements added an antiforeign element and guerrilla warfare. Guerrilla warfare, pioneered by the Nien, foreshadowed the People's Liberation Army,* at least in terms of gaining and sustaining support from the Chinese peasantry by utilizing a code of conduct that proscribed mistreatment of the masses.

The name *Nien* probably refers either to the torchlights made of twisted oiled paper that were sometimes carried on raids, or to the Nien's grouping in a band consisting of a few men or of several score. Geographically, the Nien's base was the area between the Huai and the Yellow rivers. This locale, which is comprised of parts of Honan, Anhwei, and Kiangsu provinces, contained vast expanses of land unsuitable for rice cultivation. There were also frequent floods and droughts, which added to the peasantry's rather miserable life. In addition, several rather unique aspects of the region benefited the Nien. The river systems frequently created marshy areas around the villages, which were used to advantage by the Nien who were much more familiar with the topography than were the pursuing government troops. In addition, the earthen or brick walls of the larger villages in the locale provided protection. Next, the region possessed an abundant supply of horses, which permitted the development of mobile cavalry units. Finally, there was a vigorous salt-smuggling trade in the area. This activity, which supposedly involved brave and aggressive men who were always prepared to flout authority, was the chosen profession of several Nien leaders.

The history of the Nien can be divided into four relatively distinct stages. The first, dating from the late eighteenth century to 1852, can be characterized as localized, decentralized, and sporadic as far as the Nien are concerned. Prompted by several years of bad harvests, a large number of men from the region between the Huai and the Yellow rivers had earlier joined existing rebel sects. When the government was finally able to disband these rebels, the men, made arrogant and bold by their previous adventures, turned to a life of drinking and gambling. Soon they organized into small bands, and began engaging in salt-smuggling, pillaging, kidnapping, and looting to support their new lifestyle. Incompetent and/or corrupt officials in the area allowed for the continuation of this activity.

The second phase, covering the period from 1853 to 1855, is marked by the transition of the Nien from what was essentially a small pillaging movement of roaming bandits, with virtually no organizational structure, to a substantial revolutionary enterprise. The contributing factors to this transformation appear to be twofold. The years 1851 and 1852 witnessed a widespread famine in the area, greatly increasing the number of men who claimed Nien membership. In February 1853 the Taipings took Anch'ing, releasing Nien who had been held prisoner by the government. These newly freed rebels returned to Nien bastions full of praise for their liberators. Shortly thereafter, connections between the Nien and Taiping were established. As a result of this linkage, the rapidly growing Nien became avowedly antigovernment and anti-Manchu. As an outward display of this revolutionary evolution, the Nien began the practice of keeping their hair long.

In the third era of the Nien, 1856–1864, Nien units fought alongside the Taipings as separate entities. The relationship was much more an alliance than an amalgamation. The Nien retained their independence and their rather unique form of warfare. Relying on a strong cavalry and skillful guerilla tactics, the Nien, who numbered between 30,000 and 50,000, were able to win numerous victories against much larger government forces. Popular support by the local peasantry, fostered both by a widespread resentment against the Manchu regime and by the Nien practice of treating the masses fairly, were also major factors in the Nien's success.

The end for the Nien came between 1865 and 1868. A combination of tactical mistakes on the part of the rebels, such as organizing into huge regiments and splitting their forces into two units that campaigned far beyond their home base, and superior opposition forces caused the demise. Government forces led by Tseng Kuo-fan* and Li Hung-chang* utilized larger and better fed, led, and paid army, cavalry, and navy personnel to surround and then eliminate Nien. By requiring the registration of peasants in the former Nien areas, and conducting the election of new village heads, the government was able to prevent a re-emergence of the movement.

REFERENCES: Siang-tseh Chiang, *The Nien Rebellion* (Seattle, Wash., 1954); Chiang Ti, *Ch'u-ch'i Nien-chün shih lun-ts'ung* (Essays on the early history of the Nien Army) (Peking, 1959); S. Y. Teng, *The Nien Army and Their Guerrilla Warfare, 1851–1868* (Paris, 1961).

GERALD W. BERKLEY

NINETEENTH ROUTE ARMY: One of the most famous and professional of the KMT's armies in the 1930s; fell prey to the divisive politics of the day. Best known for its heroic defense of Shanghai against Japanese attack in January 1932 and for its abortive rebellion in Fukien Province late the next year.

Formally created in the summer of 1931, the Nineteenth Route Army was a Cantonese army that grew out of the Whampoa Military Academy* and the Fourth Regiment of the KMT's Kwangtung Army's First Division. Its leading officers exhibited personal loyalties to each other above any loyalty to the Nanking government.* The Nineteenth Route Army first saw action in Fukien in the Third Encirclement Campaign* against the Communists in Kiangsi. In September 1931 it inflicted severe losses on the armies of Mao Tse-tung* and Chu Teh* at Kaohsinghsü in western Fukien. The army was transferred to Shanghai in the fall of 1931.

The army and its generals, Ts'ai T'ing-k'ai and Chiang Kuang-nai, became popular folk heroes for their stiff resistance to Japanese military attacks on Shanghai in January and February 1932. This success, however, troubled Chiang Kai-shek*, who feared the army would become too powerful for him to control. Therefore, he sent it back to Fukien to fight the Communists.

In Fukien the Army carried out some social reforms but became involved with the political intrigues of Ch'en Ming-shu (who had former connections with the army) and his Third party. Reforms were partially successful in 1932–1933, including eliminating local bandit gangs, road building, and limited land redistribution. The army was disciplined and well behaved toward the local population. However, the heavy taxation and ethnic tensions with the Cantonese "outsiders" strained support among the Fukienese.

Ultimately, Ts'ai T'ing-k'ai was drawn into the maneuvering of Ch'en Ming-shu and others dissatisfied with the Nanking government (including the Kwangtung and Kwangsi cliques and the A. B. Clique), and the army supported the ill-fated and short-lived Fukien Rebellion* of November 1933 to January 1934 (the *Min-pien* in Chinese sources). Although the rebellion established a People's government, opposed Japan and Chiang Kai-shek, and proposed social policies similar to the Chinese Communist party's* (several Communists were active in the Rebellion), the Kiangsi Red Army did not support the rebels. Mao Tse-tung later recalled this lack of assistance as a major error.

The Nineteenth Route Army stands as an example of the Nationalists' inability to achieve leadership unity and Chiang Kai-shek's distrust of any army, no matter how good, that was not completely under his control. This experience contrasts with the Chinese Communist party's success in controlling the Eighth Route Army.* Chiang was also unable to eradicate his non-Communist competitors. After the defeat of the Nineteenth Route Army by Nanking's armies, no rebel was punished. The officers were given safe passage back to Kwangtung (many joined later rebellions against Chiang), and the rank-and-file was absorbed into other KMT forces.

REFERENCES: Lloyd E. Eastman, *The Abortive Revolution: China Under Nationalist Rule, 1927–1937* (Cambridge, Mass., 1974); William F. Dorrill, "The Fukien Rebellion and the CCP: A Case of Maoist Revisionism," *The China Quarterly*, no. 37 (1969): 31–53; Parks M. Coble, *Facing Japan: Chinese Politics and Japanese Imperialism, 1931–1937* (Cambridge, Mass., forthcoming); Ch'iu Kuo-chen, *Shih-chiu lu chün hsing-wang shih* (A history of the rise and fall of the Nineteenth Route Army) (Hong Kong, 1969); Ma Hung-wu, et al., eds., *K'ang-Jih chan-cheng shih-chien jen-wu lu* (Events and personalities of the anti-Japanese war) (Shanghai, 1986).

                                                                    TIMOTHY CHEEK

NORTHERN EXPEDITION (1926–1928): KMT military campaign to unify China.

The military campaign of the Kuomintang from 1926 to 1928 carried the National Revolution from its base in Kwangtung Province northward in an attempt to replace regional warlords with a unified national government able to cast off foreign imperialism. The diverse National Revolutionary Army (NRA) absorbed a wide variety of local and provincial forces as they defected to the new nationally oriented alliance. The inclusive nature of its political objectives proclaimed a Union of All Classes seeking national unity and included an alliance with the Comintern.* Moscow ordered the Chinese Communist party to participate in the KMT movement, which in 1922 it viewed as a United Front of revolutionary, reformist elements seeking liberation from foreign imperialism.

An era of collaboration between the Chinese Communist party and the KMT under the guidance of numerous Soviet advisers began in 1923 and continued through the initial phase of the Northern Expedition into early 1927. During this period, the United Front saw the consolidation of Nationalist authority throughout the National Revolutionary Base in Kwangtung, aided by support from new unions and peasant associations in the province. The CCP, promoted by Comintern experts led by Michael Borodin,* worked through KMT organizations that specialized in organizing and recruiting workers and peasants. Through the anti-British Kwangtung–Hong Kong Strike and boycott of 1925 and 1926, both parties experienced dramatic growth and popularized both nationalistic and socialist issues. However, rent-lowering efforts and strikes brought disagreements that plagued the United Front both in Kwangtung and later in "liberated" territories. Chiang Kai-shek* became increasingly impatient both with the dictates of Soviet advisers and with the disorders that hindered the military buildup. When Chiang's Party Army, an outgrowth of the KMT's Whampoa Military Academy,* succeeded in an anti-Communist coup on March 20, 1926, the opponents of a

Northern Expedition were neutralized and the way was cleared to move out of the Revolutionary Base.

The Northern Expedition was formally launched in July 1926 from northern Kwangtung across the mountains into the territory of the Shantung warlord, Wu P'ei-fu.* The entrance into Hunan was eased by the defection of his subordinate, Hunanese T'ang Sheng-chih. This was typical of the inclusive approach of the KMT and was the result of earlier offers of promotion within the NRA ranks and considerable autonomy for T'ang over Hunan in the event the expedition against Wu succeeded. Such efforts to bring into the NRA what had been localistic warlord units did, in the short run, weaken the three existing large northern military confederations that were unable to consolidate their individual armies against the NRA offensive.

In Hunan a series of bridge-crossings on tributaries of the Hsiang River fell only after bitter battles. The NRA attack was aided by civilian carriers, friendly local guides, and food suppliers. Pressing their advantage in mobility, the NRA flanked the enemy and threatened the rail links to northern supply sources. This tactic, which was used throughout the expedition, forced Wu's troops to withdraw to the north where Wuchang fell in October after a long siege.

Chiang Kai-shek, as commander-in-chief, carried the offensive into Kiangsi where Sun Ch'üan-fang, ruler of his five United Provinces, held off and bloodied the NRA from September into November. Simultaneously, the NRA guard force in Kwangtung withstood a counterattack from Sun's allies in Fukien and pushed into that province toward Chekiang. The coastal campaign combined an offensive along coastal roads with attacks by mobile units that entered Fukien from southern Kiangsi and pushed down river valleys to threaten the flanks and rear of Sun's defenders.

Defections helped gain entrance through border passes into Chekiang where Sun's defense suffered from its northern coloration. Local units preferred a so-called national movement that included many Chekiangese and allowed for provincial self-rule to military rule under mercenaries from Shantung.

By the time the northern forces pulled out of Shanghai in March 1927 to prevent their isolation south of the Yangtze, the United Front was badly strained and the KMT had split into Chiang's faction that set up its headquarters at Nanking and a loose coalition at Wuhan of KMT civilians such as Wang Ching-wei*, the CCP, and their military allies. The era of the Wuhan government from late 1926 into May 1927 saw the Soviet advisory group and their CCP lieutenants reach a peak of authority in which tensions even with the civilian KMT left rose over peasant land confiscation, execution of landlords, and strike disorders in the cities.

Chiang's forces came into competition with CCP-led unions over control of Shanghai, which was settled in a bloody coup favoring the NRA in April 1927. When Comintern intervention and insensitivity (see M. N. Roy)* turned the KMT left against a Communist takeover of the National Revolution, the split with the CCP and the suppression of its social revolution spread in July 1927 to include Wuhan and Canton. Although the KMT was able to reunite and continue the expedition to its final victory in Peking in June 1928, the threat of internal disintegration included not only the ex-warlord local powers, but also the new Communist dissidents who became guerrilla warriors from 1927 until 1949. Patriotic feelings helped the Chinese to unite in the final phase of the Northern Expedition when Japanese Army units attacked the NRA and bombed civilian Tsi-nan as the action passed north in May 1928. Such obvious collusion between the Japanese and Manchurian warlord Chang Tso-lin defending north China merely justified the Northern Expedition's goals of reunifying China and rejecting imperialism. By 1928 the Northern Expedition under Chiang's NRA provided a nominal unity that only began the process of creating a modern national statehood.

REFERENCE: Donald J. Jordan, *The Northern Expedition: China's National Revolution of 1926–1928* (Honolulu, 1976).

DONALD A. JORDAN

O

OCTOBER SIXTH COUP (1976): The arrest of the Gang of Four by a coalition of senior Communist party and military leaders headed by Hua Kuo-feng and Yeh Chien-ying.

When Mao Tse-tung* died on September 9, 1976, the Chinese Communist party* leadership was deeply divided over two important issues: Who was to succeed Mao as party chairman, and what kind of politics was the party to pursue without Mao? The answer, according to CCP leaders who had risen to power rather recently, was the appointment of someone with the impeccable revolutionary leftist credentials of Mao's widow Chiang Ch'ing* or her protégé Wang Hung-wen* to the party chairmanship and the continuation of the Cultural Revolution.* According to most party elders, however, the answer was the purge of the Gang of Four* and their followers and the appointment to the party chairmanship of someone who would bring the Cultural Revolution to its long overdue conclusion.

While Mao Tse-tung was dying, Long March* veteran Wang Chen is said to have asked CCP Deputy Chairman Yeh Chien-ying,* "Why not just arrest the 'Gang of Four'? Certainly that would solve the problem!" The powerful Yeh, who as concurrent head of the Standing Committee of the CCP Military Affairs Commission in 1976 ranked second only to Mao within the party's military establishment, is reported to have urged caution, and suggested that one wait until Mao was dead before doing anything. After Mao's death, Chou En-lai's* widow Teng Ying-ch'ao,* Ch'en Yün,* and Li Hsien-nien* among others told Yeh that they had no objections to a radical solution to the succession crisis. The first deputy-chairman of the CCP, premier of the State Council, and concurrent minister of Public Security Hua Kuo-feng* also indicated to Yeh that he supported the idea of removing the Gang of Four from China's political stage by force.

On October 5, at a meeting of part of the CCP Politburo at the headquarters of the People's Liberation Army* General Staff, a formal decision was made to arrest the Gang of Four. The People's Liberation Army Unit 8341—the leadership's bodyguard—under the command of Politburo member Wang Tung-hsing was given the task of executing the actual arrest.

A number of contradictory accounts exist of exactly when, where, and how the Gang of Four were arrested. One official account claims that on October 6, Wang Hung-wen, Chang Ch'un-ch'iao,* and Yao Wen-yüan* were summoned to a meeting of the Politburo Standing Committee at Huai-jen Hall in Chungnan-hai. When they arrived at the meeting site at 8 P.M., they were informed by Hua Kuo-feng of the decision taken the previous day, and they were promptly taken into custody. Chiang Ch'ing, according to this account, was also arrested elsewhere at the same time. A different account claims that all the members of the Gang of Four were arrested in the early hours of the morning of October 6, in the Tiao-yü-t'ai residential compound in western Peking.

On October 7, the CCP Politburo appointed Hua Kuo-feng chairman of the party and of the party's Military Affairs Commission. Over the next few days, news of the arrest of the Gang of Four was transmitted first to party, government, and military leaders, and subsequently to ordinary party members and the public at large. On October 18, the CCP Center issued the first in a series of circulars containing detailed accounts of the alleged "crimes" of the Gang of Four—the "crimes" that were said to have justified their arrest. On October 26, Teng Hsiao-p'ing* (whose political career had been in limbo since early that year) told Hua Kuo-feng that he "welcomed" and "supported" him as Mao's successor.

The new post–Mao leadership was able to claim legitimacy mainly on the basis of two things. First, it had acted out the popular will by getting rid of the Gang of Four. The Cultural Revolutionary policies symbolized by the gang had been genuinely unpopular with broad segments of China's population. Over the next few years, and in particular after 1978, the CCP was gradually to turn its back on the Cultural Revolution. Second, Hua Kuo-feng was able to point at a curious political testament of Mao Tse-tung's—a message scribbled on a piece of paper by the dying Mao on April 30, 1976—that read "With you in charge, I am at ease!" The existence of this testament made China's post–Mao transition smoother than it might otherwise have been, since it temporarily permitted the CCP leadership to argue whenever it was convenient to do so that whoever opposed Hua was in fact opposing the Late Great Helmsman.

REFERENCE: Roderick MacFarquhar, "The Succession to Mao and the End of Maoism," in *The Cambridge History of China*, vol. 14, *The People's Republic*, Part II (London, 1987).

MICHAEL L. SCHOENHALS

"ON CONTRADICTION": An important writing of Mao Tse-tung.

Mao Tse-tung* wrote "On Contradiction" together with "On Practice" in 1937 as part of a series of lectures on Marxist philosophy given at the Anti-Japanese Military and Politics University at Yenan in August 1937.

"On Contradiction" was taken from Chapter 3 of "Dialectical Materialism (lecturing outline)" and was originally entitled "The Law of Unity of Opposites." It was renamed "On Contradiction" and revised by Mao later when it was included in Volume 2 of *Mao Tse-tung: Selected Works* in April 1952, which was also published in *Hsüeh-hsi* magazine, no. 4, April 10, 1952.

It was said that Mao wrote the piece as well as "On Practice" in order to combat "the existing serious mistakes of doctrinairism in the Party at the time." Despite their political motivation, "On Contradiction" and "On Practice" constituted the basic ideas of Mao's philosophical thinking and position.

Mao began the elaboration of his ideas of contradiction on the basis of Soviet pamphlets on Marxist philosophy and their interpretation of the ideas about contradiction as the quintessence of dialectical materialism by Marx, Engels, Lenin, and Stalin. According to some analysts, for example, French structural Marxist philosopher Louis Althusser, Mao insisted on the non-Hegelian tradition of Marx and Lenin.

In Mao's terminology, according to the viewpoint of materialist dialectics, changes in nature are due chiefly to the development of the internal contradictions in nature, human society being no exception. Universality or absoluteness of contradiction has a twofold meaning: (1) contradiction exists in the process of development of all things, and (2) in the process of the development of each thing, a movement of opposites exists from beginning to end. At the same time universality of contradiction presupposes the particularity of contradiction. In their totality, the particularity of the concrete contradictions in the process of society and nature constitutes the universality of contradiction, but it is the particularity of contradiction that defines "the quality of the process of development of things" and that makes it concrete. Since they are qualitatively different, particularly in the sense of being unique, these contradictions, and their characteristics as well, could not be treated uniformly. It underscores the principle put forth by Lenin and heartily endorsed by Mao: "the concrete analysis of concrete conditions," that is, contradictions can only be studied with respect to their particularity and thus only in a concrete way.

Mao, like Lenin, emphasized the identity and struggles of the aspects of a contradiction. Contradictions have different aspects, but all of them are on the one hand opposed to each other and on the other hand interconnected, interpenetrating, interpermeating, and interdependent. This character is named as identity. As they are opposed to each other, their identity could only be conditional, relative, temporary, and transitory. The opposites or contradictions that are united are always changing and developing, as compelled by the universality of contradiction, which presumes that contradictions and opposites exist in a process from beginning to end and define the process. This is called the struggle of opposites. The ceaseless struggles of opposites would transform the opposites themselves, going through stages of quantitative change to qualitative change, which by the end would also change the original unity of the now transformed opposites. However, the forming and the dissolution of the unity could only come "under certain conditions," which are again referred to as real and concrete.

The unity and struggles of opposites may be regarded as aspects or characteristics of a particular contradiction, or a process of contradictions. These aspects, according to Mao, have always had a principal one among them at a particular stage of the process. Either as the principal aspect of a contradiction or as the principal contradiction in a complex process of contradiction, its "existence and development determine or influence the existence and development of other contradictions" or aspects. Yet just like the transitory nature of unity, the existence or dominance of the principal aspect or contradiction is also transitory. Mao insisted that "in any contradiction, the development of the contradictory aspects is uneven." Thus, "the principal and the non-principal aspects of a contradiction transform themselves into each other," and the quality (the unity and the characteristics) changes accordingly.

Following Lenin, Mao further stated that the forms assumed by the changes to the unity of opposites in a contradiction or in a complex process of contradictions may be "antagonistic" or "nonantagonistic"; they are both the forms of the struggle of the opposites. Again like the principal and nonprincipal aspects or contradictions, they would be transformed into each other. "Based on the concrete development of things, some contradictions, originally non-antagonistic, develop and become antagonistic, while some contradictions, originally antagonistic, develop and become non-antagonistic."

The non-Hegelian nature of materialist dialectics as expounded by Mao in this essay found its best expression in his position on the deterministic relationship between economic foundation and superstructure in Marxist analysis of society and societal transformation. Mao stated: "while we recognize that in the development of history as a whole it is material things that determine spiritual things and social existence that determines social consciousness, at the same time we also recognize and must recognize the reaction of spiritual things and social consciousness on social existence, and the reaction of the superstructure on the economic foundation. This is not running counter to materialism, this is precisely avoiding mechanistic materialism, and firmly upholding dialectical materialism."

Mao's greater emphasis on dialectics than on materialism had a practical policy and strategy implication for the Chinese Communist party* in 1937, just when it had survived the adventurism of the former leadership following a Soviet-inspired doctrinairism. As a result, the CCP abandoned many of its bases in the country and went on the Long March.* At this time, too, the intensification of the Japanese invasion of China posed a new opportunity for political cooperation with the ruling Kuomintang Regime. It also inspired Mao's later political strategy and positions after the founding of the People's Republic of China*—for example, his famous thesis of the antagonistic and nonantagonistic contradiction within the Chinese people, and his thinking in the early 1960s that led subsequently to the Cultural Revolution* in 1966.

CHAN MAN-HUNG THOMAS

OPIUM WAR (1839–1842): First Sino-British War, precipitated by China's effort to suppress the illegal opium trade and ending in China's defeat; followed by humiliating unequal treaties giving Westerners special privileges in China.

The Opium War represents a clash of two cultures and the ways in which they conducted foreign relations. For the Chinese the chief issues were the maintenance of the traditional tributary system and the immediate need to suppress the opium trade. For the British the chief issues were free trade and diplomatic equality. Before the war, Chinese relations with the West were limited to trade; there were no diplomatic relations. That trade, too, was strictly controlled by the Canton System, whereby all Western commerce with China was carried out through the port of Canton and Western merchants had to deal only with a small group of Chinese firms called the Cohong. By the early nineteenth century, the Canton System had become a major source of tension between China and the West.

Opium was another major cause of tension. Although opium had been introduced into China by Arab and Turkish traders about a thousand years earlier, it was not until the eighteenth century that opium consumption had become a serious problem and the Ch'ing* emperors began outlawing it. In the meantime, in an effort to offset the trade imbalance, British merchants began importing Indian opium into China. British demands for tea and silk were tremendous, but the Chinese had little interest in purchasing British merchandise, that is, at least until the development of the Chinese market for opium. By the mid–1820s the balance of trade was reversed: the previous flow of silver into China now flowed out of the country to pay for the ever-increasing demands for opium.

After a long and heated debate among the high-ranking officials throughout China, in late 1838 the Tao-kuang emperor (r. 1821–1850) ordered a stepped-up suppression of opium trafficking. A vigorous campaign against dealers and addicts began, and soon thousands of Chinese were imprisoned and hundreds executed. This was the situation when the emperor appointed Lin Tse-hsü (1785–1850) as imperial commissioner with plenipotentiary powers to handle the opium problem at Canton. After arriving at his new post on March 10, 1839, Lin immediately put into action a three-pronged attack against addicts, Chinese dealers, and their Western suppliers. In order to force the foreigners to surrender their opium supplies, on March 24 Lin detained the foreign community of about 350 men in the foreign factories in Canton. By late June over 21,000 chests of opium had been turned over to Lin, who then destroyed the contraband.

Tensions were further strained when on July 12 a Chinese villager was killed in a brawl by British sailors. Lin demanded the surrender of the murderers. Captain Charles Elliot, the British superintendent of trade in China, refused; instead he arrested, tried, and sentenced several men to go to prison in England. Once they were returned to England, however, the prisoners were freed by the home court. Angered by Elliot's refusal to cooperate, Lin ordered the expulsion of all British residents from Macao, where the British had already retreated earlier that summer. On August 26, all British subjects moved to Hong Kong, a sparsely populated island at the mouth of the Pearl River and some 90 miles from Canton.

Actual hostilities began gradually in a series of skirmishes during the autumn of 1839. The first major clash in the war occurred on November 3, when a Chinese war junk was sunk by a British vessel in the Pearl River. This was followed on December 6 by Commissioner Lin banning all British trade in China. Finally, on January 31, 1840, the Indian government announced a formal declaration of war on behalf of the British Crown.

In June 1840 the British expeditionary force assembled off Macao, where it first blockaded Canton before the main body of the fleet moved northward up the coast. By late August the British had defeated Chinese forces near the mouth of the Yangtze River, seized Chusan Island, and were threatening Tientsin and the security of the imperial capital at Peking. At this point the emperor dismissed Lin Tse-hsü and replaced him with the Manchu prince, Ch'i-shan (d. 1854), who persuaded the British to return to Canton to negotiate.

After considerable delays and continued fighting, finally on January 20, 1841, Ch'i-shan and Elliot signed the Ch'uan-pi Convention, which would have ceded Hong Kong, given diplomatic equality and an indemnity to Britain, and reopened Canton. But both governments rejected the agreement, both Ch'i-shan and Elliot were dismissed, and hostilities were renewed. In May the British attacked Canton but withdrew after securing a "ransom" of $6 million. During the fighting around Canton, however, a British patrol was defeated by Chinese militia in the famous San-yüan-li Incident.* Although the incident was militarily insignificant, it was indicative of the strong popular antiforeign sentiment brewing in China at the time.

In August 1841 Sir Henry Pottinger relieved Elliot, and once again British forces moved north, easily capturing four coastal cities by winter. After reinforcements arrived from India, Pottinger advanced up the Yangtze threatening to attack Nanking. The Ch'ing court finally accepted the futility of continuing the war and on August 29, 1842, signed the Treaty of Nanking.

The Treaty of Nanking was a dictated settlement imposed by Britain on the vanquished Chinese. It contained the following provisions: (1) an indemnity of 21 million Mexican dollars; (2) the opening of the five ports of Canton, Amoy, Foochow, Ningpo, and Shanghai; (3) equal relations between Britain and China, with the rights of British consuls to reside in the treaty ports; (4) the abolition of the Cohong monopoly; (5) fixed tariffs on imports and exports; and (6) the cession of Hong Kong to Britain in perpetuity. The Treaty of Nanking (together with the supplementary treaties signed with France and the United States) ended the old Canton System and in its place established the basic pattern for China's foreign relations over the next hundred years. Furthermore, the opening of China to the West profoundly altered the way the Chinese thought about themselves and created internal problems that had far-reaching consequences for China.

REFERENCES: Hsin-pao Chang, *Commissioner Lin and the Opium War* (Cambridge, Mass., 1964); Peter W. Fay, *The Opium War, 1840–1842* (New York, 1976); Frederic Wakeman, Jr., "The Canton Trade and the Opium War," in John Fairbank, ed., *The Cambridge History of China*, vol. 10 (Cambridge, 1978): 163–212; Dilip Basu, "The Opium War and the Opening of China: A Historiographical Note," *Ch'ing-shih wen-t'i* 3 (1977), Supplement: 2–16.

ROBERT J. ANTONY

OVERSEAS CHINESE (*hua-chiao*): An estimated 30 million Chinese living overseas as of 1990 and intimately involved in Chinese politics.

A large number of Chinese began to emigrate to Southeast Asia as early as the fifteenth century when the Ming government undertook seven phenomenal maritime explorations. But for several decades after its conquest of China, the Ch'ing* government, fearing a possible alliance between anti-Ch'ing forces at home and overseas Chinese, refused to sanction the emigration of Chinese people. By the nineteenth century, however, population pressure, bureaucratic incompetence, and natural disasters created food shortages that led to social unrest and rebellion. Many chose to risk the perils of travel and punishment to go to Southeast Asia and America in search of greater economic opportunities. By the turn of the twentieth century, it was estimated that between 70,000 and 90,000 overseas Chinese, excluding those who lived in Hong Kong and Macao, were wooed by three political groups: the Ch'ing government, the Reformers, and the revolutionaries. When the Republic of China* was established in 1912, its government published electoral laws providing for an indirect election of 274 members of the Upper House. An additional six members would be chosen by an electoral college of overseas Chinese. Overseas Chinese would become intimately involved in domestic Chinese politics.

After the creation of the Republic of China, overseas Chinese continued to bear the burden of having to respond to political changes in China, namely, the turmoil of the warlordism* of the 1920s, the Japanese invasion of the 1930s, and the rivalry between the Communists and the Nationalists. Many prominent modern Chinese statesmen were in fact overseas Chinese, Dr. Sun Yat-sen*, Liao Ch'ung-kai, Wellington Koo*, and Eugene Ch'en, just to name a few. Following the Communist triumph and the Nationalist calamity in 1949, the uneasy coexistence of the two Chinas not only complicated their relations with their motherland, but also intensified their divided loyalty crisis. Overseas Chinese often willingly or unwillingly became pawns in China's political game, while various groups jockeyed for power and influence. In the meantime, the governments in Peking and Taiwan watched with intense interest and occasional grave concern.

After signing an agreement in 1955 with the Indonesian government, the policy of the People's Republic of China* toward overseas Chinese was to encourage naturalization on a voluntary basis. Once naturalized, however, a Chinese immigrant lost his Chinese citizenship. The Nationalist government on Taiwan, on the other hand, retained a policy of dual citizenship so that naturalized Chinese, no matter where they lived, were permitted to carry a Chinese passport and were accorded the rights of citizens of the Republic of China. Under this arrangement a number of overseas Chinese actually held offices in the Nationalist government. For instance, in December 1989 Taiwan authorities appointed twenty-nine overseas Chinese to serve in its Legislative Yuan. They represented overseas Chinese who lived in North, Central, and South America, Hong Kong and Macao, Northeast and Southeast Asia, Europe, Australia and New Zealand, and Africa.

For those who chose to remain Chinese, both Peking and Taiwan urged them to abide by local law and to respect local customs and habits. Both governments pledged to continue to protect the emigrant's legitimate rights and interests. But while the Taiwan government maintained that those who became citizens of another country were still "overseas Chinese," Peking referred to them as "naturalized Chinese" or "people of Chinese origin." While the Peking regime welcomed both overseas Chinese and naturalized Chinese to visit their homeland and their relatives, the government on Taiwan actively made contact with the Chinese living abroad, naturalized or otherwise, sponsored a variety of programs to woo their support, and briefed them about Taiwan's economic development and cultural achievements. In short, Taiwan's policy toward the overseas Chinese was one of courtship, while Peking's attitude was one of indifference and suspicion.

REFERENCES: Maurice Freedman, *Chinese Lineage and Society: Fukien and Kwangtung* (London, 1966); Lee Lai To, ed., *Early Chinese Immigrant Societies: Case Studies from North America and British Southeast Asia* (Singapore, 1988); Shih-shan Henry Tsai, *China and the Overseas Chinese in the United States* (Fayetteville, Ark., 1983); Wang Gungwu, "Sun Yat-sen and Singapore," *Journal of the South Seas Society* 15, Pt. 2 (Singapore, 1959).

SHIH-SHAN HENRY TSAI

P

PAI CH'UNG-HSI (1893–December 2, 1966): Regional militarist; member of the Kwangsi Clique.

Born into a literate Muslim farmer family near Kweilin in 1893, Pai Ch'ung-hsi received a traditional classical education and attended the Kwangsi Military Elementary School, where he was a schoolmate of Li Tsung-jen and Huang Shao-hung, the trio in the Kwangsi Clique. In the 1911 Revolution,* Pai joined the student dare-to-die squad of the Kwangsi Army and headed north. Having arrived too late and missed all the fighting, he decided to stay behind to further his military education, first in the Second Military Preparatory School in Wuchang and then in the Paoting Military Academy. He was graduated from Paoting in the third class with Huang Shao-hung.

Afterward, Pai returned to Kwangsi to join the Kwangsi Model Battalion. Soon the battalion was involved in the Constitutional Protection Movement and the interprovincial disputes between Kwangsi and Kwangtung. Injured in an inspection tour, Pai went to Canton for treatment. This gave him a chance to be the mediator between Sun Yat-sen* and the Kwangsi militarists, and subsequently led to the renaming of Huang Shao-hung's troops the Anti-Bandit Army associated with Kwangtung. After years of fighting against Lu Yung-ting and Shen Hung-ying in a civil war, the Kwangsi Clique finally emerged as victors in the province.

Prior to the Northern Expedition (1926–1928)*, Pai negotiated an alliance between Kwangsi and Kwangtung. He also won T'ang Sheng-chih over to the Nationalist side and defeated the forces of Wu P'ei-fu.* During the campaign, Pai was named deputy chief-of-staff of the National Revolutionary Army by Chiang Kai-shek.* He was then assigned the task of purging the Communists in Shanghai. As Wusung-Shanghai garrison commander, Pai moved his troops on April 12, 1927, against the labor union while Li Tsung-jen simultaneously eliminated the Communist influence in Nanking. But he released the arrested Chou

En-lai.* He later assisted Chiang in the fighting against Sun Ch'üan-fang and T'ang Sheng-chih. As field commander of the East Route Army in the northward drive toward Peking, Pai participated in the east Tientsin campaign that brought the Northern Expedition to completion. The joint forces of Pai and Yen Hsi-shan* eventually occupied the capital. Pai was also responsible for bringing Yang Yu-ting of the Northeastern Army to Chiang's side.

After the Kwangsi revolt in 1929, Pai returned to his province to reconstruct the province. He proposed a three-self-reliance and three-reservation policy (*san-tzu san-yu cheng-ts'e*) which called for streamlining the provincial government, constructing public works, reforming the military through building up the militia, and modernizing the local schools. Through Pai's conscious efforts of provincial reconstruction Kwangsi came to be known as the "model province."

During the Sino-Japanese War*, Pai Ch'ung-hsi met with Chiang Kai-shek in Kuling and received an appointment from Chiang as director of the Kweilin field headquarters. Failing to drive back the Japanese invading forces in the K'unlun pass, Pai was recalled to Chungking and served as deputy joint chief-of-staff. During this time, he devoted himself to the military education of the army.

After the war, Pai was appointed minister of war in the Nationalist government and served as director of the Strategic Advisory Commission. He fled to Taiwan in 1949 and served as deputy director in the same commission. He was a member of the Central Executive Committee of Kuomintang. On December 2, 1966, he died of a heart attack in Taipei at the age of seventy-four.

REFERENCES: Ch'eng Szu-yüan, *Pai Ch'ung-hsi ch'uan* (Biography of Pai ch'ing-hsi) (Hong Kong, 1989); Diana Lary, *Region and Nation: The Kwangsi Clique in Chinese Politics* (London, 1974).

ODORIC Y.K. WOU

PANAY **INCIDENT** (December 12, 1937): Sinking of U.S. gunboat by the Japanese in the war of aggression against China.

The *Panay* Incident took place in China during the early phase of the Second Sino-Japanese War* (July 7, 1937–August 14, 1945). On December 12, 1937, the Japanese naval bombers bombed and sank the U.S. gunboat, U.S.S. *Panay*, and three Standard Oil Company tankers, which were at anchor on the Yangtze about twenty-eight miles upstream from Nanking. As a result, three Americans were killed and forty-three crew members of the *Panay* were wounded. Furthermore, for the first time, American prestige received a heavy blow in Asia. The incident almost brought the United States and Japan to the brink of war. This was the kind of incident that Chiang Kai-shek*, the leader of Nationalist China, hoped would drag the United States into war against Japan. Chiang was in desperate straits at this time, with his troops badly beaten by the Japanese invaders, and Nanking, the capital of the Nationalist China, about to be seized. Nanking was in fact occupied on December 13.

In Washington, at a cabinet meeting held on December 17, several cabinet members, including Harold L. Ickes (secretary of the interior) and Claude A.

Swanson (secretary of the Navy) insisted that the United States should have an immediate showdown with Japan. They maintained that the war with Japan was inevitable. Naval experts also concluded that the U.S. Navy could defeat Japan at that time because Japan was preoccupied with the war with China and was heavily dependent on raw materials and military supplies from the outside world. They also concluded that the U.S. fleet was quite ready for combat operations. But neither President Franklin D. Roosevelt nor Secretary of State Cordel Hull wanted to go to war with Japan over the incident. Both leaders believed that the American public did not consider the gunboat incident a justifiable cause for war and that there was no clear evidence of the Japanese government's complicity in the incident. Nevertheless, Roosevelt wanted to impose economic sanctions on Japan if Japan failed to meet U.S. demands. Consequently, the U.S. government demanded: (1) an official apology from the Japanese government; (2) the payment of indemnities ($2.2 million); (3) assurances for the future; and (4) punishment of the officers involved. Japan met the demands promptly on December 24, 1937, for three reasons. First, Japan was tied up by the war with China and could not afford another war with the other powers. Second, Japan purchased most of its raw materials such as steel, iron, oil, aluminum, copper, and automobiles, from the United States. Without these strategic materials, Japan would find it difficult to carry out the war with China. Third, the Russians were continuously threatening Japan from the north, and there was frequent fighting between the Japanese and the Soviet forces along the Manchurian-Russian border. Over 250 Russo-Japanese clashes occurred between 1932 and 1936. From the beginning of the Sino-Japanese conflict in July 1937, the Soviet Union had been supplying China with war materials, personnel, and financial support. If Japanese relations with the United States were to be allowed to deteriorate, the Russians might increase military operations along the Manchurian-Soviet border, which would severely jeopardize Japanese operations in China.

The major cause of the *Panay* Incident was the mistaken identity of the Japanese pilots involved in the bombing mission. The Japanese naval airforce command in China was aware of the presence of the *Panay* on the Yangtze, but it had no knowledge of its exact position when the bombing planes departed their base for the bombing mission. The bombers belonged to the Twelfth and Thirteenth Air Groups under the Second Combined Air Group. They were to fly over the Taiping area, and search and destroy the steamers carrying troops escaping from Nanking. The naval planes departed their base at 1:00 P.M., on December 12. At 1:38 P.M., fifteen Japanese bombers accompanied by nine fighters reached the target area where they found the *Panay* and three Standard Oil Company tankers. They immediately began their bombing operations, destroying the vessels. In fact, the Japanese pilots who took part in the bombing operations were fresh and inexperienced flyers who had just arrived at the base in China from Japan only eight days earlier. They had never been briefed on the existing special orders that specified the policy of the Japanese naval airforce against bombing neutral vessels. It was their first mission and their first attack on real targets. When they were told that they might get a unit citation for a successful operation, they became overenthusiastic and eager to destroy the Chinese ships. Wanting to achieve a quick strike, as soon as they reached the Taiping area, they released their bombs without clearly identifying their targets. With more care, they would certainly have noticed the U.S. flags displayed on the decks of the *Panay*. This pilot negligence brought the United States and Japan to the brink of war, but actual war would await Pearl Harbor on December 7, 1941.

REFERENCES: Manny T. Koginos, *The Panay Incident: Preclude to War* (Lafayette, Ind., 1967); Masatake Okumiya, "How the Panay Was Sunk," *U.S. Naval Institute, Proceedings* 79, no. 6 (June 1956): 587–596; Hamilton D. Perry, *The Panay Incident: Preclude to Pearl Harbor* (New York, 1969).

WON Z. YOON

PAO-HUANG HUI (Emperor Protection Society) (1899–1907): The most famous reform organization in the late Ch'ing period.

The Pao-huang hui is an abbreviation of the Pao-chiu ta-Ch'ing huang-ti hui (the Society for Protecting and Saving the Emperor of the Great Ch'ing). In the wake of the abortive Hundred Day Reform Movement[*] in 1898, K'ang Yu-wei[*] went to Japan for refuge. There he formed the Pao-huang hui in an embryonic form. But he officially organized the Pao-huang hui in Victoria, British Columbia, on July 20, 1899, with the help of his supporters such as Li Fu-chi and Feng Hsiu-shih who had earlier celebrated the birthday of the deposed Kuang-hsü Emperor[*] on June 28, 1899. Its charter was composed of twenty-eight articles; its chief aims were to restore Emperor Kuang-hsü to power; to change institutions for the salvation of China and the yellow races; to urge the compatriots to respect the will of the emperor; to recruit members of the Pao-huang hui by stressing loyalty to the emperor and patriotism to their country; to establish its chapter and board of trustees; and to elect its president to take care of such tasks as fund-raising, correspondence, and propaganda. Furthermore, the Pao-huang hui should have its own newspaper and magazine in every major region to promote the cause of the Pao-huang hui. Finally, it should also create banks and businesses not only to finance these operations, but also to promote and protect Chinese commerce and industry. K'ang Yu-wei was elected president, and Liang Ch'i-ch'ao[*] and Hsü Ch'in vice-presidents, under whose leadership 11 regional headquarters and 103 chapters were operated throughout Asia and the Americas. Its propaganda organ, the *Ch'ing-i pao*, was first published in Yokohama, Japan, on December 23, 1898, under the editorship of Liang Ch'i-ch'ao.

On October 26, 1899 the regional headquarters of the Pao-huang hui was established at 629 Clay Street, San Francisco. It had an eleven-member board of trustees whose president was T'an Shu-pin (Tom She Bin); secretary was T'ang Ch'ung-ch'ang (Tong King Chong). Its articles of incorporation were filed in the Office of County Clerk of San Francisco, October 31, and in the Office of Secretary of the State of California, November 2. According to the articles of incorporation, the main purpose of the Pao-huang hui was not so much to promote the political but the social, educational, cultural, and economic interests of the members. The articles stated that the main purpose was to elevate the Chinese people to the same level of excellence achieved by the other civilized races; to cultivate their spiritual welfare so as to endow their offspring with all the advantages and privileges enjoyed by their fellow human beings in the world; and to promote commercial enterprises and social and moral education for the Chinese so as to make them happy and law-abiding citizens in the country in which they resided. The articles also touched on the reform of China, stating that to become a mighty world power both brotherhood and love should be enhanced, thus promoting better relationships among the Chinese at home and abroad. Finally, they concluded that in order to end the sorry state of political conditions in China as well as to place the Chinese people on an equal footing with the citizens of the United States, the political reform in China would be urgently needed.

The Pao-huang hui, recognized as a legitimate organization in California, carried out propaganda and fund-raising activities throughout the United States. It became increasingly active. In December 1899 K'ang Yu-wei sent Liang Ch'i-ch'ao to Hawaii from Japan to further the cause of reform. Earlier in Japan, Japanese sympathizers had urged Liang to collaborate with the revolutionary Sun Yat-sen[*] for the greater cause of China. But the Japanese mediation failed because of K'ang's refusal. As a result, Liang was sent to Hawaii to establish the chapter of the Pao-huang hui, to increase membership, to raise funds, and to propagandize the reform through the organ paper.

In the summer of 1900, while the Boxer Uprising[*] was underway in the north, an armed attempt on behalf of the Pao-huang hui was taking place in central China along the Yangtze River. General T'ang Ts'ai-ch'ang of the Tzu-li chün (the Independent Army) who planned this last military operation failed because of insufficient funds and poor coordination among the reformist leaders at home and abroad. T'ang was captured and executed by Chang Chih-tung, governor-general of the region.

In another historic event, the Pao-huang hui's organ, the Hsin-min ts'ung-pao (formerly the Ch'ing-i pao), attacked the aims of the revolutionary Sun Yat-sen and fought brilliantly against the Min-pao, the organ of the T'ung-meng hui[*] in Tokyo after 1905. Liang Ch'i-ch'ao, editor and writer of the Hsin-min ts'ung-pao, alone could not stop the rising tide of the revolutionary spirit among the young radical Chinese in Japan. When the Ch'ing government decided to draft the constitution in 1907, the Pao-huang hui cast its lot with the reigning regime in Peking and changed its name to the Kuo-min hsien-cheng hui (the National Constitutional Government Association) and finally to the Ti-kuo hsien-cheng hui (the Imperial Constitutional Government Association) on January 1, 1907.

REFERENCES: Key Ray Chong, *Americans and Chinese Reform and Revolution, 1898–1922* (Lanham, Md.; 1984); Li Chien-nung, *The Political History of China, 1840–1926* (Princeton, N.J., 1956).

KEY RAY CHONG

PARTY PURIFICATION (1927): The purge of Communists from the Kuomintang during the dissolution of the first KMT–CCP United Front.

As the Northern Expedition* swept into the Yangtze River Valley in late 1926, dissension in the KMT–CCP United Front and within the Kuomintang itself also deepened. Elements in the KMT who were dissatisfied with Chiang Kai-shek's* rapid rise to party leadership collaborated with the Chinese Communists and seized control of the new KMT headquarters and its national government at Wuhan. They soon moved to dismantle Chiang's military and political power. Feeling threatened, Chiang, then directing campaigns in Kiangsi, became increasingly hostile toward the Wuhan Regime* and the United Front it was based on. From late 1926 to early 1927, Chiang's troops clashed with pro-Wuhan KMT branches and CCP-led labor unions in a number of recently taken Yangtze cities.

In March 1927, with the help of general strikes organized by the Chinese Communist party,* Chiang's forces occupied Shanghai. Thus, coming into direct contact with the foreign and Chinese business interests in the Lower Yangtze area, which were alarmed by the radical policies of the United Front, Chiang found new support for his opposition to the Wuhan Regime. He quietly began to meet with potential allies in the party and the military to plan for an open break with Wuhan. A group of KMT veterans in the party's Central Supervisory Committee (CSC), who agreed with Chiang's plan, provided him with the necessary institutional basis to challenge Wuhan's authority. On April 2, they held a CSC plenum in Shanghai and recommended that the party take "extraordinary actions" against the Communists, whom they claimed were subverting the KMT. A week later, these CSC members issued a circular telegram denouncing the pro-Communist tendencies of the Wuhan Regime.

Throughout this period, Chiang's forces were competing with the CCP-led workers in controlling Shanghai. On April 12, his twenty-sixth Corps, assisted by the local underworld Green Gang, launched a surprise attack on the Shanghai General Labor Union and disarmed its pickets. In protest against this action, the workers organized a mass demonstration on the next day, which was brutally suppressed by the troops. Massive arrests and executions of suspected Communists and leftists followed and continued for weeks, resulting in the killing of about 5,000 workers, students, and CCP members in the city. Meanwhile, Chiang's followers took similar actions in Kiangsu, Chekiang, Anhui, Fukien, Kwangtung, and Kwangsi.

Wuhan summarily relieved Chiang of all his posts and expelled him from the KMT. Chiang, however, backed by conservative party veterans, several of his military commanders, and the foreign powers, established his own KMT headquarters and national government at Nanking on April 18. The Nanking Regime formally terminated the United Front and ordered the arrest of leading Communists. The regime organized the Central Party Purification Committee on May 7, with the task of ousting Communists as well as "local bullies and evil gentry, venal officials, opportunists, and all corrupted and degenerated elements" from the party. The committee then appointed local committees in fourteen provinces and four cities to carry out the work, but they were active only in areas under Chiang's control.

In July the KMT leaders in Wuhan, facing increasing political and military isolation and an imminent Communist takeover, also decided to end the United Front. Later, following the Communist uprising at Nanchang on August 1, Wuhan's policy changed from a peaceful separation with the CCP to the severe suppression of the CCP. The purge of Communists and leftists from the KMT thus spread into most of south and central China.

By the end of 1927, the CCP had been driven underground with a loss of 80 percent of its membership. The KMT was seriously affected as well. The regimes at Wuhan and Nanking were reunified in early 1928, with Chiang Kai-shek again emerging as the party's leader, but the radicalism that had been guiding the party for the past three years was abolished. This directly contributed to the ideological confusion within the KMT in the late 1920s.

REFERENCES: Li Yün-han, *Ts'ung jung-kung tao ch'ing-tang* (From admitting the Communists to the Party purge) (Taipei, 1966); C. Martin Wilbur, *The Nationalist Revolution in China, 1923–1928* (Cambridge, 1983); Tien-wei Wu, ''Chiang Kai-shek's April 12 coup of 1927,'' in Gilbert F. Chan and Thomas H. Etzold, eds., *China in the 1920s* (New York, 1976).

KE-WEN WANG

PEACE-PLANNING SOCIETY (CH'OU-AN HUI): Society in support of Yüan Shih-k'ai's Monarchist Movement.

In August 1915 supporters of Yüan Shih-k'ai[*] founded the notorious Ch'ou-an hui (Peace-Planning Society) in an attempt to promote Yüan's monarchical ambitions. The Hunanese political activist Yang Tu led the movement and five other eminent men—Hu Ying, Sun Yu-yun, Li Hsieh-ho, Yen Fu[*], and Liu Shin-pei—joined the effort. According to Yang Tu, the purpose of the society was to discuss and compare the relative merits of monarchism and republicanism. In a meeting on August 23, Yang and Sun were elected presidents, and the other four sponsors became members of the executive committee. They announced the formation of the society in the Peking papers and asked the provincial leaders to send delegates to Peking to discuss the ideal polity for China. They passed a resolution supporting the adoption of a monarchical system. In September 1915 the society presented a petition to the Council of State, asking Yüan Shih-k'ai to assume the title of emperor. It also urged the members to vote for monarchism against republicanism. The society made some headway in enlisting the support of military commanders and provincial gentry for the imperial cause.

The goal of the society was laid down in an article by Yang Tu entitled ''A Defense of the Monarchical Movement.'' He asserted that only a monarchical government under Yüan Shih-k'ai could save the country from political turmoil and make China strong. Yang emphasized that China lacked political experience to hold presidential elections and that the republican government could only lead to internal disturbances. In Yang's view, poverty, internal warfare, and the insufficient literacy rate all constituted conditions unfavorable to republicanism. In order to avoid periodic upheavals over presidential succession, Yang argued, China should change its system from a republic to a constitutional monarchy.

He further emphasized that only Yüan Shih-k'ai was qualified to be the monarch. Under Yüan's leadership, China would be able to become a constitutional monarchy and to command enough loyalty and respect to make the nation strong. Yang Tu's article was a manifesto of the Ch'ou-an hui.

The society's plans were frustrated by ideological opposition and organizational factionalism. In August 1915 Liang Ch'i-ch'ao* challenged Yang Tu's article in an article entitled "The Strange Problem of the Polity." An eminent scholar and a renowned political activist, Liang questioned the belief that a monarchical system would lead to constitutional government. Liang identified the monarchical system with autocracy and believed that even an imperfect republic would be better than a monarchy. The Communications Clique* under Liang Shih-i organized the National Petitioners' Association in September to promote the imperial polity. Since the society under Liang was more powerful, Ch'ou-an hui was forced to disband and came under the control of the National Petitioners' Association in October 1915. Founders of the Ch'ou-an hui did not play an important role in Yüan Shih-k'ai's administration during his short-term emperorship in 1916. Nonetheless, the Chou-an hui had provided both theoretical and organizational support in the initial phase of Yüan's monarchical attempt.

REFERENCES: Jerome Ch'en, *Yüan Shih-k'ai* (Stanford, Calif., 1972); Huang Chung-hsing, *Yang Tu yü min-chu cheng-chi* (Yang Tu and the Politics of Early Republican China [1911–1916]) (Taipei, 1986); Ernest P. Young, *The Presidency of Yüan Shih-k'ai* (Ann Arbor, Mich., 1977).

                                                                                            WING-KAI TO

PEIYANG CLIQUE: Political faction based on military control of north China which dominated Chinese politics during the first three decades of the twentieth century.

The Peiyang Clique (*Peiyang-hsi*), which literally means northern faction, originated with the creation of the modern New Army* units in 1903 by the Ch'ing dynasty* central government authorities (under the leadership of the Empress Dowager Tz'u-hsi*). The six divisions in north China under the overall command of Chihli Governor-general Yüan Shih-k'ai* were called the Peiyang Army. By 1908 the Peiyang Army numbered about 60,000 well-trained and well-armed men and was by all accounts the most effective and cohesive fighting force in the empire. Division commanders included Tuan Ch'i-jui, Feng Kuo-chang, Chang Hsün,* and Ts'ao K'un.* These generals were considered the core of a political clique of loyal supporters behind Yüan Shih-k'ai, as he maneuvered in court politics in Peking during the waning years of the dynasty. The threat of the Peiyang Army crushing Republican insurgents in Wuhan and Nanking in 1911 led to Yüan Shih-k'ai becoming president of a new Republic of China* in 1912.

With the establishment of the Republic of China in 1911–1912, the Peiyang Clique became even more powerful. Yüan used the clique to enforce stability on the citizenry, driving Sun Yat-sen* and other genuine republicans into exile in 1913. Through the clique Yüan exercised military control over north and south China and thus dominated national politics.

With Yüan Shih-k'ai's death in 1916, the cohesiveness of the clique was threatened. Each general made a play for national leadership as Yüan's successor and failed. By 1918 the national polity had disintegrated into fragmented and brutal warlord-like competition between clique members. The resulting warlord period in Chinese political history continued until the completion of the Northern Expedition* in 1928 by Chiang Kai-shek*. Thus, the term *Peiyang Clique* has become synonymous with the warlord politics of the 1916–1928 era, with roots in the political and military machine built up by strongman Yüan Shih-k'ai between 1903 and 1916.

REFERENCES: Stephen R. MacKinnon, *Power and Politics in Late Imperial China: Yuan Shikai in Beijing and Tianjin, 1901–1909* (Berkeley, Calif., 1980); Edmund S.K. Fung, *The Military Dimension of the Chinese Revolution* (Vancouver, 1980).

STEPHEN R. MACKINNON

P'ENG CHEN (alias, Peng Mao-kung, Lau Wei, 1902–): CCP Politburo member; mayor of Peking; chairman, Standing Committee of the NPC.

Born in 1902 in Ch'u-wu, Shansi Province, to a poor peasant family, P'eng grew up in hardship. He graduated from elementary school at the age of twenty-one and an old-style (four-year) normal school at twenty-five. Except for a short period as an elementary school teacher, P'eng's long life has been devoted to the Communist Revolution, first as an activist in student and labor movements and then as a party and government leader. In 1927 he married Chang Chieh-ch'ing (his second wife), the grand-daughter of Chang Hsün*. They have three sons and one daughter.

P'eng joined the Socialist (later Communist) Youth Corps and the Chinese Communist Party* in 1923 and became a confidant of Liu Shao-ch'i* in Tientsin in 1928. Jailed for over six years in 1929 by the Kuomintang, he three times led hunger strikes among prisoners. Released in 1935, P'eng worked in the CCP's Northeast Bureau in Taiyuan and was entrusted with organizational work. During the Sino-Japanese War,* he served as secretary of the CCP's Shansi-Chahar-Hopei Sub-bureau, deputy-principal of the Central Party School, head, Central Organization Department, and head, Central Urban Work Department.

Elected to the Central Committee at the Seventh Party Congress, April 1945, five months later P'eng was made the secretary of the CCP Northeast Bureau, with Lin Piao* as his deputy, and concurrently the commissar of the Northeast Democratic Allied Army, with Ch'en Yün* as his deputy. However, P'eng refused to follow Mao's advice to stress the countryside over the cities and was removed from these posts in 1946. Two years later, Liu Shao-ch'i had him appointed to the Central Organization Department again. For the next eighteen years, he was Liu's right-hand man. In 1949 he was appointed to the Peking Planning Committee, elected to the Politburo, made a CCP delegate to the Chinese People's Political Consultative Conference* (CPPCC) (which he was responsible for organizing), and, upon the establishment of the People's Republic of China,* was made a councilor of the Central People's Government Council, the vice-chairman of the State Council's Committee on Political and Legal Affairs, as well as the party secretary of Peking (succeeding Yeh Chien-ying*).

Over the next four decades, P'eng became one of the PRC's central leaders, was disgraced at the hands of the Red Guard*, and resurfaced to take charge of legislative affairs. He retired after the CCP's Thirteenth Congress in October 1987 but remains an influential elder.

Within the party, P'eng was a member of the Seventh, Eighth, Eleventh, and Twelfth Politburos. His concurrent posts included the head of the Central Organization Department, the CCP's first secretary of Peking, and member of the Central Secretariat.

In the government, P'eng served as the vice-chairman and secretary-general of the First and Second National People's Congress (NPC), the vice-chairman of the Third and Fifth NPCs, and the chairman of the Sixth NPC. Next to Tung Pi-wu, P'eng can be considered the most influential personality in the PRC legislature before 1987. Many of the PRC's laws were enacted under his leadership. It was P'eng who delivered the report on the revision of the PRC constitution in 1982. In addition, in March 1951 he succeeded Nie Jung-chen as the mayor of Peking, and he held that post until June 1966. In that capacity, P'eng also made a significant impact on the PRC capital.

Outside of party and government, P'eng had also been, inter alia, the vice-chairman of the Second, Third, and Fourth CPPCCs and a leader of the Sino-Soviet Friendship Association. During 1956 P'eng headed a delegation to the USSR and several Eastern European countries. Between then and 1966, he led a number of other PRC delegations to Romania (1960), Moscow (1960, 1961, and 1963), North Korea (1962), North Vietnam (1962), and Indonesia (1965).

P'eng was one of the earliest victims of the Cultural Revolution.* In June 1966 he was stripped of all his posts. On December 4 that year, he was "arrested" by the Red Guards and humiliated three times in public kangaroo courts. He was accused by Mao of harboring the Three-family Village Anti-Party Group and building an independent kingdom in resisting the Cultural Revolution. For some twelve years, the outside world heard practically nothing about P'eng.

In January 1979 P'eng reappeared, and a month later he became the new chairman of the NPC's Legal Committee. Within nine months, he was again the vice-chairman of the NPC and a Politburo member. In 1983 he became chairman of the NPC upon Yeh Chien-ying's retirement. During Teng Hsiao-p'ing's* reform, P'eng was closely associated with the notion of constitutionalism. Possibly because he used law to resist Teng in certain areas, he was half-forced to retire in October 1987 from all party and government posts without being given a seat in the Central Advisory Commission. Nonetheless, P'eng, now in his late eighties, is still wielding considerable power in political and legal circles. It was reported on March 7, 1990, that he had made a major speech on "the domestic and international situation" the previous day to the closing session of a national conference on politics and law. Some say that P'eng might have played a hand in the June 4, 1989, T'ienanmen Incident.

REFERENCES: Li Ku-Ch'eng, *Chung-kung tang-cheng-chün chieh-kou* (The Party, government and military structure of the PRC) (Hong Kong, 1989): 193–199; *Chung-kuo ta pai-ke ch'uan-shu: Fa hsüeh* (The great encyclopaedia of China: Law) (Peking, 1984): 451–452; Donald W. Klein and Ann B. Clark, *Biographic Dictionary of Chinese Communism, 1921–1965*, vol. 2 (Cambridge, Mass., 1971): 713–718.

BYRON SONG JAN WENG

P'ENG P'AI (October 22, 1896–August 30, 1929): Early Chinese Communist leader.

P'eng P'ai was the first prominent Chinese Communist leader to devote himself to rural issues and organization of the peasantry. He is also celebrated by the Chinese Communist party* as one of its greatest and most selfless martyrs. P'eng P'ai was born in coastal Hai-feng County, Kwangtung Province, to a wealthy landlord family. Having imbibed the currents of the New Culture Movement, P'eng P'ai spent three years (1918–1921) at Waseda University in Tokyo. There he became converted to socialism.

Back in China, P'eng joined the Chinese Communist party, and soon returned to his home district where he began organizing Peasant Associations and pressuring landlords to reduce the rent burden on tenants. Despite landlord and warlord opposition, he persisted in these efforts, which became more successful after the formal conclusion of the First United Front* between the Nationalists and the Communists in early 1924.

P'eng P'ai spent most of the next several years in Canton, headquarters of both the CCP and the Kuomintang. He helped organize the CCP's Peasant Movement Training Institute and was its first director. He also held other posts in both parties dealing with rural affairs. By late 1925 P'eng P'ai was back in the Hai-feng District, pushing the Peasant Associations, carrying out fairly radical policies against landlords, and extending his actions to neighboring Lu-feng County (hence, the combined term *Hai-lu-feng*). Peasant Associations now existed in many counties of Kwangtung Province.

During the Northern Expedition,* P'eng P'ai accompanied Communist-led units to Hankow, where the so-called Kuomintang left wing and the CCP were in uneasy alliance. After the split between the KMT and the CCP, beginning in April 1927 in Shanghai and spreading to Hankow in July, P'eng returned to Hai-lu-feng, where he reorganized the Peasant Associations into the Workers and Peasants Dictatorship, or the Hai-lu-feng Soviet. For several months, an armed peasantry and a few Communist-led military units held out against warlord commanders affiliated with the Nationalists. In late December 1927, some survivors of the Canton Commune* sought refuge in Hai-lu-feng. But in January 1928, the Hai-lu-feng Soviet was crushed by the Nationalists.

P'eng P'ai escaped from Hai-feng to Shanghai, where he continued to hold high positions in the party. At the sixth CCP Congress (held in Moscow in July 1928), P'eng was elected in absentia to the Central Committee. He operated underground in Shanghai for another year, but in late August 1929, he and several colleagues were betrayed by turncoat Communists and arrested by Nationalist authorities. A week later, he was executed.

REFERENCES: Fernando Galbiati, *Peng Pai and the Hai-Lu-Feng Soviet* (Stanford, Calif., 1985); Roy Hofheinz, *The Broken Wave: The Chinese Communist Peasant Movement, 1922–1928* (Cambridge, Mass., 1977); Donald Klein and Ann Clark, *Biographic Dictionary of Chinese Communism, 1921–1965*, vol. 2 (Cambridge, Mass., 1971).

LYMAN P. VAN SLYKE

P'ENG TE-HUAI (orig. P'eng Te-hua, alias P'eng Ch'ung-shih, 1898–Nov. 29, 1974): Commander of the Chinese People's Volunteers in the Korean War; PLA Marshal; PRC Defense Minister; CCP Politburo member.

Born into a lower-middle level peasant family, P'eng entered an old-style private school at age six where he was introduced to some of the Confucian classics. However, the family situation deteriorated so badly that he became a beggar when he was ten.

Hardship, victimization by exploitative rich peasants and coal mine owners, and heroic stories of the Taiping Revolution[*] combined to make P'eng a rebel at heart early in his life. In 1916, he enlisted in the Hunan Army and embarked upon a military career. In 1922, he received officers' training for about a year. By the time the Northern Expedition[*] began in mid–1926, P'eng was a regiment commander in the Nationalist Army.

In February 1928, P'eng joined the CCP. In 1931, he was elected one of two vice chairmen of the Revolutionary Military Council at the First Soviet Congress. Except for the period from 1934 to 1937 when Chou En-lai[*] replaced him, he occupied this post throughout until 1949. In January 1934, he was elected a CCP Central Committee Member.

During the Sino-Japanese War (1937–1945),[*] P'eng was Deputy Commander of the Eighth Route Army[*] under Chu Teh,[*] that is, the top field commander, and the Secretary of the CCP's North China Bureau (1941–1949). About this time, P'eng married P'u An-hsiu of Kiangsu province who was a Peking Normal University graduate about twenty years younger than himself. (His first wife was "lost" sometime in 1928.)

After the PRC was established, P'eng was elected to the first CPPCC, the Central People's Government Council and the People's Revolutionary Military Council. Of these, the most important (his real) post was the last as vice chairman and concurrently the deputy commander of the PLA.

In October 1950, the Chinese People's Volunteers (CPV) crossed the Yalu under P'eng's command. Although the CPV suffered very heavy casualties, P'eng claimed "victory," having forced the Americans, for the first time in their history, to sign, in July 1953, an armistice agreement without winning the war. He was decorated by the North Korean government at least three times.

In February 1954, he was made a Politburo Member. Under the first PRC Constitution, P'eng was appointed the third-ranking vice premier after Ch'en Yün[*] and Lin Piao,[*] the second-ranking vice chairman of the National Defense

Council after Chu Teh and, most notably, the minister of National Defense. In September 1955, he was made one of the ten PLA marshals and given three top awards—the Orders of August First, Independence and Freedom, and Liberation—for his long, distinguished service.

For P'eng, all went well in the ensuing years until the fateful Lushan Conference[*] of July–August 1959. In the months before the Lushan Conference, P'eng was busy tending to various military functions and leading and receiving military delegations to and from Communist countries. From April 24 to June 2, P'eng headed a twelve-member military delegation that visited seven East European countries. At the Second NPC of April 1959, while he was away, Liu Shao-ch'i[*] became chairman of the Republic and the Head of the National Defense Council in place of Mao Tse-tung[*] and Chu Teh retired from the senior vice chairmanship of the latter body. P'eng retained his three major government posts.

At the Lushan Conference, P'eng was deeply concerned that the meeting, fondly nicknamed "fairy's meeting" by its participants, might adjourn before the serious "leftist" policy and unrealistic goals set for 1959 were discussed. He decided to submit a memorandum, on July 14, to call Mao's attention to the matter. Patriotic and candid, P'eng frankly stated his reservations about the Great Leap Forward[*] and the People's Communes[*] and the way of thinking behind them. Although P'eng wanted only Mao to see the memorandum, it was issued to all participants for discussion. Opinions about P'eng's views were mixed and mild at first. Then on July 23, Mao, who reportedly was unable to sleep for three nights, gave a speech calling P'eng's letter a blueprint for a planned, organized, purposeful Rightist opportunist action. Before it ended, the Central Committee had adopted a formal resolution calling for struggles against "Rightist" assaults on the party. P'eng was denounced as the leader of a "Rightist Opportunist Anti-Party Group." Other major victims included Huang K'e-ch'eng, Chang Wen-t'ien, Chou Hsiao-chou, and Li Jui.

P'eng was made a non-person. Put under house arrest in Peking's western suburbs, P'eng was to repent. On June 26, 1962, P'eng wrote a long letter comprised of 80,000 characters to Mao in which he described his own life history in some detail. There were self-criticisms as required, but P'eng remained proud and unbending in other respects. Efforts to explain himself only invited more severe criticism against him.

During 1965 and 1966, P'eng's nominal titles in the government and the party were formally dropped. On September 23, 1965, P'eng was summoned by Mao for an audience and told to go to the southwest to help build up the strategic rear areas and prepare for war and then perhaps there would be an opportunity to recover his reputation. However, in December 1966, not long after the Cultural Revolution[*] started, P'eng was taken back to Peking on Chiang Ch'ing's[*] order and for the next eight years subjected to endless interrogations and persecutions. On November 29, 1974, P'eng died from mental and physical abuse by his interrogators. His body was secretly cremated.

In December 1978, at the Third Plenum of the eleventh CC, P'eng was posthumously exonerated and his ashes buried in the cemetery of Papaoshan in Peking after an official memorial service. Today, the people of China generally remember P'eng as one of their most respected heroes of the Maoist years. A number of books have appeared to commemorate him since then.

REFERENCES: *P'eng Te-huai chih-shu* (Self-Explanations by P'eng Te-huai), (Peking, 1981); Li Jui, *Lushan Hui-yi shi-lu* (The Actual Record of the Lushan Conference) (Peking, 1989 internal controlled edition); Li Ku-Ch'eng, *Chung-kung tang-cheng-chün chieh-kou* (The Party, Government and Military Structure of the PRC), (Hong Kong, 1989): 333–339; Donald W. Klein and Ann B. Clark, *Biographic Dictionary of Chinese Communism, 1921–1965* (Cambridge, Mass., 1971)II: 727–737.

BYRON SONG JAN WENG

PEOPLE'S ARMY (KUOMINCHÜN): Military unit of General Feng Yü-hsiang.

Kuominchün, or Chung-hua Ming-kuo Kuo-min-chün, was organized on October 25, 1924, two days after the "Capital Revolution" plotted by Feng Yü-hsiang* and others. Feng was its commander-in-chief, and his own units, numbering about 35,000 in 1924 and growing to over 100,000 a year later, constituted the best fighting power of the Kuominchün, which was famed for both its discipline and gallantry. At its inception, the Kuominchün pledged allegiance to Dr. Sun Yat-sen* supporting his endeavors for China's reunification. At Feng's insistence, Chang Tso-lin and Tuan Ch'i-jui agreed to invite Sun to Peking for deliberations on unification and other impending national issues. Soon afterward, the Kuominchün was forced out of Peking by Chang Tso-lin's army, retreating to the Nankow Pass, about 30 miles northwest of the capital. The following year saw increasing Kuominchün's contacts with the Kuomintang and Soviet Russia, thus furthering its revolutionary orientation. Both KMT and Soviet personnel were employed for the purposes of promoting revolutionary ideology and strengthening the military skill of the Kuominchün.

In May 1926, on the eve of his trip to Moscow, Feng joined the KMT, and the whole Kuominchün followed suit. Four months later, the Kuominchün merged with the Northern Expeditionary Army, officially fighting under the revolutionary banner of the KMT. The Northern Expedition* made speedy advances, reaching central China and capturing Wuhan three months after its launch, partly because Kuominchün had tied up 450,000 warlords' troops in Nankow. The following summer saw Kuominchün's influence at its apex, with both rival KMT party centrals in Wuhan and Nanking wooing its support. Conflicting views regarding revolutionary direction and the Communists' role in the revolution, among other factors, led to a KMT schism. Feng and the Kuominchün's decision to side with Nanking sealed Wuhan's fate. Furthermore, the Kuominchün then occupied the strategic Chengchow–Kaifeng region, holding the key pass to further expeditionary advances against northern warlords. In April 1928 the Northern Expedition was resumed after about one year's interruption. The Kuominchün fought splendid battles, contributing greatly to the fall of the warlord regime in Peking under Chang Tso-lin and to China's sub-sequent reunification in the same year.

No sooner had the Northern Expedition (1926–1928) been completed than internecine struggle erupted among fellow KMT generals over the issue of troop reduction. Yen Hsi-shan,* Li Tsung-jen, and Feng Yü-hsiang resented the re-duction scheme, fearing it would result in their loss of influence and Chiang Kai-shek's* rise to supreme power at their expense. Finally, in June 1930 they formed a grand coalition together with dissenting KMT politicians like Wang Ching-wei* and Tsou Lu* challenging Chiang's leadership. In the ensuing de-cisive battles of the Central Plains later in the same year, the Kuominchün was almost completely wiped out. Afterward, its remaining 30,000 troops were re-organized into the Twenty-ninth Army of the Chinese landed forces.

At the outbreak of China's war of resistance, the Twenty-ninth Army defended northern China and engaged the Japanese troops in the famed Marco Polo Bridge Incident* on July 7, 1937, and in subsequent battles. Its deputy commander, Tung Lin-ko, and one of its divisional commanders, Chao Teng-yu, both veteran Kuominchün officers, were fatally wounded while fighting the Japanese troops. Among many other former Kuominchün officers who lost their lives fighting the Japanese to the bitter end was General Chang Chih-chung. The Kuominchün had performed admirable services for China's revolutionary endeavors in both stages of the national unification and subsequent war of national survival, 1937–1945.

REFERENCES: Li T'ai-fen, *Kuo-min-chün shih-kao* (A draft history of the Kuominchün) (n.p., 1930); James E. Sheridan, *Chinese Warlord: The Career of Feng Yü-hsiang* (Stan-ford, Calif., 1966).

LAU YEE-CHEUNG

PEOPLE'S COMMUNES: Chinese experimentation to communize China, 1958–1982.

Agricultural collectivization* began in 1953 as part of China's transition to socialism, resulting in advanced producer cooperatives in 1956. The amalgam-ation of these cooperatives into People's Communes occurred during the Great Leap Forward* in 1958, as China departed from the Soviet model of the lopsided development of heavy industry embodied in the First Five-Year Plan. Instead, the new line opted for decentralization, the simultaneous development of city and countryside, and the labor-intensive strategy. Strong local units were needed to assume responsibilities such as water conservation projects and the devel-opment of small industries. Chinese leaders also deemed the elimination of the remnant rural private sector as conducive to the increase of capital accumulation and state revenue. These practical considerations were mingled with the Maoist utopian yearning for the "withering away of the state."

The first commune of an experimental nature sprang up "spontaneously" in Honan Province in April 1958. As it spread rapidly in northern China, the Maoist Ch'en Po-ta* first used the term *People's Commune* in the July issue of the *Red*

Flag to describe this new formation, with utopian overtones implying transition into communism. Upon Mao's urge, an enlarged Politburo session at Peitaiho in August approved its spread to the whole country. It also resolved, however, that the commune should be based on collective ownership and embody the socialist principle of distribution, and it was to merge with the rural administrative unit, the *hsiang*, or township. Unlike the Soviet collective and state farms, the commune was to be an all-comprehensive economic, social, political, cultural, and military unit.

Before the year was out, larger size communes, totaling 26,000, were formed, incorporating virtually all the rural population. The movement entered into its most utopian phase in the summer and fall of 1958, when many communes proceeded to introduce Communist principles and to eliminate the family system. Its momentum was spent by late autumn, owing to peasant resistance, food shortages caused by the diversion of peasant labor to industrial and irrigation projects, and the breakdown of centralized planning. The Wuhan Plenum in December shifted the level of ownership and accounting downward to the subordinate unit of the commune—the "production brigade." Mao also stepped down as head of state. Severe floods and drought in the spring and summer of 1959 undermined the communes further. The intraparty struggle over the issue of the communes came to a head in the Lushan Conference* in July-August 1959, when P'eng Te-huai* criticized Mao. While P'eng was sacked and the Lushan Plenum endorsed the Great Leap Forward, floods and drought continued to ravage the country, causing severe food shortages. It compelled the continued retreat from communization, the reemergence of material incentives and private markets, and the lowering of the unit of ownership and accounting to the "production team" level in 1961. The communes were also reduced in size and increased to 74,000 in 1963.

In 1964 Mao first presented the Ta-chai Brigade as a model. The size of the communes increased again during the early phase of the Cultural Revolution.* The poor-peasant associations were revived, and revolutionary committees were formed at the commune and brigade levels, the former combining party, management, and military functions. In many areas, attempts were made to abolish private plots and farm markets, and to ban sideline occupations. The work-point system, however, remained socialist, and the unit of account stayed with the production team. Experiments in 1969 to make the brigade or commune "the unit of account" were abortive.

After 1972, the Chinese countryside gradually returned to the pattern of the 1962–1965 period. The commune system began to erode after Mao's death. In 1978 in several provinces the production team was broken down into smaller work groups, and a responsibility system appeared, fixing production quotas to individual members. By the end of 1980 the new system of fixing output quotas directly to each household came to encompass one-fifth of the peasant households, while plots of land were put under the management of individual households on a long-term basis. The 1982 state constitution ended the all-comprehensive feature of the commune and reestablished township government as the rural local administrative unit. The communes were to be transformed into corporate business ventures.

REFERENCES: Chu-yuan Cheng, *China's Economic Development: Growth and Structural Change* (Boulder, Colo., 1982); Maurice Meisner, *Mao's China and After: A History of the People's Republic* (New York, 1986); Vivienne Shue, ''The Fate of the Commune,'' *Modern China* 10, no. 3 (July 1984): 259–283.

LUNG-KEE SUN

PEOPLE'S LIBERATION ARMY (PLA): Military system of the PRC; the largest of its kind in the world.

The term *PLA* encompasses China's ground, naval, and air forces. The leadership has never revealed its total size or the number of personnel services. Estimates suggest that there are around 3 million men in the ground forces, with the air and naval forces totaling less than half a million.

Mao Tse-tung* described the PLA as follows: ''This army is powerful because of its separation into two parts; the main forces and the regional forces with the former available for operations in any area whenever necessary, and the latter concentrating on defending their own localities and attacking the enemy there in cooperation with local militia.''

On August 1, 1927, about 30,000 soldiers led by generals Chou En-lai,* Ho Lung, Yeh T'ing, Chu Teh,* and Liu Po-ch'en revolted from the Nationalist Central government and regrouped to form the Chinese Workers and Farmers Revolution Army. After 1928, their numbers grew, and this army became the Chinese Workers and Farmers Red Army. During the Sino-Japanese War (1937–1945)* when the Chinese Communist party* and the Kuomintang agreed to cooperate, the main force of the Red Army merged with the Central government military and was referred to as the Eighth Route Army.* Other Red Army units scattered in southern China grouped to form the New Fourth Army. After the war, the Eighth Route Army and the New Fourth Army joined forces and became the Chinese People's Liberation Army.

The CCP has proclaimed that this army was ''created and led by the Chinese Communists, armed with Marxism, Leninism and Mao Tse-tung thought to serve the people with.'' Mao's two principles governing this army's role were based on the dictums that ''political power grows out of the barrel of a gun'' and ''the Party commands the gun.''

The first principle called for the PLA to destroy the KMT and the CCP to seize political power; the second principle urged the PLA to be subordinate to all party decisions. For example, the PLA waged war in Korea (1950–1953) and with Vietnam (1979) by carrying out party orders, even though it suffered tremendous casualties and was poorly equipped for those campaigns.

The PLA is organized and equipped primarily as a defensive force with little ability to project force on areas distant from China's borders. The ground forces only have conventional weapons, mostly of Russian design. Its coastal defense force, the PLA Navy, lacks cruisers and aircraft carriers. Only after the 1960s did the PLA Airforce receive funds to develop an air defense radar system and begin production of surface-to-air missiles. China has possessed the atom bomb since 1964 and the hydrogen bomb since 1967. The PLA already has the capability of projecting medium-range, intermediate-range ballistic missiles and ICBMs. The PLA military planning calls for maintaining nuclear capability only to deter would-be attackers.

Given its large size, the PLA is one of the least expensive military forces in the world to maintain. Troops grow nearly one-fourth of their own food and even operate small-scale local industries to supply their needs.

The PLA has redoubled its efforts to become a modernized, professional military force. To that end, it reduced the size of its forces during the 1980s by over a million persons. The party elders still have effective control over the PLA. Yet, future power struggles in the CCP might sever party control over the PLA.

REFERENCES: *Chung-kung tang-shih shih-chien jen-wu-lu* (Record of incidents and personage in CCP history) (Shanghai, 1984); Harvey W. Nelsen, *The Chinese Military System: An Organizational Study of the Chinese People's Liberation Army* (Boulder, Colo., 1977); *T'zu-hai* (Word book) (Shanghai, 1980).

RAMON H. MYERS

PEOPLE'S REPUBLIC OF CHINA (PRC): A socialist state established by the Communist party of China on October 1, 1949.

The People's Republic of China (PRC), according to its 1982 constitution, is "a socialist state under the people's democratic dictatorship led by the working class and based on the alliance of workers and peasants."

In general, the PRC means the state of China since 1949. However, the continuing existence of the Republic of China (ROC)* on Taiwan presents the PRC and the rest of the world with the problems of recognition and membership in international organizations. For this reason the Teng Hsiao-p'ing* regime adopted a rather imaginative, though controversial, policy of "one country, two systems."

Established on October 1, 1949, by the Chinese Communist party* after a long revolutionary struggle against the Nationalist regime, the PRC, as a member of the international Communist movement, subscribes to the doctrines of Marxism, Leninism, and Mao Tse-tung Thought.*

From the beginning, the Communist government sought to transform China from a precapitalist, semifeudal, and semicolonial society into a socialist society. But the road to Mao's version of Communist utopia has proved to be a treacherous and tortuous one. The PRC has gained some ground in economic development and in its international standing. The "sickman of East Asia" has, in the eyes of many commentators, become the world's third great political power. However, the Communist party has created a totalitarian regime and eliminated all its opposition forces. Under this one-party dictatorship, a series of socialist policies and some erratic experiments have been forced on the people. A very high price, in both human and ecological terms, has been paid. Yet, citizens of the country are denied many fundamental rights and freedoms, and a large portion of them are still living in poverty.

In the years from October 1949 to mid–1957, the PRC was fairly successful in achieving national unity. Considerable socioeconomic progress was made. This was the period of consolidation, reform, and the First Five-Year Plan. Domestically, the PRC emulated the Soviet form of government and adopted many of the known Soviet policies. This emulation is clear in the 1949 Common Program of the Chinese People's Political Consultative Conference (CPPCC)* and the Organic Laws. In the countryside, land reforms were carried out, and landlords as a class were eliminated. In the cities, a pragmatic accommodation with the petty bourgeoisie and the national bourgeoisie was considered expedient. Former capitalists and bureaucrats were temporarily retained in various organizations. Popular sympathy and support enabled the new regime to accomplish many of these revolutionary policies. At any rate, public ownership of the means of production and collectivization of agriculture, industry, and commerce were largely completed in the first half of the 1950s.

In the next two decades, from mid–1957 to October 1976, the PRC was characterized by radical experiments and devastating class struggles. In early 1957 the intellectuals' severe criticism of the Communist government during the Hundred Flowers Campaign* was a shocking disappointment to the Communist leadership. As a result, Mao launched a harsh Anti-Rightist Campaign* to silence his critics, which effectively broke the backbone of China's intellectuals.

The Peking leaders also decided to abandon the Soviet model and to embrace the idea of self-reliance in mid–1958. The Three Red Banners*—the General (more, faster, better, and more economic) Line for Socialist Construction, the Great Leap Forward,* and the People's Commune*—were hoisted. On the surface, the Three Red Banners were introducing a larger scale collective form of production and faster and more equitable redistribution of income. In reality, the ambitious but blind drive to leap forward only led to serious setbacks. At its worst, in an attempt to industrialize, backyard furnaces were built around the country which turned useful utensils into useless steel. To produce more grains, productive orchards and woodlands were turned into unproductive rice fields. In turn, these experiments caused serious soil erosion and environmental destruction.

Under the leadership of Liu Shao-ch'i,* there was a short period (1961–1965) of readjustment. Unfortunately, Mao was unhappy that his revolution was being rolled back. Determined to wrest power away from Liu Shao-ch'i in order to create new socialist men and women for his utopia, he called for a Great Proletarian Cultural Revolution* in 1966.

The Cultural Revolution was very much a power struggle between two factions within the CCP which represented two different lines. Mao and his leftist radicals were on the offensive, and Liu Shao-ch'i and his developmentalist-moderates were on the defensive. The moderates used the orthodox machinery—the party and government bureaucracies, the mass media, and other propaganda institutions controlled from Peking—to fend off the attack. The leftist radicals resorted to the media in Shanghai and other places and invented unorthodox means (such as big character posters and young Red Guards)* to "bombard the headquarters." The whole country was turned upside down in the turmoil. Many individuals, including Liu Shao-ch'i, fell victims, were ridiculed, condemned, and sent to "cow pens." Millions suffered persecution and humiliation for no reasons other than the suspicion of the regime. Some committed suicide. In January 1967, amidst runaway chaos, the armed forces were called in. As a result, Lin Piao* became Mao's "comrade in arms" and an heir-apparent. Revolutionary committees were established in place of local governments from the province downward. When order was restored and the Ninth Party Congress met in April 1969, the Red Guards* had been suppressed and the country was under the control of Mao and Lin Piao.

Before Mao's death in September 1976, life in some cities of the PRC was akin to that in George Orwell's *1984* or the world of Dostoevsky's *Grand Inquisitor*. First, Lin Piao and later the Gang of Four took control of the party and the government. Lin was keen on establishing his own dynasty. Reportedly, he plotted to assassinate Mao when Mao showed a mistrust about his intentions. Lin died in a plane crash on September 13, 1971 while trying to escape.

The Gang of Four were power-hungry relatives and servants of Mao, in the tradition of the concubines, eunuchs, and secretaries of the emperor. Their power came from, and was dependent on, their access to the ruling dictator. They were also revolutionary purists and extremists. Bent on instilling the Maoist values and way of thinking in the average Chinese, they embarked on a course of radical reform and banned everything they did not approve of. Their peculiar approach to reforms in the ideological and cultural sphere affected Chinese life in every respect. The party, the government, and the military were all subjected to their spell. Anyone suspected of possible opposition was quickly silenced one way or another. The national economy, law, education, social life, arts, music and theater, and so on—all experienced sweeping and uprooting changes that generated not exhilaration but despair among the people.

During the three dark years, 1959–1961, and again during the Cultural Revolution period (1966–1976), millions of people died from starvation and class struggles. At the 1959 Lushan plenum of the CCP Central Committee, General P'eng Te-huai* openly criticized Mao for his policy errors. P'eng and his innocent associates were purged and banished to the countryside. No real dissent was possible after then.

After Mao's death, there was a power struggle between the "whateverists" (who said, "Whatever Mao decided, we support; whatever Mao instructed, we follow") led by Hua Kuo-feng* and the reformers (who said, "Practice is the only test of truth") led by Teng Hsiao-p'ing. At the CCP's Central Committee Plenum in December 1978, Teng succeeded in establishing himself as the new leader and started a new decade of pragmatic reform.

The fourth decade of the PRC, approximately from December 1978 to June

1989, can be called the decade of Teng Hsiao-p'ing's reform. The general thrust shifted from class struggle to national modernization in a fundamental way for the first time since 1949. To enhance the four modernizations (in agriculture, industry, science and technology, and defense), a series of new policies were introduced. Economics took command, and a policy of liberalization entailing a degree of market mechanism was justified in the guise of a theory of productivity (later, a theory of the early stage of socialism). A new constitution adopted in 1982 promised to guide the country into a state of normalcy (rather than endless revolution). The national economy recorded a high growth rate of about 9 percent per annum during the 1980s.

The reform soon ran into difficulties. As soon as the urban sector reform was launched in 1984, it became quite clear that there was an innate weakness in the socialist supply system. Unless the artificial price and wage system of the centrally planned economy was dismantled, the market mechanism could not really function. Reforming the price and wage system, in turn, would mean reallocating the privileges and advantageous opportunities from the party cadres and loyalists to the meritorious managers and technocrats. Furthermore, there would need to be a concomitant political reform, a restructuring of the administrative and political setup from top to bottom.

When faced with such a challenge, Teng was neither willing nor able to do what was necessary. Teng's interest in reform never included a real political reform that might do away with the dictatorship of the CCP. In his old age, Teng proved short as a leader for the formidable task of a thorough reform. He could not trust his own protégés to do the job either. One after another, first Hu Yao-pang* and then Chao Tzu-yang*, were made the scapegoat when Teng's policy failed.

As the government alternately loosened and tightened its control mechanisms, such as foreign exchange and tax policies, a half-reformed economic system was overheated or dampened. Overheating led to inflation; dampening led to unemployment. Concurrently, a more complicated bureaucratic maze and various new opportunities for corruption developed. All these spelled popular discontent.

In the spring of 1989, a democratic movement took shape in Peking which forced the hands of the Communist regime. First, the intellectuals submitted petitions and issued open statements demanding more respect for human rights, a more open government process, and a faster reform. To China's misfortune, the hard-liners prevailed in the intraparty debate over the crisis, and the authority called in the troops which led to the June 4 massacre.

The Tengist reform was seriously jeopardized by the June 4 massacre. There was a worldwide outcry of disbelief and condemnation. The United States led the way with immediate political and economic sanctions against the Teng regime's massive violation of human rights. Foreign loans were suspended, the PRC's international business came to a sudden stop, and tourists shunned China. Domestic economic activities also experienced a recession beyond the slowdown projected by a contraction policy.

REFERENCES: Maurice Meisner, *Mao's China and After* (New York, 1986); Witold Rodzinski, *The People's Republic of China: A Concise Political History* (New York, 1989); "The People's Republic of China After 40 Years," special issue, *China Quarterly*, No. 119 (September 1989); NCNA, *China Official Annual Report* (Peking) (in Chinese).

BYRON SONG JAN WENG

PERIOD OF POLITICAL TUTELAGE (hsün-cheng shih-ch'i): A stage in the creation of republican government prescribed by Sun Yat-sen and the KMT.

China's need for a period of tutelary transition to democratic government was recognized by reformers like K'ang Yu-wei[*] and Yen Fu[*] as early as the 1890s, and was generally accepted by constitutionalists and revolutionaries alike. In his *Ko-ming fang-lüeh* (Design for revolution) of 1906, Sun Yat-sen[*] prescribed an initial three-year stage of revolutionary government by the military under martial law (*chün-fa*) immediately upon the revolutionary seizure of power, in which the people would be prepared for self-government at the local level. This was to be followed by a six-year period under a provisional constitution (*yüeh-fa*) during which the military was to continue in power, with self-government progressively introduced at the local and higher levels. At the end of this period, the third and final stage of full constitutional rule was to be introduced. Although he did not use the term at this time, Sun later referred to the *yüeh-fa* stage in this scheme as a period of *hsün-cheng*.

The overthrow of the Ch'ing[*] monarchy in 1911–1912 owed as much to nonrevolutionary elements as to the revolutionary armed forces, which were in any case not under the firm control of Sun Yat-sen or his Revolutionary party. His blueprint was simply ignored as revolutionaries, reformers, and Yüan Shih-k'ai[*] negotiated the replacement of the dynasty by an elected republican government. After Yüan's seizure of power, Sun participated in varying degrees in several short-lived military governments in south China, in none of which he was able to undertake the kind of nation-building by a revolutionary military government foreseen in his original Design. In his 1917 *Psychological Reconstruction*, however, he explicitly spoke of a "period of tutelage" (*hsün-cheng shih-ch'i*) in which a national revolutionary government of "foreknowers" would educate the people as a necessary transition from autocracy to republicanism. It is significant that here Sun stressed the responsibility of the revolutionary *party*, rather than the army, in providing tutelage. In his 1924 *Fundamentals of National Reconstruction for the Nationalist Government*, Sun presented a revised and detailed description of the three periods of revolution: military government, tutelage, and constitutional government. The period of tutelage in any province was to begin when it was fully pacified. The central government was to prepare each county for self-government, culminating in the election of county councils and representatives to a consultative organ in the central government. The period of tutelage in any province was to end, and constitutional government to begin, when all its counties had achieved self-government. When over half the provinces had attained the status of constitutional government, a national constituent assembly was to be convened, and the period of constitutional government to begin nationwide. The formula is not precise and implies overlapping stages.

After Sun's death, partly in response to T'ang Chi-yao's bid as vice-marshal to succeed Sun as grand marshal and leader, the Kuomintang discontinued the position and asserted civilian supremacy in a reorganized "national government." Not until after the formal reunification of China in 1927, however, was any serious effort made to identify institutions and policies with Sun's three stages. The national government established in October 1928 inaugurated in theory a period of tutelage under the KMT. The theory was reiterated in its Central Executive Committee's Policy Plans of the National Government during the Period of Tutelage of June 1929, which promised a transition to constitutional government after six years.

In the meantime, Nationalist party rule was formalized in the Provisional Constitution of the Republic of China for the Period of Tutelage in June 1931 (effectively superseded by the Organic Law of the National government adopted in December 1931). No realistic program for converting counties into fully self-governing units was implemented, however, and a variety of factors—nationalism, imperialism, cultural anxieties, and the attractions of fascist models—weakened the impulse for democratic government. Even so, discontent with Chiang Kai-shek's[*] largely military-based rule and one-party dictatorship fueled demands for a prompt transition to full constitutional government, and the preparation of a constitution proceeded amidst intense political struggles. A draft constitution was promulgated on May 1, 1936, to await approval by a national constituent assembly, but the Japanese invasion forced the postponement of this process.

The constitutional movement was revived briefly in 1939–1940, and in 1943. Responding to criticisms of dictatorship and repression, the government established an Association to Assist in the Inauguration of Constitutionalism. Ultimately, it was dissatisfaction with tutelage rather than the completion of its tasks that led to its formal termination after the war. Sun's conditions for constitutionalism were far from satisfied when the inauguration of a new constitutional government brought tutelage to an end in May 1948.

REFERENCES: Jürgen Domes, *Vertagte Revolution* (Berlin, 1969); Tuan-sheng Ch'ien, *The Government and Politics of China* (Cambridge, Mass., 1961); Lloyd E. Eastman, *The Abortive Revolution* (Cambridge, Mass., 1974); C. Martin Wilbur, *Sun Yat-sen* (New York, 1976).

DON C. PRICE

PO KU (CH'IN PANG-HSIEN) (1907–1946): General secretary of the CCP (1931–1935); member of Central Committee of the CCP.

Po Ku (Ch'in Pang-hsien) was one of the most influential of the Twenty-eight Bolsheviks,[*] occupying the post of party secretary from 1931 until 1935 and participating in the Long March,[*] the Sian Incident,[*] propaganda, and United Front activities. Born in Wu-hsi, Kiangsu, Po Ku was involved in the student movement as a youth in Soochow as president of the Student Union. Involved in several organizations when he went to Shanghai, Po Ku then joined the Communist party in Shanghai (1925) before he went for study at the Sun Yat-sen University in 1926. In Moscow, Po Ku showed an easy facility with the Russian language. He joined the clique known as the Twenty-eight Bolsheviks, under the leadership of Wang Ming.* With the cohort of returned Russian students, Po Ku returned to China in 1930 and was supported for high Chinese Communist party* positions by the Comintern* representative, Pavel Mif. By 1931, while in Shanghai, after the execution of Hsiang Chung-fa,* Po Ku became, at the age of twenty-four, the general secretary of the CCP.

During the early 1930s, the strategies and policies of the CCP were in transition. This was reflected in the Po Ku leadership; like Li Li-san,* he advocated urban areas as the keystone of the revolution, in contrast to the emerging strength of the rural strategy as exemplified by the CCP base in Kiangsi. Unable to avoid a retrenchment of the CCP Central Committee to the countryside (1933), Po Ku became involved in policy and power struggles in the Kiangsi Soviet.* During this period, the inadequate use of guerrilla tactics during the last KMT Encirclement Campaign,* and the inability to capitalize on the Fukien Incident* in 1933, have been attributed to the leadership of Po Ku and the Russian returned group. However, the facts have not yet fully emerged. It is clear that Po Ku was a truly powerful leader, using his strong linkages with the Russian-sent representatives. This power base, together with Po Ku's genuine belief that he was a better Marxist theoretician than Mao Tse-tung,* who became his chief nemesis, was important in his maintaining power, even after the Long March began in 1934. It is significant that the CCP Fifth Plenum (January 1934) reconfirmed Po Ku as general secretary.

Po Ku was replaced by his fellow Russian returned cohort, Lo Fu (Chang Went'ien),* during the Tsunyi Conference* in January 1935. This marked the beginning of Mao Tse-tung's rise to preeminence in the CCP. However, it did not mark a total eclipse for Po Ku, such as occurred with other deposed general secretaries like Ch'en Tu-hsiu* or Ch'ü Ch'iu-pai.* Po was able to retain a position on the Central Committee, and more importantly, he was deeply involved in further consequential party activities. In 1936 he was one of the negotiators during the Sian Incident. After the formation of the Second United Front,* Po Ku served in important organizational and propaganda work. In 1941, located in Yenan, he managed the newly created *Chieh-fang jih-pao* (Liberation Daily). Upon concluding the successful negotiation for the release of Yeh T'ing in 1946, Po Ku, together with Yeh T'ing and Wang Jo-fei, died in a plane crash.

Po Ku represented an important category of CCP leadership. His close linkages with the Comintern advisers, his advocacy of urban-centered revolution, and the need for more theoretical grounding for the CCP leadership decidedly placed Po Ku, like Wang Ming, in the ranks of the internationalists. Yet, Po Ku was not just a theoretician. He braved the harsh living of the Soviets, the deprivations of the Long March, and the dangers of liaison work for the United Front. Although Po Ku lost the leadership battle with Mao Tse-tung, he still retained several positions of power for the remaining decade before his death.

REFERENCES: Otto Braun, *A Comintern Agent in China, 1932–1939* (Stanford, Calif., 1982); Chou En-lai, *Chou En-lai hsüan-chi* (Selections from the writings of Chou En-lai) (Peking, 1980); Helen Foster Snow, *The Chinese Communists: Sketches and Autobiographies of the Old Guard* (Westport, Conn., 1972).

MARILYN LEVINE

POTSDAM CONFERENCE (July 17–August 2, 1945): The last of the Big Three summits during World War II.

Before Japan's defeat but after Germany's surrender, U.S. President Harry S Truman, British Prime Minister Winston Churchill (replaced by Clement Attlee after the British elections), Soviet Premier Joseph Stalin, and their top diplomatic and military advisers met to discuss issues related to postwar Europe and the defeat of Japan. They fixed the terms of German occupation, set the Oder–Neisse line as the temporary western boundary of Poland, accepted Italy as a member of the United Nations, and established the Council of Foreign Ministers to continue discussion on issues not resolved at Potsdam, such as German reparations, peace terms for Italy, Romania, Bulgaria, Austria, Hungary, and Finland, the withdrawal of Allied troops from Iran, and peace settlement in the Far East.

With respect to the Far East, Britain and the United States issued the Potsdam Declaration to Japan, demanding unconditional surrender or face destruction. The declaration also reaffirmed that all the territories Japan had stolen from China, such as Manchuria, Formosa, and the Pescadores, should be restored to the Republic of China,* as stipulated by the Cairo Declaration (December 1, 1943). Stalin renewed his pledge to enter the war against Japan in early or mid-August.

At Potsdam, the United States made two efforts on China's behalf. One was the Chinese membership in the Council of Foreign Ministers. Upon Truman's insistence, Churchill and Stalin agreed that China could take part in the work of the council when it was dealing with "problems concerning the East or problems of worldwide significance." This was the United States' last effort to elevate China to great power status. Another was Washington's support of the Nationalists' positions in the negotiation of the Sino-Soviet Treaty of Friendship and Alliance.*

At the Yalta Conference* (February 4–11, 1945), Stalin had promised to enter the war against Japan and to support the Nationalist government instead of the Communists in China. In return, President Franklin D. Roosevelt had agreed that, in addition to other terms, the Russians could regain the "preeminent interests" in Manchuria which they lost to the Japanese during the war of 1904. Since Manchuria was China's territory, the concurrence of the Chinese government was required to validate the accord. The content of the Yalta Agreement was revealed to the Nationalist government in June, and the negotiations of a Sino-Soviet treaty began at the end of that month. Stalin demanded the creation of a naval base area surrounding Port Arthur and Dairen, along with exclusive ownership of the Eastern and Southern Manchurian railroads as well as connected enterprises. These demands went far beyond the specific provisions of the Yalta

Agreement. The negotiations reached an impasse before Stalin departed for the Potsdam Conference. China thus suspended the negotiations in the hope that, at Potsdam, Truman could persuade Stalin to work out a compromise acceptable to the Chinese.

State Department officials at Potsdam, particularly the chief of the Division of Chinese Affairs John Carter Vincent, advocated that the United States should support China in resisting excessive Soviet demands. Yet, while discussing the Manchurian problem with Stalin on July 17, Truman seemed to be satisfied with Stalin's verbal assurance that Soviet demands would negate neither Chinese sovereignty nor the Open Door in Manchuria. In reply to China's plea for support, the president merely stated that he had asked the Nationalists to carry out, but not to exceed, the Yalta Agreement, and that negotiations with the Russians should be resumed. News of the successful testing of the atomic bomb reached Potsdam on July 21. American officials began to consider Soviet entry into the war against Japan unnecessary, and even undesirable. Consequently, they strongly urged U.S. support of Chinese resistance of Soviet demands in Manchuria. On August 5, Secretary of State James Brynes instructed Averell Harriman, the U.S. ambassador to Moscow, to tell Stalin that the American government considered the Nationalist positions had met the terms of the Yalta Accord fairly, and to obtain Stalin's written assurance that the Open Door principle would be observed in Manchuria.

Although the discussions were fairly cordial, signs of Soviet-American rifts were apparent at Potsdam. Some historians contend that the Americans' awareness of their possession of the atomic bomb had created a new mood of assertiveness and impatience on the part of the United States. The toughening attitude, as illustrated by the handling of the Manchurian problem, contributed to the rapid unfolding of the cold war after the Potsdam Conference.

REFERENCES: Department of State, *Foreign Relations of the United States: The Conference of Berlin* (the Potsdam Conference), Parts I & II (Washington, D.C., 1960); Charles L. Mee, *Meeting at Potsdam* (New York, 1975); Michael Schaller, *The U.S. Crusade in China, 1938–1945* (New York, 1979); Tsou Tang, *America's Failure in China, 1941–1950* (Chicago, 1963).

SU-YA CHANG

P'U-I (Aisin-Gioro P'u-i or Henry Pu-Yi, 1906–1967): Last Ch'ing emperor (Emperor Hsüan-t'ung, r. 1908–1912).

Crowned emperor three times in his life, Henry Pu-Yi, as he was known to Westerners, was the last to sit on the Chinese imperial throne. At the age of two, the Empress Dowager Tz'u-hsi* selected him to succeed the Kuang-hsü emperor.* With his father Prince Chun serving as regent, P'u-i reigned as the Hsüan-t'ung emperor until the fall of the Ch'ing dynasty* in 1912. The revolutionary settlement arranged by Yüan Shih-k'ai* allowed the young former emperor to remain within the Forbidden City Complex with a large budget supplied by the new Chinese Republic. Thereafter, excluding a brief restoration in July 1917 at the hands of a traditionalist warlord, he was allowed to live in the Forbidden City until driven from the complex in 1924. Much of the deposed emperor's early life was taken up with attempts to regain the throne. When the Japanese, bent on expanding their holdings in north China, eventually offered their assistance, he readily agreed to accept the throne of Manchuria (Manchukuo)* in 1934. In Manchuria his willingness to act as a puppet emperor served superficially to hide the reality of the Japanese occupation.

Captured by the Russians in 1945, P'u-i was eventually returned to the authorities of the People's Republic of China* in 1950. He was then imprisoned until 1959 when he was released and allowed to become a citizen. His last years were spent working as a horticulturist and writing his memoirs which appeared in 1964. He died of cancer in a hospital during the Cultural Revolution.*

REFERENCES: Aisin-Gioro Pu Yi, *From Emperor to Citizen: the Autobiography of Aisin-Gioro Pu Yi*, 2 vols. (Peking, 1964–1965); Arnold C. Brackman, *The Last Emperor* (New York, 1975).

STEVEN A. LEIBO

Q

QUOTATIONS FROM CHAIRMAN MAO: A palm-size red book; during the Cultural Revolution, people called it the *Hung-pao-shu* (the precious red book).

In 1959 Lin Piao* replaced P'eng Te-huai* as China's minister of defense. He coined the slogan "everyone must study Chairman Mao's writings, follow his teachings, act according to his instructions and be his good soldiers." In 1960 he also said, "In Chairman Mao's writings, one sentence is worth ten thousand sentences; by learning Mao's works, one can profit ten thousand times." As a result, in May 1961 the *Chieh-fang chün-pao* (the Liberation Army Newspaper) started publishing Mao's quotations on the front page of every issue. These quotations were to help soldiers with little education to learn Mao's doctrine.

In May 1964 the General Political Department (GPD) of the Liberation Army assembled these quotations and consolidated them, after making some editorial changes, into a single booklet with a red cover entitled *Quotations from Chairman Mao* for circulation throughout the army. The Little Red Book contained thirty-three chapters with a total of 427 quotations.

When the Cultural Revolution* erupted in June–July 1966, the GPD reprinted the *Quotations* for nationwide circulation. Vast numbers of people soon waved their Little Red Book in public everywhere in China. This scene of a "red ocean" eventually became a horrible nightmare for millions of innocent Chinese people who lost their families, their dignity, and even their lives during the Cultural Revolution. From 1966 through 1969 approximately 1 billion copies of the Little Red Book were probably printed and distributed.

During those years, the people in China were ordered to bow to Mao's picture and recite the Little Red Book before starting their daily activities each morning. Before they retired each evening, they had to join a group and discuss the contents of the book. When a child started talking, he was taught to wave the Little Red Book and to cry with the adults: "Chairman Mao is the reddest, reddest, reddest sun in our heart! He is the greatest leader, the greatest teacher, and the greatest helmsman!'' ''The great Chairman Mao will live ten thousand, a hundred thousand years!''

This method used during the Cultural Revolution for studying Mao's thoughts was called *t'ien-t'ien-tu* (daily reading). By doing this for many years, 800 million people perhaps worshiped Mao Tse-tung* more devoutly than most religious people worship their God. Many truly believed in the sacredness of the Little Red Book far more than many Christians believed in their Bible.

This Little Red Book contained the distilled essence of Mao Tse-tung's thoughts and presented a cross section of his basic ideas which permeated virtually all discussions in China in those years. The book's didactic quality can be observed in its great repetition. Most of the 427 quotations are short—about five to fifteen lines, with a few of only one or two lines. Their syntax ranges from the simple colloquial to the semiliterary, including some classical Chinese and Marxist terminology as well.

After the Cultural Revolution ended in 1976, the Little Red Book also lost its glory and soon vanished. People now refer to it only as a reminder of one of the darkest and cruelest ten years in China's history.

REFERENCES: *A Comprehensive Glossary of Chinese Communist Terminology* (Taipei, 1978); *Jen-min jih-pao* (People's Daily), June–November 1966; *Mao Chu-hsi yü-lu* (Quotations from Chairman Mao) (Peking, 1964); Yen Chia-ch'i and Kao Kao, *Chung-kuo wen-ko shih-nien-shih* (Ten years' history of Cultural Revolution) (Taipei, 1987).

RAMON H. MYERS

R

RECTIFICATION CAMPAIGN (1942–1945): A study campaign designed to establish ideological orthodoxy, unify the Communist party, elevate Mao Tse-tung to a position of undisputed leadership, and induce mass conformity.

The Rectification Campaign of 1942–1945 would define one of the key operational tactics of the Chinese Communist party* for many decades. On the surface, it was a study campaign designed to establish a single orthodoxy for Communist party members and all cadres, to unify the party organizationally, and to strengthen leadership, particularly that of Mao Tse-tung.* In the process, it entailed developing and applying methods of thought reform, weeding out unreliable cadres, drafting activists, who would do the bidding of the party leadership, and fostering mass conformity through inducements and intimidation.

The immediate goals of the campaign at its inception were to eradicate "subjectivism, sectarianism, and stereotyped Party writing" among party members. Subjectivism was described as the inability to comprehend "objective reality" and therefore to formulate and implement policies commensurate with it. A premise of the campaign was that only Mao Tse-tung had successfully done that, and therefore his thought should constitute the ideological orthodoxy of the CCP.

Sectarianism was defined as the organizational manifestation of subjectivism—lacking unity of thought, there could be no unity of organization. Varieties of sectarianism were said to be the result of leftist and rightist opportunistic deviations from the correct ideological line.

Stereotyped party writing was designated as a propaganda tool in the service of subjectivism and sectarianism. By speciously asserting the authority of the Marxist-Leninist classics, it masked the subjectivity and sectarian propensities of dogmatists, fostering their illegitimate aspirations for power.

Behind these abstract formulations was a concrete need, from the Communist's perspective, to strengthen the unity and leadership of the party in 1942. Failure to do so would risk the very existence of the Communist movement. In the previous two years the party had suffered serious military reverses. Half the territory under its control in 1940 had been taken by Japanese troops and their Chinese collaborators by 1942, reducing the population on the CCP tax registers from 100 million to 50 million. In addition, an economic blockade by Chiang Kai-shek's* Nationalist forces had increased hardship and suffering in the Communist base areas, as had three years of exceptionally bad weather, causing both drought and flood.

To deal with the crisis, the leadership prescribed a unified set of policies to strengthen the United Front of all forces opposed to Japanese imperialism, and to improve the lives of the common people and gain their allegiance. Implementation would require a disciplined, informed cadre—one that could function reliably in the dispersed Communist base areas where communication and control were difficult.

The immensity of the task of educating such a cadre is apparent in the statistics of party growth. Between 1937, when the war with Japan began, and 1940, party membership grew from 40,000 to 800,000. Most of the new members were peasants and urban youth who had little knowledge of CCP ideology. Many of those who did, and many older party members, according to party history, had been influenced by the policies of Wang Ming,* Mao Tse-tung's chief rival for leadership, thus threatening party unity and Mao's supremacy. Mao's remedy was to "rectify" their thinking.

Twenty-two documents, most of them written by Mao or by the party Central Committee under his direction, were prescribed as the basic content of the campaign. They were to be read, discussed in small groups, and provide the basis for criticism and self-criticism assessments of party members' lives and work. Participants were instructed to expose completely their shortcomings in "thought autobiographies."

Little headway was made in the campaign until an example was made of a recalcitrant party member and writer, Wang Shih-wei. Wang's insistence on a degree of independence from party control led to harsh criticism, imprisonment, and eventually execution. The intimidation evoked by this, and similar cases, became an integral part of the methodology of rectification, inseparable from the positive inducements of belonging to a tightly knit organization and movement; one dedicated, in its pronouncements, to improvement of the lives of the suffering and oppressed.

The campaign, scheduled to last a few months, was extended over several years. It reached its height in mid–1943 during a phase of "investigating cadres" and "rooting out traitors and spies." Mass accusations and denunciations implicated many of the common people, as well as cadres and party members. Eventually the party leadership itself condemned the climate of terror that had led to "overinclusiveness" and to the widespread practice of "using coercion, forcing confessions, and believing them." These tactics had led to many thousands of "false, unjust, and incorrect verdicts."

Although such verdicts were said to have been reversed and remedied later, the "excesses" of the Rectification Campaign became a standard characteristic of every subsequent mass campaign throughout Mao Tse-tung's tenure of power. Victimizing the innocent was an invariable result of methods the party would repeatedly use to attain conformity to its wishes.

The results of the campaign were considered worth the regrettable excesses. It succeeded remarkably well in establishing a well-defined ideology and work methodology; it made the Communist party more disciplined and responsive; it provided an effective process for weeding out undesirable party members and drafting new members from among activists identified among the populace; and almost certainly it did help the Communists organize effective resistance to the Japanese, gain control over much rural area behind enemy lines, and implement policies that engendered significant public support. It also succeeded in strengthening party leadership and elevating Mao Tse-tung to a position of unprecedented ideological and political power, reducing the influence of his rivals in the process.

On the other hand, it introduced oppressive, intimidating procedures that would stifle initiative and creativity and turn the new orthodoxy into stale dogma maintained by an unreproachable personality cult. This was the foundation for such Maoist-inspired disasters as the Great Leap Forward* and the Great Proletarian Cultural Revolution.*

REFERENCES: Mao Tse-tung, *Selected Works of Mao Tse-tung*, vol.3 (Peking, 1965); Peter J. Seybolt, "Terror and Conformity: Counter Espionage Campaign, Rectification, and Mass Movements, 1942–1943," *Modern China* 12, no. 1 (January 1986): 39–73.

PETER J. SEYBOLT

RED GUARDS: Students told to make revolution on the street as Mao's revolutionary successors during the early years of the Cultural Revolution (1966–1976).

The Red Guard movement represented a dramatic aspect of the Cultural Revolution (1966–1976).* A popular image was one of rampaging and unruly students bent on overturning the establishment, the Chinese Communist party.* It was evident that the authorities had lost control, Mao seemingly had gone mad and sent millions of young students to make revolution in the streets. At the beginning of the Cultural Revolution, the Maoists praised these students as "Little Generals" who wanted to gain revolutionary experience to prepare themselves as successors to the revolution.

Explanations for the rise of the Red Guard movement include generational politics, the Marxist theory of alienation, manipulation of the young in the power struggle by the top leaders, a reaffirmation of the ideals of a Maoist society, and a massive reaction against historical and foreign influences. The Red Guards generally refer to those high school and university students who organized themselves as Mao's revolutionary successors to wage battle against the establishment: veteran party leaders and organizations. They took upon themselves the role of investigator and judge of the cadres' behavior and attitude. Too often this role gave them the opportunity not only to air their grievances against school officials and teachers, but also to vent their frustration with the educational system which stipulated during that time that normal schooling had to be abandoned. Mass criticisms led by the Red Guards against the party leaders and apparatus became an everyday occurrence. Party leaders were dragged out into the streets for failure to provide the answers sought by students. To counter the roaming Red Guards organized by the university students, party leaders in many localities formed their own Red Guard groups. During 1966 and 1967, China was in the midst of utter chaos and rampant violence as warring Red Guard groups competed and feuded with each other. Finally, Mao ordered military intervention to restore order. The Red Guard movement was crushed and ended in tragedy and disillusionment.

REFERENCES: Gordon Bennett and Ronald N. Monteperto, *Red Guards: The Political Biography of Dai Hsiao-ai* (New York, 1972); Victor Nee, *The Cultural Revolution at Peking University* (New York, 1969); William Hinton, *Hundred Day War: The Cultural Revolution at Tsinghua* (New York, 1972); Liang Heng and Judith Shapiro, *Son of Heaven* (New York, 1983).

JAMES C.F. WANG

RED VERSUS EXPERTISE: The attempt to strike a balance between technical competence and ideological correctness in China's search for political and economic development.

The perennial controversy between "red" versus "expertise" began during the summer of 1957 in the Chinese Communist party's* debate on cadre policy. The party was then criticized by the rightists, the so-called bourgeois intellectuals, for placing people in governmental positions based not on merit or ability (*ts'ai*), but on political reliability or political "virtue" (*te*). Subsequently, an ideological rectification or Anti-Rightist Campaign* was launched to correct the political orientation and to raise the ideological level of the bourgeois intellectuals. The 1957–1958 Anti-Rightist Campaign resulted in widespread persecution and purge of party and nonparty cadres.

The controversy was revived in 1959 at the Lushan Conference* where Marshal P'eng Te-huai* issued his dissent and protest against the ruinous party policy of placing reliance on the mass mobilization strategy rather than on technical knowledge and expertise. Marshal P'eng charged that the party was mistaken to emphasize guerrilla warfare and politics-in-command in the military rather than military professionalism during the Great Leap,* which brought economic disaster to China from 1958 to 1960. Marshal P'eng was purged in 1959 for his outspoken criticism of the party's reliance on "ideological redness" at the expense of "technical competence" for both the military and party cadres.

The Cultural Revolution (1966–1976)* replayed the earlier policy of placing greater emphasis on political reliability than on technical knowledge and competence.

The "red" versus "expert" controversy engulfed the Chinese higher education system in 1952, with shifting emphasis from a professionally and technologically oriented university education to a more revolutionary and egalitarian one. From

1952 to 1956 Chinese university education was based on the Soviet model, with emphasis on academic excellence and acquisition of technical knowledge. Then the emphasis shifted to work-study programs, with stress on manual labor and the *hsia-fang* (downward transfer)[*] movement to the countryside to be close to the peasants. The 1960–1963 economic recovery following the Great Leap fiasco saw a reemphasis on technical expertise, intellectual elitism, and academic excellence. This emphasis on academic excellence created a dilemma for students from the countryside because of their poor academic preparation and their feeling of inferiority in competition with those whose class origin provided cultural and intellectual advantages for academic work. It was against this background that the Cultural Revolution came to the universities.

Since the Cultural Revolution sought radical transformation of the people, intellectuals—the bearers of knowledge—became the first target for attack by the radicalized Red Guards.[*] To ensure the Maoist concept of education stressing political ideology and manual labor, the administration and management of education during the Cultural Revolution was taken out of the hands of professional educators. Scientists and technicians were criticized and purged for their professionalism, for their aloofness and disinterest in politics, and for their research unrelated to solving practical problems.

It was not until 1977 when Teng Hsiao-p'ing[*] returned to power that reform in science and technology was instituted to bridge the decade-long gap from neglect in order to catch up with the world's advanced industrial powers by the year 2000. Similarly, the Open Door policy of the 1980s was designed to assist the adoption of the world's advanced technology and to acquire modern equipment and, according to the December 1978 party communique, "greatly strengthen scientific and educational work to meet the needs of modernization."

Viewed from the perspective of the shifting emphasis on the red versus expert dichotomy, China's retrenchment by the hard-liners following the June 4, 1989 T'ienanmen crackdown on the students may be read as another possible sign for reemphasis on ideological-political reliability over technological expertise. The retrenchment has understandably generated fear at the universities and among intellectuals.

REFERENCES: Joseph Levenson, "Communist China in Time and Space: Roots and Rootlessness," *The China Quarterly*, No. 39 (July-September 1969): 1–11; Richard D. Baun, "The Politico-Ideological Factors of the Chinese Great Leap Forward," *Asian Survey* 4, no. 9 (September 1964): 1048–1057; and D. J. Waller, "China: Red or Expert? *The Political Quarterly* (April-June 1967): 122–131.

JAMES C.F. WANG

REORGANIZATIONISTS (kai-tsu-p'ai): Left-wing faction within the KMT, 1928–1931.

The Reorganizationists, or members of the Society for the Reorganization of the Kuomintang, led a left-wing opposition to Chiang Kai-shek's[*] party leadership during the late 1920s. Founded in Shanghai in late 1928, the society called for a revival of the spirit of the KMT's 1924 reorganization and a new reorganization of the party. It also supported Wang Ching-wei,* then in exile in France, to be the party's leader. The most important person behind the organization of the society was Ch'en Kung-po,* Wang's major assistant, who since early 1928 had written a series of articles criticizing Chiang and his Nanking government. While in agreement with the party's decision to purge the Communists, Ch'en deplored the abandoning of mass movement and anti-imperialism by Chiang's leadership as a betrayal to the National Revolution. His writings attracted wide support from idealistic KMT members and helped to shape the ideological stand of the forthcoming society.

The society supported a group of Central Committee members of the KMT, headed by Wang, as its nominal leadership, while daily operations at its headquarters at Shanghai were supervised by Ch'en and two other followers of Wang, Ku Meng-yü and Wang Lo-p'ing. Branches and sub-branches were established in more than a dozen provinces and overseas, often working within the existing KMT branches. A university founded by Ch'en at Shanghai, Ta-lu University, was used as a recruiting and training organ for the Society. Its membership was said to have exceeded 10,000 by late 1928.

In early 1929, the society mobilized nearly half of the KMT branches in an impressive operation to boycott the Third Party Congress convened by Chiang Kai-shek, which the society denounced as undemocratic and reactionary. Nevertheless, the Congress was opened under Chiang's iron hand, and leaders of the society received severe punishments for this opposition.

From mid–1929 to late 1930 the society instigated and coordinated a series of armed uprisings, relying mainly on the support of anti-Chiang militarists, in an attempt to topple the Nanking government. None of the uprisings was successful. Meanwhile, Wang Ching-wei returned from France, assuming more direct control over the society. After the assassination of Wang Lo-p'ing by Chiang's secret police in early 1930, the society intensified its attack on Nanking. Later that year Wang and the entire leadership of the society played a leading role in the organization of a rival KMT headquarters and national government at Peip'ing (Peking). When Chiang again crushed this opposition, Wang fled the country and announced the dissolution of the society in early 1931. Throughout the 1930s, however, political observers still occasionally used the term *Reorganizationists* in referring to Wang's factional following.

Opposing both the Chinese Communist party* and the conservative leadership of the KMT, the Reorganizationists were seeking a middle-of-the-road position for the KMT. Their effort, and the influence they briefly enjoyed, reflected the ideological confusion within the KMT and the Chinese people generally.

REFERENCES: Cha Chien-yü, ed., *Kuo-min-tang kai-tsu-p'ai tzu-liao hsüan-pien* (Selected historical materials concerning the reorganizationists of the Kuomintang) (Hunan, 1986); N. Lee, W.S.K. Waung, and L.Y. Chin, eds., *Bitter Smile: Memoirs of Ch'en*

Kung-po, 1925–1936 (Hong Kong, 1979); Wang Ke-wen, "The Left Kuomintang in Opposition, 1927–1931," *Chinese Studies in History* 20, no. 2 (Winter 1986–1987).

KE-WEN WANG

"REPORT ON THE PEASANT MOVEMENT IN HUNAN": Polemics of Mao Tse-tung.

This article was a reply to criticisms inside and outside both the Kuomintang and Chinese Communist parties* to oppose the peasants' revolutionary struggles in 1926–1927. Mao Tse-tung* wrote this report after he went to Hunan and spent thirty-two days investigating the local conditions. It first appeared in the *Hsiang-tao Chou-pao (Guidance Weekly)* in March 1927. The first book edition was published in April of the same year in Hankow, Hupeh Province, by the Ch'ang-chiang Book Store. When the *Selected Works of Mao Tse-tung* first appeared in 1951, major changes had been introduced for at least forty items in this article to accommodate the shifting winds of ideological change.

In 1926 Mao Tse-tung "personally started and led the peasant movement in Hunan" and made Hunan "the center of a national peasant movement." What was this movement? According to Mao:

When the peasants become organized, there is action. Their major targets are local bullies, bad gentry, lawless landlords, patriarchal ideologies and institutions, corrupt officials in the cities and evil customs in the rural areas. In force and momentum, the attack is like a tempest or a hurricane; those who submit to it survive and those who resist it perish. As a result, the privileges which the feudal landlords have enjoyed for thousands of years are being shattered into pieces. The dignity and prestige of the landlords are dashed to the ground.

Mao criticized the KMT leaders, especially Chiang Kai-shek,* by claiming: "they totally mishandled this movement." He also excoriated the CCP leaders, headed by Ch'en Tu-hsiu,* because "They totally misunderstood the movement." Mao then wrote the following:

A revolution is not the same as inviting people to dinner, or writing an essay, or painting a picture, or doing fancy needlework; it can not be any thing so refined, so calm and gentle, or so mild, kind, courteous, restrained and magnanimous. A revolution is an uprising, an act of violence whereby one class overthrows another.

In the 1920s the peasant movement led by Mao Tse-tung created a campaign called the red terror which reflected an intense struggle between the KMT and the CCP. These two parties had been cooperating between 1924 and 1927, but this new movement drove a great wedge between the two sides. This report sheds light on why cooperation between these two parties could never be maintained.

Mao's "Report on the Peasant Movement in Hunan" was quoted extensively in the 1960s, when a heavy black turbulent cloud swept over China and many innocent people were injured and even killed. The following slogans from that report inflamed the violence of those years:

"A revolution is not the same as inviting people to dinner."

"To right a wrong it is necessary to exceed the proper limits, and the wrong cannot be righted without the proper limits being exceeded."

"Trample the landlords underfoot after knocking them down."

"Every revolutionary comrade must support this action, or he will be taking the counter-revolutionary stand."

All these slogans are from Mao's article.

The peasant movement in the 1920s and the Cultural Revolution[*] in the 1960s were created by one person—Mao Tse-tung. This 7,000-word article has haunted China for more than fifty years.

REFERENCES: Chang Hsin-ju, *Kuan-yü Mao Tse-tung t'ung-chih tsai ti-i-tz'u kuo-nei ko-ming chan-cheng shih-ch'i ti liang-p'ien chu-tso* (Two articles by Mao Tse-tung during the first civil war) (Peking, 1953); Ch'en Po-ta, *Tu "Hu-nan nung-min yün-tung k'ao-ch'a pao-kao"* (Read the "Report on the Peasant Movement in Hunan") (Peking, 1951); *Selected Works of Mao Tse-tung* (New York, 1954).

RAMON H. MYERS

REPUBLIC OF CHINA (ROC): A republican form of government based on Dr. Sun's Three People's Principles following the success of the 1911 Revolution and the collapse of the imperial system.

The name the "Republic of China" is given to the Chinese state created by the overthrow of the Ch'ing dynasty[*] in 1911–1912. Until 1949 it encompassed all of China; now it consists only of Taiwan and some much smaller islands, including several belonging to Fukien Province. The capital of the Republic of China was at Peking from 1912 to 1927; at Nanking and (during World War II) Chungking; and has been at Taipei since 1949. Polities called the Republic of China have operated under six constitutional documents (1911, 1912, 1914, 1923, 1931, and 1946). In 1990 discussions about further constitutional revision began in Taipei.

The first proclamation of a republic followed a military uprising in central China in October 1911 and was confirmed the following year when the Ch'ing general Yüan Shih-k'ai[*] forced the Manchu ruling house to abdicate. Although Sun Yat-sen[*] was named provisional president of the Republic, he was quickly succeeded by Yüan himself, who made Peking the capital, and while maintaining certain republican appearances, he acted as a centralizing autocrat (albeit a modernizer), even attempting, near the end of this life, to become emperor himself. After Yüan's death in 1916, the Peking government fell into increasing chaos during the period of so-called warlordism.[*]

The name "Republic of China" was maintained after the victory of the Nationalists over the Peking government in the late 1920s, and the move of the capital to Nanking. The new national government there, effectively under the authority of Chiang Kai-shek,[*] proved reasonably successful during the brief period between its own establishment and the beginning of the Japanese onslaught in 1931. Thereafter intractable military problems sapped its energy and led indirectly to its collapse in the face of the Communists in the civil war of 1945–1949.[*]

Defeated on the Chinese mainland, the government then withdrew to the island of Taiwan, which had returned to the sovereignty of the Republic of China following the surrender of the Japanese in 1945. The first Nationalist Chinese officials then sent to the island were welcomed as liberators, but their corrupt and autocratic ways soon enraged the population, leading, in February 1947, to riots that were bloodily suppressed by troops. Since 1949 when it moved to Taipei, the central government of the Republic of China has maintained itself as a rival national government to that of the People's Republic of China,* proclaimed in the same year by the Communists at Peking.

The early years of the Republic of China on Taiwan were extremely difficult. Nearly 2 million soldiers and refugees had arrived with the government on an island only 14,000 square miles in size. Although the former Japanese colonial rulers had developed basic agricultural and other infrastructure, Taiwan was still very poor. In the postwar period it was also divided internally by the tension between its earlier settlers—the "Taiwanese" (of mostly Fukienese and Hakka origin)—and the "Mainlanders" who had just arrived. Moreover, it was militarily insecure, threatened by attack at any time from across the Taiwan strait.

The situation stabilized after the outbreak of the Korean War in 1950. The American President Truman ordered the Seventh Fleet into the strait, and American policy, which until then had been inclined eventually to recognize Peking, turned to support for Taipei. A mutual defense treaty between Taipei and Washington was concluded in 1954, and military cooperation between the two countries grew. In 1958 American support, including the threatened use of nuclear weapons, helped Taipei to prevail in the Formosa Straits Crisis.

Among the most important steps taken by the Republic of China during this early period were economic reforms. Prospects for the island were not good: it had a substantial population, and it lacked resources. Furthermore, government policies were initially statist, protectionist, and directed toward self-sufficiency and import substitution. By the mid–1950s the economy was stagnant. Two sets of measures reversed this state of affairs. The first was the land-to-the-tiller program, completed in 1958, in which tenant farmers were given their fields and landlords were compensated with the assets of former Japanese industrial enterprises. The second was a basic shift in economic philosophy toward export-led growth, encouragement of local entrepreneurship, and the welcoming of foreign investment into special export processing zones—policies developed by a brilliant group of economists and administrators, including K. Y. Yin, K. C. Yeh, and K. T. Li.

By the 1960s such measures were beginning to pay off in an economic miracle that rapidly transformed the island of Taiwan, until then known for its sugar and pineapples, into a major exporter first of textiles and simple consumer goods, and then of mechanical, electrical, and electronic products of ever-increasing sophistication. Steady growth in the decades that followed, with the proceeds largely reinvested in capital, infrastructure, and an inclusive educational system of very high quality, rapidly lifted Taiwan from Third World Status to become one of the "little dragons," or New Industrializing Economies of East Asia. All of this was done while maintaining a strikingly even income distribution. By 1990 the Republic of China on Taiwan had become a major economic power and model for developing countries, with a higher volume of trade and greater foreign exchange reserves than the whole People's Republic of China, and one of the highest standards of living in Asia.

For most of this period of economic advance, however, the Republic of China changed little politically. Although elections were held at the local level, the Parliament elected on the mainland in 1948 was effectively frozen in place, press and media were controlled, and all dissent was crushed. President Chiang Kai-shek, who held unchallenged executive power in the island until his death in 1975, showed himself remarkably open to the advice of economists and technical specialists, but he brooked no political rivalry. Those who challenged him or even threatened to do so—whether Mainlanders like Governor Wu Kuo-chen and General Sun Li-jen, or Taiwanese such as Professor P'eng Ming-min—were arrested or exiled.

On the senior Chiang's death, the presidency passed first to Yen Chia-kan,* and then to his son Chiang Ching-kuo,* who had long handled military and internal security matters for his father. In office, however, the younger Chiang proved a reformer. His modest and approachable personal style contrasted with the austere and distant atmosphere that had surrounded his father. While continuing economic reform, he began political change as well by bringing local people into government, while in the civil service he promoted an impressive cadre of younger officials, many holding advanced degrees from leading foreign universities. By 1988, when Chiang Ching-kuo died, significant progress had been made in reconciling Taiwan society, improving the quality of government, and moving toward democracy.

At the same time, the Republic of China on Taiwan had been fighting a long retreat in the international community. Both Taipei and Peking insisted that they alone were the legitimate Chinese government: to recognize one thus required breaking with the other. More and more countries did so with Taipei, slowly at first, but then in a flood after 1971 when the Republic of China was voted out of the United Nations, and the American President Richard Nixon announced his intention to visit the People's Republic. When the American President Jimmy Carter broke diplomatic relations with Taipei and abrogated the mutual defense treaty in 1979, many people thought the Republic of China on Taiwan had reached the end of the road. However, relations between Taipei and Washington were continued in substance through the framework of a law called the Taiwan Relations Act, while the Republic of China itself proved remarkably resilient.

After Chiang Ching-kuo's death the presidency passed to his protégé, Lee Teng-hui, a Taiwanese expert on agricultural economics with a doctorate from Cornell. Under President Lee, the pace of change in Taiwan has accelerated. An official opposition, the Democratic Progressive party, has contested elections and won some important victories, and the frozen Parliament is in the process of being completely reelected. Long-neglected issues of environmental protection and human rights have received new attention, political prisoners have been released, exiles are returning home, and contacts and travel between the two sides of the strait have greatly increased.

International status is the great imponderable in the future of the Republic of China on Taiwan. East Asia and the world are faced with the anomaly of an economic powerhouse and substantial military power—without embassies, diplomats, or even clear legal status. The search for a way out of this incongruous situation has led, within Taiwan, to calls on the one hand for independence— that is, for giving up any proclaimed relationship with China—and on the other, for unity with China, through federal or associational plans. The People's Republic, for its part, denies any legal status to the Republic of China government; it considers Taiwan simply a renegade province that force may be required to recover.

When he was near death, Mao Tse-tung* is reported to have stated that abolishing the "Republic of China" title was one of his biggest mistakes: had he kept it (as Chiang did when he defeated his rivals) the Kuomintang party would have been denied a national basis for their resistance to communism. Ironically enough, that basis has perhaps acquired a new significance since the T'ienanmen massacre of 1989, with mainland Chinese increasingly looking back to the earlier Republic and across the strait at the contemporary one for clues to their own situation.

REFERENCES: Ralph Clough, *Island China* (Cambridge, Mass., 1978); Lloyd E. Eastman, *The Abortive Revolution: China Under Nationalist Rule, 1927–1937* (Cambridge, Mass., 1974); Martin L. Lasater, *U.S. Policy Toward China's Reunification* (Washington, D.C., 1988); William L. Tung, *The Political Institutions of Modern China* (The Hague, 1964); Walter Galenson, ed., *Economic Growth and Structural Change in Taiwan: The Postwar Experience of the Republic of China* (Ithaca, N.Y., 1979).

ARTHUR WALDRON

RESEARCH CLIQUE: Early republican political faction consisting mainly of parliamentary politicians, journalists, and intellectuals.

Research Clique members came from two main backgrounds: (1) expatriate intellectuals and students in Japan around the turn of the century; (2) prominent parliamentarians in the first provincial and national assemblies of the same era. What they shared was a commitment to constitutionalism, colored with a liberal or "reformist" bent that sought some median path between Republican Revolution and reactionary militarism in the early republican period.

Following Yüan Shih-k'ai's* death in mid–1916, "parties" that had been ineffectual in resisting his power gave way to a plethora of cliques, clubs, and societies. One casualty was the Progressive party (Chin-pu-tang). From its fragments Liang Ch'i-ch'ao* and his close associates formed a broader organization, the Association for Constitutional Research (Hsien-fa yen-chiu hui), popularly simplified as the Research Association or Clique. This latter label belonged more correctly to a much smaller core of a dozen or so around Liang and almost an equal number attached to his allies, T'ang Hua-lung and Lin Ch'ang-min. Never tightly structured, the clique can be traced only vaguely through its individual members' activities.

The Research Clique supported, but had little influence over, Tuan Ch'i-jui's early cabinets. Although their proposals for the draft 1917 constitution were ignored, they seconded Tuan's call for war on Germany, arguing its necessity to give China a voice in the postwar world. In the consequent confrontation of President Li Yüan-hung* with several military governors over Tuan Ch'i-jui's dismissal, the Research Clique boycotted Parliament, helping prevent a quorum that might support the president.

In late 1917 the clique's prominence reached its zenith. Liang Ch'i-ch'ao served briefly as minister of finance, and in the same cabinet were T'ang Hua-lung as minister of the interior, Lin Ch'ang-min as minister of justice, and Fan Yuan-lien as minister of education. Wang Ta-hsieh, minister of foreign affairs, was also an associate of the group. Particularly in Parliament, they were the articulate voices answering the pro-Kuomintang members' opposition to Tuan's government.

Their resignations in concert with Tuan Ch'i-jui's in late 1917 played into the hands of Tuan's emerging Anhwei Clique.* To some historians, their support for Tuan's new elections delivered Parliament into the control of the Anfu* militarists, making war with Sun Yat-sen* and southern *tu-chüns* inevitable. It certainly proved the undoing of the clique's hope to improve their political influence. In the 1918 "Anfu election," Anfu Club politicians captured the Research Clique's Kiangsu base, reducing their parliamentary representation to barely twenty members.

The Research Clique's coherence was over. Liang Ch'i-ch'ao retreated into scholarly isolation, foreign travel, and periodic lecturing until his death in 1929. T'ang Hua-lung went abroad in early 1918 and was assassinated in Victoria, British Columbia, later that same year. A few clique figures did continue in public roles. Lin Ch'ang-min had been perhaps the group's most prominent parliamentarian since serving as secretary general of the first republican provisional Senate and the First National Assembly in 1912. After 1918 he concentrated on other projects such as the Chinese League of Nations Association, and he helped organize the famous lectures of Dewey, Russell, and Tagore. He served on various constitutional drafting committees until his death in 1925. A small group recongregated under the Research Clique label in the Parliament of 1922–1924, but the spark was gone. They were still identifiable in Wellington Koo's* cabinet of early 1926 which served mainly as a cover for Chang Tso-lin's dominance of the capital.

In the end, the Research Clique served mainly as useful parliamentary allies to political figures with less respectable aims. Their moderate reformist views brought association with Yüan Shih-k'ai and later Tuan Ch'i-jui in the forlorn hopes of protecting republican constitutional values. They paid the price of that association when their allies proved little inhibited by the constitutionalism that motivated their engagement in politics. In short, the clique was a voice of

constitutional liberalism for a small band of sincere conservative intellectuals who suffered the fate of being used by those they sought to influence.
REFERENCES: Howard L. Boorman and Richard C. Howard, eds. *Biographical Dictionary of Republican China* (New York and London: 1967–71), 2:346–351, 368–372; 3:230–232; Hsi-sheng Ch'i, *Warlord Politics in China, 1916–1928* (Stanford, Calif., 1976); Andrew J. Nathan, *Peking Politics, 1918–1923: Factionalism and the Failure of Constitutionalism* (Berkeley, Calif., 1976).

PETER M. MITCHELL

REVIVE CHINA SOCIETY (Hsing-Chung hui): Revolutionary society and early political party, established in 1894, dissolved into the T'ung-meng hui around 1905.

The Revive China Society was founded in 1894 by Sun Yat-sen* while he was staying in Hawaii. It was a secret, pro-revolutionary society whose purpose was to overthrow the Manchu Ch'ing dynasty.* When Sun returned to China in 1895, he used the Revive China Society to organize an antigovernment attempt in Kwangtung Province in alliance with local secret societies, but this uprising failed and Sun fled overseas. There, he organized more branches of the Revive China Society to raise money and, secondarily, manpower for further revolutionary attempts. With its overseas roots, the Revive China Society developed into a political party—China's first—dedicated primarily to replacing government by the Manchus with government by Han Chinese (Han being the majority ethnic group), and secondarily to establishing a republican form of government, "modernizing" China's institutions and society, and perhaps addressing questions of rural poverty.

Between 1895 and 1900, although Sun Yat-sen and his partisans were able to establish small branches of the Revive China Society among Chinese in Hong Kong, Japan, the United States, Canada, and South Africa (as well as south China), the response to Sun's summons was far less than he had expected. In the meantime, certain gentry–literati in China, particularly those associated with the iconoclastic scholar K'ang Yu-wei,* were becoming increasingly concerned about China's fate. They became convinced that very radical reforms were needed. Between 1895 and 1897, several attempts were made to bring together Sun's partisans and those of K'ang Yu-wei, but the efforts failed. After the conservative coup d'état in 1898 against the Kuang-hsü Emperor* and K'ang Yu-wei's policies, Sun hoped that his Revive China Society and his revolutionary cause would attract more interest, but he was again disappointed. Certain Japanese pan-Asian activists, however, interested themselves in Sun and from time to time provided arms and other aid to him and to the Revive China Society.

In 1900 the Boxer Rebellion* led the Western powers and Japan to send an expeditionary force to relieve the siege of the legations in Peking, and it looked as if China might be dismembered. Sun rushed back to China to try again to start a revolution. Once again, Sun worked partly through the Revive China Society, but also sought alliances with secret societies in south and southeastern Kwangtung. Through intermediaries, Sun even approached the moderate Governor-General Li Hung-chang* and tried again to join his forces with K'ang Yu-wei's. Neither of these last two met with success, even though K'ang's supporters were organizing an uprising at the same time. Disappointed again, Sun launched his second revolutionary attempt in October 1900. After a couple of early successes, it was rapidly put down.

After the dramatic events of 1900, concern over China's fate and activist sentiment increased tremendously. Revolutionary organizations and nationalist societies sprang up in many quarters. The line between radical reform and revolution became increasingly blurred, as did the specific programs called for by the various revolutionary parties. The Revive China Society lost its position as the leading organized proponent of revolution for China. In the Americas, where after 1899 supporters of K'ang Yu-wei far outnumbered backers of Sun Yat-sen, leadership in the revolutionary cause for a time went to K'ang's adherents (without K'ang's approval), and the Revive China Society became practically moribund. In Kwangtung, pro-revolutionaries loosely associated with Sun Yat-sen, the Canton, and certain overseas branches of the Revive China Society, some supporters of K'ang Yu-wei, and an important secret society leader organized an unsuccessful revolutionary attempt in 1902 without Sun Yat-sen's advance knowledge. In Japan, new revolutionary societies formed by overseas Chinese students, while cooperating with Sun and the Revive China Society, soon outstripped the society in number of adherents and political importance.

In 1905 Sun and certain revolutionaries in Japan decided to join forces in one, unified organization called the T'ung-meng hui.* With the founding of the T'ung-meng hui, all branches of the Revive China Society were to turn themselves into T'ung-meng hui branches. There was some resistance to this call on the part of former Revive China Society local leaders and members, exacerbated by jealousy and suspicion within the leadership of the T'ung-meng hui itself. In the end, however, between 1905 and 1909, the Revive China Society disappeared into the T'ung-meng hui.

REFERENCES: L. Eve Armentrout Ma, *Revolutionaries, Monarchists and Chinatowns: Chinese Politics in the Americas and the 1911 Revolution* (Honolulu, 1990); Harold Z. Schiffrin, *Sun Yat-sen and the Origins of the Chinese Revolution* (Berkeley, Calif., 1968).

L. EVE ARMENTROUT MA

REVOLUTION OF 1911: Repulican Revolution that overthrew the imperial Ch'ing dynasty.

The Revolution of 1911 is also known as the Republican Revolution or the Wuchang Revolution of October 10, 1911, which overthrew the Manchu dynasty. The revolutionary movement may be roughly divided into three stages. The first stage (1894–1900) was marked by the founding of the Hsing-Chung hui (Revive China Society)* by Sun Yat-sen* in Honolulu in 1894 and then in Hong Kong in 1895. The movement in the second stage (1901–1905) had no unified organization and no single dominant figure. The most important groups in this period were Kuang-fu hui (the Recovery Society) and the Hua-hsing Hui (China Revival

Society)* founded by Huang Hsing* in Changsha, Hunan, in 1903. The establishment of the T'ung-meng hui* (Chinese United League) by Sun Yat-sen and Huang Hsing in Tokyo in 1905 was a milestone of the revolutionary movement. This third stage was marked by accelerated armed struggles led by Huang Hsing.

In many ways Sun and Huang were ideal collaborators. Sun was a Cantonese with connections abroad and ability, actual or potential, for raising funds. Huang, as a Hunanese of the literati class, belonged to the elite of the society. He had closer contacts with Chinese intellectuals and military circles than did Sun, and he was a leader among the Japan-educated Chinese students who were active in the revolutionary movement.

The revolutionary movement relied mainly on three groups: students, overseas Chinese, and the New Army.* Secret society members played a significant part in the early stage of the movement, but their role was a minor one after the successful infiltration of the revolutionaries in the New Army in 1910. Moreover, the elite of the society, as represented by the provincial reformers, also helped to hasten the collapse of the Manchu regime when many of them went over to the revolutionary side.

The 1911 Revolution was the culmination of many decades of growing discontent among the people. It was caused in part by the decay of Manchu rule, foreign aggression, and the interplay of internal and external forces. It succeeded in overthrowing the Manchu dynasty, and it established a republican form of government for the first time in China's history. However, it failed to establish a viable democratic political system. Sun Yat-sen, who held the provisional presidency for six weeks, stepped down in February 1912 in favor of Yüan Shih-k'ai,* the military strong man of the last empire. Party politics came to an end with the assassination of Sung Chiao-jen* in March 1913. This led to the Second Revolution* of that summer of the year. Yüan's attempt to become an emperor did not materialize. The so-called first phase of the revolution ended with his death in June 1916.

REFERENCES: Chün-tu Hsüeh, *Huang Hsing and the Chinese Revolution* (Stanford, Calif., 1961); Chün-tu Hsüeh, ed., *The Chinese Revolution of 1911: New Perspectives* (Hong Kong, 1986); Chün-tu Hsüeh, ed., *Revolutionary Leaders of Modern China* (New York, 1971), particularly Section II.

CHÜN-TU HSÜEH

REVOLUTIONARY COMMITTEES: Legacy of the Cultural Revolution originally established as temporary organs to replace the regular party structure dismantled by the Cultural Revolution; finally abolished in 1979 as a grass-roots administrative organization for local government.

There is no evidence to show that the revolutionary groups in the Cultural Revolution (1966–1976)* had a deliberate plan to provide some sort of temporary power structure after the seizure of power had taken place. It is even highly doubtful that a temporary power structure was a part of Chairman Mao's* grand design for the Cultural Revolution. The mere fact that there was no uniform term for the temporary power structures formed after the power seizures in

January 1967 demonstrates the spontaneous and confused state of development. The term *revolutionary committee* was first used by the Heilungkiang Provincial Red Rebel Revolutionary Committee for the "Three-in-One united power seizure." This new provisional power structure, which served as a model for all, was made up of representatives of three groups: (1) mass revolutionary rebel groups (Red Guards[*] and other rebel organizations of the peasants and workers); (2) military district command of the People's Liberation Army[*] (PLA) and militia; and (3) Maoist revolutionary cadres, including officials and bureaucrats from the former party and government administration who had repented or were acceptable to the PLA. Representatives of all three groups had to be included in order to organize any provisional revolutionary authority in provinces, cities, factories, commerce, and education. This "Three-way Alliance" was workable, according to Mao's radical supporters, because the masses trusted the PLA.

While the Central Cultural Revolution Group stressed that the revolutionary committees as "provisional organs of power" must have "proletarian authority" by accepting representatives of the mass organizations, the key element in the formation of the revolutionary committees was the PLA. The success in the formation of revolutionary committees was dependent on the military's active intervention on behalf of the Maoists in Peking. There were frequent confrontations between the military in power in the provinces and the central authority in Peking. Order was gradually restored in the provinces as new revolutionary committees, purged and cleansed of "revisionist" tendencies, were formed to operate as party committees. From 1969 to 1977 the revolutionary committees in the party, government units, factories, and schools acted as grass-roots organizations through which the masses could participate directly in making decisions. However, it became evident that, with the gradual reestablishment of the party structure in the early 1970s, many functions of the regular party were duplicated by the revolutionary committees. Then, when the Gang of Four[*] was arrested in the fall of 1976, the status of the revolutionary committees at the basic levels became unclear and confusing. At the Fifth National People's Congress (1978), it was decreed that the revolutionary committees were to become executive organs of the local people's congresses and "local organs of state administration." The local party committees were responsible only for decisions concerning the party's general line. But confusion remained as to the delineation of responsibilities of the revolutionary committees. A large part of the confusion stemmed from the appointment of individuals to hold concurrent chairmanship of both the party and revolutionary committees. The revolutionary committees, which could no longer meet the needs of socialist modernization, were finally abolished in June 1979 at the second session of the Fifth National People's Congress. This action removed one of the last vestiges of the Cultural Revolution.
REFERENCES: Parris H. Chang, "The Revolutionary Committee in China: Two Case Studies: Heilungkiang and Honan," *Current Scene* 6, no. 9 (June 1, 1968): 1–37; *The Cultural Revolution in the Provinces* (1971); Paul Hyer and William Heaton, "The

Cultural Revolution in Inner Mongolia,'' *The China Quarterly* 36 (October–December 1968): 114–128.

JAMES C.F. WANG

ROY, M. N. (Manabendra Nath, 1887–1954): Comintern agent to China in 1927.

In 1927 Roy was sent to China by the Comintern,[*] which in 1923 had promoted the First United Front[*] between the Kuomintang and the Chinese Communist party[*] in the Chinese National Revolution. Roy was born into a landed Brahmin family in Bengal, and his earliest political objective had been Indian independence from British rule and modernization. This objective stimulated his interest in communism and anti-imperialism. From his experience with promoting revolution against colonial rule in India, he became disillusioned with what he felt was an Indian middle class coopted by its British rulers into a conservative force. While fleeing an aborted coup against the British, Roy met Communist International agent Michael Borodin[*] in Mexico who convinced him that communism was the means to achieve broad-based revolutionary power via mass organizations. Borodin also gave Roy entry into the Comintern where he rose as a pioneer among Asian revolutionaries.

By 1920 Roy was the Indian representative at the Second Comintern Congress where he debated with Lenin over the reliability of any middle class among anti-imperialist revolutionary social elements in national liberation movements. Lenin saw such national revolutions in India and China as the means of isolating British capitalism from vital markets and raw materials. During Roy's years in Moscow with the Comintern, he tried to create an Indian Communist party. He came under the influence of Trotsky who idealized the potential of the proletariat and peasantry. Great political strength would come through their mobilization and organization for revolutionary struggle against capitalists and oppressive landlords, and against the foreign rule of imperialists.

Following his efforts to organize Indians against the British, the Comintern assigned Roy to China in 1927 to support the National Revolution that was underway. By that time, the Comintern had promoted and funded the CCP and its United Front with the nationalistic KMT as an indirect weapon against British and Japanese capitalism. Earlier, the policy from Moscow had pressured the CCP into accepting a subordinate role in the National Revolution under KMT leadership, which aimed at overthrowing both the rule of warlords internally and the domination of foreign imperialism from abroad. Whether the CCP should develop its own supportive base of unions and peasant associations for a social revolution, or channel its energies into a KMT-directed military campaign to reunite China became a source of conflict among CCP and KMT colleagues, as well as Comintern and Soviet advisers such as M. N. Roy and Michael Borodin. Upon his arrival in Wuhan, China, in February 1927, Roy found himself in an extremely complex situation where part of the United Front had already broken

away from Chiang Kai-shek[*] and his KMT allies at Nanking. In basic disagreement with Borodin who had Stalin's backing and funds to finance a temporary alliance of antiwarlord, anti-imperialist forces to gain immediate military
results, Roy fell back on Trotsky's theories on social revolution. He exemplified
a Comintern weakness in trying to apply universal theories of social revolution
to societies regardless of the current situation or cultural differences.

Concluding quickly that the flimsy unity at Wuhan would be strengthened by
armies of radicalized peasants, Roy rejected the approach of his former mentor,
Borodin, who had used finances to glue together a hodgepodge of ex-warlord
militarists, capitalistic KMT civilian opponents of Chiang Kai-shek, and Communist unions and peasant associations. Instead, Roy wanted to show the KMT
left that the Communist masses were a stronger, more committed shield and
weapon. When the contest, in May 1927, between Trotskyite Roy and Borodin
over how to deal with the threat of an anti-Communist coup by the local KMT
generals ended with Borodin's control of needed funds, Roy telegraphed Stalin
and the Comintern in desperation to order an agrarian revolution to check the
rightist allied militarists. When Stalin's telegram of June 1, 1927, backed Roy's
proposal for a CCP-led mass uprising, Borodin rejected it as ludicrous and
untimely since units of the Wuhan military were already using armed force to
suppress peasant land confiscation and punishment of landlords. As a last resort,
Roy showed Stalin's message to KMT leftist Wang Ching-wei.[*] Wang was
shocked by Stalin's order to the CCP to use its 20,000 cadres to steer 50,000
armed peasants and proletariat to take over the KMT leadership of the National
Revolution and the Northern Expedition.[*] Although the Wuhan KMT was already
backing away from the CCP and its agrarian revolution, Roy's action apparently
supplied the perfect justification for anti-Communist action. Thus, through its
efforts to guide the Chinese Revolution, the Comintern contributed to the breakup
of the United Front. By mid-July 1927 Roy had been sent back to Moscow, and
the violent split between the KMT and its former Communist colleagues was
complete, both in Wuhan and in Nanking. Thus, 1927 saw the end of the Soviet
Union's dominance since 1923 over the Chinese Revolution and the beginning
of a long phase of bloody competition between the KMT and CCP for total
control of China. Roy was made a scapegoat for the Comintern failure in China
and was purged by Stalin as a Trostkyite in the late 1920s. Roy dedicated his
energies to the problems of his native India until his death in 1954.

REFERENCES: *M. N. Roy's Memoirs* (1964); Robert C. North and Xenia J. Eudin,
M. N. Roy's Mission to China (1963); Chang Kuo-t'ao, *The Rise of the Chinese Communist
Party, 1921–27*, 2 vols. (Lawrence, 1971–72).

DONALD A. JORDAN

S

SAN-YÜAN-LI INCIDENT (May 29–31, 1841): Sino-British clash during the Opium War.

San-yüan-li was a village marketing center about 2.5 kilometers to the north of Canton, where on May 29–31, 1841, Chinese irregulars skirmished with British troops. Although only one foreign soldier was killed, the Chinese hail the incident as an important victory and the first strong expression of popular resistance to foreign imperialism.

After a lull in the fighting during the Opium War, the Tao-kuang emperor (r. 1821–1850) appointed his nephew, I-shan, as the new imperial commissioner in Kwangtung with orders to aggressively suppress the foreign barbarians. The British troops, under the command of Captain Charles Elliot, however, seized the initiative in the early part of 1841 to advance into the Pearl River and begin a siege of Canton. In March the British troops occupied the city's foreign factories and threatened to overrun the entire city.

The prefect of Canton, She Pao-shun, and the hong merchants (Chinese merchants dealing with foreign merchants) hastily offered to "ransom" the city with a payment of $6 million. On May 27, 1841, Elliot accepted and agreed to a truce on the following conditions: (1) payment of the $6 million to the British within one week; (2) withdrawal of Chinese troops to sixty miles outside of Canton within six days; (3) withdrawal of British forces from the Bogue in the Pearl River; (4) exchange of war prisoners; and (5) postponement of the cession question of Hong Kong.

In the meantime Major General Sir Hugh Gough's forces had occupied the hills just north of Canton, where they remained awaiting the final outcome of the negotiations. In this situation with British troops roaming the countryside, trouble was inevitable. There were reports that foreign soldiers had looted several homes, desecrated graves, and molested Chinese women. The most serious incident occurred on the morning of May 29, 1841, near the village of San-yüan-li. Several thousand angry peasants armed with pikes, knives, bamboo poles, and an occasional matchlock attacked a British patrol. By the next day the local gentry from a dozen nearby villages had assembled some 5,000 to 8,000 peasants into a militia under such banners as "Quell the British Corps" (p'ing-ying-t'uan). Although skirmishes continued throughout the day, by night General Gough reported that only one private had been killed and fifteen men wounded.

As news of the "victory" spread to other villages around Canton, by the following day (May 31) between 10,000 and 12,000 more villagers had gathered to fight the British. That morning General Gough, outraged that the Chinese had broken the truce, warned She Pao-shun that he would attack Canton. The prefect immediately went out to the scene of the incident to order the gentry leaders to disband their militia. The peasants dispersed, convinced that they could have defeated the barbarians had the officials not intervened.

Although the British viewed the incident only as a minor skirmish, the Chinese have seen it ever since as a great popular victory. Not long afterward the San-yüan-li Incident became a part of popular legend, a sort of Chinese "Bunker Hill," in which some 25,000 peasants had assembled and several hundred barbarian soldiers had been killed. Later Marxist historians have depicted the incident as the first sign of Chinese nationalism. The incident had politicized the people in both their hatred of foreigners and their distrust of the alien Manchu rulers. What began as a spontaneous mass movement against foreign imperialism ended in popular resentment against the Ch'ing officials who had capitulated and appeared to have sold out the country to the foreigners. Seen in this way, the San-yüan-li Incident was but the first in a long series of popular disturbances that eventually ended in the anti-Manchu nationalism that overthrew the Ch'ing dynasty* in the Revolution of 1911.*

REFERENCES: Frederic Wakeman, Jr., *Strangers at the Gate: Social Disorder in South China, 1839–1861* (Berkeley, Calif., 1966); Peter Ward Fay, *The Opium War, 1840–1842* (New York, 1976); Mou An-shih, *Ya-p'ien chan-cheng* (The Opium War) (Shanghai, 1982).

ROBERT J. ANTONY

SECOND REVOLUTION (July–September 1913): The military attempt to remove Yüan Shih-k'ai from the presidency of the Republic.

During the first year of the Chinese Republic, the T'ung-meng hui* was reorganized from a conspiratorial group into a legitimate political party named the Kuomintang, which scored a decisive majority in the parliamentary election that took place in the fall of 1912. Though nominally headed by old revolutionaries such as Sun Yat-sen* and Huang Hsing,* the Kuomintang in actuality came under the sway of Sung Chiao-jen,* a shrewd politician and able organizer who provided much direction and vision for this new and grand political alliance. Just as Sung was savoring the electoral triumph of his fledgling party and was getting ready to offer checks and balances to Yüan Shih-k'ai's* presidential power, he was shot down by an assassin at the Shanghai train station on March

20, 1913, and died two days later. The investigation into his assassination implicated Premier Chao Ping-chang, and even President Yüan himself. This created an uproar in the newly formed National Assembly, especially among some Kuomintang members who became convinced that only the removal of Yüan Shih-k'ai could guarantee true republicanism in China.

Meanwhile, the National Assembly was rocked by the discovery of irregularity with which Yüan floated a large foreign loan with a five-nation consortium in the amount of 25 million British pounds. The president had secured the loan without parliamentary debate and explicit approval. It was further believed that the loan was going to be used to further Yüan's private interests rather than the public good. This also caused great agitation in the Kuomintang-dominated legislature.

The Kuomintang was by no means the only voice in the National Assembly, nor was it united in its response. The other non-Kuomintang political parties had by now coalesced into another alliance under the name of the Progressive party, which consisted primarily of former constitutional monarchists who were far more tolerant of Yüan's excesses. They blocked every attempt in the National Assembly to remove or even censure Yüan. The Kuomintang itself was also plagued by disunity within. Some members advocated the use of legal maneuvers to chastise and impeach the president, while others, Sun Yat-sen included, opted to use military force to eliminate him.

The military option was unrealistic, however, and was doomed from the start. Many of the provincial military commanders (*tu-tu*) were either irresolute or incapable of rallying their troops to offer a real challenge to Yüan. Yüan had bought off some of them. Only Li Lieh-chün of Kiangsi was adamant and determined enough to oppose him militarily. Aware of this disunity within the Kuomintang and reassured by the support of the Progressive party as well as the foreign powers, not to mention the financial well-being brought about by the large loan, President Yüan decided that the time was right to launch a first strike against his opponents.

Using the pretext that Li Lieh-chün and two other *tu-tu* had disobeyed the central government by voicing their opposition to the great loan, he dismissed them in June 1913. He further prepared for war by dispatching his henchmen Tuan Ch'i-jui to lead the First Army and Feng Kuo-chang the Second Army to move against Kiukiang in Kiangsi and Nanking in Kiangsu, respectively. After some hesitancy, Li Lieh-chün responded by declaring Kiangsi's independence on July 12, and occupied the Hukow battery. His troops immediately clashed with Yüan's Peiyang Army at Kiukiang. Three days later, Huang Hsing succeeded in forcing Kiangsu's *tu-tu* Ch'eng Te-ch'üan to declare his support for Li in opposing Yüan. Other military commanders in Anhwei, Kwangtung, Fukien, Hunan, and Szechwan also voiced their support for the movement to oust Yüan. But the bulk of the fighting was concentrated in Kiangsi and Nanking.

The Hukow anti-Yüan forces were routed by the Peiyang Military Clique[*] from both land and water in less than two weeks. By August 18, even the provincial capital of Nanchang was lost to Yüan's army, who quickly took control of the entire province. In Nanking, Huang Hsing was double-crossed by Ch'eng Te-ch'üan, who escaped to Shanghai and rescinded his declaration of independence. But Huang fought on until July 29, when he was forced to flee Nanking. He was succeeded by Ho Hai-ming, a revolutionary colleague, who resisted the Peiyang troops' advance until Nanking's fall on September 1. In the meantime, skirmishes at Shanghai and Woosung also resulted in the defeat of the anti-Yüan forces, as did others in Anhwei, Kwangtung, Fukien, Hunan, and Chungking. Thus, the entire Yangtze River Valley, as well as southern China, came under the domination of Yüan's Peiyang Army. The Second Revolution collapsed less than two months after it was hastily and confusedly launched. In its aftermath, Yüan emerged as the uncontested ruler of China, with no legislature or military to keep him in check.

REFERENCES: Li Chien-nung, *The Political History of China, 1840–1928* (Stanford, Calif., 1956); Immanuel Hsü, *The Rise of Modern China* (New York, 1970).

RICHARD SHEK

SECOND UNITED FRONT (1937–1945): Second KMT–CCP collaboration, this time against Japan's invasion of China.

The Second United Front refers to the later of two periods of alliance between the Chinese Communist party[*] and Chiang Kai-shek's[*] Nationalists. It evolved in 1935 and 1936, crossed a watershed with the Sian Incident[*] (December 1936), and came into formal being with the Japanese invasion of China in July and August 1937. It continued through the Sino-Japanese War[*] until 1945, but all effective cooperation between the two parties had ended by 1940.

During this period, "united front" also became part of Mao Tse-tung's[*] revolutionary strategy, along with "armed struggle" and "party leadership." In theory, united front aimed to isolate the principal enemy of the moment; armed struggle was used to overcome that enemy; and party leadership ensured that a correct line would always be followed. This concept was thus much broader than the First United Front[*], which was limited exclusively to relations with the KMT. A second major difference is that during this period, the CCP had its own military force and territorial base, and it took care not to lose absolute control over these assets. In the 1920s the CCP was without these guarantees of independent existence.

After several years of ruthless conflict between the KMT and the CCP after 1927, rapprochement between these blood enemies seemed unthinkable, but by 1935–1936 important new influences were at work. (1) Japanese imperialism, which seemed to threaten China's very survival, accelerated the growth of Chinese nationalism, including the demand that all Chinese patriots join hands to protect the motherland. (2) Japanese collaboration with Germany and Italy led Stalin to urge the formation of antifascist united fronts in many countries (at the Seventh Comintern Congress, August 1935). Wishing to distract Japan, Stalin promoted Chiang Kai-shek as the leader of Chinese resistance and urged the CCP to follow suit. (3) The CCP was vulnerable following the Long March,* particularly if Nationalist agreements with Japan gave Chiang Kai-shek a free hand domestically. At the same time, the CCP could capitalize on nationalist fervor by calling for an end to civil war and unified resistance to Japan.

Mao Tse-tung and the CCP did not easily accept the directives of the Comintern to form a United Front with the KMT, and finally did so in mid–1936 more because of their own calculations than because of orders from Moscow. But it was one thing to call for a United Front, and quite another to get Chiang Kai-shek to accept it.

The Sian Incident (December 12–25, 1936) was the watershed that made the United Front possible. As a result of the kidnap of Chiang Kai-shek in Sian by Chang Hsüeh-liang,* the CCP agreed to end its efforts to overthrow the Nationalists and Chiang Kai-shek promised to end civil war. The United Front was formally announced after the Marco Polo Bridge Incident* in July 1937.

For the first couple of years of the war, CCP–KMT cooperation was better than many had expected, but by 1939 the Nationalists were seeking to restrict unauthorized Communist expansion in north and central China. The CCP charged in return that the Nationalists were impeding the war effort and avoiding resistance to the Japanese. In what amounted to a war within a war, the two forces frequently clashed, with sometimes the one and sometimes the other being the instigator. These clashes culminated in the New Fourth Army Incident* (January 1941), when Nationalist forces in southern Anhwei Province attacked and decimated the headquarters units of the New Fourth Army.

Neither side, however, wished to touch off full-scale civil war, and the level of direct violence declined thereafter. In this struggle, the CCP prevailed more often than did the Nationalists. From mid–1943 until the end of the war, the CCP progressively expanded its territories and populations.

The breakdown of KMT–CCP cooperation did not mark the end of the Second United Front, as many have thought. First, a major goal of the United Front was to prevent the Japanese and the Nationalists from making peace at the expense of the Communists, and this goal was achieved throughout the war. Second, the United Front was used in many social and political circumstances, for example, to enlist support from intellectuals, landlords, merchants, secret society leaders, and so on, through moderate reformist policies, as long as these elements fully accepted CCP leadership and supported its vision of the anti-Japanese war effort. This United Front did much to enlist support or encourage neutrality, in many settings, among those who might otherwise have opposed the CCP.

Long after the end of the Sino-Japanese War* in 1945 and the onset of civil war* with the Nationalists, the CCP continued to proclaim and to practice this broad United Front as a major element of its revolutionary strategy.

REFERENCES: John W. Garver, *Chinese-Soviet Relations, 1937–1945: The Diplomacy of Chinese Nationalism* (Oxford, 1988); Tetsuya Kataoka, *Resistance and Revolution in*

China: The Communists and the Second United Front (Berkeley, Calif., 1974); Lyman
P. Van Slyke, *Enemies and Friends: The United Front in Chinese Communist History*
(Stanford, Calif., 1968).

LYMAN P. VAN SLYKE

SELF-RELIANCE: One of the underlying moral themes of micro- and macro-
political economy during much of the Mao era.

The slogan "self-reliant regeneration" (*tzu-li keng-sheng*) was used to pop-
ularize a moral way of life free of heterodoxy and alien ideas. Mao Tse-tung*
is said to have invoked the notion as early as December 1935, but at that time
the concept was subordinated to the call for domestic and international alliances.
It was only in 1939, with the rupture of the KMT–CCP alliance, that the concept
began being applied strictly, and thereafter greater attention was paid to the
theoretical underpinnings. In 1945 during a discussion of how to overthrow the
KMT, Mao declared that the Communists' policies "should rest on our own
strength, and that means self-reliant regeneration. Although we are not alone,
and all the countries and people in the world opposed to imperialism are our
friends, we nevertheless stress regeneration through our own efforts. Relying on
the forces we ourselves organize, we can defeat all Chinese and foreign reactionaries." The general notion was popularized in the fable that Mao recounted,
"The Foolish Old Man Who Removed the Mountains." Similar themes were
occasionally repeated during the 1950s, but only during the Cultural Revolution*
did the term become ubiquitous. For example, in November 1969 the phrase
appeared in headlines in twenty-two out of thirty issues of the *People's Daily*,
often more than once in an issue. The "Little Red Book" (*Quotations from
Chairman Mao Tse-tung*)* contained a chapter devoted to the subject.

Self-reliance went out of favor in 1949, but in 1957 it was revived and would
remain the rationale for many domestic and foreign policies until the 1970s.
China looked inward, with the cities suspending their overseas connections and
reorienting themselves toward China's hinterland. This was the period of Sino-
Soviet estrangement, delegitimization of professional expertise, and decentralized economy. A difficulty such as shortage of raw materials was supposed to
constitute "a driving force" for efficiency and productivity. But in its extreme
form, the theory meant that units should try to get along even without integrating
horizontally, that is, without relying on other units or areas for inputs. There
was little pretense that efficiency and output would thereby be maximized; rather,
the advantages of autarky and diversification were seen as essentially social,
psychological, ecological, and political. Post–1958 Maoist economics was, in
effect, a self-declared victory of microeconomics over macroeconomics. In reality, when practiced on the lowest levels (villages, factories) the economic costs
were too high to be sustained. A better case could be made for self-sufficient
communes, and of course many provinces could be made reasonably self-sufficient. During the period of national isolation, Mao proved that China as a whole
could indeed get along without help from and trade with foreign countries.

Tzu-li keng-sheng was bolstered by related ideas, old and new. The term is redolent of the conservative Chinese idea of internally generated transformation, rejecting everything foreign except strictly for *yung* (utility, opposed to *t'i*, essence). The aspect of self-cultivation may hark back to Confucianism. *Tzu-li* also has Buddhist roots, being opposed to *t'a-li* (exogenous strength). *Keng-sheng* carries the sense of "achieving a new life," which is also related to the newer concepts such as *hsiu-yang* (nurturing), *fan-shen*, and "walking on two legs" (combining the traditional Chinese with the modern Western). Since China was unable to utilize the most modern means of development, it was seen as appropriate to rely in part on nonmodern methods. The backyard iron furnaces were an example, as was traditional Chinese medicine. Another example pertained to education; Mao's early ideas about education were spelled out in a speech of October 30, 1944. He favored a system that consisted of modern schools and also part-time institutions for workers, who might eventually go on to "red and expert colleges" (as distinguished from real universities for the better trained students). But in the 1960s "walking on two legs" in this sense fell afoul of Mao's ideal of egalitarianism.

In terms of international relations, self-reliance was a departure from the old tribute system and the more recent clientism. Now China was intent on getting along without strategic alliances, foreign aid, and commerce. In terms of economic relations, the theory had five components: reliance on China's own manpower resources (labor and intellectual skills), internal generation of capital rather than borrowing abroad, full utilization of domestic material resources, emphasis on experiences suited to Chinese conditions (avoidance of mimicking foreign experiences), and autarky. In military theory, it bolstered the concept of guerrilla tactics and "people's war." As for China's relations with the Third World, the theory permitted China to provide only moral support to revolutionary movements, advising that they were best off eschewing foreign material support (which China was in no position to provide).

Although there was little obvious opposition to the policy of self-reliance, there was much foot-dragging. "There are a few units," the party journal noted in 1970, "which look passively to higher authorities for supplies. This kind of thinking should be overcome." Later ideological pragmatists (or at any rate opportunists) declared that Mao went overboard here and that unreasonable demands had been placed on the localities. For example, Hu Ch'iao-mu[*] blamed China's slow technical progress on the practice of self-reliance. "Many enterprises," he complained in 1978, "have been established as make-everything-you-need concerns."

Although scholars have debated the point, Mao's adherence to self-reliance is probably to be explained less by its philosophic roots than by the isolated situation in which the Chinese Communists so often found themselves during the Yenan period, after the break with the West in 1949, and especially after the Sino-Soviet schism. Thus, self-reliance had its *faute de mieux* quality. Although doubtless Mao genuinely believed in its moral superiority, it was also a convenient philosophy when the world was not interested in helping China anyway. Thus, part of its virtue was necessity. This was certainly true after the 1989 crackdown, when China's isolated leaders once again reemphasized self-reliance.

REFERENCES: James D. Seymour, *China: The Politics of Revolutionary Reintegration* (New York, 1976); Edgar Snow, *The Other Side of the River: Red China Today* (New York, 1961); Carl Riskin, *China's Political Economy: The Quest for Development since 1949* (New York, 1987).

JAMES D. SEYMOUR

SELF-STRENGTHENING MOVEMENT (1861–1894): China's early modernization.

The idea of the Self-Strengthening Movement originated partly from Chinese thought on statecraft (*ching-shih*). However, late Ch'ing* statecraft thought aimed at developing the "wealth and power" (*fu-ch'iang*) of the Chinese (or Ch'ing) state following Western challenges and the Taiping Uprising.* Beginning in the early 1860s, the phrase "self-strengthening" (*tzu-ch'iang*) was frequently used in memorials, edicts, and the private writings of scholar-officials. Feng Kuei-fen's *Chiao-pin-lu k'ang-i* (Protests from the Chiao-pin Studio) was among the best known of such writings.

The 1861 coup d'état, planned by Prince Kung (I-hsin, 1833–1898) and the Empress Dowager Tz'u-hsi* (1835–1908), allowed greater flexibility in government policies during the T'ung-chih reign (1862–1874) and the early years of the Kuang-hsü* (1875–1908) period. A number of senior ministers and provincial leaders, including Wen-hsiang, Tseng Kuo-fan,* Li Hung-chang,* Tso Tsung-t'ang,* and Ting Jih-ch'ang advocated a series of proposals for self-strengthening, including the establishment of the Tsungli Yamen in March 1861 to handle diplomatic affairs, an Interpreters' College (T'ung-wen kuan) in Peking in 1862, arsenals and shipyards, as well as schools for Western learning. A small number of Chinese students were sent to the United States, England, and France to study Western technology. Meanwhile, state-sponsored enterprises were organized for the steamship, coal and iron mining, textile manufacturing, and the telegraph. All such modern enterprises as well as the handling of diplomatic matters were also referred to as "Western affairs" (*yang-wu*).

In the first phase of the Self-Strengthening Movement during 1865–1872, such regional officials as Li Hung-chang, through their Chinese and foreign advisers, attempted to extend the logistical mobilization in the Taiping war. Revenues acquired during the anti-Taiping campaigns were used to buy Western weapons. The most important undertakings of this period were the Kiangnan Arsenal in Shanghai, the Foochow Navy Yard, and the Tientsin Arsenal.

The second stage of the Self-Strengthening Movement (1872–1894) saw the development of a wide range of undertakings under the formula of *kuan-tu shang-pan* (official supervision and merchant operation). Li Hung-chang, the principal innovator, hoped to solve both problems of capital and management by "recruiting merchants" (*chao-shang*). Such modern enterprises involving the use of Western machinery included the China Merchants' Steam Navigation Company (Lun-ch'uan chao-shang chü). Although such projects remained under government supervision, profit and loss were to be "entirely the responsibility of the merchants." Capital in joint stock form was to be owned by the merchants, and the company was to be administered according its own rules and regulations. The model of the China Merchants' Steam Navigation Company was followed by other government-sponsored enterprises: coal mining (the Hupei Coal Mining Company, 1875, and the Kaiping Mining Company, 1877), textiles (the Shanghai Cotton Cloth Mill, 1878), the telegraph (Tientsin-Shanghai line, 1881), the railroad (thirteen miles at Kaiping Mines, 1882), and iron and steel (Hanyang Ironworks, 1896). The last project was sponsored by Chang Chih-tung. Another major innovation of the Self-Strengthening Movement in the 1870s and 1880s was the establishment of the Peiyang Navy by Li Hung-chang.

Although China established some modern enterprises as early as 1872, most scholars still claim that there was no fundamental change in China's national economy and that the self-strengthening reform was never put into effect on a national scale. But the key problems of the movement were also fiscal and political. First, the taxes collected at the time were not sufficient to launch the modernization programs effectively. Second, the reform itself was influenced by vested economic or bureaucratic interests and other institutional, social, and ideological factors. The comparative failure of the modernization effort should be attributed mainly to the fact that the Chinese state did not relinquish its control when the industries were ready to stand on their own. This is in contrast to Meiji Japan, whose government collected all it could from the farmers to pay for its initial industrialization efforts, and then decided to let independent entrepreneurs run the industries after the government had built a foundation for these industries.

The importance of the Self-Strengthening Movement lies in its contribution to the beginnings of China's modernization, inspired by a search for wealth and power.

REFERENCES: Albert Feuerwerker, *China's Early Industrialization: Sheng Hsüan-huai, 1844–1916 and Mandarin Enterprise* (Cambridge, Mass., 1958); Chi-kong Lai, "Tzu-ch'iang yun-tung"(Recent historiography on the Self-Strengthening Movement) *Studies of Modern Chinese History*, vol. 2 (Taipei, 1989): 691–718; Kwang-Ching Liu, "The Ch'ing Restoration," in John K. Fairbank, ed., *The Cambridge History of China*, vol. 10, *Late Ch'ing, 1800–1911, Part 1* (Cambridge, 1978): 409–490; Kwang-Ching Liu and Ting-yee Kuo, "Self-Strengthening: The Pursuit of Western Technology," in ibid: 491–542; *Proceedings of the Conference on the Late Ch'ing Self Strengthening Movement* (Taipei, 1988).

CHI-KONG LAI

SERVICE, JOHN STUART (b. August 3, 1909–   ): Foreign Service officer; author.

John Stuart Service was born in Chengtu, Szechwan. His parents, Robert and Grace Service, were missionaries, and his early education was in China. At fifteen he traveled for the first time to the United States, graduating several years later from Berkeley High School in California.

Service graduated from Oberlin College in 1931 with a major in economics and art history. In 1933 he passed the Foreign Service examination, after which he returned to China to a clerkship in the U.S. Consulate at Kunming. In the fall of 1935 Service received a commission as a Foreign Service officer and moved to Peking as a language attaché.

Before being transfered to Shanghai in 1938, Service became fluent in Chinese and deepened his knowledge of Chinese history, law, and economics. In 1941 he was again transferred, this time to Chungking as the Embassy's third secretary. Within a month of the transfer, Clarence A. Gauss was appointed ambassador. Gauss summed up his opinion of Service before the State Department Loyalty Security Board in 1950: "He was outstanding. I don't know of any officer in my whole thirty-nine years of service who impressed me more favorably than Jack Service. . . . We had constantly before us as to what was going on in China and he did a magnificent job at it." In part, Service's knowledge was due to travel and observation beyond the wartime capital. He spent half of his time in the field, going to central Szechwan, the northeast, the Indochina border, Burma, and Yenan.

After August 1943 Service was attached to the staff of the commander general of the China–Burma–India theater. In this capacity he made two fateful trips to Yenan as part of the U.S. Army Observer Mission (Dixie Mission)[*]. Service went to Yenan with the initial group that left on July 22, 1944, under the leadership of Colonel David D. Barrett.

Service's experience in Yenan and his past observations regarding the Nationalists led him to argue for a realistic appraisal of China and a practical policy based on that assessment. Many of his reports contained vivid descriptions of life in Yenan and provided a stark contrast with reports of life under the Nationalists. He also reported his observations about the relationship between political conditions, popular support, and military success. On August 23 Mao Tse-tung[*] met with Service for eight hours. The interview was wide ranging, covering the Chinese Communist party[*], the Kuomintang, and U.S. activity in China. Mao exhorted Service to understand that the KMT would launch a civil war in China unless the United States acted to prevent it. Mao also stressed that conflict between the United States and the CCP was not inevitable; in fact, he told Service, the United States was the only country suited to aid in China's development.

On February 28, 1945, the counselor of the American Embassy sent a telegram to the State Department. Although this telegram was signed by every political officer of the embassy, Service initially drafted it. The officers recommended that "the President inform the Generalissimo in definite terms that military necessity requires that we supply and cooperate with the Communists . . . [through] such policy . . . we could expect to hold the Communists to our side rather than throw them into the arms of Russia."

When Patrick Jay Hurley* discovered the telegram he was livid, vowing to John Carter Vincent that "I know who drafted the telegram. Service! I'll get that son of a bitch if its the last thing I do." On March 30, 1945, Hurley ordered Service to return to the United States. Service would not return to China until 1971.

From April 1945 until he was exonerated by the U.S. Supreme Court in 1957, Service faced constant challenge to his loyalty. Critics, full of vitriol and riding a wave of mendacity that crested with Joseph McCarthy, falsely accused Service of disloyalty, of contributing to America's "failure" in China, and of being friendly with "suspected Communists." The years of harassment began with the "*Amerasia* Affair." On June 6, 1945 the New York office of the leftist Asian affairs journal, *Amerasia*, was raided by the FBI. Service was arrested on espionage charges for passing classified documents to *Amerasia* magazine. Subsequently cleared by a grand jury and a State Department review, Service faced loyalty and security hearings in 1946, 1947, 1949, 1950, and 1951. All investigations attested to his loyalty. But in December 1951 the Civil Service Review Board reversed the State Department's Loyalty Security Board's favorable reviews of Service. That same day Secretary of State Dean Acheson dismissed him.

After his dismissal, Service worked in New York for a steam engineering firm, fighting for a reversal of the unfavorable decision. In 1957 the Supreme Court ruled in his favor in the case, *Service* v. *Dulles*. Soon after, he returned to active duty in the Foreign Service, retiring in 1962. He settled in Berkeley, California where he obtained an M.A. from the University of California; subsequently, he took a position with the Center for Chinese Studies.

REFERENCES: Joseph Esherick, *Lost Chance in China: The World War II Dispatches of John S. Service* (New York, 1974); E. J. Kahn, Jr., *The China Hands: America's Foreign Service Officers and What Befell Them* (New York, 1975); John S. Service, *The Amerasia Papers: Some Problems in the History of U.S.–China Relations* (Berkeley, Calif., 1971).

EDWIN CLAUSEN

SHANGHAI COMMUNIQUE (1972): The first official joint statement for normalizing relations between the United States and the PRC.

President Richard Nixon visited the People's Republic of China* on February 21–28, 1972, at the invitation of Premier Chou En-lai.* Nixon met Chairman Mao Tse-tung* in the afternoon of February 21 in Peking, and the two leaders had a serious and frank exchange of views on Sino–U.S. relations and world affairs.

Nixon's visit heralded a new stage in American–East Asian relations after a period of intense U.S.–PRC hostility from 1949 to 1971. On February 27, the day before his departure, the two sides agreed on a joint communique, signed by the two heads of state. The joint communique signaled the American recognition of a Communist government in China.

Why is the communique called the Shanghai Communique instead of the

Peking Communique? Before the president's visit, both governments had agreed that if discussions went on smoothly, they should announce a communique to record this historical event. Officials from different levels of the two governments had held intensive discussions about the contents of the communique but they could not reach a mutual agreement until the very last moment when Nixon was in Shanghai and ready to go home.

The opening paragraph of the communique notes the benefits to be derived from direct contact between the two nations and admits that some important differences could not be resolved at that time. The most noticeable differences between the two sides related to Taiwan and issues concerning the Sino–Soviet–American triangular relationship.

The paragraph dealing with Taiwan is a masterpiece of ambiguity, deliberately designed to permit both the United States and the PRC to enter into a new relationship without compromising their differences over the status of Taiwan. Every word of the paragraph was carefully chosen to give away no more than what was necessary to achieve the purpose of opening up direct relations between the two nations.

To establish a stable balance of power, the two sides stated that neither should seek hegemony in the Asia-Pacific region and each opposed the efforts by any other country or group of countries to establish such hegemony.

Normalizing U.S. and PRC relations required the passing of seventeen years of difficult times for both parties before the signing of the Shanghai Communique. Beginning in the 1950s, numerous ambassador-level meetings between both sides had been held in Geneva and Warsaw. In 1971 American table tennis players were invited to visit China, and the so-called round of Ping Pong diplomacy began. In July 1971 Secretary of State Henry Kissinger secretly visited the PRC. In February 1972 President Nixon visited China and announced the breakthrough Shanghai Communique. In 1973 liaison offices were established in both capitals. George Bush also served as the U.S. delegate to Peking. On December 16, 1978, both governments announced that they would establish a normal diplomatic relationship as of January 1, 1979.

REFERENCES: *Hsin-hua Monthly* (February 1972): 19–31; *Jen-min jih-pao* (*People's Daily*), February 28, 1972; Yu-ming Shaw, *ROC–U.S. Relations: A Decade after the "Shanghai Communique"* (Taipei, 1983).

                                                                    RAMON H. MYERS

SHEN-KAN-NING BORDER REGION: The major Communist rural soviet in northwest China covering portions of Shensi, Kansu, and Ninghsia provinces and the seat of the CCP's central governing bodies from October 1935 to March 1947. Famous for its capital, Yenan, and the social and military policies codified there under Mao Tse-tung.

At the conclusion of the Long March* in October 1935, the Red Army and the Central Committee settled in northern Shensi Province. There it revived and expanded the previously small Shen-Kan Revolutionary Base Area, settling a dispute among local Communists and freeing the independent-minded Liu Chih-tan from prison. Mao Tse-tung's* forces soon extended Communist control into the neighboring provinces of Kansu and Ninghsia. Chinese Communist party* leadership was seriously divided between Mao Tse-tung and Chang Kuo-t'ao,* and the Nationalist forces missed an opportunity to destroy the Communist forces during the ensuing struggle that ended in Mao's favor. The CCP first called the area the Northwest Bureau of the Central Soviet Government but soon changed the name to the Shen-Kan-Ning Revolutionary Base Area. The capital was moved south from Pao-an to Yenan in January 1937. Following the resumption of United Front policies with the KMT, the area was recognized by the Nationalist government and changed its name on September 6, 1937, to the Shen-Kan-Ning Border Region. The base area received financial support from the Nationalist government during the late 1930s, but as relations worsened this support was cut off and the base area faced severe economic hardship. The Central Committee occupied the area until March 1947 during the civil war* when they abandoned it in the face of advancing Nationalist troops; it never returned. The border region government was officially disbanded in January 1950.

The Shen-Kan-Ning Border Region became a model of the party's social, economic, military, and ideological programs. These are also associated with the Yenan Period*. Social and economic programs were drawn from the experience of the neighboring Chin-Ch'a-Chi Border Region* and especially the 1941 report by P'eng Chen* on that border region's experiences. With the growing glorification of Mao, the Chin-Ch'a-Chi's experience was not publicized, and its policies were adapted and propagandized as the product of Shen-Kan-Ning. The result was a series of highly practical reforms organized as mobilization campaigns or movements (*yün-tung*): the movement for crack troops and simple administration, the strengthening of party leadership in local administration ("dual rule"), the "To the Village" transfer of cadres, the "three-thirds" organization of local government (limiting CCP cadres to one-third of official positions), rent reduction (as opposed to land confiscation), the cooperative movement among farmers, and the 1943 production movement which stressed efforts by military and government units to achieve self-sufficiency by growing their own food. These policies were highlighted by propaganda on "labor heroes" exemplifying their goals. One of the most famous models was the military brigade at Nan-ni-wan. These policies helped relieve the economic pressure of a renewed KMT blockade in the 1940s and strengthened the Communist administration. Mao would harken back to these policies in the Great Leap Forward* in 1958 and later.

While Shen-Kan-Ning absorbed social policy from other areas, it was the seat of military orthodoxy through the Resistance University (K'ang-ta). K'ang-ta served more successfully than its predecessor, the Whampoa Military Academy* in Canton in the 1920s, in unifying the military under civilian control and in enforcing a consistent military policy. Founded in 1936, K'ang-ta expanded to fifteen branches and trained some 10,000 cadres a year. Its dean was Lin Piao,* and its deputy dean was Lo Jui-ch'ing. In 1937 it was moved to Yenan where in May 1938 Mao expounded his ideas "On Protracted War." Between 1939 and 1943 the university was moved out of Yenan and into various branches throughout the CCP's north China base areas. After 1945 it became the Political and Military Institute of the People's Liberation Army.*

The core of the ideological success of Shen-Kan-Ning was the 1942–1944 Rectification Campaign.* This was an extended study movement aimed at unifying thought among CCP cadres. It trumpeted Mao Tse-tung's "Sinification of Marxism" and provided effective and (for cadres with little education) simple rules of behavior under the rubric of democratic centralism.* Rectification is widely credited with providing the unity, discipline, and morale that contributed to CCP success later in the 1940s. Rectification also had a troubling dark side that returned to haunt the Communists after 1949. The campaign included harsh and unreasonable attacks on intellectuals, as laid down by Mao in his famous "Talks at the Yenan Forum on Art and Literature." It also led to a virtual witch-hunt for spies in the 1943–1944 "rescue movement" (now blamed rather simplistically on K'ang Sheng). Finally, the deification of Mao as supreme leader and font of orthodoxy directly contributed to the party's inability to control him in later years.

REFERENCES: Mark Selden, *The Yenan Way in Revolutionary China* (Cambridge, Mass., 1971); Frederick C. Teiwes, *Politics and Purges in China: Rectification and the Decline of Party Norms, 1950–65* (White Plains, N.Y., 1979); *Shen-Kan-Ning pien-ch'ü ta-shih chi* (Chronology of major events in the Shen-Kan-Ning Border Region) (Sian, 1986); *Shen-Kan-Ning pien-ch'ü cheng-fu wen-chien hsüan-pien* (Selected documents from the Shen-Kan-Ning government) (Peking, 1982).

TIMOTHY CHEEK

SHIH TA-K'AI (1831–1863): Military commander and leader of the Taiping Revolution.

Shih Ta-k'ai was born into a wealthy Hakka peasant family in Na-pang Village, Kuei-p'ing County, Kwangsi. His family had moved from Ho-p'ing County, Kwangtung.

Shih was one of the best educated leaders of the Taiping Revolution.* Before the age of twenty, he had already acquired a reputation for extraordinary talent in both civil and military affairs. He took the civil service examination in an attempt to enter the scholar class. However, like Hung Hsiu-ch'üan,* he failed. Thereafter he joined his older brothers in the management of the family business and estate.

In 1849, following an ethnic clash in which the Hakkas were routed by the natives, Shih led his clan to join the God Worshippers* and thereby obtain protection. At this stage, Shih donated all his wealth, an estimated 100,000 *taels* of silver, to the common military fund, and also convinced thousands of people to join the rebellion.

On January 1, 1851, Shih participated in the Taiping Revolutionary Movement, and the Heavenly King, Hung Hsiu-ch'üan, appointed him "commander" (*chu-chiang*) of the Right Army Corps. In September 1851 the Taipings occupied their first walled city, Yung-an chou. Hung declared the founding of the *T'ai-ping t'ien-kuo* and bestowed on Shih the title of assistant king (*I Wang*) on December 17, 1851.

At first, the Westerners supported this apparently Western and Christian movement. Sir Samuel George Bonham, governor of Hong Kong and the highest British representative in China from 1848 to 1854, was the first foreign visitor to the Taiping territory. In conversations on May 11, 1853, with Shih and the North King, Wei Ch'ang-hui,* they discussed such issues as religious beliefs and Taiping foreign policies. Seeking an alliance with the British government, Shih and Wei emphasized that the Taiping people and the British worshiped the same God. Bonham notified the two kings that the British government intended to remain perfectly neutral during the Taiping Revolution.*

In September 1853 Shih went to An-ch'ing to take over the command of the Western Expedition from Hu I-huang, assuming responsibility for the Western provinces along the Yangtze River—Anhwei, Kiangsi, Hupeh, Hunan, and Szechwan. Shih ruled his subjects with justice and treated them with consideration, winning widespread popular support. In An-ch'ing, robbers were brought under control, and peace and order were restored. Shih also enjoyed a brilliant reputation in military affairs. He was never defeated in battle, and once he even captured Tseng Kuo-fan's* flagship on the occasion when he retook Wuchang in 1855.

But the bloody struggle within the Taiping leadership in 1856 evolved into a disaster for the Taiping Movement. Growing conflict between the Heavenly King and the East King, Yang Hsiu-ch'ing,* resulted in Yang's assassination by Wei Ch'ang-hui, who later also murdered Shih's mother, wife, and many of his relatives. Returning to Nanking to deal with Wei, Shih finally received Wei's head from Hung Hsiu-ch'üan.

Shih Ta-k'ai stayed at the Taiping capital from the end of November 1856 to the end of May 1857. Originally, Shih was the Assistant King. The Heavenly King announced Shih's promotion from Assistant King to Righteous King, but Shih was unwilling to accept it. In fact, Shih and the Heavenly King distrusted each other. Although Shih became the full commander of the whole Taiping Army, Shih was dissatisfied with court politics at the capital. When Shih found himself under increasing suspicion by the Heavenly King and his two brothers, Hung Jen-fa and Hung Jen-ta, he left Nanking in June 1857 with an enormous number of followers, said to number 200,000 soldiers. Shih left An-ch'ing and proclaimed that he would continue an independent campaign in Szechuan. When Tseng Kuo-fan learned of Shih's departure, he invited Shih to join the Ch'ing government, but Shih refused to surrender. Shih made his way through Kiangsi, Chekiang, Fukien, and Hunan. However, after reaching Kwangsi in the autumn of 1859, Shih's force began to collapse. In early 1862 he finally arrived in Szechwan.

After extensive campaigning with a large army, cut off from the Taiping government, Shih was captured by Lo Ping-chang, governor-general of Szechwan on June 13, 1863, and executed as a traitor on August 6, 1863.

Shih Ta-k'ai has been recognized as the best leader of the Taiping Movement based on his administrative virtues and unquestioned military genius. He was obviously an able military leader, and his break with the Heavenly King was a crucial setback to the Taiping Movement.

REFERENCES: C. A. Curwen, *Taiping Rebel: The Deposition of Li Hsiu-ch'eng* (Cambridge, 1977); Ssu-yu Teng, "Shih Ta-k'ai," in Arthur W. Hummel, ed., *Eminent Chinese of the Ch'ing Period* (Washington, D.C., 1943): 655–658; *Shih Ta-k'ai lun-chi* (Essays on Shih Ta-k'ai) (Szechwan, 1983).

CHI-KONG LAI

SIAN INCIDENT (1936): Kidnap of President Chiang Kai-shek by the Manchurian Army.

The Tungpei (Northeastern) Army led by Young Marshal Chang Hsüeh-liang* was driven out of the northeast (Manchuria) by the Japanese who engineered the September 18 Incident in 1931. By 1936, however, the Tungpei Army with about 200,000 strong was still a force to be reckoned with, when it was dispatched to the northwest to fight the Red Army which had just completed its 6,000-mile Long March* from Kiangsi and settled in northern Shensi in October 1935. Despite its initial victory over the Tungpei Army, the Red Army and the newly established Soviet base remained far from secure; constantly threatening were the ongoing Kuomintang campaigns of Encirclement and Suppression* and the hostile natural environment. Above all, the Communists faced Chiang Kai-shek's* determination to eradicate them, which was the core of his policy of "internal pacification before resistance against external aggression" (*an-nei jang-wai*).

The young marshal had always hated civil war, especially since experiencing his personal tragedy; his father was murdered by the Japanese, and he himself was driven out of the northeast. Chang's primary concern was how to fight the Japanese and recover his homeland. Having found Chiang's policy increasingly repugnant, Chang sought to make contact with the Chinese Communist party.* By December 1935 the CCP adopted the resolution to implement the anti-Japanese United Front policy formulated by the Seventh Congress of the Comintern* at Moscow in August 1935. By February 1936 Chang was successful in making contact with the CCP, and about the same time General Yang Hu-cheng, leader of the Hsipei (Northwest) Army, who had a long history of association with the CCP and as late as 1933 reached a secret agreement with the Fourth Front Red Army in northern Szechwan, accepted the CCP overture for a truce. What was left to be done was to smooth the strained relations between the host Hsipei Army and the guest Tungpei Army, which was readily achieved so as to make possible the formation of a triune alliance between the Tungpei and Hsipei Armies and the Red Army. In early April 1936 Chang had a conference with Chou En-lai* at Yenan which cemented the alliance. On Chang's insistence, the CCP changed its United Front policy from opposing Chiang to allying with and supporting him, which also paved the way for the CCP to appeal directly to Chiang to suspend the civil war and form a United Front against Japan.

Ironically, Chiang Kai-shek secretly instructed his right-hand man, Ch'en Li-fu, to negotiate with the CCP, and some progress had been made. Such movement could not have escaped the attention of the Young Marshal, because the CCP emissary had to obtain permission from him to travel back and forth between his zone and the Soviet area. The first fruit of Chang's alliance with the CCP was to rejuvenate his Tungpei Army by establishing an officers' training school in June 1936, to which he gave the revolutionary ideology that "The Only Future of China Is Resistance against Japan." On the one hand, he openly protected the student movement and lent his support to the national salvation movement, thereby transforming Sian into the center of the anti-Japanese United Front. On the other hand, to solidify the anti-Japanese base in the northwest, he twice visited the Soviet ambassador in Shanghai to seek Soviet support and sent representatives to Sinkiang to approach Sheng Shih-ts'ai for cooperation.

Unless Chiang accepted Chang and Yang's appeal to suspend the civil war and form a United Front against Japan, there really was no way of return. That the plot against Chiang was hatched by Yang as suggested by Chang himself was not so crucial, for Chang may have thought of taking drastic action against Chiang following the celebration of Chiang's birthday at Loyang. Even though Chiang was aware of the situation in Sian, he went there in early December 1936 for a high-level military conference. At the meeting he laid down his plan for what he thought would be the delivery of a coup de grace to the Red Army, and he drastically reshuffled his military commands in preparation for the "final campaign," including the appointment of Chiang Ting-wen to replace the Young Marshal and the transfer of the Tungpei Army to the east. Unexpectedly, on the eve of his departure from Sian, Chiang was seized and put under house arrest by Chang and Yang, who presented eight demands:

1. Reorganize the Nanking government,* and admit all parties to share the joint responsibility of saving the nation.

2. Stop all kinds of civil war.

3. Immediately release the patriotic leaders arrested in Shanghai.

4. Release all political prisoners throughout the country.

5. Emancipate the patriotic movement of the people.

6. Actually carry out the will of Dr. Sun Yat-sen.*

7. Safeguard the political freedom of the people to organize and call meetings.

8. Immediately call a national salvation conference.

The Nanking leaders were divided over the issue of how to save Chiang and resolve the Sian Incident; as a result, the "carrot and stick" policy was unconsciously employed. In recounting the negotiations, Madame Chiang Kai-shek had the following comment: "Mr. [W. H.] Donald [an adviser] had laid the foundation, T. V. [Soong]* had built the walls, and it would be I who would have to put up the roof.'' Undoubtedly, personal diplomacy played an important role in releasing Chiang, especially his being escorted by Chang back to Nanking, an act that to this day is generally believed to have cost him his freedom.

The CCP had no foreknowledge of the incident, nor did it play a decisive role in the decision to release Chiang. Nevertheless, Chou En-lai did mitigate opposition to the release by persuading Yang Hu-cheng to accept it without a written pledge from Chiang.

No sooner had the news of Chang's detention at Nanking become known at Sian than his return became such an intractable issue that it split the ranks of both the Tungpei and the Hsipei armies. With the issue of war with Nanking hanging in the balance, the radicals staged the February 2 coup to force the big generals to declare war on Nanking, in which General Wang I-che was killed. The coup caused the collapse of unity within the Tungpei Army and shattered the three-army alliance. More importantly, Chiang saw no need to release the Young Marshal in order to avert a war with Sian.

REFERENCES: Tien-wei Wu, *The Sian Incident: A Pivotal Point in Modern Chinese History* (Ann Arbor, Mich., 1976); James Bertram, *Crisis in China* (New York, 1937); Tien-wei Wu, "New Materials on the Xi'an Incident," *Modern China* 10, no. 1 (January 1984); *Sian shih-pien ch'in-li chi* (A collection of eyewitness accounts of the Sian Incident) (Peking, 1986).

TIEN-WEI WU

SINO-JAPANESE WAR (1894–1895): A war between China and Japan over the control of Korea which broke out on July 24, 1894, but was officially declared on August 1, 1894, and ended on April 17, 1895, with the signing of the Treaty of Shimonoseki.

After the Meiji Restoration (1868) Japan engaged vigorously in modernization programs under the leadership of such capable leaders as Itō Hirobumi and Yamagata Aritomo. The success of the Meiji modernization not only brought economic prosperity by the 1880s, but also made Japan a viable military power in East Asia. In order to test its new rise in military strength, Japan tried to exert its influence on Korea, the closest Asian mainland to Japan.

The Treaty of Kanghwa (1876), resulting from Japan's protection of Japanese fishermen in the Pusan area of Korea, was the first Japanese attempt to impose its new military strength on China. The treaty unilaterally declared Korea's "independence" from China. In the 1880s Russia, Italy, Germany, Great Britain, and the United States also signed separate treaties with Korea. In 1882 General Yüan Shih-k'ai,* appointed China's resident governor-general in Seoul by Li Hung-chang,* arrived in Korea with 3,000 reinforcement troops to try and avert the deteriorating situation there. In December 1882 an antigovernment riot broke out, led by Korean radical Kim Ok-kyun and supported by Japan. Responding to an appeal for help from Korea's Queen Min, Yüan Shih-k'ai fired on Korean rioters as well as Japanese troops in Seoul. Conflicts between China and Japan over Korea were now out in the open. A similar incident occurred in 1884, which was settled on April 18, 1885, by Li Hung-chang and Itō Hirobumi in the Treaty of Tientsin by officially recognizing Japan as China's equal in Korea. It also stated that in the event of any future problems there, China and Japan would have to consult each other before taking any action. Unhappy with this capitulation to Japan, the Chinese public severely criticized Li Hung-chang for signing the treaty. As far as Japan was concerned, however, the treaty only whetted its appetite for more, and the country began to press for total control over Korea. Japan also feared that the other European powers might try to exert their own power in Korea, thus threatening Japan's security in East Asia.

Utilizing a domestic uprising in Korea in the spring of 1893 (the Tonghak Rebellion), Japan sent troops to Korea immediately after China had done so. Although the rebellion was soon suppressed, Japan refused to withdraw its troops from Korea. Itō Hirobumi and Japanese Foreign Minister Mutsu Munemitsu seized this opportunity to challenge China. On July 24, 1894, Japan opened fire and sank a chartered ship carrying Chinese troops to Korea in the Chihli Sea. On August 1, 1894, Japan, in full control of the situation, declared war on China.

The ensuing battles between China and Japan humiliated China completely. Japan destroyed China's entire Northern Fleet at Weihaiwei on February 12, 1895, forcing China to ask for a settlement. Before the negotiations, Japan demanded that only Li Hung-chang be allowed to represent China and that he be granted "credentials to cede territory" by the Ch'ing court. China had no choice but to concede to these demands. Li was dispatched to Shimonoseki in March 1895 to negotiate for a settlement treaty. Negotiations dragged on for weeks without any result until Li was shot and wounded on March 24 by a Japanese fanatic. Only then did Japan soften its demands somewhat. Key provisions of the treaty included (1) the independence of Korea; (2) the cession of Taiwan, the Pescadores, and the Liaotung Peninsula to Japan; and (3) the payment of an indemnity of 300 million *taels* to Japan. However, on April 23, 1895, Russia, in a joint letter co-signed by France and Germany, "advised" Japan to drop its demand for China's Liaotung Peninsula, which Russia also had its eye on. Facing pressure from these three powerful European powers, Japan had no choice but to accept their "advice" and retrocede the Liaotung Peninsula in return for an additional indemnity of 30 million *taels*.

For opposite reasons, the effect of the Sino-Japanese War of 1894–1895 was significant for both China and Japan. To China, the war revealed the total impotence and weakness of the Chinese government, which later gave rise to many antigovernment activities, such as K'ang Yu-wei's[*] reform movement and Sun Yat-sen's[*] revolutionary movement. It marked the beginning of the end for the Ch'ing dynasty.[*] To Japan, the war demonstrated the success of the Meiji modernization, especially in its military programs. Japan had indeed become a power to reckon with in Asia. The territorial gains from China only whetted the resource-conscious nation's appetite. After the war, Japan's desire for more territory became insatiable. The pressure from Russia, France, and Germany over Liaotung also made Japan even more wary of the West in its quest for land, prompting the rise of Japanese militarism in Asia.

REFERENCES: Grant Goodman, *Imperial Japan and Asia* (New York, 1976); Akira Iriye, *The Chinese and Japanese* (Princeton, N. J., 1980).

ANTHONY Y. TENG

SINO-JAPANESE WAR (1937–1945): War between China and Japan, which initiated World War II in the Pacific and facilitated the Communist rise to power.

Full-scale war between China and Japan erupted with the July 7, 1937, Marco Polo Bridge Incident[*], culminating more than a decade of conflicts between the two powers. At first the war was confined to China, but the involvement of the United States in the Pacific War following the Japanese attack on Pearl Harbor on December 7, 1941, incorporated the Sino-Japanese War into the China–Burma–India (CBI) theater of World War II. The war momentarily quelled the domestic strife between the Chinese Communists and the Kuomintang (the Chinese Nationalist party[*]), but ultimately it created the opportunity for the Communists to carve out independent base areas and to challenge the Nationalists in the civil war, 1945–1949.[*]

The war originated in the nominal unification of China in 1928 by the Kuomintang and the expansion of Japan into Manchuria in the 1930s. In 1928 at least two-thirds of China still lay outside the Nationalists' direct control. Manchuria remained under the control of the warlords and the Japanese, who since 1894 had sought to make Manchuria a colony.

Tensions between the Japanese and the Kuomintang increased between 1928 and 1931 and culminated in the Manchurian Incident of September 18, 1931, which the Japanese Kwantung Army used as a pretext for expansion throughout Manchuria. The Japanese created the puppet state of Manchukuo[*] on March 9, 1932, and subdued China's four northern provinces by the end of 1936. The Marco Polo Bridge Incident of 1937 continued this pattern of aggression.

The Japanese armies quickly overran vast portions of China in 1937 and 1938. Unable to stop the Japanese in northern China, Chiang Kai-shek[*] decided to make a stand at Shanghai. Hostilities began in the lower Yangtze on August 13, 1937. After some early successes, the Chinese retreated toward Nanking in September. The mechanized Japanese columns turned the Chinese retreat into slaughter, culminating in the Rape of Nanking in December, in which Japanese troops attacked the Chinese civilian population with unprecedented brutality. By the end of 1937, China had lost most of its important urban centers to the Japanese. At least 450,000 Chinese perished in these early months of the war.

During 1938 the Kuomintang government retreated to Chungking and prepared for a protracted war. By October the Japanese had conquered most of the Yellow River Basin, the central Yangtze metropolis of Wuhan, and Canton. Hoping for a negotiated peace on their terms, they set up puppet regimes in north and central China and attempted to demoralize the Kuomintang by massive air attacks against strategic population centers. Chinese strategists, believing the Japanese lacked the resources and the willpower to vanquish all of China and hoping for eventual assistance from the Western powers, traded space for time.

After a Chinese offensive failed in the winter of 1939, the war settled into a stalemate. Kuomintang troops tied up approximately 2 million Japanese forces along relatively static battle lines, and Communist forces employed guerrilla tactics to harass the Japanese troops and create popular support for their movement.

The United States' entrance into World War II in the Pacific altered the character of the Sino-Japanese War by providing some external aid to the Kuomintang and diverting Japan's energies from East Asia to the Pacific. The United States' China policy was designed to keep the Chinese in the war to tie up Japanese resources but to win the war by attacking Japan from the Pacific side. Consequently, only 3 percent of U.S. wartime aid to its allies went to China. American efforts under General Joseph Stilwell* to reorganize and train Kuomintang armies ran afoul of intractable political problems and failed.

In contrast, Communist forces under Mao Tse-tung* grew numerically during the war and expanded their areas of control. It is estimated that the Maoist troops numbered 900,000 regulars and controlled a population of at least 50 million by 1945. Moreover, they carried out party reform, land reform, and educational programs that had wide appeal among the Chinese. Successes in guerrilla actions helped them to emerge from the war identified with nationalism and sociopolitical reform. In contrast, the Kuomintang's morale and popular support deteriorated during the war. In essence, the Sino-Japanese War created a political and military environment that altered the prewar balance of power between the Communists and Nationalists and made the outcome of the civil war between the two problematic.

REFERENCES: Hsi-sheng Ch'i, *Nationalist China at War* (Ann Arbor, Mich., 1982); Chalmers Johnson, *Peasant Nationalism and Communist Power* (Stanford, Calif., 1962); Michael Schaller, *The United States Crusade in China, 1938–1945* (New York, 1979); Mark Selden, *The Yenan Way in Revolutionary China* (Cambridge, Mass., 1971).

LOREN W. CRABTREE

SINO–SOVIET SPLIT: Division in the USSR–PRC alliance beginning in the late 1950s.

After about six years of apparent unity since 1950, the Sino-Soviet alliance began to sour. The early symptoms of the schism began to be slightly visible to the non-Communist world in the wake of Nikita Khrushchev's famous secret de-Stalinization speech at the twentieth Congress of the Communist party of the Soviet Union (CPSU) in February 1956. As early as 1954, Khrushchev relates in his somewhat self-serving but still revealing memoirs, he told his colleagues in Moscow after his official state visit to Peking that "conflict with China is inevitable." By 1959 this "prophecy" was taking a life of its own, gradually becoming self-fulfilling. The alliance, in Khrushchev's calculation, was one-sided, dangerous, and perhaps even beyond repair, as he pushed vigorously for peaceful coexistence and peaceful competition with the capitalist world in general and with the United States in particular as the general line of Soviet foreign policy.

The official Chinese account in 1964–1965 (and also in the post–Mao era) generally accepts the Twentieth CPSU Congress in 1956 as "the root from which stems all the evils done by the Khrushchev revisionists" and situates the main causes of the split in (1) Soviet demands that would have harmed Chinese sovereignty (meaning Khrushchev's request to set up a Sino-Soviet joint fleet and radio station for Soviet submarines in the Pacific in 1958), (2) Soviet hegemonic behavior in the management of intersocialist relations within the Communist bloc, and (3) Soviet pressures and sanctions against China, ranging from breaching contracts, withdrawing experts, and pressing for the repayment of debts to beefing up military forces along the border. Actually, during the 1954–1956 period preceding the Twentieth CPSU Congress, Moscow's attitude and behavior toward Peking changed discernibly from that of a hegemon to that of relatively equal alliance partners. The irony is that the split became the unavoidable consequence of growing equality in the Sino-Soviet alliance. The widening gap between Peking's rising demands and expectations and Moscow's inability and unwillingness to satisfy them undermined the alliance rooted in shared values and shared fears.

The Sino-Soviet conflict in the post–Stalin era was a drawn-out process, evolving by fits and starts in several phases before its purported final rupture in 1964. Khrushchev's de-Stalinization speech opened a Pandora's box, introducing polycentric tendencies to the Communist world hitherto united by the ultimate ideological authority and supreme leadership in the Kremlin. In addition, Khrushchev introduced several doctrinal innovations (e.g., the demise of the inevitability of war and peaceful coexistence as the general foreign policy line) that were to set the parameters for the Sino-Soviet conflict that would rage for the next twenty-five years. Still, Sino-Soviet differences in 1956–1958 were confined to esoteric intrabloc communications.

From mid–1958 onward, the dispute began to escalate from ideological to national security issues in direct proportion to the radicalization of Chinese domestic and foreign policy. Particularly rankling to Peking were Moscow's failures to meet expected alliance obligations in the 1958 Taiwan Strait crisis, the 1959 Sino-Indian border clashes, and the 1959 "perfidious" Soviet letter calling off the 1957 New Defense Technical Accord. In Peking's perception, then, not just the extent but the very credibility of the Soviet alliance commitments were now in serious doubt. Peking's growing realization of Moscow's unwillingness to maintain Sino-Soviet unity at China's own terms, coupled with the rise of an independent set of Chinese domestic and foreign policy concerns in 1957–1958, precipitated the move toward a rupture.

In the article, "Long Live Leninism" published in the spring of 1960 in the *Red Flag*, China launched its first ideological counterattack, raising the dispute to the highest level of Marxist principles of international relations, especially concerning imperialism, war, and peace. Moscow retaliated a few months later with economic sanctions (e.g., withdrawing 1,390 Soviet experts working in China and canceling 257 projects of scientific and technical cooperation). By

August 23, 1960, Moscow had completely withdrawn the last of its technical experts from the Chinese nuclear program. The Moscow Conference in November 1960 produced a temporary compromise, papering over differences by condemning both revisionism and dogmatism. Until the end of 1962, both parties engaged in a proxy war, refraining from attacking the other directly. With the Cuban Missile Crisis and the Sino-Indian War, however, the dispute became increasingly more public, more direct, and more explicit, dominating the pages of the official propaganda organs of both parties. With the 1963 Nuclear Test Ban Treaty and the failure of another Sino-Soviet meeting to resolve the conflict in July 1963, the dispute now acquired another rung of escalation, increasingly transcending its original struggle revolving largely around Sino-Soviet bilateral relations and their respective authority in the international Communist movement to subsume all aspects of contemporary world politics. On August 3, 1963, the *People's Daily* charged that the test ban treaty "is a U.S.-Soviet alliance against China pure and simple." By early 1964 the conflict reached the point of no return, even though CCP–CPSU relations were not severed until the spring of 1966, as Peking began to churn out a series of putative Soviet violations of alliance commitments and obligations. What followed is an eighteen-year period of Sino-Soviet enmity, followed by a seven-year long process of normalization talks, culminating in the Sino-Soviet renormalization in May 1989.

REFERENCES: G. F. Hudson, Richard Lowenthal, and Roderick MacFarquhar, eds., *The Sino-Soviet Dispute* (New York, 1961); Donald Zagoria, *The Sino-Soviet Conflict, 1956–1961* (Princeton, N.J., 1962); William E. Griffith, *The Sino-Soviet Rift* (Cambridge, Mass., 1964); Lowell Dittmer, *Sino-Soviet Normalization* (Seattle, Wash., 1991).

SAMUEL S. KIM

SINO–SOVIET TREATY OF FRIENDSHIP AND ALLIANCE (1945): Treaty signed in Moscow on August 14, 1945; defined the postwar Soviet position in China.

In essence, the Sino-Soviet Treaty concluded that neither country would enter into an alliance or a coalition against the other while guaranteeing a full military alliance against Japan. Although signed jointly by the two foreign ministers, Wang Shih-chieh and V. M. Molotov, the real basis of the agreement had been thrashed out by Franklin D. Roosevelt and Joseph Stalin at Yalta.* This prior agreement limited the Chinese capacity for maneuver.

While China quickly agreed to Soviet possession of the Kuriles and southern Sakhalin, and the Soviet Union agreed to Chinese sovereignty over Manchuria and to limit support to the Chinese Communist party,* there was disagreement on a number of other issues. These were the questions of Outer Mongolia, the Southern and Eastern Manchurian Railways, and the ports of Dairen and Lu-hsün (Port Arthur).

On the Lu-hsün naval base, the Soviet Union renounced demands for exclusive military control and agreed to a joint Sino-Soviet committee. A verbal agreement was made that the military facilities there would not be leased to any third power.

Initially, Stalin proposed that Dairen harbor be owned and managed jointly by China and the Soviet Union with a Chinese chairman and a Soviet chief executive. The United States acknowledged Soviet "preeminence" but was particularly concerned that Dairen might be included in a Soviet military zone. Eventually, Stalin renounced the need for the establishment of a joint committee.

The Soviet Union got its way with the Southern and Eastern Manchurian railways. Both railways would be headed by Soviet appointees but, in a face-saving gesture, it was also agreed that a Chinese chairman of the Southern Manchurian Railway board of directors would be allowed two votes.

Outer Mongolia formed the main stumbling block in the negotiations. For Chiang Kai-shek* to be seen to be giving in to Soviet demands on this issue could undermine his prestige as the leader of the nationalist struggle. However, for Stalin this was a crucial issue, for he felt that the "independence" of the Mongolian People's Republic was necessary for Soviet security. For the United States, the issue of who controlled Outer Mongolia was not as important as limiting Soviet influence in Manchuria.

China's initial tack was to argue that Outer Mongolia could retain a high degree of independence as long as it was clearly recognized that de jure sovereignty remained with China. Stalin was not willing to accept this position. Despite proposing face-saving measures, the Chinese were forced to concede. Thereafter, Chiang Kai-shek was anxious to ensure that an agreement on the correct borders took place before independence was recognized. Chiang was anxious that the Altai region be classified as part of Sinkiang rather than as coming within the jurisdiction of Outer Mongolia. To pave the way for the final agreement, China dropped this demand while the Soviet Union agreed to an exchange of notes specifying that existing boundaries would be maintained.

China's bargaining position was undermined by the fast pace at which events unfolded. On August 6, the United States dropped the atomic bomb on Hiroshima, on August 8 Soviet Russia declared war on Japan, and on August 10 the Japanese indicated that they were willing to surrender unconditionally. Some Chinese negotiators now argued that it was imperative to reach an agreement swiftly to prevent Soviet occupation of Manchuria and strong support for the CCP. This move toward accommodation was aided by the resignation of Tse-Ven Soong* as foreign minister and his replacement by the more pliant Wang Shih-chieh on July 30.

The treaty also affected the CCP. First, U.S. and Soviet interests in China led to further attempts to bring the two Chinese parties together. Mao Tse-tung* was invited to Chungking for talks, and the CCP began to moderate its public criticism of the Kuomintang. At the same time, the CCP rushed to fill the vacuum left by the retreating Japanese troops, and numerous clashes occurred with the Kuomintang. The Kuomintang asked the Soviet Union to delay its troop withdrawal to give its troops more time to reach the area; during negotiations a period of three months after the Japanese surrender had been agreed upon.

On August 29, the CCP circulated internally its response to the treaty. It acknowledged that the Soviet desire for peace in the Far East meant that it would have to turn Manchuria over to Kuomintang control. Yet the three-month with-drawal period for Soviet troops gave the CCP an excellent opportunity to win over the three provinces. CCP strategy was to concentrate on gaining control of the countryside and the smaller cities where there was no Soviet presence. This strategy proved vital to eventual Communist success in the northeast.

REFERENCES: Liang Chin-tung, "The Sino-Soviet Treaty of Friendship and Alliance of 1945: The Inside Story," in Paul K. T. Sih, ed., *Nationalist China during the Sino-Japanese War, 1937–1945* (New York, 1977); John W. Garver, *Chinese-Soviet Relations 1937–1945* (Oxford, 1988).

TONY SAICH

SINO–SOVIET TREATY OF FRIENDSHIP, ALLIANCE, AND MUTUAL ASSISTANCE (1950): Treaty signed by Mao Tse-tung and Joseph Stalin that formally established the Sino–Soviet Alliance.

On February 14, 1950, the Soviet Union and the newly established People's Republic of China[*] concluded six agreements. The first was the Sino-Soviet Treaty of Friendship, Alliance, and Mutual Assistance, the linchpin of the new Sino-Soviet alliance system, signed by Chinese Foreign Minister Chou En-lai[*] and Soviet Foreign Minister Andre Yanuaryevich Vyshinsky. The treaty can be said to have entered into force on April 11, 1950 by which time both Moscow and Peking ratified it (as Article 6 provides that it will come into effect "immediately upon its ratification"), even though instruments of ratification were not exchanged until September 30, 1950. The treaty was supposed to remain in force for thirty years—and for another five years—unless either of the contracting parties gave a one-year notice of renunciation before the expiration of this thirty-year term. Although the treaty was a dead letter for both parties by early 1964, Peking complied with the legal requirement by informing Moscow on April 3, 1979, of its decision not to renew the treaty (and simultaneously offering normalization talks).

The main objective of this six-article treaty was to forge a socialist solidarity in East Asia as a counterweight against the clear and continuing possibility of a Japanese-American anti-Communist alliance network in East Asia. In both the Preamble and Article 1, the central driving force was stated in terms of preventing the rebirth of aggression and imperialism on the part of Japan "or any other state which would unite with Japan directly or any other form in acts of aggression." This was a regional, not a global, military pact with its focus on Japan and East Asia. At the same time, it was not purely military in nature and scope, for it also promised the development and consolidation of economic and cultural ties.

Mao Tse-tung[*] made his first foreign trip to Moscow on December 16, 1949, and stayed nine weeks personally negotiating the terms of this treaty with Stalin. That it would require nine weeks of Mao's precious time in Moscow when it should have taken no more than a few days to complete such a short agreement suggests that this was indeed "another struggle" (Mao's 1962 recollection)—and indeed, the "foreign policy struggle"—that Mao had to go through in his

"continuing revolution." Mao had few bargaining chips. Strategically and ideologically, he had already cast New China's lot with the socialist camp led by
the Soviet Union, as there was no "third road." Apparently, Stalin refused to
satisfy many of Mao's requests. Moreover, Stalin, according to Mao's 1962
recollection, "was not willing to sign" the treaty, suspecting Mao's China of
being another Yugoslavia. It was not until China's intervention in the Korean
War in the winter of 1950 that Stalin was finally persuaded that Mao was not
another Tito—and that China was not another Yugoslavia.

Despite the relatively short life cycle of the treaty and Mao's weak bargaining
position, the treaty was not entirely one-sided. Article 5 promised the development of Sino-Soviet economic and cultural cooperation "in conformity with
the principles of equality, mutual interests, and also mutual respect for state
sovereignty and territorial integrity and noninterference in the internal affairs of
the other party." Indeed, Article 5 stands out as the most surprising (and most
overlooked) provision of this so-called asymmetrical alliance treaty system between the strong and the weak, as it presaged and embodied what came to be
known in 1954 as the Five Principles of Peaceful Coexistence.[*]

After about six years of apparent harmony and cooperation, the treaty began
to lose its legal and practical value. From 1956 to 1964 Sino-Soviet disputes on
a wide range of ideological and foreign policy issues undermined the foundation
of the alliance treaty beyond repair. On February 4, 1964, Peking publicly
accused Moscow of having violated the Sino-Soviet Treaty of Friendship, Alliance, and Mutual Assistance with the unilateral decision to withdraw (in 1960)
1,390 Soviet experts working in China, to tear up 343 contracts and supplementary contracts on the employment of experts, and to cancel 257 projects of
scientific and technical cooperation. This marks the denouement of the 1950
Sino-Soviet alliance treaty.

REFERENCES: Howard L. Boorman et al., *Moscow–Peking Axis: Strengths and Strains*
(New York, 1957); O. Edmund Clubb, *China and Russia: The "Great Game"* (New
York, 1971); Jerome A. Cohen and Hungdah Chiu, *People's China and International
Law*, 2 vols. (Princeton, N.J., 1974); Douglas M. Johnston and Hungdah Chiu, *Agree-
ments of the People's Republic of China 1949–1967: A Calendar* (Cambridge, Mass.,
1968).

SAMUEL S. KIM

SIX MARTYRS (of the Hundred Day Reform of 1898): Six men (K'ang Kuang-
jen, T'an Ssu-t'ung, Yang Shen-hsiu, Yang Jui, Lin Hsü, and Liu Kuang-ti)
executed without trial on September 28, 1898, because of their association with
K'ang Yu-wei and the Hundred Day Reform program launched through the
Kuang-hsü Emperor.[*]

Reacting to China's repeated defeats by the Western powers and a further
defeat by Japan in the Sino-Japanese War of 1894–1895,[*] by the late 1890s
many of China's gentry-literati became convinced that only radical reform could
save China from dismemberment. K'ang Yu-wei,[*] an iconoclastic scholar from
Kwangtung Province, soon became a leader of the radical reform movement.

Five of the Six Martyrs were men who by the fall of 1898 considered themselves K'ang's disciples. The sixth, though not a disciple, was still an enthusiastic supporter.

K'ang's policies had come to be espoused by the Kuang-hsü Emperor by late July 1898, after reform-minded officials managed to bring K'ang to the personal attention of the emperor. Conservatives at court, led by the Empress Dowager Tz'u-hsi* and the aristocrat/general Jung-lu, strongly objected to K'ang, preventing the Kuang-hsü Emperor from giving him a substantive position in the government. Instead, the emperor promoted four of those who were later martyred (T'an Ssu-t'ung,* Lin Hsü, Yang Jui, and Liu Kuang-ti) to be secretaries of the Grand Council, from which position they sent proposed reform measures to the emperor. (Measures were often written by K'ang Yu-wei but submitted under the name of the secretary in question.) Among the reforms proposed which the emperor subsequently approved were abolition of the existing examination system (which relied on the "Eight-Legged Essay"), a push to seek knowledge from abroad, measures to lead to the early convening of a Parliament, and an overhaul of foreign relations pointing toward an alliance with Great Britain and Japan.

Finding the empress dowager and conservatives increasingly antagonistic to their reforms, the radical reformers along with the emperor feared a coup d'état. To forestall this threat, the reformers tried to arrange for then-General Yüan Shih-k'ai* to protect the emperor, arrest the empress dowager, and execute Jung-lu. Instead, Yüan revealed the reformers' plans to the empress dowager who did, indeed, execute a coup with the result that the emperor was imprisoned, the empress dowager took over direction of the government, and the chief reformers were either forced to flee (K'ang Yu-wei and others) or were arrested and executed (the Six Martyrs).

As for the martyrs as individuals, K'ang Kuang-jen (1867–1898) was K'ang Yu-wei's younger brother. For most of his life, he associated himself with his brother's reform schemes. Kuang-jen was particularly interested in reform of education and the examination system, and the proposed alliance with Great Britain and Japan. At one time, he also tried to bring together the group around K'ang Yu-wei and those associated with Sun Yat-sen.* He was a managing editor of Macao's *China Reporter* (*Chih-hsin pao*) and, in addition to a classical Chinese education, had studied medicine for three years under an American surgeon.

T'an Ssu-t'ung (1866–1898) of Hunan was the son of an official. Raised primarily in the north and northwest, at an early age he acquired an interest in horsemanship and swordsmanship, seeing himself as something of a knight-errant. As an adult, he failed at the examinations and purchased degree status. He wrote an eclectic philosophical treatise combining elements of Western learning with the Confucian tradition, and he negotiated with Japanese military officers to promote an alliance between China and Japan. In 1898, before the start of the Hundred Day Reform,* T'an had been an expectant intendant for Kiangsu Province. He was particularly close to K'ang Yu-wei during the summer of 1898, and he was one of those promoted by the emperor to be secretary of the Grand Council to help promote K'ang's reform policies. He went personally to see Yüan Shih-k'ai to try to secure Yüan's support in the critical days before the late September coup, tried to rescue the emperor from imprisonment after the coup had occurred, and chose martyrdom to flight.

Yang Shen-hsiu (1849–1898) of Shansi, was a *chin-shih* and secretary to the Board of Punishments in 1898. Though not a disciple of K'ang Yu-wei, Yang was an enthusiastic supporter of K'ang and K'ang's reform program. He was also involved in the effort to persuade Yüan Shih-k'ai to come to the emperor's aid. He was arrested and executed with the other five primarily because, after the coup, he presented a memorial asking that the empress dowager *not* resume power.

Yang Jui (1857–1898) of Szechwan was a *chü-jen* closely associated with Chang Chih-tung before he came under K'ang Yu-wei's influence. In the early part of 1898, when K'ang organized a Kwangtung Study Society to promote interest in radical reform, Yang Jui organized a similar society for Szechwanese, and in May of 1898 when K'ang organized the Society to Preserve the Nation (Pao-kuo hui), Yang Jui became one of its founding members. Yang, then a reader for the National Academy, was another of those the emperor promoted to be secretary of the Grand Council in the summer of 1898 so as to facilitate reform.

Lin Hsü (1874–1898) of Fukien passed the examinations to enter the bureaucracy four years before the Hundred Day Reform, and by 1898 he had become a secretary in the Grand Secretariat. As part of the reform movement, the emperor made him secretary of the Grand Council. Liu, associated with K'ang by early 1898, organized a pro-reform Fukien Study Society within two weeks of the founding of K'ang's Kwangtung Study Society. Of the Six Martyrs, he was considered the one with the greatest literary ability.

Liu Kuang-ti (1859–1898) of Szechwan was a *chin-shih* who had served on the Board of Punishments and then temporarily retired to his native area upon the death of one of his parents. When he returned to Peking, K'ang Yu-wei was on the ascendancy and Liu enthusiastically joined the radical reform cause. Liu along with Yang Jui was a signatory to the founding of K'ang's Society to Preserve the Nation. When K'ang came to the emperor's personal attention, Liu was one of those made secretary to the Grand Council.

REFERENCES: Luke S.K. Kwong, "Reflections on an Aspect of Modern China in Transition: T'an Ssu-t'ung (1865–1898) as a Reformer," in Paul A. Cohen and John E. Schrecker, eds., *Reform in Nineteenth-Century China* (Cambridge, Mass., 1976): 184–193; Jung-pang Lo, ed. and trans., *K'ang Yu-wei: A Biography and a Symposium* (Tucson, Ariz., 1967).

L. EVE ARMENTROUT MA

SNOW, EDGAR PARKS (July 19, 1905–February 15, 1972): Well-known American journalist who visited the Yenan Communist base.

Edgar Parks Snow is the most famous journalist to cover China in the twentieth century. During his lifetime he wrote eleven books, over 200 magazine articles, and hundreds of newspaper articles. His *Red Star over China* is, arguably, the most influential book on China in this century.

Ed Snow was born into a middle-class family in Kansas City, Missouri, enjoying a typical Midwest childhood during which he became an eagle scout and a choir boy before graduating from high school in 1923. He attended a local junior college and the University of Missouri's School of Journalism before leaving for New York in 1926.

In New York Snow worked for an advertising agency and attended classes at Columbia University's School of Journalism. But New York, while exciting, was not enough of an adventure for Snow, and so in February 1928 he embarked on what he expected would be an eighteen-month trip around the world. He traveled through the Panama Canal to Hawaii (from where he sold his first article to *Harper's Bazaar*), to Japan (by stowing away), and finally to China where the plan called for a six-week stay.

Using his University of Missouri connection, Snow got a job on the *China Weekly Review*, edited by another Missourian graduate, J. B. Powell. One of his first assignments was to travel and report on the railways of China. These travels included visits to areas of extreme famine; young Snow's shock at the suffering he witnessed was to have a profound effect on him all his life.

Snow's work as a journalist was so good that Powell offered him the job of assistant editor. Snow loved the job, which meant running the paper when Powell was out of Shanghai. But Snow had not yet lost his wanderlust, so in September 1930 he took a job as roving reporter for the Consolidated Press Association. He spent the next year traveling to Taiwan, Hong Kong, Indochina, Burma, Singapore, and British India.

Snow familiarized himself with the peoples, cultures, and politics of South and East Asia, but it was China that most captivated him. In 1934 Snow and his wife, Helen Foster Snow, moved to Peip'ing (Peking) where he continued to report and also teach journalism at Yenching University.[*]

Snow's growing anger at China's poverty brought him into contact with members of the progressive student movements (some of whom were his students at Yenching University), leftist foreigners, Chinese authors like Lu Hsün[*] and others like Soong Ching-ling,[*] the widow of Sun Yat-sen.[*] These contacts gave Snow a great deal of access to the underground political activities of Chinese opposed to the Kuomintang government. Plans for the student movement in Peip'ing, for example, were hatched in his living room. Those contacts were to give Snow the "scoop of the century." In June 1936, accompanied by an American doctor, George Hatem, Snow went behind the Communist lines and became the first foreign journalist to live with the Communist forces. He interviewed all the important figures and got Mao Tse-tung[*] to tell his life story.

When he left the Communist area, Snow wrote *Red Star over China* which remains a classic history of the Chinese Revolution and the only autobiography of Mao Tse-tung. The book made Snow a worldwide celebrity and influenced countless Chinese and foreigners. Chinese students deluged Snow with requests for him to arrange their travel to the Communist bases.

Until Snow left China in 1941, he remained in touch with people struggling for change there. He was one of the founding editors of a magazine called *Democracy* in Peip'ing until the Japanese closed it down. He was also one of the founders of the Chinese Industrial Cooperative Movement (INDUSCO) [see Rewi Alley*); he harbored political refugees in his house and helped them escape from Peip'ing] and he encouraged and helped translate and publish modern Chinese authors such as Lu Hsün—all the while continuing to report and making a second trip to the Communist areas in 1939.

Snow left China when the Japanese and the United States went to war and spent the next four years writing for the *New York Herald Tribune* and the *Saturday Evening Post* from Russia, Europe, and India. After the war he became an editor at the *Saturday Evening Post*.

The specter of McCarthyism that hung over the United States in the late 1940s brought Snow under suspicion because of his ties to the Communists in China and because he was one who had predicted they would win the Chinese civil war. Unable to work, he and his second wife, Lois Wheeler Snow, moved to Switzerland.

In 1960 Snow was invited to the People's Republic of China* spending several months traveling 12,000 miles—an unprecedented opportunity—and wrote *The Other Side of the River: Red China Today*. He returned to the PRC in 1964–1965 and again in 1970 when the Chinese leadership chose him to be the conduit through which they expressed their willingness to host U.S. President Richard Nixon. Premier Chou En-lai* told Snow "the door is open," and on October 1, China's National Day, Snow and his wife were asked to stand next to Mao Tse-tung atop of the main gate to the Forbidden City as they watched the festivities.

Snow was the natural person to act as a liaison, and his dream of bringing together the two nations he loved seemed to be coming true. President Nixon accepted the invitation and went to China in 1972. Snow had been commissioned by *Life* magazine to cover the visit, but several months earlier he became ill. The Chinese government rushed a special medical team to his side in Switzerland, but there was nothing to be done. Edgar Snow died the very week that President Richard Nixon arrived in China.

Snow's ashes, according to his wishes, are buried at Peking University where he taught and on the Hudson River in New York symbolizing his devotion to two nations.

REFERENCES: Edgar Snow, *Journey to the Beginning* (New York, 1958); Lois Wheeler Snow, *Edgar Snow's China: A Personal Account of the Chinese Revolution Compiled from the Writings of Edgar Snow* (New York, 1981); John Maxwell Hamilton, *Edgar Snow, A Biography* (Bloomington, Ind., 1989).

A. TOM GRUNFELD

SOCIALIST EDUCATION MOVEMENT (*she-hui chu-i chiao-yü yün-tung*, 1962–1966): Rural forerunner of the Great Proletarian Cultural Revolution.

At the Chinese Communist Party's* Eighth Central Committee's Tenth plenum (September 1962), Chairman Mao Tse-tung* warned "never forget class struggle" and insisted that "we must carry out socialist education." Evidently he was determined to resume his political offensive to further revolutionize China after "three hard years" of setbacks. He succeeded in having the party issue (May 1963) a "Decision on Certain Problems in the Present Rural Work (Draft)," known as the Former Ten Points, to lay out specifics.

Notable among these specifics were (1) an emphasis on "four cleanups" (workpoints, accounts, supplies, and granaries) to reverse a trend toward weakening the five-year-old agricultural communes; (2) an emphasis on "reeducation" of privileged officials, mainly by having them engage in common labor; and (3) an emphasis on Poor and Lower-Middle Peasants' Associations, as distinct from local party organs, as the voice of farmers. Mao's apparent strategy was to rejuvenate the party, starting with a popularly rooted campaign to reaffirm the value of People's Communes.* The peasant's ambivalence about communes, however, provided an opening for Mao's rivals to deflect his thrust.

The first deflection (September 1963) was embodied in the Provision of Certain Concrete Policies of the CCP CC Concerning the Socialist Education Movement in the Rural Areas (Draft), known as the Latter Ten Points. The second deflection (September 1964) was a revision of this draft known as the Revised Latter Ten Points. Both removed all mention of peasant associations, substituting "work teams" sent by the party to run the campaign in rural villages.

Mao countered (January 1965) by eliciting from the Central Committee "Some Current Problems Raised in the Socialist Education Movement in the Rural Areas," known as the Twenty-three Points. This new document escalated intra-elite conflict. The new "four cleanups" (politics, economics, organization, and ideology) were more far-reaching than the old. Peasant associations were favored again, and work teams were explicitly criticized: problems were to be judged by "the masses" and not "decided from above." Ominously, the CCP elites themselves were targeted: "those persons in positions of authority within the Party who take the capitalist road," or capitalist roaders.*

The Socialist Education Movement did not succeed for Mao. Communes were not reorganized; no re-registration of party members took place; rural officials were not made less corrupt; and peasant associations enjoyed no new powers. The three-year struggle had merely reaffirmed for Mao that he could no longer hope to achieve his ambitions with familiar tactics. Even such a major ideological mass campaign as socialist education could be taken over and made harmless by party leaders hostile to its thrust. To defeat his opponents in the party, he would need a stronger formula, which eighteen months later would prove to be the Cultural Revolution.*

The Decision of the CCP CC Concerning the Great Proletarian Cultural Revolution (August 1966) contained as Point Thirteen discussion of how to integrate the new movement with socialist education, effectively drawing the curtain on the predecessor campaign.

REFERENCES: Richard Baum and Fredrick C. Teiwes, *Ssu-Ch'ing: The Socialist Education Movement of 1962–1966* (Berkeley, Calif., 1968); M. Meisner, *Mao's China and After: A History of the People's Republic* (New York, 1986).

GORDON BENNETT

SOCIETY FOR THE DIFFUSION OF CHRISTIAN AND GENERAL KNOWLEDGE AMONG THE CHINESE (SDK) (Kuang-hsüeh hui): The most influential missionary study association in the late Ch'ing period.

Founded in Shanghai in 1887, the Society for the Diffusion of Christian and General Knowledge Among the Chinese (SDK) aimed at transmitting Western learning to the educated Chinese elite through the publication of books and periodicals. Its predecessor was the Book and Tract Society, a publishing association in Glasgow which was founded by the Reverend Alexander Williamson in 1884. After the Book and Tract Society was dissolved in 1887, Dr. Williamson transferred its printing press and other property to the SDK. The initial object of the SDK was "the circulation of literature based on Christian principles throughout China." After Timothy Richard became the secretary of the Society in 1891, he further stressed the need to persuade the Chinese elite of the value of Western culture. Instead of emphasizing direct evangelical missionary efforts, the SDK missionaries became enthusiastic advocates of enlightenment in China.

The SDK published a great variety of writings and translations pertaining to Western learning and current issues. Timothy Richard's translation of Mackenzie's *History of the Nineteenth Century* (1894) and Young J. Allen's compilation on the Sino-Japanese War[*] (*Chung-Tung chan-chi pen-mo*, 1896) were the most popular books read by reform-minded literati in the late Ch'ing[*] period. Both books were popular enough to be pirated repeatedly by Chinese booksellers. Moreover, the missionaries of the SDK took advantage of the periodic convening of candidates for the state examinations to distribute books on Western learning. They also set up centers in different provinces for the promotion and sale of books. The yearly income from SDK sales of books and magazines increased rapidly from about $800 in 1889 to over $18,000 in 1898. However, the most influential publication of the SDK continued to be the renowned monthly periodical entitled *Wan-kuo kung-pao* (*International Review*).

Originally an independent newspaper under the management of Young J. Allen, *Wan-kuo kung-pao* was revived in 1889 after its suspension in 1883 and came under the sponsorship of the SDK. The magazine retained its former format and style, but it now concentrated more on Western knowledge and world affairs. The missionaries formulated topics about Western culture and offered monetary rewards to attract the literati to submit articles to the journal. Prior to journalism organized by Chinese reformers after the Sino-Japanese War,[*] *Wan-kuo kung-pao* appealed to the literati as a major vehicle for Western learning and a forum for discussing current issues. The SDK also published a monthly magazine entitled *The Christian Church Review* which was far less influential. The facilities of the SDK in Shanghai also included a library and a reading room.

SDK publications and activities became an important channel for transmitting new ideas and values in late Ch'ing China. The missionaries introduced science, mathematics, history, and international law which broadened the horizons of the Chinese literati. The promotion of Western techniques, ideas, and world-views had an effect on the intellectual outlook of Chinese reformers like K'ang Yu-wei[*] and Liang Ch'i-ch'ao.[*] The SDK's newspapers and magazines as vehicles of Western learning further stimulated the growth of new Chinese journalism that emerged after the Sino-Japanese War of 1894–1895. As an association, the SDK set an example for Chinese study societies after 1895. After this date, the proliferation of the Chinese periodical press gradually overshadowed the importance of the SDK in introducing Western culture and the study of current affairs. The SDK shifted its emphasis to the secularization of religious knowledge during the republican period.

REFERENCES: Liang Yüan-sheng, *Lin Yao-chi chai-hua shi-yeh yü Wan-kuo kung-pao* (Young J. Allen in China: His Careers and the *Wan-kuo kung-pao*) (Hong Kong, 1978); Timothy Richard, *Forty-five Years in China* (New York, 1960); Wang Shu-huai, *Wai-jen yü wu-hsu pien-fa* (Foreigners and the 1898 Reform) (Taipei, 1965); Wang Shu-huai, "Ch'ing-chi te Kuang-hsüeh hui" (Society for the Diffusion of Christian and General Knowledge Among the Chinese in Ch'ing China), *Bulletin of the Institute of Modern History* (Academia Sinica) 4, no. 1(1973): 193–227.

WING-KAI TO

SOONG, CH'ING-LING (January 27, 1893–May 29, 1981): Wife of Sun Yat-sen; revolutionary; vice-chairman of the PRC.

Soong was born in Shanghai. Her father, Charlie Soong, a Methodist minister, started the Commercial Press. Ch'ing-ling received her early education at the McTyeire School for Girls at Shanghai and later studied at Wesleyan College for Women at Macon, Georgia, graduating with a B.A. in 1913.

Upon her return to China, Soong became secretary of Dr. Sun Yat-sen,[*] leader of the Chinese Republican Revolution. Her admiration for Sun turned into love, and despite her father's strong opposition, Ch'ing-ling married Sun in Japan in October 1914.

In 1917, during the Second Revolution,[*] Sun and Soong moved their base to Canton to join the warlord Ch'en Chiung-ming. Sun was elected president extraordinaire in 1921. However, Ch'en was content with enlarging his base in Kwangtung rather than national unification. Their conflict soon induced Ch'en to stage a mutiny on June 16, 1922, whereupon he ordered firing on the presidential headquarters. Soong pleaded with Sun to escape first. Ten hours later, disguised as a country woman and mixing with the crowd, she fled to the gunboat *Yung-feng* after an arduous journey. The ordeal, resulting in a miscarriage, had the paradoxic consequence of turning her into a heroine, and would take on a significance similar to Sun's London kidnap.

Throughout the years of their marriage, up to Sun's death, Soong remained supportive of his ideas and ideals. After Ch'en's mutiny, Sun was determined to reorganize the party. Soong fully agreed with his decision to accept Soviet aid, having been impressed by Soviet renunciation of all Tsarist gains in China from unequal treaties and territorial expansion. In 1924 Soong accompanied Sun to Peking to discuss the prospect of reconciliation and national unification with the warlords. However, he was extremely ill and passed away on March 25, 1925.

The assassination of Liao Chung-k'ai in 1925 and the party purges before the Northern Expedition* of 1926 convinced Soong that she should carry the banner for her late husband. At the Second National Congress of the KMT in 1926, she was elected to the Central Executive Committee and was reelected at every subsequent congress until 1945. When the Northern Expedition reached Wuhan in November 1926, she moved there with her brother Tse-Ven Soong,* Soviet adviser Michael Borodin,* and KMT leftists to form the Nationalist government. As a result of Chiang's purges of Communists and KMT leftists in Shanghai, she revoked with others Chiang's emergency powers granted for the Northern Expedition, charging him with "massacre of the people." Soong also denounced the subsequent purge of Communists by Wuhan to avert the prospect of civil war with Nanking as "violence to Sun's ideals." She then returned to Shanghai to persuade T. V. Soong to join her, but T. V., having been won over to Chiang, advised her to join Chiang's Nanking Regime. She refused. Her attempt to win General Feng Yü-hsiang's* help in dealing with Chiang also failed.

In August, Soong went to Moscow in an act of defiance to Chiang. Moreover, she openly opposed her sister Mei-ling's marriage to Chiang in 1927. After the International Anti-imperialist Convention in Brussels, she went to Berlin to meet Teng Yen-ta, a general who had turned against Chiang. Together, they organized a Third Force as an alternative to the KMT and the Chinese Communist Party.* In May 1929 she returned to attend the state burial of Sun in the mausoleum erected in Nanking. While back in China, she issued further condemnations of the Nanking Regime. Her outspokenness caused Chiang to keep her house under constant surveillance. As a result of Chiang's execution of Teng Yen-ta in 1931, she organized the China League for Civil Rights with Ts'ai Yüan-p'ei* and others, demanding the release of dissidents and Communists arrested by the government, condemning the excesses of the New Life Movement,* and calling for freedom of speech. But more executions followed.

After the outbreak of the Sino-Japanese War,* Soong moved to Hong Kong and founded the China Defense League in 1938 to channel medical relief to Communist bases in the hinterland. At this time the International Peace Hospital was set up in Shensi by Canadian surgeon Dr. Norman Bethune.* During the war, Chiang as well as Soong's family stopped her from accepting invitations to visit the United States, for fear that she would stop Lend-Lease diversions at the source. However, in the spirit of wartime patriotism, a rapprochement with her sisters was effected. She supported the industrial cooperative movement organized by her sisters to set up small factories in rural areas. In April 1940 she and her sister flew from Hong Kong to wartime capital Chungking and subsequently organized welfare in Szechwan. However, Ch'ing-ling's vociferous attack of the regime kept her in relative isolation. She was considered a Communist by most Westerners, though she was not a member. In the second half of 1944, after a period of relative silence, she showered attacks on Chiang in a chorus of demands for reforms. In 1945, she and T. V. went to Moscow to conclude a Sino-Soviet treaty for KMT–USSR cooperation. In 1948 she attempted to revive the Third Force, but to no avail. In September 1949 she was invited to Peip'ing as a delegate to the People's Political Consultation Conference leading to the formation of the People's Republic of China.* She became one of the three non-Communist vice-chairpersons of the government.

Other posts were offered to her up to her death in 1981. She continued with welfare work and led delegations abroad. During the Cultural Revolution,* her house was stormed by Red Guards,* and she was branded a bourgeois liberal, but Chou En-lai* saved her from disgrace. After she had developed leukemia in 1960, she remained in a weakened state but lived nearly twenty more years. She was named honorary president of China in 1981 and was inducted into the CCP before her death on May 29. Mei-ling, the only sister to survive her, refused to attend her funeral.

REFERENCES: Sterling Seagrave, *The Soong Dynasty* (London, 1985); Helen F. Snow, *Women in China* (The Hague, 1967); Howard L. Boorman and Richard C. Howard, eds., *A Biographical Dictionary of Republican China* (New York, 1968).

TERENCE T.T. PANG

SOONG, MEI-LING (known in the West as Soong May-ling, March 5, 1897–): Wife of Chiang Kai-shek.

A native of Hainan Island, but born in Shanghai into an Americanized Christian family, Soong Mei-ling learned English at home and at McTyeire School, a Methodist School for wealthy girls in Shanghai. In 1908, she went to the United States and was enrolled at Wesleyan College in Macon, Georgia, as a special student, because she was under age. In 1913, she transferred to Wellesley College in Massachusetts where she graduated in 1917 with honors. Thoroughly Americanized, she returned to Shanghai and devoted herself to philanthropic work in the YMCA.

Her marriage to Chiang Kai-shek* was viewed as a political move on both sides. Her sister Ai-ling, married to K'ung Hsiang-hsi (H. H. Kung),* was the matchmaker and prevailed on her mother to give consent. Chiang, being ten years her senior, a non-Christian, and married, did not appear to be a suitable suitor. Soong Ch'ing-ling,* the elder sister, reportedly remarked that "the marriage was opportunism on both sides." For Chiang, the marriage would bring him into the respectable financial circle in Shanghai where hitherto he was known as an upstart through his linkage with the notorious Green Gang, the most powerful underworld group in Shanghai during that time. The marriage would also bring him Western connections through the Kungs and Soongs. Mei-ling was to prove herself invaluable as a public relations person and a fund-raiser in the years to come. She did convert Chiang to Christianity in 1931. Persuaded by Australian adviser W. H. Donald, she toured the country with him, and thus started the image-building efforts of the regime with help from American journalists like Henry Luce. In 1934 she initiated the Chinese New Deal and named it the New Life Movement,* venerating Confucian virtues and exhorting good manners. In 1936 Soong was appointed secretary-general of the National Aeronautical Affairs Commission and devoted herself to the creation of a modern airforce for China. In the Sian Incident* of December 1936, she remained calm and counseled General Ho Ying-ch'in* not to bomb Sian to avoid a civil war. With her brother Tse-Ven,* she successfully negotiated Chiang's release. Paradoxically, the incident gained publicity for the regime and *Time* labeled Chiang and Soong, "Man and wife of the year." During the Second Sino-Japanese War (1937–1945), she was engaged in philanthropic work and together with other family members, including her politically alienated sister Ch'ing-ling, established cooperative factories in rural aréas. In 1937, when her her stepson Chiang Ching-kuo* returned from study in Moscow, the two began to vie for political power.

Through her propaganda publications and transoceanic broadcasts to the United States, Soong Mei-ling was well received on her U.S. tour in 1942–1943. She went to the White House as President Roosevelt's guest, and on February 18, 1943, she addressed a joint session of Congress. Afterward, she went on a cross-country fund-raising tour and obtained U.S. $17 million for United China Relief. Accompanying Chiang to the Cairo summit in 1943, she helped to promote China's image as one of the Big Four.

Soong Mei-ling was alleged to have manipulated government bonds and obtained huge profits in silver speculation. She was under constant attack for involvement in corruption with sister Ai-ling and brother-in-law, H. H. Kung. The two sisters' waning influence surfaced in 1944 when Mei-ling, accompanied by Ai-ling, went to Brazil ostensibly for "medical reasons," but reportedly made substantial investments in South American banks and stocks in oil, minerals, and shipping. It was rumored that she made her visit to avoid the embarrassment of a formal breakup with Chiang. In 1945, at the news of nephew David Kung's arrest by her stepson Chiang Ching-kuo, for appropriation of goods, she hurried back to China to arrange David Kung's release.

Despite her diminished political influence after World War II, in 1948 she tried to obtain U.S. aid for fighting the Communists and obtained U.S. $1 million from Congress. However, her influence ended after Harry Truman was elected to the U.S. presidency. Meanwhile, a full-scale FBI investigation into her personal wealth and that of Ai-ling, T. V., and H. H. Kung, was underway. A lot of investments in property and other areas were uncovered. Even so, she remained in the United States until January 1950, by which time the KMT forces had already retreated to Taiwan.

In Taiwan, Soong Mei-ling was inactive politically, and her influence declined with the rise of her stepson Chiang Ching-kuo. She resumed her charity work, including establishing orphanages, and she made occasional unofficial visits to the United States, usually in the name of medical treatment. In 1965 she went

to Washington as First Lady and was welcomed by the White House. After
Chiang's death in 1975, she went into exile, having given up hope of contesting
power with Chiang Ching-kuo. Today she lives in Taiwan, and is still considered
a force behind the conservative vanguards of the KMT in Taiwan.
REFERENCES: Sterling Seagrave, *The Soong Dynasty* (London, 1985); Helen F. Snow,
Women in Modern China (The Hague, 1967); Howard L. Boorman, and Richard C.
Howard, eds., *A Biographical Dictionary of Republican China* (New York, 1968).

TERENCE T.T. PANG

SOONG, TSE-VEN, PAUL (better known as T. V. Soong, December 4, 1894–
April 24, 1971): Financier; diplomat; premier and finance Minister of the ROC.
    A native of Hainan Island, Kwangtung, but born in Shanghai, T. V. Soong
received his education at St. John's University, Shanghai, before entering Harvard, where he graduated in 1915 with a B.A. degree. He later did graduate
work at Columbia University. In 1917 he returned to China to join the Han-
Yeh-P'ing Coal and Iron Works Ltd., as secretary. Dr. Sun Yat-sen* asked him
to join the Nationalist government at Canton, and T. V. handled financial planning for the Northern Expedition.* He also reformed the taxation system of
Kwangtung Province, setting up the Central Bank and obtaining funds from
Soviet Russia. For his efforts, he was appointed finance minister. During the
Northern Expedition, however, he moved to Wuhan with his sister Ch'ing-ling*,
Soviet adviser Michael M. Borodin*, and KMT leftists. In 1927, failing to
persuade Chiang Kai-shek* to treat the Communists leniently, he did a turnabout,
acting as Chiang's envoy to the Wuhan government and demanding to eradicate
the Communists and reunite with Nanking.
    As finance minister, Soong was dedicated to rehabilitating the Chinese econ-
omy. The bond market he started was favored because of his reputation, but it
fluctuated depending on his relationship with Chiang. His proposals, including
cuts in military expenditure, adoption of a budget, and establishment of a Central
Bank, won him support from the Shanghai financial circle. The bond market
plummetted when he resigned with Chiang after Chiang was criticized during
the Manchurian Incident. When Chiang returned to office, Soong was rewarded
with the vice-premiership while staying on as finance minister. The destruction
of Shanghai and the annihilation of Soong's Salt Protection Brigade by Japanese
forces in 1932 convinced him that the government should defend the country
against foreign invasion before settling accounts with the Communists. This view
was not shared by Chiang and would soon cost Soong his vice-premiership.
    Despite difficulties, Soong managed to score a few credits as finance minister,
including the unprecedented balanced budget in 1932, the establishment of the
Central Bank serving as the government treasury in 1928, and a loan of U.S.
50 million from the U.S. Farm Board in 1933. However, the huge military
spending, rendering budgetary balance impossible, was a source of constant
attrition between him and Chiang. Finally, a huge debt of $60 million run up
during Soong's attendance of the World Economic Conference in London led

him to resign in October 1933. He was succeeded by his brother-in-law, H. H. Kung.*

Afterward, Soong occupied his time with building up his personal wealth. In 1935 he became the chairman of the nationalized Bank of China. Despite his rift with Chiang, he was instrumental in arranging Chiang's release during the Sian Incident* of 1936 and forming the second KMT–CCP alliance. Since 1940, as Chiang's personal representative to the United States and as foreign minister from 1942 to 1944, he had repeatedly requested loans and aid from the United States. He actually succeeded in gaining sizable funds by exploiting Roosevelt's pro-China sentiments and utilizing his friendship with the president's aid, Thomas G. Corcoran. Allegedly he embezzled a sizable portion of U.S. aid and supplies, which his brothers T. A. and T. L. sold.

In 1944 Soong was reinstated as vice premier and finance minister after H. H. Kung was accused of corruption by the Ko-hsin (Reform) group, only to face enormous deficits and an empty treasury. Continuing to press the United States for loans and aid, Soong set up the China National Relief and Rehabilitation Administration to oversee the distribution of relief supplies. He was also active in wartime diplomacy. In July 1945, as premier, Soong went to Moscow to negotiate Soviet Russia's entry into the China theater and succeeded in gaining Stalin's promise to recognize Chinese sovereignty in Manchuria. But a month later, he resigned in protest at the conclusion of the Sino-Soviet Treaty of Friendship* which recognized the independence of Outer Mongolia. Ultimately, his power rested on his relationship with Chiang. The two quarreled in 1947 when military expenditures reached 80 percent of the budget. Reluctantly, Soong resorted to the printing press approach normally associated with Kung's name. In despair, he imposed import restrictions and stopped gold sales, causing a gold panic; he finally stepped down amid attacks from his former supporters in the Ko-hsin group.

In 1948 Soong was appointed governor of Kwangtung. His last-minute attempt to rescue the government's finances with a currency conversion plan also failed. Before the Nationalist government collapsed, he refused the demand to yield half his personal fortune to the state. His relations with the Kungs and his sister Mei-ling became strained when they began to suspect that he had amassed a greater fortune than other family members. Upon his retirement, he was rumored to be the richest man in the world. After Chiang's withdrawal to Taiwan, he fled to the United States and refused Chiang's invitation to official posts in 1950. He died in the United States in 1971.

REFERENCES: Sterling Seagrave, *The Soong Dynasty* (London, 1985); Howard L. Boorman and Richard C. Howard, eds., *A Biographical Dictionary of Republican China*, (New York, 1970); Arthur N. Young, *China's Nation-Building Effort, 1927–1937: The Financial and Economic Record* (Stanford, Calif., 1971).

TERENCE T.T. PANG

STILWELL, JOSEPH WARREN (March 19, 1893–October 12, 1946): U.S. general; chief-of-staff to Chiang Kai-shek; commander of U.S. forces in the China–Burma–India theater.

Joseph Stilwell was born in Palatka, Florida. An excellent officer with a gritty personality, he was often referred to as "Vinegar Joe." A soldier at Fort Benning had drawn a cartoon of him, his face floating from a vinegar bottle with the poisonous triple X on it. The nickname, which Stilwell took with humor, stuck throughout his life.

After graduation from West Point, Stilwell was assigned to a post in the Philippines in October 1904. Following a second tour in the Philippines, in 1911 he made his first of many visits to China. He returned to the United States in January 1912, having experienced the immediate aftermath of the first Chinese Revolution.

In 1919 Stilwell was appointed the first army language officer of China. He sailed for China on August 5, 1920 and spent the next three years there before returning to the United States. In 1926 Stilwell was again assigned to China, and after another stint in the country, one colonel concluded that Stilwell knows "China and the Far East better, in my opinion, than any other officer in the service."

In January 1942 Chiang Kai-shek[*] accepted the Allied position of supreme commander of the China theater of World War II. Chiang asked President Franklin D. Roosevelt to send an American officer to be chief of the General Staff. Roosevelt, at the urging of General George Marshall, selected Stilwell. Stilwell's orders, as supreme commander of the China–Burma–India theater and chief of the Joint General Staff under Chiang, mandated that he "supervise and control all United States defense-aid affairs for China" and "improve, maintain, and control the Burma Road in China." He was also to improve the combat effectiveness of the Chinese soldiers, enabling them to make better use of U.S. aid.

Conflict immediately arose between the two men, when Stilwell pushed for the defense of Burma and the maintenance of the Burma Road as a chief supply route. Chiang promoted the Himalayan air route, known none too affectionately as the "Hump." After Burma fell in what he claimed was "a hell of a beating," Stilwell worked toward his goal of creating an army that could reclaim Burma and provide the core of an army powerful enough to battle the Japanese in China. Stilwell also suggested that Chiang lift the military blockade of the Communist areas in the northeast.

Stilwell blamed Chiang Kai-shek for most of his frustrations and for the conditions he found in China, writing that the "cure for China's troubles is the elimination of Chiang Kai-shek." When President Franklin Roosevelt asked him what he thought of Chiang, he responded: "He's a vacillating, tricky, undependable old scoundrel who never keeps his word."

Despite this assessment, Roosevelt maintained the status quo. When Claire Lee Chennault,[*] with whom Stilwell had chilly relations, began the air offensive against the Japanese in late 1943, Stilwell's worst fears were realized. The offensive was disastrous, and as such played some part in Roosevelt's decision to reassess the overall situation. Also contributing to Roosevelt's review were Stilwell's return to Burma in April 1944 and Chiang's refusal to allow the bulk of the new troops to enter Burma. Chiang finally relented in the face of Roosevelt's threat to cut off aid, but he continued to use his best troops for the blockade of the Communists. By June 1944 Roosevelt, convinced that the situation had become untenable, sent Vice-President Henry Wallace to investigate the situation. Wallace filed a report that cast continued doubt on the viability of the Nationalists and their leader: "Chiang, at best is a short-term investment. It is not believed that he has the intelligence or political strength to run post-war China." By July 4, 1944, Roosevelt approved a telegram requesting that Stilwell be given command of both American and all Chinese forces. Chiang requested that the president send someone to China to help improve relations with Stilwell. The president selected Republican and former Secretary of War Patrick Jay Hurley,* who arrived in Chungking on September 6, 1944.

Events moved quickly. Kweilin in Kiangsi was taking a pounding, and Stilwell boiled over: "It's a mess . . . what they ought to do is shoot the G-mo [Chiang] . . . and the rest of the gang." As relations between the two men worsened, Stilwell received a telegram from Roosevelt on September 19, 1944, instructing Chiang to comply with his wish that Stilwell command all forces.

Stilwell's elation was short-lived, as Hurley, with the support of Chiang and T. V. Soong,* sent a message to Roosevelt decrying the action. Hurley pressed the issue, sending two more messages. Accepting warnings that as Chiang went so did China and that it was impossible to work with Stilwell, the president then reversed his decision. On October 18, 1944, he issued the order to recall Stilwell. Stilwell returned to the United States, and died of cancer nearly two years later in Letterman General Hospital.

REFERENCES: Herbert Feis, *The China Tangle: The American Effort in China from Pearl Harbor to the Marshall Mission* (New York, 1967); Michael Schaller, *The United States and China in the Twentieth Century* (New York, 1979); Michael Schaller, *The United States Crusade in China, 1938–1945* (New York, 1979); Joseph Stilwell, *The Stilwell Papers*, ed. Theodore H. White (New York, 1948); Barbara Tuchman, *Stilwell and the American Experience in China, 1911–1945* (New York, 1971).

EDWIN CLAUSEN

STRONG, ANNA LOUISE (November 24, 1885–March 29, 1970): Communist sympathizer and well-known American writer.

Anna Louise Strong was born in Friend, Nebraska, in a family that traced its ancestors to seventeenth-century New England. Her father was a Congregationalist minister, and Strong was a gifted writer and poet, being first published at age nineteen.

Graduating early from high school, Strong went to Europe for eighteen months at the age of fifteen. Upon her return to the United States in 1902, she entered Bryn Mawr College and soon transferred to Oberlin from where she graduated at the age of twenty.

Strong went to Chicago and worked for a magazine, writing poetry and contributing to their children and women's pages. She also enrolled at the University of Chicago where, working at odd jobs to support herself, she graduated three years later with a Ph.D. in philosophy magna cum laude. Her dissertation was later published.

The next few years were spent in different parts of the United States working with social welfare agencies and writing for periodicals. When World War I broke out, she also worked for pacifist organizations. But Strong's political ideology was not set until she got involved with the labor struggles in the Pacific Northwest. She was active in the Seattle General Strike of 1919.

Disenchanted with many things in the United States, she began to look to the Soviet Union as a model for change. Because Americans were not permitted to travel to the Soviet Union then, she went first to Poland as a representative of the American Friends Service Committee in the spring of 1921. By summer she was working in refugee relief in the Volga region, and by October she had arrived in Moscow.

Strong was immediately impressed with the social experiment being carried out in the Soviet Union. She began writing from Russia for several American labor newspapers and for Hearst's International News Service.

In 1925 Strong returned to the United States via China where she spent two months in Peking, Shanghai, and Canton. By 1927 she was back in Moscow, only to leave almost immediately for China again, this time to go specifically to Hankow where Soviet advisers were working with the left-wing Kuomintang government. When that government fell, Strong managed to escape with the Soviets across China and the Gobi Desert, at one point almost getting lost from the caravan.

Anna Louise Strong's life settled into a routine. She was based in Moscow but traveled extensively throughout the Soviet Union and elsewhere such as Spain to cover the civil war and to China once again, this time to the Communist headquarters in Yenan where she interviewed all the major leaders including Mao Tse-tung.[*] Beginning in 1930, the major outlet for her writing was the English-language *Moscow Daily News*. She also made frequent trips back to the United States where she lectured widely.

In February 1949 Strong was suddenly arrested in Moscow, accused of being an American spy. She spent some days in jail and was deported on February 22. After Stalin's death, in March 1955, the Soviet government admitted it had made a mistake and withdrew the charges.

Meanwhile, Strong had been waging a protracted struggle to get a passport from the U.S. government. In July 1958 Washington finally relented, and she immediately left for Moscow revisiting old haunts and friends. However, her destination was now China where she arrived in September. She had become disillusioned with the Soviet Union and saw China as a better model for society.

At the age of seventy-three Anna Louise Strong made her permanent home in Peking from where she continued to travel to places such as North Korea, Tibet, and Southeast Asia. From Peking she continued her prolific writing of articles and books and began a pamphlet series entitled *Letter from China* (1961–1970). It was in Peking that she died at the age of eighty-five. Anna Louise Strong had written some forty books, over 500 magazine articles, and a countless number of newspaper articles. For many in the United States and Europe she was the authoritative voice on events in the Soviet Union and, later, in the People's Republic of China.[*]

REFERENCES: Anna Louise Strong, *I Change Worlds: The Remaking of an American* (New York, 1935; reprinted Seattle, 1979); Tracy B. Strong and Helene Keyssar, *Right in Her Soul* (New York, 1983); Robert William Pringle, Jr., "Anna Louise Strong: Propagandist for Communism" (Ph.D. dissertation, University of Virginia, 1967).

A. TOM GRUNFELD

SUN FO (October 20, 1891–September 13, 1973): Son of Sun Yat-sen; head of the Legislative Yuan and premier of the ROC in China.

Sun Fo was born in Hsiangshan *hsien*, Kwangtung. Educated in America and long active in Kuomintang politics and government service, he served as president of the Executive Yuan for four months after holding the presidency of the Legislative Yuan from June 1932 to November 1948. After 1949 Sun Fo lived for a period in France and then in the United States. In 1964 he moved to Taiwan, became a senior adviser to the presidential office in 1965, and took up the post of president of the Examination Yuan in May 1966.

In 1896 Sun Fo left China with his mother to join Sun Yat-sen[*] in Hawaii. He was educated in Honolulu and graduated from St. Louis College, a Catholic institution, in 1910. From 1908 to 1910 he worked on the Chinese-language newspaper, the *Liberty News*.

Sun Fo went to the United States in 1911 to study at the University of California. After the Revolution of 1911,[*] he returned to China to join the new republican government. Dr. Sun Yat-sen sent his son back to study in America where he graduated from the University of California in 1916; Sun Fo went on to receive an M.A. in economics from Columbia University in 1917. He returned to China in 1917 where he worked in the Rump Parliament at Canton and in the Ministry of Foreign Affairs. In 1919 Sun Fo became associate editor of the English-language *Canton Times* but moved the following year to Hong Kong.

From 1921 to 1925 Sun Fo served as mayor of Canton where he oversaw projects in road building, street widening, sewage system construction, and the introduction of modern public utilities. He played a part in drafting a Kuomintang constitution, and he went on to Kuomintang posts such as membership in the Central Executive Committee and the Political Council. He also became commissioner of reconstruction and active governor of Kwangtung.

After the Northern Expedition[*] of 1926, Sun Fo was associated with the government established in Wuhan in opposition to Chiang Kai-shek[*] and his anti-Communist supporters who established a government at Nanking.[*] Sun Fo was a key figure in the Wuhan government as a member of the five-man Standing Committee of the Government Council, director of the party youth ministry, a member of the presidium of the Central Political Council, and a member of the Military Council.

With the advent of a newly unified national government at Nanking in October 1928, Sun Fo became a member of the State Council, minister of railroads, and vice-president of the Examination Yuan. In 1929 he established China's first civil aviation company, the China National Aviation Corporation.

As president of the Legislative Yuan from 1932 to 1948, Sun Fo directed the drafting of modern laws for the Republic of China.* While in this position, he opposed as too soft Chiang Kai-shek's policies toward Japan and urged instead immediate military opposition to Japan's invasion. In 1937 he represented China in secret negotiations with the Soviet Union, which resulted in a Sino-Soviet nonaggression pact. In 1938 and 1939 he represented Chiang Kai-shek in Moscow for talks that led to loans from Stalin and a Sino-Soviet Commercial Treaty in 1939. Early in the Sino-Japanese War,* Sun Fo frequently lectured on world affairs. A collection of his speeches titled *Ch'ien-tu* was published in 1942, followed in 1944 by an English version published in the United States under the title *China Looks Forward*.

As president of the Legislative Yuan Sun Fo played a major part in shaping the 1947 constitution which eliminated the Kuomintang's twenty-year monopoly on power. From 1947 to 1948 he held the newly created post of vice-president. REFERENCE: Howard L. Boorman and Richard C. Howard, eds., *Biographical Dictionary of Republican China*, vol. 3 (New York, 1970).

                                                                     PARRIS H. CHANG

SUN YAT-SEN (November 12, 1866–March 12, 1925): Founding father and first president of the Republic of China.

Born in 1866 into a peasant family in Tsui-heng Village, Hsiang-shan County, near Canton, some fifteen miles from the Portuguese colony of Macao, Sun Yat-sen received traditional primary education in village schools as a child, studying primers on Chinese classics. In 1879, when he was thirteen, his mother took him to Hawaii to join his emigrant elder brother. During the next four years, Sun studied at missionary schools and graduated from Oahu College in 1883, at the age of seventeen. This early exposure to the outside world helped influence his future career as a revolutionary.

Returning to China, Sun found himself unable to adjust to the restricted life in his native village now that his horizons had been broadened. After an arranged marriage to a girl at age eighteen, he went to Hong Kong, first to study English and then to study medicine, eventually graduating from the College of Medicine for Chinese in Hong Kong in 1892. During his years in Hong Kong, he also did further studies in Chinese history and classics. Therefore, upon his graduation, he was not only a modern professional, but also had considerable Western and Chinese education, as well as twelve years of experience living in Hawaii and Hong Kong. The Western impact on him was profound.

During his maturing years in Hong Kong, like many other young intellectuals, Sun was intensely concerned about the fate of his country. Each humiliation China suffered at the hands of foreign powers only served to further radicalize him. He repeatedly petitioned local officials for reform, and in 1894, he also traveled to Tientsin to petition Viceroy Li Hung-chang*, presenting in detail his ideas for strengthening China in the face of foreign encroachment. When his petition fell on deaf ears, a thoroughly disappointed Sun, now twenty-eight, went to Hawaii and made a daring move: he organized the first revolutionary group, the Hsing-chung hui (Revive China Society),* aimed at overthrowing the Manchu government and establishing a republic in China, a goal from which he was never to deviate for the rest of his life.

With the help of the anti-Manchu secret society members, he launched an uprising in southern China in 1895. The uprising ended in failure, and Sun became an exile with a price on his head. The next year, he narrowly escaped death, when the Chinese Legation in London kidnapped him and tried unsuccessfully to ship him back to China. After his release, he stayed in London for the next two years, spending much time at the British Museum. It was during this crucial period that he developed his famous Three People's Principles:* nationalism, democracy, and people's livelihood.

In 1905 Sun traveled to Japan, where he formed the T'ung-meng hui* (Chinese United League) by merging his followers with several other groups, thus greatly strengthening the revolutionary ranks. Between 1907 and 1911, more uprisings were attempted in China. After the Wuchang Uprising in October 1911, many provinces declared independence from Peking, and on January 1, 1912, Sun was chosen president of the Republic of China* in Nanking.

In February 1912, in an effort to promote national unification, Sun resigned the presidency in favor of Yüan Shih-k'ai*, the strongman in the Peking government. In the next several years, Yüan decimated Sun's followers, now known as the Kuomintang, in order to return China to a monarchy and install himself as emperor. Sun was again in exile abroad. Yüan died in 1916, after the demise of his short-lived monarchy, leaving the country in chaos with warlords fighting for control.

Without a base and without his own military forces, Sun sought in vain for help from Western powers to regroup his revolutionary followers. In 1923 he received help from the Soviet Union, which led to the collaboration with the Chinese Communists and the founding of the Whampoa Military Academy* to train the Nationalist revolutionary forces. In the winter of 1924, already in poor health, he traveled north from his base in Canton, hoping to secure peace with the warlord government in Peking. On March 12, he died in Peking at the age of fifty-nine with his goal of unifying the country unfulfilled.

Sun left behind many writings concerning his ideas on the reconstruction of China, published as different editions of his complete works. He is universally respected as the founding father of the Republic.

REFERENCES: Lyon Sharman, *Sun Yat-sen, His Life and Its Meaning* (New York, 1934); Harold Schiffrin, *Sun Yat-sen and the Origins of the Chinese Revolution* (Berkeley, Calif. 1968); C. Martin Wilbur, *Sun Yat-sen, Frustrated Patriot* (New York, 1976).

TA-LING LEE

SUN–JOFFE MANIFESTO (January 26, 1923): An agreement between Sun Yat-sen, leader of the KMT, and Adolf Joffe, high-ranking Soviet diplomat.

The Sun–Joffe Manifesto was an agreement of Soviet support for the Kuomintang between Dr. Adolf Joffe, a high-ranking Soviet diplomat, and Dr. Sun

Yat-sen[*], leader of the KMT. Issued on January 26, 1923, the manifesto stated the conditions of cooperation between the KMT and the Soviet Union. The two men agreed that because of the dismal political and economic conditions in China it was not possible to establish communism or even a more limited Soviet system. In addition, the manifesto stated Joffe's primary concern that China's most pressing problems were the completion of national unification and attainment of independence from foreign powers in China.

The manifesto later became the basis for negotiations between Joffe and Liao Chung-k'ai, a labor leader and an ardent representative of the KMT leftwing. The Sun–Joffe Manifesto strengthened the KMT and eventually forced the Communists to ally with the Chinese Nationalists.

Preparation for the manifesto began in August 1922, with a series of correspondence between Joffe in Peking and Sun, who had sought refuge in Shanghai from warlord Ch'en Chiung-ming. Spurred on by the prospects of negotiation, fifty KMT representatives met in Shanghai on September 4, 1922. The majority of these representatives agreed with Sun's plan to reorganize the party. Hu Han-min[*] and Wang Ching-wei[*] were elected by the representatives to draft a manifesto, which Sun Yat-sen revised and approved on December 16. Joffe advised Dr. Sun on the reformation of his party and on making the Three People's Principles[*] specifically anti-imperialist.

In order to prepare for negotiations with the Comintern's[*] representative, the KMT announced its new political platform on January 1, 1923. Provisions were made in the party constitution for holding annual party congresses and monthly meetings for leaders of party committees and departments, establishing party branches in major cities. While the Comintern had made a negative assessment of the Chinese Communist party[*] and had previously failed to persuade Sun to form an alliance with the CCP, both sides accepted a Comintern compromise allowing CCP members to join the KMT as individuals, with the understanding that they could retain their Communist affiliations.

On January 17, 1923, Joffe met with Sun in Shanghai to discuss the conditions for Soviet aid. Joffe had offered Soviet moral and financial support to Sun and the KMT on the conditions that they agree (1) to establish diplomatic relations with Moscow and to recognize the Soviets as the legitimate government of Russia; (2) to form an open alliance with the Soviet government; and (3) to place no restriction on Bolshevik revolutionary propaganda in China. The first two conditions were acceptable to Dr. Sun, but he rejected the last condition for fear of alienating wealthy and conservative KMT supporters. A compromise was finally reached, and the two men agreed that Dr. Sun and the KMT would recognize the Soviet government once they achieved supremacy in China; in return, the Soviet government would give Sun moral and financial support.

On January 26, 1923, a joint statement was issued in English as a warning to American and British imperialists, outlining broad agreement between Sun and Joffe. But the document did not mention any agreement on Soviet aid for Sun and the KMT. The manifesto had significant foreign and domestic implications. For Sun and the KMT, the statement is written as a state paper between a Chinese leader responsible for foreign policy matters and a foreign envoy. The agreement was Sun's attempt to undercut the legitimacy of the Peking government, and the Soviets' growing ties with northern warlord Wu P'ei-fu.* To achieve this purpose, Sun Yat-sen inserted the provision that the Russians should consult with northern warlord Chang Tso-lin on any new arrangement for the operation of the Chinese Eastern Railway. Chang Tso-lin and Dr. Sun were quasi-allies against the Peking government and Wu P'ei-fu. The railway was important because it ran through territory controlled by Chang. This insertion signaled that Dr. Sun had not forgotten his ally's interest.

For the Soviets, the agreement was the third leg of its foreign policy tripod. The Foreign Office wanted State relations with Peking and the northern warlords. The Comintern wanted to support revolutionary groups whose goal was to advance the anti-imperialist struggle. Finally, the Soviet Union wanted to protect its interest in the Chinese Eastern Railway. As Lenin explained in his essay, "Left-wing Communism," the objective of revolutionary work was to minimize the number of one's enemies and maximize the number of allies and friends. However, the overlapping alliances with the KMT, the Chinese Communist party, the warlords, and the government in Peking were fraught with contradictions and would result in violent struggles between the Communist and Nationalist forces.

REFERENCES: Shinkichi Etō, "China's International Relations 1911–1931," *The Cambridge History of China: Republican China, 1912–1949*, part 2 (London, 1986); C. Martin Wilbur, *Sun Yat-sen: Frustrated Patriot* (New York, 1976); C. Martin Wilbur and Julie Lien-ying How, *Documents on Communism and Nationalism, and Soviet Advisors in China, 1918–1927* (New York, 1972).

RICHARD C. KAGAN

SUNG CHIAO-JEN (April 5, 1882–March 22, 1913): Late Ch'ing revolutionary and early republican statesman.

Sung Chiao-jen was born into a lower gentry household in T'ao-yüan County, Hunan. At the local Chang-chiang Academy, he is reported to have shown interest in statecraft, textual criticism, and neo-Confucian self-cultivation. In 1901 he won the *sheng-yüan* degree.

Precocious, strong-willed, and fond of physical exercise as a youth, Sung was exposed to a variety of anti-Manchu influences. China's traumatic defeat by Japan, the reform movement, the empress dowager's coup, the Boxer* fiasco, and the Independence Army Uprising (in which he was briefly involved) confirmed him as an anti-Manchu revolutionary. In 1902 he entered a modern school, the Wen-p'u-t'ung hsüeh-hsiao, in Wuchang. When Huang Hsing* returned from Japan in 1903 to organize an uprising, Sung Chiao-jen became one of the founding members of Huang's revolutionary organization and took over coordination of the forces in his native area of northwestern Hunan.

The exposure of the plot in 1904 forced Sung to flee to Japan, where he spent most of the next six years. There he immediately organized and published a new

revolutionary journal, *Erh-shih shih-chi chih Chih-na* (Twentieth-century China).
His earliest extant writings on public affairs date from this period, and show
him to have been deeply, and favorably, impressed by Japanese nationalism and
militarism. At the same time, Sung entered, and passed, a college preparatory
course at Waseda University. Upon Sun Yat-sen's* return to Tokyo in 1905,
Sung was involved in the founding of the T'ung-meng hui* and was made an
officer in its Judicial Department. His journal, which had been suppressed by
the Japanese authorities, was converted into an organ of the new revolutionary
party under the name *Min-pao*.

Keenly interested in Manchuria, especially in news of a bandit kingdom in
the area known as Chien-tao on the Korean border, Sung went there in March
of 1907 to enlist the mounted bandits into the revolutionary cause, and to prepare
simultaneous northern and southern uprisings. Although this undertaking failed,
Sung learned details of Japanese machinations to falsify the border and claim
Manchurian territory for Korea. Recording these findings in a book, he made
the manuscript available to the Ch'ing government,* and is credited thereby with
a major contribution to the successful rejection of Japan's demands. From this
time until the end of 1910, Sung apparently read widely in world affairs, constitutional law, and finance, translating and publishing Kobayashi Ushisaburô's
massive, two-volume *Comparative Public Finance*.

Sung returned to Shanghai in early 1911 and became a major writer for Yü
Yu-jen's revolutionary newspaper, *Min-li pao*, criticizing the Ch'ing regime's
incompetence in finance and foreign policy and its spurious program for constitutional government. His articles on Chinese, Japanese, and English politics
during this year show a strong commitment to the principles and institutions of
representative government, a position that is sharply at variance with his earlier
militarism.

Sung went to Hong Kong to participate in the abortive Canton uprising of
April 1911. Frustrated by its failure and long dissatisfied with Sun Yat-sen's
leadership, he organized a nearly independent Central Branch of the T'ung-meng
hui to begin plans for an uprising in the Yangtze region. After the outbreak of
the Wuchang Uprising in October, he joined Huang Hsing there to undertake
the organization of provincial and national revolutionary governments. Strongly
favoring a parliamentary form of government, he clashed with Sun when Sun
returned to China and insisted on the presidential system. Sun's views prevailed
for the time, and in January 1912 Sung was appointed attorney general of the
Legislative Bureau. Shortly before Yüan Shih-k'ai's* election to the presidency
of the new Republic, the provisional assembly, hoping to limit his power, adopted
a constitution with many features of a parliamentary system. Sung was appointed
minister of Agriculture and forestry in the new cabinet.

Yüan's disregard of constitutional constraints confirmed Sung's worst fears
about him, and after the cabinet's resignation in July, Sung, convinced of the
need for a responsible cabinet under a majority party, spearheaded a drive to
amalgamate several parties around the T'ung-meng hui as a contender for par-

liamentary dominance. The Kuomintang was established in August and won an impressive victory in the Republic's first general elections the following winter. Now openly critical of Yüan's government, Sung was rumored to be a likely choice for the premiership; he also seems to have approached Li Yüan-hung* as a candidate to displace Yüan in the presidency. On March 20, 1913, departing for Peking for consultations with Yüan and the opening of the new Assembly, Sung was shot by Ying K'uei-hsing at the Shanghai railroad station, in an assassination generally accepted to have been ordered by Yüan Shih-k'ai.

REFERENCES: K. S. Liew, *Struggle for Democracy* (Berkeley, Calif., 1971); Don C. Price, "Sung Chiao-jen, Confucianism and Revolution," *Ch'ing-shih wen-t'i* 3, no. 7 (November 1977): 40–66; Wu Hsiang-hsiang, *Sung Chiao-jen* (Taipei, 1964).

DON C. PRICE

T

TAIPING REVOLUTION (1851–1864): First revolutionary movement in modern China.

The Taiping Movement, though not the only significant Chinese uprising of the nineteenth century, was certainly the first of the modern era which drew its inspiration as much from outside foreign influences as indigenous Chinese conditions. The uprising, which originated from a host of tensions stemming from demographic, economic, and religious issues, eventually engulfed the majority of Chinese provinces and literally destroyed the lives of untold millions. Some have estimated the death toll at more than 20 million people.

Literally dwarfing the American Civil War which it partly paralleled, the Taiping Movement set off a civil war that eventually overwhelmed large portions of China. The rebellion itself was sparked by a proclamation by Hung Hsiu-ch'üan,* a failed examination scholar, of a Kingdom of Heavenly Peace based on a newly devised version of the Christianity trinity, a modification that included himself as the younger brother of Jesus.

Taiping society was quite puritanical and outlawed alcohol, opium, and gambling. While few gentry joined the effort, large numbers of southern Chinese, from the poorer classes of Kwangtung and Kwangsi provinces and especially Hakka, were drawn to the movement. Attracted to images of a primitive communism reminiscent of both purported Chou dynasty (1123–249 B.C.) practices and early Christianity, the movement proved well able to inspire large numbers of Chinese. For women, the Taipings proclaimed sexual equality and outlawed both footbinding and concubinage, although in practice Taiping society often deviated from its own stated goals regarding sexual equality. The principal leaders, for example, maintained large harems.

The Taiping Revolution was as great a challenge as Confucian society was to meet before the twentieth century, and many of their practices foreshadowed more recent developments. Rejecting the use of classical Chinese, the Taipings worked to introduce more simply written material in the vernacular. They also carried out an iconoclastic attack on Chinese traditional culture. Both developments are familiar to students of twentieth-century China and especially movements like the May Fourth Era* and the Cultural Revolution.*

By 1853 the movement led by Hung and a group of exceptional leaders, now titled Taiping Wangs, or princes, swept north into the historic southern capital of the Ming dynasty: Nanking. Tremendous momentum had developed, and it looked for a time like the Ch'ing dynasty* itself was about to totter. Unfortunately for the Taipings, however, their leadership at Nanking, so impressive in the early years, soon flagged. Worse, by 1856 the Taiping leadership almost destroyed itself in a series of bloody internecine struggles. Only rarely was the Heavenly Kingdom later able to muster the forces necessary to fundamentally threaten the Ch'ing dynasty. By 1864, under the leadership of gentry militia leaders like Tseng Kuo-fan* and others, the Taipings were destroyed. Nevertheless, the movement played a significant role in inspiring later leaders from Sun Yat-sen* to Mao Tse-tung.* Among contemporary Chinese leaders, the Taipings are often cited as the first peasant revolutionaries of modern Chinese history.

REFERENCES: Yu-wen Jen, *The Taiping Revolutionary Movement* (New Haven, Conn., 1973); Franz Michael, *The Taipings*, 3 vols. (Seattle, Wash., 1966–1977); Prosper Giquel, *The Journal of the Chinese Civil War*, edited by Steven A. Leibo (Hawaii, 1985); S. Y. Teng, *The Taiping Rebellion and the Western Powers* (Oxford, 1971); Richard J. Smith, *Mercenaries and Mandarins, the Ever-Victorious Army in Nineteenth Century China* (Milwood, N.Y., 1978).

STEVEN A. LEIBO

T'AN SSU-T'UNG (1865–1898): Reformer, philosopher, activist, and martyr of the One Hundred Day Reform.

T'an Ssu-t'ung, a native of Hunan, was an important philosopher and activist in modern China, who, though his life was exceedingly short, played a significant role in Chinese history. He is often remembered as a heroic figure for his martyrdom in the coup d'etat of 1898 and as a great thinker for the ideas he expressed in the *Jen-hsüeh* (An Exposition of Benevolence.)

T'an was born into a scholar-gentry family in Peking in 1865. At the age of five, he began to gain some knowledge of traditional Chinese learning from Pi Ch'un-chai. Five years later, he studied under Ou-yang Chung-ku, a well-known Hunanese scholar. In 1876 a diphtheria epidemic in Peking took the lives of six of his relatives, among them his most beloved mother. This was a great shock to him which was to have an immense impact on his life. T'an also fell victim to the epidemic but was miraculously cured after three days. His father therefore gave him the name of Fu-sheng, or "Restored to Life."

From 1878 to 1889, when his father was intendant of the Circuit of Kansu, T'an began to explore the writings of Mo Tzu and Chuang Tzu, and it was during these years that such ideas as "love without discrimination" and "chivalry" began to take shape. With his father's promotion to the governorship of

Hupeh in 1889, T'an moved to Wuchang where he was exposed to new influences that opened up his horizons. He fraternized with intellectuals who had firsthand knowledge of the West, and he also met Europeans, John Fryer in particular whose influences brought him a new vision of Western culture. At the same time, he spent a great deal of his time on scholarly pursuits in traditional Chinese learning. Nevertheless, the years 1894 to 1896 may be viewed as the most crucial years during which T'an Ssu-t'ung, deeply agitated by the bankruptcy of superficial reforms as demonstrated by China's defeat in the Sino-Japanese War,[*] reexamined many of his previous opinions and attitudes and began to search for a new identity. He therefore dropped most of his ideas and adopted a new name "Chuang-fei" (meaning "fly high") to mark his resolution to start anew.

In 1896, in deference to his father's wishes, T'an accepted an official position as expectant prefect in Nanking. It was the corruption of officialdom, among other things, which had prompted T'an to study Buddhism with a leading Buddhist layman Yang Wen-hui. It was during the summer of 1896 and the spring of 1897 that he began to think through all that he had observed and studied to write his most widely recognized work, *An Exposition of Benevolence*. This treatise grew out of an awakening that resulted from China's disastrous defeat in the Sino-Japanese War and from the realization that, without rectifying the deep-rooted misconceptions and parochialism of the Chinese people, China was doomed to disaster. The work was not published until three months after T'an's death in the *China Discussion* (*Ch'ing-i pao*) in thirteen installments between 1898 and 1901. It not only had enormous influence on T'an's fellow patriots, but it also uplifted the revolutionary morality of many who followed in his footsteps to fight for national independence at the turn of the twentieth century. On the score of this theoretical work, he has been extolled by Liang Ch'i-ch'ao[*] as "a meteor of the late Ch'ing intellectual world"; by Ts'ai Shang-ssu as "a vanguard, a bombshell, a Wang Ch'ung of modern China"; by Ch'en Po-ta[*] as "a forerunner of May Fourth iconoclasm"; by one of his biographers, Yang T'ing-fu, as "an enlightening thinker of the modern bourgeois movement, a democrat and a vanguard of materialism in nineteenth-century China"; and by various other historians as "a radical thinker of the 1890's."

In 1897 Ch'en Pao-chen, the governor of Hunan, urged T'an to return to Changsha to take part in the reform of the province. T'an immediately resigned his position and returned to Hunan. In the Hunan Reform Movement, he made a number of proposals that were instrumental in sweeping aside the conservative atmosphere of the province. The following year, with the promulgation of the Reform Decree, upon the recommendation of Hsü Chih-cheng, T'an was summoned for an audience with Emperor Kuang-hsü[*] and was later appointed a fourth-rank secretary in the Grand Council to help with the work of carrying out far-reaching reforms. But the reform incurred great enmity from the empress dowager Tz'u hsi[*] and her ministers which, in less than ten days, led to a coup d'etat. T'an was arrested on September 25, and was beheaded at Ts'ai-shih-k'ou three days later.

REFERENCES: Chan Sin-wai, *T'an Ssu-t'ung: An Annotated Bibliography* (Hong Kong, 1980); Chan Sin-wai, trans., *An Exposition of Benevolence: The Jen-hsüeh of T'an Ssu-t'ung* (Hong Kong, 1984).

CHAN SIN-WAI

T'ANG SHAO-YI (Tzu Shao-ch'uan, 1860–September 30, 1938): First premier of the Chinese Republic, long associated with Yüan Shih-k'ai; generally aligned with elements within the Kuomintang opposing Chiang Kai-shek.

T'ang Shao-yi was born in Hsiangshan (now Chungshan), Kwangtung Province, into a family with an uncle (T'ang T'ing-shu) well known for his entrepreneurial activities as comprador for Jardine Matheson and as director of such enterprises as the China Merchants' Steam Navigation company and the K'aip'ing Mining Company. Through this uncle's friendship with Yung Wing* (Jung Hung), T'ang was put on the third contingent of youngsters to be sent to America in 1874 to obtain a Western eduction under the China Educational Mission program. T'ang returned to China in 1881, before obtaining his B.A. from Columbia University. His subsequent political career saw repeated appreciative use of Chinese with foreign training—a trait of entrepreneurial and compradorial openness long identified with Hsiangshan people.

Beginning his career as a minor official sent to Korea, T'ang Shao-yi witnessed the major events of the late nineteenth century and met and worked with some of the era's great figures: the Korean crises leading to the Li-Itō Agreement and later the Sino-Japanese War of 1894–1895*, and persons such as Li Hung-chang* and Yüan Shih-k'ai*. Yüan especially liked T'ang and helped him gain posts of growing importance. T'ang therefore played major roles in such early twentieth-century events as quelling the Boxers* in Shantung, serving as customs *tao-t'ai* in the same province when Yüan was governor, and negotiating with the British over the status of Tibet.

Prior to the 1911 Revolution,* T'ang held high positions in the Imperial Maritime Customs, the Peking–Hankow and Nanking–Shanghai railways, the Board of Communications, Opium Abolition Regulations, and the politics of building and financing the Canton–Kowloon Railway. His penchant for hiring foreign-trained personnel earned him considerable conservative opposition.

When Yüan Shih-k'ai, T'ang's former mentor, came out of retirement after the outbreak of the Republican Revolution in October 1911, T'ang's star rose once more. He headed the team appointed by Yüan to negotiate with the revolutionaries on behalf of the Manchus. Through the many about-faces of early republican politics, T'ang was ultimately appointed premier by Yüan when Yüan assumed office as the first president of the Chinese Republic in March 1912. This height of power was short-lived, however, for by June of the same year, Tang and Yüan became openly estranged. Tang's gravitation toward Sun Yat-sen's* cause was one of the causes of this rift. After Yüan made known his monarchical ambitions, T'ang joined forces with the reforming Kuomintang to oppose him.

T'ang participated in the many internal strifes of the Kuomintang before its reorganization in 1919. In October of that year, he returned to Hsiangshan to retire in his Kung-le-yüan (Garden of Shared Happiness), refusing several of Sun Yat-sen's offers of high posts in Sun's revolutionary government. In October 1925 T'ang issued a statement opposing tariff talks in Peking, favoring general constitutional revision, local self-government, and reinstatement of the Chinese civil service system, and demanding an end to warlordism* and imperialism.

Oriented to south China culturally and politically, T'ang spurned Chiang Kai-shek's* entreaty for him to be an elder statesman and, when Chiang exiled Hu Han-min,* T'ang joined forces with the southern elements of the KMT composed of Wang Ching-wei* and Sun Fo*. Moreover, he had always given his support to the semi-independent Southwest Executive Headquarters of the Kuomintang and the Southwest Political Council. He became more nationalistic and supported the Nanking government,* especially after the Manchurian Incident of 1931.

Details of T'ang's assassination on Sept. 30, 1938 remain opaque. He was assassinated by four men whose identities and motive remain mysterious. T'ang chose to remain in Shanghai during the Japanese occupation. Married twice and served by two concubines, he sired four sons and several daughters. Son Liu (Tong Lao) served as consul-general in Singapore and Honolulu. One daughter married Wellington V.K. Koo (Ku Wei-chün),* and another had married a son of K. C. Lee, noted business leader of Singapore.

REFERENCES: *Biographical Dictionary of Republican China*, Howard L. Boorman and Richard Howard, eds., vol. 3 (New York, 1970): 232–236; Mary C. Wright, ed. *China in Revolution: The First Phase, 1900–1913* (New Haven, Conn., 1968); James E. Sheridan, *China in Disintegration* (New York, 1975).

D.W.Y. KWOK

TENG HSIAO-P'ING (1904–   ): Chairman of the CCP Military Commission; member of the CCP Politburo Standing Committee.

Teng Hsiao-p'ing, one of the most important leaders in China since the early 1950s, was born into a family of landlords in Kuang-an in southwestern Szechwan Province in 1904. After middle school education, he left home at sixteen to study as a work-study student in France, where he became a close friend of Chou En-lai.* In Paris he joined the Chinese Socialist Youth League in 1922 and the Chinese Communist party* in 1924. He studied briefly in Moscow before his return to China in 1926, and he became a very active CCP member in China's Communist movement.

During the Long March* of 1934–1935, Teng served as a political officer in the First Front Army. After the Sino-Japanese War* broke out in 1937, he was appointed political commissar of the 129th Division under the command of General Liu Po-Ch'eng, with whom he worked closely for the next fifteen years. In the postwar years, Teng, who was elected a member of the CCP Central Committee by the Seventh CCP Congress in 1945, played a decisive role in the final elimination of Chiang Kai-shek's* Nationalist forces from the mainland.

After the establishment of the People's Republic of China* government in

Peking in 1949, Teng held several posts in Szechwan and southwest China in the early 1950s. Appointed vice-premier in 1952, he became the CCP's secretary-general in 1954. From 1952 to 1966 he held a number of important posts, including those of finance minister, vice-chairman of the National Defense Council, member of the ruling Politburo of the CCP and its Standing Committee, and acting premier. Responsible for the operations of the CCP Central Committee as its secretary-general, he also played a significant role in drafting the PRC constitution in 1954. As the sixth ranking member in the CCP hierarchy, he delivered important speeches at CCP meetings on such important issues as the denunciation of the Kao Kang-Jao Shu-shih anti-Party block in 1955, the Anti-rightist Campaign* of 1957, and the problems and issues dividing the Communist parties of China and the Soviet Union in the late 1950s and early 1960s. He led several delegations to Moscow in the early 1960s and played a key role in the growing conflict between Peking and Moscow. In 1963 he held tough ideological talks with the Soviet ideologue M. A. Suslov, which led to the open rift between China and the Soviet Union.

Purged in 1966 at the beginning of the Cultural Revolution,* Teng was forced to undergo self-criticism on the charge of following Liu Shao-ch'i's* bourgeois-reactionary line as number two capitalist roader.* Rehabilitated by Premier Chou En-lai, Teng reappeared in public as vice-premier in 1973. Groomed as ailing Chou's successor, Teng was elected vice-chairman of the CCP Central Committee in 1975. Soon after Chou's death in January 1976, the radical Gang of Four* engineered Teng's dismissal from all party, government, and army posts. It was only after the purge of the Gang of Four upon the death of Mao Tse-tung* in September 1976 that Teng, a durable figure with a forceful personality, regained his former status and power to push forward China's modernization drive.

Soon afterward, Teng shunted aside Mao's handpicked successor, Hua Kuo-feng*, and installed his associates Hu Yao-pang* and Chao Tzu-yang* to replace Hua. He emerged more clearly than ever as China's most powerful leader following his election as chairman of the CCP's Military Commission in 1981. In the late 1970s and early and mid–1980s, the CCP and PRC government, under his energetic leadership, downgraded Mao's personal legacy and launched economic reforms and the modernization drive. They adopted such pragmatic policies as accepting Western technology and investment, sanctioning higher wages and other benefits for workers, and giving greater scope to individual initiative. These and other policies helped China achieve some economic prosperity and substantially improved the average income and living standard.

After his return to power in 1973, Teng stressed stability, production, economic modernization and growth, and pragmatism rather than ideology. He played a vital role in establishing formal diplomatic relations between China and the United States in 1979 and in normalizing Sino-Soviet relations in 1989. His realistic approach to China's economic problems, and as well as his emphasis on higher wages and other incentives for workers and for a rise in the Chinese living standard, won him wide support among the Chinese people in the early 1980s. He refused, however, to accept the growing demand for democratization and political reforms in the mid- and late 1980s.

The 1989 military suppression of the growing student democracy movement was a serious setback to Teng's personal reputation and modernization drive. Even though he relinquished all his official posts in 1989–1990, he remains the most powerful and influential leader in China today.

REFERENCES: A. Doak Barnett and Ralph N. Clough, eds., *Modernizing China: Post-Mao Reform and Development* (Boulder, Colo., 1986); David Wen-Wei Chang, *China under Deng Xiaoping* (New York, 1988); Han Shan-pi (Han Wen-fu), *Teng Hsiao-p'ing p'ing-ch'uan* (A critical biography of Teng Hsiao-p'ing), 3 vols. (Hong Kong, 1984–1988); Donald W. Klein and Anne B. Clark, *Biographic Dictionary of Chinese Communism 1921–1965*, vol. 2 (Cambridge, Mass., 1971): 819–825; Teng Hsiao-p'ing, *Selected Works of Deng Xiaoping (1975–82)* (Peking, 1984); Winston L.Y. Yang, "Deng Xiaoping," *Encyclopaedia Britannica 1982 Book of the Year* (Chicago, 1982): 73.

WINSTON L.Y. YANG

TENG YING-CH'AO (1903–   ): Member of Central Committee and Politburo; vice-chairman, NPC; chairman, National Committee of the CPPCC; honorary president, National Women's Federation of China.

Teng Ying-ch'ao was born in Hsin-yang, southern Honan. Her widowed schoolteacher mother sent Teng to study successively in Peking and Tientsin. By the time of her graduation from middle school in Tientsin in 1920, she had become deeply immersed in the May Fourth Movement.* She had already helped found the Tientsin Students' Union and was a leading participant in the Tientsin Women's Patriotic Association. It was during a street demonstration that she reportedly first met her future husband, Chou En-lai.* She and Chou contributed to the initial radical journals that were published at the time, and she was jailed at least once for her activities.

During the five years that Chou En-lai was abroad, Teng continued to live mostly in Tientsin where she taught primary school and provided leadership in women's rights activities, including the founding of a society for progressive women and the publication of a newspaper. She joined the Socialist Youth League in 1924, and the following year she became a member of the Chinese Communist Party* and head of its Women's Department in Tientsin. She also joined the KMT. In late 1925 she went to Canton where she married Chou En-lai who had just returned from Europe.

In January 1926 Teng was elected to the KMT Central Executive Committee (being its only woman member). She moved to Wuhan with the KMT government when that urban center became secured, and served as vice-chairman of the Woman's Department under Liao Chung-k'ai's widow, Ho Hsiang-ning. But when the left-wing KMT foreclosed on the CCP in July 1927, Teng moved to Shanghai where she worked underground. She did, however, attend the Sixth CCP Congress in Moscow in mid–1928, at which time she was appointed head of the party's Women's Department.

In 1932 Teng went to the Chinese Soviet Republic that had been established in Kiangsi in November of the preceding year; there she continued to be very active, sometimes taking positions opposed to Mao Tse-tung.* She was reportedly made an alternate member of the Central Committee, and soon thereafter she became a member of the Soviet Republic's Central Executive Committee. However, that fall the Communists were forced out of their Kiangsi base, and Teng was one of the very few women who took part in the Long March.* She stayed in Shensi, the terminus of the Long March, only a short-time, and this stay was interrupted by a trip in 1937 to Japanese-occupied Peking for medical attention. Her safe departure from Peking was facilitated by American correspondent Edgar Snow.*

In 1938 Teng was sent with Chou En-lai to Hankow, the temporary provisional capital, to serve as CCP representatives to the Nationalist government in the new United Front. Shortly afterward, they evacuated with the government to Chungking, where she was a representative of the Eighth Route Army* (the designation of the Red Army during the Second United Front* period). Aside from another trip, this time to Moscow in 1939, Teng resided for the most part in Chungking until 1943. However, following the New Fourth Army Incident* in January 1941, in which the Nationalists killed thousands of Communist troops, Teng boycotted most of the meetings of the People's Political Council. She returned to Yenan in 1943, where she was active in women's organizing work. She was named an alternate member of the Central Committee in 1945.

After the war of resistance against Japan, Teng was again sent to Chungking as a delegate to the Political Consultative Conference, a new body agreed upon by Mao Tse-tung and Chiang Kai-shek,* and then moved to Nanking when the Nationalist government returned to its prewar capital. However, as the situation deteriorated toward civil strife, Teng and Chou returned to Yenan in late 1946. During the civil war* she remained active in women's organizational work and in the land reform program. She was elected a vice-chairman of the All-China Federation of Democratic Women (renamed the National Women's Federation of China in 1957) in April 1949, a position she would hold for many years, becoming its honorary president in September 1978.

Teng was very active in the work of establishing the new government and has had an impressively active career ever since. In October 1949 she was appointed a member of the Committee of Political and Legal Affairs in the Government Administration Council until October 1954. She was deeply involved in the drafting and difficult implementation of the Marriage Law, the People's Republic of China's* first major legislation and in many ways a capstone of her years of women's rights work, adopted on May 1, 1950. She was elected a delegate from Honan to the first National People's Congress (NPC) in August 1954, and re-elected in subsequent elections; she was also elected a member of the Standing Committee of the NPC in September 1954 and in subsequent elections. She was appointed vice-chairman of the Standing Committee of the NPC in December 1976, a post she held until June 1983, when she was elected chairman of the

National Committee of the Chinese People's Political Consultative Conference,* the leading United Front organization of the PRC. In this role, her call at a 1984 New Year's tea party for reunification with Taiwan was briefly publicized.

She delivered the major report to the Second Women's Congress in April 1953. She became a full member of the Central Committee sometime prior to the Eighth Party Congress in 1956, at which she gave a speech outlining the achievements and shortcomings in women's work.

Teng was a member of Kuo Mo-jo's delegation to the Second World Peace Congress in Warsaw in November 1950, and in March 1961 she led a delegation to Hanoi to attend a women's congress.

Teng was elected to the Politburo in December 1978 and again in September 1982. Along with 130 other elderly party veterans, however, she resigned from her party positions, including membership on the Central Committee and Politburo in September 1985.

REFERENCES: Donald W. Klein and Anne B. Clark, *Biographical Dictionary of Chinese Communism*, vol. 2 (Cambridge, Mass., 1971): 838–843; Wolfgang Bartke and Peter Schier, *China's New Party Leadership: Biographies and Analysis of the Twelfth Central Committee of the Chinese Communist Party* (Armonk, N.Y., 1985): 101–102.

STEPHEN UHALLEY, JR.

THOUGHT OF MAO TSE-TUNG: A term officially defined as equivalent to the Union of Marxism-Leninism with the practice of Chinese Revolution, that is, the application of Marxism-Leninism to the concrete practice of the Chinese Revolution.

Officially, the Thought of Mao Tse-tung is not considered to be coextensive with the actual thoughts of Mao Tse-tung* the man during his entire revolutionary career, but only that part of his thoughts that has been validated by the revolutionary practice of the Chinese Communist party.* On the other hand, the ordinary definition of the Thought of Mao Tse-tung would include all elements of the actual thoughts of Mao Tse-tung, the man. Here we will use the term in this sense.

The development of Mao's thought can be roughly divided into two periods— starting either with the downfall of the Kuomintang and the establishment of the people's democratic dictatorship in 1949 as a political dividing line, or with the complete annexation of private enterprises into the public sector in 1956 as an economical dividing line. In the first period, Chairman Mao struggled mainly against left deviation or adventurism and avoided taking risks in socialist reform and reconstruction. In the first period he was realistic in thought and action and achieved brilliant successes in both political revolution and economic reforms. In the second period, on the other hand, he struggled mainly against the right deviationism or opportunism as he saw it in the carrying through of the socialist revolution and reconstruction. He was not credited with the same success as in the first period.

Chairman Mao's most important insight was that a people's revolution in China must liberate peasants who are the most oppressed and exploited in a semifeudal and semicolonial society such as China from their bondage to the traditional landowning system. Based on his knowledge of many great peasant revolts in Chinese history, which were as a rule the motive power in dynastic changes, he realized the tremendous revolutionary potential of the peasant masses once driven to a desperate situation. Therefore, he advocated revolutionary strategies that were appropriate to these social conditions, and he opposed any doctrinaire copying of revolutionary strategies in Western capitalist countries. But the doctrinaire party chiefs, one after the other, had blindly obeyed directives from the Third International and staged military uprisings in big or medium cities. After they suffered calamitous defeats and brought about heavy losses to the Red Armies and the party, Mao Tse-tung was propelled to the position of party chairman. Under Mao's guidance, the CCP grew steadily and became increasingly stronger in the favorable circumstances of the war against the Japanese invasion.

Mao's successful strategies consisted in

1. Establishing a state apparatus in the hinterland of China and training a large number of both military and administrative personnel.

2. Strengthening the bases in the countryside and creating conditions to eventually adopt the famous strategy of encircling cities by occupying all the countryside.

3. Employing the strategy of people's war, that is, using numerically huge and courageous troops to overcome the mechanized armies of the Kuomintang in a favorable lay of the ground, and eventually driving out the Kuomintang from the mainland in 1949. All these stupendous military feats occurred in the first period.

The second period lasted about twenty years (1957–1976). Beginning from 1957 until the start of the Great Proletarian Cultural Revolution* in 1966, Mao Tse-tung repeatedly emphasized the class struggle within the nation and the party, and he urged the people, on the one hand, to "attend to class struggle yearly, monthly, and even daily," and on the other, to exert their utmost in reconstructing socialism, "to do more and better, and quicker, and (be) more parsimonious" in performing their duties on all points. But these two admonitions often worked at cross-purposes inasmuch as a person has to be suspicious of everybody when attending to class struggle, and no well-functioning and smooth operation of any system can be hoped for when everyone is in such a mood.

The first ten years of this period witnessed the Anti-Rightist Campaign* in the beginning and the starting of the Cultural Revolution* at the end, a series of intermittent class struggles. In the interim, roughly from 1959 to 1961, another series of stupendous struggles against nature was launched. By these struggles Chairman Mao dared to hope that the direction of rivers and the position of mountains could be changed in the process of a people's war against nature. The Three Red Banners*—the General Line of Socialist Reconstruction, the Great Leap Forward,* and the People's Communes*—were raised high, and few, however high their rank in the party hierarchy, dared to express a doubt. The consequence was three consecutive years of so-called natural calamity (by which the at least partially manmade disaster was whitewashed) which brought about widespread hunger and starvation, especially in the countryside. Mao's sanguine hope that this declaration of war on nature would bring communism near at hand was dashed, and he began to be suspicious that the right-deviationists were giving only lukewarm support to his policies or even that the capitalist roaders[*] within the party would sabotage his program. Then he declared war on his former comrades-in-arms and started the Great Proletarian Cultural Revolution. At this time, as a result of the personality cult, Mao became overly self-confident and ambitious, oblivious to any mistake he might be making. He blamed others, and even human nature itself, for all these frustrations and failures. He had always hoped to eradicate individualism and egoism by education, but it would be a protracted process. Now, through the Cultural Revolution, he believed human nature could be transformed all at once, and thus eventually root out these obstacles to communism. Apparently, Chairman Mao never recognized his own failings. In this second period he was idealistic rather than realistic, and what was allotted to him now was not success, but bafflement and frustration. Failures he did not admit.

REFERENCES: *Selected Works of Mao Tse-tung*, 5 vols.; Stuart R. Schram, *The Political Thought of Mao Tse-tung* (New York, 1969); Frederick Wakeman, Jr., *History and Will: Philosohpical Perspectives of Mao Tse-tung's Thought* (Berkeley, Calif. 1973).

                                                                    TIANJI JIANG

THOUGHT REFORM: Indoctrination program, particularly in the early 1950s.

Known colloquially as brainwashing (*hsi-nao*), the term *thought reform* (*ssu-hsiang kai-tsao*) refers to one of the methods the Communists used to achieve political socialization. Tapping traditional Chinese notions of the people's educability, thought reform was designed to alter the social and political outlook of citizens previously unsympathetic to communism. The methods used were physically less brutal than those employed by Stalin, though the Chinese Communist party's[*] methods could be very unpleasant. The psychological techniques were developed in the early 1940s, primarily by Mao Tse-tung[*] and Liu Shao-ch'i.[*] They were applied during the 1942 Rectification[*] Campaign and more extensively after 1949. Unlike mass campaign and media blitzes, thought reform was aimed at the *individual* (though at first, whole social groups—landlords, intellectuals, and so on, were involved).

The idea that thought reform was necessary would seem to be at odds with the materialistic dogma that existence determines consciousness. However, philosophers like Ai Ssu-ch'i rejected the mechanistic approach to political socialization, and they argued that, material conditions notwithstanding, thought tends to have an independent existence and therefore people have to be helped along.

In the early 1950s thought reform was officially deemed the fifth of the Five Major Campaigns[*] (along with land reform, "resist America aid Korea," suppression of counterrevolutionaries, and *San-fan Wu-fan*). However, it was inextricably linked to the other four, and the term can be used in a general sense, meaning to persuade anyone to embrace the current line. In this benign form, people were simply persuaded to support and contribute to socialist construction. In the early 1950s, however, those targeted for thought reform had already been deemed guilty of deviance and were in for rough treatment. The beliefs and even personality of the individual were transformed through programmed criticism and often humiliation.

When carried to extremes, the result was a cataclysmic emotional experience. Typically, people were placed in highly structured situations that permitted no evasion of the issues. Official norms were prescribed, and the reluctant were "struggled against," often by peers in group settings. People were required to criticize themselves and others, and profess allegiance to the new order. The sessions were long and frequent, making it impossible to get by with lip-service or pro forma declarations. The recalcitrant were set up as negative models. One was obliged to confess (often many times, if the first recantations were deemed insincere), after which one underwent the process of reeducation. The results could be psychologically devastating, and resulted in many suicides and nervous breakdowns.

The party often had to admit that the process had gone too far and that those in charge had mislabeled people or applied political standards to intellectuals which were appropriate only for party members. But by that time the unreconstructed had usually been sent off for labor reform (i.e., highly coercive thought reform) or at least the milder labor education. A shift in party line did not necessarily effect their release. For those who were not incarcerated, however, after the early 1950s the process became more relaxed, formalistic, and sometimes even perfunctory. Even in prison, in-depth psychological techniques were largely abandoned after 1957.

The process undoubtedly achieved results for the regime, and to some extent people's beliefs really were changed. In the early 1970s leading intellectuals like Fei Hsiao-t'ung and Feng Yu-lan did indeed sound as though they had been persuaded to throw in their lot with China's rulers. However, the post–Mao thaw revealed what the Hundred Flowers Campaign* had already suggested: that conversions induced by thought reform were usually shallow and that transformations were more behavioral than attitudinal. Certainly, the impact on the acumen of the targets was usually temporary, but there was usually a long-run legacy of demoralization and alienation.

After the 1950s there was less resort to the total-immersion psychological techniques, and the term *thought reform* was heard less often. By the Cultural Revolution (1966–1976)* it was replaced by the slogan "struggle against selfishness and criticize revisionism" (*tou-ssu p'i-hsiu*). However, there would often be sharp echoes of the old methods, particularly in penology. For those not deemed criminals, the most that had to be endured were occasional spasms of "ideological study," such as after the crackdown following the democracy movement in 1989.

REFERENCES: Ai Ssu-ch'i, et al., *Lun ssu-hsiang kai-tsao wen-t'i* (The question of thought reform) (Peking, 1951); Robert Jay Lifton, *Thought Reform and the Psychology of Totalism* (New York, 1961); *Tsen-yang kai-tsao ssu-hsiang* (How to reform thought) (Chungking 1952).

JAMES D. SEYMOUR

THREE-ANTI (*SAN-FAN*) CAMPAIGN: A mass movement to counter corruption, waste, and bureaucracy.

In late 1951 the recently formed People's Republic of China* had essentially completed two of the three major tasks set by the Communist party for its early years—land reform and suppression of counterrevolutionaries. The third major task, to "resist America, aid Korea" was far from complete and was a serious drain on the new nation's resources. In October 1951 party Chairman and President of the State Council Mao Tse-tung* announced that the major effort in the future must be to "increase production and economize." As more attention shifted to the economy, it became apparent that problems of "corruption, waste, and bureaucratism" were endemic and seriously hindering economic growth. In his New Year's address in 1952 Mao called for a nationwide campaign to "wash clean the poisonous residue of the old society."

On January 4, the Party Central Committee ordered every official organization in the party and government to "mobilize the masses to participate in the Three-Anti struggle. In the early stages of this struggle, attention was increasingly focused on China's indigenous entrepreneurs, the national bourgeoisie who owned the private sector of the economy, but they soon became the target of a separate campaign, the Five-Anti, which dealt more directly with problems attributed particularly to them (see Five-Anti Campaign*). The Three-Anti campaign remained focused on party and government cadres.

A Party Central Committee directive of February 3, 1952, called for reregistration of all party members, expulsion of "corrupt and degenerate" elements, and replacement of officials who were "arrogant, lazy, fatigued, or completely incompetent." Directives by the Central People's government in March and April established criteria for punishing those judged to be guilty of unlawful acts. It stipulated lenient treatment for the majority, "those whose transgressions are relatively minor, who have fully confessed, and who have performed meritorious deeds"; and harsh treatment, including execution, for "the small minority whose cases are serious and who refuse to confess."

The government demonstrated its commitment, and set the tenor of the campaign early by staging two huge public rallies at which it tried and immediately executed four high-level officials accused of gross corruption. As the campaign proceeded, hundreds of thousands of party members and nonparty cadres were investigated. No available figures indicate how many were expelled from the party, removed from official posts, or punished more severely.

The purpose of such rectification campaigns orchestrated by the Chinese Communist party* is always the same. There is every reason to believe that the ostensible problems addressed are indeed real and need to be remedied. Beyond that, however, the party leadership uses rectification to affirm the reliability of its cadres and to gain popular support by demonstrating its integrity and its power. In the process of the campaign, unreliable, inept, and corrupt cadres are weeded out, activists among the masses are drafted to replace them, and the whole public is educated in the current policies and values of the leadership. It is also warned that nonconformance will not be tolerated.

The methods employed to achieve those aims are also standard and can be traced back to the first Rectification Campaign,* launched in 1942. First, policy documents are issued for study. They then become the basis for accusation and denunciation by the masses, and the standard for criticism, self-criticism, and reform. A relatively few people are always chosen as special targets to serve as negative examples. Their harsh treatment serves to intimidate those who might not take the campaign seriously. In dealing with transgressors, the party always stipulates "combining strictness with magnanimity," severely punishing a few and forgiving and reinstating the many who have confessed and recanted.

Invariably, such campaigns lead to excesses that are eventually "discovered" by the highest authorities who admit that "accusations have been too inclusive, errors have been made, confessions have been coerced, and good people have been hurt." Such excesses are always reported to have been remedied later when "unjust verdicts" have been overturned. The formulaic repetition of these statements in every one of the numerous campaigns the party has launched makes it evident that "excesses" are expected and tolerated in the interest of realizing the party's objectives.

Rectification campaigns usually precede or coincide with a major new policy initiative. In the case of the Three-Anti Campaign, the party leadership was preparing its cadres for implementing the socialist transformation of the economy during the First Five-Year Plan, 1953–1957. The Three-Anti Campaign had basically run its course by June 1952 and was officially declared "victoriously concluded" by the Party Central Committee in October.

                                                                          PETER J. SEYBOLT

THREE PEOPLE'S PRINCIPLES (*san-min chu-i*): The social and political ideology that Sun Yat-sen devised for China's revolution and national reconstruction.

According to his own recollection, Sun Yat-sen* was committed to the principles of nationalism and democracy as early as 1894, but during his subsequent European sojourn (1896–1898), moved by his observations of social injustice and unrest, he recognized the need for a third principle—social reform or revolution. Partly inspired by the ideas of Henry George, he began to talk of land nationalization as a solution to such social problems. In an oath administered to revolutionary military students in Japan in 1903, the third principle, people's livelihood, was adumbrated in the call for equalizing land rights, and this became part of the T'ung-meng hui* oath when the new party was established in 1905. The collective term *san-min chu-i* may not have been used before 1912, but in the first issue of the new party organ, *Min pao*, Sun proclaimed the "three great principles'' of modern Western revolutions, and of the Chinese, to be nationalism (*min-tsu chu-i*), people's rights (*min-ch'üan chu-i*, or democracy), and people's livelihood (*min-sheng chu-i*, or socialism). At this time nationalism for China meant primarily the liberation of the Han Chinese from Manchu rule, and democracy was equated with the elimination of autocracy. Sun Yat-sen himself conceived of socialism as a state of economic justice which might require a violent revolution to achieve in the environment of gross inequity and class antagonism generated by industrialization in the West, but not so in less industrialized China.

While opponents of revolution took issue with both the anti-Manchu revolution and the rejection of monarchy, even revolutionaries did not always support Sun's principle of people's livelihood. The central China branch of the T'ung-meng hui omitted it in 1911, and the successor party, the Kuomintang, abandoned it in 1912, over the objections of Sun's supporters. Anti-Manchu nationalism seemed irrelevant after the end of the dynasty, and for a decade little attention was paid to the Three People's Principles.

In the January 1, 1923, Kuomintang manifesto, the principles were redefined and proclaimed to be the ''basic principles of our nation.'' Nationalism was now interpreted as the unification of the races inside China and the achievement of national equality with the other nations in the world; democracy would entail universal suffrage and various political rights including the rights of initiative, recall, and referendum; and the people's livelihood would involve limits on landholding, the nationalization of various enterprises, and fiscal and other measures to ensure material security and the equitable distribution of wealth. Sun elaborated on the content and significance of these principles in a series of lectures that he gave in Canton in 1923. Published in book form, they became the authoritative, if often ambiguous, statement of the KMT ideology. In these lectures, Sun further fleshed out the content of nationalism by reference to the past greatness and present potential of the Chinese tradition and the threat to China's national survival posed by modern (mainly Western) imperialism, which had reduced China to semicolonial status and threatened its people with biological extinction. In this connection Sun praised the Soviet Union as a champion of oppressed peoples.

Under the heading of democracy Sun focused on the problem of reconciling expert leadership with popular control, explained his formula for a five-power government, and explicitly subordinated individual liberty to the imperative of national liberation. In discussing the people's livelihood, he reiterated his view that with state regulation of capital and control and promotion of economic development China could achieve prosperity and avoid the social ills that had attended uncontrolled industrialization, stressing the importance of the land tax as the key. He said that communism and the people's livelihood were fundamentally the same; he accepted Marx's analysis of the ''pathology'' of modern industrial society, but he rejected the materialistic theory of history and in particular, he rejected class struggle in China.

In 1937, as a condition for the United Front, the Communists pledged to fulfill the Three People's Principles, and in 1938 the KMT created a Three People's Principles Youth Corps. *"San-min chu-i"* is the title of the national anthem of the Republic of China.* The Three People's Principles have remained the ideology of the KMT and a compulsory subject of study in the schools in Taiwan, where calls from the mainland for reunification are met with the insistence that it be on the basis of the Three People's Principles. On the mainland, interest in the Three People's Principles has lately been revived largely in connection with the emphasis on Sun Yat-sen as a symbol of cooperation between the CCP and the KMT.

REFERENCES: Paschal M. d'Ella, *The Triple Demism of Sun Yat-sen* (Wuchang, 1931); Michael Gasster, *Chinese Intellectuals and the Revolution of 1911* (Seattle, Wash., 1969); Harold Z. Schiffrin, *Sun Yat-sen and the Origins of the Chinese Revolution* (Berkeley, Calif., 1968); *Sun Chung-shan hsüan-chi* (selected works of Sun Yat-sen) (Peking, 1981 reprint); C. Martin Wilbur, *Sun Yat-sen* (New York, 1976).

DON C. PRICE

THREE RED BANNERS CAMPAIGN: A political campaign in China referring to the three major, radical economic policies in the late 1950s—the General Line for Socialist Construction, the Great Leap Forward, and the People's Communes.

The General Line or General Line for Socialist Construction, is embodied in the slogan "go all out, aim high, and achieve greater, faster, better and more economical results in building socialism." Mao Tse-tung* initially advanced this concept in his article "Handling People's Internal Contradictions Correctly," published in June 1957. The Second Session of the Eighth Chinese Communist party* National Congress in May 1958 officially endorsed this concept, in which the goal was "to construct a greater socialist country with modern industries, modern agriculture and modern science as soon as possible."

At first, the Great Leap Forward* was a campaign designed only to increase industrial and agricultural products. By 1958–1959 it had expanded to cover the entire national economy. Mao Tse-tung conceived the Great Leap Forward policy in the winter of 1957. It represented a movement to implement the General Line. Under the slogans of "overtaking Britain within fifteen years," "overtaking the United States within twenty years," "one day equals twenty years," "working morale up to the sky," "red flowers all over the earth," this campaign vigorously promoted the construction of backyard steel furnaces and numerous water conservation projects. The Great Leap Forward movement ended in 1960 and was later considered to be a failure by the Communist party leadership in 1977–1978.

The People's Communes* were political and economic organizations that integrated all forms of agricultural cooperation and was also a new institution produced by implementing the General Line strategy.

On August 4, 1958, Mao Tse-tung inspected Hsu-shui-hsien, Hopei Province, and he established the first People's Commune there that same day. Then on August 29, the CCP Central Committee adopted the Resolution for Establishing

People's Communes in the Rural Areas. Within two months, more than 740,000 agricultural cooperations were absorbed into 26,000-odd People's Communes.

The principles for establishing People's Communes were: *"i-ta-erh-kung"* (to make larger in size and create a higher degree of public ownership); the "three combinations" (to combine within the commune all political, economic, labor, and military affairs); the four changes (militarize organizations, infuse action with combat energy, collectivize everyday life, and socialize household labor).

By the end of 1958, People's Communes were being created throughout China's rural areas. This institution was eliminated in December 1982, however, when the CCP amended the nation's constitution.

The people greatly disliked Mao Tse-tung's Three Red Banners Movement. P'eng Te-huai,[*] a member of the CCP Central Politburo, went to the rural areas to inspect how these campaigns were carried out. He reported to Mao that the people had suffered greatly because of the Three Red Banners Movement. Mao did not like P'eng's frankness. In the Lushan Conference (1959)[*] Mao condemned P'eng and others who opposed the movement as right-wing opportunists and purged them from the party.

As a result of the Three Red Banners Campaign, several hundred million people starved and perhaps as many as 20 to 30 million died between 1960 and 1962, the so-called three years of hardship. This movement must stand as one of the great disasters in modern Chinese history.

REFERENCES: *A Comprehensive Glossary of Chinese Communist Terminology* (Taipei, 1978); *Hsin-hua Bimonthly*, No. 138–140 (August–September 1958); *Jen-min shou-tse* (People's handbook) vols. 1–2, (1959).

RAMON H. MYERS

T'IENANMEN SQUARE INCIDENT (April 5, 1976): A mass demonstration in Peking against Mao's rule.

On the occasion of the traditional gravesweeping festival in early April 1976, tens of thousands of Peking students, workers, and citizens went to the centrally located T'ienanmen Square for several days to place wreaths, banners, and poems commemorating the recently deceased prime minister, Chou En-lai.[*] Many of the banners and poems indirectly attacked Mao Tse-tung[*] and his radical supporters. On April 5 the crowd swelled to an estimated 100,000. On the orders of the mayor of Peking, Wu Te, armed police dispersed the crowd with water cannon and nightsticks and arrested over 300 of the demonstrators.

Labeling the event a counterrevolutionary incident, the authorities blamed it on Teng Hsiao-p'ing,[*] a Chou ally who had been purged during the Cultural Revolution[*] and who had recently returned to office to serve as vice-premier and administer the economy. The Politburo dismissed Teng from his official posts and promoted Hua Kuo-feng[*] to serve as prime minister and first vice-chairman of the Central Committe, marking Hua's designation as Mao's successor.

The incident became a major symbol in the struggle over China's future that unfolded after Mao's death. The official reversal of verdict on the incident in

November 1978 marked an important step in Teng's return to power and the
gradual erosion of Hua's power base. On this occasion, all those who were
arrested during the incident were released, and some of the leaders were promoted
to prestigious positions in the Communist Youth League. However, the incident
was in turn claimed as a symbol by Teng's critics in the Chinese Democracy
Movement, for whom the date April 5 became as freighted with historical significance as May 4. Just as "5.4" stands for the May Fourth Movement* of
1919 and its advocacy of science and democracy, so "4.5" today stands in the
Chinese mind for the beginning of the many-phased democratic movement that
has demanded fundamental reform of Chinese communism.

ANDREW J. NATHAN

TING WEN-CHIANG (April 13, 1887–January 5, 1936): Scientist, journalist,
and secretary general of the Academia Sinica (1934–36).

Born into a declining gentry family in T'ai-hsing County, Kiangsu, Ting Wen-
chiang was educated in the Chinese classics until age fifteen. In 1902 he went
to Japan to study for a year and a half. From there he went to England in 1904.
In 1908 he enrolled at the University of Glasgow, from which he graduated in
1911 with a degree in geology and zoology.

Arriving back in China immediately before the Republican Revolution, Ting
spent a year teaching middle school in Shanghai. Then, in early 1913, he took
the post of head of the Geology Department in the newly established Ministry
of Commerce and Industry [Kung-shang pu] of the republican government. This
department, largely through Ting's efforts, led to the establishment of the China
Geological Survey (Chung-kuo ti-chih tiao-ch'a-so) in 1916. In 1914 he took
part in his first geological fieldwork, a geological investigation of Yunnan,
Kweichow, and parts of Szechwan in southwestern China. His resulting survey
reports contained not only material on mineral resources of the area, but also
information on fossil remains and the customs of minority peoples of the area.
Ting formally headed the China Geological Survey from its founding until 1921,
and he continued to involve himself with its activities until his death. Throughout
its existence, the China Geological Survey trained competent geological personnel, conducted geological surveys, and published numerous scientific reports.

In the winter and spring of 1919, together with Chang Chia-sen, Chiang Fang-
chen, and Hsu Hsin-liu, Ting accompanied Liang Ch'i-ch'ao* to postwar Europe
as a semiofficial advisory delegation to the Versailles Peace Conference. On his
way back to China at the beginning of 1920, Ting officially offered geology
Professor A.W. Grabau a teaching post at Peking University. Grabau accepted,
and during his long sojourn in China, Grabau also directed paleontology research
for the China Geological Survey, helping make China a world-class center for
this type of research.

A mining survey Ting conducted in southeastern Jehol province in the 1910s
indicated that the abandoned Pei-p'iao coal mine could be operated profitably.

In 1921 Ting resigned his directorship to become general manager of a new Pei-p'iao Coal Mining Company, which soon grew into a flourishing enterprise.

In the same year, writing under the pen-name Tsung-yen, Ting began to involve himself in the world of letters with several articles on his travels and local political affairs. He suggested to Hu Shih* the establishment of a liberal journal to voice the political concerns of Chinese intellectuals. In May 1922 *Endeavor* (*Nu-li chou-pao*) was established. When a group of liberal intellectuals in Peking published a manifesto proclaiming their concern for reform in government, Ting joined them in signing it and a few months later, in a *Nu-li chou-pao* article, elaborated on one of the points: that "good" men of moral integrity and talent should become actively involved in government.

In April 1923 Ting provoked what was perhaps the most lively intellectual controversy of the decade when he replied to Carsun Chang's lecture on "Philosophy of Life" *(jen-sheng kuan)* published in the *Tsing-hua Weekly* of February 1923. Ting interpreted Chang's lecture as an attack on science. His counterattack, titled "Hsüan-hsüeh yü k'o-hsüeh" (Science and metaphysics), sought to defend the value of science for human life and in education. Ting contended that science can know everything that is knowable. Adopting the philosophical stance of critical positivism similar to that of Karl Pearson and Ernst Mach, Ting insisted that science was characterized by its way of knowing, not by any specific (material) class of things known; nature was uniform, and therefore, the organizations of perception that make up one person's knowledge can be taken as true for all normal human beings. Chang, Ting declared, was a "metaphysical ghost" relying on the obscurantist tradition of European idealism. Many of China's famous intellectuals joined the resulting "Science and Metaphysics" fray, so defined and designated by Ting's initial article. At the end of 1923, a collection of the essays written by the participants was published under the title *K'o-hsüeh yü jen-sheng-kuan* (Science and philosophy of life).

By 1925 Ting's travel and journal articles had established him as knowledgeable scientific analyst of Chinese political and intellectual matters. As often happened to such men, he was drawn into the patronage network of regional militarists. In July 1925 he met with Wu P'ei-fu*, and the next month he consulted with Sun Ch'uan-fang. About a year later, after resigning his post in the Pei-p'iao Coal Company, Ting went to Shanghai to serve as the director of the Port of Woosung and Shanghai, in which capacity Ting organized the Chinese-administered parts of the city into one entity as part of building a "greater Shanghai." He also introduced modern sanitation to the city. Such actions enabled the Chinese to gain control of the Shanghai Mixed Court and extended Chinese jurisdiction into the International Settlement, thus setting the stage for the eventual end of extraterritoriality in 1943.

Because of his "collaboration" with a regional militarist, the Nationalist Northern Expedition* forced Ting to flee Shanghai and quit politics at the end of 1926. In late 1929, the China Geological Survey commissioned Ting to do a geological investigation of China's southwest. He not only surveyed mineral resources of the region, planned the Szechwan–Canton railroad route, and compiled geological maps, but he also collected anthropological materials on the various non-Han minority peoples of the region.

In the summer of 1930, his work completed, Ting returned to Peking, whereupon Peking University appointed him professor of geology. During his three-year tenure in this post, he produced a number of important publications, both scientific and political. The Japanese occupation of Manchuria in the latter half of the year stimulated Ting, Hu Shih, Chiang T'ing-fu, and other Peking scholars to launch another political journal, *The Independent Critic (Tu-li p'ing-lun)*, in May 1932. Ting contributed extensively to this periodical, and in the process shaped a political position that called for nonmilitary resistance to Japanese aggression with a simultaneous scientific modernization of China that would strengthen it against Japan. In the prewar public discussion of dictatorship versus democracy, Ting tended to argue for a Chinese dictatorship for development while deploring the armed insurrection of the Chinese Communists as destructively divisive at a time when China needed unity against a powerful external threat. His visit to the USSR in 1933 reinforced both his anti-communism and his support for a modernizing dictatorship that would utilize a scientific elite for effecting a modernization program.

Perhaps perceiving himself as a member of the tiny Chinese scientific elite, Ting resigned from Peking University in June 1934 in order to accept the post of secretary general of the Academia Sinica in Nanking. Shortly thereafter Ting was also appointed as an adviser to the national government in the area of natural resources. It was in performing this duty that he met his death. Investigating the coal fields in Hunan, he spent the night of December 8 in a small inn near a colliery in Hsiang-t'an County. During the night he was overcome by carbon monoxide poisoning because of the fumes of a coal stove. The resulting mismanaged medical attention he received first in the Heng-yang hospital and a few days later in a Changsha hospital resulted in his death on January 5, 1936.

Aside from his many journal articles in *Endeavor* and *Independent Critic*, Ting's writings include collections of travel essays and a posthumously published draft chronology of Liang Ch'i-ch'ao. He is also responsible for a large number of technological publications in geology and related disciplines as well as the atlas of China (*Chung-hua min-kuo hsin ti-t'u*) published in 1934.

REFERENCES: Charlotte Furth, *Ting Wen-chiang: Science and China's New Culture* (Cambridge, 1970); D.W.Y. Kwok, *Scientism in Chinese Thought, 1900–1950* (New Haven, Conn., 1965); Hu Shih et al., *Ting Wen-chiang che-ke jen* (This Man Ting Wen-chiang) (Taipei, 1967).

GUY S. ALITTO

TS'AI AO (1882–1916): Military general who opposed Yüan Shih-k'ai.

Ts'ai Ao, a leading commander of the National Protection Army which ended Yüan Shih-k'ai's[*] monarchical dream, was a native of Shao-yang, Hunan Province. In his short life of thirty-four years, Ts'ai had a brilliant military career, first as a supporter of the 1911 revolutionary forces, and then as the military governor of Yunnan and Szechwan. Most significant of all, Ts'ai is known for outmaneuvering Yüan Shih-k'ai in a series of political intrigues that have since been dramatized, as well as romanticized, in Chinese plays and films.

Ts'ai was educated in Confucian learning at a very early age, but the reformist spirit of the times steered him away from participating in the civil service examination. In 1897 he studied under Liang Ch'i-ch'ao* at the Shih-wu Hsüeh-t'ang, an institution started by T'an Ssu-t'ung*. There Ts'ao was exposed to ideas of constitutional government and the vital question of China's national survival. The failure of the 1898 Reform Movement encouraged Ts'ai to participate in anti-Manchu activities, but probably because of a sense of loyalty to Liang Ch'i-ch'ao, Ts'ai never joined any of Sun Yat-sen's* political groups. During this period, Ts'ai was also preoccupied with plans for modernizing China's military institutions. In the *Hsin-min ts'ung-pao* he argued that, in order for China to regain wealth and power, it must give higher status to the soldier; military training must also be organized in a more systematic manner.

In 1902 Ts'ai graduated from Japan's Seijo Military Preparatory School, where he gained a reputation for extreme physical endurance, such as swimming in the ocean during winter days. In 1904 Ts'ai completed his training at the Shikan Gakkō Military Academy and returned to serve in China. He was first posted in the Kwangsi region where he helped to establish military schools and trained cadets for the New Army*. He kept a close relationship with members of the T'ung-meng hui,* however, and after the October Tenth Uprising in Wuchang, Ts'ai, who was now in Yunnan, quickly set up a provisional government there. He was soon elected military governor of Yunnan.

To a large extent, Ts'ai's belief in strict discipline and political order explain why he was able to remain on friendly terms with Yüan's Peking government. In 1913 Ts'ai refused to endorse Sun's call for a Second Revolution.* Yüan, probably distrustful of Ts'ai's early association with the Sun faction, decided to invite Ts'ai to Peking, allegedly so that Ts'ai could play a more prominent role in promoting military education. By late 1915, however, Yüan's surrender to Japan's Twenty-One Demands and his secret preparations for establishing a new dynasty finally prompted Ts'ai to break with Yüan. Secretly, he contacted his former teacher, Liang Ch'i-ch'ao, and Huang Hsing,* and prepared for the next course of action.

What happened next is one of the more dramatic episodes of republican history. Ts'ai pretended that he had lost all interest in matters of state, and instead he visited all the well-known brothels in Peking. Ostensibly, Ts'ai had become so obsessed with Hsiao Feng-hsien that he was ready to abandon his wife and family for this "notorious courtesan." The coverup was so successful that some historians question Ts'ai's overall intentions at this time. Nevertheless, the scandal did not prevent Yüan's spies from discovering Ts'ai's association with the other plotters. In late 1915 Ts'ai traveled back to Yunnan incognito, and declared the province independent on December 25. In the next three months, battles between Ts'ai's hastily called army and Yüan's Peiyang forces demonstrated Ts'ai's strategic abilities. Although his troops were outnumbered ten to one, Ts'ai managed to defeat the government forces in every campaign. On March 22, 1916, Yüan renounced his imperial pretensions, but most provinces insisted on their independence, until Yüan's death in June. For a short time, Ts'ai was appointed governor of Szechwan, but in November he died in Japan, after seeking treatment for throat cancer.

Political reformer, soldier, patriot, and educationalist, Ts'ai was a man of many dimensions. Unlike some of his contemporaries, his commitment to republicanism remained steadfast. At the same time, for Ts'ai, traditional values of obedience and loyalty were important even in the new China. On the one hand, he supported Liang's call for democracy and freedom, and on the other, he was an admirer of Tseng Kuo-fan* and Hu Lin-i, loyal officials of the T'ung-chih Restoration. He consistently praised them for their insistence on self-cultivation and personal sacrifice.

In terms of his other contributions to modernizing China's military establishments, Ts'ai proposed the need for universal conscription. He also made many proposals for reorganizing China's national forces; some of his ideas may have affected both the Nationalist and Communist military arrangements later.

In his obituary, Liang Ch'i-ch'ao, the man who introduced Ts'ai to concepts of nationhood and democracy, said of Ts'ai, that he had buried his own needs, for the sake of serving his own country.

REFERENCE: Howard Boorman, and Richard Howard, eds. *Biographical Dictionary of Republican China*, vol. 3 (New York, 1970): 286–290.

JOHN D. YOUNG

TS'AI YÜAN-P'EI (January 1868–March 5, 1940): Scholar and educator.

Ts'ai was born into a merchant family in Shanyin County of Chekiang's Shaohsing Prefecture. His father, a manager of a traditional banking house (*ch'ien-chuang*), died when Ts'ai was only ten, and the task of raising him and his two brothers fell to his mother and his uncle, Ts'ai Ming-en, a *chü-jen* scholar who introduced his nephew to the classics. Ts'ai's rise up the imperial examination ladder was meteoric. He not only passed all three levels of civil service exams (*hsiu-ts'ai*, 1883; *chü-jen*, 1889; *chin-shih*, 1890) by the age of twenty-two, but he also went on to gain the highest academic honor of the imperial system—Hanlin scholar (1892).

After China's humiliating defeat at the hands of the Japanese Navy in 1895, Ts'ai (with most other progressive intellectuals of the time) turned to Western learning as a source of much needed internal reform. Though not a direct participant in the Reform Movement of the summer of 1898, Ts'ai was moved by its failure to resign his position as Hanlin compiler and return to his native Shaohsing to devote himself to education, which was to remain his lifelong occupation. He directed the Shaohsing *Chung-hsi hsüeh-t'ang* (Sino-Western School), a school with a progressive Western curriculum. Among its students was Chiang Meng-lin* (who later replaced Ts'ai as temporary chancellor of

Peking University). From Shaohsing, Ts'ai went to Shanghai where he taught
first at the Nan-yang kung-hsüeh (Nanyang Public School) and then at the progressive Ai-kuo hsüeh-she (Patriotic Study Society) which was under the auspices
of the revolutionary Chung-kuo chiao-yü hui (China Education Society). The
Patriotic Study Society, of which Ts'ai was principal, was partially funded by
the anti-Manchu newspaper *Su-pao* (*Kiangsu Tribune*) for which members of
the teaching staff (Chang T'ai-yen, Wu Chih-hui*) wrote inflammatory articles
as compensation. When the Ch'ing* court banned the *Su-pao* in 1903, Ts'ai and
others on the staff of the school were implicated. After a brief exile in German-
held Tsingtao, Ts'ai returned to Shanghai and founded and edited the *Ching-
chung jih-pao* (*The Alarm*) which openly published anti-Manchu material. Ts'ai's
revolutionary sentiments took political shape in 1904 when he helped found the
Kuang-fu hui (Recovery Society) with other Chekiang revolutionaries (Ch'iu
Chin,* Chang T'ai-yen, and Hsü Hsi-lin). The Kuang-fu hui was subsumed in
1905 into Sun Yat-sen's* larger T'ung-meng hui,* of which Ts'ai became a
member. Ts'ai's faith in political revolution, however, lacked resolve, and in
1906 he returned to Peking in hopes of foreign study.

Ts'ai was offered a scholarship to study in Germany. After a year of language
training in Berlin, he transferred to the University of Leipzig where from 1908
to 1911 he immersed himself in Western studies, with particular interest paid to
philosophy, experimental psychology, and aesthetics.

Ts'ai returned to China shortly after the fall of the Ch'ing court in 1911 and
became the first minister of education of the new Republic. Political infighting
led to the resignation of the entire Yüan Shih-k'ai* cabinet in June 1912, and
Ts'ai had no time in which to execute his plans for developing a democratic
educational system. Nonetheless, his short tenure as minister was a catalyst for
educational reform in China.

Except for a brief return to China in 1913, Ts'ai spent the next four years in
Europe, mostly in France where he was active in organizing Chinese workers
sent to France during World War I. At the same time he wrote works on Western
art and aesthetics, philosophy, and his famous scholarly foray into fiction, the
Shih-t'ou chi suo-yin (Revelations of the story of the stone). Ts'ai returned to
China in late 1916 when he was offered the chancellorship of Peking University,
which had a notorious reputation as a den of gambling and debauchery for those
awaiting civil service postings. He attempted to reform the morals of the school's
students and instill in them the modern liberal notion of disinterested study. He
reorganized the administration along democratic lines and hired as professors
young progressive intellectuals (Li Ta-chao,* Ch'en Tu-hsiu,* Hu Shih,* et al.)
who were intent on the pursuit of ''scientific'' research. Although he resigned
on several occasions (most notably during the May Fourth* demonstrations in
protest of the Peking government officials' handling of his students), he retained
the post until 1926. Under his tutelage, Peking University became the center for
the intellectual iconoclasm of May Fourth and the first Marxist study groups in
China.

Ts'ai contributed to the KMT revolution (1925–1927) by engaging in under-ground activities in Chekiang and Kiangsu. He later supported the right wing of the KMT in its purge of left-wing radicals, and in 1928 he joined the KMT government as head of the *Ta-hsüeh yuan* (Education Yuan) which he attempted to reform without success. Disillusioned with the political world, he resigned all government posts in 1929. In 1928 he helped found and became president of the Academica Sinica, a post he held until his death at seventy-two in 1940. Ts'ai was also a co-founder (with Soong Ch'ing-ling[*]) of the League for the Protection of Civil Rights (Chung-kuo min-ch'üan pao-chang t'ung-meng) in 1932.

Though himself a brilliant product of the imperial educational system, Ts'ai Yüan-p'ei did more than any single educator to undermine that system and develop a modern notion of the autonomy of intellectuals from politics. During his tenure as chancellor of Peking University (1916–1926), Ts'ai was largely responsible for fostering the intellectual climate that gave birth to the May Fourth Movement.

REFERENCES: Ts'ai Shang-ssu, *Ts'ai Yüan-p'ei hsien-sheng hsüeh-shu ssu-hsiang chuan-chi* (The scholarship, thought and biography of Ts'ai Yüan-p'ei) (Shanghai, 1950); William J. Duiker, *Ts'ai Yüan-p'ei: Educator of Modern China* (University Park, Md., 1977).

KIRK A. DENTON

TS'AO K'UN (December 12, 1862–May 17, 1938): Militarist, warlord politi-cian, president of the ROC.

Ts'ao worked his way up from street peddler to instructor of the Tientsin Military Academy, and, after 1895, the Peiyang Army's elite young officer corps. From 1906 until 1918 he commanded the Third Division. This unit's "mutiny" in February 1912 aided Yüan Shih-k'ai's[*] move of the capital back to Peking. Subsequently, the Third Division served in the middle Yangtze. Shortly after Yüan Shih-k'ai's death in June 1916, Ts'ao became military governor of his native Chihli. Combined with the Yangtze military connections, Chihli remained his power base for the next few years.

For a time, Ts'ao avoided Peking politics, although he helped crush the Manchu Restoration in mid-1917. However, Tuan Ch'i-jui's military and po-litical strengthening led Ts'ao to join the opposing combination of Kiangsu-area military and Peking civilian bureaucrats coalescing around Feng Kuo-chang. This realignment of old Peiyang relationships during late 1917 and early 1918 marked the emergence of the Chihli[*] and Anhwei[*] factions. When Feng died in late 1919, Ts'ao became the new Chihli faction leader.

In the Chihli–Anhwei War of mid-July 1920, Ts'ao's group allied with Chang Tso-lin's Fengtien troops to decimate Tuan Ch'i-jui's rival coalition. This victory owed much to Ts'ao's able assistant, Wu P'ei-fu,[*] who had succeeded Ts'ao as commander of the Third Division and now gradually overshadowed his cautious patron as Chihli's most effective military leader. In 1921 Wu turned from south-central regions to confront Chang Tso-lin's increasing ambitions in north China, provoking the Chihli–Fengtien War of late April 1922. Victory left the Chihli coalition dominant in north and central China.

Ts'ao K'un tried to parlay this coalition victory into personal gain. The Chihli military dominance had benefited mostly Wu's Loyang faction. Gradually, the Tientsin and Paoting factions of Ts'ao's family members and close associates outmaneuvered their rivals, engineering the resignation of President Li Yüan-hung[*] in mid–1923. Ts'ao then set out to purchase (at $5,000 to $7,000 a head) sufficient parliamentary votes to "legitimize" his new power. On October 10, he took office as president and promulgated a new constitution.

It was a precarious ambition. Most Chihli members accorded only token support. Ts'ao's security rested with Wu P'ei-fu whose Loyang faction had opposed Ts'ao assuming the presidency. Demonstrations in several cities evidenced widespread public disgust over this particularly blatant example of ambitious militarists' manipulating republican constitutionalism. Chang Tso-lin publicly labeled Ts'ao a puppet for Wu P'ei-fu and developed links with both the remnant Anhwei faction and Sun Yat-sen's[*] southern forces.

Caution delayed the Second Fengtien–Chihli War until September 1924. Very rapidly, the strong Chihli position was fatally undermined. As his troops moved north with Wu P'ei-fu's forces to meet Chang Tso-lin, Feng Yü-hsiang[*] suddenly reversed direction, occupied Peking, and captured Ts'ao K'un on October 23. Unable to rally other Chihli militarists, Wu fled to central China. By November 2, Feng forced Ts'ao to declare peace and resign the presidency.

Ts'ao remained under house arrest in Peking until April 1926. Thereafter he sojourned in Honan and then Dairen before ultimately settling down to obscurity in his native Tientsin. The Chihli Clique survived for a few years under Wu P'ei-fu in the Honan–Hupeh region, before succumbing to Northern Expedition[*] troops in 1926. In the beginning of his central prominence, Ts'ao and his associates had used Tuan Ch'i-jui's pro-Japanese policies as justification for their rival political coalition. Ts'ao remained true to that sentiment, in his last few months refusing to cooperate with the Japanese occupation forces.

One may look at Ts'ao K'un in two lights—as representing a corrupt, upstart militarist typical of the warlord era, or as marking a transition stage from fragmentation toward a greater unity. In the former view, Ts'ao contributed to the Chinese Revolution primarily by intensifying popular disillusionment with Peking militarist politics. The more recent perspective notes that Feng Yü-hsiang's defection made necessary some years of revolutionary struggle to achieve a degree of national reunification significantly greater than that which the Ts'ao-Wu combination briefly achieved in mid–1924.

REFERENCES: Howard L. Boorman and Richard C. Howard, eds., *Biographical Dictionary of Republican China*, vol. 3 (New York and London, 1967–1971): 302–305, 444–450; Andrew J. Nathan, "A Constitutional Republic: The Peking Government, 1916–1928," in *The Cambridge History of China*, vol. 12: *Republican China 1912–1949, Part*

424 TSENG KUO-FAN

I, ed. by John K. Fairbank (Cambridge, 1983): 259–283; Odoric Y.K. Wou, *Militarism in Modern China: The career of Wu P'ei-fu, 1916–1939* (Dawson, Australia, 1978).

PETER M. MITCHELL

TSENG KUO-FAN (November 26, 1811–March 12, 1872): (posthumous title Wen-cheng) imperial official; militia leader; governor–general; imperial commissioner for the suppression of the Taiping Rebellion.

Tseng Kuo-fan was born into a landowning family in the Hsiang-hsiang District of Hunan Province. Educationally ambitious, Tseng achieved the *chin-shih*, the highest degree in the civil service examination system, in 1838. In the same year he became a member of the Han-lin Academy, China's leading academic institution. Tseng Kuo-fan married a member of the Ou-yang family of the Heng-yang District of Hunan; they had three sons and six daughters, two sons and five daughters surviving to adulthood. His oldest son, Tseng Chi-tse, served as China's ambassador to Britain, France, and Tsarist Russia. Tseng Kuo-fan held various offices in the six boards of the imperial government until 1849 when he was named acting vice-president of the Board of Rites. During his education and subsequent service in the imperial government, Tseng was influenced by the practical concerns of the neo-Confucian School of Statecraft, the moral authoritarianism of the orthodox Sung School of neo-Confucianism and the strict literary standards of the T'ung-ch'eng School. He was intellectually eclectic, at once deeply conservative with respect to the traditional social order but practical in the measures he advocated for protecting it.

In December 1852, the imperial government ordered Tseng, who had returned to his home in Hunan to mourn the passing of his mother, to mobilize militia forces to defend the province against the advancing Taiping* revolutionary army. During the first half of 1853, he welded together a congeries of local defense forces to form the provincially based and locally financed Hunan Army.

In 1854 Tseng's Hunan Army turned back the western campaign of the Taipings in Hunan. During 1855 and 1856, however, it suffered serious setbacks on land and in naval engagements in the central Yangtze Valley. From the spring of 1855, as a result of strategic blunders, Tseng was isolated in Kiangsi with a small force of ships and troops of the Hunan Army. Reinforcements finally reached his Kiangsi headquarters in the summer of 1856. By September an internecine power struggle paralyzed the Taiping leadership, affording Tseng the opportunity to take the offensive against the Taipings in Kiangsi. Tseng left his command in Kiangsi in early 1857 to return to Hunan to mourn the death of his father.

Tseng emerged from retirement in May 1858 responding to an imperial edict to halt the recent Taiping invasion of Chekiang. After resuming command of the Hunan Army, Tseng reorganized the command structure and established logistical units in preparation for an effort to retake the upper Yangtze Valley. In late 1858, while directing operations in southern Kiangsi against Taiping forces in Fukien and Kiangsi, Tseng was devastated by news of the massacre of Hunan Army forces and the death of his brother Tseng Kuo-hua at San-ho in northern Anhwei. By July 1859 the Hunan Army had cleared the Taipings from Kiangsi. Tseng moved his headquarters to Wuchang in late September 1859 where he formulated plans for the recapture of Anking, capital of Anhwei and key to control of the upper Yangtze Valley.

To execute these plans, in July 1860 Tseng shifted his command post to Ch'i-men in southern Anhwei where he was invested by Taiping forces defending Anking. Meanwhile, in May 1860, the Imperial Army's Great Camp of Kiangnan in the suburbs of Nanking, the Taiping capital, collapsed before the onslaught of rejuvenated Taiping forces, as did the imperial forces east of Nanking. A desperate imperial government revamped its command structure and, on June 8, 1860, named Tseng governor-general of the Liangkiang provinces and imperial commissioner for suppression of the Taipings, giving him the administrative authority and access to financial resources that he had long held were essential to successful prosecution of the war. However, Tseng did not escape from the Taiping investment at Ch'i-men until the spring of 1861, when Taiping forces were diverted from Ch'i-men and defeated by Hunan Army forces commanded by Tso Tsung-t'ang.

In June 1861 Tseng directed Hunan Army units against Taiping forces in southern Anhwei from a new headquarters afloat on the Yangtze. On September 5, 1861, his strategy for recapture of the upper Yangtze achieved a decisive victory: Anking fell to the relentless attack of Hunan Army troops commanded by his younger brother Tseng Kuo-ch'üan. Tseng moved his headquarters to Anking on September 11 whence he began a drive to clear the Taipings from southern Anhwei to open the way for the advance on Nanking.

A palace coup in the winter of 1861 put power in the hands of Prince Kung and the Empress Dowager Tzu-hsi* and eliminated most in the court who had opposed Tseng's rise to command. In addition to his governor-generalship of Kiangsi, Kiangsu, and Anhwei, he was given control of military affairs in Chekiang.

Following the destruction of the Imperial Army's Great Camp of Kiangnan in May 1860, a rejuvenated Taiping Army commanded by Li Hsiu-ch'eng* advanced eastward, reaching the outskirts of Shanghai in August 1860 where they were repulsed by British and French forces. In response to a request for aid from Shanghai merchants in 1861 and fearing the further intervention of foreign forces, Tseng ordered Li Hung-chang,* who had joined his staff in early 1859, to raise a force similar to the Hunan Army in Li's home province, Anhwei. In April 1862, Li's Anhwei Army was transported from Anking down the Yangtze to the beleaguered city of Shanghai in steamships rented from foreign companies. On Tseng's recommendation, Li was named governor of Kiangsu on May 13. Li's forces, equipped with foreign firearms and assisted by the Sino-Western Ever Victorious Army, cleared the Taipings from the environs of Shanghai by December 5, 1863.

After the fall of Hangchow, provincial capital of Chekiang, to the Taipings in December 1861, Tseng succeeded in having Tso Tsung-t'ang* placed in charge of military affairs for the province and named governor in January 1862. During the next two years, Tso cleared Taiping forces from Chekiang, retaking Hangchow on April 1, 1864.

Meanwhile, Tseng Kuo-ch'üan's forces had advanced from Anking, reaching the outskirts of Nanking in June 1862. They were unable to complete encirclement of the city until February 1864 and did not penetrate its defense until July 19.

The fall of Nanking marked the destruction of the Taiping Revolutionary Movement, though scattered resistance continued until 1866. In a move calculated to demonstrate loyalty to the court, over the next two years Tseng demobilized 120,000 troops of the Hunan Army. In recognition of Tseng's pivotal role in suppressing the Taipings, the court named him marquis of the first class, the first civil official so honored.

After the fall of Nanking, Tseng moved his headquarters to that city and assumed his duties as governor-general of the Liangkiang provinces, directing postwar reconstruction. In June 1865 he was named imperial commissioner for suppression of the Nien* rebels in Chihli, Shantung, and Honan. Previously unsuccessful efforts by government forces to suppress the Nien rebels culminated in an alarming crisis in May 1865 when the imperial army battling the Nien was virtually annihilated at Tsao-chou in southwestern Shantung; Peking was threatened. Tseng directed units of Li Hung-chang's Anhwei Army equipped with Western firearms, employing the traditional strategies of strengthening village walls, clearing adjacent countryside, blockading key areas, and fortifying natural barriers to restrict the movements of the highly mobile Nien. The results were disheartening. In early October 1866 Tseng, in deteriorating health, recommended that Li Hung-chang, who had replaced him as acting governor-general of the Liangkiang provinces, replace him as imperial commissioner for suppression of the Nien. Tseng resumed his governor-generalship of the Liangkiang provinces, with the additional responsibility of keeping the Anhwei Army supplied with modern arms and ammunition.

Recognizing the efficacy of Western ordnance and steamships, Tseng preferred domestic production to prolonged dependence on foreign purchase, the difficulties of which became clear during the ill-fated attempt to incorporate British vessels of the Lay Osborn flotilla under Li's command in Kiangsu in 1863. Tseng was instrumental in establishing arsenals at Anking in 1862 and Shanghai in 1865, and the early development of the Nanking Arsenal which Li had established in 1865. Both the Nanking Arsenal and the Kiangnan Arsenal in Shanghai were important suppliers of modern ordnance to the Anhwei Army forces battling the Nien.

In 1867 Tseng was named grand secretary; the following year he became governor-general of the metropolitan province of Chihli. In 1870 he rose from a sickbed to investigate the Tientsin Massacre in which Chinese residents of that city had rioted in protest of the activities of French missionaries and the arrogance of French diplomats with resultant loss of French lives and property. Tseng's conciliatory approach seemed calculated to avoid war with France, a war that China could ill afford to pursue. Summoned back to the governor-generalship of the Liangkiang provinces in 1871 following the assassination of Governor-General Ma Hsin-i, Tseng collaborated with Li Hung-chang, who replaced him in Chihli, in sending the first Chinese educational mission to the United States in 1872. Tseng died while incumbent in the Liangkiang governor-generalship in March 1872.

Tseng Kuo-fan's position in history as the principal architect of the Ch'ing dynasty's[*] victory over the Taiping Revolutionary Movement is secure. As an individual, he was complex; his complexities influenced the nature and conduct of his activities in suppressing the revolution. He was the epitome of Confucian self-cultivation: frugal, filial, loyal to the ruling dynasty, disdainful of personal gain, and devoted to classical scholarship and traditional morality. At the same time, he was ruthless, authorizing or condoning the slaughter of hundreds or thousands when necessary to attain his objectives. He was a poor strategist and a worse tactician but a superb judge of human talent. The major victories over the Taipings were planned and executed by his subordinates. His irrational determination to persevere in the face of adversity carried him, on occasion, to suicidal despair.

Tseng's great contributions derive from his capacity for institutional innovation in defense of the traditional social order. The Hunan Army's victories gave the Ch'ing dynasty a half century lease on life. The establishment of the domestic ordnance industry opened the door—albeit only a crack—to the introduction of machine production and the gradual transformation of China's economy.

REFERENCES: Chu Tung-an, *Tseng Kuo-fan Chuan* (Biography of Tseng Kuo-fan) (Cheng-tu, 1985); Ho I-k'un, *Tseng Kuo-fan P'ing-chuan* (Critical biography of Tseng Kuo-fan) (Taipei, 1979); Arthur W. Hummel, ed., *Eminent Chinese of the Ch'ing Period* (Washington, D.C., 1944): 751–775; Ts'ai Kuan-lo, ed., *Ch'ing-tai ch'i-pai ming-jen-chuan* (Biographies of seven hundred famous people of the Ch'ing period) (Peking, 1984): 1036–1047.

THOMAS L. KENNEDY

TSINGHUA UNIVERSITY: One of China's premier national universities.

The history of Tsinghua University is inextricably linked to the development of Sino-American relations in the twentieth century. It was founded in 1908 when the United States remitted nearly $12 million of its share of the Boxer[*] indemnity, and its initial purpose was to prepare young Chinese for study in the United States. The Americans hoped to nurture Chinese leaders who would share Western values and cooperate with the United States.

The funds provided a secure financial base for Tsinghua, enabling it to become one of China's premier national universities by the mid–1930s. It remained the nation's most Americanized secular university until 1949 and retained some of its American characteristics even during the Communist era.

Between 1909 and 1911, the Ch'ing[*] government used the Boxer funds to establish Tsinghua School, a foreign-staffed school preparing students for study in the United States. By 1929 a total of 1,268 talented students had been sent to America.

Between 1911 and 1929, Tsinghua developed an American-style curriculum, emphasizing general liberal arts at the introductory level followed by specialization in a major. Students entered the school by examination, took eight years of course work, and then went to the United States to work on advanced degrees. Tsinghua's regulations and procedures were based on American models. Virtually all students and teachers spoke and read English, and Western learning took precedence over Chinese subjects. In 1926 the preparatory school became Tsinghua College, with a full four-year baccalaureate program.

During 1928–1937 Tsinghua became China's leading scientific and engineering institution, as well as one of its outstanding liberal arts institutions. In 1928 the new Kuomintang government designated it National Tsinghua University and appointed Lo Chia-lun as its first president. During his brief, tumultuous tenure, Lo moved to add a College of Engineering to the three colleges already at Tsinghua (Letters, Sciences, and Law), and encouraged graduate studies and advanced research. He attempted to mold the curriculum into conformity with official Kuomintang ideology. This assailed Tsinghua's tradition of self-governance and political independence, and led to frequent clashes between Lo and his faculty and students.

Lo's successor, the quiet and conciliatory Mei I-ch'i (Y. C. Mei), served as president between 1931 and 1948. Although the problem of Kuomintang political control was never resolved, Tsinghua nonetheless developed into one of China's finest universities. It strengthened its liberal arts, introduced graduate training, developed a strong library, set up specialized research institutes, published its own academic journals, and continued to teach Western liberal values.

Tsinghua students and faculty were somewhat insulated from the chaotic domestic and international environment of the early 1930s. By 1935, however, Japan's threat to China could no longer be ignored, and Tsinghua students began to protest Japanese aggression. When the Sino-Japanese War* erupted in July 1937, the university withdrew first to Changsha and then to Kunming, where it joined Nankai University and Peita to form Southwest Associated University in 1938.

The wartime period was extremely difficult for all of China's universities, including Tsinghua. The academics wished to preserve the prewar quality of education, particularly their political independence. The Kuomintang, however, attacked the universities, and Tsinghua thus had to cope not only with material deprivation but also with the Kuomintang's political intrusions.

Following the war, Tsinghua attempted to reestablish itself on its devastated Peking campus and to recover its independence. However, autonomous higher education of the Tsinghua variety could not survive in revolutionary China.

After 1949 the Communists stripped Tsinghua of its liberal arts and converted it into a polytechnical institution. Periodic government campaigns against intellectuals and educational institutions culminated in the closing of Tsinghua during the Cultural Revolution,* when its campus became a Red Guard* battleground. Despite these traumas, Tsinghua retained its excellence in science and technology, and even the old American ties resurfaced after 1976.

Tsinghua's history reveals that Sino-American cooperation in higher education could not survive nationalism's attack on imperialism. Its graduates nonetheless played leading roles in introducing Western learning to China, and Tsinghua scholars pioneered important studies of China's past and present. Tsinghua's influence on Chinese higher education was surpassed only by Peita.

REFERENCES: John Israel, ed., "Draft History of Qinghua University," *Chinese Education* 15, no. 3–4 (Fall–Winter 1982–1983): iii–xvi, 1–185; John Israel, "Southwest Associated University: Survival as an Ultimate Value," in Paul K.T. Sih, ed., *Nationalist China During the Sino-Japanese War, 1937–1945* (Hicksville, N.Y., Exposition Press, 1977): 131–154; E-tu Zen Sun, "The Growth of the Academic Community, 1912–1949," in John K. Fairbank and Albert Feuerwerker, eds., *The Cambridge History of China*, vol. 13, *Republican China, 1912–1949*, Part 2 (Cambridge, 1986): 361–420.

LOREN W. CRABTREE

TSO TSUNG-T'ANG (posthumous title Wen-hsiang, November 10, 1812– September 5, 1885): Governor-general; military leader.

Tso Tsung-t'ang was born to a family of modest means in the Hsiang-yin District of Hunan. He passed the provincial civil service examinations for the degree of *chü-jen* in 1832. Subsequently, he took and failed the metropolitan examination for the degree of *chin-shih* three times. In 1832 Tso married Chou I-tuan, and they had four sons. By the age of thirty-nine, in 1851, he had served as a private teacher, acquired and managed his own farm, and organized local defense forces, all in Hunan.

From 1852 until 1860 Tso served on the military staffs of several governors of Hunan Province, gaining a reputation as an able strategist in defensive operations against Taiping[*] revolutionary forces. In 1860, on the recommendation of Tseng Kuo-fan,[*] Tso was placed in charge of military affairs in southern Anhwei Province. After recruiting a force of 5,000 from the depleted manpower reserves of Hunan, he led his troops into Kiangsi where, in April 1861, he defeated Taiping forces commanded by Li Shih-hsien at Lo-p'ing, recaptured Ching-te-chen in southern Anhwei, and forced Li to withdraw into Chekiang. This victory enabled Tseng kuo-fan to escape from Ch'i-men in southern Anhwei where his headquarters had been invested by Taiping forces.

Early the following year, 1862, after the fall of Hangchow, provincial capital of Chekiang, the court named Tso governor of that province, again on the recommendation of Tseng Kuo-fan. During the next two years Tso's troops (known as the Ch'u Army) cooperated with the Sino-French Ever Victorious Army commanded by Prosper Marie Giquel[*] in clearing Chekiang of Taiping forces. While the campaign was in progress, Tso was named governor-general of Chekiang and Fukien in May 1863. His forces finally recaptured Hangchow after a siege that lasted from the fall of 1863 until April 1864. Tso was rewarded with an earldom of the first rank.

After the fall of Hangchow, the Taiping capital at Nanking was cut off from relief forces and fell to the Hunan Army troops of Tseng Kuo-ch'üan on July 19, 1864. Tso subsequently pursued Taiping remnants in Fukien and directed the operations that finally crushed the last rebel forces at Chia-ying-chou in Kwangtung in 1866.

Impressed by the speed and efficiency of Western steamships in military operations, Tso tested an experimental vessel constructed by Chinese engineers at West Lake near Hangchow in 1864. Disappointed but not discouraged by its mediocre performance, he determined to construct steamships in China using Western methods and technology. This led to the establishment, in 1867, of the Foochow Dockyard at Mawei on the Min River near Foochow. Under the directorship of French advisers, Prosper Giquel and Paul d'Aiguebelle, the Foochow Dockyard was one of China's earliest modern industries.

While engaged in securing imperial approval for the establishment of Foochow, on September 25, 1866, Tso was named governor-general of Shensi and Kansu where the Muslim minority, goaded by the discriminatory political and social policies of the Han Chinese, had begun armed rebellion in 1864. In 1867 with an imperial appointment as commissioner for military affairs in the two provinces, Tso determined first to launch an all-out attack on the Western Nien and then to move against the Muslims. The Nien* were a loose aggregation of mounted bands who had ravaged the economically depressed countryside of Shantung, Honan, Kiangsu, and Anhwei since 1853. In 1866 Nien bands moved westward into Shensi where they made contact with the Muslim rebels. There, they came under attack by Tso's forces in the northern watershed of the Wei River, east of Sian. The Nien withdrew northeastward recrossing the Yellow River into Shansi late in 1867, with Tso leading a force of 5,000 in hot pursuit. He chased the Nien through Shansi, Honan, and into the metropolitan province of Chihli where they approached Pao-ting, causing grave alarm in Peking. For this action Tso was stripped of his imperial rank. He finally joined forces with Li Hung-chang* who had been campaigning against the Eastern Nien; their combined armies forced the Nien into a trap in northern Shantung where they were annihilated in July 1868.

With his imperial rank restored, Tso turned westward to attack the Muslim rebels who, since 1864, had controlled most of Shensi, Kansu, Ninghsia, and Sinkiang. He directed an army (assembled from various provincial militia and financed in part by international loans) in a coordinated attack on the stronghold of Muslim leader Ma Hua-lung at Chin-chi-pao in Kansu. By the spring of 1869, Tso's troops had cleared Shensi of Muslim rebels, but Chin-chi-pao did not fall to the relentless attacks of Tso's army until January 1871. By August 1872, eastern Kansu was sufficiently pacified to allow Tso to establish his headquarters at Lanchow. From there he directed the pacification of northwestern Kansu, which was essentially completed with the recapture of Su-chou, at the head of the Kansu corridor, on October 24, 1873. While in Shensi and Kansu, Tso pursued his interest in industrial development, establishing arsenals at Sian in 1869 and Lanchow in 1872 and China's first modern woolen mill at Lanchow in 1877.

In 1864 the Muslim population in Sinkiang had rebelled, smarting from a century of occupation and exploitation by Manchu military forces. Preoccupied with the Taiping, Nien, and Muslim uprisings, the Manchu government was unable to move against the Sinkiang Muslims until 1873 when Shensi and Kansu were secured. In the intervening years, the Muslim chieftain Yakub Beg had consolidated his rule over most of Sinkiang by 1870 and gained international recognition in 1872 from Great Britain, which regarded Sinkiang as a buffer area between the expanding Russian Empire and British India. Russian forces also occupied the fertile and strategic Ili River Valley in extreme northwestern Sinkiang in July 1871, giving public assurances that their occupation was temporary and was intended only to insure the stability of Russian Turkestan, while Sinkiang experienced unrest. In 1872, however, Russia extended official recognition to the Yakub Beg regime.

This was the situation that Tso faced in 1873 as he readied his forces for the reconquest of Sinkiang. His request for imperial authorization and allocation of resources for the campaign gave rise, in 1874, to a debate over national priorities and the allocation of resources. On one side were the advocates of maritime defense led by the governor-general of Chihli, Li Hung-chang, who cautioned against the future aggression of Japan; on the other were the advocates of frontier defense led by Tso, who saw the loss of Sinkiang to Russia as China's foremost international concern. Not until April 1875 was an imperial decision made to allocate the necessary resources and proceed with the reconquest of Sinkiang.

Tso's logistical preparations were not completed until March 1876 when he moved his advance headquarters to Su-chou from whence he struck rapidly into Sinkiang securing the northern half of the territory before the end of the year. He then turned south crushing Yakub Beg's regime, bringing all of Sinkiang, save the Russian occupied Ili River Valley, under Chinese rule by the end of 1877.

Although the uprising of the Sinkiang Muslims had been suppressed and Chinese authority had once more been extended over Sinkiang, Russia proved reluctant to relinquish its hold on the Ili region. Ch'ung-hou, the Manchu emissary sent to St. Petersburg in 1879 to secure the return of Ili, was manipulated by the Russians into signing the Treaty of Livadia which, while it appeared to return Ili to China, actually ceded 70 percent of the territory to Russia. Because of this and the other provisions of the treaty damaging to Chinese sovereignty, the court disavowed Ch'ung-hou's signature, condemned him to death (though this sentence was later rescinded owing to international pressure), and in 1880 named Tseng Chi-tse to head a second mission to St. Petersburg to renegotiate the return of Ili.

Tso was among the many Chinese officials who recoiled at the terms of the treaty. Seeing the fruits of his victories in Sinkiang about to slip away through the diplomatic ineptitude of Ch'ung-hou, Tso called for war with Russia if Tseng Chi-tse's diplomatic initiative failed. Tso responded to the court's urging to increase military preparedness during the first half of 1880, moving his forces first to Su-chou and then to Hami. Russia reinforced its army in the Ili Region and dispatched a fleet toward Chinese waters. In a move presumably calculated to lessen the likelihood of actual hostilities, in the late summer of 1880, the court recalled Tso to Peking. He arrived in the capital on February 24, 1881, the very day that Tseng Chi-tse signed the Treaty of St. Petersburg restoring the Ili territory to China on more favorable terms. Tso's conquest of Sinkiang and his military preparations during the negotiations for the return of the Ili region strengthened the resolve of those at court who were determined not to compromise with foreign power. It also led to the incorporation of Sinkiang as a province of China in 1884, a move that Tso had proposed after his initial conquest of the region in 1877.

After a short stint in Peking during which he served on the Grand Council and the Tsungli Yamen, Tso was named governor-general of the Liang-kiang provinces, taking up his new post in Nanking on February 12, 1882. Although he was in declining health and his vision was now impaired, he devoted his efforts to the suppression of secret societies, to administrative reform, and to economic development.

When fighting broke out between Chinese and French forces in Vietnam in 1883, Tso was called to Peking and placed in charge of military affairs. The following year, on August 23, the French fleet sunk eleven Chinese vessels on the Min River in Fukien and destroyed the Foochow Dockyard. China declared war on France and named Tso imperial commissioner in charge of military affairs in Fukien. He arrived in Foochow at the end of 1884 and immediately began preparing a force to relieve Taiwan which had also come under French attack. China accepted French terms for peace in June 1885; Tso died a few months later on September 5, 1885, in Foochow.

Tso's role in nineteenth-century China has been subject to differing interpretations. Some Marxist historians have emphasized the ruthlessness and brutality with which Tso suppressed the Muslim uprisings in the northwest. Of equal significance, however, were his policies of administrative reconstruction, agricultural development, industrial modernization, and the promotion of education which laid the foundation for the incorporation of Sinkiang as a province of China.

Tso's meteoric rise to the office of governor-general during the final years of the Taiping Revolution seems to have cast him in a competitive nexus with his earlier sponsor Tseng kuo-fan. Parallel postwar activities, Tseng's in Shanghai and Tso's in Foochow, marked them as competitors for prestige and resources. But it was only after Tseng's death in 1872, when the national debate over frontier versus maritime defense pitted Tso against Tseng's protégé Li Hung-chang, that the lines of policy difference were clearly drawn. Although Tso's advocacy of frontier defense ultimately prevailed, it is uncertain, in view of China's defeat in 1895 in a naval war with Japan, whether this turn of events strengthened the dynasty against its most formidable potential enemy.

REFERENCES: Gideon Chen (Ch'en Ch'i-t'ien), *Tso Tsung-t'ang: Pioneer Promoter of the Modern Woolen Mill in China* (Peking, 1938); Arthur W. Hummel, ed., *Eminent Chinese of the Ch'ing Period* (Washington, D.C., 1944):762–767; Tai I and Lin Yen-chiao, eds., *Ch'ing-tai jen-wu chuan-kao* (Draft biographies of figures from the Ch'ing period), Second Collection, II (Shenyang, 1984):67–75; Ts'ai Kuan-lo, ed., *Ch'ing-tai chi'i-pai ming-jen chuan*, vol. 2 (Biographies of seven hundred famous people of the Ch'ing period) (Peking, 1984):1399–1412.

THOMAS L. KENNEDY

TSOU LU (February 20, 1885–February 13, 1954): Republican revolutionary, military commander, statesman, and educator.

Born into a poor tailor's family in Tapu, Kwangtung, Tsou Lu received a thorough classical education before enrolling in Canton's School of Law and Politics in 1906. There he became acquainted with Ch'iu Feng-chia and Chu Chih-hsin, under whose influence Tsou embarked on his career. Upon his graduation he served as secretary of the provincial assembly whose deputy speaker was Ch'iu. Soon Tsou joined the T'ung-meng hui* through Chu's introduction, and became involved in Kwangtung's uprisings. He was instrumental in converting the provincial garrison to the revolutionary cause, leading to the rebels' capture of the province in November 1911. Tsou was subsequently appointed superintendent for provisioning the expeditionary army marching to the front in the Yangtze Delta. After the founding of the Republic, Tsou was elected to China's first Parliament, where he fought against the five-power banking consortium loan, one of many illegalities under the Yüan Shih-k'ai* administration. When the Second Revolution* failed to overthrow Yüan's dictatorship, Tsou continued his anti-Yüan efforts by contributing articles to the revolutionary organ *Min-kuo tsa-chih* or *The Republic Journal*, which he helped edit, and raising funds in Hong Kong and Southeast Asia.

Tsou's close links with the army in Kwangtung and Kwangsi previously established during the Republican Revolution helped Dr. Sun Yat-sen* in the early 1920s to secure the region as the base challenging warlord-controlled central government in the north following Yüan's demise in June 1916. Tsou was appointed Kwangtung's finance commissioner and then chancellor of National Kwangtung University, later renamed Sun Yat-sen University, in 1924. Tsou was a pioneer in China's modern education, having earlier founded a middle school and a normal school in Tapu and Canton, respectively. Meanwhile, he also edited the scripts of Dr. Sun's lectures on the Three People's Principles* delivered at his university.

The Kuomintang, in 1923, then allied with the Soviet Russia and admitted members of the Chinese Communist party* in overthrowing warlords and their foreign backers. Soon Tsou was alarmed by the CCP's rapid expansion at the KMT's expense. In November 1925 he and seven other members of KMT's central executive committee held a special meeting in Peking's Western Hills, proposing the Communists' peaceful withdrawal from the KMT. These eight men and their sympathizers, dubbed the Western Hills Faction,* then set up a separate party center in Shanghai in rivalry against the one in Canton, thus beginning the perennial KMT schism. Following KMT's general split with the CCP in 1927, Tsou and others endeavored to forge party unity by forming a special central committee. It failed to achieve genuine party solidarity because of the lack of sincerity and good-will among KMT leaders of various factions. The KMT remained ever schismatic, losing both its vigor and vitality as a revolutionary and then a ruling party.

Tsou then traveled abroad touring twenty-nine countries in Asia, North America, Europe, and Africa. During his eleven-month trip he took special interest in educational matters in the countries he visited. Upon his return to China in November 1928, he completed and published *A Draft History of the Kuomintang*, which among other works on the KMT and Chinese Revolution, helped establish him as an authority in the field. Meanwhile, the Chiang Kai-shek-*led Nationalist government in Nanking was challenged by fellow KMT leaders who formed a grand coalition and founded a rival regime in Peip'ing in June 1930. Tsou became involved in it, playing a key role in producing a draft provisional constitution, which became a major reference for the Chinese constitution later promulgated in January 1947. The Japanese invasion of Manchuria in 1931 drew the KMT leaders together, and Tsou emerged as the spokesman for the southwestern region at that time. In 1932 he was also appointed chancellor of Sun Yat-sen University in Canton. He served in that position until 1940, when he had to resign to tend to more urgent national defense matters. His chancellorship transformed the university into a highly esteemed institution both at home and abroad. In acknowledging his contribution to China's modern education, Germany's Heidelberg University awarded him an honorary doctorate at its 550th anniversary in 1936.

Tsou contributed greatly to his country's resistance war efforts after July 1937 as a Standing Committee member of China's Supreme National Defense Council, offering good advice and sound judgment on military affairs and defense strategy. In March 1945 he published *My Past and Present Views on Education*, reiterating his earlier belief in the idea that educational philosophy should be based on *jen-ai*, or benevolent love, in achieving lasting peace in the postwar world. He urged governments all over the world to invest generously in education, providing free education through the tertiary level in order to eliminate illiteracy and ignorance which Tsou considered the roots of struggle among men. After the war, Tsou was elected a member of China's Supervisory Yuan in 1948. Two years later he went to Taiwan, becoming involved in restructuring the KMT there and serving on its advisory council until his death in 1954.

REFERENCES: Tsou Lu, *Wo-ti hui-ku* (My reminiscences), 4 vols. (Chungking, 1943); Ch'en Chieh-san, *Tsou Lu Yen-chiu ch'u-chi* (A collection of essays on Tsou Lu) (Taipei, 1980).

LAU YEE-CHEUNG

TSUNYI CONFERENCE: CCP meeting in January 1935 during the Long March, in which Mao Tse-tung tried to gain control of party leadership.

The Tsunyi Conference was a Politburo meeting of the Chinese Communist party* held at Tsunyi, in Kweichow Province. Convened on January 6–8, 1935, during the Long March,* this meeting was one of the most important conferences in the history of the CCP and of the Chinese Revolution. At Tsunyi Mao Tse-tung* took an initiative to gain control of the party leadership by challenging the Russian-returned student group which controlled the party's policymaking machinery since the Fourth Plenum of the party's Central Committee in January 1931. However, Chang Wen-t'ien (Lo Fu),* one of the Russian-returned student group, retained the party's position as the general secretary, perhaps with the support of Mao himself.

Leaders attending the Tsunyi Conference included such Politburo members and alternates as Ch'in Pang-hsien (Po Ku),* Chang Wen-t'ien, Chou En-lai,* Ch'en Yün,* Chu Teh,* and K'ai Feng. The party's Central Committee members like Mao Tse-tung, Liu Shao-ch'i,* Li Wei-han, and P'eng Te-huai* and alternates Liu Po-ch'eng, Li Fu-ch'un, and six others were also present at the conference. Comintern* military adviser Otto Braun (alias Li T'e)* also attended the meeting as an observer. Ch'in Pang-hsien, until then general secretary of the party's Central Committee, chaired the conference, and Chou En-lai, as director of the party's Military Affairs Committee, delivered the keynote address. The meeting reviewed the mistakes of the party's military strategy in countering the series of five Encirclement Campaigns* that the KMT army carried out against the Kiangsi Soviets.*

At the Tsunyi Conference the CCP leadership was reorganized when Mao Tse-tung took the key position of director of the Military Affairs Committee of the party's Central Committee, replacing Chou En-lai. Mao was also elected to the Standing Committee of the Politburo, as a secretary of the Central Committee's Secretariat, and continued as chairman of the Central Executive Committee of the Central Soviet government, to which he was elected at the Second National Congress of the Chinese Soviet Republic in January 1934. Some controversy has arisen over whether or not Mao Tse-tung took control of the party's policymaking power at the Tsunyi Conference. Recent research findings show that Mao was not able to control the party's leadership and decision-making process, and he therefore had to share the power and policymaking of the party's Central Committee with the segment of the Russian-returned student group led by Chang Wen-t'ien at the Tsunyi Conference.

REFERENCES: Benjamin Yang, "The Zunyi Conference as One Step in Mao's Rise to Power: A Survey of Historical Studies of the Chinese Communist Party," *The China Quarterly* 106 (June 1986): 235–271; Richard C. Thorton, *China, the Struggle for Power, 1917–1972* (Bloomington, Ind., 1973).

ILPYONG KIM

TUNG PI-WU (1886–April 2, 1975): Party "elder"; vice-chairman, PRC; member, Standing Committee of the Politburo of the Central Committee; secretary, CCP Central Control Commission.

Tung was born in Huang-an hsien, Hupeh, of a "landless gentry" family, his father was a degree-holder in the late Ch'ing* period. Tung himself studied the Confucian classics and earned the *hsiu-ts'ai* degree when he was fifteen, perhaps in 1901, following which he pursued a modern education, initially at a middle school in Wuchang. He began a teaching career in 1911, but when the revolution began he enlisted in the revolutionary army, marking the beginning of a lifelong revolutionary career. He joined the T'ung-meng hui* in 1911, but fled to Japan in 1913 when Yüan Shih-k'ai* suppressed the revolutionary organization. In 1914 he joined Sun Yat-sen's* newly organized Chung-hua ko-ming tang (Chinese Revolutionary party),* while studying law in Tokyo. In 1915 Tung returned to Hupeh at Sun Yat-sen's request, to undertake secret work in the Chinese military, in the course of this work he was arrested and jailed for half a year. On his release in 1916, Tung returned to Japan to complete his studies. For a time, in 1917–1918, Tung, back in China, did propaganda work in western Hupeh. But in the spring of 1919 he went to Shanghai and began to study Marxism. He was converted to Marxism by late 1919 or early 1920.

Tung returned to Wuhan where he opened a middle school, which, along with a bookstore founded by his friend Yun Tai-ying became gathering places for left-oriented intellectuals. He soon founded a Communist group in Hupeh, and in July 1921 Tung was one of two delegates from Hupeh to attend the First Congress of the Chinese Communist party* in Shanghai. (He was thus one of the founding members of the CCP.) Tung then returned to Hupeh where he continued to develop party organizations, although he is said to have spent a year in Szechwan working on tactics among the military. During the period of cooperation with the Nationalists, Tung served in a KMT branch in Hupeh. In 1924 he went to Chin-chai hsien with two colleagues to begin a peasant movement, which apparently was a first such effort in this area. In early 1925 he traveled in the northwest and northeast of China looking for recruits. In January 1926 he attended the Second KMT Congress in Canton and was elected an alternate member of the Central Executive Committee. Tung, together with other colleagues, succeeded in persuading T'ang Sheng-chih, who at the time, was in Hunan, to side with the revolutionaries just before the Northern Expedition* was launched. Tung claims to have helped in the capture of Wuhan by the Northern Expeditionary forces, and remained in Wuhan during the remaining turbulent period of CCP–KMT cooperation until mid–1927. Following the termination of the alliance Tung narrowly escaped and made his way to the French Concession in Shanghai and then to Japan where he stayed for eight months. Next he went to Moscow, arriving there in September 1928. He attended either Sun Yat-sen University or the University of the Toilers of the East or the Comintern-run Lenin School (the latter according to his own account to Nym Wales). He completed his studies in 1931 and returned to China in 1932.

During the period of the agrarian revolutionary war he served as president of the Party School, secretary of the Party Affairs Commission, member of the Soviet Republic's Central Executive Committee, president of the Supreme Court, and vice-chairman of the Workers' and Peasants' Procuratorial Committee in the Kiangsi Central Revolutionary Base. He took part in the Long March* from Kiangsi to Shensi in 1934–1935. In Shensi he continued to be president of the

Party School and became acting chairman of the Shensi-Kansu-Ninghsia Border Regional Government.*

Tung also assisted Chou En-lai* in negotiations with Chiang K'ai-shek* and his captors during the famous Sian Incident* of December 1936. Beginning in September 1937, Tung again went to Sian to work as a liaison officer with the KMT during the renewed CCP–KMT cooperation. He continued in this role for much of the following decade, moving as circumstances demanded to Hankow, Chungking, and Nanking. After Chou En-lai returned to Yenan in June 1943, Tung was the chief Communist representative in Chungking for most of the remaining period of the war against Japan. In March 1945 Tung was appointed by the Nationalists as the only Communist on the ten-member delegation sent by China to the conference in San Francisco to establish the United Nations Organization. Tung subsequently toured the United States for several months, returning to China in December 1945. He served as Chou En-lai's top assistant during the negotiations with the KMT at the time of General George C. Marshall's mission to China in 1946–1947. After the failure of the Marshall Mission* Tung returned to Yenan just as the Communist capital was about to fall into Nationalist hands in the resumed civil war.*

Prior to the establishment of the People's Republic of China* in 1949, Tung also served as a member of the Secretariat of the party's North China Bureau, director of the North China Commission of Finance and Economy, and chairman of the North China People's Government. During 1949 he was busily involved with a number of assignments in preparation for the new government about to come into being.

Following the establishment of the People's Republic of China, Tung served as director of the Central Commission of Finance and Economy, vice-premier of the Administration Council of the Central People's government, director of the Committee of Political and Legal Affairs, president of the Supreme People's Court, vice-chairman of the Second National Committee of the Chinese People's Political Consultative Committee, secretary of the party's Control Commission, vice-chairman and acting chairman of the PRC, and vice-chairman of the Standing Committee of the National People's Congress. In the early 1950s Tung appeared at numerous public functions and produced a steady flow of reports for various government organs and national conferences.

He traveled abroad again only in 1954 and 1958, respectively, leading delegations to Sofia on both occasions, adding visits to Prague and to East Berlin on the second trip.

Tung appears to have played an important role in the purge of Kao Kang* and Jao Shu-shih in 1954–1955. He was named chairman of the new Central Control Commission that was established in 1955 specifically to prevent a recurrence of a Kao-Jao "antiparty plot."

Tung was elected a member of the party's Central Committee at the Sixth, Seventh, Eighth, Ninth, and Tenth National Party Congresses. He was a member of the Politburo since the Sixth Plenary Session of the Sixth Central Committee, and was elected to the Standing Committee of the Politburo at the First Session of the Tenth Central Committee in August 1973.

Tung died of illness on April 2, 1975, at the age of ninety. Marshall Yeh Chien-ying[*] gave the eulogy at the memorial ceremony at the Great Hall of the People in Peking on April 7, 1975. His ashes were interred at Papaoshan Cemetery. He was survived by his third (or fourth) wife, Ho Lien-chih, and three children.

REFERENCES: Donald W. Klein and Anne B. Clark, *Biographic Dictionary of Chinese Communism, 1921–1965*, vol. 2 (Cambridge, Mass. 1971): 874–880; Yeh Chien-ying, "Memorial Ceremony Speech," *Peking Review* (April 11, 1975): 7–8.

STEPHEN UHALLEY, JR.

T'UNG-MENG HUI (Chinese United League): Chinese revolutionary organization founded by Sun Yat-sen in Tokyo in 1905.

The formation of the T'ung-meng hui (Chinese United League) in Tokyo in 1905 marked an important milestone in Dr. Sun Yat-sen's[*] revolutionary career. For eleven years, since he first organized the Hsing-Chung hui (Revive China Society)[*] in Hawaii in 1894 and subsequently failed in an uprising against the Manchus on the south China coast, Sun had been in exile, traveling the world and preaching his revolutionary cause before Chinese groups that were often less than enthusiastic. It was not until he toured North America in 1904 and European capitals in early 1905 that he began to pick up support from Chinese students studying abroad.

Japan in 1905 was a center of Chinese students and political exiles, with several thousand of them concentrating in the Tokyo–Yokohama area. They ranged in their political persuasion from favoring constitutional monarchy to advocating revolution against the Manchus. Many, in fact, had escaped to Japan after failing in insurrectional attempts in China. They were loosely grouped by their native places. Among many such groups, three stood out: the Hsing-Chung hui with members predominantly from south China, the Hua-hsing hui (China Revival Society[*]) from central China, and the Kuang-fu hui (Recovery Society) from the east coast. Sun Yat-sen, commanding great prestige among the students, succeeded in merging the three into one by forming the T'ung-meng hui, thus greatly enhancing the cause of revolution. The new organization became the mainstay of the revolutionary movement under Sun Yat-sen which culminated in the Wuchang Uprising in October 1911.

At its inception, the T'ung-meng hui made clear that its objectives were the overthrow of the Manchu dynasty and the establishment of a republic. In the political field, the revolutionaries consistently stressed nationalism and republicanism as the dual guideposts; in the economic field, they advocated moderate socialism. To defend their cause, in 1905–1907 they carried out the celebrated great debate with the Pao-huang Hui[*] (Emperor Protection Society), headed by K'ang Yu-wei[*] and Liang Ch'i-ch'ao.[*] K'ang and Liang supported Emperor Kuang-hsü[*] and championed constitutional monarchy. The debate showed that,

while the royalists were primarily conservative in their outlook, the revolutionaries were dedicated to what they believed to be the world's most advanced
political system.

The T'ung-meng hui expanded rapidly after its formation in 1905. The revolutionaries used different methods and adapted to local conditions in organizing
branches, such as wooing overseas Chinese leaders abroad and allying themselves
with the secret societies at home. While members inside China planned and
carried out revolts, overseas members played an important role in providing
financial support.

Between 1907 and 1911, no fewer than eight uprisings were staged in south
China. Since the T'ung-meng hui had no military force of its own, it relied
heavily in these uprisings on the secret societies and the New Army,* which the
revolutionaries had succeeded in infiltrating, particularly at the lower echelon.
While their military importance may be limited, these uprisings were significant
as a political demonstration against the Manchu rule, hastening its downfall.

The most significant result of the 1911 Revolution* was the overthrow of the
centuries-old monarchical system and the establishment of a republic in China.
Both in providing ideological leadership and in guiding the actual course of
action, the role of the T'ung-meng hui was crucial in the revolution. Indeed, it
may be said that had it not been for the T'ung-meng hui, there would have been
no Revolution of 1911.

REFERENCES: Chün-tu Hsüeh, *Huang Hsing and the Chinese Revolution* (Stanford,
Calif., 1961); Ta-ling Lee, *Foundations of the Chinese Revolution, 1905–1912* (New
York, 1970).

TA-LING LEE

TWENTY-EIGHT BOLSHEVIKS: The name for a group of returned students
from the Soviet Union, who during the early 1930s were able to control central
power within the CCP.

The Twenty-eight Bolsheviks were an important political faction within the
Chinese Communist party.* They were a political clique who had studied at Sun
Yat-sen University in Moscow from the mid–1920s to 1930, when they returned
to China. Led by Wang Ming* (Ch'en Shao-yü), the ranks of the returned students
included Po Ku* (Ch'in Pang-hsien), Lo Fu* (Chang Wen-t'ien), Shen Tse-min,
Wang Chia-hsiang, Ho Tzu-shu, Ch'en Ch'ang-hao, Ch'en Wei-ming, K'ai
Feng, and Sun Chi-ming.

Amidst the Stalin–Trotsky struggle for power (1927), the Chinese studying
in the Soviet Union were also forming cliques. The Twenty-eight Bolsheviks,
a group gathered around Wang Ming, were supportive of the rector of Sun Yat-
sen University, Pavel Mif, who in turn backed them for important party duties
upon their return to China in 1930. After the failure of urban uprisings in 1930,
during the Fourth Plenary session of the Sixth Central Committee in January
1931, they were able to oust Li Li-san* from his dominant position in the party,
maneuver positions on the Central Committee and Politburo, and gain de facto

control of the CCP. The height of power for the Twenty-eight Bolsheviks was the early 1930's, but members of their clique such as Po Ku, Lo Fu, and Wang Chia-hsiang were able to hold key CCP positions throughout their careers.

There were important differences between the Twenty-eight Bolsheviks and other CCP factions. After the April 12 coup in 1927, the CCP began having struggles in tactical and theoretical areas. However, most of the leadership had been tested through dangerous and demanding situations. The Twenty-eight Bolsheviks were resented as a returned student clique who had "theory without practice." They had not taken the risks, but were promoted for leadership, in large part, because of their Communist International backers. For many of the veteran CCP leaders, this principle of leadership imposed from the top did not generate deep loyalty to the Twenty-eight Bolsheviks.

Besides issues of personal political power, the Twenty-eight Bolsheviks represented the most "international" of the CCP factions. They espoused the idea of the Chinese Revolution as part of the world revolution, which had to follow the leadership of the Soviet Union. This meant that there were some important differences in revolutionary strategy and theory. The Twenty-eight Bolsheviks contended that the Chinese Revolution had to be led by the proletariat and that to rely on nonworkers was not following the Marxist-Leninist route to revolution. Thus, while appreciating the red bases, consolidated in the countryside by leaders such as Chu Teh* and Mao Tse-tung,* Wang Ming and his cohorts believed that the revolution should be based in the urban centers. When it was no longer feasible to maintain the CCP Central Committee in Shanghai, the Wang Ming-led faction retreated to the Kiangsi Soviet* and kept supreme political control. According to Communist historians, the Twenty-eight Bolshevik clique argued for set battles with the Kuomintang during the Fifth Encirclement Campaign,* instead of guerrilla tactics, which successfully repelled the first four campaigns. This led to the need to abandon the Kiangsi Soviet and to the Long March.* However, both the military and the political circumstances were more complex than this scenario suggests, and questions such as the role of the Twenty-eight Bolsheviks, before and during the Long March, the issue of when power actually devolved on Mao Tse-tung, and the force of other factions are under investigation as new sources become available. The cohesion of the Twenty-eight Bolsheviks is an area which itself needs exploration, as leaders such as Shen Tse-min and Lo Fu changed their loyalties.

The internationalist perspective of the Twenty-eight Bolsheviks was also evident in their attitude toward the United Front with the Kuomintang. They strictly followed the line of the Soviet Union, and they tried to emulate Soviet policies elsewhere, such as the United Front in France. They were more willing to cooperate and assimilate within the Kuomintang than other CCP leaders. Similar to the debacle of the stress on the proletariat basis of the Chinese Revolution, the lack of a Sinocentric vision of the United Front in China further eroded the legitimacy of leadership for the Twenty-eight Bolsheviks.

The Twenty-eight Bolsheviks represented a fundamental and powerful countercurrent within the CCP leadership. Although other cohorts based on associational linkages or foreign experience existed they were the strongest internationalists, as displayed by their dependence on, and allegiance to, the Communist International.

REFERENCES: Otto Braun, *A Comintern Agent in China, 1932–1939* (Stanford, Calif., 1982); Chin Chün, "Kung-chan kou-chi ho Wang Ming 'tsuo' hsiang mao-chien chu-i" (The Communist International and the Left Adventurism of Wang Ming), in *Chung-Kung tang-shih yen-chiu lün-wen hsüan*, vol. 2 (Hunan, 1983): 479–494; Thomas Kampen, "Changes in the Leadership of the Chinese Communist Party during and after the Long March," *Republican China* 12, no.2 (April 1987): 28–36; Robert C. North, *Moscow and the Chinese Communists* (Stanford, Calif., 1953).

MARILYN LEVINE

TZ'U-HSI, EMPRESS DOWAGER (November 29, 1835–November 15, 1908): Wife of Emperor Hsien-feng (the seventh emperor of the Ch'ing dynasty, r. 1850–1861); power figure in Ch'ing politics.

Tz'u-hsi, born as Yehonala, daughter of Hui-cheng of the Manchu Bordered Blue Banner, was chosen in 1851 to enter the imperial court as a concubine of Emperor Hsien-feng when her father was an intendant of circuit of southern Anhwei. Tz'u-hsi was not, however, the emperor's senior consort at this time. Because of her beauty, intelligence, and powers of manipulation, however, she became Hsien-feng's favorite concubine, especially after she gave birth to Hsien-feng's only son, Tsai-ch'un (later Emperor T'ung-chih), in 1856. Thenceforth, Hsien-feng's favoritism of Ts'u-hsi made her a very influential member of the court. Reportedly, she was even asked to assist the emperor in dealing with state affairs. Thus, Tz'u-hsi quickly learned the intricacies of court politics.

Emperor Hsien-feng died in 1861. Prince Tsai-ch'un succeeded his father, becoming Emperor T'ung-chih, the eighth emperor of the Ch'ing dynasty,[*] at the age of five. Empresses Tz'u-hsi and Tz'u-an (Hsien-feng's senior consort) were appointed to be Tsai-ch'un's co-regents. Under this arrangement, Tz'u-hsi was naturally the more powerful regent. For the first time in her life, Tz'u-hsi was able to fully experience the sweet taste of power. Yet she knew that if she wanted more control of the court, she had to cooperate closely with her brother-in-law, Prince Kung (Hsien-feng's younger brother and prince counselor of the Ch'ing court), who had helped China through one of its most serious crises, the invasion of British and French Joint Expedition Forces. It was he who successfully negotiated with the French and the British over the Treaty of Peking in 1860. Thus, in Peking, Prince Kung was popular, influential, and powerful, but he knew that he had to rely on the support of Tz'u-hsi in order to manage court affairs smoothly.

The power balance between Tz'u-hsi and Prince Kung in the 1860s and the 1870s created an atmosphere of openness that brought new strength to China, as open-minded southern Chinese leaders such as Tseng Kuo-fan,[*] Tso Tsung-t'ang,[*] and Li Hung-chang[*] became increasingly important decision makers in the government's national affairs. This able group of statesmen suppressed the

Taiping Uprising* in 1864, and they quelled the many Muslim uprisings in 1873. Under their guidance, many Self-Strengthening* programs began to take shape, such as developing the Foochow Shipyards, the Kiangnan Arsenal, and the T'ung-wen Kuan (or foreign language schools). Although the success of these developments, known as the T'ung-chih Restoration, formed a base for future industrialization and modernization in China, it also signified that China needed to open its doors to the West even further. Conservatives such as Tz'u-hsi and Wo-jen opposed such liberal change. Thus, a power struggle developed between Tz'u-hsi and Prince Kung.

In 1872 Emperor T'ung-chih came of age. Although Tz'u-hsi's regency officially ended the following year, she remained powerful and became even more ambitious in the years after 1873. When Emperor T'ung-chih died in 1875, Tz'u-hsi, by manipulating the court, was able to place her nephew, Tsai-tien, on the throne. Since the new Emperor Kuang-hsü* was only four at the time, this arrangement guaranteed power to Tz'u-hsi, although nominally she was still a co-regent with Empress Dowager Hsiao-chen, the young emperor's mother.

Tz'u-hsi controlled Emperor Kuang-hsü's government in the same way that she had Emperor T'ung-chih's, through fear and intimidation. When Kuang-hsü came of age in 1886, Tz'u-hsi did not relinquish her regency until Kuang-hsü's marriage in 1889, and even then, Tz'u-hsi still maintained tight control over the court and the government. By this time, she had completely edged Prince Kung out of power in the court.

Tz'u-hsi's domination of power after 1875 weakened China considerably. Internally, its corruption, which included the embezzlement of public funds, not only paralyzed many modernization programs but also discouraged the southern Chinese leaders such as Tseng Kuo-fan from participating in making national decisions. In 1898 even Emperor Kuang-hsü rebelled against Tz'u-hsi to recruit the young and dynamic K'ang Yu-wei* to launch the Hundred Day Reform* (June 11–September 10, 1898). But he found Tz'u-hsi too powerful. Emperor Kuang-hsü failed; K'ang Yu-wei was expelled, and Tz'u-hsi resumed her regency by the end of 1898.

Externally, Tz'u-hsi's ultraconservatism worried foreign powers in China, and their encroachments on China reached new heights, bringing on the Sino-French War of 1884–1885, the Sino-Japanese War of 1894–1895,* and the territory-lease treaties with France, Germany, Russia, and Great Britain in 1898–1899. As a result, Tz'u-hsi became increasingly more antiforeign, and yet she was immensely frustrated at failing to find effective ways to cope with foreign powers. The greatest expression of her frustration came in the form of the Boxer Rebellion* of 1900, the most infamous antiforeign act in China, which resulted in humiliating China, alienating the southern Chinese leaders, and stimulating liberal intellectuals such as Dr. Sun Yet-sen to engage in anti-Manchu revolutionary movements.

After the Boxer Rebellion, Tz'u-hsi never regained her power in Peking, for her association with the Boxers was too politically damaging for both herself and for China. Her control over the Ch'ing court, however, was still pervasive; she died on November 15, 1908, a day after the Emperor Kuang-hsü, giving credence to the rumor that Tzu-hsi had "arranged" Kuang-hsü's death for being an "unfilial child" during his anti-Tz'u-hsi involvement in the Hundred Day Reform.

REFERENCES: Charlotte Haldane, *The Last Great Empress of China* (Indianapolis, Ind., 1967); Immanuel C.Y. Hsü, *The Rise of Modern China*, 4th ed. (New York, 1990); Harry Hussey, *Venerable Ancestor: The Life and Times of Tz'u-hsi, Empress of China*, (Westport, Conn., 1970).

ANTHONY Y. TENG

U

ULANFU (December 23, 1906–December 8, 1988): Top Mongolian CCP cadre, member of the CCP Central Committee and Politburo; member of the Central People's Government Council, vice-premier of the PRC; chairman of the Nationalities Affairs Committee.

Ulanfu, often known also by his Han name of Yün Tse, was born in 1906 to an agricultural family in the Tumet Banner of the Bayan Tala League in Inner Mongolia. Little is known about Ulanfu's childhood and his early youth, except that both he and his elder brother, known by his Han name of Yün Jen, attended the primary school in the Tumet Banner, located west of today's Huhehot, the capital of the Inner Mongolia Autonomous Region. Around 1922, Ulanfu and his brother went to Peking where they enrolled in the middle school division of Peiping Mongolian—Tibetan School, which had been established for the purpose of providing a Chinese-oriented education for young Tibetans and Mongols. At this time, Li Ta-chao* was the director of the North China Bureau of the fledgeling Chinese Communist party,* and Li, with his exceptional charismatic appeal to young students and his particular concern for the unity of nationalities, found fertile opportunities for recruiting CCP members among university students at the capital. It was during this time, in the spring of 1924, that Ulanfu became a member of the Communist Youth League, and in the following year he joined the CCP. He and other Mongol students participated actively in the Peking student demonstrations in reaction to the May Thirtieth Incident* in Shanghai in 1925. This was Ulanfu's first significant participation in mass political movements.

In the summer following the May Thirtieth Incident, Ulanfu returned to Inner Mongolia, where, under the leadership of Pai Yün-t'i, a number of progressive young Mongols set about transforming the National Revival Association (NRA), which had been established two years earlier. The association was apparently influenced by the movement toward autonomy in Outer Mongolia and the establishment of the Mongolian People's Republic in November 1924. Stirred by this activity, the Mongols in Inner Mongolia reorganized the NRA into the Inner Mongolia People's party (IMPP) to unite themselves and to give greater and clearer definition to their political aspirations. The opinions within the IMPP, though commonly based on a platform for greater autonomy from China and resisting absorption by China as a province, were quite divided, however. They ranged from a proposal to unite with the Mongolian People's Republic to the option of setting up a Mongol government within a federated Republic of China. This latter opinion was demonstrated as more favorably (though not decisively) preferred in the manifesto of the First Congress of the IMPP that was held in October 1925 at Kalgan. However, there is no documentary evidence of what specific position Ulanfu held at this time, although he was most certainly an active participant of the Congress.

Soon thereafter, Ulanfu went to Moscow with his brother, and both enrolled in schools there for the next few years. Ulanfu entered Sun Yat-sen University (later renamed the Communist University of the Toilers of China), and Yün Jen in the University of the Toilers of the East. Ulanfu became classmate and friend to Wang Jo-fei, who would eventually be his superior in underground work in Suiyuan Province in the early 1930s. After graduation, Ulanfu remained in Moscow and worked for a short time as an interpreter before enrolling in the Infantry School.

Ulanfu returned to China in 1930 and joined the Communist underground in Suiyuan. He barely escaped arrest in October 1931 when Wang Jo-fei, his superior, was arrested and incarcerated. At the time, northern China was under the control of the warlords Feng Yü-hsiang* and Yen Hsi-shan,* who were allied with the KMT leaders Wang Ching-wei* and Li Tsung-jen who were feuding with Chiang Kai-shek.* As a result of these subtle political alignments, Ulanfu found himself a secretarial position under Fu Tso-yi,* who at that time was a lieutenant of Yen Hsi-shan, and served as a section chief in the Political Department of Fu's Third Cavalry Regiment.

In 1932 Japanese forces, having overrun Manchuria the previous year, began to penetrate Jehol and threaten Chahar. Ulanfu became involved in organizing Mongol anti-Japanese guerrilla forces, taking part in a rebellion against the Japanese in 1934. In April 1934 a Mongolian Regional Autonomy Political Council was formed. The leadership of this council soon divided, with two Mongol princes, Te Wang and Yün Wang, going over to the Japanese side. In February 1936, at a policy meeting of the Council at Pai-ling-miao, the anti-Japanese group split off and soon thereafter established the Suiyuan-Mongolian Local Autonomous Political Council, which continued to operate against the Japanese with the support of the Nationalists and was specifically supported and supplied by Fu Tso-yi. During this time, Ulanfu was operating underground against the Japanese in the Pai-ling-miao region.

After the Sian Incident* of December 1936 and with the outbreak of the war of resistance against Japan, Ulanfu served as a political commissar of Pai Hai-feng's Suiyuan-Mongolian Peace Preservation Corps, which was later reorganized as an independent Mongol brigade of the Nationalist Army under the auspices of the Ikechao League. Meanwhile, Ulanfu continued to promote Communist organizations. In the winter of 1939, he was nearly arrested by Chang Yi-ting, director of the Political Department of the forces under Fu Tso-yi who at that time took over command of Pai Hai-feng's troops. Afterward, in 1941, Ulanfu fled to Yenan, the wartime headquarters of the Communist party, and became head of the Nationalities' Institute of the Anti-Japanese Military and Political University under Kao Kang.* He also assumed the positions of chairman of the Nationalities Affairs Committee of the Shensi-Kansu-Ninghsia Border Region government* and president of the Mongolian Culture Association. In 1944 Ulanfu returned to northern Suiyuan to organize a Communist base under the aegis of the Shensi-Suiyuan Border Region government, and thus became the chairman of the Suiyuan-Mongolian government. After the Japanese surrender in 1945, Communist forces moved from Jehol into Chahar and took control of Kalgan, where, in November, the Inner Mongolia Independence Movement Association (IMIMA) was formed with Ulanfu as its chairman. Earlier that year, Ulanfu was elected as an alternate member of the Seventh Central Committee of the CCP at the Seventh National Congress of the party, and appointed deputy secretary of the CCP's Minority Nationalities Affairs Committee. In the spring of 1946, the IMIMA merged with the Ulanhot Mongols who had sought to set up an Eastern Mongolian autonomous government. This was propitious, since Kalgan soon fell to the Nationalists in the KMT–CCP civil war* that erupted in 1946, and Ulanfu could move the IMIMA to Ulanhot where it came under the protection of Lin Piao's* Communist forces that soon controlled Manchuria. On May 1, 1947, the Inner Mongolia People's Congress was held at Ulanhot, and Ulanfu was elected as chairman of the People's government of the Inner Mongolia Autonomous Region (IMAR). Subsequently, in the same year, he was appointed secretary of the CCP's Inner Mongolia Sub-bureau and commander and political commissar of the Inner Mongolia Self-Defense Army (later reorganized as the CCP's Inner Mongolia Military District). This made him the ranking CCP cadre in Inner Mongolia, as well as the top-ranking Mongol within the CCP.

In September 1949 Ulanfu was named to the Standing Committee of the Preparatory Committee of the Chinese People's Political Consultative Conference (CCPCC),* and on the convening of the CPPCC was named as a delegate from the IMAR to the Standing Committee of the Presidium, and to the First National Committee of the CPPCC which served nominally as the People's Republic of China's (PRC's)* national representative assembly at the time. At the same time, he also participated in the formation of the new central government as a member of the committee to draft the Common Program (the organic law that served as the PRC's constitution until the first constitution was formally promulgated in 1954). In October 1949 he became a member of the Central People's Government Council, the PRC's chief executive body until 1954. He also held the positions of vice-chairman of the Nationalities Affairs Commission of the CCP and was a member of the CCP's Political and Legal Affairs Committee. When the military districts structure of the CCP government was formed, and the Inner Mongolia People's Self-Defense Army became the Inner Mongolia Military District, he continued as its commander and political commissar. In 1952 Suiyuan was incorporated to form the Suiyuan-Inner Mongolia Military District, and Ulanfu held on to the top positions, as well as becoming the chairman of the Suiyuan People's government. He held all these posts (among others) until 1954, when the governmental structure of the PRC was reorganized, while adding the membership on the North China Administrative Council in 1951.

In restructuring the PRC government (and promulgating the PRC constitution, in whose drafting he took part), Ulanfu was elected as a delegate of the IMAR to the First National Congress, in August, and became a vice-premier of the State Council, chairman of the Nationalities Affairs Commission, and member of the National Defense Committee. In April 1955 he became chairman of the IMAR People's Committee and secretary of the IMAR Party Committee (first secretary after 1956). Ulanfu was subsequently reelected to his national positions in 1959 and in 1965.

Furthermore, Ulanfu became one of the top CCP leaders in 1956 when he was elected to full membership in the Central Committee after the CCP's Eighth National Congress, and as alternate member of the Politburo at the subsequent First Plenum of the Eighth Central Committee. When the regional bureaus of the CCP were reinstated in 1961 by the Ninth Congress, he became second secretary of the North China Bureau.

In 1967, in the Cultural Revolution[*] period, Ulanfu was attacked by Maoists and deposed by the CCP army that entered Inner Mongolia under the command of T'eng Hai-ch'ing. He was rehabilitated in 1973 and was elected to the Tenth Central Committee of the CCP in August of that year. In January 1975 he was elected a vice-chairman of the Standing Committee of the Fourth National People's Congress. In 1977 he was head of the CCP's United Front Department, and in August of that year he was elected a member of the CCP's Eleventh Central Committee and a member of the Politburo. In 1978 he became a vice-chairman of the Fifth Chinese People's Political Consultative Conference, and in 1982, at the Twelfth CCP Congress he was reelected to the CCP Central Committee and Politburo. In 1983 he was elected a vice-president of the PRC.

Throughout most of his political career, Ulanfu had been the key Communist cadre in Inner Mongolia, and arguably the top-ranking non-Han in the CCP governmental structure. He also claimed the longest tenure in dominant positions in any one autonomous region or province in PRC and CCP history. Ulanfu passed away on December 8, 1988.

REFERENCES: Wolfgang Bartke, *Who's Who in the People's Republic of China* (Armonk, N.Y., 1981): 353–354; *Chung-kung jen-ming-lu* (Biographies of Chinese Communists) (Taipei, 1978): 495–496; *Chung-kung jen-wu-chih* (Who's Who in Communist China), vol. 2 (Hong Kong, 1970): 657–659; Donald W. Klein and Ann B. Clark, *Biographic Dictionary of Chinese Communism*, vol. 2 (Cambridge, Mass., 1971): 880–885; Yang Chih-lin et al., eds., *Wang Jo-fei tsai yu chung* (Wang Jo-fei in Prison) (Peking, 1961).

JOHN KONG-CHEONG LEUNG

W

WANG CHING-WEI (May 4, 1883–November 10, 1944): Leader of the KMT; head of the collaborationist regime at Nanking during the Sino-Japanese War.

Born in 1883 into a poor scholarly family in Canton, Wang had received a classical education and passed the provincial examination with distinction before going to Japan for study on a government scholarship in 1904. While in Japan, Wang came into contact with the emerging anti-Manchu movement among overseas Chinese students, and in 1905 he became a leading member of the T'ungmeng hui* founded by Sun Yat-sen.* He subsequently participated in the polemic between the revolutionary journal *Min Pao* and the constitutionalist publications under Liang Ch'i-ch'ao.* In 1910 Wang led an abortive attempt to assassinate the Manchu regent prince at Peking. He was arrested and sentenced to life imprisonment. The incident made him a national hero.

Released after the outbreak of the 1911 Revolution,* Wang worked briefly for a compromise between the revolutionaries and Yüan Shih-k'ai.* When a settlement was reached and Yüan became the first president of the new Republic, Wang temporarily retired from politics and devoted his attention to cultural and educational affairs. In 1917 Wang returned to the entourage of Sun Yat-sen, who was then organizing a regime at Canton in opposition to the Peking government controlled by warlords. For the next seven years Wang was a major assistant to Sun, and when Sun reorganized his Kuomintang in 1924, Wang became a member of the powerful Central Executive Committee.

Sun's death in 1925 made Wang a leading contender for the succession to KMT leadership. He was elected head of the party and the government in July, and as such he continued Sun's policy of allying with the Soviet Union and cooperating with the Chinese Communists. In March 1926 he was ousted by Chiang Kai-shek*. after the *Chung-shan* Gunboat Incident. He left the country for France in April. When the Nanking–Wuhan split emerged in early 1927, halfway in the Northern Expedition,* Wang was welcomed back by his supporters in the KMT to head the Wuhan Regime* in opposition to the Nanking government* under Chiang Kai-shek.* The two regimes joined hands later that year after both had purged the Communists. However, in the following struggle for leadership of the reunified KMT, Wang again lost to Chiang.

From 1928 to 1931, while spending most of his time in exile overseas, Wang led a powerful opposition to Chiang's national government. He became known as the leader of the left KMT, an ideological-political movement claiming to represent the party's radical line of 1924–1927. With the assistance of his factional followers (the Reorganizationists*) and some anti-Chiang militarists, he directed a series of political and military attacks aimed at toppling the Nanking government. All of them ended in failure. In early 1932, following the Japanese invasion of Manchuria, Wang finally decided to cooperate with Chiang Kai-shek.

From 1932 to 1935 Wang served as head of the Administrative Yuan (i.e., prime minister) at Nanking, interrupted only by a leave from late 1932 to early 1933. In appearance he was sharing equal power with Chiang, but in effect his influence diminished rapidly as Chiang's control over the party and the government continued to increase. In late 1935 Wang was wounded in an assassination attempt and was forced to resign his position. He took another trip to France and did not return until early 1937.

Shortly after Wang's return, the Sino-Japanese War* began. During the first year of the war, Wang served as the number two man in the KMT and its wartime government, a position reaffirmed by his election as the party's deputy-leader (with Chiang as leader) in 1938. In part disappointed by his continued loss of power to Chiang, and in part pessimistic about China's ability to fight against Japan, Wang was soon involved in an effort initiated by a group of middle-ranking KMT officials and Japanese Army officers to end the war peacefully. In December 1938 Wang left Chungking, the wartime capital, and went to Hanoi. There he announced his intention to lead a "peace movement," and then he went to Shanghai to negotiate a separate peace with Japan. In March 1940, with the help of the Japanese, he established a new national government at the Japanese-occupied Nanking. For the next four years Wang tried to restore effective Chinese rule over the occupied territories, while limiting the military and economic domination of these territories by Japan. Neither of these efforts was successful, and Wang was regarded by most Chinese as a puppet and a traitor. He died in Japan in 1944 while seeking treatment for an illness caused by the wound he received in the 1935 assassination attempt.

REFERENCES: Howard L. Boorman, "Wang Ching-wei: A Political Profile," in Chün-tu Hsüeh, ed., *Revolutionary Leaders of Modern China* (Oxford, 1971); "Wang Ching-wei," in Huang Mei-chan, ed., *Wang-wei shih han-chien* (Ten Traitors in the Wang Ching-wei puppet regime) (Shanghai, 1986); Lei Ming, *Wang Ching-wei hsien-sheng chuan* (A biography of Mr. Wang Ching-wei) (Shanghai, 1943).

KE-WEN WANG

WANG CH'UNG-HUI (December 1, 1881–March 15, 1958): Jurist, diplomat, participant in the Republican Revolutionary Movement, holder of numerous official posts.

Wang Ch'ung-hui's reputation rests largely on his legal work and on the distinguished career that he built in jurisprudence, but his role in modern Chinese history was many-sided, and he made distinctive contributions to the Revolution of 1911* and to the Republic it created. An early follower of Sun Yat-sen,* he worked closely with him but only sporadically as an active revolutionary. After the revolution, he held many high positions in both government and the Kuomintang. He also served in many capacities dealing with international affairs, notably as the first judge from China to sit on the Permanent Court of International Justice at the Hague and as a member of the Chinese delegation to the UN Conference on International Organization in 1945.

Wang was born in Hong Kong, where the family had moved in 1849, two years after his grandfather became a Christian. His father was also active in religious work. The family lived near the medical school where Sun Yat-sen studied. Sun and Ch'en Shao-pai visited the Wang home frequently, and Wang recalled hearing much talk of how revolution could save the nation and Christianity could save humanity.

Until the age of fourteen, Wang studied in Hong Kong, gaining fluency in English while also being rigorously tutored in Chinese. In 1895 he went to Tientsin and entered the law program at Peiyang University, from which he graduated at the top of his class in 1900. His political consciousness began to be shaped in this period. Strongly influenced by China's defeat at Japan's hands in 1894–1895 and by the disasters of the next five years, Wang was also deeply impressed by the young revolutionary Shih Chien-ju, whom he met through Ch'en Shao-pai. Shih's martyrdom is said to have helped convince Wang to work for the revolution. He went to Shanghai to teach in the Nanyang College, a center of anti-Ch'ing ferment. While there, he sheltered a fleeing revolutionary, Ch'in Li-shan, and helped him escape to Japan. Wang soon followed him there and went to work on the monthly revolutionary journal *Kuo-min-pao*, of which Ch'in was an editor. In this work Wang met Feng Tzu-yu, Chang Chi, and other revolutionaries. He edited an English-language section of the journal, translating into Chinese the United States Declaration of Independence and some materials on the French Revolution and the thought of Montesquieu. Wang also participated in the founding of the Kwangtung Independence Association, a Chinese student group that formed in Japan when reports circulated that France might detach the province from China.

While in Japan, Wang studied Japanese and resumed his legal education. Late in 1902 he decided to go to the United States for further study, which he pursued mainly at Yale from 1903 to 1905. During this period Sun Yat-sen came to the United States and, while there, he consulted with Wang on a wide range of matters, notably Sun's plans for a "five-power constitution" (a government with five branches) and the importance of gaining foreigners' support for the Chinese Revolution. Together Sun and Wang worked out a declaration to the outside world called "The True Solution of the Chinese Question," which Wang drafted in English. Written while the Russo-Japanese War was being fought, the essay stressed that China was the scene of a dangerously explosive international struggle, and that "the root of all these difficulties . . . lies in the weakness and corruptness of the Manchu government." It is the Manchus who try to shut out foreigners, Wang and Sun wrote; the Chinese have always welcomed foreign traders and missionaries, and under Chinese rule "the whole country would be open to foreign trade." The manifesto closed with a plea for American help: "We hope we may find many Lafayettes among you."

In 1905 Wang moved to Europe to continue his studies, which Sun Yat-sen helped to finance on the grounds that a jurist with international training and contacts would be valuable in the Republic. Wang returned to China shortly before the outbreak of the revolution in October 1911. Learning of the Wuchang Uprising while in Tientsin, he proceeded to Shanghai and served as an adviser to Ch'en Ch'i-mei in the local revolutionary military government. He then joined a group of T'ung-meng hui* leaders in planning the organization of a provisional republican government and, as a representative from Kwangtung, participated in the convention at Nanking that elected Sun Yat-sen provisional president. When the Nanking Provisional government was formally established, Sun named Wang his minister of foreign affairs. After Sun yielded the presidency to Yüan Shih-k'ai,* Wang served in T'ang Shao-yi's* cabinet as minister of justice, resigning shortly after T'ang stepped down in June 1912.

For all practical purposes Wang's role as a revolutionary ended in 1912. His subsequent career saw frequent involvement in domestic politics, but his major work was concentrated on legal and constitutional matters.

REFERENCES: *Wang Ch'ung-hui hsien-sheng wen-chi* (A collection of essays by Mr. Wang Ch'ung-hui) (Taipei, 1981); Yü Wei-hsiung, *Wang Ch'ung-hui yü Chung-kuo* (Wang Ch'ung-hui and China) (Taipei, 1987).

MICHAEL GASSTER

WANG HUNG-WEN (b. 1935 [?]): Worker leader during the Cultural Revolution; member of the Gang of Four.

Very little is known of Wang Hung-wen's life before his rise to prominence during the Cultural Revolution.* One source records that he was born into a poor peasant family in 1935 in Su-pei County in northern Kiangsu; another source places his birth as 1932 in Mukden (then in Liaoning Province). It is also recorded that he joined the "Little Red Soldiers" organization as a young man. In any case, he was in his late teens or very early twenties when he joined a unit of the Chinese People's Volunteers in 1953 during the war to resist U.S. aggression and aid Korea. It was at this time that Wang became a member of the Communist party. At the end of the war, Wang was given a job as a worker at the No. 17 National Cotton Mill Factory in Shanghai, a major factory under the jurisdiction of the State Council's Ministry of Textile Industries. Wang soon became a member of the personnel security department in the factory and a workshop party committee secretary.

Wang was still a relatively low-ranking worker on the eve of the Cultural Revolution. In June 1966, in response to Mao Tse-tung's* May 16 Bulletin that identified the targets of the Cultural Revolution, Wang was instrumental in stirring up the "revolutionary" fever in the No. 17 Cotton Mill and wrote the first big-character poster denouncing the party secretary at the factory. Mao later acclaimed this to be the first significant big-character poster of the Cultural Revolution. Wang then expanded the attack, including among his targets the municipal-level party cadres in Shanghai such as First Municipal Party Secretary Ch'en P'i-hsien, and Mayor of Shanghai Ts'ao Ti-ch'iu. At first, such rebellious activities were suppressed by the work groups sent by the CCP Central Committee, which was still momentarily controlled by Liu Shao-ch'i* and Teng Hsiao-p'ing.* After the Eleventh Plenum of the Eighth Central Committee in August 1966, however, the Maoist faction began to take control in Peking, and Cultural Revolution groups elsewhere began to emerge and redouble their attack on local party cadres that were still identified with the Liu-Teng faction. Sometime during this period, Wang and others in his group went to Peking where they received strong support from the Central Cultural Revolution Group headed by Chiang Ch'ing,* Mao's wife, and from Mao himself.

Back in Shanghai in September 1966, Wang organized the Shanghai Workers Revolutionary Rebellion General Headquarters (SWRRGH). On November 8, several thousand delegates of the SWRRGH besieged the CCP headquarters in Shanghai, making five demands on Ch'en P'i-hsien and other party cadres for self-criticism. On November 11, delegates of the SWRRGH, rebuffed by the Shanghai CCP organization, mustered a massive petition group to go to Peking. This group was detained at the An-t'ing Railroad Station some twenty miles outside of Shanghai. With this incident resulting in some bloodshed, the CCP Central Committee sent Chang Ch'un-ch'iao* to Shanghai to mediate. Wang organized a mass gathering of the "revolutionary rebellious faction" in Shanghai to greet Chang, and in response, Chang recognized the SWRRGH as a legitimate "revolutionary organization" in the name of the Central Cultural Revolution Group. From that moment on, the SWRRGH became the backbone of the Cultural Revolution in south and central-south China.

Wang then returned to Peking as a member of the petition group, and there he gained the support of the Central Cultural Revolution Group, including people such as Ch'en Po-ta,* and Lin Piao.* In January 1967 the power struggle over Shanghai was intensified, with the rebellious factions taking over control of the newspaper Wen-hui pao. Meanwhile, there was also an internal struggle within the SWRRGH from which Wang emerged triumphant. With a second open letter to the citizens of Shanghai, Wang demanded a confession from Ch'en P'i-hsien and Ts'ao Ti-ch'iu, and urged the workers to return to normal work schedules. In early February, under Chang Ch'un-ch'iao and Wang's leadership, a new power organization, the Provisional Committee of the Shanghai People's Commune, was formed. Following another general, and violent, political struggle in the city that month, the Maoist faction, under Chang Ch'un-ch'iao, reorganized the Provisional Committee into the Shanghai Revolutionary Committee, with Wang as the vice-chairman. Wang also became the chairman of the No. 17 Cotton Mill Revolutionary Committee. In the remainder of 1967 and in 1968,

Wang published, variously in the *Jen-min jih-pao* (*People's Daily*), the *Ta-kung pao* (in Hong Kong) and through the Hsin-hua News Agency, several essays extolling Maoism and calling on the people to study Mao's writings. In April 1969, Wang was elected as a delegate to attend the Ninth CCP Congress in Peking, where he was elected chairman of the presidium of the congress and subsequently a member of the Ninth CCP Central Committee.

In January 1971 Wang Hung-wen became secretary of the reconstructed Shanghai Municipal party secretariat, under Chang Ch'un-ch'iao (first secretary) and Yao Wen-yüan[*] (second secretary). Since Chang and Yao remained in Peking, Wang was actually the active leader in the Shanghai CCP organization. He remained in this position until September 1972 when he returned to Peking and took up more important leadership roles in the Central Committee. In August 1973, at the Tenth CCP Congress, Wang became vice-chairman of the presidium of the congress, and read the political report proposing the outline of the new party constitution. He was elected to membership in the Tenth Central Committee and in the Politburo. On August 30, at the First Session of the Tenth Central Committee, he was elected its second vice-chairman.

Wang's position in the post–Cultural Revolution CCP remained high as a vice-chairman of the Central Committee's Military Affairs Council, although he was clearly considered a junior member of the top-ranking power structure. At the Fourth National People's Congress in January 1975, he was elected vice-chairman of the presidium, but he no longer held significant positions in the State Council. Despite his meteoric rise as a Maoist during the Cultural Revolution and his performance as an effective worker organizer during that time, Wang had little long-term experience in the basic CCP organization, and few personal connections among veteran and backbone CCP cadres. His functional capacity in the post–Cultural Revolution stabilization period was therefore quite slim. Many of his activities after 1975 were ceremonial, culminating with ritual duties during funeral services for Chou En-lai[*] in January 1976 and the same after the death of Mao Tse-tung in September of that year. With the demise of his chief protectors and supporters, Wang's position became perilous in late 1976. On October 6, Wang, along with his former Cultural Revolution cohorts Chang Ch'un-ch'iao, Chiang Ch'ing, and Yao Wen-yüan, were labeled the Gang of Four[*] by Hua Kuo-feng,[*] Mao's successor as chairman of the Central Committee, charged with antiparty conspiracy, arrested, and removed from all his positions in the CCP. Wang and the others in the Gang of Four were subsequently placed on public trial in the fall of 1980, and he was purged from the party.

REFERENCES: *Chung-kung jen-ming-lu* (Biographies of Chinese Communists) (Taipei, 1978), appendix 3–7; Wolfgang Bartke, *Who's Who in the People's Republic of China*, (Armonk, N.Y., 1981): 586–587.

JOHN KONG-CHEONG LEUNG

WANG MING (CH'EN SHAO-YÜ) (1901–1974): Leader of the Twenty-eight Bolsheviks; member of the CCP Central Committee; Chinese representative for the Executive Committee of the Communist International.

As the leader of the Twenty-eight Bolsheviks,[*] also known as the Russian returned students, Wang Ming was one of the most important Chinese representatives of the Soviet-controlled Communist International. Born Ch'en Shao-yü in Chin-sai, Anhwei Province, Wang Ming was a politically active youth during the 1920s, editing a student newspaper in Wuchang and later becoming an important leader in the Wuchang and Hupei Associated Student Organizations after the eruption of the May Thirtieth Incident[*] in 1925.

Wang Ming joined the Chinese Communist party[*] in 1925 and represented the Hupei party branch in attendance at Sun Yat-sen University in Moscow. Wang quickly mastered Russian and became a protégé of the increasingly powerful Pavel Mif, which supported Stalin during the power struggle with Trotsky. Mif gave Wang Ming important tasks as his personal translator, including the right to attend the sixth meeting of the Communist International. Among the students at Sun Yat-sen University in Moscow, Wang Ming was able to gain ascendancy for his growing clique, and with the backing of Pavel Mif he was able to rise rapidly in the CCP hierarchy when he returned to China in 1930. With the failure of urban insurrection in 1930 and the fall of Li Li-san,[*] Wang Ming and the Twenty-eight Bolsheviks[*] were able to take control of the CCP Central Committee. Wang Ming was elected to both the Central Committee and the Politburo at the Fourth Plenum of the CCP in January 1931.

The resentment which other powerful leaders within the CCP felt because of the nature of "outside" support for a group of CCP members, not tested in the fire of revolutionary action, was exacerbated in Wang Ming's case because he was physically distanced from the Chinese Revolution in contrast to others of the returned Russian students such as Po Ku,[*] Lo Fu,[*] or Shen Tse-min. Wang returned to Moscow in late 1931 for several years. While in the Soviet Union, he became an important authority on Chinese affairs and served as a representative on the Executive Committee of the Communist International (ECCI).

Wang Ming was a prolific writer. Between 1928 and 1930 he wrote over thirty essays analyzing and often criticizing the CCP revolutionary directions, especially the Li Li-san[*] line of urban-centered revolt. Yet, Wang Ming's emphasis on the need to develop the Chinese proletariat as a revolutionary force was not far afield from the strategy of Li Li-san, whom he energetically criticized. This kind of inconsistency, as well as his continued stay in Moscow, during a period when the Central Committee had to escape to the countryside, led other leaders to label Wang Ming an opportunist.

Before the Sian Incident,[*] Wang Ming was an important promoter of the United Front with the Kuomintang. His growing association with the interests of the Soviet Union and the Communist International, together, with his detachment from the realities of revolutionary hardship, made him more willing to accept an accord with Chiang Kai-shek.[*] In 1937 Wang Ming returned to China where he administered the Wuhan Defense Committee. According to Communist sources, Wang was criticized for being too conciliatory toward the KMT. As Lyman Van Slyke has mentioned, in an era of United Front promotion, this charge is sometimes difficult to assess. However, there appear to have been some differences between Wang Ming and the growing CCP strategy of guerrilla warfare. In 1938 Wang had written that *only* regular land troops could overcome the Japanese Army. This belief was more in line with the KMT wartime approach. Moreover, Wang wanted to merge CCP and KMT troops, a view that other CCP leaders did not widely support.

Wang Ming's power within the CCP declined after 1945, and plummeted further after the establishment of the People's Republic of China* in 1949. He was consistently appointed to the Central Committee, but in the mid–1950s he left for the Soviet Union, where he remained until his death in 1974.

Wang Ming's position in CCP history is unique because his impact on the internal politics of the CCP was greater than his distance from CCP action warranted. His support stemmed in large part from the Communist International and at times from cohort identification, but for the most part it depended little on actual revolutionary activity inside China. His areas of influence included the stress on urban centers of revolution, the necessity to be cooperative in the United Front with the KMT, and the generation of political factionalization within the CCP. The other area of Wang Ming's influence was his impact as a representative of the ECCI and the question of his portrayal of Chinese political realities to the Communist International. Wang Ming's influence on the Soviets' perception of the Chinese Revolution may have been more significant than his direct impact on revolutionary activity within China.

REFERENCES: Chou Wen-ch'i, ''Wang Ming te tsuo-hsiang tsuo-wu ho kung-chan kuo-chi'' (The leftist mistakes of Wang Ming and the Communist International), *Chin-tai shih yen-chiu* 2 (1987): 249–262; Helen Foster Snow, *The Chinese Communists: Sketches and Autobiographies of the Old Guards* (Westport, Conn., 1972) [Originally published in 1952]; Lyman P. Van Slyke, *Enemies and Friends: The United Front in Chinese Communist History* (Stanford, Calif., 1967).

MARILYN LEVINE

WARD, FREDERICK TOWNSEND (1831–1862): Mercenary; founder of the Ever-Victorious Army.

Ward was an American mercenary and founder of the Ever-Victorious Army, a hybrid Sino-foreign military contingent that aided the Ch'ing* cause against the Taipings.* Working with Chinese merchants desirous of protecting Shanghai, Ward in 1860 initially organized his new military contingent using foreign sailors and Filipinos. Eventually, however, the hybrid mercenary contingent recruited Chinese troops, thus introducing Western military skills to Chinese soldiers. In addition, Ward's army, along with the other Sino-foreign contingents that were themselves modeled after the Ever-Victorious Army, had access to Western military ordance, and thus served to demonstrate to China's future leadership, men like Li Hung-chang* and Tso Tsung-t'ang,* the superiority of Western military skills. Certainly, this exposure spurred Chinese leadership to begin its efforts to transfer Western technology to China most notably during the Self-Strengthening Movement* which dominated the late 1860s through the 1880s.

REFERENCES: Richard C. Smith, *Mercenaries and Mandarins* (Millwood, N.Y., 1978); Jonathan Spence, *To Change China, Western Advisers in China 1620–1960* (New York, 1964); Hallett Abend, *The God from the West* (Garden City, N.Y., 1947); Holger Cahill, *A Yankee Adventurer: The Story of Ward and the Taiping Rebellion* (New York, 1930)
STEVEN A. LEIBO

WARLORDISM: The dominance of regional military authorities over the central government, particularly from 1916 to 1928.

After the death of Yüan Shih-k'ai[*] in 1916, a protracted struggle for control of the central government began among the regional military commanders, or *tu-chün*. As these wars became more costly and chaotic, both Chinese and foreigners began to think of them not simply as military succession struggles, but rather as a new social pathology, "warlordism," and of their protagonists not just as generals, but rather as "warlords," or *chün-fa*.

During this period of governmental weakness in Peking, power at the local level increasingly fell into the hands of military groupings of varying size. The only major contenders for national power, however, were the Chihli and Fengt'ien cliques,[*] which fought major wars in 1922 and 1924. But because their campaigns weakened both of them while yielding no winner, their most important consequence was to prepare the way for Chiang Kai-shek's[*] Northern Expedition,[*] whose successful completion in 1928 is generally considered to have ended the era of warlordism.

Although often thought of as uniquely Chinese, the idea of the warlord is in fact of foreign origin. The Chinese word *chün-fa* was borrowed in about 1919, perhaps by Ch'en Tu-hsiu,[*] from the Japanese *gunbatsu* (military clique), a term that had become common in discussions of Japan's internal politics during the Taishō period (1912–1926). The coinage (which parallels in structure such terms as *hanbatsu* and *zaibatsu*—respectively, regional and financial cliques) reflects the influence in Japan of European (and particularly German and Marxist) theories of militarism, a term translated into Japanese as *gunkokushugi* (first appearing in about 1911) and then borrowed into Chinese (*chün-kuo-chu-yi*) a few years later. With this vocabulary came an analytical approach that saw warlordism more as a social than as a military phenomenon, and therefore (following Lieb-knecht, Luxembourg, Hilferding, and Bukharin) sought its roots in class structures and the economy rather than the military per se.

Although much scholarship, both Chinese and Western, has adopted this approach, it has been difficult to sustain. Often thought of as regionalists, the major generals (if not the local strongmen) of the 1916–1928 period in fact had their eyes firmly set on the goal of national conquest, and, like Chang Tso-lin in Manchuria, they repeatedly proved willing to sacrifice a secure regional kingdom for the possibility of dominance over all China. Thus, they lacked any specific constituencies beyond their armies and their allies. Links with foreign powers, often asserted, have proved equally difficult to confirm. So the once dominant social and economic approach that gave us the term *warlord* has recently been fading in popularity.

The word has continued to be used as a term of abuse, however. The Communists regularly call the Nationalists the new warlords, and since the massacre of June 4, 1989, some democratic activists have labeled the Peking authorities fascist warlords.

REFERENCES: Volker R. Berghahn, *Militarism: The History of an International Debate, 1861–1979* (New York, 1982); Jerome Ch'en, *The Military-Gentry Coalition: China Under the Warlords* (Toronto, 1979); Hsi-sheng Ch'i, *Warlord Politics in China 1916–1928* (Stanford, Calif., 1976); Arthur Waldron, "Warlordism Versus Federalism: The Revival of a Debate?" *The China Quarterly*, No. 121 (March 1990): 116–128.

ARTHUR WALDRON

WEDEMEYER, ALBERT COADY (July 9, 1897–December 17, 1989), U.S. Army general; chief-of-staff to Chiang Kai-shek; commander of the U.S. forces in the China Theater of World War II.

Albert Wedemeyer was born in Omaha, Nebraska, and graduated from West Point in 1918. Following a successful career, including the receipt of the Distinguished Service Medal, Wedemeyer replaced General Joseph Stilwell,* commander of U.S. forces in the China–Burma–India Theater and chief-of-staff to Chiang Kai-shek.* Wedemeyer, as Stilwell's replacement, commanded all U.S. forces in the newly designated China Theater. While Stilwell considered Wedemeyer to be the "world's most pompous prick," Patrick Jay Hurley* convinced President Franklin D. Roosevelt that Wedemeyer could work effectively with Chiang Kai-shek.

Wedemeyer arrived in the Nationalist wartime capital of Chungking on October 31, 1944. His responsibilities, according to his orders, were to advise and assist the Chinese in the conduct of military operations and to direct U.S. forces to carry out air operations from China. Following the Dixie Mission's* report about the Communists in Yenan, and the inefficacy demonstrated by the Nationalist troops, Wedemeyer in early December 1944 ordered his chief-of-staff, General Robert McClure, to devise a plan to strengthen the Chinese Communist party's* role in the war against Japan. McClure did so, sending it to Yenan with Colonel David D. Barrett. Barrett made a second trip to Yenan with a revised plan, suggesting a much larger American presence in north China. When Ambassador Patrick Hurley discovered these plans, he called for a full investigation, protesting that his efforts were being subverted. As a result, Wedemeyer ended direct contact with the CCP.

Following a return to the United States where he promoted the Kuomintang, Wedemeyer outlined the parameters of what became American policy in China during the transfer of rule from the Japanese to the Kuomintang. In August 1945 Wedemeyer told American reporters that the United States recognized Chiang Kai-shek as the supreme allied commander in the China theater, that the United States would invite the Nationalist government to take control of territory recovered by American forces, and that America would help transport Nationalist troops to areas held by the Japanese.

Wedemeyer's projections became reality with the orders issued by the Joint

Chiefs of Staff on August 10 and reinforced by President Harry S Truman's General Order Number One issued five days later. The Joint Chiefs' order committed U.S. assistance to KMT forces in their quest to acquire liberated territory and gave Wedemeyer permission to transport Chiang's troops to northern China. The American forces were to avoid any involvement in "fratricidal warfare." Truman's order named the Nationalists as the only group authorized to accept Japanese surrender.

Following these mandates, the United States intervened in China's civil war,* moving Nationalist troops to north China. Even with this assistance, however, Wedemeyer remained pessimistic about the Nationalists' chances because of their corrupt and ineffective government. By the end of 1945, he concluded that the United States had three options in China. It could withdraw completely, it could become massively involved militarily, or it could devise a trusteeship over Manchuria and Korea and allow the United Nations to repatriate the Japanese.

General George Marshall arrived in China in mid-December 1945. His task was to try to find a way to get KMT–CCP cooperation. At first, he appeared stunningly successful. But soon after Marshall's departure, fighting between the CCP and the KMT resumed, bringing Marshall back for a second time. He continued to work for an American-defined solution until failure and frustration resulted in his recall in January 1947.

While Marshall negotiated, Wedemeyer returned to the Untied States in the summer of 1946. The following summer Truman sent him back to China, asking him to look into "the political, economic, psychological, and military situations" in the country. On August 27, 1947, Wedemeyer strongly criticized the Nationalist government for corruption and inefficiency.

When he returned to the United States, Wedemeyer filed his report. In the report he recommended that the United States provide military aid for China, while encouraging internal reform. He also recommended that the military assistance be under the supervision of 10,000 American officers and men. The report suggested a five-power guardianship of Manchuria and, if this failed, a United Nations trusteeship.

Wedemeyer did not return to China, and he remained an advocate for the KMT. He continued to adhere to the belief that communism was globally aggressive; this belief and his activities were recognized by the Council Against Communist Aggression in April 1973. The Council cited Wedemeyer and others for their steadfast fight "for the freedom of the Chinese people for over a quarter of a century."

REFERENCES: Michael Schaller, *The U.S. Crusade in China, 1938–1945* (New York, 1979); Immanuel C.Y. Hsü, *The Rise of Modern China*, 3rd ed. (New York, 1983); Paul A. Varg, *The Closing of the Door: Sino-American Relations, 1936–1946* (East Lansing, Mich., 1973); James Readon-Anderson, *Yenan and the Great Powers: The Origins of Chinese Communist Foreign Policy, 1944–1946* (New York, 1980).

EDWIN CLAUSEN

WEI CH'ANG-HUI (1823–September 1856): Leader of the Taiping Revolution. Wei Ch'ang-hui was formerly known as Wei Cheng or Wei Chih-cheng. He was born into one of the wealthiest clans in Chin-t'ien Village, Kuei-p'ing County, Kwangsi.

Recent studies have shown that Wei Ch'ang-hui had wealth but not honor. Although the Wei clan owned a large amount of land and operated a pawnshop, Wei suffered from his Chuang minority origins. Having been a *yamen* lictor (a Chinese government officer), Wei was disbarred from the civil service examinations. This frustration led Wei to purchase the academic degree of *chien-sheng* (Student of the Imperial Academy) for his father in order to raise the prestige of his clan. During a celebration of this event on the night of his father's birthday, Wei was threatened by the regular gentry. Wei appealed to Feng Yün-shan,* founder of the God Worshippers Society,* and Feng later helped Wei to pillage the offending gentry.

Wei joined the society in the winter of 1848. Because he belonged to a large clan, he became one of the prominent leaders of the organization. During the preparation for the uprising, Wei donated tens of thousands of silver *taels* to the organization. The wealthy Wei clan had contributed an immense quantity of grain, enough to sustain the rebellion over several months. The Wei family also opened a shop in the nearby commercial center of Chiang-k'ou and bought iron for making weapons.

On January 1, 1851, Wei joined the Taiping Revolutionary Movement,* and the Heavenly King, Hung Hsiu-ch'üan,* appointed him "commander" (*chu-chiang*) of the Left Army Corps. With his best Holy Soldiers, Wei succeeded in eluding the local militia. In September 1851 the Taipings occupied their first walled city, Yung-an chou. Hung declared the founding of the T'ai-ping t'ien-kuo and bestowed on Wei the Co-Deputy Marshal (Yu fu Chün-shih) and the North King (Pei Wang) on December 17, 1851.

After the founding of the Heavenly capital at Nanking, Wei was the operational commander of the central area, which included Nanking and Chenkiang in the south, and the region north of the Yangtze River. He appointed Ch'in Jih-kang and Lo Ta-kang as his field commanders. Between 1855 and 1856, Wei took charge of political and military affairs in Kiangsi. His small troops, many times outnumbered, made three courageous triumphant attacks to break through Hsiang Yung's imperial forces, called the Great Camp of Kiang-nan (Kiang-nan Ta-ying).

Sir Samuel George Bonham, governor of Hong Kong and the highest British representative in China from 1848 to 1854, was the first foreign visitor to the Taiping territory. In conversations on May 11, 1853, with Wei and the Assistant King, Shih Ta-k'ai,* they discussed such issues as religious beliefs and Taiping's foreign policies. In order to make an alliance and have a friendship with the British government, Wei and Shih emphasized that both the Taipings and the British worshiped the same God. Bonham notified the two kings that the British government intended to remain perfectly neutral in the Chinese civil war. Wei was not a good diplomat, and the visitors concluded that Wei "was quite ignorant of the relative positions of foreign countries."

The power struggle of the Taiping leadership in 1856 was very complex and was a great disaster to the Taiping Revolutionary Movement. Growing conflict between the Heavenly King and the East King, Yang Hsiu-ch'ing,* resulted not only in Yang's assassination but also in the beheading of Wei. At midnight on September 1, 1856, Wei and Ch'in Jih-kang murdered Yang Hsiu-ch'ing, and wiped out all Yang's relatives and all his staff in Nanking. Over 20,000 of Yang's followers, civil and military, young and old, men and women, were executed in this horrible massacre. When the Assistant King, Shih Ta-k'ai, heard about this tragic news, he attempted to stop the killing, but Wei later killed all the members of Shih's family. Later, Wei was purged by the Heavenly King, who ordered the execution of Wei together with his whole family and followers.

The background on the assassination of Yang Hsiu-ch'ing is still unclear. The key question is: what was the intention of the assassination? Did Wei kill Yang on his own ambition, or did he do so on Hung Hsiu-ch'üan's instructions? Regardless of who planned it, the assassination has been blamed on Wei Ch'ang-hui alone. After the Nanking Massacre, his title of the North King was rescinded, and he was never again mentioned in Taiping texts.

REFERENCES: C. A. Curwen, *Taiping Rebel: The Deposition of Li Hsiu-ch'eng* (Cambridge, 1977); Lo Erh-kang, "Wei Ch'ang-hui ts'an chia Chin-t'ien ch'i-i ti chi-chien-shih" (A few remarks on Wei Ch'ang-hui's participation on the Chin-t'ien rebellion) in *T'ai-ping t'ien-kuo shih ts'ung k'ao chia chi* (Peking, 1981): 68–73; Su Shuang-pi, "Ping Wei Ch'ang-hui" (An Evaluation of Wei Ch'ang-hui) in Yüan Shu-i and Liu Yen-chiao, eds., *T'ai-ping t'ien-kuo jen-wu yen-chiu* (Collected studies on Taiping Leaders) (Chengtu, 1987): 315–338.

CHI-KONG LAI

WEN I-TO (November 24, 1899–July 15, 1946): Poet, scholar.

Wen I-to was the eldest son of a renowned scholar family of Hsi-shui County in Hupei Province. At an early age he was trained in the classics by a disciplinarian father, and at ten he was sent to Wuchang (a day's trip from Hsi-shui) to study at a modern grade school. Soon after the 1911 Revolution* cut short Wen's studies in Wuchang, he wrote and passed a special government examination to select candidates for overseas study. He would spend the next nine years at the Tsing Hua School (later Tsing Hua University)* in Peking in preparatory study.

Typical of young well-to-do intellectuals of the time, Wen remained politically conservative until the May Fourth* demonstrations (in which he was actively involved but did not march) liberalized his thought. He was, however, a reluctant convert to the use of the vernacular in literature, not adopting its use in poetry until 1920. During his years at the Tsing Hua School, Wen was exposed to an array of Chinese and Western subjects, but poetry and art emerged as his keenest interests. Wen was also a regular contributor to and editor of various school journals.

In 1922 Wen began study at the Art Institute of Chicago. But his work in art was secondary to his primary interest—poetry. His passion for the Western romantics (particularly Keats) developed into a mature aesthetic theory of the unity of beauty and truth which found expressions in his own vernacular poetry, collected in his acclaimed *Hung chu* (Red candle, 1923).

A year of loneliness and homesickness in this uncultured city was enough for Wen I-to, and when his good friend from Tsing Hua, Liang Shih-ch'iu, asked him to accompany him to Colorado College he eagerly accepted. The natural beauty of Colorado Springs revived his interest in art but failed to provide an outlet for his growing nationalism. In 1924 Wen traveled to New York where he joined the Arts Student League. Ever the eclectic, drama (particularly the re-staging of traditional Chinese plays) became Wen's newest focus of creative attention. His growing cultural nationalism expressed itself in the formation of the Chung-hua hsi-chü kai-chin she (Chinese Drama Reform Society) and the Ta-chiang she (Great River Society), founded with Lo Lung-chi and Liang Shih-ch'iu as a patriotic and anti-Communist organization.

In June 1925 Wen I-to returned to China, without a degree, to teach at the Peking School of Fine Arts. At this time he was the active spokesman for the Great River Society and co-founder (with Hsü Chih-mo) of the short-lived, but influential, *Shih-k'an* (*Poetry Journal*), the unofficial organ of the Hsin-yueh she (Crescent Society), a group of poets who promoted an aesthetic approach of literature in reaction to the sentimentalism and didacticism they saw a dom-inating contemporary literature. During this period Wen developed the first po-etics of vernacular verse, decrying the lack of attention to form in most *pai-hua* poetry. He also wrote many of the poems that in 1928 would be collected into what some consider the finest body of vernacular poems ever written in China—*Ssu shui* (Dead Water). It wasn't until March 1928 that the Crescent Society established its first official literary journal, for which Wen was an editor and frequent contributor until his break with the group in 1929.

Wen left the Peking School of Fine Arts in 1926 and throughout 1927 taught English literature at a variety of universities. In 1928 he transferred to Wuhan University where he became head of the Chinese Department, thus marking a conscious move from Western literature toward the teaching and research of Chinese classical literature. Wen taught at Tsingtao University from 1930 to 1932, at which point he transferred to Tsing Hua University where he remained as a teacher of Chinese until his death. He devoted the last fourteen years of his life to classical scholarship, creatively combining Ch'ing philological techniques with Western socio-anthropological perspectives. Wen's biographical study of Tu Fu and his philological analysis of the *Shih-ching*, the *Ch'u-tz'u*, and *Erh-ya* are highly respected works of literary scholarship.

With the outbreak of the Sino-Japanese War,* the Tsing Hua campus was moved south, first to Ch'angsha and then to Kunming where it became incor-porated into the National Southwest Associated University (Lien-ta). For Wen the "march" from Changsha to Kunming was both a pastoral journey into the Chinese hinterland and an eye-opening revelation of China's poverty and back-wardness.

The journey to K'unming invigorated Wen who became active in the university community and highly productive in his scholarship. Much of the war period was spent in dire poverty, wartime inflation had made Wen's meager salary barely adequate to support his wife and five children. The deteriorating war effort sparked his dormant political sentiments, and by 1943 Wen had abandoned his hermetic scholarly life for one involving contemporary affairs. He reversed his negative opinion about Lu Hsün[*] (whom he felt had sacrificed literature for politics) and praised the propaganda poems of T'ien Chien. In 1944 he joined the China Democratic League and became increasingly critical of the KMT's feeble resistance to the Japanese. Wen's open and vociferous opposition to the civil war[*] was criticism the KMT could not bear; he was assassinated by KMT henchmen in 1946.

REFERENCES: Kai-yu Hsu, *Wen I-to* (Boston, 1980); Mian Zhi, *Wen I-to* (Hong Kong, 1949).

KIRK A. DENTON

WESTERN HILLS FACTION (Hsi-shan p'ai): Right-wing faction within the KMT, 1925–1931.

The Western Hills Faction, which originated in a meeting of conservative Kuomintang leaders at the Western Hills near Peking, was the first organized dissent within the KMT in opposition to the party's alliance with the Chinese Communists.

Following the death of Sun Yat-sen[*] in March 1925, conflicts within the KMT–CCP United Front intensified and were complicated by the succession struggle in the KMT leadership. In July Wang Ching-wei[*] and Liao Chung-k'ai, in a bloodless coup, deposed Hu Han-min[*] and seized control of the KMT and its government at Canton. The next month Liao was assassinated, allegedly by the order of a group of KMT politicians close to Hu. Thus implicated, Hu was sent into exile by the party in September.

Since both Wang and Liao were supportive of the United Front and since Michael Borodin,[*] the Soviet adviser, was extremely powerful in Canton, the turn of events convinced a group of party veterans, many of whom sympathized with Hu, that the current KMT leadership had fallen prey to Soviet and CCP manipulation. In November, the group gathered at the Western Hills near Peking, where the body of Sun Yat-sen was temporarily placed, and held what they described as the Fourth Plenum of the First Central Committees of the KMT. The meeting, presided over by Lin Shen and Tsou Lu,[*] denounced the KMT headquarters at Canton as illegitimate and decided to terminate the United Front. Wang was reprimanded and Borodin dismissed. These party veterans subsequently organized their own KMT headquarters at Shanghai.

This move caused fierce retaliation from Canton. Most of the participants of the Western Hills meeting were punished by the Second Party Congress convened at Canton in January 1926. Meanwhile, a few others, such as Tai

Chi-t'ao and Wu Chih-hui,* began to disassociate themselves from the opposition. Yet the Shanghai headquarters, now known as the Western Hills Faction, continued to exist and held its own Second Party Congress there in March.

During the following months, when Canton's Northern Expedition* swept over half of China and was then halted by the Nanking–Wuhan split, the faction was somewhat demoralized and inactive. It found an opportunity for a political comeback in September 1927 when both Wuhan and Nanking terminated the United Front. The faction, now praised for its foresight, participated enthusiastically in the ensuing negotiation to reunify the party. It dominated the Special Committee at Nanking which was created by the negotiation to assume temporary party leadership. Although supported by the Kwangsi militarists, the committee lasted only three months since both Wang Ching-wei and Chiang Kai-shek,* the two most influential KMT leaders at the time, opposed it. When Chiang returned to power in early 1928, the faction was again ostracized.

From 1928 to 1931 the faction, still based at Shanghai, bitterly attacked the KMT leadership under Chiang. Its position remained unchanged even after Hu Han-min agreed to cooperate with Chiang's Nanking government in late 1928. In early 1930, Chiang arrested Chü Cheng, one of the faction's top leaders. This action further angered the faction. Later that year, it joined hands with the Reorganizationists* under Wang Ching-wei in forming a rival KMT headquarters and government at Peip'ing (Peking). In 1931 it again featured prominently in an opposition at Canton, this time cooperating with both Wang and Hu. After these anti-Nanking efforts ended in failure, the Western Hills ceased to function as a faction and its name gradually disappeared from the Chinese scene.

REFERENCES: Li Yün-han, *Ts'ung jung-kung tao ch'ing-tang* (From admitting the communists to the party purge) (Taipei, 1966); Shen Yün-lung, *Min-kuo shih-shih yü jen-wu lun-ts'ung* (Essays on the events and personalities of the republican period) (Taipei, 1981); Tsou Lu, *Hui-ku lu* (Memoirs) (Nanking, 1946).

KE-WEN WANG

WHAMPOA MILITARY ACADEMY: Premier KMT military college.

Founded near Canton in 1924 with Chiang Kai-shek* as its first commandant, the Whampoa Military Academy trained the early Nationalist officer elite. Its graduates, particularly those from the first four classes, were fiercely loyal to Chiang Kai-shek and later constituted an informal but influential group known as the Whampoa Clique.

The name is derived from Huang-p'u, on the island of Ch'ang-chou, about ten miles south of Canton, and the site of earlier provincial military and naval academies. Chiang Kai-shek was appointed principal on May 2, 1924. The first class numbered 350 and followed a six-month course combining both military training and political indoctrination. Soviet funds and advice were important in the academy's early years, and the early faculty in-cluded several Soviet members.

In 1927, following the establishment of the new National government, the academy was moved to Nanking and renamed the Central Military Acad-emy.

REFERENCES: Lloyd E. Eastman, "Whampoa Military Academy," in Ainslie T. Em-bree, ed., *Encyclopedia of Asian History*, vol. 4 (New York, 1988): 217; C. Martin Wilbur and Julie Lien-ying How, *Missionaries of Revolution: Soviet Advisers and Na-tionalist China 1920–1927* (Cambridge, Mass., 1989).

ARTHUR WALDRON

WU CHIH-HUI (March 25, 1865–October 30, 1953): Longtime KMT loyalist, cultural critic-iconoclast, and spokesman for philosophical materialism.

A quirky essayist, an activist, and a scholar, seen by some as a superficial dilettante, a dabbler in ideas whose main contributions were as a wit and gadfly rather than a serious thinker, and by others as the quintessential Chinese intel-lectual of his time, Wu Chih-hui played a major role in countless aspects of Chinese life. Although not one of Sun Yat-sen's[*] earliest supporters, once he enlisted in Sun's cause he devoted himself faithfully to it, and after Sun's death he remained active in Kuomintang affairs. On balance, Wu's contributions to China's revolution lie less in the relatively visible areas of politics and socio-economic transformation, and more in the rather intangible realms of values and culture. A vigorous critic of Chinese tradition, he is perhaps most famous for his belief in the "omnipotence of science" and his attack on religion, meta-physics, and the "national essence."

Wu Chih-hui was classically trained and earned *sheng-yüan* and *chü-jen* titles. He failed three times to win the *chin-shih*, the last failure coming in 1895. In the next few years he began to recognize the need for reform along the lines advocated by Chang Chih-tung, but he was not an active reformer. He sympa-thized with K'ang Yu-wei's[*] call for the abolition of eight-legged essays, foot-binding, and opium-smoking, but he did not support the Reform Movement of 1898. Indeed, Wu wrote at the time that the movement violated traditional ideas of loyalty to the throne; five years later he critcized himself for this and renounced what he had written.

Wu's evolution into a revolutionary occurred chiefly abroad, in Japan and Europe. When he first went to Japan in 1901, he refused a friend's invitation to meet Sun Yat-sen, dismissing Sun as an uneducated rebel. On a second trip to Japan, leading a group of students, Wu found that defending the students' in-terests embroiled him in a drawn-out conflict with the Ch'ing minister to Japan and the Japanese authorities. The experience seems to have had a major effect on him. About to be deported, while en route to the boat Wu attempted suicide, and a valedictory he had written was revealed. In it he pleaded dramatically for the salvation of China via reforms, democracy, and freedom. The incident drew the attention of many Chinese in Tokyo. A large crowd saw him off, and Ts'ai Yüan-p'ei[*] decided to escort Wu back to China. The two then plunged into anti-

Ch'ing activity, joining with others in Shanghai to establish the Chinese Education Association and the Patriotic Academy and to write for *Su-pao*. When the Ch'ing cracked down in 1903, Wu fled, first to Hong Kong and then to Europe. By 1904 he had settled in London, where a year later he met with Sun Yat-sen and joined the European branch of the T'ung-meng hui.[*]

Wu was a diligent student of his surroundings, and he was fascinated by life abroad. He studied English, observed politics, learned printing, and read widely. He was especially impressed by science, technology, and China's relative backwardness. In 1906 he moved to Paris, joining several old friends including Li Shih-tseng. There he developed an interest in anarchosyndicalism, and the friends soon began publishing a journal called *The New Century* (*Hsin Shih-chi*) which was devoted primarily to introducing the ideas of Kropotkin and Bakunin. Wu formed a utopian vision based on advances in science and technology and rooted in theories of evolution. The journal lasted three years, 1907–1910, and its 121 issues included a variety of articles and translations on a range of subjects embracing all social questions of the time. A major concern, for example, was to encourage the use of Esperanto, and for Wu and problem of language reform became a lifelong preoccupation.

After the 1911 Revolution[*] broke out, Wu returned to China and worked for the Ministry of Education on the problems of standardizing Chinese pronunciation and developing a system of phonetic symbols, tasks to which Wu devoted many years and made significant contributions. He was also a major force in organizing a work-study program for sending students to Europe, and eventually he managed to establish an Institut Franco-Chinois in France which he headed from 1920 to 1923. When he returned to China, he joined the famous 1923 debates on science and philosophy, during which he published what is perhaps his most famous article, "A New Belief's Cosmology and Philosophy of Life." Although Wu had written for some years about the importance of science and technology, he now launched what became a campaign of many years' duration in behalf of the idea that only knowledge gained via the scientific method could be regarded as valid. Wu also stressed that science is the foundation of industrial society, and he came to be famous for the idea of "saving the nation with motors."

In politics, Wu went along with Sun Yat-sen's policies on the First United Front, but after Sun's death he opposed the Kuomintang's links with the Chinese Communists. For the remainder of his life he was a strong supporter of Chiang Kai-shek[*] and a vigorous opponent of the Communists, calling for a purge of the Communists in 1927 and subsequently serving Chiang in many different capacities. He accompanied the National government to Taiwan in 1949 and spent his last years there.

REFERENCES: Ch'en Hung and Ch'en Ling-hai, eds., *Wu Chih-hui hsien-sheng ta-chuan* (A biography of Wu Chih-hui) (Taipei, n.d.); Michael Gasster, *Chinese Intellectuals and the Revolution of 1911* (Seattle, Wash., 1969).

MICHAEL GASSTER

WU P'EI-FU (April 22, 1874–December 4, 1939): Chihli warlord.

Wu P'ei-fu was born in 1874 in P'englai into a poor family. He first received a classical education at the local school and at the age of fourteen was sent to the naval barracks of Tengchou Prefecture to serve as a sailor. Following the traditional path to success, Wu took the district examination in 1897 and obtained the *sheng-yüan* degree at the age of twenty-three. He then joined Nieh Shih-cheng's Wu-wei Army as a clerk. Later he enrolled in the K'aiping Military Preparatory School and Yüan Shih-k'ai's* Paoting (or Peiyang) Military Academy. During the Russo-Japanese War (1904–1905), Wu was assigned to work with a Japanese officer, Morita Rien, in several reconnaissance works in Manchuria for which he was awarded a medal by the Meiji emperor.

After the Wuchang revolt broke out, Shansi declared independence from the Ch'ing.* Yen Hsi-shan,* the elected military governor of Shansi, met with Wu Lu-chen, commander of the imperial Sixth Division, in Shih-chia-chuang to work out a plan for a joint assault of Peking. Unfortunately, Wu Lu-chen was killed. Yüan Shih-k'ai then ordered Ts'ao K'un* and Wu P'ei-fu to attack the Niang-tzu and suppress the revolution in Shansi. But Commander Liu, Wu's superior, had worked out an arrangement with the revolutionaries to have the Third Division delivered to the revolutionary camp. The plan was discovered by Wu, and Liu was immediately arrested. Yen was forced back into Shansi. Ts'ao K'un and Wu P'ei-fu also played an important role in staging a ''mutiny'' in support of Yüan in his maneuver against the provisional government in Nanking. In the Nan-yuan riot, Wu played the part of suppressor. For his role, Wu was duly awarded a promotion to the rank of chief adjutant of the Third Division. Ts'ao K'un and Wu remained loyal to Yüan to the very end. They faithfully carried out Yüan's instruction and obstructed the advance of the Yunnan Army in Szechwan during the National Protection Movement.

Following the death of Yüan Shih-k'ai, the Peiyang Clique* was divided into the Anhwei* (Tuan Ch'i-jui) and the Chihli* (Ts'ao K'un and Wu P'ei-fu) rival factions. In a competition for political power, Wu led the Chihli group in a war against Tuan's Anfu clique. With the support of the Manchurian warlord Chang Tso-lin, Wu brought Tuan down in the Chihli–Anfu War of July 1920. But the ensuing political rivalry between Chang and Wu led them into direct political conflict in 1922. With Chang defeated in the first Chihli–Fengt'ien War, Wu and the Chihli Clique became the de facto ruler in China.

In 1922 Wu had an opportunity to join Sun Yat-sen* in the revolutionary camp. Wu's nationalistic pronouncement against Japanese encroachment in China, his liberal policy of peaceful unification of the country, and particularly his support for an ''able-men cabinet'' headed by Wang Ch'ung-hui, a follower of Sun Yat-sen, put him in favorable standing in the revolutionary camp. His protection of labor policy was equally well received by the Communists. Through the efforts of Li Ta-chao,* the co-founder of the Chinese Communist party,* and some of the pro-Kuomintang parliamentarians, a movement was launched to bring Sun Yat-sen and Wu P'ei-fu together. The plan called for the unification of the country backed by the Soviet Union, in which Sun was to assume political leadership while Wu would be the head of the military. In December 1922 Sun sent Ch'en

Chung-fu to meet with Wu in Loyang. For whatever reasons, either his unquestioned loyalty to Ts'ao K'un or his underestimation of Sun's political power, Wu was not interested in Sun's proposal. The subsequent conflict between Wu's troops and the Communist-organized labor union in the Peking–Hankow Strike on February 7, 1923, put an end to what remained of the so-called Sun-Wu Entente. Later, when the Second Chihli-Fengt'ien War broke out in 1924, the Canton government was decidedly on the side of Wu's opponent, Chang Tsolin. But it was Feng Yü-hsiang's[*] defection that finally put the Chihli faction out of power.

Wu made a comeback in 1926 and dominated Hupeh and Honan for a couple of months before the the Northern Expeditionary forces[*] invaded from the South. In fact, Wu's dispute with T'ang Sheng-chih over Hunan drove T'ang into the revolutionary camp. Later, T'ang led the revolutionary forces to attack southern Hupeh. Wu's troops, however, failed to stem the revolutionary advance and, with some of his subordinates defected to the South, Wu's rule in central China collapsed. He fled to Chengchow and afterward to Szechwan. At the time of the Sino-Japanese War,[*] General Doihara Kenji of the Japanese Kwantung Army made several attempts to recruit Wu to head a puppet regime in north China. Although pressured by his former subordinates who worked closely with the Japanese, Wu refused the Japanese offer. He later died of an infected tooth in Peip'ing (Peking) in December 1939.

REFERENCES: Odoric Y.K. Wou, *Militarism in Modern China: The Career of Wu P'ei-fu, 1916–39* (Dawson, Australia, 1978); T'ao Chu-yin, *Wu P'ei-fu chiang-chün chuan* (A biography of General Wu P'ei-fu) (Shanghai, 1941).

ODORIC Y.K. WOU

WUHAN REGIME (1927): Leftist government under the first KMT–CCP United Front during the Northern Expedition.

In October 1926 the Northern Expeditionary forces[*] of the Kuomintang captured Wuhan—the tricity of Wuchang, Hankow, and Hanyang. Acting on a previous party decision, the KMT headquarters and its national government in Canton began to move to Wuhan. In December the first group of KMT leaders arrived in Wuhan and, guided by the Soviet adviser Michael Borodin,[*] organized the Provisional Joint Council of the KMT Central Executive Committee and the National Government Committee for assuming temporary leadership of the party–government. Hsü Ch'ien was elected its chairman and Borodin its adviser.

The second group of KMT leaders traveling from Canton to Wuhan, however, was persuaded by Chiang Kai-shek[*] to stay at his military headquarters at Nanchang. They organized the Provisional Central Political Council of the KMT in January 1927, challenging the authority of the Wuhan Council. During the following months, the two sides denounced each other as illegitimate while a personal conflict developed between Chiang and Borodin. In early March the majority of the Nanchang group finally rejoined their comrades at Wuhan where they held the Third Plenum of the KMT's Second Central Executive Committee.

In the absence of Chiang and some of his supporters, the plenum nullified most of Chiang's political and military power and replaced it with a form of collective leadership. The Wuhan leaders also strengthened the KMT–CCP United Front, vowing to carry out the Three Great Policies of the late Sun Yat-sen*—allying with the Soviet Union, allying with the Chinese Communists, and assisting workers and peasants. In April, Wang Ching-wei* returned from exile in Europe and became the top leader of the party–government at Wuhan. Meanwhile, Chiang's Northern Expeditionary forces entered the lower Yangtze Valley and began to move against the United Front. Following a bloody massacre of the CCP-led workers and students at Shanghai, Chiang established his own party headquarters and national government at Nanking.* Wuhan immediately expelled Chiang from the KMT.

From April to July the Wuhan Regime, which controlled the three provinces of Hunan, Hupeh, and Kiangsi, faced increasing political and economic difficulties. Chiang's Nanking Regime was winning support from the foreign powers, who were alienated by Wuhan's anti-imperialist stand, as well as from many KMT commanders. Military threat and economic blockade by pro-Nanking forces in the lower Yangtze seriously crippled Wuhan's ability to survive. In addition, the radical worker and peasant movements directed by the Chinese Communist party* in Wuhan-controlled areas disrupted social order, shrank the regime's revenue, and caused widespread dissatisfaction among officers in the Wuhan military, who often came from landed families.

In May Wuhan resumed its Northern Expedition and captured Honan. After a meeting between the Wuhan leaders and Feng Yü-hsiang* at Cheng-chou, the regime decided to let Feng control the province while withdrawing its forces back to the middle Yangtze, in preparation of a military showdown with Nanking. Partly instigated by Nanking and partly a reaction to CCP's radical policies, a series of rebellions occurred in the Wuhan military. Feng also voiced his opposition to Borodin and the CCP in June.

As tensions within the United Front grew, Borodin and the CCP, both under instructions from Moscow, wavered between helping the left wing of the KMT and developing the independent strength of the CCP. In early June Comintern* representative M. N. Roy* revealed to Wang Ching-wei a telegram from Moscow ordering the CCP to organize its own armed forces. This further convinced the KMT leaders at Wuhan of their precarious condition. On July 16 the regime announced the termination of the United Front. The CCP was crushed, and Borodin was sent back to the Soviet Union.

Agreement with Chiang Kai-shek on the United Front issue, however, did not reduce Wuhan's hostility toward Chiang, and in late July the regime launched an Eastern Expedition against Nanking. Two weeks later Chiang was forced to step down by the Kwangsi Clique, his partner in the Nanking Regime, and negotiation for the peaceful reunification of the two regimes soon began. In late August the Wuhan leaders decided to move the party–government to Nanking. Wang and the majority of the Wuhan leadership arrived in Nanking in early

September, and the KMT leaders from all sides agreed to organize a Special Committee at Nanking to preside over the party's reunification. The Wuhan Regime thus came to an end.

REFERENCES: Chiang Yung-ching, *Pao-luo-t'ing yü Wu-han cheng-ch'uan* (Borodin and the Wuhan regime) (Taipei, 1972); Liu Chi-tseng, Mao Lei, and Yüan Chi-ch'eng, *Wu-han kuo-min cheng-fu shih* (A history of the Nationalist government at Wuhan) (Hupei, 1986); C. Martin Wilbur, *The Nationalist Revolution in China, 1923–1928* (Cambridge, 1983).

KE-WEN WANG

Y

YALTA CONFERENCE (February 4–11, 1945): Big Three conference on issues affecting Europe and East Asia during World War II.

As World War II began to wind down in Europe and Germany's defeat appeared imminent, the Allies focused on the aftermath in Europe and the defeat of Japan. The United States decided to attack Japan directly, eschewing any idea of launching the attack from the Chinese mainland. With this strategy in mind Joseph Stalin, Franklin D. Roosevelt, and Winston Churchill gathered at Yalta in the Soviet Crimea from February 4 to February 11, 1945.

When the three men met, they discussed the future of a liberated Europe and the war against Japan. Specifically, there were four basic agenda items: what was then called the Far East, the governments of Poland and other Eastern European countries, the future of Germany, and the organization of the United Nations.

While agreement was reached on issues affecting the organization and function of the United Nations, some differences over Europe proved more divisive and less amenable to resolution. Questions about the nature of the Polish government, the land to be "returned" to the Soviet Union, and German reparations caused tempers to flare and vague agreements to be accepted. Discussions reflected reality, and future accusations that Roosevelt did poorly in negotiations with Stalin are not accurate.

Less confrontational was the discussion about East Asia. Roosevelt was convinced that Soviet participation in the defeat of Japan was essential. General Douglas MacArthur estimated that up to sixty Soviet divisions were needed to defeat Japan in Manchuria. Many advisers shared this estimation of the Japanese strength on the Chinese mainland and concurred that Soviet involvement would speed up the defeat and save American lives. Roosevelt also wanted to set the conditions for Soviet participation, try to induce the Soviet leader to help maintain a Nationalist China, and reduce the possibility of direct support to the Chinese Communist party.*

Stalin and Roosevelt hammered out the agreement without much input from Churchill. Essentially, Roosevelt accomplished his objective, committing the Soviet Union to war against Japan within three months of Germany's defeat. The USSR also agreed to support Chiang Kai-shek* as the leader of China, respect Chinese sovereignty in Manchuria, and begin to evacuate its troops three weeks after Japan's surrender. The withdrawal was to be completed within three months.

The support of the USSR was conditional. Stalin had divulged his price for war against Japan six weeks prior to the conference. When the Allies reached agreement at Yalta, the Soviets defined their stipulations in the Draft of Marshall Stalin's Political Conditions for Russia's Entry in the War against Japan. The Kurile Islands would be transfered to the USSR, the Soviet Union would control Outer Mongolia, and territory lost to Japan in 1905 at the end of the Russo-Japanese War would be returned to Russia. The Allies also agreed that the port at Dairen would be internationalized, while safeguarding Russia's "preeminent interest," Russia's lease at Port Arthur as a naval base would be restored, and there would be a joint Soviet-Chinese operation of the Chinese Eastern and South Manchurian railroads.

Implementation of the agreement involved negotiations with Chiang Kai-shek. At this point events moved quickly. On April 5, 1945, the Soviet Union notified Japan that it was abrogating the 1941 neutrality pact. Seven days later Franklin Roosevelt died. Chiang Kai-shek sent his brother-in-law, Tse-Ven Soong,* to Moscow to negotiate the details of an agreement, and Stalin basically affirmed what had been decided while he was in Yalta. But before the final documents could be signed, Stalin left for the conference at Potsdam.

By July 26, 1945, the completion of the atomic bomb led many Americans to conclude that the Soviet Union's participation was not imperative to Japan's eventual defeat. These same people also felt that Soviet troops could hasten the end of the war and save lives. They also acknowledged that, short of war, Soviet involvement could not be stopped. On August 8, two days after the first atomic bomb was dropped on Japan, Soviet forces entered the war.

On August 14, 1945, the promise of Yalta was consummated by an agreement between China and the Soviet Union. The Soviet Union agreed to give the Nationalists, as the government of China, moral, military, and material aid, to respect Chinese sovereignty in Manchuria, to evacuate troops within three months, to eschew intervention in Sinkiang, and to acknowledge the territorial integrity of Outer Mongolia. In turn, the Chinese allowed for self-determination in Outer Mongolia through a plebiscite, approved joint operations of the Chinese Eastern and Southern Manchuria Railroads for thirty years (then to revert to China), stipulated that Dairen would be a free port for thirty years for all treaty nations, and agreed that Port Arthur would become a naval base used jointly by China and the Soviet Union.

REFERENCES: Diane Clemens, *Yalta* (New York, 1970); Herbert Feis, *The China Tangle: The American Effort in China from Pearl Harbor to the Marshall Mission* (New York, 1967); Walter LaFeber, *The American Age: United States Foreign Policy at Home and Abroad Since 1750* (New York, 1989); Immanuel C.Y. Hsü, *The Rise of Modern China*, 3rd ed. (New York, 1983).

EDWIN CLAUSEN

YANG HSIU-CH'ING (former name Szu-lung, d. September 2, 1856): East King of the Taiping Revolutionary government from December 1851 and principal political officer from March 1853.

Yang Hsiu-ch'ing, of Hakka ancestry, was a native of P'ing-ai-shan in the Kuei-p'ing District of Eastern Kwangsi Province. Orphaned at an early age, he lived with an uncle with whom he pursued farming and charcoal making; he had no formal education. In the 1840s, Yang along with other members of his family joined the God Worshippers Society, an evangelical Christian revolutionary organization led by Hung Hsiu-ch'üan and Feng Yün-shan. Yang subsequently gained great influence in the society through his claim to be a spokesman of God and the possessor of miraculous healing powers.

In addition to an unquenchable thirst for power, Yang gave evidence of considerable military talent. After the initial victory of the God Worshippers over imperial troops at Chin-t'ien Village early in 1851, Hung Hsiu-ch'üan proclaimed the establishment of the T'ai-p'ing T'ien-kuo (Heavenly Kingdom of Great Peace) and in a formal designation of military responsibilities named Yang as commander-in-chief of the Central Army Corps. The Taipings, then, advanced toward the northeast by a circuitous route capturing the walled city of Yung-an on September 25, 1851. While besieged in Yung-an during the next six months, Hung elaborated the structure of the Taiping central government, the court, and the armed forces, conferring the title of East King and Chief Marshal (commander-in-chief) on Yang.

The Taiping Army slipped through the imperial encirclement of Yung-an on the night of April 5, 1852, and advanced northward. After a futile effort to capture Kweilin, they crossed into southern Hunan in early June, occupying the district city of Tao-chou on June 12. There, Yang and West King Hsiao Ch'ao-kuei jointly issued a proclamation to the entire nation calling on all Chinese to rid themselves on Manchu misrule and to establish peace and prosperity in the name of God.

In the summer of 1852, with the Taiping advance stalled in southern Hunan, the leadership contemplated a withdrawal into Kwangsi, but Yang persuaded his comrades to push north toward Changsha, the provincial capital of Hunan. In the fall of 1852, when West King Hsiao Ch'ao-kuei succumbed from wounds sustained during the unsuccessful siege of Changsha, the delicate balance of power between the subordinate kings shifted further in favor of the power-hungry Yang.

The Taipings abandoned Changsha on November 30, 1852, and moved rapidly northward into the Yangtze Valley. Moving eastward, they seized Nanking, seat of the Liangkiang provincial government, on March 19, 1853. There, the Tai-pings established their capital. Yang exhorted the residents to accept the rule of Hung, the Heavenly King, to enjoy the blessings it would bring, and to be mindful of his divine sanction.

As commander-in-chief of the armed forces, Yang launched two major military campaigns from Nanking. The Northern Campaign (1853–1855), calculated to take the imperial capital at Peking, crossed the Yangtze and moved through Kiangsu, Anhwei, Honan, Shansi, and southern Chihli but was turned back at the gates of Tientsin on November 1, 1853. Yang's inability to deliver timely reinforcements led to the withdrawal and annihilation of the Taiping force in western Shantung in May 1855.

The Western Campaign (1853–1856) was intended to recapture Wuchang and the upper Yangtze Valley through which the Taipings had passed in early 1853. By June 1854 the Taiping forces had not only retaken Wuchang but had also extended their control into southern Hupeh and northeastern Hunan. By the end of the year, however, the recently organized Hunan Army commanded by Tseng Kuo-fan* forced the Taipings to abandon Wuchang and withdraw to the port city of Kiukiang on the Yangtze near the entrance of Po-yang Lake. They held Kiukiang stubbornly, bottling up a large portion of Tseng's naval forces in Po-yang Lake and recapturing Wuchang from April of 1855 until December 1856.

The high point of Yang's military success came in June 1856 when he directed the overall strategy that resulted in the collapse of the imperial forces guarding Nanking in the Great Camp of Kiangnan, freeing the Taiping capital from the threat of imperial military forces.

This victory fed Yang's overwhelming ambition and touched off a round of internecine struggle among the Taiping leaders. Over the years, Yang had in-creasingly used his status as divine spokesman to enhance his own authority and limit the access of other Taiping kings to Hung. After the victory over the Imperial Great Camp at Kiangnan, Yang's arrogance betrayed his intent to usurp Hung's leadership. When Hung realized Yang's aims, he recalled the two sur-viving subordinate kings Wei Ch'ang-wei* and Shih Ta-k'ai,* whom Yang had conveniently dispatched from the capital, and ordered Wei to assassinate Yang. Wei killed Yang on September 2, 1856, also slaughtering numerous relatives and retainers. Wei's excesses precipitated a retaliatory strike directed by Hung, which resulted in Wei's death. Shih Ta-k'ai, realizing the hopelessness of the divisions among the leaders, fled Nanking.

Yang's career—marked by military genius, overwhelming personal ambition, manipulative leadership, and religious charlatanism—culminated in a violent death that precipitated a general purge of Taiping royalty, opening the way in 1856 for a new generation of leaders.

REFERENCES: Chien Yu-wen, T'ai-p'ing T'ien-kuo Ch'üan-shih (Complete history of the Heavenly Kingdom of Great Peace), vol. 1 (Hong Kong, 1960): 134–136; Arthur W. Hummel, ed., *Eminent Chinese of the Ch'ing Period* (Washington, D.C., 1944): 886–888; Yu-wen Jen (Chien), *The Taiping Revolutionary Movement* (New Haven, Conn.,

1973); Ts'ai Kuan-lo, ed., *Ch'ing-tai ch'i-pai ming-jen chuan* (Biographies of seven hundred famous people of the Ch'ing period), vol. 3 (Peking, 1984): 1863–1868.

THOMAS L. KENNEDY

YAO WEN-YÜAN (1931–   ): Member of the Politburo of the CCP; one of the Gang of Four; purged in October 1976.

A native of Chu-chi County, Chekiang Province, Yao Wen-yüan is the son of the leftist writer Yao P'eng-tze. He joined the Chinese Communist party* while attending middle school in Shanghai in 1948. After the Communist take-over of the city, he became a resident correspondent for the *Literary Gazette*, the official organ of the Chinese Writers' Union, and began a career that two decades later was to make him one of China's most powerful censors.

During the CCP's 1955 campaign to denounce the prominent left-wing writer Hu Feng,* Yao emerged as a representative of a new breed of young and fierce party polemicists and literary critics. Over the next few years, his relentless attacks on allegedly bourgeois, revisionist, or decadent writers and works of literature appeared frequently in Shanghai newspapers like the *Wen-hui Pao* and *Liberation Army Daily* as well as in major national literary journals. By March 1957 he had attracted the attention of Mao Tse-tung,* who found his essays "quite convincing."

In the early 1960s Yao continued to publish in the fields of literary criticism, theory, and aesthetics. Many of the ideas he developed in his writings at this time later became cornerstones of Cultural Revolutionary literary orthodoxy. Around 1963, he, together with Chang Ch'un-ch'iao,* became close to Mao Tse-tung's wife Chiang Ch'ing,* who was attempting to reform traditional Peking opera, using Shanghai as her base. With Chiang as his patron, Yao took part in some of the preparations for what eventually was to become the Cultural Rev-olution.* On November 10, 1965, the publication of his article "On the New Historical Play 'Hai Jui's Dismissal from Office' " in the *Wen-hui Pao* triggered a series of events that eventually led to the downfall of Peking's mayor P'eng Chen.*

In May 1966 Yao was made a member of the CCP Politburo's Cultural Revolution Small Group, of which Chiang Ch'ing and Chang Ch'un-ch'iao were vice-directors. In February 1967 he became vice-chairman of the Shanghai Rev-olutionary Committee. At the National Day celebrations in Peking in 1968, he ranked number eight among the party and government leaders present. With the backing of Mao Tse-tung, he soon became one of the party center's chief ide-ological watchdogs, and it was primarily in his capacities as censor and ghost-writer for the CCP Central Committee that he was to exercise power over the following years.

In April 1969 the Tenth CCP Central Committee elected him to its Politburo. He was reelected to this position in August 1973, when the Eleventh CCP Central Committee held its first plenary session. On March 1, 1975, the *People's Daily* published his highly significant article "On the Social Base of Lin Piao's Anti-

Party Clique,'' in which, using the ideological jargon of the time, he explained the correctness of the politics pursued by the CCP since the beginning of the Cultural Revolution. In the spring of 1976, he together with Chiang Ch'ing and Chang Ch'un-ch'iao was largely responsible for orchestrating a nationwide media campaign intended to disgrace Teng Hsiao-p'ing[*] and mobilize public opinion against a departure from Cultural Revolution policies and practices after the already anticipated impending death of Mao Tse-tung.

On October 6, 1976, four weeks after Mao's death, Yao was arrested on the orders of a coalition of senior government and military leaders opposed to the Cultural Revolution. Together with Chiang Ch'ing, Chang Ch'un-ch-iao, and Wang Hung-wen[*] (see also Gang of Four[*]), he was accused of counterrevolutionary crimes and of having attempted to usurp state power. The party press he had once controlled now heaped abuse on him and compared him to the Nazi Propaganda Minister Joseph Goebbels. On January 23, 1981, at a major show trial in Peking, he was sentenced to twenty years in prison.

REFERENCE: Lars Ragvald, *Yao Wen-yüan as a Literary Critic and Theorist: The Emergence of Chinese Zhdanovism* (Stockholm, 1978).

MICHAEL L. SCHOENHALS

YEH CHIEN-YING (1898?–1985): Top-ranking military cadre of the CCP; member of the CCP Politburo; vice-chairman of CCP Central Military Council; marshal of the PRC.

Born to a Hakka family in Yen-yang-pao of Mei County in eastern Kwang tung Province, Yeh received a prematurely ended traditional education at Tung-shan Middle School before he accompanied his merchant father to Singapore and Hanoi in 1917. On returning from that brief sojourn, he enrolled at the Yunnan Military School from which he graduated as a member of the twelfth class in 1919. From there he joined the army of the Kwangtung warlord Ch'en Chiung-ming. Subsequently, he was promoted to administrative positions as magistrate of Chung-shan County and later of Mei County. Not long afterward, however, he went to Canton to work with Sun Yat-sen.[*] When the Whampoa Military Academy[*] was founded in 1924, Yeh was hired as an instructor and at one time served as an assistant to the KMT General Ho Ying-ch'in,[*] dean of Whampoa. On July 9, 1926, the Northern Expedition[*] was launched, and Yeh served as the chief-of-staff of Ho's First Army. As the Northern Expedition got underway, he joined the Nationalist Fourth Army, which was commanded first by Li Chi-shen and then by Chang Fa-k'uei. When Wu-ch'ang fell to the Nationalist forces in October 1926, the Fourth Army, redesignated the Second Front Army, was placed in control of the critical Wuhan area. During this time Yeh was chief-of-staff of the important Twenty-fourth Division of the Second Front Army.

In the summer of 1927 Chang Fa-k'uei moved his headquarters to Chiu-chiang, near Nanchang, the capital of Kiangsi Province. When their relations with the Nationalists began deteriorating, Communist leaders in the military plotted an uprising. Yeh participated in a meeting on July 18, which Chu Teh* once described as the initial planning meeting for the Nanchang Uprising* of August 1, 1927. Apparently, Yeh was also elected to the Front-line Committee that directed that unsuccessful coup, in which the Twenty-fourth Division of the Second Front Army took part. After the defeat at Nanchang, Yeh fled to Hong Kong, where he and Yeh T'ing took care of Chou En-lai,* who had taken ill. It was during this time (in September 1927) that Yeh officially became a member of the Chinese Communist party.* By October, Yeh had surreptitiously returned to Canton, and was instrumental in mobilizing the Workers' Red Guard Unit that played a key role in the also unsuccessful Canton Uprising of December 11. Afterward, Yeh made his way to Shanghai, where he worked briefly in the CCP organization before going to Moscow, in time to attend the CCP's Sixth Congress held there in mid–1928. Yeh remained in the Soviet Union for about two years as a student in Sun Yat-sen University, and then did some traveling in Europe (mainly in Germany) before returning to China in 1931.

In late 1931 Yeh was elected a member of the Central Revolutionary Military Council by the Central Executive Committee of the CCP, and in early 1932 he made his way to the southern Kiangsi area where Chu Teh and Mao Tse-tung* had established a rural base for the revolution. There he became chief-of-staff of the Military Council and alternated in this position with Liu Po-ch'eng whom he succeeded as the commander of the garrison of Jui-chin. Yeh also assumed the presidency of the Red Army School and held it for a number of years. By late 1933 Yeh also became chief-of-staff of Chu Teh's First Front Army, which was the backbone of the Communist forces in the Kiangsi region. At the Second Congress of Soviets in January 1934, Yeh was elected to the Central Executive Committee of the Chinese Soviet Republic.

In October 1934, as the Long March* set out, Yeh served as deputy chief-of-staff of the Military Council under Liu Po-ch'eng, as well as chief-of-staff of the Shensi-Kansu division of the Communist forces. In June 1935 the Communist forces under Chang Kuo-t'ao,* made up largely of the Fourth Front Army, and those under Chu Teh and Mao Tse-tung rendezvoused in northwest Szechwan. In August, the conference at Mao-erh-kai was held in which the differences between Chang and Mao came to a head over the strategic decision of where the destination of the Long March would be. As a result of the conference, the two leaders went their separate ways. Mao headed north toward Shensi, and Chang went to Tibet, taking with him Chu Teh and Liu Po-ch'eng. In this split, Yeh took Mao's side.

As Mao's forces arrived in northern Shensi, they came into periodical conflict with the KMT troops of generals Chang Hsüeh-liang* and Yang Hu-ch'eng. However, Yang and Chang had stronger inclinations toward uniting all Chinese forces against Japan's increasing expansion in China, and the clashes soon gave way to friendlier relations. During this time, Yeh often shuttled between the Communist headquarters at Pao-an and Sian, Chang's seat of power, and gained Chang's favor as a strategic consultant. In December 1936, during the Sian

Incident* Yeh was selected as one of the Communist negotiators with Chiang Kai-shek,* who had been kidnapped by Chang and Yang for the purpose of forcing a mediated settlement between the KMT and the Communists. The kidnapping had led to the formation of the Second United Front* against Japan.

In 1937, when the national war of resistance against Japan broke out, Yeh became chief-of-staff of the Communist Eighth Route Army.* His active duties, however, were mainly to serve as a chief liaison officer between the Communists and the KMT, first in Sian, then in the Nanking office, and after the fall of Nanking in October 1937, in Hankow. When Hankow fell to the Japanese in late 1938, Yeh followed Chiang Kai-shek's government in its evacuation to Chungking. During this transition, Yeh became the chief officer of the Nationalists' Guerrilla Warfare Training Center, which was established to infuse the KMT forces with the Communists' experience in guerrilla fighting. In 1939 Yeh served under Chou En-lai in the Communist liaison mission in Chungking. In 1941 he returned to Yenan, the new Communist headquarters in northern Shensi, resuming his position as chief-of-staff of the Eighth Route Army. Although this was a staff position, Yeh distinguished himself as a chief military analyst for Mao and Chou En-lai.

At the CCP's Seventh Congress in mid–1945, held at Yenan, Yeh was elected to the party's Seventh Central Committee. Later that year he was appointed a member of the delegation to the Political Consultative Conference which was held in Chungking in January 1946. Yeh was subsequently appointed the Communist representative in the executive headquarters, based in Peking, established to coordinate the KMT–CCP ceasefire agreement that had been signed through the mediation efforts of U.S. Special Envoy George Marshall as the Political Consultative Conference was convened. The ceasefire broke down in just a few months, however, and in February 1947 Yeh and his group were airlifted by American aircraft to Yenan, within days of the KMT's capture of that Communist capital. From this time until the CCP forces captured Peking in January 1949, Yeh served as deputy chief-of-staff of the People's Liberation Army* (PLA) units in northern China.

When KMT General Fu Tso-yi* surrendered in January 1949 and Peking fell to the Communists, Yeh became chairman of the Peking Military Control Commission and of the Peking Joint Administrative Office, as well as the city's mayor, taking charge of the negotiations with Acting Nationalist President Li Tsung-jen in April of that year. In September, negotiations having ended with the KMT's refusal of Communist terms, Yeh joined the PLA forces in Kwangtung and was made commander of the PLA's Kwangtung Military District. As a native of Kwangtung, Yeh was a natural choice to assume leadership of the CCP government apparatus in the South as the People's Republic of China* was established. Consequently, in October 1949 he became the chairman of the Canton Military Control Commission and the mayor of Canton, while also holding the positions of commander and political commissar of the South China Military District, secretary of the South China Sub-bureau of the Central Committee of the CCP, and secretary of the Canton Party Committee. In November, he became chairman of the Kwangtung People's government. In March 1950 he became a vice-chairman of the newly established Central-South China Military and Administrative Commission (later, in 1953, the Central-South Administrative Council). At the national level he was a member of the Central People's Government Council and the Central People's Revolutionary Military Council (PRMC). Yeh held these positions until 1954. In the South for the majority of the time from 1950 to 1954, Yeh was primarily involved in the socialist revolutionary programs there, such as the land reform and the suppression of counterrevolutionaries. In 1951 he became secretary of the Kwangtung CCP committee. In mid–1952 he was dispatched to Wuhan, under the nominal leadership of the ailing Lin Piao,* to serve as the acting commander of the Central-South Military District and acting secretary of the Central-South CCP Bureau, while retaining the titles appertaining to his role as chief CCP cadre in Kwangtung.

In 1954, with the purging of the Kao Kang-Jao Shu-shih faction and the abolition of the regional administration structure, Yeh was promoted to vice-chairman of the PRMC (in June) and in September to a similar position on the National Defense Council which replaced the PRMC. He was also elected to membership on the Standing Committee of the National People's Congress (NPC). In November 1954 he became director of the Armed Forces Supervision Department. Awarded various top-level military decorations, Yeh was also made a marshal of the PLA in September 1955.

In the post–1949 period in general, Yeh held many top-ranking military positions and headed a large number of military delegations to foreign countries. He had been an outspoken advocate of the PRC's military modernization, especially in the armaments area. He served as an influential member of the Standing Committee of the Military Affairs Council, which was the top-ranking military body of the CCP, and in 1961 he was identified as chairman of that committee's Regulations Examination Subcommittee.

In the early stages of the Cultural Revolution,* Yeh's position in the CCP hierarchy rose even further. In mid–1966 he became the only active military personnel in the CCP General Secretariat, and in 1967 he was a member of the Politburo. He also played a very significant part in the criticism against People's Liberation Army* chief-of-staff Lo Jui-ch'ing in early 1966 as a member of the CCP Central Committee Work Group. However, Yeh himself began to come under attack by the Red Guards* in August 1966, which reached a crescendo in the riotous March of 1967. Yeh survived the assault largely because Chou En-lai vouched for his loyalty to the Maoist cause. In 1969 Yeh was reelected to the CCP Central Committee and the Politburo at the Ninth CCP Congress. Nonetheless, his activities remained minimal until the purging of Lin Piao* in 1971, after which he was reactivated as the first vice-chairman of the Military Affairs Council and took over the day-to-day leadership of the operations of that committee. In 1976, in Hua Kuo-feng's* purging of the Gang of Four* following

Mao Tse-tung's death, Yeh came out on the side of the new power-holders, and in 1977 he was elected to the Eleventh CCP Central Committee. Like most veteran cadres of his generation, Yeh remained largely inactive except in nominal roles after Teng Hsia-p'ing's* third rise to power in 1978.

REFERENCES: Wolfgang Bartke, *Who's Who in the People's Republic of China* (Armonk, N.Y., 1981): 474–475; *Chung-kung jen-ming lu* (Biographies of Chinese Communists) (Taipei, 1978): 815–817; *Chung-kung shou-yao shih-lueh hsü-p'ien* (Chronology of Chinese Communist leaders, II) (Taipei, 1972): 551–562; Donald W. Klein and Anne B. Clark, *Biographical Dictionary of Chinese Communism, 1921–1965*, vol. 2 (Cambridge, Mass., 1971), 1004–1009.

JOHN KONG-CHEONG LEUNG

YEN CHIA-KAN (October 23, 1905–   ): Governor of Taiwan; minister of finance, premier, vice-president and president of the ROC on Taiwan.

Yen Chia-kan, also known as C. K. Yen, was born into a gentry family in Soochow, Kiangsu. He built his reputation as a financial expert and government official who played a major part in stabilizing Taiwan's economy after assuming a variety of financial posts there beginning in 1946. After becoming premier in 1963, he was elected vice-president of the Republic of China* in 1966 and was reelected in 1972. He took over as president on April 6, 1975—less than twelve hours after the passing of President Chiang Kai-shek.* He held that position until 1978 when Chiang Ching-kuo* gave up his position as premier to become president.

C. K. Yen gained recognition for the important part he played in stabilizing China's economy during World War II. The experience and skills he accumulated, readied him for the task of stabilizing Taiwan's economy after some 2 million Nationalist refugees fled there in 1949. His economic and financial policies helped spur Taiwan's economic growth and make it strong enough to withstand the shock of the termination of U.S. economic aid in July 1965.

As a boy, C. K. Yen studied Chinese classics at home with his grandfather and father, both of whom were classical Chinese scholars. He also attended modern schools in Soochow, where he graduated from the Tao-wu Middle School, a missionary institution. He began his career as director of supplies for the Nanking–Shanghai railroad bureau in Shanghai following his graduation in 1926 from St. John's University in Shanghai, where he majored in theoretical chemistry.

After the Sino-Japanese War* began, C. K. Yen gained prominence, first as commissioner of reconstruction in the Fukien provincial government (1938) and then as commissioner of finance there (1939). He helped restore the province's self-sufficiency by reforming land taxes. The system he devised was known as land levies in kind. Implemented beginning in 1941, it did away with the old system of collecting land taxes in paper currency that had been rendered increasingly valueless by rapid inflation. The new system collected land taxes in grain, much like the taxes collected in pre-Ming China.

The National government judged the reform in Fukien a success and extended

it to other provinces. Rice and wheat collections strengthened the financial situation of both provincial and national governments. They are credited with the
government's increased ability to regularly supply food and supplies to soldiers
at the front.

In 1945 C. K. Yen took over as director of procurement of the War Production
Board. In this capacity he supervised all procurement under the United States
Lend-Lease and the British and Canadian loan programs. At war's end, he took
part in economic planning for the takeover of Japanese-occupied areas by the
Chinese Army. After the war he went to Nanking as a member of the army
general headquarters planning committee for taking over party and political
offices and as a standing member of the Ministry of Economic Affairs' committee
for reorganizing industrial and mining enterprises in Japanese-occupied areas.

Yen went to Taiwan in December 1945 as communications commissioner,
and he also served as minister of economic affairs representative in taking over
railroad, telecommunications, and navigations facilities from the Japanese. As
finance commissioner and board chairman of the Bank of Taiwan, he issued
bank notes for exclusive use in Taiwan, thus helping spare Taiwan the inflation
that was troubling Mainland China. Yen helped stabilize Taiwan's economy with
a currency reform to fix the exchange rate of Taiwan and United States dollars.
He became minister of finance in 1950 and governor of Taiwan in 1955. In 1958
he again became minister of finance before moving up to be premier in 1963.
REFERENCE: Howard L. Boorman and Richard C. Howard, eds., *Biographical
Dictionary of Republican China*, vol. 4 (New York, 1971).

PARRIS H. CHANG

YEN FU (January 8, 1854–October 27, 1921): Translator and interpreter of
Charles Darwin, Herbert Spencer, John Stuart Mill, and other Western thinkers.

As China's earliest and most devoted advocate of Darwinian-Spencerian evolution, Yen Fu was a vigorous spokesman for gradualist reform and an opponent
of both radical reform and revolution. But his ideas were far from consistent,
and he took stands that at least by implication could be understood at times to
favor revolution. Above all, he introduced to China ideas from the West that
profoundly influenced reformers and revolutionaries from K'ang Yu-wei[*] to Mao
Tse-tung.[*] His translations were often summaries, abridgments, or paraphrases
rather than literal renderings of the originals, and even when translating, he
added commentaries of his own. Elegantly written, his work provided Chinese
readers with a wealth of striking new concepts.

Between the ages of five and twelve, Yen Fu received a classical education.
In 1866, because his father's death led to economic hardship, Yen took the
entrance examination for a newly established naval school in Foochow. The
school offered free tuition, room and board, and a stipend that included a subsidy
for his family. Yen won first place and chose to attend the School of Navigation,
where instruction was in English.

Upon graduation in 1871, Yen served in several advanced training positions that took him to Japan and Singapore, among other places. In 1877 he was sent to England for two years of further study. Then twenty-three years old, he was full of curiosity and excitement, burning to answer the questions that plagued his generation—why was China, despite its size and glorious history, so weak? And why were countries such as England, though small, so strong?

Yen's answers to these questions only began to appear in 1895 when, after more than a decade of filling minor posts and experiencing mounting frustration at his own and China's failures, he published four major essays. These essays contain the themes that ran through most of his life's work. Yen marveled, for example, that British society managed both to encourage individual effort and to channel those efforts toward the national good. Somehow, he observed, the pursuit of individual interests was conducted in Britain with a certain "public spirit" (*kung-hsin*) that promoted national interests. Freedom and democracy seemed to foster a correspondence between individual and group interests, between public and private concerns. Unless China reformed itself so as to head in this direction, he wrote, the country would die; one specific step would be to establish a deliberative national assembly made up of representatives from all parts of China.

As the four essays appeared, Yen was already at work on a translation of Thomas Henry Huxley's *Evolution and Ethics*, which he published in 1898 to huge acclaim. In the course of the next ten years he issued translations of Smith's *Wealth of Nations*, Mill's *On Liberty* and *A System of Logic*, Montesquieu's *Spirit of the Laws*, and other major translations as well as some writings that were entirely his own.

Yen Fu was critical of the Republican Revolutionary Movement both as a matter of practical politics and from a more broadly philosophical perspective. He believed that the Chinese people were not ready to rule themselves and that a premature attempt to found a republic would do more harm than good. Evolution, he tended to argue, must proceed at its own pace. But he was not altogether consistent on this point, and at times he suggested that human effort, even to the extent of engaging in struggle, was necessary if human evolution was to reach its highest potential. Moreover, in Western history he found proof that the pace of change can quicken: "The power the West now has represents a rapid change of only the last fifty to two hundred years. Why then cannot we rouse ourselves to do the same?"

Yen Fu shared the spirit of eagerness for rapid change that came to characterize radical movements in modern China. He was outspoken about the failings of China's imperial system, and he berated rulers and philosophers alike for holding China back. For a moment in 1911, he even sounded eager for the revolution to come, hinting in a poem that it was imminent and would be a good thing, but the moment passed. Still, his attack on China's past sages foreshadowed the New Culture Movement, and his translations inspired its leaders. Hu Shih* once wrote that Yen's Darwinian language became "a kind of clarion call" to an entire generation of young Chinese intellectuals. The seventeen-year-old Lu

Hsün[*] read Yen's translation of Huxley and could not put it down; the book was a voyage of discovery for him. And Mao Tse-tung, thanks to Yen Fu and Liang Ch'i-ch'ao,[*] knew Darwin before he knew Marx.

In the end, Yen Fu could accept neither the 1911 Revolution,[*] the Republic, nor the May Fourth Movement.[*] In the last decade of his life he worked for Yüan Shih-k'ai,[*] reconsidered many criticisms he had made of past rulers and ideas, and in 1913 even supported a proposal to make Confucianism a state religion. But whatever his inconsistencies and reversals, Yen Fu's work remains indispensable to an understanding of the intellectual sources of China's revolution. He called into question virtually the entire Chinese world-view, and he provided China's new intelligentsia with some of the key ideas they needed in their search for national regeneration.

REFERENCES: James Reeve Pusey, *China and Charles Darwin* (Cambridge, Mass., 1983); Benjamin Schwartz, *In Search of Wealth and Power: Yen Fu and the West* (Cambridge, Mass., 1964).

MICHAEL GASSTER

YEN HSI-SHAN (1883–May 24, 1960): Shansi warlord.

Born into a small banker's family, Yen Hsi-shan studied Chinese classics and in his early years served as an apprentice at the bank. At eighteen, he was elected the village leader. During the Boxer Uprising[*] (1900), he effectively organized the villagers to put up a defense against the marauding Ch'ing[*] troops. He later enrolled in the provincial Military Preparatory School. Having received a government scholarship to study in Japan, Yen went to the Shimbu Gakko and then the Japanese Military Officers' Academy (Shikan Gakko).

In Japan, Yen joined the T'ung-men-hui[*] and the Dare-to-Die Corps, a small tightly knit group of revolutionary military. In 1907, carrying a bomb, he went back to Shansi to make preparations for the coming revolution. In 1909 Yen became a teacher in the Shansi Military Primary School and was later appointed the training officer of the Second Regiment of the Shansi Army. He organized a Hsin-hai Recreation Club to rally his fellow revolutionaries for the purpose of overthrowing the Ch'ing.

When the Wuchang revolt broke out, Yen and the Shansi revolutionaries were supposed to wait until the revolutionary armies reached Honan before mobilizing their forces out of Shih-chia-chuang to participate in the fighting. However, in a move to suppress the revolution in Shansi, Governor Lu Ch'ung-ch'i dispersed the New Army[*] and sent part of the German-made rifles to Honan. Lu's actions compelled Yen and the revolutionaries to rebel. The revolutionary forces attacked Taiyuan, and the provincial assembly declared independence of the Ch'ing government. After taking over Shansi, Yen conferred with Wu Lu-chen, the revolutionary commander of the imperial forces, at Niang-tzu Pass in an attempt to join forces to oppose Yüan Shih-k'ai's[*] coming north to assist the Manchus. But with Wu assassinated and the

Third Division of Ts'ao Kun* and Wu P'ei-fu* assaulted at the Niang-tzu Pass, Yen and his army retreated to Suiyuan. Yüan subsequently appointed Yen the military governor of Shansi. During his rule, Yen undertook a social reform in Shansi to make it into a "model province."

During the Nationalist Revolution, both the Kuomintang and Chang Tso-lin solicited Yen's support. At the outset, Yen was rather apprehensive of the radical leaning of the left-Kuomintang. But with the Nanking–Wuhan split, Yen and Feng Yü-hsiang* lent their support to Chiang Kai-shek.* The subsequent purge of the Communists and the reconciliation between the two factions in the Kuomintang paved the way for Yen to participate in the Northern Expedition,* accepting the appointment as commander-in-chief of the Northern Route Revolutionary Army. The Shansi Army was assigned to stall Chang Tso-lin's southward movement but would have been almost decimated by Chang's troops had it not been for the intercession of the Kuominchün. With Chang out of the way, Yen and Feng then competed in their drive toward Peking. Whether it was due to the Japanese intervention or to his appointment by Chiang as the commander of the Nationalist Garrisons in Peking and Tientsin, Yen's army was allowed to enter Peking first. For his decisive role in the Nationalist Revolution, Yen was given the governorship of Shansi.

Relations between Yen, Feng Yü-hsiang, and Chiang Kai-shek were greatly strained over the question of disbandment of troops. Allied with the Kuominchün, the Kwangsi Clique, and Wang Ching-wei's* Reorganizationists,* in 1930 Yen openly opposed Chiang in the Honan Campaign. The rebellion was crushed only with the military support of the Manchurian warlord, Chang Hsüeh-liang,* who remained loyal to Chiang Kai-shek.

After the rebellion, Yen retreated to Shansi. In 1930 he drew up a Ten-Year Plan for reconstructing the province. In a couple of years, he had gathered data through the Village Inspection Committees, developed iron mining and light industry, constructed roads and railways, reclaimed and redistributed land, remodeled the education system, established government monopoly, and curbed the power of the gentry. By the time of the Sino-Japanese War,* Shansi is said to have invested CH $100 million in its industrial enterprises.

With the Communist invasion of Shansi in 1936 and the subsequent Japanese encroachment into the province during the war, Yen's territorial base greatly shrank into a small area east of the Yellow River in western Shansi. During the War, he received an appointment as commander of the Second War Zone from Chiang. The clash between Yen and the Communists forced him to make friends with the Japanese. After the Japanese surrendered, Yen took up the "bandit suppression" of north China in Taiyuan. Forced out of his province in 1949, he flew to Taipei. He later served as a member of the Central Advisory Committee in the National government in Taiwan. He died on May 24, 1960.

REFERENCES: Donald G. Gillin, *Warlord: Yen Hsi-shan in Shansi Province, 1911–1949* (Princeton, N.J., 1967); Yen Po-ch'uan hsien sheng chi nien chi pien chi wei-yüan hui, *Yen Hsi-shan tsao-nien hui-i lu* (Yen Hsi-shan's memoirs of his early years) (Taipei, 1960).

ODORIC Y.K. WOU

YEN YANG-CHU, JAMES (October 26, 1893–January 17, 1990): Educator, reformer, and head of Mass Education Movement.

Born in Szechwan, Yen received both a classical and modern education. When he was seventeen years old, he graduated from a missionary high school in Chengtu and entered the University of Hong Kong. Two years later, he decided to go to the United States, and in 1916 he was admitted to the junior class of Yale. At that time, World War I was ongoing in Europe, and the Allies recruited Chinese laborers to work in the front in France. The Chinese Labor Corps, as they were called, dug trenches, built roads and railways, worked in mines, factories, and ordnance workshops, and exhumed and reburied the war dead. By the end of 1918, about 140,000 Chinese laborers, including some students, who joined as interpreters, were recruited. After Yen graduated, he accepted an invitation from the National War Work Council of the YMCA to go to France to help the Chinese laborers at an encampment near Boulogne.

Yen was horrified by the conditions at the camp. Working conditions were often dangerous; there were little or no organized recreational activities; and above all, the men were homesick. At the request of some of the laborers, Yen began to write letters to their families in China. Later, he decided to organize evening classes to teach the laborers how to read and write. He used the vernacular and began with several hundred commonly used characters. This approach proved to be very successful, and Yen was asked by the YMCA to direct an educational program for all the Chinese laborers in France.

After the Chinese Labor Corps was disbanded in 1920, Yen returned to China after a brief stay in the United States. The following year, he married Alice Huie whom he had met while he was at Yale. Under the auspices of the YMCA, Yen began to develop a program of popular education to tackle the illiteracy problem. He and his collaborators devised simple primers: *People's Thousand Character Texts*, whose lessons included only the most frequently used words in the vernacular. With the help of a group of specially trained teachers, Yen launched the project in Changsha. Each course lasted four months, a period in which Yen believed the average person would be able to master about 1,000 words, working only an hour a day. The project gradually developed into a system not only of literacy education, but also of organization, supervision, and teacher training. The success of the experiment attracted the attention of other reformers, and in August 1923 a National Association of the Mass Education Movement was founded.

In 1926 Yen with his colleagues and their families moved to Ting Hsien, a county south of Peking, to demonstrate the feasibility of establishing a model *hsien* for his Mass Education Movement. Ting Hsien, with its 472 villages and 397,000 people, was to be the laboratory for Yen's ideas of *hsien*-unit based rural life research. Initially, the focus was on the literacy program, but by 1929 the project became an integrated program of rural reconstruction, encompassing livelihood, health, education, and self-government. The objective was to eradicate the "four fundamental problems of rural China—poverty, disease, ignorance, and civic inertia." The emphasis was on study and practical experimentation based on actual conditions in the county. The local population was mobilized and local resources were used.

The educational aspect of the reconstruction program included the setting up of People's Schools in which subjects such as Chinese history and literature, agriculture, and health were taught. The economic aspect was concerned with improving the standard of living through agricultural research to increase production, village industries, and rural economics. The health division, headed by Dr. C. C. Chen, a graduate of Peking Union Medical College, sought to provide basic medical relief and health protection for the people through sanitary improvements, communicable disease control, school health, and maternity and child health care. In 1936 the Ting Hsien experiment joined with such institutions as the Peking Union Medical College, Tsing Hua and Nankai universities to promote rural reconstruction through the North China Council of Rural Reconstruction. These efforts, however, were cut short by the Japanese invasion in 1937. Despite his attempts to continue his program after the war, the Civil War* and the Communist victory effectively ended his work in China.

Yen established his new base in the United States and, securing a source of funds, began to implement his ideas of rural reform again—this time in the Philippines. The success of his work led to the founding of the International Institute of Rural Reconstruction (IIRR) in 1960.

REFERENCES: P. S. Chin, *Ding Xian* (New York, 1984); James Yen, *The Ting Hsien Experiment in 1934* (Peip'ing, 1934).

KA-CHE YIP

YENAN PERIOD (1936–1947): Key period in the Chinese Communist movement during which the CCP regrouped after the Long March and formulated its organizational, leadership, and ideological programs.

This period is named after the Communists' seat of government, Yenan, a county town in Shensi Province and capital of the Shen-Kan-Ning Border Region*. It is best known as the source of the mass-line*, the Rectification Movement* and the rise to power of Mao Tse-tung,* and the formulation of Mao Tse-tung Thought*. To the present day, the Yenan period has had great symbolic significance for Chinese Communists and scholars.

At the end of the Long March*, the Chinese Communist party* was at a low point. Military errors in the Kiangsi Soviet* and organizational failures in the "White Areas" (underground party work in KMT-administered regions) during the 1930s had almost led to the destruction of the CCP. During the Yenan period, the CCP addressed these failures by strengthening its organization and focusing policy on local and practical issues. After the Sian Incident* of December 1936, this approach included United Front policies that ameliorated leftist excesses. Cadre screening and education provided a coherent organizational culture, and a panoply of committees put into practice Lenin's ideas about democratic centralism.* These reforms were instituted during the 1942–1944 Rectification Campaign, and their immediate fulfillment was the "mass-line"—a series of concrete policies for administering and developing the local economy which stressed equal relations between peasants and cadres and glorified self-reliance. They were largely successful in the 1940s.

Key to the CCP's successful organizational reforms were leadership unity and a clear ideology. During this period Mao Tse-tung rose to dominance as the representative of these two goals. The early Yenan period saw a bitter competition for power between Mao and Chang Kuo-t'ao* for military control and with Wang Ming (Ch'en Shao-yü)* for political leadership. Mao defeated both. He offered guerrilla warfare tactics and the Sinification of Marxism as alternatives to his competitors' ideas. Leadership finally coalesced around a triumvirate: Mao, Liu Shao-ch'i* with constituencies in the White Areas and south China, and Kao Kang* who controlled the local area in Shensi.

The CCP successfully domesticated Marxism-Leninism* during this period in the form of Mao Tse-tung Thought which became the CCP's official ideology at the Seventh Party Congress in 1945. Mao provided an earthy and appealing expression of the utopian goals of Marxism, along with symbols and assumptions congenial to the traditional Chinese respect for "great leaders." This ideology was articulated and inculcated in party cadres in the Rectification Movement (cheng-feng yün-tung) and appealed to sufficient numbers of soldiers, peasants, and intellectuals to organize public support for the CCP. Recent studies have shown that the party leadership permitted Mao's dominance in public as a pragmatic way of combatting Chiang Kai-shek's* leadership cult and of motivating the culturally backward rural population, but Mao's colleagues assumed that behind closed doors Mao would defer to collective leadership. In addition, rectification required subservience of literary and technical intellectuals to party leadership, as was demonstrated in the purge of Wang Shih-wei. These tensions would explode later in the People's Republic of China.*

Finally, the Yenan period has been a powerful symbol for those interested in the Communist Movement. Mao called on the spirit of Yenan during the Great Leap Forward* in 1958, and Teng Hsiao-p'ing* revived Yenan rectification in the 1980s. Yenan has had symbolic significance for Western scholars as well. Mark Selden saw it as a hopeful answer to a Third World problem, and recently, comparative scholars such as David Apter have sought to analyze the power and function of the "symbolic capital" the CCP accumulated in Yenan.

REFERENCES: Mark Selden, *The Yenan Way in Revolutionary China* (Cambridge, Mass., 1971); Raymond F. Wylie, *The Emergence of Maoism* (Stanford, Calif., 1980);

David E. Apter, "Mao's Republic," *Social Research* 54, no. 4 (Winter 1987): 691–729; *Yenan cheng-feng yün-tung shih-chi* (Chronology of the Yenan Rectification Movement) (Peking, 1982); Tai Ch'ing, "Wang Shih-wei yü *Yeh pai-ho-hua*" (Wang Shih-wei and "Wild Lilies"), *Ming-pao yueh-k'an* (Hong Kong), (May 1988): 3–16 and (June 1988): 24–33.

TIMOTHY CHEEK

YENCHING UNIVERSITY: Leading missionary institution, 1916–1952.

Yenching University, a leader among China's Christian colleges, emphasized the liberal arts, study of China's cultural heritage, and Sino-Western cooperation. Yenching's social gospel approach to reform in China reflected early twentieth-century Western optimism that education and social change could redeem "backward" societies. Although Yenching's ideology conformed for a time to the revolutionary forces remaking China, it ultimately failed to adapt to the rising demands of nationalism.

Yenching was founded between 1915 and 1920 by American missionaries and Chinese Christians who were members of the Life Fellowship (Sheng-ming she), which sought to domesticate Christianity to China. The Chinese intellectuals who had been trained in both the Confucian classics and Western subjects stood astride two cultures as few men ever have. They were firmly committed to their common Christian experience, to China's national salvation, and to Sino-Western cooperation in the remaking of Chinese society. Five influential members of the Life Fellowship who taught at Yenching and shaped the university were Liu Ting-fang, Wu Lei-ch'uan, Hsü Pao-ch'ien, Chao Tzu-ch'en, and Hung Yeh.

They were joined by missionary educators such as John Leighton Stuart, Henry W. Luce, Lucius C. Porter, Howard S. Galt, and John Stewart Burgess. They believed in the immanence of God and the humanity of Jesus and disassociated themselves from the narrow proselytizing of their fundamentalist colleagues. They thought that Christianity and the Western liberal arts tradition could be rooted in Chinese society and become tools for gradually reforming Chinese society along Western lines. By uniting Christianity with Chinese nationalism, they hoped to contribute to international peace and amity.

The university grew rapidly during the years of the New Culture Movement and the Kuomintang Revolution, 1916–1928. Located on a beautiful campus just outside Peking, it was noted for its English-language training, its program in Chinese studies, and the publications of its Harvard–Yenching Institute. It emphasized the liberal arts ideals of general competence, character building, and moral discipline. The school's idealism and commitment to service appealed to patriotic Chinese, and its high-quality curriculum and faculty attracted excellent, bilingual students.

When the Kuomintang established its new national government in 1928, it required foreign-sponsored universities to become more Chinese by registering with the government, including Chinese on their boards of trustees, hiring more Chinese faculty, and equalizing the pay and benefits of Chinese and Western faculty. When Yenching complied, it became less Christian, and more Chinese but its Western liberal arts orientation did not change.

As revolution and war engulfed China after 1931, Yenching faculty and students had to come to terms with the encroachment of Japan upon China, the sharpening of militant nationalism, and the appeals of the emerging Communist movement. Yenching had to resolve three dilemmas if it were to survive in this tumultuous environment.

First, what was the proper role of intellectuals? Yenching planned that its students would earn an excellent education and then fan out into society to lead positive change. By the mid–1930s, however, students began to sense the futility of gradual change and to demand complete catharsis of the old order. Patriotism led many students to abandon the gradualist alternative and join revolutionary movements.

A second problem was the relationship of Yenching to the masses. How could an elite liberal arts university help to alleviate the misery of China's rural masses? Many faculty and students participated in rural reconstruction movements in the 1930s, but others argued that reconstruction was too slow and that nothing less than revolutionizing the rural power structure could save China. Eventually, concern for the masses translated into support for the Communists' revolutionary activities in the countryside.

A third problem was the internationalist stance of the university in the context of Chinese resistance to Japanese aggression and pervasive American influence. When the prospect of a new political order free from outside influence emerged under communism, Yenching's commitment to internationalism could not be sustained.

These problems caused many to question the essential Yenching ideology and mission and to consider synthesizing Christianity and communism. While this was not accomplished by 1949, it was clear that Yenching's confidence in the efficacy of gradual social reform was waning.

The Communist Revolution was greeted enthusiastically on the Yenching campus in 1949, but given Communist ideology, the school could not long continue in its bicultural, cosmopolitan mode. The onset of the Korean War in June 1950 intensified Chinese nationalism and antiforeignism. In 1952 the institution was abolished, and its campus became part of Peking University.

In the long run, Yenching's style of gradual reform and Western liberal arts education failed to galvanize lasting support from the Chinese. Marxism, which effectively blended ideology and revolutionary strategy, held a more powerful appeal. Chinese nationalism, the Communist Revolution, and war with the United States in Korea doomed Yenching's internationalist vision.

REFERENCES: Dwight Edwards, *Yenching University* (New York, 1959): Jessie G. Lutz, *China and the Christian Colleges, 1850–1950* (Ithaca, N.Y., 1971); Philip West, *Yenching University and Sino-Western Relations, 1916–1952* (Cambridge, Mass., 1976).

LOREN W. CRABTREE

YÜAN SHIH-K'AI (September 16, 1859–June 6, 1916): Statesman and controversial strongman of Chinese politics, 1895–1915.

Born into an aristocratic family from Honan Province (Hsiang-cheng County), Yüan Shih-k'ai eschewed the traditional examination route to high office. He first rose to prominence as a military aide to Li Hung-chang* in Korea between 1885 and 1894. Thereafter Yüan emerged as a military reformer and supporter of the Kuang-hsü Emperor until the One Hundred Days Reform* of the summer of 1898. It was at that point (September 1898) that Yüan chose to betray the emperor and his advisers including K'ang Yu-wei* in favor of the Empress Dowager Tz'u-hsi.* Yüan refused to use his small, Western-trained and-armed New Army* to protect the young emperor against the coup d'etat led by the empress dowager and her adviser Prince Jung-lu. The next year Yüan was rewarded with the governorship of neighboring Shantung Province, where he carried out reforms and brutally suppressed the peasant-based, anti-foreign Boxer Rebellion*—driving the Boxers into the neighboring province of Hopei and toward Peking.

The Boxer debacle of 1900–1901, which included the occupation of Peking and Tientsin by foreign troops, the exiling of the empress dowager to Sian, and the bankrupting of the Ch'ing dynasty,* was a turning point in Yüan Shih-k'ai's career. In the new, reform-minded and foreign-dominated government of the last decade of the Ch'ing dynasty (1901–1911), Yüan emerged as the strongman of the period. He was the Bismarck of his time. Yüan led a vigorous effort to effect fundamental reforms of the Chinese bureaucratic, educational, and economic institutions. These reforms included for the first time sending a significant number of students recruited from China's elites to study abroad.

Yüan Shih-k'ai's reforms were part of the Ch'ing dynasty's last-ditch effort led by the empress dowager to save itself, but politically the reforms had the reverse effect. Expectations had been raised. The students abroad, most of whom were in Japan, rallied around Sun Yat-sen* and plotted with elites at home to force the overthrow of the dynasty and the establishment of a parliamentary democracy. The result was a bloodless coup d'etat that toppled the dynasty during the winter of 1911–1912. By the spring of 1912 Yüan Shih-k'ai emerged as president of the new Republic of China.* Yüan continued the economic and bureaucratic modernization program of the previous decade and negotiated major foreign loans to keep his government solvent. But as president he ignored the new Parliament and exercised increasingly dictatorial powers.

Yüan Shih-k'ai's basic maintenance of political power was control of the military. The key to Yüan's rise and maintenance of power was his control of a reform army that by 1908 numbered 60,000 men and was called the Peiyang Army (or Northern Army). As president, Yüan was hailed in the West as a reformer and strongman who was committed to modernization of the Chinese economic and social system. Yüan's children were being educated in the West, and his top American adviser in 1914, Frank Goodnow, was a friend of the American President Woodrow Wilson and a future president of Johns Hopkins University. For Yüan Shih-k'ai the situation changed dramatically in 1915 when his inability to accommodate genuine political reform with economic and social reforms caught up with him. Under pressure from the Japanese over their demands for territorial concessions in Manchuria and elsewhere, Yüan suddenly faced widespread demonstrations against him in the cities. Overcome by a sense of losing control, Yüan reacted in the worst way imaginable. He tried to use military power to restore a Confucian monarchy with himself as emperor and founder of a new dynasty. The results of his political rigidity were disastrous. Yüan's own generals refused to remain loyal in the face of the popular outcry against his Monarchical Movement. Within a year Yüan fell from power and died in June 1916 in disgrace as the subject of ridicule.

As for the Chinese political system as a whole, the effects of Yüan Shih-k'ai's rigidity and failure were devastating. In 1916 Yüan's generals fell immediately to squabbling over national leadership so that central authority disintegrated quickly. The warlordism[*] that plagued China until 1949 was the product of the failure of Yüan's presidency of the Republic of China and short-lived Monarchical Movement. History has largely forgotten Yüan's earlier successes as an effective late Ch'ing reformer.

REFERENCES: Stephen R. MacKinnon, *Power and Politics in Late Imperial China: Yuan Shikai in Tianjin and Beijing* (Berkeley, Calif., 1980); Jerome Ch'en, *Yüan Shih-k'ai: Brutus Assumes the Purple* (Stanford, Calif., 1972); Ernest Young, *The Presidency of Yüan Shih-k'ai: Liberalism and Dictatorship in Early Republican China* (Ann Arbor, Mich., 1977).

STEPHEN R. MACKINNON

YUNG WING (JUNG HUNG) (November 17, 1828–April 21, 1912): The first Chinese graduate from an American university (Yale, 1854) and advocate of the Chinese reform and revolution.

Born in the village of Nan-p'ing (the present-day Shu-chu-hai) in the district of Hsiang-shan (now Chung-shan) near Macao as the third in a family of four children, Yung Wing studied at Western-style Christian mission schools. In 1835 he first entered a school in Macao and later in 1841, the Morrison Educational Society school in Hong Kong. In 1847 the retiring principal of the school, Samuel Robbins Brown, took him to America. He was admitted to Monson Academy at Monson, Massachusetts. In 1852 he became a naturalized American citizen. He entered Yale in 1850 from which he graduated in 1854 as the first Chinese in America and returned to China in April 1855.

Because of his American education, Yung worked as secretary to Dr. Peter Parker, the U.S. commissioner at Canton, interpreter for the Supreme Court in Hong Kong, and translator for the Imperial Customs in Shanghai. He also worked as an agent of the British firm, Dent & Company, to purchase silk and tea in the interior of China in 1859, and later in 1861 he went into the same kind of business for himself and became successful accumulating $25,000 at one time. In 1859 he journeyed to Soochow and Nanking to visit the Taiping[*] rebel chiefs and to learn more about their movement. In talks with the rebel chief, Hung Jen-kan,[*] in Nanking, he proposed a seven-point reform measure for the military, government, finance, and education. None of his reform measures was adopted, nor was he offered any important position.

Yung's career took a different turn when the great leader of the time, Tseng Kuo-fan,* summoned him in 1863. At Tseng's urging, Yung presented a plan for introducing of Western machinery into China. When the plan was adopted, he was sent to America in 1863 to purchase the machinery for the Kiangnan Arsenal. In 1865 he was made Expectant Taotai, the first official position he had ever held, first with the fifth rank and subsquently the fourth. In 1867 Yung helped establish a school for the training of mechanics for Tseng.

In 1872 Yung went back to the United States as head of the Chinese Educational Mission sponsored by the Ch'ing* government. He had supervised 120 Chinese youngsters until the study abroad program was suspended in 1881. In 1874–1875 he was briefly engaged in a journalistic stint for the *Hui-pao* (the *Source Report*, later renamed the *Collective Report*) and the *I-pao* (*Beneficial Report*) until its operation came to an end when chief editor Chu Lien-sheng resigned. He contributed a series of articles to this newspaper and discussed the merits of the reform in response to the *Shen-pao* (the *Detailed Report*). In 1875 he married Mary Louis Kellogg, the daughter of a New England physician, and in 1878–1881 he was appointed joint minister to the United States, Spain, and Peru with Ch'en Lan-pin in Washington. He returned to China in 1882 shortly after the students had left. He came back to Hartford in 1883 and remained there until 1895. His American wife died in 1886, leaving two sons, Morrison Brown Yung and Bartlett B. Yung.

In 1895 Chang Chih-tung, a powerful leader of the Ch'ing regime, asked Yung to negotiate a $15 million loan in London to help China defend itself against Japan. Although his negotiations were not fruitful, he accepted Chang's invitation to return to China. He first worked in Nanking as a secretary and later went to Peking to work on projects to establish a national bank and a railway patterned after the American counterparts, but again with no results. During the Hundred Day Reform Movement* of 1898 he was also involved with K'ang Yu-wei* and Liang Ch'i-ch'ao,* but he deemed it wise to leave Peking for safety. Until 1903 he had sojourned in Shanghai, Hong Kong and Taiwan. In 1900 T'ang Ts'ai-ch'ang, a reform leader, held the so-called Chinese National Assembly in Shanghai to discuss the critical issues of China's reform. Yung Wing was named leader of this gathering. As a result, the Ch'ing government put a price on his head, and he fled the country. Upon his return to the United States in 1903, he unsuccessfully tried to establish an independent kingdom called the "Heavenly Kingdom of Great Brightness and Prosperity (Ta-ming-shun t'ien-kuo)" in south China, along with Hsieh Tsuan-t'ai, Hung Ch'uan-fu, Li Chi-t'ang, and Ou Ch'u-chia. For this movement Yung unsuccessfully tried to obtain moral and material support from the Americans and Chinese in America. Nevertheless, he continued to maintain ties with the reformists. He received Liang Ch'i-ch'ao in Hartford in 1903. In 1905–1906, when K'ang Yu-wei met President Roosevelt twice in the White House, Yung served as an interpreter in the second meeting.

In 1908 Yung sided with the revolutionary Sun Yat-sen.* For the following three years, he worked with Sun's American collaborators, Homer Lea,* W. W. Allen, and Charles B. Boothe. Despite his commitment to the new cause, the American colleagues often questioned Yung's integrity, largely because of his earlier connections with the Taipings for personal glory and partly because of his inordinate interest in financial gains through the American collaborators. He was ultimately branded undesirable. The American collaborators promised and yet failed to provide financial and/or military aid to the Chinese revolutionaries. In early 1912 Sun, then provisional president of the Republic of China,* asked Yung to return home and serve his mother country. But he was too old to do so; at age eighty-four he died of apoplexy in his adopted land in late April 1912.

REFERENCES: Key Ray Chong, *Americans and Chinese Reform and Revolution, 1898–1922* (Lanham, Md., 1984); Edmund H. Worthy, Jr., "Yung Wing in America," *Pacific Historical Review* 34, no. 3 (August 1965): 265–287; Yung Wing, *My Life in China and America* (New York, 1909).

KEY RAY CHONG

CHRONOLOGY OF REVOLUTIONARY CHINA, 1839–1976

1839	Nov. 3–13	Chinese war junks clash with British warship at Ch'uan-pi near Canton. Opium War breaks out in Canton areas.
1840	June	British forces under Rear Admiral George Elliot blockade Canton and then sail north.
1841	May 29–31	San-yüan-li Incident occurs in Canton.
1842	Aug. 24	The Opium War ends with the signing of the Treaty of Nanking.
1843		Hung Hsiu-ch'üan begins to preach Christianity in his native village in Hua County, Kwangtung. His followers include cousin Hung Jen-kan and Feng Yün-shan.
1844		Hung Hsiu-ch'üan and Feng Yün-shan travel and preach in Kwangtung and Kwangsi.
1845	July 10	The Governor-general of Chihli reports that there are many Nien rebels in Kiaochow, Shantung.
1847	July 21	Hung Hsiu-ch'üan and Feng Yün-shan set up the Pai Shang-Ti hui (God Worshippers Society).
	Aug.	Hung Hsiu-ch'üan arrives at Tzu-ching-shan, Kwangsi, where Feng Yün-shan has been preaching since 1845. The number of "God Worshippers" has grown to 2,000. Hung is joined by Yang Hsiu-ch'ing, Hsiao Ch'ao-kuei, Wei Ch'ang-hui, and Shih Ta-k'ai.
1851	Jan. 11	Hung Hsiu-ch'üan declares revolution against the Ch'ing dynasty and establishes the T'ai-p'ing t'ien-kuo (Heavenly Kingdom of Great Peace) at Chin-t'ien Village, Kuei-p'ing County, Kwangsi.

	Sept. 25	Taiping armies capture Yung-an, Kwangsi, and make the first reorganization and policy proclamation.
	Dec. 17	Hung Hsiu-ch'üan proclaims that Yang Hsiu-ch'ing is to be the Tung Wang, Hsiao Ch'ao-kuei the Hsi Wang, Feng Yün-shan the Nan Wang, Wei Ch'ang-hui the Pei Wang, and Shih Ta-k'ai the I Wang.
1852	April 5	The Taipings break the Ch'ing government's siege of Yung-an and head north.
	June 10	Nan Wang, Feng Yün-shan, who is one of the original founders of the Pai Shang-Ti hui, dies at So-Yi-Tu, Kwangsi.
	Sept. 11	Hsi Wang, Hsiao Ch'ao-Kuei, dies in the battle of Changsha.
1853		The Nien rebellion breaks out in Shantung, Honan, Kiangsu, and Anhwei.
	Jan. 12	Taiping armies capture Wuchang.
	March 20	Taiping armies capture Nanking and designate it as the capital.
	May 8	Northern Expedition of the Taipings is launched to topple the Ch'ing dynasty.
	May 19	Concurrent with the Northern Expedition, a second expedition is sent up the Yangtze River.
	Oct. 30	The Northern Expedition of the Taipings moves close to Tientsin.
1854	Feb. 25	The Hunan Army (Hsiang-chün), established under the command of Tseng Kuo-fan, sets out for Hupeh to meet the Taipings.
1855		The Muslim (Panthay) Rebellion breaks out in Yünnan. It lasts eighteen years and finally is pacified by Ts'eng Yü-ying.
	May 31	Taiping's Northern Expedition ends with its collapse.
	Aug.	Nien's leader, Chang Lo-hsing, reorganizes the poorly coordinated bands into five banners and rejuvenates their strength.
1856	Sept. 2	Civil strife reaches a climax in Taiping's capital, T'ien-ching (Nanking). Tung Wang, Yang Hsiu-ch'ing, as well as his subordinates, are slaughtered by Wei Ch'ang-hui (Pei Wang).
	Oct. 8	Twelve Chinese crew members of the *Arrow* are arrested. The British consul at Canton protests against the arrest.
	Nov.	Wei Ch'ang-hui is put to death by Hung Hsiu-ch'üan.
1857	June 2	I Wang, Shih Ta-k'ai, deviates from the main Taiping forces.

	Dec. 28	Anglo-French forces storm Canton.
1858	June 26	The Treaty of Tientsin is signed.
1859	April 22	Hung Jen-kan arrives at T'ien-ching and is appointed as the prime minister. Hung and Li Hsiu-ch'eng, a talented general, are responsible for upholding the Taiping movement in the last phase until 1864.
1860	Aug.-Oct.	The Anglo-French forces attack Peking, burn the Summer Palace, and Emperor Hsien-feng flees to Jehol. Prince Kung takes charge of the peace settlement and signs the Convention of Peking.
1861	March 11	The Tsungli Yamen (Office for General Management) is established at the suggestion of Prince Kung. This action marks the first step of the Self-Strengthening Movement.
	Nov.	Empress Dowager Tz'u-hsi and Prince Kung initiate a coup. They become co-regents of Emperor T'ung-chih (r. 1862–1874).
1862		The Tungan (Muslim) rebellion breaks out in Shensi, Kansu, and Ninghsia. It lasts twelve years until it is suppressed by Tso Tsung-t'ang.
1863	March	Charles G. (Chinese) Gordon, an English officer, is named commander of the "Ever-Victorious Army." He battles with the Taipings in the lower Yangtze areas until May 1864.
1864	June 1	T'ien Wang, Hung Hsiu-ch'üan, commits suicide at age fifty-two. His eldest son, Hung T'ien Kuei-fu, succeeds to the throne.
	July 19	After a two-year siege by Tseng Kuo-ch'üan, T'ien-ching falls to the Ch'ing Army. The Taiping Revolution comes to an end.
1865		Yakub Beg invades Sinkiang and controls Kashgaria (southern Sinkiang) as well as part of northern Sinkiang.
	May 18	The Nien Army and Taiping remnants annihilate Seng-ko-lin-ch'in's army and kill him.
1868	Aug.	Under attack of the Ch'ing Army, commanded by Li Hung-chang and Tso Tsung-t'ang, the Nien Rebellion is suppressed.
1870	June	The Tientsin Massacre occurs.
	Aug. 29	Li Hung-chang is promoted to be the governor-general of Chihli. He becomes the pivot of the Self-Strengthening Movement and foreign policy.
	Nov. 12	Li Hung-chang is appointed the high commissioner of the Northern Ocean.

1871	July 4	Russian general K. P. von Kaufman occupies the Ili Valley. Russia asserts that it will return Ili as soon as Ch'ing's authority is reassumed in Sinkiang.
1872	Aug.	For the first time, on the recommendation of Tseng Kuo-fan and Li Hung-chang, thirty teenage students are sent to the United States to study.
1874	May	Japan sends expeditionary forces to Formosa (Taiwan) to punish the aborigines who killed shipwrecked Ryūkyū and Japanese sailors. The Ch'ing government orders Shen Pao-chen, director of Foochow Dockyard, to defend the island.
1875	Jan. 8	Emperor Kuang-hsü succeeds to the throne (r. 1875–1908). Two dowagers continue to serve as co-regents.
1877	Feb.	The first Chinese Embassy is set up in London with Kuo Sung-t'ao as ambassador to England.
1878	Jan.	The Ch'ing Army, under the command of Tso Tsung-t'ang and Liu Chin-t'ang, recovers Sinkiang except the Ili Valley.
1879	April	Japan annexes Ryūkyū.
1881	Feb. 24	The Treaty of St. Petersburg is signed, with Russia agreeing to return Ili.
1882	July 23	Domestic insurrection erupts in Korea, and Yüan Shih-k'ai is ordered to station there. Li Hung-chang begins to follow a positive policy to counter Japanese influence in Korea.
1883	Dec.	The Sino-French War breaks out over the question of Annam (Vietnam).
1884	Aug. 23	French warships destroy the Foochow Dockyard and the Fukien fleet.
	Dec. 4	In Korea, the Japanese minister and pro-Japanese group stage a coup. Yüan Shih-k'ai puts down this rebellion and rescues the king of Korea.
1885	March	The French Army at Langson, Kwangsi, suffers a major defeat by the Ch'ing Army.
	April 18	In the Tientsin Convention, China confirms Japan's right to dispatch troops to Korea, and Korea's status is reduced to a co-protectorate of China and Japan.
	June	China and France conclude a treaty to end the war. Annam becomes a protectorate of France.
1886	July	Burma, a former tributary state of China, becomes a British protectorate.

1887	Nov.	Kuang-hsüeh hui (the Society for the Diffusion of Christianity and General Knowledge among the Chinese, SDK) is established by missionaries and foreigners in Shanghai.
1894		The Tonghaks rebel against the Korean government. Both China and Japan send troops to suppress the uprising. After this incident, Japan refuses to withdraw its troops and further asks to reform Korean internal administration.
	July 25	Japanese warships sink the steamer *Kaosheng* which carries Chinese soldiers to Korea.
	Aug. 1	China and Japan declare war on each other.
	Sept. 17	The Peiyang fleet is defeated by the Japanese Navy in the Yellow Sea. Later, the surviving Chinese warships surrender, and the admiral commits suicide.
	Oct. 24	Japanese troops cross the Sino-Korean border into Manchuria.
	Nov. 24	Dr. Sun Yat-sen organizes the first revolutionary group, the Revive China Society (Hsing-Chung hui), in Honolulu.
1895		The Japanese Army moves to Liaotung, Shantung, as well as the Pescadores.
	April 17	The Treaty of Shimonoseki is concluded between China and Japan. It includes the cession of Taiwan, the Pescadores, and the Liaotung Peninsula to Japan. Korea is also recognized as an independent state. Japanese are granted the privilege of manufacturing in China.
	April 23	Russia, France, and Germany intervene in the cession of Liaotung Peninsula. Japan finally gives up.
	May 25	The Republic of Taiwan is established with T'ang Ching-sung as president. Taiwanese organize militia to resist the Japanese takeover.
	Aug.	Ch'iang hsüeh-hui (the Society for the Study of National Strengthening) is set up by K'ang Yu-wei in Peking to promote reform movement.
	Oct. 26	The Canton uprising, the first of its kind that is led by Dr. Sun Yat-sun, fails.
	Dec.	Yüan Shih-k'ai is ordered to train a new army at Hsiao-chan, Tientsin. Leaders of this army become the forebears of Peiyang Clique.
1896	June 2	The Sino-Russian secret alliance is concluded. China agrees to the building of the Chinese Eastern Railway by Russia in Manchuria. Russia agrees to defend China against Japanese aggression.

	Oct. 11–23	Dr. Sun Yat-sen is kidnapped by officials of the Ch'ing Embassy in London. After release, he gains a reputation as the leader of the Chinese Revolutionary party.
1897	May–Aug.	During his exile in Europe, Dr. Sun Yat-sen develops the theory of the Three People's Principles (San Min Chu I)—the Principle of the People's National Consciousness (Min-tsu), the Principle of the People's Rights (Min-ch'üan), and the Principle of the People's Livelihood (Min-sheng).
	Oct. 30	Shih-wu hsüeh-t'ang (the School of Current Affairs) is founded in Changsha by reform-minded gentry and provincial government officials. Liang Ch'i-ch'ao is invited to be the chief instructor.
	Nov. 14	Germans, who make an excuse of protecting missionaries in Shantung, seize Kiaochow Bay as their naval base.
	Dec. 15	Russians occupy Port Arthur and Dairen in response to Germany's action in Shantung.
1898	Feb. 10	Great Britain asks for the Yangtze Valley as its sphere of influence. Later, Weihaiwei and Kowloon are leased to the British.
	April 9	France asks for Kwangtung, Kwangsi, and Yünnan as its sphere of influence, as well as the lease of Kwangchow Bay. Japan asks for Fukien as its sphere of influence.
	June 11	The Hundred Day Reform begins. At the urging of K'ang Yu-wei and Liang Ch'i-ch'ao, Emperor Kuang-hsü issues edicts to reform the government, education, industry, and international cultural exchange.
	Sept. 21	The Hundred Day Reform ends with a coup that is instigated by Empress Dowager T'zu-hsi and the conservatives. K'ang Yu-wei and Liang Ch'i-ch'ao flee to Japan. Six Martyrs—Yang Shen-hsiu, K'ang Kuang-jen, Yang Jui, Lin Hsü, Liu Kuang-ti, and T'an Ssu-tung—are executed.
1899		I-ho ch'üan (the Righteous and Harmonious Fists) is encouraged by the governor of Shantung, Yü-hsien, and changes its name to I-ho t'uan (the Righteous and Harmonious Militia, Boxers). Under his aegis, Boxers carry the goal of supporting the Ch'ing and exterminating the foreigners.
	July 15	K'ang Yu-wei establishes the Emperor Protection Society (Pao-huang hui) in Canada.
	Sept. 6	U.S. Secretary of State John Hay declares the Open Door policy on China.

	Dec. 6	Yüan Shih-k'ai replaces Yü-hsien as the governor of Shantung and suppresses the Boxers. Part of their members move to Chihli.
1900	May–June	Under the influence of the conservatives, Empress Dowager T'zu-hsi secretly summons the Boxers to Peking.
	June	The secretary of the Japanese legation, Sugiyama Akira, and the German minister, Clemens von Ketteler, are killed by the Boxers. The foreign legations in Peking are under heavy attacks.
	June 21	The Ch'ing government declares war on all foreign powers.
	June 26	The governors-general of southeastern China take an independent stance against the court order and reach an informal pact with foreign consuls to protect foreign subjects.
	July 6	Taking the chance of a Boxer uprising, Russia invades Manchuria.
	Aug. 9	Tzu-li chün (Independence Army) launches an uprising in Tatung and fails on August 21.
	Aug. 14	The Allied forces of eight countries break into Peking. The emperor and empress dowager flee to Sian.
	Oct. 8–22	The Huichou (Waichow) Uprising, led by Hsing-Chung hui member Cheng Shih-liang, fails because of a shortage of supplies.
	Dec. 24	The Ch'ing government agrees on a joint note of twelve articles, presented by the Allies. Later, it is finalized into the Boxer Protocol, signed on September 7, 1901.
1901	April 21	The Superintendency of Political Affairs (Tu-pan cheng-wu chü) is formed to initiate political reform by the Ch'ing government.
	Nov. 7	Li Hung-chang dies. Yüan Shih-k'ai succeeds Li's post of governor-general of Chihli.
1902	April 27	Chung-kuo Chiao-yü hui (the China Education Association) is set up by Ts'ai Yüan-p'ei and Chang Ping-lin.
1903	June	The *Kiangsu Tribune* (*Su-pao*) case occurs. Its editor, Chang Ping-lin, and the author of *The Revolutionary Army* (*Ko-ming chün*), Tsou Jung, are under arrest. Tsou Jung later dies in prison.
	Nov.	Huang Hsing and Sung Chiao-jen organize the China Revival Society (Hua-hsing hui) at Changsha.
1904	Feb. 6	The Russo-Japanese War breaks out in Manchuria. The Ch'ing government stays neutral.

	Nov.	Ts'ai Yüan-p'ei organizes the Recovery Society (Kuang-fu hui) in Shanghai.
1905	Aug. 20	In order to unify different revolutionary groups including the Hsing-Chung hui, Kuang-fu hui, and Hua-hsing hui, the Chinese United League (Chung-kuo T'ung-meng hui) is formed in Japan. Dr. Sun Yat-sen is elected chairman, and Huang Hsing becomes chief of the executive department.
	Aug.	The Ch'ing government announces the abolition of the civil service examination.
	Nov. 26	*Min Pao* is founded in Japan and serves as the official organ newspaper of the T'ung-meng hui.
	Dec.	The Ch'ing government sends a mission to investigate constitutionalism around the world.
1906	Sept.	The Ch'ing government announces preparations for the establishment of a constitutional monarchy.
	Dec.	Members of T'ung-meng hui and Ko-lao hui as well as coal miners in Ping-hsiang (Kiangsi) and Li-ling (Hunan) revolt against the Ch'ing government. They fail within a month.
1907	May 22–Dec.	Uprisings of Ch'aochou (Huang kang), Huicho (Ch'i-nü hu), An-ch'ing, Ch'inchou, Lienchou, Fang-ch'eng, and Chen-nan kuan, almost all located in southern China and border areas, fail.
1908	March	Uprisings of Ch'inchou, Lienchou, and Ho-k'ou fail again.
	Aug. 27	The Ch'ing government issues the Outline of Constitution.
	Dec. 2	Emperor P'u-i succeeds to the throne.
1909	Oct. 14	Provincial assemblies are established. Because of the Ch'ing government's insincerity toward constitutionalism, some constitutionalists—members of provincial assemblies—begin to sympathize with the revolutionaries.
1910	Feb. 12	The Canton Uprising, instigated by T'ung-meng hui members in the New Army (Hsin chün), takes place.
1911	April 27	The Canton Uprising, led by Huang Hsing, fails and results in the death of Huang-hua kang 72 martyrs.
	May 9	The Ch'ing government formally pronounces the policy of nationalization of railways. This policy stirs up a common resentment of gentry as well as merchants in Hupeh, Hunan, Kwangtung, and Szechwan.
	July 31	T'an Jen-feng, Sung Chiao-jen, and Ch'en Ch'i-mei set up the central China headquarters of the T'ung-meng hui in Shanghai.

	Sept. 7	In Chengtu, a mass of people demand that Viceroy Chao Erh-feng release the leaders arrested in the Railway Protection Movement. Viceroy Chao orders to open fire, and thirty-two people are killed.
	Oct. 10	Revolutionaries in the New Army succeed in taking Wuchang. Hanyang and Hankow fall during the following days. Li Yüan-hung is drafted to be the military governor of Hupeh. Within one and a half months, fifteen provinces declare independence.
	Oct.	Yüan Shih-k'ai is ordered by the Ch'ing government to suppress the rebellion. He adopts the strategy of killing two birds with one stone, that is, putting pressure on both revolutionaries and Manchu aristocrats.
	Dec.	Under the influence of Russia, Outer Mongolia secedes from China.
1912	Jan. 1	The Republic of China is established in Nanking, and Dr. Sun Yat-sen is inaugurated as provisional president.
	Jan. 28	A provisional Senate is established in Nanking.
	Feb. 12	Ch'ing Emperor P'u-i announces abdication of the throne.
	Feb. 13	Dr. Sun Yat-sen tenders his resignation to the provisional Senate.
	Feb. 15	Yüan Shih-k'ai is elected provisional president by the provisional Senate.
	March 10	Yüan Shih-k'ai is inaugurated as provisional president in Peking.
	March 11	The provisional constitution is promulgated.
	Aug. 25	T'ung-men hui, allied with four other small parties, is reorganized into the Kuomintang (the Nationalist party) with Dr. Sun Yat-sen as its chairman and Sung Chiao-jen as its deputy chairman.
1913	March 20	Afraid of the domination of Parliament by the Nationalist party, Yüan Shih-k'ai orders the assassination of Sung Chiao-jen in Shanghai.
	July 12	Li Lieh-chün, military governor of Kiangsi, declares independence. The Second Revolution, instigated by the Nationalist party against Yüan Shih-k'ai, breaks out.
	Sept.	The Second Revolution fails, and Dr. Sun Yat-sen goes into exile to Japan.
1914	Jan. 10	Yüan Shih-k'ai dissolves the Parliament.
	July 8	Dr. Sun Yat-sen reorganizes the Nationalist party into the Chinese Revolutionary party (Chung-hua ko-ming tang) in Japan and continues fighting against Yüan Shih-k'ai.

	Sept.	Taking the opportunity of World War I, Japan invades Shantung—Germany's former sphere of influence.
1915		Hu Shih and Chao Yüan-jen promote the *Pai-hua* (plain language) movement while they are students in the United States.
	Jan. 18	The Japanese minister delivers the Twenty-one Demands to Yüan Shih-k'ai. They contain five groups that grant special privileges to Japan in Shantung, Manchuria, Inner Mongolia, coastal areas, and the steel industry. They require that China employ Japanese advisers in domestic administration and purchase more than 50 percent of its munitions from Japan.
	May 9	Yüan Shih-k'ai accepts the first four groups of the Twenty-one Demands.
	Aug.	Dr. Frank J. Goodnow publishes an article to endorse Yüan's monarchical movement.
	Aug.	Yang Tu organizes the Peace-Planning Society (Ch'ou-an hui) to promote constitutional monarchy.
	Sept. 15	Ch'en Tu-hsiu founds the *Youth Magazine (Ch'ing-nien tsa-chih)* in Shanghai. It is renamed the *New Youth (Hsin Ch'ing-nien)* the next year.
	Nov. 20	The National People's Representative Assembly, manipulated by Yüan, disregards the constitution and unanimously approves monarchy.
	Dec. 12	Yüan Shih-k'ai accepts the throne.
	Dec. 25	Ts'ai Ao and other revolutionaries organize the National Protection Army (Hu-kuo chün) to oppose the Monarchical Movement and declare independence of Yünnan.
1916	March 22	Under pressure from revolutionaries and his own generals, Yüan Shih-k'ai gives up the monarchy.
	June 6	The warlord period begins with the death of Yüan Shih-k'ai. The Peiyang Clique later splits into two: the Anhwei Clique under Tuan Ch'i-jui and the Chihli Clique under Feng Kuo-chang.
	Dec.	Ts'ai Yüan-p'ei is appointed chancellor of National Peking University, which becomes the center of intellectual ferment.
1917	July 1–12	Chang Hsün, military governor of Anhwei, who is summoned by President Li Yüan-hung to counterbalance the power of Prime Minister Tuan Ch'i-jui, restores the abdicated Ch'ing emperor, P'u-i, to the throne. Under attacks from the warlords, the Restoration Movement ends within twelve days.

	Aug.	Dr. Sun Yat-sen establishes a military government in Canton and starts the Constitution Protection Movement (Hu-fa yün-tung, protecting the 1912 provisional constitution).
1918	May 4	Dr. Sun Yat-sen is forced out of the military government and lives in Shanghai where he devotes himself to writing the *Outline of National Reconstruction* (*Chien-kuo fang-lüeh*).
	May 15	Lu Hsün publishes the "Diary of a Madman" in the *New Youth*.
	Autumn	The New Tide Society (Hsin-ch'ao she) is founded. Among its members are Li Ta-chao, Ch'ü Ch'iu-pai, Chang Kuo-t'ao, and Mao Tse-tung.
1919	May 4	Students in Peking rally to protest the decision of the Versailles Peace Conference on the issue of Shantung. Mass demonstrations break out throughout China.
	Sept. 16	Chou En-lai organizes the Awakening Society (Chüeh-wu she) in Tientsin.
	Oct. 10	Dr. Sun Yat-sen reorganizes the Chinese Revolutionary party into the Chinese Nationalist party (Chung-kuo kuo-min tang, KMT).
1920	March	The Third Comintern sends Grigorri Voitinsky to China to help with the founding of the Chinese Communist party (CCP).
	July	War between the Anhwei Clique and the Chihli Clique breaks out. The Anhwei Clique is defeated, and Tuan Ch'i-jui resigns.
1921	April	A republican government, headed by Dr. Sun Yat-sen, is established in Canton versus the government in Peking, which is dominated by the Chihli and the Feng-t'ien cliques.
	July 23–31	The First Congress of the Chinese Communist party is held in Shanghai and Chia-hsing. The party is led by Ch'en Tu-hsiu, as general secretary, and Li Ta-chao. Chang Kuo-t'ao, Li's student, is head of the Department of Organization.
	Dec.	Lu Hsün publishes the "True Story of Ah Q."
1922	April	War between the Chihli Clique and the Fengt'ien Clique breaks out. The Chihli Clique, under Ts'ao K'un and Wu P'ei-fu, defeats Chang Tso-lin. Chang retains his independent control of Manchuria.
	June 16	Ch'en Chiung-ming leads a mutiny, and Dr. Sun Yat-sen is forced out of Canton.

	Aug.	The CCP Central Committee concludes the policy of permitting individual Communists to join the KMT. Li Ta-chao becomes the first CCP member to join the KMT. This is the first United Front between CCP and KMT.
	Sept.	KMT leaders approve the policy of "alliance with the Soviet Union, admission of the Communists" (Lien-O yung-Kung).
1923	Jan. 26	Dr. Sun Yat-sen and Adolf Joffe, the Soviet representative, issue a joint manifesto. In this manifesto, both of them agree that the Communist organization and the Soviet system are not suitable for China. But China can rely on Soviet assistance to achieve the goal of national unification and independence.
	Aug. 10	Chiang Kai-shek leads a KMT delegation to visit the Soviet Union.
	Oct. 5	Ts'ao K'un is elected president of the Peking government by bribing members of the Parliament.
	Oct.	Michael Borodin arrives at Canton and serves as political adviser of the KMT to reorganize the party.
1924	Jan. 20–30	The First National Congress of KMT is held in Canton. Communists are appointed to several key positions of the reorganized KMT.
	May 3	The Whampoa Military Academy is founded. Chiang Kai-shek is appointed principal and Liao Chung-k'ai, party representative. CCP members, like Chou En-lai and Yeh Chien-ying, serve as acting director of the Political Education Department and instructor, respectively.
	Sept.	The second Chihli–Fengt'ien War breaks out. Feng Yü-hsiang's mutiny causes the defeat of the Chihli Clique. Feng welcomes Dr. Sun to Peking to hold a conference for national unification and reconstruction.
	Dec. 31	Dr. Sun Yat-sen proceeds to Peking.
1925	March 12	Dr. Sun Yat-sen dies in Peking. The KMT leadership falls to Wang Ching-wei and Hu Han-min.
	May 30	A mass demonstration by students and workers in Shanghai to protest British and Japanese brutality ends with the killing and arrest of Chinese.
	July 1	The Nationalist government is established in Canton with Wang Ching-wei as chairman.
	Nov.	Fifteen rightist KMT Executive and Supervisory committee members form a Western Hills (Hsi-shan) Faction in Peking against the Lien-O yung-Kung policy.
1926	March 20	The warship *Chung-shan* incident occurs, and that is Chiang Kai-shek's first break with the Communists.

	July	Chiang Kai-shek is appointed commander-in-chief of the Northern Expedition Army. The Nationalist government begins the mission to unify China.
	Sept.	Feng Yü-hsiang's National People's Army takes the pledge to ally with Chiang's army against the warlords.
	Sept.	The Northern Expedition Army occupies Wuhan and crushes the major forces of Wu P'ei-fu.
	Nov.	Sun Ch'uan-fang's army is defeated by the Northern Expedition Army at Nanch'ang.
1927	Jan.	The Nationalist government moves to Wuhan.
	March	The Northern Expedition Army takes Shanghai and Nanking.
	April 12	Chiang Kai-shek orders the purge of Communists. With the help of Hu Han-min, he establishes another Nationalist government in Nanking. The Wuhan government is controlled by leftist KMT members (headed by Wang Ching-wei), Soviet advisers (like Michael Borodin), and the CCP.
	July 15	The Wuhan Nationalist government announces its split with the CCP. It reunites with the Nanking government afterward. The First United Front between the KMT and the CCP ends.
	Aug. 1	The Communist Nanch'ang Uprising fails.
	Aug. 7	In a provisional Politburo meeting, Ch'ü Ch'iu-pai replaces Ch'en Tu-hsiu as general secretary of the CCP. The CCP adopts a new policy of riot and uprising.
	Sept.–Oct.	Mao Tse-tung leads the Autumn Harvest Uprising in Hunan and Hupeh. He then retreats to the Ching-kang Mountain in the border areas of Hunan and Kiangsi.
	Oct.	P'eng P'ai establishes the first soviet government in Hai-feng and Lu-feng, Kwangtung.
	Dec. 11	The Canton Uprising by the CCP fails.
1928	Feb.	With the support of Feng Yü-hsiang and Yen Hsi-shan, Chiang Kai-shek resumes the Northern Expedition.
	April	Chu Teh and Ch'en Yi join Mao Tse-tung's forces at Ching-kang Mountain and form the Fourth Red Army.
	June 4	Chang Tso-lin is assassinated by the Japanese Kwantung Army at Huangkut'un while fleeing to Manchuria.
	June-July	The Sixth Party Congress of the CCP is held in Moscow. Because of the failure of many uprisings, Ch'ü Ch'iu-pai is replaced by Hsiang Chung-fa and Li Li-san.

	Oct.	An Outline of Political Tutelage and the five-yüan structure are proclaimed. Chiang Kai-shek is elected president of the Nationalist government in Nanking.
	Dec. 29	Chang Hsüeh-liang announces his support of the Nationalist government. Major parts of China are now united.
1929	June	In the Second Plenum of the Sixth CCP Central Committee, the Li Li-san line is formed. Li recognizes the coming of a new tide of revolution and urges CCP members to instigate strikes and military attacks in the cities.
	Dec. 28	Mao Tse-tung makes his report on the "Rectification of Incorrect Ideas in the Party" at the Kut'ien Conference in Fukien.
1930	April–Nov.	Yen Hsi-shan, Feng Yü-hsiang, and Li Tsung-jen rebel against the Nationalist government. Civil war erupts in north and central China.
	Dec.	Mao Tse-tung strikes down large number of opponents during the Fut'ien Incident, but formal party leadership bestowed elsewhere.
1930 1931	Dec.– Jan.	Chiang Kai-shek launches the First Campaign of Encirclement and Extermination against the Communists in Kiangsi.
	Jan.	After criticism of the failure of the Li Li-san line in the Fourth Plenum of the Sixth CCP Central Committee, Ch'en Shao-yü (Wang Ming), Ch'in Pang-hsien (Po Ku), and the so-called Twenty-eight Bolsheviks take over the Politburo.
	April–May	The Second Campaign of Encirclement and Extermination is launched.
	July–Sept.	The Third Campaign against the Communists is cut short by the Mukden Incident.
	Sept. 18	The Japanese Kwantung Army attacks Chinese military camps and occupies Mukden. Manchuria is occupied by Japan.
	Nov. 7–20	The First All-China Congress of the Soviets is held in Juichin, Kiangsi. A Soviet Republic is established with Mao Tse-tung as chairman of the Central Executive Committee of the All-China Soviet Government, as well as chairman of the Council of People's Commissars.
1932	Jan. 28	The Japanese Army invades Shanghai. The Nationalist Nineteenth Route Army resists fiercely.
	March 9	Manchukuo, headed by the last Ch'ing Emperor P'u-i, is established by the Japanese.

	Nov.	The Communist Army, under Chang Kuo-t'ao, retreats from Hupeh and Anhwei to northern Szechwan and southern Shensi.
1933	Jan.–April	The Fourth Campaign of Encirclement and Extermination is launched against the Communists in Kiangsi.
	Jan.	The CCP Central Committee moves from Shanghai to Kiangsi.
1933 1934	Oct.– Oct.	The last and Fifth Campaign of Encirclement and Extermination is launched.
1933 1934	Nov.– Jan.	The Nineteenth Route Army rebels against the Nationalist government and establishes the People's Revolutionary government at Foochow, Fukien.
1934	Jan.	In the Second All-China Congress of the Soviets, Mao Tse-tung loses his power to the Twenty-eight Bolsheviks. Chang Wen-t'ien takes Mao's chairmanship of the Council of People's Commissars.
	July–Sept.	Mao Tse-tung is under house arrest by the Twenty-eight Bolsheviks at Yü-tu, Kiangsi.
1934 1935	Oct.– Oct.	The Long March begins. Because of Comintern representative Li T'e's incorrect military strategy, the CCP starts a 25,000 *li* (6,000 miles) retreat, along southwest and west China, and finally reaches northern Shensi.
1935	Jan.	In the Tsunyi (Kweichow) Conference, with the support of Chu Teh and other military commanders, Mao Tse-tung criticizes the current leadership and regains power from the Twenty-eight Bolsheviks.
	July	In the Maoerhkai Conference, at the border of Szechwan, Tsinghai, Sikang, and Kansu, the First Front Red Army, under Mao Tse-tung and other Central Committee members from the Kiangsi Soviet, splits with the Fourth Front Red Army, which is led by Chang Kuo-t'ao. Mao heads north, and Chang heads west.
	Aug. 1	CCP issues a manifesto of the Anti-Japanese United Front and begins to show a willingness to cooperate with the Nationalist government against Japanese aggression.
	Oct.	Mao's forces finally arrive in Wuch'i-cheng, Paoan County, Shensi.
	Dec.	In order to counterbalance the Autonomous Movement of North China sponsored by the Japanese, the Nationalist government establishes a Hopeh-Chahar Political Council.
1936	Dec. 12	The Sian Incident occurs. Chang Hsüeh-liang and Yang Hu-ch'eng end the campaign against the Red Army and kidnap Chiang Kai-shek in Sian.

	Dec. 25	Upon the intervention of the Soviet Union and the CCP, Chiang Kai-shek is released and Chang Hsüeh-liang is put under house arrest by Chiang. The war against the Communists in northern Shensi is terminated.
1937	July 7	The Japanese Army attacks the Chinese garrison and occupies Wanping, Hopeh. It is called the Marco Polo Bridge (Lukouchiao) Incident. The Sino-Japanese War begins.
	July 15	The CCP issues a Together We Confront the National Crisis (Kung-fu kuo-nan) manifesto and pleads for cooperation with the KMT.
	Aug. 13	The Japanese Army invades Shanghai and opens the second battle front.
	Aug.	The Communist Red Army in Shensi is reorganized into the Eighth Route Army, led by Chu Teh and P'eng Te-huai.
	Dec.	Nanking is taken by the Japanese Army. The Rape of Nanking takes place when Japanese soldiers massacre more than 200,000 Chinese civilians. The Nationalist government retreats to Chungking.
	Dec.	The Communist Red Army south of the Yangtze River is reorganized into the New Fourth Army, and is led by Yeh T'ing and Hsiang Ying.
1938	March 25– April 6	The Chinese Army defeats the Japanese Army at Tai-erh-chuang, Shantung.
	Oct. 21	Canton is lost to the Japanese Army.
	Oct. 25	The Nationalist government orders the evacuation of Wuhan. The fall of Wuhan ends the first phase of the war.
	Dec. 18	Wang Ching-wei issues a statement in Hanoi and starts the peace movement with Japan.
1939	Dec.	The Chinese Army launches a winter offensive, but it dies down until April of the next year.
1940	March	Wang Ching-wei establishes a puppet government in Nanking.
1941	Jan.	The frictions between CCP and KMT forces in Japanese-occupied areas reach a climax. The New Fourth Army is disbanded by the KMT. The New Fourth Army Incident ends the Second United Front between the two parties.
	Dec. 7	The Japanese Navy attacks Pearl Harbor. The Pacific War begins.
	Dec. 9	The Nationalist government officially declares war on Japan, Germany, and Italy.

1942	Feb.	A Rectification Movement, which is designed to correct the subjectivism, sectarianism, and formalism in ideology, party organization, and literature, begins in Communist-controlled areas.
	May 2–23	A Forum on Art and Culture is convened at Yenan and Mao Tse-tung postulates several guidelines that literary people are to follow.
1943	Dec. 1	After the meeting of Chiang Kai-shek, Winston Churchill, and Franklin D. Roosevelt in Cairo, a declaration is issued to demand the unconditional surrender of Japan and the return of Manchuria and Taiwan to China.
1944	April	The Honan Campaign of Operation Ichigo begins. Loyang and Chengchou are taken by the Japanese Army. The defense line of the Chinese Army along the Yellow River collapses.
	May	The Hunan Campaign of Operation Ichigo is launched after the conclusion of the Honan Campaign. Changsha is occupied on June 18.
	Aug. 8	After a forty-seven-day siege, Hengyang (Hunan) is lost.
	Sept.–Dec.	Owing to the difficulty of logistics, the Kwangsi-Kweichow Campaign of Operation Ichigo is finally halted.
1945	Feb.	In the Yalta Conference, President Franklin D. Roosevelt signs away Manchurian sovereignty to Russia in exchange for Russia's entry into the Pacific War against Japan.
	April 23	The Seventh National Party Congress of the CCP is held in Yenan. Mao Tse-tung's leadership is firmly consolidated at this meeting.
	Aug. 8	Russian troops march into Manchuria.
	Aug. 10–11	Chu Teh orders the PLA to accept Japanese surrender and to seize military strongholds. Civil war breaks out in China.
	Aug. 14	Japan officially surrenders.
	Aug. 14	The Sino-Soviet Treaty of Friendship and Alliance is signed granting Russia the privileges of railways and ports in Manchuria.
	Aug. 28–Oct. 10	Mao Tse-tung leads a delegation to Chungking to negotiate with Chiang Kai-shek about postwar political and military arrangements.
	Dec.	General George C. Marshall arrives in China to mediate between the KMT and the CCP.

1946	Jan. 10–31	The Political Consultative Conference is convened in Chungking. All participants agree on forming a multiparty State Council, a cabinet system, and a provincial government.
	July–Oct.	Nationalist forces advance and win major battles against the Communist PLA.
	Nov. 25	Defying the CCP's nonrecognition, the National Assembly is held in Nanking. A new constitution is adopted on December 25 the same year. Later, the National Assembly elects Chiang Kai-shek as president and Li Tsung-jen as vice-president.
1947	Jan. 6	U.S. mediation fails, and General George C. Marshall is recalled by President Harry Truman.
	Feb. 28	The Taiwanese rebel against the KMT ruling in Taiwan.
	March	Nationalist forces capture Yenan.
	July	From this point on, the PLA advances to Honan, Hopeh, and gets an upper hand in the civil war.
	Oct.	The Outline of Agrarian Law is promulgated by the CCP, and land reform is formalized in "liberated areas."
	Oct.–Dec.	Lin Piao's forces gain a major victory in Manchuria.
1948	Sept.	The PLA, under Ch'en Yi, occupies Shantung.
1948 1949	Oct.–Jan.	The battle of Huai-Hai (Anhwei) is a major defeat of the Nationalist forces.
1948	Nov.	The Manchurian campaign ends with the victory of the Communists.
1949	Jan.	The garrison of Peking and Tientsin surrenders to the PLA.
	Jan. 21	Chiang Kai-shek resigns from the presidency.
	April 21	The PLA crosses the Yangtze River.
	April 23	Nanking is taken by the PLA. The Nationalist government, headed by acting president Li Tsung-jen, moves to Canton.
	Sept. 21	The People's Political Consultative Conference is held by the CCP and pro-Communist parties in Peking. An Organic Law of the Central People's Government and a Common Program are adopted.
	Oct. 1	Mao Tse-tung proclaims the formal inauguration of the People's Republic of China.
	Dec. 16	Mao Tse-tung visits Soviet Union and announces his "lean to one side" policy.

1949–53		Land reform in Taiwan is sponsored by Governor Ch'en Ch'eng. This reform is divided into three stages—37.5 percent rent reduction, sales of public land, and land to the tillers.
1950	Feb. 14	The Sino-Soviet Treaty of Friendship, Alliance, and Mutual Assistance is signed. The Moscow–Peking Axis is established.
	March 1	Chiang Kai-shek resumes the presidency of The Republic of China in Taiwan. Taipei becomes the temporary capital.
	April 30	The Marriage Law is promulgated in Mainland China.
1950 1952	June 14–	The Land Reform Law is promulgated, and the Land Reform Movement is pushed for the whole of China. Landlord and rich peasant classes are eliminated.
1950	Oct. 14	The PLA under P'eng Te-huai crosses the Yalu River and participates in the Korean War. The U.S.–China relationship is severed.
1950 1953	Nov.–	The Resist-America Aid-Korea Campaign is launched.
1951	Feb. 23	The Campaign for the Elimination of Counterrevolutionaries begins.
1952	May–	Criticism of the movie *Wu Hsün Chuan* (Biography of Wu Hsün) starts the thought reform of the intellectuals.
1952	Jan. 1	The Three-Anti (*San-fan*) Movement against corruption, waste, and bureaucratism in the Communist party commences.
	Jan.	The Five-Anti (*Wu-fan*) Movement against bribery, tax evasion, theft of state property in carrying out government contracts, theft of state economic secrets, against cheating on workmanship and materials targets the business community.
1953		The First Five-year Plan officially starts. Actually, it is not put into practice until two and half years later.
	Feb.	Semisocialist agricultural producers' cooperatives begin to form in the rural areas.
1954	Feb.	Kao Kang and Jao Shu-shih, two senior party leaders, are charged with antiparty activities and are expelled from office.
	April 26	Chou En-lai leads a delegation to the Geneva Conference to discuss the issues of Korea and Indochina.
	Sept. 15–28	The First National People's Congress is convened in Peking and adopts a state constitution.

	Oct.	A campaign against *A Study on the Dream of the Red Chamber*, which involves its author Yü P'ing-po as well as Hu Shih and other scholars, is launched.
1955	Jan.	The Hu Feng Affair erupts and brings another purge in the cultural and educational circle.
	Apr. 18–24	A Chinese delegation headed by Chou En-lai participates in the Bandung Conference in Indonesia. The peaceful coexistence policy is posted.
	July	Mao Tse-tung pushes forward the once-slackened cooperative movement by rallying support from provincial party leaders.
1955 1956	Oct.–	Socialization of private-owned enterprise begins. Capitalists are virtually transformed into managers of their own shops and factories.
1956	May 2	Mao Tse-tung declares the "Let One Hundred Flowers Blossom, Let One Hundred Schools Contend" policy and asks intellectuals as well as "democratic" party members to criticize state policy.
	June 15–30	The Model Ruling for a Socialist Agricultural Producers' Cooperative is promulgated at the third session of the First National People's Congress. By the end of this year, more than 90 percent of rural households join the cooperatives.
	Sept. 7–27	The Eighth Party Congress is convened. A retrenchment policy of agricultural collectivization and collective leadership is formulated.
1957	June	The Hundred Flowers Campaign ends with the Anti-Rightist Movement against intellectual dissidents.
	Sept.	The Socialist Education Movement is launched in the countryside.
1958	May 5–23	In the Second Plenum of the Eighth Party Congress, a General Line of Socialist Construction, that is, construction based on the principle of more, faster, better, and more economically is established.
	Aug. 4–13	After Mao Tse-tung inspects and praises several model communes, the People's Communes mushroom all over China.
	Oct.	A movement to build backyard furnaces is promoted by the government.
	Nov.	In order to free women from traditional household works, mass dining halls and nurseries are built in the People's Communes.

1958–60		The period of the Great Leap Forward begins. A new strategy of development—Walking on Two Legs—is put into practice.
1959	March 17–31	Tibetans rebel against the Chinese Communists' ruling. The Dalai Lama goes into exile to India.
	April 27	At the Second National People's Congress, Liu Shao-ch'i is elected state chairman.
	Aug.	Defense minister P'eng Te-huai criticizes Mao's policy of the Great Leap Forward and the People's Communes in the Lushan Conference of the Politburo.
	Sept. 17	P'eng Te-huai is dismissed from the Ministry of Defense and is replaced by Lin Piao.
1959–61		Owing to the dislocation of economic resources, which is caused by the policy of the Three Red Banners (the Great Leap Forward, the General Line, and the People's Communes) and bad weather, China experiences a severe economic depression.
1960	Aug.	General Secretary Nikita Khrushchev recalls all Soviet technical advisers in China. The Sino-Soviet relationship is severed over the issues of Communist ideology, leadership in the Communist bloc, as well as China's internal politics.
	Sept.	In order to cope with the country's economic disarray, the Politburo adopts a new guildline of Adjustment, Consolidation, Strengthening, Uplift.
1961		Wu Han first publishes the story "Hai Jui Scolds the Emperor" in the *People's Daily* in June 1959. It is rewritten into a historical play, "Hui Jui Dismissed from Office," and is put on stage in the early part of the year.
1962	Jan.	Two policies—Three Privates and One Guarantee (*San-ssu i-pao*) and Three Reconciliations and One Reduction (*San-ho i-shao*)—are endorsed and implemented by Liu Shao-ch'i and Teng Hsiao-p'ing.
	Sept. 24–27	The Tenth Plenum of the Eighth Central Committee is held in Peking. In this meeting, Mao Tse-tung reminds his fellow comrades: "Never forget class struggle." His concern is about the present development of ideology toward the restoration of "capitalism, feudalism, and revisionism."
1962 1965	Sept.–	Another Socialist Education Movement is launched in the countryside. This campaign aims at corrupt local cadres and capitalist tendency. But it is resisted by local as well as central officials, such as P'eng Chen, mayor of Peking.

516

	Oct.–Nov.	Military clashes along Sino-Indian borders over the sovereignty of Aksai–Chin occur.
1963	Feb.	The Learn from Lei Feng Campaign begins. Later, Mao Tse-tung even asks the entire country to learn from the PLA. Lin Piao emerges as a strong supporter of Mao Tse-tung.
1964	June	In the Peking Opera Festival on Contemporary Themes, Chiang Ch'ing promotes her revolutionary drama.
	June	A cultural Rectification Campaign is launched but is blocked by P'eng Chen, head of the Five-Person Cultural Revolution Group.
	Dec.	At the Third National People's Congress, Chou En-lai proposes the Four Modernizations scheme.
1965	Nov. 10	Under the direction of Mao Tse-tung, Yao Wen-yüan publishes an article entitled "Comment on the Newly Composed Historical Play 'Hai Jui Dismissed from Office' " in *Wen-hui Pao* in Shanghai. This article starts the Great Proletarian Cultural Revolution.
	Dec.	Because of the disagreement with Lin Piao's people's war thesis, Lo Jui-ch'ing is dismissed as PLA chief-of-staff and becomes the first victim of the Cultural Revolution.
1966	Feb.	P'eng Chen brings forward the February Outline Report and tries to counter the allegation from the Maoists. But this report is opposed by another document from the Forum on the Work in Literature and Art for the Armed Forces in April.
	April 18	The *Liberation Army Daily* publishes "Hold High the Great Red Banner of Mao Tse-tung's Thought and Actively Participate in the Great Socialist Cultural Revolution." This shows the PIA's support of Mao.
	May	Several articles attacking Wu Han, Teng T'o, and Liao Mo-sha—the so-called Three Family Village (San Chia Ts'un)—are published.
	May 16	In the enlarged Politburo meeting, the February Outline Report is overruled, P'eng Chen is dismissed, and a new Central Cultural Revolutionary Committee is formed, with Ch'en Po-ta as its chairman and Chiang Ch'ing as vice-chairwoman.
	June	Peking University Nieh Yüan-tzu posts a wallposter that attacks the school authority. This action is manipulated by the Maoists to arouse other students to stand up against their school authorities.

	Aug. 1–12	In the Eleventh Plenum of the Eighth Central Committee, Mao Tse-tung attacks those who are "taking the capitalist road," namely, Liu Shao-ch'i and Teng Hsiao-p'ing, and he also announces the creation of the Red Guards (Hung wei-ping).
	Aug. 1	Lin Piao is promoted to the first vice-chairmanship of the party.
	Aug. 5	Mao Tse-tung writes his own first wall poster: "Bomb the Headquarters."
	Aug. 18	A Decision Concerning the Great Proletarian Cultural Revolution (Sixteen Points) is issued.
	Aug. 18–31	A campaign aimed at destroying Four Olds (old thoughts, old culture, old customs, old habits) is launched.
	Nov.	Liu Shao-ch'i and Teng Hsiao-p'ing become the known targets of wallposter attacks.
1967	Jan.	Under the Maoists' support, the Shanghai worker coalition, headed by Wang Hung-wen, seizes control of the city and establishes the Shanghai Commune in February. Later, it is changed into the Shanghai Revolutionary Committee.
	Jan.	The PLA intervenes in the Cultural Revolution to restore order. Revolutionary Committees, including regional PLA commanders, party cadres, and radicals, are formed.
	Feb.	Top-ranking leaders of the party criticize the policy of the Cultural Revolution, which is known as the "February Countercurrent."
	March	A case of sixty-one renegades in which Liu Shao-ch'i is involved is revealed.
	July	Local radicals rob the ammunition depots and start large-scale bloody fighting throughout China.
	July 20	Wuhan garrison troops and local worker coalition—The Army of One Million Heroes—mutiny and arrest negotiators from the central government.
	July–Aug.	Liu Shao-ch'i and Teng Hsiao-p'ing are subject to intensified mass-struggle meetings and, finally, are placed under house arrest.
	Aug.	A campaign aimed at the May 16 Antirevolutionary Corps is launched against the ultraleftist tendency of some Maoists. Wang Li, Kuan Feng, and Ch'i Pen-yü are purged.
1968	Aug. 12– Sept. 25	Mao Tse-tung's Thought Worker Propaganda Teams begin to move into university campuses and restore order.

	Sept.	By now, Revolutionary Committees have seized the power of all provinces, autonomous regions, and large municipalities.
	Oct. 13	May 7 cadre schools are established to reeducate party cadres as well as intellectuals through hard labor.
	Oct.	The Twelfth Plenum of the Eighth Central Committee confirms that Liu Shao-ch'i has been ousted from all party and government posts. He dies in humiliation one year later.
	Dec.	Mao Tse-tung decides to reduce the disturbances of the Red Guards; they are sent down to the countryside to learn from the peasants.
1969	March 2	Sino-Soviet border clashes take place on Chen-pao Island (Damansky Island) in the Ussuri River.
	April	In the Ninth Party Congress, military commanders and leaders of the Cultural Revolutionary Group gain power in the Central Committee. Lin Piao is designated as Mao's successor.
1970	Aug.	In the Second Plenum of the Ninth Central Committee at Lushan, Mao Tse-tung and Lin Piao openly split on the issues of state chairmanship and the thesis of genius.
	Dec.	Mao Tse-tung, allying with Chou En-lai, launches a campaign to criticize Ch'en Po-ta as well as other Lin Piao's supporters.
1971	March	Lin Li-kuo, Lin Piao's son, and other conspirators gather in Shanghai and plan the "5–7–1 Engineering Outline" for armed uprising.
	July 9	Dr. Henry Kissinger visits Peking. U.S. President Richard Nixon announces that he will visit China.
	Aug.–Sept.	Mao Tse-tung inspects the central and southern provinces to dissuade regional PLA commanders from supporting Lin Piao.
	Sept. 13	When Lin's plot is discovered, he and his conspirators fly to the Soviet Union, but the airplane crashes in the Mongolian People's Republic.
	Oct. 15	The People's Republic of China is admitted into the United Nations and replaces the seat of the Republic of China.
	Dec.	The Anti-Lin Piao Campaign is launched. More than a hundred central and provincial party as well as military leaders are purged.
1972		Yen Chia-kan, vice-president of the Republic of China in Taiwan, and Chiang Ching-kuo, the premier and eldest son of Chiang Kai-shek, begin a process of power transfer within the KMT.

	Feb. 21	President Richard Nixon visits China. The Shanghai Communiqué opens a new page of Sino-American relations.
	Sept. 25	Japanese Prime Minister Tanaka Kakuei visits China. China and Japan agree to establish diplomatic relations.
1973	March	Owing to Chou En-lai's failing health, Teng Hsiao-p'ing is rehabilitated to the vice-premiership to help Chou.
	Aug. 24–28	In the Tenth Party Congress, Chiang Ch'ing, Chang Ch'un-ch'iao, Yao Wen-yüan, and Wang Hung-wen, later called the Gang of Four, are elected into the Politburo.
1973 1974	Aug.– Jan.	The Anti-Lin, Anti-Confucius Campaign is launched. The Cultural Revolutionary Group uses this movement to harass Chou En-lai who represents the group of moderate party cadres.
1975	Jan. 13–17	In the Fourth National People's Congress, struggle between the moderate party elders and the Cultural Revolutionary Group continues. A plan of Four Modernizations is revealed.
	April 5	Chiang Kai-shek dies in Taiwan, and Yen Chia-kan succeeds the presidency.
	Aug.	The campaign criticizing the novel *Water Margin* is launched. The Cultural Revolutionary Group attacks Chou En-lai and Teng Hsiao-p'ing.
1976	Jan. 8	Chou En-lai dies.
	April 5	The T'ienanmen Square Incident breaks out in Peking. The Cultural Revolutionary Group violently suppresses demonstrators who support Teng Hsiao-p'ing and oppose the Gang of Four.
	April 7	Hua Kuo-feng, the former party chairman of Hunan Province and minister of public security, is appointed premier to succeed Chou En-lai. At the same time, Teng Hsiao-p'ing is dismissed from all party and government posts.
	July 6	Chu Teh dies.
	July 28	The Tangshan (Hopeh) earthquake causes more than 700,000 casualties.
	Sept. 9	Mao Tse-tung dies, and the succession crisis reaches its climax.
	Oct. 6	Chiang Ch'ing, Chang Ch'un-ch'iao, Yao Wen-yüan, and Wang Hung-wen are under arrest in a coup that is initiated by Hua Kuo-feng, Teng Hsiao-p'ing, and Yeh Chien-ying. Hua Kuo-feng becomes chairman of the CCP and chairman of the party's military commission. The Great Proletarian Cultural Revolution officially ends.

BIBLIOGRAPHY

Academy of Sciences of the USSR, Institute of Far Eastern Studies. *Noveĭsaia istoriia Kitaia, 1917–1927.* (Modern history of China, 1917–1927.) Moscow: Nauka, 1983.

———. *Noveĭsaia istoriia Kitaia, 1928–1949.* (Modern history of China, 1928–1949.) Moscow: Nauka, 1984.

Anderson, Marston. *The Limits of Realism: Chinese Fiction in the Revolutionary Period.* Berkeley: University of California Press, 1989.

Andors, Phyllis. *The Unfinished Liberation of Chinese Women, 1949–1980.* Bloomington: Indiana University Press, 1983.

Anschel, Eugene. *Homer Lea, Sun Yat-Sen, and the Chinese Revolution.* New York: Praeger, 1984.

Armstrong, J. D. *Revolutionary Diplomacy: Chinese Foreign Policy and the United Front Doctrine.* Berkeley: University of California Press, 1977.

Bailey, Paul John. *China in the Twentieth Century.* Oxford: Basil Blackwell, 1988.

Barnett, A. Doak. *China on the Eve of Communist Takeover.* Boulder, Colo.: Westview Press, 1985.

Bartke, Wolfgang. *A Biographical Dictionary and Analysis of China's Party Leadership, 1922–1988.* New York: K. G. Saur, 1990.

———. *Who's Who in the People's Republic of China.* 2nd ed. Munich: K. G. Saur, 1987.

Bastid, Marianne. "Histoire de la fin de la dynastie des Qing et de la révolution de 1911." (History of the late Ch'ing and the 1911 Revolution.) *Missions en Chine, 1980–1981.* Paris: École des Haute Études en Sciences Sociales. 12–28.

Baum, Richard. *Prelude to Revolution: Mao, the Party, and the Peasant Question, 1962–66.* New York: Columbia University Press, 1975.

Baum, Richard, with Louise B. Bennett, eds. *China in Ferment: Perspectives on the Cultural Revolution.* Englewood Cliffs, N.J.: Prentice-Hall, 1971.

Bays, Daniel H. *China Enters the Twentieth Century: Chang Chih-tung and the Issues of a New Age, 1895–1909.* Ann Arbor: University of Michigan Press, 1978.

Bergère, Marie-Claire. *La République Populaire de la Chine de 1949 a Nos Jour.* (The PRC from 1949 to the present.) Paris: Armand Colin, 1987.

Berton, Peter, and Eugene Wu. *Contemporary China: A Research Guide.* Ed. Howard Koch, Jr. Stanford, Calif.: Hoover Institution on War, Revolution and Peace, Stanford University, 1967.

Bianco, Lucien. *Origins of the Chinese Revolution, 1915–1949.* Trans. Muriel Bell. Stanford, Calif.: Stanford University Press, 1971.

Bilancia, Philip R. *Dictionary of Chinese Law and Government (Chinese-English).* Stanford, Calif.: Stanford University Press, 1981.

Boorman, Howard L., and Richard C. Howard, eds. *Biographical Dictionary of Republican China.* 5 vols. New York: Columbia University Press, 1967–1979.

Bown, Colin, and Tony Edwards. *Revolution in China, 1911–1949.* Portsmouth, N.H.: Heinemann Educational Books, 1974.

Brandt, Conrad, Benjamin Schwartz, and John King Fairbank. *A Documentary History of Chinese Communism.* New York: Atheneum, 1967.

Buck, David D., ed. *Recent Chinese Studies of the Boxer Movement.* Armonk, N.Y.: M. E. Sharpe, 1987.

Buss, Claude A. *The People's Republic of China.* Princeton, NJ: D. Van Norstrand, 1962.

Cambridge History of China. (See Vol. Editors: Vol. 10: Fairbank, John King, ed.; Vol. 11: Fairbank, John King, and Kwang-Ching Liu, eds.; Vol. 12: Fairbank, John King, ed.; Vol. 13: Fairbank, John King, and Albert Feuerwerker, eds.; Vol. 14 and Vol. 15: MacFarquhar, Roderick, and John King Fairbank, eds.)

Cameron, Meribeth E. *The Reform Movement in China, 1898–1912.* Stanford, Calif.: Stanford University Press, 1931.

Catchpole, Brian. *A Map History of Modern China.* London: Heinemann Educational Books, 1976.

Chai, Winberg, ed. *Essential Works of Chinese Communism.* New York: Bantam Books, 1969.

Chan, F. Gilbert. "Sun Yat-sen and the Chinese Revolution: An Historical Survey." *Chinese Republican Studies Newsletter* 2, no. 2 (February 1977): 20–29.

Chan, F. Gilbert, and Thomas H. Etzold, eds. *China in the 1920's: Nationalism and Revolution.* New York: New Viewpoints, 1976.

Chang Chu-hung, ed. *Chung-kuo hsien-tai ko-ming-shih shih-liao-hsüeh.* (A study of historical materials in contemporary Chinese revolutionary history.) Peking: Chung-kung tang-shih tzu-liao ch'u-pan she, 1987.

Chang Hai-p'eng, ed. *Chung-kuo chin-tai shih-kao ti-t'u chi.* (A map history of modern China.) Shanghai: Chung-kuo ti-t'u ch'u-pan she, 1987.

Chang Hao. *Chinese Intellectuals in Crisis: The Search for Order and Meaning, 1890–1911.* Berkeley: University of California Press, 1987.

Chang Hsi-k'ung, and T'ien Yüan, eds. *Chung-kuo li-shih ta-shih pien-nien, ti wu chi: Ch'ing, chin-tai.* (An annual chronicle of major events in Chinese history, vol. 5: Ch'ing and the modern period [up to 1919].) Peking: Peking ch'u-pan she, 1987.

Chang Hsien-wen, ed. *Chung-hua min-kuo shih-kang.* (Outline history of the ROC.) Cheng-chou: Ho-nan jen-min ch'u-pan she, 1985.

———. *Chung-kuo hsien-tai-shih shih-liao hsüeh.* (The study of historical materials in modern Chinese history.) Chi-nan: Shan-tung jen-min ch'u-pan she, 1985.

Chang K'ai-yüan, and Lin Tseng-p'ing, eds. *Hsin-hai ko-ming.* (The Revolution of 1911.) 3 vols. Peking: Jen-min ch'u-pan she, 1980–1981.

Chang King-Yuh, ed. *Ideology and Politics in Twentieth Century China.* Taipei: Institute of International Relations, 1988.

Chang Kuang-hsin, and Yang Shu-chen, eds. *Chung-kung tang-shih shih-chien ming-tz'u jen-wu chien-shih.* (An annotation of events, terms, and people in CCP history.) Shan-hsi: Jen-min ch'u-pan she, 1985.

Chang, Maria H. *The Chinese Blue Shirt Society: Fascism and Developmental Nationalism.* Berkeley: Institute of East Asian Studies, University of California, 1985.

Chang P'eng-yüan. *Li-hsien-p'ai yü Hsin-hai ko-ming.* (The constitutionalists and the Revolution of 1911.) Taipei: Chung-kuo hsüeh-shu chu-tso chiang-chu wei-yüan-hui, 1969.

———. *Liang Ch'i-ch'ao yü Ch'ing-chi ko-ming.* (Liang Ch'i-Ch'ao and the late Ch'ing revolutionary movement.) Taipei: Chung-yang yen-chiu yüan chin-tai-shih yen-chiu so, 1964.

Chang Yü-fa. *Ch'ing-chi ti ko-ming t'uan-t'i.* (Revolutionaries of the Late Ch'ing Period: an Analysis of Groups in the Revolutionary Movement 1894–1911.) Taipei: Chung-yang yen-chiu yüan chin-tai-shih yen-chiu so, 1982.

———. *Ch'ing-chi ti li-hsien t'uan-t'i.* (Constitutionalists of the Ch'ing Period: An Analysis of Groups in the Constitutional Movement, 1895–1911.) Taipei: Chung-yang yen-chiu yüan chin-tai-shih yen-chiu so, 1971.

———. *Chung-kuo hsien-tai-shih.* (History of contemporary China, [1911–1949].) 2 vols. Taipei: Tung-Hua shu-chu, 1986.

———. ed. *Chung-kuo hsien-tai-shih lun-chi.* (Essays on contemporary Chinese history.) 10 vols. Taipei: Lien-ching ch'u-pan shih-yeh kung-szu, 1980–1983.

———. *Min-kuo ch'u-nien ti cheng-tang.* (Political parties in the early Republic of China, 1911–1913.) Taipei: Chung-yang yen-chiu yüan chin-tai-shih yen-chiu so, 1985.

Chang Yü-fa, and Chang Jui-te, eds. *Chung-kuo hsien-tai tzu-chuan ts'ung-shu.* (A collection of contemporary Chinese autobiographies.) 1 vol. published to date. Taipei: Chung-yang yen-chiu-yüan san-min chu-i yen-chiu so, 1989.

Ch'en, Jerome. *Mao and the Chinese Revolution.* London: Oxford University Press, 1965.

Ch'en Jung-hua, Yen Chung-heng, and Ho Yu-liang, eds. *Chung-kuo ko-ming-shih shou-ts'e.* (Handbook of the history of the Chinese Revolution, [1919–1949].) Wuhan: Hua-chung shih-fan ta-hsüeh ch'u-pan she, 1986.

Ch'en Kung-lü. *Chung-kuo chin-tai-shih tzu-liao kai-shu.* (An introduction to materials on Chinese modern history.) Peking: Chung-hua shu-chu, 1982.

Ch'en Ming-hsien. *Hsin Chung-kuo szu-shih-nien.* (Forty years of the New China.) Peking: Kung-jen ch'u-pan she, 1989.

Ch'en Pao-t'ing, and Tsou Ming-te, eds. *Chung-kuo ko-ming, 1840–1956.* (The Chinese Revolution, 1840–1956.) Shanghai: Shanghai she-hui k'o-hsüeh ch'u-pan she, 1988.

Chen, Theodore H. *Thought Reform of the Chinese Intellectuals.* Westport, Conn.: Hyperion Press, 1984.

Ch'en Yung-fa. *Making Revolution: The Communist Movement in Eastern and Central China, 1937–1945.* Berkeley: University of California Press, 1986.

———. *Moral Economy and the Chinese Revolution.* Amsterdam: Universiteit van Amsterdam, Antropologisch-Sociologisch Centrum, 1986.

Cheng Jin. *A Chronology of the People's Republic of China, 1949–1984*. Peking: Foreign Languages Press, 1986.

Cheng, Peter. *A Chronology of the People's Republic of China from October 1, 1949*. Totowa, N.J.: Rowan and Littlefield, 1972.

———. *A Chronology of the People's Republic of China, 1970–1979*. Metuchen, N.J.: Scarecrow Press, 1986.

Chesneaux, Jean. *China: The People's Republic, 1949–1976*. Trans. Paul Auster and Lydia Davis. New York: Pantheon, 1979.

———. *The Chinese Labor Movement, 1919–1927*. Trans. H. M. Wright. Stanford, Calif.: Stanford University Press, 1968.

———. *Peasant Revolts in China, 1840–1949*. Trans. C. A. Curwen. London: Thames and Hudson, 1973.

———, ed. *Popular Movements and Secret Societies in China, 1840–1950*. Rev. translation. Stanford, Calif.: Stanford University Press, 1972.

Chesneaux, Jean, Françoise Le Barbier, and Marie-Claire Bergère. *China from the 1911 Revolution to Liberation*. Trans. Paul Auster and Lydia Davis. New York: Pantheon, 1977.

Chesneaux, Jean, Marianne Bastid, and Marie-Claire Bergère. *China from the Opium Wars to the 1911 Revolution*. Trans. Anne Destenay. New York: Pantheon, 1976.

Chevrier, Yves. "Mort et transfiguration: le modèle russe dans la révolution chinoise." (Death and transfiguration: the Russian model in the Chinese Revolution.) *Extrême-Orient Extrême-Occident* 2 (1983): 41–108.

Ch'i Hsi-sheng. *Nationalist China at War: Military Defeat and National Collapse, 1937–45*. Ann Arbor: Center for Chinese Studies, University of Michigan, 1982.

———. *Warlord Politics in China, 1916–1928*. Stanford, Calif.: Stanford University Press, 1976.

Chi-lin shih-fan ta-hsüeh Chung-kuo chin-tai-shih chiao-yen shih, ed. *Chung-kuo chin-tai-shih shih-chi*. (Record of historical events in modern China.) Shanghai: Jen-min ch'u-pan she, 1961.

Chi Ping-feng. *Ch'ing-mo ko-ming yü chün-hsien ti lun-cheng*. (Debate between the revolutionaries and constitutionalists in the late Ch'ing period.) Taipei: Chung-yang yen-chiu yüan chin-tai-shih yen-chiu so, 1966.

Chi Wen-shun. *Ideological Conflicts in Modern China: Democracy and Authoritarianism*. New Brunswick, N.J.: Transaction Books, 1986.

Chiang Ping-cheng. *Yen-chiu T'ai-p'ing T'ien-kuo shih chu-shu tsung-mu*. (A comprehensive bibliography of publications for research on the history of the Taiping Kingdom.) Peking: Shu-mu wen-hsien ch'u-pan she, 1984.

Ch'iao Chin-ch'iang. *Hsin-hai ko-ming ch'ien ti shih-nien*. (The decade prior to the 1911 Revolution.) T'ai-yüan: Shan-hsi jen-min ch'u-pan she, 1987.

Ch'ih Ching-te. "Kuo-shih kuan tien-ts'ang cheng-fu tang-an shih-liao chieh-shu." (An introduction to government archival materials in the Academia Historica.) *Chin-tai Chung-kuo shih yen-chiu t'ung-hsün* 4 (September 1987): 154–157.

Chih-shih ch'u-pan she, ed. *Chung-kuo chin hsien-tai-shih ta-shih chi, 1840–1980*. (A historical record of major events in modern and contemporary China, 1840–1980.) Shanghai: Chih-shih ch'u-pan she, 1984.

Chin Hsiao-yi. "An Introduction to the Historical Commission of the Kuomintang." *Chinese Republican Studies Newsletter* 8, no. 2 (February 1983): 16–22.

Chin Te-hsing, ed. *Chung-kuo ko-ming-shih, 1840–1956.* (History of the Chinese Revolution, 1840–1956.) Cheng-chou: Ho-nan ta-hsüeh ch'u-pan she, 1987.

Chin Te-hsing, and Ch'en Wan-an, eds. *Chung-kuo ko-ming-shih tz'u-tien.* (Dictionary of Chinese revolutionary history.) Cheng-chou: Ho-nan ta-hsüeh ch'u-pan she, 1986.

Ch'ing-chu Lo Erh-kang hsüeh-shu yen-chiu liu-shih-nien pien-chi wei-yüan-hui, ed. *Lo Erh-kang yü T'ai-p'ing T'ien-kuo shih.* Ch'eng-tu: Szuchuan-sheng she-hui k'o-hsüeh yüan, 1987.

Ch'iu Chin-cho, ed. *Chung-kung tang-shih jen-ming lu.* (Biographies from CCP history.) Chungking: Chungking ch'u-pan she, 1986.

Chiu Hungdah, and Leng Shao-chuan, eds. *China: Seventy Years after the 1911 Hsin-hai Revolution.* Charlottesville: University of Virginia Press, 1984.

Chong, Key Ray. *Americans and Chinese Reform and Revolution, 1898–1922: The Role of Private Citizens in Diplomacy.* Lanham, Md.: University Press of America, 1984.

Chow Tse-tsung. *The May Fourth Movement: Intellectual Revolution in Modern China.* Cambridge, Mass.: Harvard University Press, 1960.

———. *Research Guide to the May Fourth Movement: Intellectual Revolution in Modern China, 1915–1924.* Cambridge, Mass.: Harvard University Press, 1963.

Chu Chien-hua, ed. *Chung-kuo ko-ming-shih tz'u-tien.* (Dictionary of Chinese revolutionary history.) Ha-erh-pin: Hei-lung-chiang jen-min ch'u-pan she, 1989.

Chu Chien-hua, and Kuo Pin-wei, eds. *Chung-hua jen-min kung-ho-kuo shih tz'u-tien.* (Dictionary of PRC history.) Ch'ang-ch'un: Chi-lin wen-shih ch'u-pan she, 1989.

Chuan-chi wen-hsüeh tsa-chih she, ed. *Min-kuo ta-shih jih-chih.* (A daily chronology of the ROC.) 3 vols. Taipei: Chuan-chi wen-hsüeh, 1988.

Chung-hua min-kuo k'ai-kuo wu-shih-nien wen-hsien pien-tsuan wei-yüan-hui, comp. *Ch'ing-t'ing chih kai-ko yü fan-tung.* (Reform and reactionary movements of the Ch'ing Court.) 2 vols. Taipei: Cheng-chung shu-chü, 1967.

———, comp. *Ko-ming chih ch'ang-tao yü fa-chan.* (The advocacy and development of the Revolution.) 8 vols. Taipei: Cheng-chung shu-chu, 1970.

———, comp. *Ko-ming yüan-yüan.* (The origins of the Revolution.) 2 vols. Taipei: Cheng-chung shu-chu, 1968.

Chung-kung chung-yang tang-shih yen-chiu shih, ed. *Chung-kung tang-shih ta-shih nien-piao.* (A chronology of major events in CCP history.) Hupeh: Jen-min ch'u-pan she, 1981.

Chung-kuo chin pai-nien li-shih t'u-chi pien-chi wei-yüan-hui, ed. *Chung-kuo chin pai-nien li-shih t'u-chi, 1840–1975.* (A pictorial history of modern China, 1840–1975.) Hong Kong: Ch'i-shih nien-tai tsa-chih she, 1976.

Chung-kuo chin-tai-shih chih-shih shou-ts'e pien-hsieh tsu, ed. *Chung-kuo chin-tai-shih chih-shih shou-ts'e.* (A handbook of modern Chinese history.) Peking: Chung-hua shu-chü, 1980.

Chung-kuo chin-tai-shih tz'u-tien. (Dictionary of modern Chinese history.) Shanghai: Tz'u-shu ch'u-pan she, 1984.

Chung-kuo hsien-tai-shih tz'u-tien pien-chi wei-yüan-hui, ed. *Chung-kuo hsien-tai-shih tz'u-tien.* (Dictionary of contemporary Chinese history.) Taipei: Chin-tai Chung-kuo ch'u-pan she, 1985.

Chung-kuo she-hui k'o-hsüeh yüan chin-tai-shih yen-chiu so. *Wu-szu ai-kuo yün-tung.*

(The patriotic May Fourth Movement.) 2 vols. Peking: Chung-kuo she-hui k'o-hsüeh yüan ch'u-pan she, 1979.

Chung-kuo she-hui k'o-hsüeh yüan chin-tai-shih yen-chiu so fan-i shih. *Chin-tai lai-Hua wai-kuo jen-min tz'u-tien.* (A biographic dictionary of foreigners in modern China.) Peking: Chung-kuo she-hui k'o-hsüeh yüan ch'u-pan she, 1981.

Chung-yang yen-chiu yüan chin-tai-shih yen-chiu so k'ou-shu li-shih ts'ung-shu. (The oral history collection of the Institute of Modern History, Academia Sinica.) 18 vols. to date. Taipei: Chung-yang yen-chiu yüan chin-tai-shih yen-chiu so, 1982–

Clarke, Prescott, and J. S. Gregory, eds. *Western Reports on the Taiping: A Selection of Documents.* Canberra: Australian National University Press, 1982.

Clubb, O. Edmund, *Twentieth Century China.* 3rd ed. New York: Columbia University Press, 1978.

Cohen, Paul A. *Between Tradition and Modernity: Wang T'ao and Reform in Late Ch'ing China.* Cambridge, Mass.: Harvard University Press, 1974.

———. *Discovering History in China: American Historical Writing on the Recent Chinese Past.* New York: Columbia University Press, 1984.

Cohen, Paul A., and John E. Schrecker, eds. *Reform in Nineteenth-century China.* Cambridge, Mass.; East Asian Research Center, Harvard University, 1976.

Compton, Boyd, trans. *Mao's China: Party Reform Documents, 1942–1944.* Seattle: University of Washington Press, 1966.

Crane, Daniel M., and Thomas A. Breslin. *An Ordinary Relationship: American Opposition to Republican Revolution in China, 1919–1937.* Gainesville: University Presses of Florida, 1986.

Croizier, Ralph. *Art and Revolution in Modern China: The Lingnan (Cantonese) School of Painting, 1906–1951.* Berkeley: University of California Press, 1988.

———. "Chinese Art in the Chiang Ch'ing Era." *Journal of Asian Studies* 38 (1979): 303–11.

Croll, Elisabeth. *Feminism and Socialism in China.* London: Routledge & K. Paul, 1978.

Davis, Fei-ling. *Primitive Revolutionaries of China: A Study of Secret Societies in the Late Nineteenth Century.* Honolulu: University of Hawaii Press, 1977.

Davis-Friedman, Deborah. *Long Lives: Chinese Elderly and the Communist Revolution.* Cambridge, Mass.; Harvard University Press, 1983.

Dietrich, Craig. *People's China: A Brief History.* New York: Oxford University Press, 1986.

Dillon, Michael. *A Dictionary of Chinese History.* Totowa, N.J.: Biblio Distribution Ctr., Division of Littlefield, Adams and Co., 1979.

Dirlik, Arif. *The Origins of Chinese Communism.* New York: Oxford University Press, 1989.

———. *Revolution and History: The Origins of Marxist Historiography in China, 1919–1937.* Berkeley: University of California Press, 1987.

Dittmer, Lowell. *China's Continuous Revolution: The Post-Liberation Epoch, 1949–1981.* Berkeley: University of California Press, 1987.

———. *Liu Shao-ch'i and the Chinese Cultural Revolution: The Politics of Mass Criticism.* Berkeley: University of California Press, 1974.

Domes, Jürgen. *Die Kuomintang-Herrschaft in China.* (KMT rule in China.) Hannover: Niedersächsische Landeszentrale für Politische Bildung, 1970.

———. *Vertage Revolution: Die Politik der Kuomintang in China, 1923–1937.* (Deferred revolution: KMT politics in China, 1923–1937.) Berlin: De Gruyter, 1969.

Donovan, Peter. *The Red Army in Kiangsi, 1931–1934*. Ithaca, N.Y.: China-Japan Program, Cornell University East Asian Program, 1976.

Doolin, Dennis, and Robert C. North. *The Chinese People's Republic*. Stanford, Calif.: Hoover Institution Press, 1966.

Eastman, Lloyd E. *The Abortive Revolution: China Under Nationalist Rule, 1927–1937*. Cambridge, Mass.: Harvard University Press, 1974.

———. *The Nationalist Era in China, 1927–1949*. Cambridge, Mass.: Harvard University Press, 1990.

———. *Seeds of Destruction: Nationalist China in War and Revolution, 1937–1949*. Stanford, Calif.: Stanford University Press, 1984.

Embree, Ainslie T., ed. *Encyclopedia of Asian History*. 4 vols. New York: Scribner, 1988.

Esherick, Joseph W. "1911: A Review." *Modern China 2* (April 1976): 141–184.

———. *The Origins of the Boxer Uprising*. Berkeley: University of California Press, 1987.

———. *Reform and Revolution in China: The 1911 Revolution in Hunan and Hupei*. Berkeley: University of California Press, 1976.

Etō, Shinkichi. *Contemporary China since 1949*. Tokyo: Centre for East Asian Cultural Studies, 1974.

Etō, Shinkichi, and Harold Z. Schiffrin. *The 1911 Revolution in China: Interpretive Essays*. Tokyo: University of Tokyo Press, 1948.

Evans, Paul M. *John Fairbank and the American Understanding of Modern China*. New York: Basil Blackwell, 1988.

Fairbank, John King, ed. *The Cambridge History of China: Vol. 10: Late Ch'ing, 1800–1911, Part 1*. Cambridge: Cambridge University Press, 1978.

———, ed. *The Cambridge History of China: Vol. 12: Republican China, 1912–1949, Part 1*. Cambridge: Cambridge University Press, 1983.

———. *The Great Chinese Revolution, 1800–1985*. New York: Harper and Row, 1986.

Fairbank, John King, Masataka Banno, and Sumiko Yamamoto. *Japanese Studies of Modern China: A Bibliographical Guide to Historical and Social-Science Research on the Nineteenth and Twentieth Centuries*. Cambridge, Mass.: Harvard University Press, 1971. (See also Kamachi, Noriko, John K. Fairbank, and Chūzō Ichiko, eds. *Japanese Studies of Modern China Since 1953*.)

Fairbank, John King, and Albert Feuerwerker, eds. *The Cambridge History of China: Vol. 13: Republican China, 1912–1949, Part 2*. Cambridge: Cambridge University Press, 1983.

Fairbank, John King, and Kwang-Ching Liu, eds. *The Cambridge History of China: Vol. 11: Late Ch'ing, 1800–1911, Part 2*. Cambridge: Cambridge University Press, 1980.

Fairbank, John King, and Edwin O. Reischauer. *China: Tradition and Transformation*. Boston: Houghton Mifflin, 1978.

Fan, K. H., ed. *The Chinese Cultural Revolution: Selected Documents*. New York: Grove Press, 1968.

Feng Chün-shih, ed. *Chung-kuo li-shih ta-shih nien-piao*. (A chronology of Chinese history.) Shen-yang: Liao-ning jen-min ch'u-pan she, 1985.

Feuerwerker, Albert. *Economic Trends in the Republic of China, 1912–1949*. Ann Arbor: Center for Chinese Studies, University of Michigan, 1977.

———, ed. *History in Communist China*. Cambridge, Mass.: M.I.T. Press, 1968.

————. *Rebellion in Nineteenth-Century China*. Ann Arbor: Center for Chinese Studies, University of Michigan, 1975.

Feuerwerker, Albert, and S. Cheng. *Chinese Communist Studies of Modern Chinese History*. Cambridge, Mass.: East Asian Research Center, Harvard University, 1967.

Fitzgerald, Charles P. *Communism Takes China: How the Revolution Went Red*. New York: American Heritage Press, 1971.

————. *Mao Tse-tung and China*. New York: Holmes and Meier, Div. of IUB, Inc., 1976.

Fitzgerald, John. "The Misconceived Revolution: State and Society in China's Nationalist Revolution, 1923–26." *Journal of Asian Studies* 49 (May 1990): 323–343.

————, ed. *The Nationalists and Chinese Society, 1923–1937: A Symposium*. Melbourne: Melbourne University History Monographs, 1989.

————. "A Rival to Mass and Military Activities: Parliamentary Politics and the Guomindang, 1919–1925." *Papers on Far Eastern History* 25 (March 1982): 45–97.

Fogel, Joshua A., ed. and trans. *Recent Japanese Studies of Modern Chinese History*, [1978–1982]. *Studies in Chinese History* (Special Issue) 18.1–2 (Fall–Winter 1987–1985). Armonk, N.Y.: M. E. Sharpe, 1984.

————, ed. and trans. *Recent Japanese Studies of Modern Chinese History (II): Translations from* Shigaku zasshi *for 1983–1986*. Armonk, N.Y.: M. E. Sharpe, 1989.

Forbes, Andrew D.W. *Warlords and Muslims in Chinese Central Asia: A Political History of Republican Sinkiang, 1911–1949*. Cambridge: Cambridge University Press, 1986.

Forster, Keith. *Rebellion and Factionalism in a Chinese Province: Zhejiang, 1966–1976*. Armonk, N.Y.: M. E. Sharpe, 1990.

Franke, Wolfgang. *A Century of Chinese Revolution, 1851–1949*. Trans. Stanley Rudman. Columbia: University of South Carolina Press, 1980.

Friedman, Edward. *Backward Toward Revolution: the Chinese Revolutionary Party*. Berkeley: University of California Press, 1974.

Frolic, B. Michael. *Mao's People: Sixteen Portraits of Life in Revolutionary China*. Cambridge, Mass.: Harvard University Press, 1980.

Fung, Edmund S.K. "The Chinese Nationalists and the Unequal Treaties, 1924–1931." *Modern Asian Studies* 21 (October 1987): 793–819.

————. *The Military Dimension of the Chinese Revolution: The New Army and Its Role in the Revolution of 1911*. Vancouver: University of British Columbia Press, 1980.

————. "Revolution and the Chinese Army, 1912–1913." *Papers on Far Eastern History* 19 (March 1979): 13–53.

Furth, Charlotte, ed. *The Limits of Change: Essays on Conservative Alternatives in Republican China*. Cambridge, Mass.: Harvard University Press, 1976.

Furuya, Keiji. *Chiang Kai-shek: His Life and Times*. Abr. English ed. by Chun-ming Chang. New York: St. John's University Press, 1981.

Gasster, Michael. *China's Struggle to Modernize*. New York: Alfred A. Knopf, 1972.

————. *Chinese Intellectuals and the Revolution of 1911: The Birth of Modern Chinese Radicalism*. Seattle: University of Washington Press, 1969.

Gittings, John. *China Changes Face: The Road from Revolution, 1949–1989*. Oxford: Oxford University Press, 1989.

Goldman, Merle. *China's Intellectuals: Advise and Dissent*. Cambridge, Mass.: Harvard University Press, 1981.

Goldstein, Steven M., et al. *The People's Republic of China: A Basic Handbook.* 4th ed. New York: Learning Resources in International Studies, 1984.

Gray, Jack, ed. *Modern China's Search for Political Form.* London: Oxford University Press, 1969.

———. *Rebellions and Revolutions: China from the 1800s to the 1980s.* New York: Oxford University Press, 1990.

Greider, Jerome B. *Hu Shih and the Chinese Renaissance: Liberalism in the Chinese Revolution, 1917–1937.* Cambridge, Mass.: Harvard University Press, 1970.

———. *Intellectuals and the State in Modern China: A Narrative History.* New York: Free Press, 1981.

Hamrin, Carol Lee, and Timothy Cheek, eds. *China's Establishment Intellectuals.* Armonk, N.Y.: M. E. Sharpe, 1986.

Hartford, Kathleen, and Steven M. Goldstein. *China's Rural Revolutions.* Armonk, N.Y.: M. E. Sharpe, 1989.

Herbert, P. A., and T. Chiang. *Chinese Studies Research Methodology.* Hong Kong: Chinese Materials Center, 1982.

Hinton, Harold C., ed. *Government and Politics in Revolutionary China: Selected Documents, 1949–1979.* Wilmington, Del.: Scholarly Resources, 1982.

———. *The People's Republic of China, 1949–1979: A Documentary Survey.* 5 vols. Wilmington, Del.: Scholarly Resources, 1980.

Ho Kan-chih. *Chung-kuo hsien-tai ko-ming-shih.* (A history of the modern Chinese revolution.) Shanghai: Jen-min ch'u-pan she, 1985.

———. *A History of the Modern Chinese Revolution.* Peking: Foreign Languages Press, 1960.

Ho Li, ed. *Chung-hua jen-min kung-ho-kuo shih.* (History of the PRC.) Peking: Tang-an ch'u-pan she, 1989.

Ho Ping-ti. *Studies on the Population of China, 1368–1953.* Cambridge, Mass.: Harvard University Press, 1959.

Ho Tung. *Chung-kuo hsien-tai-shih shih-liao hsüeh.* (A study of historical materials in contemporary Chinese history.) Peking: Ch'iu-shih ch'u-pan she, 1987.

Hofheinz, Roy, Jr. *The Broken Wave: The Chinese Communist Peasant Movement, 1922–1928.* Cambridge, Mass.: Harvard University Press, 1977.

Holubnychy, Lydia. *Michael Borodin and the Chinese Revolution, 1923–1925.* Ann Arbor, Mich.: Published for the East Asian Institute, Columbia University by University Microfilms International, 1979.

Hooper, Beverley. *China Stands Up: Ending the Western Presence, 1848–1950.* Sydney: Allen and Unwin, 1986.

Hsia, C. T. *A History of Modern Chinese Fiction, 1917–1957.* New Haven, Conn.: Yale University Press, 1961.

Hsia Tsi-an. *The Gate of Darkness: Studies on the Leftist Literary Movement.* Seattle: University of Washington Press, 1968.

Hsiao Ch'ao-jan. *Pei-ching ta-hsüeh yü wu-szu yün-tung.* (Peking University and the May Fourth Movement.) Peking: Peking ta-hsëh ch'u-pan she, 1986.

Hsiao Hsiao-ch'in, ed. *Chung-kuo ko-ming-shih, 1840–1956.* (A history of the Chinese Revolution, 1840–1956.) Peking: Chung-kung tang-shih tz'u-liao ch'u-pan she, 1988.

Hsiao I-p'ing, et al., eds. *Chung-kuo kung-ch'an-tang k'ang-Jih chan-cheng shih-ch'i ta-shih chi.* (A chronology of the CCP during the period of anti-Japanese war.) Peking: Jen-min ch'u-pan she, 1988.

Hsiao Kung-chuan. *Rural China: Imperial Control in the Nineteenth Century.* Seattle: University of Washington Press, 1960.

Hsieh I, and Wang Hsiao-ch'iu, eds. *Chin-hsien-tai Chung-kuo ti ko-ming.* (Revolution in modern and contemporary China.) Peking: Peking ch'u-pan she, 1987.

Hsieh Shu-sen, ed. *Chien-ming Chung-kuo ko-ming-shih tz'u-tien.* (A concise dictionary of the Chinese Revolution.) Ch'ang-sha: Hu-nan ta-hsueh ch'u-pan she, 1986.

Hsieh, Winston. "At the Threshold of a New Era." *Chinese Republican Studies Newsletter* 8, no. 2 (February 1983): 2–8.

————. *Chinese Historiography on the Revolution of 1911: A Critical Survey and a Selected Bibliography.* Stanford, Calif.: Hoover Institution Press, 1975.

Hsü, Immanuel C.Y. *China Without Mao: The Search for a New Order.* New York: Oxford University Press, 1983.

————, ed. *Readings in Modern Chinese History.* New York: Oxford University Press, 1971.

————. *The Rise of Modern China.* 4th ed. New York: Oxford University Press, 1990.

Hsü Shan-kuang, and Liu Chien-p'ing. *Chung-kuo wu-cheng-fu chu-i shih.* (A history of Chinese anarchism.) Hupeh: Hupeh jen-min ch'u-pan she, 1989.

Hsüeh Chün-tu. *The Chinese Communist Movement: An Annotated Bibliography of Selected Materials in the Chinese Collection of the Hoover Institution on War, Revolution and Peace.* 2 vols. Stanford, Calif.: Hoover Institution on War, Revolution and Peace, Stanford University, 1960–1962.

————. *Huang Hsing and the Chinese Revolution.* Stanford, Calif.: Stanford University Press, 1961.

Hu Hua, ed. *Chung-kung tang-shih jen-wu chuan.* (Biographies of persons from CCP history.) 37 vols. to date. Sian: Shan-hsi jen-min ch'u-pan she, 1980–.

Hu P'ing-sheng. *Min-kuo ch'u-ch'i ti fu-p'i p'ai.* (Restoration factions in the early Republic.) Taipei: T'ai-wan hsüeh-sheng shu-chü, 1985.

Hu Sheng. *Imperialism and Chinese Politics.* Peking: Foreign Languages Press, 1981.

Hu Sheng, et al. *The 1911 Revolution: A Retrospective After Seventy Years.* Peking: New World Press, 1983.

Hu Sheng-wu, and Chin Ch'ung-chi, eds. *Ts'ung Hsin-hai ko-ming tao wu-szu yün-tung.* (From the 1911 Revolution to the May Fourth Movement.) Ch'ang-sha: Hu-nan jen-min ch'u-pan she, 1983.

Huang Hsiu-yung. *Ti-i tz'u kuo-kung ho-tso.* (The first KMT–CCP collaboration.) Shanghai: Jen-min ch'u-pan she, 1986.

Hummel, Arthur William, ed. *Eminent Chinese of the Ch'ing Period (1644–1912).* 2 vols. Washington, D.C.: U.S. Government Printing Office, 1943–1944.

Hung Chang-tai. *Going to the People: Chinese Intellectuals and Folk Literature, 1918–1937.* Cambridge, Mass.: Harvard University Press, 1986.

Ichiko, Chūzō. *Kindai Chūgoku no seiji to shakai.* (The politics and society of modern China.) Tokyo: Tokyo Daigaku, 1971.

International Colloquium on the 1911 Revolution and the Founding of the Chinese Republic: A Retrospective after 70 Years. Papers presented at the 34th Annual Meeting of the Association for Asian Studies, Chicago, April 2, 1982. Washington, D.C.: Center for Chinese Research Materials, Association of Research Libraries, [1982?]

Israel, John. *Student Nationalism in China, 1927–1937*. Stanford, Calif.: Stanford University Press, 1966.

Issacs, Harold R. *The Tragedy of the Chinese Revolution*. 2nd rev. ed. Stanford, Calif.: Stanford University Press, 1961.

Jacobs, Dan N., and Hans H. Baerwald, eds. *Chinese Communism: Selected Documents*. New York: Harper and Row, 1963.

Jen Yu-wen. *The Taiping Revolutionary Movement*. New Haven, Conn.: Yale University Press, 1973.

Johnson, Chalmers A., ed. *Ideology and Politics in Contemporary China*. Seattle: University of Washington Press, 1973.

———. *Peasant Nationalism and Communist Power: The Emergence of Revolutionary China*. Stanford, Calif.: Stanford University Press, 1962.

Johnson, Kay A. *Women, the Family and Peasant Revolution in China*. Chicago: University of Chicago Press, 1985.

Jordon, Donald A. *The Northern Expedition: China's National Revolution of 1926–1928*. Honolulu: University of Hawaii Press, 1976.

Jung Meng-yuan. *Chung-kuo chin pai-nien ko-ming shih-lüeh*. (A concise history of the Chinese Revolution in the last hundred years.) Peking: Sheng-huo, tu-shu, hsin-chih san-lien shu-tien, 1954.

Kallgren, Joyce K., ed. *The People's Republic of China after Thirty Years: An Overview*. Berkeley: University of California, Institute of East Asian Studies, 1979.

Kamachi, Noriko, John K. Fairbank, and Chūzō Ichiko, eds. *Japanese Studies of Modern China Since 1953: A Bibliographical Guide to Historical and Social Science Research on the Nineteenth and Twentieth Centuries: Supplementary Volume for 1953–1969*. Cambridge, Mass.: East Asian Research Center, Harvard University, 1975. (See also Fairbank, John King, Masataka Banno, and Sumiko Yamamoto. *Japanese Studies of Modern China*.)

Kao Chün, ed. *Wu cheng-fu chu-i tsai Chung-kuo*. (Anarchism in China.) Ch'ang-sha: Hu-nan jen-min ch'u-pan she, 1984.

Kaplan, Fredric M., and Julian M. Sobin. *Encyclopedia of China Today*. 3rd ed. New York: Eurasia Press, 1981.

Kapp, Robert A. *Szechuan and the Chinese Republic: Provincial Militarism and Central Power, 1911–1938*. New Haven, Conn.: Yale University Press, 1973.

Kataoka, Tetsuya. *Resistance and Revolution in China: The Communists and the Second United Front*. Berkeley: University of California Press, 1974.

Keenan, Barry. "The Republican History Project in the People's Republic of China and Scholarly Communication." *Chinese Republican Studies Newsletter* 5 no. 2 (February 1980): 1–4.

———. "The Republican History Project in Peking: An Update." *Chinese Republican Studies Newsletter* 6, no. 1 (October 1980): 18–19.

Keishu, Saneto. *Chung-kuo jen li-hsüeh Jih-pen shih*. (A history of Chinese students in Japan, [1896–1937].) Trans. Tam Yue-him and Lam Kai-yin. Hong Kong: Chinese University Press, 1982.

Kim, K. H. *Japanese Perspectives on China's Early Modernization: A Bibliographical Survey*. Michigan Abstracts of Chinese and Japanese Works on Chinese History. Ann Arbor: Center for Chinese Studies, University of Michigan, 1974.

Klein, Donald W., and Anne B. Clark. *Biographic Dictionary of Chinese Communism, 1921–1965*. 2 vols. Cambridge, Mass.: Harvard University Press, 1971.

Kuhn, Philip A. *Rebellion and Its Enemies in Late Imperial China: Militarization and Social Structure, 1796–1864*. Cambridge, Mass.: Harvard University Press, 1980.

K'ung Hsiang-chi. *Wu-hsü wei-hsin yün-tung hsin-t'an*. (A new study of the 1898 Reform Movement.) Ch'ang-sha: Hu-nan jen-min ch'u-pan she, 1988.

Kuo Heng-yü. *Kung-ch'an kuo-chi yü Chung-kuo ko-ming*. (The Communist International and the Chinese Revolution.) Taipei: Tung-ta t'u-shu kung-szu, 1989.

Kuo Hua-lun. *Chung-kung shih-lun*. (History of the CCP.) 4 vols. Taipei: Chung-hua min-kuo kuo-chi kuan-hsi yen-chiu so, 1969.

Kuo-shih-kuan chuan-chi tsu, ed. *Kuo-shih-kuan hsien-ts'ang Kuo-min jen-wu chuan-chi shih-liao hui-pien*. (A classified compilation of Nationalist biographical source materials currently in Academia Historica.) 1 vol. to date. Taipei: Kuo-shih-kuan, 1988–

Kuo Tai-chun, and Ramon H. Myers. *Understanding Communist China: Communist China Studies in the United States and Republic of China, 1949–1978*. Stanford, Calif.: Stanford University Press, 1986.

Kuo T'ing-i. *Chin-tai Chung-kuo shih*. (History of modern China.) Taipei: Shang-wu, 1966.

———. *Chin-tai Chung-kuo shih-kang*. (An outline of modern Chinese history.) 2 vols. Hong Kong: Chung-wen ta-hsüeh ch'u-pan she, 1979.

———. *Chin-tai Chung-kuo shih-shih jih-chih (Ch'ing chi, 1829–1911)*. (A daily chronology of modern Chinese history [Ch'ing period, 1829–1911].) 2 vols. Taipei: Chung-cheng shu-chü, 1963.

———. *Chin-tai Chung-kuo ti pien-chü*. (The changing situation of Modern China.) Taipei: Lien-ching ch'u-pan she, 1987.

———. *Chung-hua min-kuo shih-shih jih-chih*. (A daily chronology of the history of the ROC.) 4 vols. Taipei: Chung-yang yen-chiu yuan chin-tai-shih yen-chiu so, 1979–1985.

———. *T'ai-p'ing T'ien-kuo shih-shih jih-chih*. (A daily chronology of the history of the Taiping Kingdom.) 2 vols. Shanghai: Hsin-Hua shu-tien, 1986.

Kwong, Luke S. K. *A Mosaic of the Hundred Days: Personalities, Politics, and Ideas of 1898*. Cambridge, Mass.: Council on East Asian Studies, Harvard University, 1984.

Lan Hsü-nan. "Chung-yang yen-chiu yüan chin-tai-shih yen-chiu so shou-ts'ang pao-chih chien-chieh." (A brief introduction to the newspaper holdings of the Institute of Modern History, Academia Sinica.) *Chin-tai Chung-kuo shih yen-chiu t'ung-hsün 3* (March 1987): 174–182 and 5 (March 1988): 158–180.

Lary, Diana. *Warlord Soldiers: Chinese Common Soldiers, 1911–1935*. Cambridge: Cambridge University Press, 1985.

Lee, Chong-sik. *Revolutionary Struggle in Manchuria: Chinese Communism and Soviet Interest, 1922–1945*. Berkeley: University of California Press, 1983.

Lee, Hong Yung. *From Revolutionary Cadres to Party Technocrats in Socialist China*. Berkeley: University of California Press, 1990.

———. *The Politics of the Chinese Cultural Revolution: A Case Study*. Berkeley: University of California Press, 1978.

———. *A Research Guide to Red Guard Publications, 1966–1969*. Armonk, N.Y.: M. E. Sharpe, 1987.

Leung, Edwin Pak-wah. *Ethnic Compartmentalization and Regional Autonomy in the*

People's Republic of China. Chinese Law and Government (Special volume) 14, no. 4 (Winter 1981–1982).

———. "Chiang Kai-shek, 1887–1975." in *Read More About It: An Encyclopedia of Information Sources on Historical Figures and Events*. (Ann Arbor, Mich.: The Pierian Press, 1989), Vol. III: 111–113.

———. "Regional Autonomy Versus Central Authority: The Inner Mongolian Autonomous Movement and the Chinese Response, 1925–1947." *Journal of Oriental Studies* 25 (1987): 49–62.

Levenson, Joseph Richmond. *Confucian China and Its Modern Fate*. Berkeley: University of California Press, 1965.

———. *Revolution and Cosmopolitanism: The Western Stage and the Chinese Stages*. Berkeley: University of California Press, 1971.

Levine, Stephen I. *Anvil of Victory: The Communist Revolution in Manchuria, 1945–1948*. New York: Columbia University Press, 1987.

Levy, Marion Joseph. *The Family Revolution in Modern China*. Cambridge, Mass.: Harvard University Press, 1949.

Lew, Roland. "L'intelligentsia chinois: du mandarin au militant, 1898–1927." (The Chinese intelligentsia: from mandarin to militant, 1898–1927.) *Le Mouvement Social* 133 (October–December 1985): 53–77.

Lewis, Charlton M. *Prologue to the Chinese Revolution: The Transformation of Ideas and Institutions in Hunan Province, 1891–1907*. Cambridge, Mass.: Harvard University Press, 1976.

Lewis, John Wilson, ed. *Party Leadership and Revolutionary Power in China*. Cambridge: Cambridge University Press, 1970.

Leys, Simon. *The Chairman's New Clothes: Mao and the Cultural Revolution*. New York: St. Martin's Press, 1978.

Li Chien-nung. *The Political History of China, 1840–1928*. Ed. Ssu-yü Teng and Jeremy Ingalls. Stanford, Calif.: Stanford University Press, 1956.

Li Chin-hsiu. *Chung-kuo chin-tai cheng-chih chih-tu shih-kang*. (An outline history of modern Chinese political institutions.) Peking: Ch'iu-shih ch'u-pan she, 1988.

Li En-han. "China's Restoration of the British Hankow and Kiukiang Concessions in 1927: A Study of the Chinese Nationalist Party's Revolutionary Diplomacy During the Northern Expedition Period." Pei-fa hou Chung-kuo "ko-ming wai-chiao" ti yen-chiu, 1. (Chinese "revolutionary diplomacy" following the Northern Expedition, 1.) *Chung-yang yen-chiu yüan Han-hsüeh hui lun-wen chi*. (1981): 1431–1464.

———. "Chiu-i-pa shih-pien ch'ien Chung-Mei ch'e-fei ling-shih ts'ai-p'an ch'üan ti chiao-she." Pei-fa hou Chung-kuo "ko-ming wai-chiao" ti yen-chiu, 3. (Sino-American negotiations over the relinquishment of extraterritoriality in China, 1928–1931. Chinese "revolutionary diplomacy" following the Northern Expedition, 3.) *Chung-yang yen-chiu yüan chin-tai-shih yen-chiu so chi-k'an* 15.shang ts'e (1986): 335–369.

———. "Pei-fa ch'ien hou shou-hui kuan-shui tzu-chu ch'üan ti chiao-she." Pei-fa hou Chung-kuo "ko-ming wai-chiao" ti yen-chiu, 2. (Negotiations for the return of sovereignty over maritime customs before and after the Northern Expedition. Chinese "revolutionary diplomacy" following the Northern Expedition, 2.) *Chung-hua min-kuo chien-kuo shih t'ao-lun chi* 3 (1981): 358–405.

Li Hsin, and Jen I-min. *Hsin-hai ko-ming shih-ch'i ti li-shih jen-wu*. (Historical figures during the period of the 1911 Revolution.) Peking: Chung-kuo ch'ing-nien ch'u-pan she, 1983.

Li Hsin, and Sun Szu-pai, eds. *Min-kuo jen-wu chuan*. (Biographies of Republican China.) 2 vols. Peking: Chung-hua shu-chü, 1978–1980.

Li Hsing-hua, ed. *Chin-tai Chung-kuo pai-nien-shih tz'u-tien*. (Dictionary of the hundred-year history of modern China.) Chekiang: Jen-min ch'u-pan she, 1987.

Li-shih Yen-chiu pien-chi pu, ed. *Chung-kuo chin-tai-shih yen-chiu chuan-t'i shu-p'ing*. (A review of topics in research on modern Chinese history.) Peking: Jen-min ch'u-pan she, 1986.

Li Shih-yüeh. *Chin-tai Chung-kuo fan-yang-chiao yün-tung*. (The movement in opposition to foreign religions in modern China.) Peking: Jen-min ch'u-pan she, 1985.

Li Sung-lin, et al., eds. *Chung-kuo Kuo-min-tang ta-shih chi, 1894.11–1986.12*. (A record of major events of the KMT, November 1894–December 1986.) Peking: Chieh-fang-chün ch'u-pan she, 1988.

Li Xin, and Chen Tiejian. "Preface to the Multi-Volume Edition of *The History of the Chinese New Democratic Revolution* and the Epilogue to Volume One." Trans. Wu Tien-wei. *Republican China* 9, no. 2 (February 1984): 48–57.

Li Yen-chiao, and Li Hsi-so, eds. *Chung-kuo chin-tai jen-wu yen-chiu hsin-hsi*. (Research news on biographical studies of modern China.) Tientsin: Chiao-yu ch'u-pan she, 1988.

Li Yü-ming, ed. *Chung-hua jen-min kung-ho-kuo shih tz'u-tien*. (Dictionary of PRC history.) Peking: Chung-kuo kuo-chi kuang-po ch'u-pan she, 1989.

Li Yu-ning, and Chang Yü-fa, eds. *Chin-tai Chung-kuo nü-ch'üan yün-tung shih liao, 1842–1911. (Documents on the Feminist Movement in Modern China, 1842–1911.)* 2 vols. Taipei: Chuan-che wen-hsüeh she, 1975.

Li Yün-han. *Ts'ung yung-kung tao ch'ing-tang*. (From the admission of the Chinese Communists into the KMT to the purge.) Taipei: Chung-kuo hsüeh-shu chu-tso chiang-chu wei-yüan-hui, 1966.

Li Zongyi. "On the Cataloging and Publication of the Archives of the 1911 Revolution." *Chinese Republican Studies Newsletter* 8, no. 2 (February 1983): 8–15.

———. "The Role of Bourgeois Revolutionaries in the Late Qing Rights Recovery Movement." *Social Sciences in China* 1 (March 1983): 127–154.

Liang Han-ping, and Wei Hung-yüan, eds. *Chung-kuo hsien-tai-shih ta-shih chi*. (A record of major events in contemporary Chinese history [1919–1949].) Ha-erh-pin: Hei-lung-chiang jen-min ch'u-pan she, 1984.

Liang Po-hua (Edwin Pak-wah Leung). *Chung-kuo chin-tai wai-chiao ti chü-pien*. (Modern changes in Chinese diplomacy.) Hong Kong: Shang-wu Publisher, 1990.

Liao Kuang-sheng. *Antiforeignism and Modernization in China, 1860–1980: Linkage Between Domestic Politics and Foreign Policy*. Hong Kong: Chinese University Press, 1984.

Lieberthal, Kenneth G. *Revolution and Tradition in Tientsin, 1949–1952*. Stanford, Calif.: Stanford University Press, 1980.

Lieberthal, Kenneth G., and Bruce J. Dickson. *A Research Guide to Central Party and Government Meetings in China, 1949–1986*. Rev. and expanded ed. Armonk, N.Y.: M. E. Sharpe, 1989.

Lin Mou-sheng, Weng Wei-li, and Wang Kuei-lin. *Chung-kuo hsien-tai cheng-chih szu-hsiang shih, 1919–1949*. (A history of Chinese political thought, 1919–1949.) Hei-lung-chiang: Jen-min ch'u-pan she, 1984.

Lin Tseng-p'ing, and Li Wen-hai, eds. *Ch'ing-tai jen-wu chuan kao: hsia pien, ti 3 chüan: Wu-hsü pien-fa hou tao Hsin-hai ko-ming shih-ch'i.* (Draft biographies from the Ch'ing period: final part, Vol. 3: From the Reform Movement to the 1911 Revolution.) Shenyang: Liao-ning jen-min ch'u-pan she, 1987.

Lin Yu-sheng. *The Crisis of Chinese Consciousness: Radical Antitraditionalism in the May Fourth Era.* Madison: University of Wisconsin Press, 1979.

Lindbeck, John M. H., ed. *China: Management of a Revolutionary Society.* Seattle: University of Washington Press, 1971.

Link, E. Perry. *Mandarins, Ducks and Butterflies: Popular Fiction in Early Twentieth Century Chinese Cities.* Berkeley: University of California Press, 1981.

Liu Delin, and He Shuangsheng. "A Brief Account of the Publications of Historical Source Materials on the 1911 Revolution since 1949." *Chinese Studies in History* 16, no. 3–4 (Spring–Summer 1983): 201–233.

Liu Guokai. *A Brief Analysis of the Cultural Revolution.* Trans. John Hsu. Ed. Anita Chan. Armonk, N.Y.: M. E. Sharpe, 1984.

Liu-shih-nien lai ti Chung-kuo chin-tai-shih yen-chiu. (Research in modern Chinese history over the past sixty years.) 2 vols. Taipei: Chung-yang yen-chiu yüan chin-tai-shih yen-chiu so, 1988–1989.

Liu Ta-nien. *Chung-kuo chin-tai-shih chu wen-t'i.* (Problems in modern Chinese history.) Peking: Jen-min ch'u-pan she, 1965.

Liu Wen-chieh. *Li-shih wen-shu yung-yü tz'u-tien: Ming, Ch'ing, Min-kuo pu-fen.* (Dictionary of terminology of historical documents: Ming, Ch'ing and Republican China.) Ch'eng-tu: Szechuan jen-min ch'u-pan she, 1988.

Liu Yü-t'ien, Li Kung, and Hsü Chien-kuo, eds. *Chung-kuo ko-ming shih chien-ming tz'u-tien.* (A concise dictionary of Chinese revolutionary history.) Peking: Chieh-fang-chün ch'u-pan she, 1986.

Lo Erh-kang. *T'ai-p'ing T'ien-kuo shih-shih kao.* (A study of historical events of the Taiping Kingdom.) Peking: San-lien shu-tien, 1979.

Loh, Pichon P.Y. *The Early Chiang Kai-shek: A Study of His Personality and Politics, 1887–1924.* New York: Columbia University Press, 1971.

Lorenz, Richard, ed. *Umwälzung einer Gesellschaft: Zur Sozialgeschichte der chinesischen Revolution (1911–1949).* (Transformation of a society: concerning the social history of the Chinese Revolution, 1911–1949.) Frankfurt: Suhrkamp, 1977.

Lötveit, Trygve. *Chinese Communism, 1931–1934: Experience in Civil Government.* Sweden: Studentlitteratur, 1973.

Louie, Kam. *Inheriting Tradition: Interpretations of the Classical Philosophers in Communist China, 1949–1966.* Hong Kong: Oxford University Press, 1986.

Lü Fang-shang. *Ko-ming chih tsai-ch'i: Chung-kuo Kuo-min-tang kai-tsu ch'ien tui hsin szu-ch'ao chih hui-ying, 1914–1924.* (Resurge of revolution: A response to the new current of thought prior to the reorganization of the KMT, 1914–1924.) Taipei: Chung-yang yen-chiu yüan chin-tai-shih yen-chiu so, 1989.

Lubot, Eugene. *Liberalism in an Illiberal Age: New Culture Liberals in Republican China.* Westport, Conn.: Greenwood Press, 1982.

Ma Chi-pin, et al., eds. *Chung-kuo Kuo-min-tang li-shih shih-chien jen-wu tzu-liao chi-lu.* (A record of materials on KMT events and biographies.) Peking: Chieh-fang-chun chan-shih ch'u-pan she, 1988.

Ma Hung-wu, Wang Te-pao, and Sun Ch'i-ming, eds. *Chung-kuo ko-ming-shih tz'u-*

tien. (A dictionary of the history of the Chinese Revolution.) Peking: Tang-an ch'u-pan she, 1988.

Ma, L. Eve Armentrout. *Revolutionaries, Monarchists, and Chinatowns: Chinese politics in the Americas and the 1911 Revolution*. Honolulu: University of Hawaii Press, 1990.

McDonald, Angus W. *The Urban Origins of Rural Revolution: Elites and the Masses in Hunan Province, China, 1911–1927*. Berkeley: University of California Press, 1978.

MacFarquhar, Roderick. *The Origins of the Cultural Revolution: Vol. 1: Contradiction Among the People, 1956–1957*. New York: Columbia University Press, 1987.

———. *The Origins of the Cultural Revolution: Vol. 2: The Great Leap Forward, 1958–1960*. New York: Columbia University Press, 1987.

MacFarquhar, Roderick, and John King Fairbank, eds. *The Cambridge History of China: Vol. 14 and Vol. 15: The People's Republic, Part I and Part II*. London: Cambridge University Press, 1987, 1991.

Mackerras, Colin, ed. *China: The Impact of Revolution: A Survey of Twentieth Century China*. Hawthorn, Victoria: Longman Australia, 1976.

———. *Modern China: A Chronology from 1842 to the Present*. San Francisco: W. H. Freeman, 1982.

Mancall, Mark. *China at the Center: Three Hundred Years of Foreign Policy*. New York: Free Press, 1984.

Martin, Edwin W. *Divided Counsel: The Anglo-American Response to Communist Victory in China*. Lexington: University Press of Kentucky, 1986.

Meisner, Maurice. *Li Ta-chao and the Origins of Chinese Communism*. New York: Atheneum, 1970.

———. *Mao's China and After*. (Updated ed. of *Mao's China*.) New York: Free Press, 1986.

———. *Marxism, Maoism and Utopianism: Eight Essays*. Madison: University of Wisconsin Press, 1982.

Melby, John F. *The Mandate of Heaven: A Record of Civil War in China, 1945–49*. Toronto: University of Toronto Press, 1968.

Meyer, Hektor. *Die Entwicklung der kommunistischen Streitkrafte in China von 1927–1949: Dokumente and Kommentar*. (The development of Communist armed forces in China, 1927–1949: documents and commentary.) Berlin: de Gruyter, 1982.

Michael, Franz. *The Taiping Rebellion*. Vol. 1. Seattle: University of Washington Press, 1966.

Min, Tu-ki. "Kankoku ni okeru Chūgoku gendaishi kenkyū ni tsuite." (Korean research on modern Chinese history.) *Chikaki ni arite* 10 (1986): 2–9.

Mirovitskaya, R. "The Great October Revolution and the Development of Revolutionary Movement in China." *Far Eastern Affairs* [Moscow] 1 (1983): 14–22.

Miu Ch'u-huang. *Chung-kuo kung-ch'an-tang chien-yao li-shih, ch'u-kao*. (A brief history of the CCP, first draft.) Peking: Hsüeh-hsi tsa-chih she, 1956.

Mo An-shih. *T'ai-p'ing T'ien-kuo*. (The Taiping Kingdom.) Shanghai: Jen-min ch'u-pan she, 1979.

Mohr, Ernst Günther. *Die unterschlagenen Jahre: China vor Mao Tse-tung*. (The suppressed years: China before Mao Tse-tung.) Esslingen: Bechtle, 1985.

Moise, Edwin E. *Modern China: A History*. London: Longman, 1986.

Moseley, George. *China Since 1911*. New York: Harper and Row, 1968.

Myers, James T., Jürgen Domes, and Erik Groeling, eds. *Chinese Politics: Documents and Analysis: Vol. 1: Cultural Revolution to 1969.* Columbia: University of South Carolina Press, 1986.

————, eds. *Chinese Politics: Documents and Analysis: Vol. 2: Ninth Party Congress (1969) to the Death of Mao (1976).* Columbia: University of South Carolina Press, 1989.

Nakayama, Yoshihiro. *Kindai Chūgoku ni okeru josei kaiho no shisō to kōdo.* (Thought and action in the liberation of women in modern China.) Kitakyūshū-shi: Kitakyūshū Chūgoku shoten, 1983.

"Nan-ching Chung-kuo ti erh li-shih tang-an kuan so-ts'ang tang-an chien-chieh." (A brief introduction to documents in the Second Historical Archives of China, Nanking.) *Chin-tai Chung-kuo shih yen-chiu t'ung-hsün* 7 (March 1989): 116–132.

Nathan, Andrew J. *China's Crisis: Dilemmas of Reform and Prospects for Democracy.* New York: Columbia University Press, 1990.

————. *Chinese Democracy.* New York: Alfred A. Knopf, 1985.

————. *Modern China, 1840–1972: An Introduction to Sources and Research Aids.* Ann Arbor: Center for Chinese Studies, University of Michigan, 1973.

————. *Peking Politics, 1918–1923: Factionalism and the Failure of Constitutionalism.* Berkeley: University of California Press, 1976.

Nee, Victor, and James Peck, eds. *China's Uninterrupted Revolution: From 1840 to the Present.* New York: Pantheon, 1975.

Ni, Chung-wen, and T'an Mu-hsüeh, eds. *Chung-hua jen-min kung-ho-kuo chien-kuo-shih shou-ts'e.* (A handbook on the history of the PRC as a nation, [1949–1985].) Peking: Hsin-shu ch'u-pan she, 1989.

Niu Lien-hai, Ch'en Wan-an, and Wei Kuan-sung, eds. *Chung-kuo ko-ming-shih.* (History of the Chinese Revolution.) Wuhan: Hua-chung shih-fan ta-hsueh ch'u-pan she, 1988.

North, Robert C. *Chinese Communism.* New York: McGraw–Hill, 1966.

Ono, Kazuko. *Chinese Women in a Century of Revolution, 1850–1950.* Trans. Kathryn Bernhardt et al. Ed. Joshua Fogel. Stanford, Calif.: Stanford University Press, 1989.

Opitz, Peter J., ed. *Chinas grosse Wandlung; Revolutionare Bewegungen im 19. und 20. Jarhundert.* (China's great change: revolutionary movements in the 19th and 20th centuries.) Munich: Beck, 1972.

Pei-ching shih-fan hsüeh-yüan li-shih hsi Chung-kuo chin hsien-tai-shih chiao-yen shih. *Chien-ming Chung-kuo chin hsien-tai-shih tz'u-tien.* (A concise dictionary of modern and contemporary Chinese history.) 2 vols. Peking: Chung-kuo ch'ing-nien ch'u-pan she, 1985.

P'eng Shu-Tse. *The Chinese Communist Party in Power.* Ed. Leslie Evans. New York: Anchor Foundation, 1980.

Pepper, Suzanne. *Civil War in China: The Political Struggle, 1945–1949.* Berkeley: University of California Press, 1978.

Perry, Elizabeth. *Rebels and Revolutionaries in North China, 1845–1945.* Stanford, Calif.: Stanford University Press, 1980.

Pickowicz, Paul G. *Marxist Literary Thought in China: The Influence of Ch'ü Ch'iu-pai.* Berkeley: University of California Press, 1981.

A Pictorial History of the Republic of China: Its Founding and Development. 2 vols. Taipei: Modern China Press, 1981.

Pong, David, and Edmund S.K. Fung. *Ideal and Reality: Social and Political Change in Modern China, 1860–1949*. Lanham, Md.: University Press of America, 1985.

Powell, Ralph L. *The Rise of Chinese Military Power, 1895–1912*. Princeton, N.J.: Princeton University Press, 1955.

Price, Don C. *Russia and the Roots of the Chinese Revolution, 1896–1911*. Cambridge, Mass.: Harvard University Press, 1974.

Rankin, Mary Backus. *Early Chinese Revolutionaries: Radical Intellectuals in Shanghai and Chekiang, 1902–1911*. Cambridge, Mass.: Harvard University Press, 1971.

———. *Elite Activism and Political Transformation in China: Zhejiang Province, 1865–1911*. Stanford, Calif.: Stanford University Press, 1986.

Reardon-Anderson, James B. *Yenan and the Great Powers: The Origins of Chinese Communist Foreign Policy, 1944–1946*. New York: Columbia University Press, 1980.

Rhoads, Edward J.M. *China's Republican Revolution: The Case of Kwangtung, 1895–1913*. Cambridge, Mass.: Harvard University Press, 1975.

Ristaino, Marcia. *China's Art of Revolution: The Mobilization of Discontent, 1927 and 1928*. Durham, N.C.: Duke University Press, 1987.

Robinson, Thomas W., ed. *The Cultural Revolution in China*. Berkeley: University of California Press, 1971.

Robottom, John. *China in Revolution: From Sun Yat-sen to Mao Tse-tung*. New York: McGraw–Hill, 1969.

———. *Modern China*. London: Longman, 1967.

———. *Twentieth Century China*. New York: G. P. Putnam's Sons, 1971.

Rodzinski, Witold. *The People's Republic of China: A Concise Political History*. New York: Free Press, 1988.

Rong, Tiesheng. ''The Women's Movement in China Before and After the 1911 Revolution.'' *Chinese Studies in History* 16, no. 3–4 (Spring–Summer 1983): 159–200.

Rosen, Stanley, and John P. Burns, eds. *Policy Conflicts in Post-Mao China: A Documentary Survey with Analysis*. Armonk, N.Y.: M. E. Sharpe, 1986.

Rosenberg, William G., and Marilyn B. Young. *Transforming Russia and China: Revolutionary Struggle in the Twentieth Century*. New York: Oxford University Press, 1982.

Rowe, David Nelson. *Modern China*. Princeton, N.J.: D. Van Nostrand, 1959.

Rozman, Gilbert, ed. *The Modernization of China*. New York: Free Press, 1982.

Salisbury, Charlotte Y. *Long March Diary: China Epic*. New York: Walker, 1986.

Salisbury, Harrison Evans. *China: One Hundred Years of Revolution*. New York: Holt, Rinehart and Winston, 1983.

Scalapino, Robert A., and George T. Yu. *The Chinese Anarchist Movement*. Westport, Conn.: Greenwood Press, 1980.

———. *Modern China and Its Revolutionary Process: Recurrent Challenges to the Traditional Order, 1850–1920*. Berkeley: University of California Press, 1985.

Schiffrin, Harold Z. *Sun Yat-sen and the Origins of the Chinese Revolution*. Berkeley: University of California Press, 1968.

Schram, Stuart, ed. *Chairman Mao Talks to the People*. New York: Pantheon, 1974.

———. *The Political Thought of Mao Tse-tung*. Rev. ed. New York: Praeger, 1969.

———. *The Thought of Mao Tse-tung*. Cambridge: Cambridge University Press, 1989.

Schurmann, Franz. *Ideology and Organization in Communist China.* 2nd ed. Berkeley: University of California Press, 1968.

Schurmann, Franz, and Orville Schell, eds. *The China Reader.* 4 vols. New York: Random House, 1967.

Schwarcz, Vera. *The Chinese Enlightenment: Intellectuals and the Legacy of the May Fourth Movement of 1919.* Berkeley: University of California Press, 1986.

Schwartz, Benjamin I. *Chinese Communism and the Rise of Mao.* Cambridge, Mass.: Harvard University Press, 1951.

Seagrave, Sterling. *The Soong Dynasty.* New York: Harper and Row, 1986.

Selden, Mark, with Patti Eggleston, eds. *The People's Republic of China: A Documentary History of Revolutionary Change.* New York: Monthly Review Press, 1979.

———. *The Yenan Way in Revolutionary China.* Cambridge, Mass.: Harvard University Press, 1971.

Shanghai jen-min ch'u-pan pien-hsieh tsu, ed. *Chung-kung tang-shih shih-chien jen-wu lu.* (Records of events and people in CCP history.) Shanghai: Jen-min ch'u-pan she, 1983.

"Shanghai-shih tang-an kuan k'ai-fang tang-an ch'üan-tsung mu-lu." (Complete catalog of documents accessible in the Shanghai Municipal Archive.) *Chin-tai Chung-kuo shih yen-chiu t'ung-hsün* 6 (September 1988): 160–168 and 8 (September 1989): 128–142.

Shao, Ming-huang. "Chung-kuo Kuo-min-tang chung-yang wei-yüan-hui tang-shih wei-yuan-hui chien chieh." (A brief introduction to the Party History Committee of the KMT Central Committee.) *Chin-tai Chung-kuo shih yen-chiu t'ung-hsün* 5 (March 1988): 129–134.

Sharman, Lyon. *Sun Yat-sen, His Life and Its Meaning: A Critical Bibliography.* Stanford, Calif.: Stanford University Press, 1968.

Shaw, Yu-ming, ed. *Reform and Revolution in Twentieth Century China.* Papers from the Third Sino-European Conference, Taipei, September 1–6, 1986. Taipei: Institute of International Relations, National Chengchi University, 1987.

Shen Yün-lung. *Min-kuo shih-shih yü jen-wu lun ts'ung.* (Collected essays on Republican events and persons.) 2 vols. Taipei: Chuan-chi wen-hsüeh ch'u-pan she, 1981–1988.

Sheridan, James E. *China in Disintegration: The Republican Era in Chinese History, 1912–1949.* New York: Free Press, 1975.

Shieh, Milton J.T. *The Kuomintang: Selected Historical Documents, 1894–1969.* New York: St. John's University Press, 1970.

Shimpen Tōyōshi jiten. (Dictionary of Far Eastern history, new edition.) Tokyo: Tokyo Sogensha, 1980.

Sih, Paul K.T., ed. *Nationalist China During the Sino-Japanese War, 1937–1945.* Hicksville, N.Y.: Exposition Press, 1977.

———, ed. *The Strenuous Decade: China's Nation-Building Efforts, 1927–1937.* Jamaica, N.Y.: St. John's University Press, 1970.

Simone, Vera, ed. *China in Revolution: History, Documents, and Analyses.* Greenwich, Conn.: Fawcett Publications, 1968.

Singer, Martin. *Educated Youth and the Cultural Revolution in China.* Ann Arbor: Center for Chinese Studies, University of Michigan, 1971.

Skinner, G. William, ed. *Modern Chinese Society: An Analytical Bibliography: 1. Pub-*

lications in Western Languages, 1644–1972. Stanford, Calif.: Stanford University Press, 1973.

Skinner, G. William, and Winston Hsieh, eds. *Modern Chinese Society: An Analytical Bibliography: 2. Publications in Chinese, 1644–1969.* Stanford, Calif.: Stanford University Press, 1973.

Skinner, G. William, and Shigeaki Tomita, eds. *Modern Chinese Society; An Analytical Bibliography: 3. Publications in Japanese, 1644–1971.* Stanford, Calif.: Stanford University Press, 1973.

Skocpol, Theda. *States and Social Revolutions: A Comparative Analysis of France, Russia, and China.* Cambridge: Cambridge University Press, 1979.

Snow, Edgar. *Red Star over China.* Rev. ed. New York: Grove Press, 1968.

Soloman, Richard H. *Mao's Revolution and the Chinese Political Culture.* Berkeley: University of California Press, 1971.

Spence, Jonathan. *The Gate of Heavenly Peace: The Chinese and their Revolution, 1895–1980.* New York: Viking Press, 1981.

———. *The Search for Modern China.* New York: W. W. Norton, 1990.

Starr, John Bryan. *Continuing the Revolution: The Political Thought of Mao.* Princeton, N.J.: Princeton University Press 1979.

Strand, David. *Rickshaw Beijing: City, People and Politics in the 1920s.* Berkeley: University of California Press, 1989.

Strong, Anna L. *China's Millions: The Revolutionary Struggles from 1927–1935.* Freeport, N.Y.: Books for Libraries Press, 1973.

T'ao Hsi-sheng. *Chung-kuo she-hui yü Chung-kuo ko-ming.* (Chinese society and the revolution.) Shanghai: Hsin-sheng-ming ch'u-pan she, 1929.

Teng Ssu-yü. *Historiography of the Taiping Rebellion.* Cambridge, Mass.: Harvard University Press, 1962.

———. *Protest and Crime in China: A Bibliography of Secret Associations, Popular Uprisings, Peasant Rebellions.* New York: Garland, 1981.

Teng Ssu-yü, and John King Fairbank. *China's Response to the West: A Documentary Survey, 1839–1923.* New York: Atheneum, 1967.

Thomas, S. Bernard. *Labor and the Chinese Revolution: Class Strategies and Contradictions of Chinese Communism, 1928–1948.* Ann Arbor: Center for Chinese Studies, University of Michigan, 1983.

———. *"Proletarian Hegemony" in the Chinese Revolution and the Canton Commune of 1927.* Ann Arbor: Center for Chinese Studies, University of Michigan, 1975.

Thomson, James C., Jr. *While China Faced West: American Reformers in Nationalist China, 1928–1937.* Cambridge, Mass.: Harvard University Press, 1969.

Thorton, Richard C. *China: A Political History.* Boulder, Colo.: Westview Press, 1981.

Thurston, Anne F. *Enemies of the People: The Ordeal of the Intellectuals in China's Great Cultural Revolution.* Cambridge, Mass.: Harvard University Press, 1988.

Tien Hung-mao. *Government and Politics in Kuomintang China, 1927–1937.* Stanford, Calif.: Stanford University Press, 1972.

———. *The Great Transition: Political and Social Change in the Republic of China.* Stanford, Calif.: Hoover Institution Press, 1989.

Ting Hsiao-ch'un, ed. *Chung-kuo ko-ming-shih, 1840–1987.* (Chinese revolutionary history, 1840–1987.) Peking: Chung-kung tang-shih tzu-liao ch'u-pan she, 1988.

Townsend, James R., and Richard C. Bush, comps. *The People's Republic of China: A*

Basic Handbook. New York: Council on International and Public Affairs, in cooperation with the Council of the Asia Society, 1981.

Tsai, David. "Modern Chinese Government Publications, 1912–1949: An Overview." *Chinese Republican Studies Newsletter* 1, no. 2 (February 1976): 1–8.

Tsai Jung-fang. "Reflections on Some Chinese Reformers' and Conservatives' Views of Freedom (Tzu-yu) in Late Ch'ing Times." *Proceedings of the 5th International Symposium on Asian Studies, 1983.* Hong Kong: Asian Research Service, 1983. 99–118.

Tseng Fan-kuang, ed. *Chung-kuo ko-ming-shih piao-chieh, 1840–1956.* (Explanatory tables of China's revolutionary history, 1840–1956.) Ch'angsha: Hunan jen-min ch'u-pan she, 1988.

Tsou Tang. *The Cultural Revolution and Post-Mao Reforms: A Historical Perspective.* Chicago: University of Chicago Press, 1986.

Tuan Pei-lung. "Chinese Students in Japan." *Sino-American Relations* 10 (Spring 1984): 38–56.

Tuchman, Barbara W. *Stilwell and the American Experience in China, 1911–1945.* New York: Macmillan, 1970.

Tung, William L. *The Political Institutions of Modern China.* The Hague: Martinus Nijhoff, 1964.

Uhalley, Stephen. *A History of the Chinese Communist Party.* Stanford, Calif.: Hoover Institution Press, 1988.

———. *Mao Tse-tung: A Critical Biography.* New York: Franklin Watts, 1975.

University of California (Berkeley), Center for Chinese Studies. *Guide to Early Chinese Communist Historical Materials: The Keio [University] Collection.* Berkeley: Center for Chinese Studies, University of California, 1972.

Van Slyke, Lyman, ed. *The Chinese Communist Movement: A Report of the United States War Department, July 1945.* Stanford, Calif.: Stanford University Press, 1968.

Vohra, Ranbir. *China's Path to Modernization: A Historical Review from 1800 to the Present.* Englewood Cliffs, N.J.; Prentice-Hall, 1987.

Wakeman, Frederic E., Jr. *The Fall of Imperial China.* New York: Free Press, 1975.

———. *History and Will: Philosophical Perspectives of Mao Tse-tung's Thought.* Berkeley: University of California Press, 1973.

Wakeman, Frederic E., Jr., and Carolyn Grant, eds. *Conflict and Control in Late Imperial China.* Berkeley: University of California Press, 1975.

Wang Ch'eng-jen, et al., eds. *Chung-kuo chin-pai-nien-shih tz'u-tien.* (A dictionary of the last hundred years of Chinese history.) Wuhan: Hupeh jen-min ch'u-pan she, 1986.

Wang Chin-ming, and Ch'en Jui-yün, eds. *Chung-kuo hsien-tai-shih tz'u-tien.* (Dictionary of contemporary Chinese history.) Ch'ang-ch'un: Chi-lin wen-shih ch'u-pan she, 1988.

Wang Chüeh-yüan. *Chung-kuo tang-p'ai shih.* (The history of political parties and factions in China.) Taipei: Cheng-chung shu-chü, 1983.

Wang Chung-ch'i. *T'ai-p'ing T'ien-kuo ko-ming-shih.* (History of the Taiping Revolution.) 2nd ed. Taipei: Shang-wu, 1969.

Wang Erh-min. *Wan-Ch'ing cheng-chih szu-hsiang shih-lun.* (History of political thought in the late Ch'ing period.) Taipei: Hsüeh-sheng shu-chü, 1969.

Wang Erh-min, and Chan Sin-wai, comps. *Letters of Prominent Figures in Modern China.* Hong Kong: Chinese University Press [1989?].

542

BIBLIOGRAPHY

Wang, James C.F. *The Cultural Revolution in China: An Annotated Bibliography*. New York: Garland, 1976.

Wang Kung-an, and Mao Lei. *Kuo-Kung liang-tang kuan-hsi shih*. (History of the relationship between the KMT and CCP.) Wuhan: Wuhan ch'u-pan she, 1988.

Wang Te-chao. *Ts'ung kai-ko tao ko-ming*. (From reform to revolution.) Peking: Chunghua shu-chu, 1987.

Wang T'ing-k'o. *Kung-ch'an kuo-chi yü Chung-kuo ko-ming yen-chiu shu-p'ing*. (A research commentary on the Communist International and the Chinese Revolution.) Ch'eng-tu: Szechuan-sheng she-hui k'o-hsüeh yüan, 1988.

Wang, Y. C. *Chinese Intellectuals and the West, 1872–1949*. Chapel Hill: University of North Carolina Press, 1966.

Wang Ya-fu, and Chang Heng-chung, eds. *Chung-kuo hsüeh-shu-chieh ta-shih chi, 1919–1985*. (A record of major events in Chinese academic circles, 1919–1985.) Shanghai: Shanghai she-hui k'o-hsüeh yüan ch'u-pan, 1988.

Warshaw, Steven, et al. *China Emerges*. Rev. ed. Berkeley, Calif.: Diablo Press, 1987.

Wei, William. *Counterrevolution in China: The Nationalists in Jiangxi During the Soviet Period*. Ann Arbor: University of Michigan Press, 1985.

———. "Research Note: Documents on the Kiangsi Soviet Period at the Historical Archives Commission of the Kuomintang." *Chinese Republican Studies Newsletter* 2, no.1 (October 1976): 15–20.

Weston, Anthony. *The Chinese Revolution*. Ed. Malcolm Yapp et al. St. Paul, Minn.: Greenhaven Press, 1980.

Who's Who in Communist China. 2nd ed. 2 vols. Hong Kong: Union Research Institute, 1969.

Wiethoff, Bodo. *Gründzuge der neueren chinesischen Geschichte*. (Introduction to China's modern history.) Darmstadt: Wissenschaftliche Buchgeschellschaft, 1977.

Wilbur, C. Martin. "Columbia University's Chinese Oral History Project." *Chinese Republican Studies Newsletter* 5, no. 2 (February 1980): 4–10.

———. "Documentary Collections on Republican China at Columbia." *Chinese Republican Studies Newsletter* 5, no. 2 (February 1980): 11–15.

———. *The Nationalist Revolution in China, 1923–1928*. New York: Columbia University Press, 1984.

———. "Up-dating on Columbia's Manuscripts on the Chinese Republican Period." *Republican China* 14, no. 1 (November 1988): 90–92.

Wilbur, C. Martin, and Julie Lien-ying How. *Documents on Communism, Nationalism, and Soviet Advisers in China, 1918–1927*. New York: Columbia University Press, 1956.

———. *Missionaries of Revolution: Soviet Advisors and Nationalist China, 1920–1927*. Cambridge, Mass.: Harvard University Press, 1989.

Wilson, Dick, ed. *Mao Tse-tung in the Scales of History*. Cambridge: Cambridge University Press, 1977.

Wong, Young-tsu. *Search for Nationalism: Zhang Binglin and Revolutionary China, 1869–1936*. Hong Kong: Oxford University Press, 1989.

Wright, Mary Clabaugh, ed. *China in Revolution: The First Phase, 1900–1913*. New Haven, Conn.: Yale University Press, 1968.

———. *The Last Stand of Chinese Conservatism: The T'ung-chih Restoration, 1862–1874*. New York: Atheneum, 1966.

Wu Hsiang-hsiang. *Chung-kuo hsien-tai jen-wu*. (China's contemporary personalities.) Taipei: Tzu-yu T'ai-p'ing-yang wen-hua shih-yeh kung-szu, 1965.

———. *Min-kuo jen-wu lieh-chuan*. (Biographies from the Republican period.) Taipei: Chuan-chi wen-hsüeh she, 1986. A sequel to *Min-kuo pai-jen chuan*.

———. *Min-kuo pai-jen chuan*. (One hundred biographies of Republican China.) 4 vols. Taipei: Chuan-chi wen-hsüeh she, 1971.

Wu Tien-wei. *Lin Biao and the Gang of Four: Contra-Confucianism in Historical and Intellectual Perspective*. Carbondale: Southern Illinois University Press, 1983.

———. *The Sian Incident: A Pivotal Point in Modern Chinese History*. Ann Arbor: Center for Chinese Studies, University of Michigan, 1976.

Yang Hsien-ts'ai, et al., eds. *Chung-kuo ko-ming-shih*. (History of the Chinese Revolution.) Peking: Chung-kuo jen-min ta-hsüeh ch'u-pan she, 1987.

Young, Arthur N. *China's Nation-Building Effort, 1927–1937: The Financial and Economic Record*. Stanford, Calif.: Hoover Institution Press, 1971.

Young, Ernest P. *The Presidency of Yüan Shih-k'ai: Liberalism and Dictatorship in Early Republican China*. Ann Arbor: University of Michigan Press, 1977.

Zarrow, Peter. *Anarchism and Chinese Political Culture*. New York: Columbia University Press, 1990.

Zhang, Kaiyuan. "A General Review of the Study of the Revolution of 1911 in the People's Republic of China." Trans. Alan T. Wood. *Journal of Asian Studies* 39 (May 1980): 525–529.

Ziring, Lawrence, and C. I. Eugene Kim. *The Asian Political Dictionary*. Santa Barbara, Calif.: ABC–CLIO, 1985.

SELECT GLOSSARY

Aisin-Gioro P'u-i 愛新覺羅
溥儀

Anfu 安福

Anhwei 安徽

Chang Ch'un-ch'iao 張春橋

Chang Chün-mai 張君勱

Chang Fa-k'uei 張發奎

Chang Hsien-p'ei 張先培

Chang Hsüeh-liang 張學良

Chang Hsün 張勳

Chang Kuo-t'ao 張國燾

Chang Ping-lin 章炳麟

Chang Tso-lin 張作霖

Chao Shih-yen 趙世炎

Chao Tzu-yang 趙紫陽

Ch'en Ch'eng 陳誠

Ch'en Chi-t'ang 陳濟棠

Ch'en Chia-keng 陳嘉庚

Ch'en Ching-yueh 陳敬岳

Ch'en Chiung-ming 陳炯明

Ch'en Kung-po 陳公博

Ch'en Kuo-fu 陳果夫

Ch'en Li-fu 陳立夫

Ch'en Po-ta 陳伯達

Ch'en Shao-pai 陳少白

Ch'en Tu-hsiu 陳獨秀

Ch'en Yün 陳雲

cheng lung-t'ou 正龍頭

Cheng-feng 整風

Chiang Ch'ing 江青

Chiang Ching-kuo 蔣經國

Chiang Kai-shek 蔣介石

Chiang Meng-lin 蔣夢麟

Ch'iang-hsüeh hui 強學會

Chih-kung t'ang 致公堂

Chihli 直隸

Chin-Ch'a-Chi 晉察冀

Chin-na an-sha-t'uan 支那暗殺團

chin-shih 進士

Ch'ing 清

Ch'ing-i pao 清議報

Ch'ing-nien tsa-chih 青年雜誌

ching-shih chih-yung 經世致用

ch'ing-tang 清黨

Chingkangshan 井崗山

Ch'iu Chin 秋瑾

Chou En-lai 周恩來

Chou Fo-hai 周佛海

Ch'ü Ch'iu-pai 瞿秋白

Chu Teh 朱德

Chu-chiang 主將

chü-jen 舉人

Ch'uang-tsao she 創造社

chuang-yüan 狀元

chün-fa 軍閥

Chün-kuo chu-i 軍國主義

Chung Ming-kuang 鍾明光

Chung-hua fu-hsing yün-tung 中華復興運動

Chung-kuo Kung-ch'an-tang 中國共產黨

Erh-yüeh ni-lu 二月逆流

Feng Kuei-fen 馮桂芬

Feng Kuo-chang 馮國璋

Feng Yü-hsiang 馮玉祥

Feng Yün-shan 馮雲山

Feng-t'ien 奉天

Foochow 福州

Fu Ssu-nien 傅斯年

Fu Tso-yi 傅作儀

fu-ch'iang 富強

Fu-t'ien 富田

Fukien 福建

Hai-lu-feng 海陸豐

Hakka 客家

Ho Kai (Ho Ch'i) 何啟

Ho Ying-ch'in 何應欽

hsi-nao 洗腦

Hsi-shan p'ai 西山派

hsia-fang 下放

hsia-hsiang 下鄉

Hsiang Chung-fa 向中發

Hsiao Ch'ao-kuei 蕭朝貴

Hsien-fa yen-chiu hui 憲法研究會

Hsin-ch'ao she 新潮社

Hsin ch'ing-nien 新青年

Hsin-chün 新軍

Hsin-hai ko-ming 辛亥革命

Hsin-min hsüeh-hui 新民學會

Hsin-min ts'ung-pao 新民叢報

Hsin-yüeh she 新月社

Hsing-Chung hui 興中會

Hsipei chün 西北軍

hsiu-ts'ai 秀才

Hsü Hsiang-ch'ien 徐向前

Hsü Shih-ch'ang 徐世昌

Hsün-cheng shih-chi 訓政時期

Hu Ch'iao-mu 胡喬木

Hu Feng 胡風

Hu Han-min 胡漢民

Hu Li-yüan 胡禮垣

Hu Shih 胡適

Hu Yao-pang	胡耀邦	Kiangsi	江西
Hu-kuo chün	護國軍	Ko-lao hui	哥老會
Hua Kuo-feng	華國鋒	ko-ming	革命
hua-chiao	華僑	Ko-ming fang-lüeh	革命方略
Hua-hsing hui	華興會	Ku Wei-chün	顧維鈞
Huai-Hai	淮海	kuan-tu shang-pan	官督商辦
Huang Chih-meng	黃之萌	Kuang-fu chün	光復軍
Huang Hsing	黃興	Kuang-fu hui	光復會
Huanghuakang	黃花崗	Kuang-hsü	光緒
Hui-chou	惠州	Kuang-hsüeh hui	廣學會
Hung Hsiu-ch'üan	洪秀全	Kuo Sung-tao	郭嵩燾
Hung Jen-kan	洪仁玕	Kung, Hsiang-hsi	孔祥熙
Hung-hua kang	洪花崗	Kung-t'ung Kang-ling	共同綱領
hung-pao-shu	紅寶書	K'ung-tzu kai-chih k'ao	
I Wang	翼王		孔子改制考
I-ho ch'üan	義和拳	Kuo-chia she-hui-tang	
Jao Shu-shih	饒漱石		國家社會黨
Jen-hsüeh	仁學	Kuo-ts'ui hsüeh-p'ai	國粹學派
Jen-min jih-pao	人民日報	Kuominchün	國民軍
Kai-tsu p'ai	改組派	Kuomintang	國民黨
Kan Wang	干王	Kwangsi	廣西
K'ang Kuang-jen	康廣仁	Kwangtung	廣東
K'ang Yu-wei	康有為	Lee Teng-hui	李登輝
K'ang-ta	抗大	Lei Feng	雷鋒
Kao Kang	高崗	Li Hsien-nien	李先念
Kiang-nan Ta-ying	江南大營	Li Hsiu-ch'eng	李秀成

548

Li Hung-chang	李鴻章	Lu Hsün (Chou Shu-jen) 魯迅 (周樹人)
Li Li-san	李立三	Lu Ting-i	陸定一
Li Lieh-chün	李烈鈞	Lukouchiao	盧溝橋
Li Shih-tseng	李石曾	Lushan	盧山
Li Ta-chao	李大釗	Manchukuo	滿州國
Li T'e	李德	Mao Tse-tung	毛澤東
Li Tsung-jen	李宗仁	Mao Tun	茅盾
Li Yüan-hung	黎元洪	min-chu	民主
Liang Ch'i-ch'ao	梁啟超	Min-chu t'ung-meng	民主同盟
Liang Shih-ch'iu	梁實秋	min-chu chi-chung-chih 民主集中制
Liang Shih-i	梁士詒	
Liang Shu-ming	梁漱溟	Min-chu tang	民主黨
Liao Chung-k'ai	廖仲凱	min-ch'üan	民權
Liao Mo-sha	廖沫沙	Min-kuo tsa-chih	民國雜誌
Lin Hsü	林旭	Min-pao	民報
Lin Kuan-tz'u	林冠慈	min-sheng	民生
Lin Tse-hsü	林則徐	Miyazaki Tōten	宮崎滔天
Lin Piao	林彪	Nanking	南京
Liu Jen	劉仁	Nien	捻
Liu Kuang-ti	劉光弟	O-Yü-Wan	鄂予皖
Liu Po-ch'eng	劉伯承	Pa Chin	巴金
Liu Shao-ch'i	劉少奇	Pa-lu chün	八路軍
Liu Shih-p'ei	劉師培	Pai Ch'ung-hsi	白崇禧
Lo Chia-lun	羅家倫	Pai Shang-Ti hui	拜上帝會
Lo Fu (Chang Wen-t'ien) 洛甫 (張聞天)	

pai-chia cheng-ming 百家爭鳴

pai-hua 白話

pai-hua ch'i-fang 百花齊放

pang-yen 榜眼

pao-chia 保甲

Pao-huang hui 保皇會

Pao-lu hui 保路會

Peiyang-hsi 北洋系

P'eng Chen 彭真

P'eng Chia-chen 彭家珍

P'eng P'ai 彭湃

P'eng Te-huai 彭德懷

P'ing-Ying-t'uan 平英團

Po Ku (Ch'in Pang-hsien) 博古 (秦邦憲)

San-chia ts'un 三家村

San-fan 三反

San-min chu-i 三民主義

San-min chu-i ch'ing-nien t'uan 三民主義青年團

San-yüan-li 三元里

She-hui chu-i chiao-yü yün-tung 社會主義教育運動

Shen-Kan-Ning 陝甘寧

sheng-yüan 生員

Shih Chien-ju 史堅如

Shih Ta-k'ai 石達開

Sian 西安

Soong Ai-ling 宋靄齡

Soong Ch'ing-ling 宋慶齡

Soong Mei-ling 宋美齡

Soong Tse-ven 宋子文

ssu-hsiang kai-tsao 思想改造

Su-pao 蘇報

Sun Ch'uan-fang 孫傳芳

Sun Fo 孫科

Sun Yat-sen 孫逸仙

Sung Chiao-jen 宋教仁

sze-ke fu-ts'ung 四個服從

Ta-chai 大寨

Tai Chi-t'ao 戴季陶

T'ai-p'ing T'ien-kuo 太平天國

T'an Ssu-t'ung 譚嗣同

t'an-hua 探花

T'ang Hua-lung 湯化龍

T'ang Shao-yi 唐紹儀

T'ang T'ing-shu 唐廷樞

T'ang Ts'ai-ch'ang te 唐才常德

Teng Hsiao-p'ing 鄧小平

Teng T'o 鄧托

Teng Yen-ta 鄧演達

Teng Ying-ch'ao 鄧穎超
t'i-t'ien hsing-tao 替天行道
Tieh-hsüeh chün 鐵血軍
Tieh-hsüeh hui 鐵血會
T'ien Wang 天王
t'ien-ming 天命
t'ien-t'ien-tu 天天讀
T'ienanmen 天安門
Ting Ling 丁玲
Ting Wen-chiang 丁文江
tou-ssu p'i-hsiu 闘私批修
ts'ai 才
Ts'ai Ao 蔡鍔
Ts'ai Yüan-p'ei 蔡元培
Ts'ao Ju-lin 曹汝霖
Ts'ao K'un 曹琨
Tseng Chi-tse 曾紀澤
Tseng Kuo-fan 曾國藩
Tsinghua 清華
Tso Tsung-t'ang 左宗棠
Tsou Lu 鄒魯
tsou-tzu-p'ai 走資派
Tsunyi 遵義
Tu-li p'ing-lun 獨立評論
tu-tu 都督
Tuan Ch'i-jui 段祺瑞

Tung Pi-wu 董必武
T'ung-chih 同治
T'ung-meng hui 同盟會
Tungpei chün 東北軍
"Tzu-cheng hsin-pien" 資政新篇
tzu-ch'iang 自強
Tz'u-hsi 慈禧
Tzu-li chün 自立軍
tzu-li keng-sheng 自力更生
Ulanfu 烏蘭夫
Wan-kuo kung-pao 萬國公報
Wan-sheng yüan 萬生園
Wang Ching-wei 汪精衞
Wang Ch'ung-hui 王寵惠
Wang Hung-wen 王洪文
Wang Ming (Ch'en Shao-yü)
王明（陳紹禹）
Wang Tung-hsing 汪東興
Wei Ch'ang-hui 韋昌輝
Wen I-to 聞一多
Wen Sheng-ts'ai 溫生才
wen-yen 文言
Whampoa 黃埔
Wu Chih-hui 吳稚暉
Wu P'ei-fu 吳佩孚
Wu-fan 五反

551

Wu-hsu pien-fa 戊戌變法
Wu-san tsan-an 五卅慘案
Yang Hsiu-ch'ing 楊秀清
Yang Hu-cheng 楊虎城
Yang Jui 楊銳
Yang Shen-hsiu 楊深秀
Yang Tu 楊度
Yang Yu-ch'ang 楊禹昌
yang-wu 洋務
Yao Wen-yuan 姚文元
Yeh Chien-ying 葉劍英
Yeh T'ing 葉挺
Yen Chia-kan 嚴家淦
Yen Fu 嚴復
Yen Hsi-shan 閻錫山
Yen Yang-chu 晏陽初
Yen-chiu hsi 研究系
Yenan 延安
Yenching 燕京
Yüan Shih-k'ai 袁世凱
Yung Wing (Jung Hung) 容閎

INDEX

Based on both the Wade-Giles and *Hanyu pinyin* romanization systems. Dictionary entries appear in bold.

About the Editor

EDWIN PAK-WAH LEUNG is associate professor in the Department of Asian Studies and senior fellow of the Asia Center at Seton Hall University. He is the author of *Adaptability of the Chinese in America* (1988), *Modern Change in Chinese Diplomacy* (1990), and several articles, and the editor of special editions of *Chinese Law and Government* and *Asian Profile*.